Red Dot Design Yearbook 2019/2020

Edited by Peter Zec

reddot award

product design

About this book

"Enjoying" presents award-winning products where aspects such as enjoyment and the experience play a special role. All of these products are of outstanding design quality and have been successful in one of the world's largest and most renowned design competitions, the Red Dot Design Award. This book documents the current results in the field of "Enjoying", and presents the most important players – the design team of the year, the designers of the best products and the jury members.

Über dieses Buch

„Enjoying" präsentiert ausgezeichnete Produkte, bei denen Aspekte wie Genuss und Erleben eine besondere Rolle spielen. All diese Produkte sind von herausragender gestalterischer Qualität, ausgezeichnet in einem der größten und renommiertesten Designwettbewerbe der Welt, dem Red Dot Design Award. Dieses Buch dokumentiert die aktuellen Ergebnisse im Bereich „Enjoying" und stellt zudem die wichtigsten Akteure vor – das Designteam des Jahres, die Designer der besten Produkte und die Jurymitglieder.

Contents

Inhalt

6 **Preface of the editor**
Vorwort des Herausgebers

8 **Red Dot: Design Team of the Year 2019**
9 **Flavio Manzoni and Ferrari Design Team**

28 **The designers of the Red Dot: Best of the Best and their award-winning products**
Die Designer der Red Dot: Best of the Best und ihre ausgezeichneten Produkte
30 Sebastian Meinecke – Urwahn Engineering GmbH
32 Adrien Roose, Tanguy Goretti, Karim Slaoui – COWBOY
34 Flavio Manzoni – Ferrari Design
36 Yasutake Tsuchida – Mazda Motor Corporation
38 Centro Stile Ducati
40 Masahiro Yasuda – Yamaha Motor Co., Ltd. Shogo Kinoshita – GK Dynamics Inc.
42 Oep Schilling, Vincent Beekman, Sander Ejlenberg – Cabiner
44 Philips Design Signify Design Team
46 Dr. Paolo Cattaneo – MOMODESIGN
48 Mark van Roon, Jasper den Dekker – REV'IT! Sport International B.V.
50 Fiskars Finland Oy Ab
52 Oliver Schweizer – Schweizer Design Consulting
54 Kunihiko Tanaka – FUJIFILM Corporation
56 Seonkyu Kim, Cheolwoong Shin, Minjae Lee, Hyunbyung Cha, Yunjoo Kim, Young Kyung Kim – LG Electronics Inc.
58 Stefan Hohn – Noto GmbH
60 Yujin Morisawa – Sony Corporation, Creative Center
62 Drew Walcott, Peter Michaelian, Lucas Saule, Vince Voron, Grayson Byrd, Cody Proksa – Dolby Laboratories
64 Robert Suchy, Veronika Suchy, Patrick Suchy – clearaudio electronic GmbH
66 Pinakesh De, Mikiyasu Ishikura – Panasonic Corporation

68 Ryan Mario Yasin – Petit Pli
70 Samsonite Design Team
72 Roland Heiler, Christian Schwamkrug, Manuel Röck – Studio F. A. Porsche
74 Saloni Kaushik – Titan Company Limited

The award-winning products of "Red Dot: Best of the Best", "Red Dot" and "Honourable Mention" distinctions
Die Siegerprodukte der Auszeichnungen „Red Dot: Best of the Best", „Red Dot" und „Honourable Mention"
76 Bicycles
Fahrräder
96 Vehicles
Fahrzeuge
150 Sports and outdoor
Sport und Outdoor
186 Leisure and games
Freizeit und Spiel
204 Entertainment
Entertainment
274 Spas and personal care
Wellness und Personal Care
302 Fashion, lifestyle and accessories
Mode, Lifestyle und Accessoires
332 Watches and jewellery
Uhren und Schmuck

The jurors of the Red Dot Award: Product Design
Die Juroren des Red Dot Award: Product Design
350 David Andersen
352 Prof. Masayo Ave
354 Martin Beeh
356 Gordon Bruce
358 Gisbert L. Brunner
360 Rüdiger Bucher
362 Prof. Jun Cai
364 Vivian Wai-kwan Cheng

366 Mårten Claesson
368 Vincent Créance
370 Martin Darbyshire
372 Katrin de Louw
374 Saskia Diez
376 Stefan Eckstein
378 Robin Edman
380 Prof. Lutz Fügener
382 Hideshi Hamaguchi
384 Prof. Renke He
386 Prof. Carlos Hinrichsen
388 Simon Husslein
390 Qiong Er Jiang
392 Prof. Cheng-Neng Kuan
394 Steve Leung
396 Dr. Thomas Lockwood
398 Wolfgang K. Meyer-Hayoz
400 Prof. Jure Miklavc
402 Adriana Monk
404 Prof. Dr. Ken Nah
406 Alexander Neumeister
408 Ken Okuyama
410 Simon Ong
412 Dr. Sascha Peters
414 Dirk Schumann
416 Prof. Song Kee Hong
418 Dick Spierenburg
420 Leon Sun
422 Kazuo Tanaka
424 Nils Toft
426 Prof. Danny Venlet
428 Dr. Joseph Francis Wong

Alphabetical index
Alphabetisches Register
430 Manufacturers and distributors
Hersteller und Vertrieb
432 Designers
Designer
440 Imprint
Impressum

Professor Dr. Peter Zec
Preface of the editor
Vorwort des Herausgebers

Dear reader,
The Red Dot Design Yearbook with its four volumes "Living", "Doing", "Working" and "Enjoying" provides a comprehensive overview of the latest developments in product design. As you leaf through the books, you will notice some trends that run through all of the categories. In the competition year 2019/2020, one such trend is the clearly recognisable move toward more eco-friendly and sustainable products on the one hand and products that are more and more intelligent on the other. Other developments unfold within the narrow framework of a certain product segment or geographical region. Frequently, such developments are no less ground-breaking. On the contrary, they often indicate where future trends might lead. Embark on a journey of discovery, and be inspired by the many excellently designed products.

This year once again saw many well-known brands enter their products in the competition. This may come as an initial surprise, as one could be forgiven for thinking that these manufacturers don't need any more awards in order to sell their products or assure themselves of their own expertise. But the lesson to be learned from these companies that are successful as a brand through design is that this success has to be carefully earned – year after year. That's because the credibility of a brand is established by a company being visible over a longer period and also demonstrating a high level of continuity in its products, their design and quality. Many of the best-known brands internationally in the field of consumer and luxury goods have also been winning distinctions in the Red Dot Design Award for years, including Ferrari, Bosch, Apple, hansgrohe, Fiskars, LG Electronics, Lenovo and Sony. Not only are they some of this year's Red Dot: Best of the Best laureates, they can also look back at a consistent brand development. They have a striking corporate design, and above all else they stand for products with outstanding design and high quality.

In order to underscore and enhance the relevance of a comprehensive brand strategy (and ideally a related design strategy), brands have been accorded a larger platform in this year's Red Dot competition for communication design. Within an industry, companies can now enter the running for the distinction "Red Dot: Brand of the Year" in the Red Dot Award: Brands & Communication Design.

Without further ado, allow me to wish you an entertaining read!

Yours sincerely,
Peter Zec

Liebe Leserin, lieber Leser,
das Red Dot Design Yearbook gewährt Ihnen mit seinen vier Bänden „Living", „Doing", „Working" und „Enjoying" einen umfassenden Überblick über die neuesten Entwicklungen im Produktdesign. Wenn Sie durch die Bücher blättern, werden Sie den einen oder anderen Trend erkennen, der sich durch sämtliche Kategorien zieht – im Wettbewerbsjahr 2019/2020 ist dies etwa eine klar erkennbare Tendenz zu umweltfreundlicheren und nachhaltigeren Produkten einerseits sowie zu immer intelligenteren Produkten andererseits. Andere Entwicklungen spielen sich im engen Rahmen eines bestimmten Produktsegments oder einer geografischen Region ab, sind deswegen aber häufig nicht weniger richtungsweisend, sondern zeigen ganz im Gegenteil oft schon an, wohin der Trend in den nächsten Jahren gehen wird. Gehen Sie auf Entdeckungsreise und lassen Sie sich von den vielen ausgezeichnet gestalteten Produkten inspirieren.

Auch in diesem Jahr haben wieder viele bekannte Marken ihre Produkte zum Wettbewerb eingereicht. Auf den ersten Blick mag dies verwundern, denn man sollte meinen, dass diese Hersteller keine Auszeichnung mehr benötigen, um ihre Produkte zu verkaufen oder sich ihres eigenen Könnens zu versichern. Doch kann man von diesen Firmen, die als Marke mit Design erfolgreich sind, lernen, dass auch dieser Erfolg sorgfältig erarbeitet werden muss – Jahr für Jahr aufs Neue. Denn die Glaubwürdigkeit einer Marke kommt erst dadurch zustande, dass ein Unternehmen über einen längeren Zeitraum hinweg sichtbar ist und auch in seinen Produkten, deren Design und Qualität eine hohe Beständigkeit zeigt. Viele der international bekanntesten Marken im Bereich der Konsum- und Luxusgüter sind auch seit Jahren beim Red Dot Design Award erfolgreich, darunter Ferrari, Bosch, Apple, hansgrohe, Fiskars, LG Electronics, Lenovo oder Sony. Sie gehören nicht nur zu den diesjährigen Red Dot: Best of the Best-Preisträgern, sondern können auch auf eine kontinuierliche Markenentwicklung zurückblicken. Sie haben ein Corporate Design, das prägnant ist; vor allem aber stehen sie für Produkte mit herausragendem Design und hoher Qualität.

Um die Relevanz einer umfassenden Marken- und einer damit im Idealfall einhergehenden Designstrategie zu unterstreichen und zu stärken, erhalten Marken bei Red Dot ab diesem Jahr eine größere Plattform im Wettbewerb für Kommunikationsdesign: Beim Red Dot Award: Brands & Communication Design können sich Unternehmen jetzt innerhalb einer Branche um die Auszeichnung „Red Dot: Brand of the Year" bewerben.

Und nun wünsche ich Ihnen viel Vergnügen bei der Lektüre!

Ihr
Peter Zec

The title "Red Dot: Design Team of the Year" is bestowed on a design team that has garnered attention through its outstanding overall design achievements. This year, the title goes to Flavio Manzoni and the Ferrari Design Team. This award is the only one of its kind in the world and is extremely highly regarded even outside of the design scene.

Mit der Auszeichnung „Red Dot: Design Team of the Year" wird ein Designteam geehrt, das durch seine herausragende gestalterische Gesamtleistung auf sich aufmerksam gemacht hat. In diesem Jahr geht sie an Flavio Manzoni und das Ferrari Design Team. Diese Würdigung ist einzigartig auf der Welt und genießt über die Designszene hinaus höchstes Ansehen.

In recognition of its feat, the Red Dot: Design Team of the Year receives the "Radius" trophy. This sculpture was designed and crafted by the Weinstadt-Schnaidt based designer, Simon Peter Eiber.

Als Anerkennung erhält das Red Dot: Design Team of the Year den Wanderpokal „Radius". Die Skulptur wurde entworfen und angefertigt von dem Designer Simon Peter Eiber aus Weinstadt-Schnaidt.

2019	Flavio Manzoni & Ferrari Design Team
2018	Phoenix Design Team
2017	Canyon Design Team
2016	Blackmagic Industrial Design Team led by Simon Kidd
2015	Robert Sachon & Bosch Home Appliances Design Team
2014	Veryday
2013	Lenovo Design & User Experience Team
2012	Michael Mauer & Style Porsche
2011	The Grohe Design Team led by Paul Flowers
2010	Stephan Niehaus & Hilti Design Team
2009	Susan Perkins & Tupperware World Wide Design Team
2008	Michael Laude & Bose Design Team
2007	Chris Bangle & Design Team BMW Group
2006	LG Corporate Design Center
2005	Adidas Design Team
2004	Pininfarina Design Team
2003	Nokia Design Team
2002	Apple Industrial Design Team
2001	Festo Design Team
2000	Sony Design Team
1999	Audi Design Team
1998	Philips Design Team
1997	Michele De Lucchi Design Team
1996	Bill Moggridge & Ideo Design Team
1995	Herbert Schultes & Siemens Design Team
1994	Bruno Sacco & Mercedes-Benz Design Team
1993	Hartmut Esslinger & Frogdesign
1992	Alexander Neumeister & Neumeister Design
1991	Reiner Moll & Partner & Moll Design
1990	Slany Design Team
1989	Braun Design Team
1988	Leybold AG Design Team

Red Dot: Design Team of the Year 2019
Flavio Manzoni and Ferrari Design Team

This year's "Red Dot: Design Team of the Year" title goes to Flavio Manzoni and the Ferrari Design Team in Maranello. Flavio Manzoni became Senior Vice-President for Design at Ferrari in 2010. Since the Italian car manufacturer was founded in 1947, he is the first head designer to have succeeded in building a successful Ferrari Design Team.

This achievement is reflected not only in the new Centro Stile that opened in Maranello in 2018 but also in the Red Dot Award: Product Design. In the last five years, Manzoni and the Ferrari Design Team have won an accolade at the Red Dot Award 14 times and have five times been awarded the highest distinction the competition has to bestow, the Red Dot: Best of the Best.

Ferrari is the first car manufacturer in the history of the competition to win the top distinction five times in a row. Thanks to this achievement, the brand now also leads the Red Dot Ranking in the Automotive Design category for the first time. This is an outstanding accomplishment that will be recognised this year with the honorary title "Red Dot: Design Team of the Year".

Die Auszeichnung „Red Dot: Design Team of the Year" geht in diesem Jahr an Flavio Manzoni und das Ferrari Design Team in Maranello. 2010 wurde Flavio Manzoni Senior Vice-President for Design bei Ferrari. Seit der Gründung des italienischen Automobilherstellers im Jahr 1947 ist er der erste Chefdesigner, dem es gelungen ist, für Ferrari ein erfolgreiches Designteam aufzubauen.

Diese Leistung spiegelt sich nicht nur im neuen Centro Stile wider, das 2018 in Maranello eröffnet wurde, sondern auch im Red Dot Award: Product Design. Manzoni und das Ferrari Design Team wurden in den letzten fünf Jahren 14 Mal im Red Dot Award ausgezeichnet und erhielten fünf Mal die höchste Auszeichnung im Wettbewerb, den Red Dot: Best of the Best.

Ein Novum in der Geschichte des Wettbewerbs: Ferrari ist es als erstem Automobilhersteller gelungen, die höchste Auszeichnung fünf Mal in Folge zu gewinnen. Mit dieser Leistung führt die Marke erstmals auch das Red Dot Ranking im Automotive Design an. Eine herausragende Leistung, die in diesem Jahr mit der Ehrenauszeichnung „Red Dot: Design Team of the Year" gewürdigt wird.

Flavio Manzoni and the Ferrari Design Team of the Monza SP1 and Monza SP2.
Flavio Manzoni und das Ferrari Design Team des Monza SP1 und Monza SP2.

Flavio Manzoni, Senior Vice-President for Design; Matteo De Petris, Responsible Advanced Design;
Francesco Russo, Senior Exterior Designer; Alain Abramo, Senior Exterior Designer; Federico Acuto, Senior Exterior Designer;
Emanuel Salvatore, Responsible Virtual Modelling; Salvo Della Ventura, Responsible Advanced Virtual Modelling;
Luca Casarini, Responsible Interior Design; Fabio Massari, Senior Interior Designer; Guglielmo Galliano, Responsible Graphic & Visual

Designing Dreams
Flavio Manzoni and Ferrari Design Team

Maranello. The small Italian town in the Emilia-Romagna region is synonymous around the world with the brand and the myth that is Ferrari. This is where the dream cars of tomorrow are made, which feature technical innovations that shape our idea of the future and whose timeless language of form endures for generations. Ferrari's company premises are more than a mere ensemble of production halls, workshops and administrative buildings. Since the mid-1990s, site has transformed into a centre of modern industrial architecture. On Viale Enzo Ferrari, the campus street that bears the name of the company founder, a new dream factory that makes customers' dreams come true has emerged between the architectural gems designed by Jean Nouvel, Massimiliano Fuksas, Renzo Piano and Marco Visconti. Its name: Ferrari Centro Stile.

The dream factory

The architectural project of the new design centre was directed by the Ferrari Design Team under the guidance of architect Flavio Manzoni while the engineering project was developed in collaboration with the Design International studio of London and the Planning studio of Bologna. The building has brought together all design-related tasks and activities under one spectacular roof: a structure made from triangular glass and aluminium modules, the exterior of which is decorated with the cavallino rampante or 'prancing horse'. The geometric modules combine to form powerful and elegant areas reminiscent at their points of intersection of the dynamic lines of a Ferrari and that overlie the four-storey building like a wave.

What was once an old warehouse for prototypes is now a design dream factory. On a space of 5,000 square metres, a modern studio has been created for the designers and employees of the in-house design team in addition to a presentation room with a terrace for presenting new models and a Tailor Made area where the company's customers can configure their own customised dream car.

The Tailor Made area turns each Ferrari into a unique piece for its owner. The designers use virtual previews to show the customer his or her individually made vehicle in real time. For example, the aesthetic of the exterior and interior can be previewed on the display. With all of these possibilities for personalising their own Ferrari, customers are given a level of exclusivity that is unparalleled in the automotive sector.

The first floor of Centro Stile houses the Virtual Modelling department, where digital Ferrari models are created in 3D. Modelling involves using software to transform surface data into three-dimensional objects. Although the designers cannot touch or feel the virtual lines and edges, digital cavities and volumes with their hands, their professional eye takes

Maranello. Die kleine italienische Stadt in der Region Emilia-Romagna ist weltweit ein Synonym für die Marke und den Mythos Ferrari. Hier entstehen die Traumautos von morgen, deren technische Innovationen unsere Vorstellung von der Zukunft prägen und deren zeitlose Formensprache Generationen überdauert. Ferraris Betriebsgelände ist nicht nur ein Ensemble aus Fabrikhallen, Werkstätten und Verwaltungsgebäuden: Es hat sich seit Mitte der 1990er Jahre zu einem Zentrum moderner Industriearchitektur entwickelt. Auf dem Campus ist an der Viale Enzo Ferrari, der Straße, die den Namen des Firmengründers trägt, zwischen den architektonischen Glanzstücken von Jean Nouvel, Massimiliano Fuksas, Renzo Piano und Marco Visconti eine neue Traumfabrik entstanden, die die Wünsche der Kunden Wirklichkeit werden lässt: Ferrari Centro Stile.

Die Traumfabrik

Das architektonische Projekt für das neue Designzentrum wurde von dem Ferrari Design Team unter der Leitung des Architekten Flavio Manzoni gesteuert, während das bautechnische Projekt in Zusammenarbeit mit dem Design International Studio in London und dem Planning Studio in Bologna entwickelt wurde. Das Gebäude vereint alle designrelevanten Aufgaben- und Tätigkeitsbereiche unter einer spektakulären Dachkonstruktion: eine Struktur aus dreieckigen Glas- und Aluminiummodulen, deren Äußeres das Cavallino rampante, das sich aufbäumende Pferdchen ziert. Die geometrischen Module verbinden sich zu kraftvollen und eleganten Flächen, die dort, wo sie aufeinandertreffen, an die dynamischen Linien eines Ferrari erinnern und sich wie eine Welle über das vierstöckige Gebäude legen.

Was früher ein altes Lager für Prototypen war, ist heute eine Traumfabrik des Designs. Auf 5.000 m² Fläche ist ein modernes Studio für die Designer und Mitarbeiter des In-house Design Teams entstanden, ein Präsentationsraum mit Terrasse für die Vorstellung neuer Modelle und ein „Tailor Made"-Bereich, welcher den Kunden des Unternehmens erlaubt, ihr Traumauto individuell ausstatten zu lassen.

Im „Tailor Made"-Bereich wird jeder Ferrari zu einem Unikat für seinen Besitzer. In virtuellen Vorschauen präsentieren die Designer dem Kunden sein individuell gefertigtes Fahrzeug in Echtzeit. So lässt sich die Ästhetik des Exteriors und Interieurs bereits am Monitor beurteilen. Mit all diesen Möglichkeiten zur persönlichen Gestaltung des eigenen Ferraris erhalten die Kunden einen Grad an Exklusivität, der in der Automobilbranche seinesgleichen sucht.

Auf der ersten Etage des Centro Stile befindet sich das Virtual Modelling. Hier entstehen digitale Ferrari-Modelle in 3D. Bei der Modellierung werden Daten der Oberflächen mithilfe von Software in dreidimensionale

in these features and 'touches' the surface with its convex and concave forms. This creative interplay with beauty, proportions, contrasts and colour hues is based on the designers' constantly alternating view of the details and the contours of the vehicle.

But alongside state-of-the-art technology, there is still a need for craftsmanship. That's because, in addition to sketches and computer models, Ferrari models are produced by hand. Flavio Manzoni places special emphasis on modelling, where scale models and original-size models are created by digitally controlled milling machines and are formed by a team of experienced artists before the meticulous manual finish. Flavio Manzoni brought the clay modelling approach from Germany in 2010. Particularly in the initial phase of the newly formed design team, Manzoni and his staff literally created new models with their hands. At that time, the Head of Design and his team worked like artists to connect surfaces with each other, to better assess forms and proportions and to refine the models step by step.

Like in many other design studios and in-house design teams, confidentiality was another top priority alongside creativity. Consequently, the geometric elements of the roof construction serve not only as an eye-catching feature but also as a privacy screen. The second skin of the roof construction works like a protective shield that allows daylight through while keeping out unwanted eyes. On the second floor of Centro Stile, which includes a terrace and a large conference and presentation room with a high-resolution LED wall, newly designed models can thus be presented in natural lighting conditions. Not only does Centro Stile make the professional work of the design team easier and more pleasant, it also makes it more effective and efficient for the company, as the draft and development phases are significantly shorter and it's possible to agree on improvements to the models with the engineers right up to the very last moment.

Start-up and warm-up

More than 100 designers work in the Centro Stile building today, but this was not always the case. When Flavio Manzoni was appointed Senior Vice-President for Design at Ferrari in 2010, there were just five people in a small team that lacked not only a structure but also tools and above all else a vision of the future of the Ferrari brand. When the decision was taken to create a dedicated in-house design team, Flavio Manzoni shared his vision with the small group of staff: "I saw their eyes light up, but nobody really believed in it," Flavio Manzoni remembers. "Everyone thought 'Manzoni is a dreamer'." Previously, the design activities were organised in collaboration with external partners such as Pininfarina.

Objekte verwandelt. Auch wenn die Designer die virtuellen Linien und Kanten, die digitalen Hohlräume und Volumen nicht mit den Händen berühren und ertasten können, fährt ihr professionelles Auge an ihnen entlang und berührt die Oberfläche aus konvexen und konkaven Formen. Das gestalterische Spiel mit der Schönheit, den Proportionen, den Kontrasten und Farbnuancen basiert auf dem ständig wechselnden Blick der Designer zwischen den Details und den Konturen des Autos.

Neben neuester Technologie ist aber nach wie vor handwerkliches Können gefragt. Denn neben Skizzen und Computermodellen werden Ferrari-Modelle von Hand gefertigt. Ein besonderes Augenmerk legt Flavio Manzoni auf den Modellbau, wo maßstabsgetreue Modelle und solche in Originalgröße von digital gesteuerten Fräsmaschinen entstehen und von einem Team aus erfahrenen Künstlern geformt werden, bevor dann das Finish sorgfältig von Hand erfolgt. Flavio Manzoni hat das Clay Modelling 2010 aus Deutschland mitgebracht. Insbesondere in der Anfangsphase des neu gebildeten Designteams formen Manzoni und seine Mitarbeiter neue Modelle buchstäblich mit ihren Händen. Der Designchef und sein Team arbeiten zu dieser Zeit wie Künstler, um Oberflächen miteinander zu verbinden, die Formen und Proportionen besser beurteilen zu können und die Modelle Schritt für Schritt weiterzuentwickeln.

Wie bei vielen anderen Designstudios und In-house Design Teams steht mit der Kreativität auch die Diskretion an oberster Stelle. Die geometrischen Elemente der Dachkonstruktion sind daher nicht nur Blickfang, sondern auch Blickschutz. Die zweite Haut der Dachkonstruktion funktioniert wie ein Schutzschild, der zwar Tageslicht hineinlässt, aber ungewünschte Blicke abhält. So können auf der zweiten Ebene des Centro Stile, wo sich eine Terrasse und ein großer Konferenz- und Präsentationsraum mit einer hochauflösenden LED-Wand befinden, neu konzipierte Modelle bei natürlichem Licht präsentiert werden. Das Centro Stile macht die professionelle Arbeit nicht nur für das Designteam angenehmer und leichter, sondern auch für das Unternehmen effektiver und effizienter, da sich die Entwurfs- und Entwicklungsphasen deutlich verkürzen und man in Abstimmung mit den Ingenieuren noch bis zur letzten Minute Verbesserungen an den Modellen vornehmen kann.

Start-up und Warm-up

In den Räumen des Centro Stile arbeiten heute mehr als 100 Designer. Das war nicht immer so. Als Flavio Manzoni im Jahr 2010 zum Senior Vice-President for Design bei Ferrari ernannt wird, bilden gerade einmal fünf Personen ein kleines Team, dem es nicht nur an Struktur fehlt, sondern auch an Werkzeugen, vor allem aber an einer Vorstellung von der Zukunft der Marke Ferrari. Als die Entscheidung fällt, ein eigenes In-house Design Team aufzubauen, teilt Flavio Manzoni mit der kleinen Gruppe von Mitarbeitern seine Vision: „Ich sah das Leuchten in ihren Augen, aber niemand glaubte wirklich daran", erinnert sich Flavio Manzoni. „Jeder dachte: Manzoni ist ein Träumer." Bisher waren Designaktivitäten in Zusammenarbeit mit externen Partnern wie Pininfarina organisiert worden.

The iconic shape of the Ferrari FXX K inspired by aircraft. The perfect fusion of form and function.
Von Flugzeugen inspirierte ikonische Form des Ferrari FXX K. Die perfekte Verschmelzung von Form und Funktion.

When Manzoni became Senior Vice-President for Design at Ferrari in 2010, an old storehouse that housed Ferrari prototypes initially had to be used as a temporary Design Center. And while Manzoni had to improvise on a daily basis, he worked tirelessly on designs for new models. Behind the scenes, he was interviewing hundreds of designers to find out who would fit in his team and be able to understand, reinterpret and transform the Ferrari brand and values.

In the beginning, it was difficult for Manzoni to judge who really understood the Ferrari brand and also fit in the team in terms of their social skills and attitudes. Manzoni quickly noticed that experience does not always pay off. Anyone who wanted to work as a designer for Ferrari would have to be able to approach the brand creatively without preconceptions and be willing to explore Ferrari's brand values again and again in a team with other designers, engineers and marketing experts. Too much experience could sometimes be a disadvantage in this regard. "It was like working in a start-up." That's how Manzoni describes the unimaginable dynamism of this new departure.

Als Manzoni 2010 Senior Vice-President for Design bei Ferrari wird, muss zunächst ein altes Lagerhaus, das Ferraris Prototypen beherbergt, als provisorisches Design Center genutzt werden. Und während Manzoni tagtäglich improvisieren muss, arbeitet er unermüdlich an Entwürfen für neue Modelle. Im Hintergrund führt er Hunderte von Bewerbungsgesprächen mit Designern, um herauszufinden, wer in sein Team passt und in der Lage sein könnte, die Marke und die Werte von Ferrari zu verstehen, sie neu zu interpretieren und zu transformieren.

Zu Beginn ist es für Manzoni schwierig zu beurteilen, wer die Marke Ferrari wirklich versteht und auch mit Blick auf seine sozialen Fähigkeiten und seine Lebenseinstellung ins Team passt. Manzoni merkt schnell, dass sich Erfahrung nicht immer auszahlt. Wer als Designer für Ferrari arbeiten will, muss in der Lage sein, sich auf die Marke einzulassen, und bereit sein, sich immer wieder aufs Neue kreativ und in einem Team mit anderen Designern, Ingenieuren und Marketingexperten mit den Werten, die Ferrari verkörpert, auseinanderzusetzen. Zu viel Erfahrung kann da bisweilen auch hinderlich sein. „Es herrschten Bedingungen wie in einem Start-up-Unternehmen", beschreibt Manzoni die unvorstellbare Dynamik des Neuanfangs.

Ferrari LaFerrari. The balance between organic form and the beauty of complexity.
Ferrari LaFerrari. Die Balance zwischen organischer Form und komplexer Schönheit.

The essence of the brand

The first model developed, designed and built entirely in-house was the LaFerrari, which was designed by the Ferrari Design Team in close cooperation with the technical and development department. The model won a Red Dot in 2015. It was the result of a sporting competition with Pininfarina, where the Ferrari Design Team ultimately emerged as the winner.

The profile of the new vehicle dipped down prominently at the nose and featured a low hood. The nose was reminiscent of the legendary shapes of the Ferrari sports prototypes from the 1960s, for example the "sharknose" of the Ferrari 156. There was a conceptual link between the two, but no formal connection. Of course Manzoni and his design team felt a loyalty to the brand and to Ferrari's mythical aura, but they didn't simply repeat individual elements nostalgically. For them, retro design was an expression of a lack of courage and creativity. With the Ferrari LaFerrari, the designers succeeded in recalling and reinterpreting milestones in the company and design history. Not only did the concave and convex surfaces provide a dramatic tension, they also ensured outstanding wind resistance and downforce values.

Manzoni and his design team have frequently been inspired by ideas and shapes from art and culture, for example the monumental sculptures and installations of the Indian-born British artist Anish Kapoor, whose Marsyas from 2002 was on display in the Turbine Hall of the Tate Modern in London. Like Anish Kapoor, Flavio Manzoni endeavours in his designs to answer the question of how to translate performance-based engineering

Die Essenz der Marke

Das erste Modell, das ausschließlich in-house entwickelt, gestaltet und gebaut wird, ist der LaFerrari, der in enger Zusammenarbeit des Ferrari Design Teams mit der Technik- und Entwicklungsabteilung entworfen wird. 2015 wird er mit dem Red Dot ausgezeichnet. Er geht aus einem sportlichen Wettbewerb mit Pininfarina hervor, bei dem das Ferrari Design Team am Ende als Sieger dasteht.

Im Profil hat das neue Fahrzeug eine scharf nach unten verlaufende Nase und eine tief sitzende Motorhaube. Die Nase erinnert an die legendären Formen der Ferrari Sport-Prototypen der 1960er Jahre, etwa an die „Haifischnase" des Ferrari 156. Zwischen beiden gibt es eine konzeptionelle, aber keine formale Verbindung. Natürlich fühlen sich Manzoni und sein Designteam der Marke und dem Mythos Ferrari verpflichtet, aber sie wiederholen nicht einfach einzelne Elemente in nostalgischer Weise. Für sie ist Retrodesign ein Ausdruck fehlenden Mutes und mangelnder Kreativität. Mit dem Ferrari LaFerrari gelingt es den Designern, Meilensteine der Unternehmens- und Designgeschichte in Erinnerung zu rufen und sie neu zu interpretieren. Die konkaven und konvexen Oberflächen sorgen nicht nur für eine wechselvolle Spannung, sie sorgen auch für herausragende Luftwiderstands- und Abtriebswerte.

Inspiriert werden Manzoni und sein Designteam nicht selten durch Ideen und Formen der Kunst und Kultur, wie etwa durch die monumentalen Skulpturen und Installationen des indisch-britischen Künstlers Anish Kapoor, dessen Marsyas aus dem Jahr 2002 in der Turbinenhalle der Tate Modern in London zu sehen war. Ähnlich wie Anish Kapoor geht

language into an aesthetic body language. "You can only design a Ferrari if you know what's under the surface." That's how Manzoni describes the interplay between technical complexity and aesthetic design.

Manzoni describes the design process as follows: "Designing a new car requires sensitivity, imagination, abstract thought and the ability to combine elements that do not appear to belong together, at least not intuitively." Ferrari endeavours to constantly redefine the limits of technology and design and to gradually push these boundaries towards the future without losing sight of the brand and its values. "Every Ferrari stands for innovation, beauty and driving thrill," says Manzoni, adding that "every model has to embody the essence of the brand."

Naturally, we always have to bear in mind the difference between a Gran Turismo and a supercar when considering the design of Ferrari models. While the Gran Turismo wins fans through its sporting elegance and luxury, a supercar that conveys the adrenaline of the racetrack calls for a higher degree of complexity. Its form hinges on the technical data and on performance. Yet what both of these models share is the idea "that a Ferrari always stems from a dream," says Flavio Manzoni.

One key difference between Ferrari and other manufacturers in automotive design is that the Italian sports car manufacturer does not feature a rhetorical evolution of form. Neither does Ferrari pursue the strategy adopted by other manufacturers that make the models belong to the brand by means of a similarity with other members of the brand family. Although there are lines that connect back to tradition, these are never for stylistic reasons. The focus is on state-of-the-art sports car technology, formal aestheticism and driving thrill. This is also exemplified by the new "Icona" model segment, the design of which draws inspiration from the open Barchettas from the 1950s that Scuderia Ferrari raced in at the time, in particular the 166 MM, but also the 750 Monza and the 860 Monza. The new limited production Monza SP1 and Monza SP2 models with their minimalistic silhouettes are the vanguard in this new series of design icons.

The Monza SP1, which won the Red Dot: Best of the Best in 2019, is designed as a single seater, while the Monza SP2 seats two. The carbon bodywork reduces the weight of the two vehicles to 1,500 kg each. The V12 6.5-litre engine has 810 hp and in both models accelerates from 0 to 100 in 2.9 seconds, reaching 200 km/h just 5 seconds later. Because neither model has a windscreen for the driver, the panelling includes a type of "bypass" that diverts the airflow away from the driver and creates a kind of "virtual windscreen" for the driver. Ferrari has registered a patent for this innovation. The two Monza models are an excellent example of how technology and design, innovation and aesthetics can all be channelled into a unique driving experience. This allows the driver to experience a feeling of speed that is otherwise known only to Formula 1 race drivers.

Flavio Manzoni bei seinen Entwürfen der Frage nach, wie eine leistungsorientierte Ingenieursprache in eine ästhetische Körpersprache umgeformt werden kann. „Man kann einen Ferrari nur gestalten, wenn man weiß, was unter der Oberfläche stattfindet", beschreibt Manzoni das Zusammenspiel von technischer Komplexität und ästhetischer Formgebung.

„Ein neues Auto zu gestalten, erfordert Einfühlungsvermögen, Vorstellungskraft, abstraktes Denken und die Fähigkeit, Elemente zu verbinden, die scheinbar nicht zusammengehören, zumindest nicht auf den ersten Blick", beschreibt Manzoni den Designprozess. Ferrari versucht, die Grenzen der Technik und Gestaltung immer wieder neu zu bestimmen und Schritt für Schritt in Richtung Zukunft zu verschieben, ohne die Marke und ihre Werte aus dem Auge zu verlieren. „Jeder Ferrari steht für Innovation, Schönheit und Fahrleidenschaft", sagt Manzoni und ergänzt, dass „jedes Modell die Essenz der Marke verkörpern muss."

Natürlich muss man bei der Gestaltung von Ferrari-Modellen immer auch den Unterschied zwischen einem Gran Turismo und einem Supersportwagen im Blick behalten. Während der Gran Turismo durch sportliche Eleganz und luxuriösen Komfort begeistert, erfordert ein Supersportwagen, der das Adrenalin der Rennstrecke versprüht, eine höhere Komplexität. Seine Form wird entscheidend von den technischen Daten und der Leistungsfähigkeit geprägt. Aber beide vereint, „dass ein Ferrari immer aus einem Traum entsteht", sagt Flavio Manzoni.

Ein wesentlicher Unterschied zwischen Ferrari und anderen Herstellern im Automobildesign besteht darin, dass es beim italienischen Sportwagenhersteller keine rhetorische Evolution der Form gibt. Ferrari folgt auch nicht der Strategie anderer Hersteller, die Markenzugehörigkeit der Modelle nach dem Vorbild von Familienähnlichkeit zu pflegen. Obgleich es Verbindungslinien zur Tradition gibt, werden diese niemals aus stilistischen Gründen gezogen. Modernste Sportwagentechnik, die Ästhetik der Form und die Fahrleidenschaft stehen im Vordergrund. So auch im neuen Modellsegment „Icona", dessen Design von den offenen Barchettas der 1950er Jahre inspiriert wurde, mit denen die Scuderia Ferrari damals an den Start ging, insbesondere von dem 166 MM, aber auch dem 750 Monza und dem 860 Monza. Die neuen Sondermodelle Monza SP1 und Monza SP2 mit ihren minimalistischen Silhouetten bilden den Auftakt zu dieser neuen Serie von Designikonen.

Der Monza SP1, im Jahr 2019 mit dem Red Dot: Best of the Best ausgezeichnet, ist als Einsitzer konzipiert, im Monza SP2 finden zwei Personen Platz. Die Karosserie aus Carbon drückt das Gewicht der beiden Fahrzeuge auf jeweils 1.500 kg. Der V12-Motor mit 6,5 Litern Hubraum leistet 810 PS und beschleunigt die beiden Fahrzeuge in 2,9 Sekunden aus dem Stand auf Tempo 100, nur 5 Sekunden später ist Tempo 200 erreicht. Da beiden Modellen eine Windschutzscheibe für den Fahrer fehlt, ist in der Verkleidung eine Art „Bypass" eingearbeitet, der den anströmenden Fahrtwind umlenkt und eine „virtuelle Windschutzscheibe" für den Fahrer erzeugt. Ferrari hat auf diese Innovation ein Patent angemeldet. Die beiden Monza-Modelle sind ein gelungenes Beispiel dafür, wie Technik und Design, Innovation und Ästhetik auf ein einzigartiges Fahrerlebnis ausgerichtet sind. So kommt der Fahrer in den Genuss eines Geschwindigkeitsgefühls, wie es sonst nur Formel-1-Fahrer erleben.

Designing values

The dream figures recorded by the sports cars from Maranello aren't limited to the race track – the company is also doing very well in terms of its profitability and share price and market value. The Italian car maker is the most profitable company in the automotive industry and the clear leader amongst premium and luxury car manufacturers. Ferrari understands better than any other company how to make luxury sports cars objects of desire by consistently focusing on the core of the brand and pursuing the strategy of always building one car less than the market requires. If ever any proof were needed that "Good design is good business," as former IBM President Thomas Watson Jr. once said, then Ferrari has delivered that proof impressively in recent years.

The models designed by Flavio Manzoni and the Ferrari Design Team won 14 awards in the Red Dot Design Award in the years 2015 to 2019 alone. Ferrari is the first car manufacturer in the history of the competition to win the top distinction five times in a row – for the Ferrari models FXX-K, 488 GTB, J50, Portofino and Monza SP1. Thanks to this achievement, the brand now also leads the Red Dot Ranking in the Automotive Design category for the first time.

By establishing a Ferrari in-house design team as well as Centro Stile in Maranello and the Ferrari models created under his leadership, Flavio Manzoni has succeeded in his pioneering work. He has created an open and trusting culture of communication, which is the basis for shared success. The further the team progresses together, the better the cars become.

Manzoni likes to compare his team to a jazz ensemble: everyone has his or her own personal strengths and individual skill set, but each person is willing to contribute his or her creativity and social skills to a shared objective and the future of the brand. As a result, the long journey from a blank sheet of paper to a finished car is a magical experience for Manzoni every single time. When a new idea is born and the first strokes and lines put an ideal scenario to paper, he dreams that this ideal and the creative fire that fanned the ideal can permeate the entire project – right through to the finished vehicle. And every new car, every new Ferrari should intuitively express the innovation and the emotion, the values and the philosophy of Ferrari. It has to be a moving sculpture that combines art and science, technology and design into something new and propels Ferrari's mythical aura into the future.

As we know, myths are stories with a significance based on uniquely lived lives that still fascinate us today. Outstanding products follow a similar pattern. They are visionary, stand out from the rest and tell us their story. Places can also carry this myth within them. Maranello is such a place.

Werte gestalten

Traumhafte Werte erzielen die Sportwagen aus Maranello nicht nur auf der Rennstrecke, traumhafte Werte erzielt das Unternehmen auch mit Blick auf die Profitabilität und seine Börsen- und Markenwerte. Der italienische Automobilhersteller ist das profitabelste Unternehmen der Autobranche und mit Abstand der Spitzenreiter unter den Premium- und Luxusherstellern. Kein anderes Unternehmen versteht es besser, luxuriöse Sportwagen zu Objekten der Begierde zu machen, indem man sich konsequent am Markenkern orientiert und der Strategie folgt, immer ein Auto weniger zu bauen, als der Markt verlangt. Wenn die Aussage „Good design is good business" des früheren IBM-Präsidenten, Thomas Watson Jr., noch irgendeines Beweises bedurft hätte, dann hat Ferrari ihn in den zurückliegenden Jahren auf eindrucksvolle Art und Weise geliefert.

Allein in den Jahren 2015–2019 werden die von Flavio Manzoni und dem Ferrari Design Team entworfenen Modelle vierzehn Mal im Red Dot Design Award ausgezeichnet. Ein Novum in der Geschichte des Wettbewerbs: Ferrari ist es als erstem Automobilhersteller gelungen, die höchste Auszeichnung fünf Mal in Folge zu gewinnen – für die Ferrari-Modelle FXX-K, 488 GTB, J50, Portofino und Monza SP1. Mit dieser Leistung führt die Marke erstmals auch das Red Dot Ranking im Automotive Design an.

Mit dem Aufbau eines Ferrari In-house Design Teams, dem Centro Stile in Maranello und den Ferrari-Modellen, die unter seiner Federführung entstanden sind, ist Flavio Manzoni eine Pionierleistung gelungen. Er hat eine offene und vertrauensvolle Kommunikationskultur geschaffen, die die Basis für den gemeinsamen Erfolg ist. Und je weiter das Team gemeinsam voranschreitet, desto besser werden die Autos.

Manzoni vergleicht sein Team gerne mit einem Jazzensemble: Jeder hat seine persönlichen Stärken und sein individuelles Qualifikationsprofil, aber jeder von ihnen ist bereit, seine Kreativität und seine sozialen Fähigkeiten für ein gemeinsames Ziel und die Zukunft der Marke einzubringen. Daher ist der lange Weg vom leeren Blatt Papier zum fertigen Auto für Manzoni jedes Mal und immer wieder ein magisches Ereignis. Wenn eine neue Idee geboren wird und die ersten Striche und Linien eine Idealvorstellung aufs Papier bringen, dann träumt er davon, dass dieses Ideal und das kreative Feuer, das dieses Ideal entfacht hat, das gesamte Projekt durchdringen kann – bis zum fertigen Auto. Und jedes neue Auto, jeder neue Ferrari sollte die Innovation und die Emotion, die Werte und die Philosophie von Ferrari wie selbstverständlich zum Ausdruck bringen. Es muss sich um eine Skulptur in Bewegung handeln, die Wissenschaft und Kunst, Technik und Design zu etwas Neuem verbindet und den Mythos Ferrari in die Zukunft trägt.

Mythen sind bekanntlich Erzählungen, deren Bedeutung auf einzigartigen Lebensgeschichten basiert, die uns heute noch faszinieren. Herausragende Produkte folgen einem ähnlichen Muster. Sie sind visionär, ragen aus der Masse heraus und erzählen uns ihre Geschichte. Auch Orte können diesen Mythos in sich tragen. Maranello ist so ein Ort.

Ferrari's premises are not just an ensemble of factory buildings, workshops and administrative buildings. It is also a center of modern industrial architecture.

Ferraris Betriebsgelände ist nicht nur ein Ensemble aus Fabrikhallen, Werkstätten und Verwaltungsgebäuden: Es ist auch ein Zentrum moderner Industriearchitektur.

Exceeding expectations
Interview with Flavio Manzoni
Senior Vice-President for Design at Ferrari

Flavio Manzoni was born in Sardinia in 1965 and studied architecture with a specialisation in industrial design at the University of Florence, where he graduated in 1993 under Professor Roberto Segoni. His first teacher, however, was his father, who taught him to draw and awakened in him a passion for art, architecture and design. He has been impressed by the approach of the Italian design masters: Bruno Munari, Joe Colombo, Achille Castiglioni, Marco Zanuso, Enzo Mari. In particular, he was fascinated by their attitude to exploring new materials and shapes, by their way of conceiving everyday objects and tools, and by the iconic power of their products. Manzoni's interdisciplinary creativity has accompanied him throughout his career in automotive design.

After graduating, he began his professional career at Lancia in Turin. In 1999, he moved to Seat in Barcelona as the Head of Interior Design before returning to Lancia as Design Director in 2001. In 2004, he took up the role of Design Director for Fiat, Lancia and LCV. From 2007 to 2010, he was Director of Creative Design in the Volkswagen Group, where he designed many of the most recent Škoda, Bentley, Bugatti and Volkswagen models and redefined the aesthetic of those brands.

Manzoni has been Senior Vice-President for Design at Ferrari since 2010. Prof. Dr. Peter Zec and Burkhard Jacob spoke with him in Maranello about design and Ferrari's brand values.

Mr. Manzoni, before joining Ferrari in 2010, you had already worked as a designer for many different automotive brands. Regardless of where and for whom you have already worked, what do you think should be important for a designer?

That's an important question, because there is one aspect that many designers fail to consider in their work, and that's respect for the brand. I think that every designer should first try to understand and interpret the brand rather than expressing himself or herself.

Flavio Manzoni, geboren 1965 auf Sardinien, studierte Architektur mit Spezialisierung auf Industriedesign an der Universität Florenz, wo er 1993 seinen Abschluss bei Professor Roberto Segoni machte. Sein erster Lehrer war indes sein Vater, von dem er das Zeichnen lernte und der in ihm die Leidenschaft für Kunst, Architektur und Design weckte. Er war beeindruckt vom Ansatz der italienischen Meister des Designs: Bruno Munari, Joe Colombo, Achille Castiglioni, Marco Zanuso und Enzo Mari. Insbesondere ihre Einstellung gegenüber neuen Materialien und Formen, ihre Art, alltägliche Gegenstände und Werkzeuge zu konzipieren, sowie die ikonische Kraft ihrer Produkte haben ihn fasziniert. Manzonis fachübergreifende Kreativität hat ihn über seine gesamte Karriere im Automobildesign begleitet.

Nach dem Studium begann Flavio Manzoni seine Laufbahn zunächst bei Lancia in Turin. Im Jahr 1999 wechselte er als Leiter Interior Design zu Seat nach Barcelona und kehrte 2001 als Design Director zu Lancia zurück. Ab 2004 übernahm er die Position des Design Directors von Fiat, Lancia und LCV. Von 2007 bis 2010 war er Director of Creative Design im Volkswagen-Konzern, wo er viele der jüngsten Autos von Škoda, Bentley, Bugatti und Volkswagen entwarf und die Ästhetik dieser Marken neu definierte.

Seit 2010 ist Manzoni Senior Vice-President for Design bei Ferrari. Prof. Dr. Peter Zec und Burkhard Jacob sprachen mit ihm in Maranello über das Design und die Markenwerte von Ferrari.

Herr Manzoni, bevor Sie 2010 zu Ferrari kamen, haben Sie als Designer bereits für viele verschiedene Automobilmarken gearbeitet. Unabhängig davon, wo und für wen Sie bereits gearbeitet haben: Was sollte aus Ihrer Sicht für einen Designer von Bedeutung sein?

Das ist eine wichtige Frage, denn es gibt einen Aspekt, den längst nicht alle Designer bei ihrer Arbeit berücksichtigen: Das ist der Respekt vor der Marke. Ich denke, dass jeder Designer zuerst versuchen sollte, die Marke zu verstehen und zu interpretieren und nicht sich selbst auszudrücken.

That's pretty surprising to hear, because it sounds very German!

Maybe it's what I learned during my time in Germany. I think it's important for a designer to experience the brand, to feel it and breathe it in, to absorb it and gauge and understand it better without being influenced by the typical design features that may have become embedded in the memory of a designer who has been in the profession for a long time. Together with my team, I try to understand, interpret and transform the Ferrari brand.

And how would you describe the Ferrari brand, its DNA?

There's a short and simple answer to that question. The Ferrari brand is based on three elements: innovation, driving thrill and beauty. These elements are key to understanding the brand. If one of the three is missing, then it's not a Ferrari.

So how do you marry these three aspects of innovation, driving enthusiasm and beauty?

If we think about very complex products like aircraft or cars, their form is heavily informed by the technical and aerodynamic conditions. The Concorde and the Ferrari FXX-K are good examples of this. They are shaped by hundreds of technical requirements, and yet there has always been and will always be a way to make these objects more beautiful without compromising on performance.

Sie sehen uns einigermaßen überrascht, denn das klingt sehr deutsch!

Vielleicht habe ich es während meiner Zeit in Deutschland gelernt. Ich denke, es ist wichtig für einen Designer, die Marke zu erleben, sie zu spüren, einzuatmen und zu absorbieren, um sie besser beurteilen und verstehen zu können, ohne dabei von den typischen Designmerkmalen beeinflusst zu werden, die sich nach einer langen Karriere vielleicht ins Gedächtnis eingebrannt haben. Zusammen mit meinem Team versuche ich, die Marke Ferrari zu verstehen, zu interpretieren und zu transformieren.

Wie würden Sie denn die Marke Ferrari, ihre DNA beschreiben?

Nun, darauf gibt es eine ebenso einfache wie kurze Antwort. Die Marke Ferrari basiert auf drei Elementen: Innovation, Fahrleidenschaft und Schönheit. Sie sind wesentlich für das Verständnis. Fehlt einer dieser drei Faktoren, ist es kein Ferrari.

Wie bringen Sie denn den Dreiklang aus Innovation, Fahrbegeisterung und Schönheit in Einklang?

Wenn wir über sehr komplexe Produkte wie Flugzeuge oder Autos nachdenken, dann wird deren Form stark von den technischen und aerodynamischen Bedingungen bestimmt. Die Concorde und der Ferrari FXX-K sind gute Beispiele dafür. Sie werden von Hunderten technischer Anforderungen bestimmt, und doch hat es und wird es immer einen Weg geben, diese Objekte schöner zu machen, ohne dass sie an Leistung verlieren.

"Every sketch already sets out a certain idea on paper."

„Mit jeder Skizze hält man bereits eine bestimmte Idee auf Papier fest."

Flavio Manzoni – Senior Vice-President for Design

This would mean that form does not necessarily follow function?

The solution has to lie in combining creativity with technology and art with science. In principle, then, form does follow function, but there will always be scope for creativity and aesthetics.

How do you manage to bridge the gap between the past and the future, between tradition and innovation?

Each new Ferrari opens up a whole new chapter and needs its own, independent form. But that doesn't mean our design team suddenly goes crazy and makes nonsensical design suggestions or interprets the product in an absurd way. There are certainly language codes that belong to the Ferrari brand and create a link between the past and the future. However, this is an unspoken, conceptual link rather than a repetition of stylistic features.

If the design of a new Ferrari means the start of a whole new design project, is it even possible to speak of a design language at Ferrari?

Absolutely. A design language does exist, but we do not pursue the strategy adopted by other car manufacturers that make their models belong to the brand by means of a similarity with other members of the brand family. We avoid this déjà vu effect. A new Ferrari always embodies our brand values, but it does not repeat any stylistic elements. That doesn't make any sense for Ferrari.

Die Form muss also nicht automatisch der Funktion folgen?

Die Lösung kann nur in der Verbindung von Kreativität und Technik, von Kunst und Wissenschaft liegen. Im Prinzip folgt die Form also der Funktion, aber es wird immer auch Raum für Kreativität und Ästhetik geben.

Wie gelingt Ihnen dann der Brückenschlag zwischen Vergangenheit und Zukunft, zwischen Tradition und Innovation?

Jeder neue Ferrari schlägt ein neues Kapitel auf und bedarf einer eigenständigen Form. Das bedeutet aber nicht, dass unser Designteam plötzlich verrücktspielt und unsinnige Gestaltungsvorschläge oder absurde Interpretationen macht. Es gibt durchaus Sprachcodes, die zur Marke Ferrari gehören und eine Verbindung zwischen Vergangenheit und Zukunft herstellen. Dies ist aber ein gedanklicher, konzeptioneller Zusammenhang, keine Wiederholung von stilistischen Merkmalen.

Wenn die Gestaltung eines neuen Ferrari gleichbedeutend mit dem Start eines neuen Designprojektes ist, lässt sich denn dann überhaupt von einer Designsprache bei Ferrari sprechen?

Absolut. Es gibt eine Designsprache. Wir folgen aber nicht der Strategie anderer Automobilhersteller, die die Markenzugehörigkeit ihrer Modelle nach dem Vorbild von Familienähnlichkeit pflegen. Wir vermeiden einen Déjà-vu-Effekt. Ein neuer Ferrari verkörpert immer unsere Markenwerte, aber er wiederholt keine stilistischen Elemente. Das macht für Ferrari keinen Sinn.

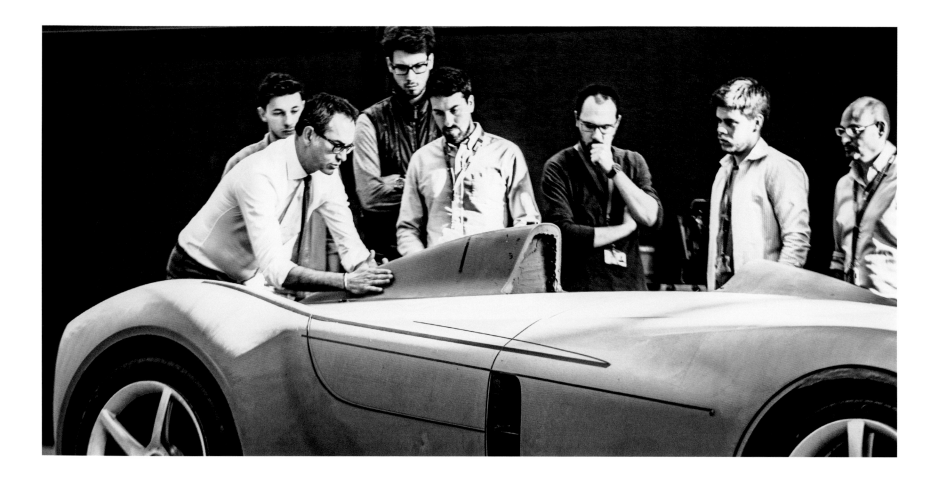

To what extent then do you even monitor the competition in your industry or compare Ferrari with other brands?

We don't compare ourselves with other brands. That's something we don't do. If we simply wanted to be different from the others, we would only have to add various distinctive elements to the interior or exterior of the car. But that's not Ferrari's approach. Otherwise I would contradict our principles and our understanding of the brand.

Can you describe to us how you and your team arrive at creative and aesthetic solutions?

The solution can either stem from the intuition of one individual or from a brainstorming session with the team. It's especially important to talk to the engineers. When we design a new Ferrari, we don't start with a blank sheet of paper, a stylistic idea or an existing form. Instead, we start with technical questions and content.

How do you start off a new project? Do you give your team a briefing, or do you use draft drawings to provide a certain direction?

Normally, I do not produce any draft drawings before my staff at the start of a new project, as I don't want to restrict the team's creativity. Because every sketch

Inwiefern beobachten Sie denn überhaupt die Konkurrenz in Ihrer Branche oder vergleichen Ferrari mit anderen Marken?

Wir vergleichen uns nicht mit anderen Marken. Das machen wir nicht. Wollten wir einfach nur anders sein als die anderen, müssten wir nur verschiedene, sich unterscheidende Elemente im oder am Auto hinzufügen. Dies ist aber nicht der Ansatz von Ferrari. Ansonsten würde ich unseren Grundsätzen und unserem Markenverständnis widersprechen.

Können Sie uns denn beschreiben, wie Sie und Ihr Team zu kreativen und ästhetischen Lösungen gelangen?

Die Lösung kann entweder in der Intuition eines Einzelnen liegen oder aus einem Brainstorming des Teams hervorgehen. Insbesondere das Gespräch mit Ingenieuren ist wichtig. Wenn wir einen neuen Ferrari gestalten, dann beginnen wir also nicht mit einem leeren Blatt Papier, einer stilistischen Idee oder einer bereits existierenden Form, sondern mit technischen Fragen und Inhalten.

Wie starten Sie in ein neues Projekt? Geben Sie Ihrem Team ein Briefing oder geben Sie durch Entwurfszeichnungen eine bestimmte Richtung vor?

Normalerweise mache ich zu Beginn eines neuen Projektes keine Entwurfszeichnungen vor meinen Mitarbeitern, weil ich die Kreativität des Teams nicht

"Every designer should first try to understand and interpret the brand."

„Jeder Designer sollte zuerst versuchen, die Marke zu verstehen und zu interpretieren."

Flavio Manzoni – Senior Vice-President for Design

already sets out a certain idea on paper. But certainly I sketch a lot, in my office, or during the development process, when it is necessary to converge and finalise ideas.

Is there internal competition in the team when designing a new model?

That's possible. But if there is internal competition, it is always fair and in good spirit. It's important to understand that the personal background and qualifications of each individual are different. That's why the composition of a team changes depending on the project.

What criteria do you use when deciding how to put a team together?

It depends on the project, the technical requirements and the timing. For example, we developed an Advanced Design Department that mainly comprises young designers and artists. Their task is to imagine the future of Ferrari and to sketch it up, far removed from technical specifications or economic restraints. They have to develop visionary ideas without any mental pressure, because the way in which they imagine the future is based on the conditions that we create here and the experiences they have here.

einschränken möchte. Denn mit jeder Skizze hält man bereits eine bestimmte Idee auf Papier fest. Aber ich fertige viele Skizzen in meinem Büro oder während des Entwicklungsprozesses an, wenn es darum geht, Ideen zusammenzuführen und zu finalisieren.

Gibt es denn innerhalb des Teams einen internen Wettbewerb, wenn es um die Gestaltung eines neuen Modells geht?

Das ist möglich. Aber wenn es einen internen Wettbewerb gibt, dann ist er immer fair und sportlich. Es ist wichtig zu verstehen, dass der persönliche Hintergrund und die Qualifikation jedes Einzelnen unterschiedlich sind. Deshalb ändert sich je nach Projekt die Zusammensetzung eines Teams.

Nach welchen Kriterien entscheiden Sie über die Zusammensetzung eines Teams?

Es hängt vom Projekt ab, den technischen Anforderungen und dem Zeitpunkt. Wir haben beispielsweise ein Advanced Design Department ins Leben gerufen, das im Wesentlichen aus jungen Designern und Künstlern besteht. Ihre Aufgabe ist es, sich die Zukunft von Ferrari vorzustellen und sie zu skizzieren, weit entfernt von technischen Vorgaben oder ökonomischen Bedingungen. Sie sollen visionäre Ideen entwickeln ohne mentalen Druck, denn die Art und Weise, wie sie sich die Zukunft vorstellen, basiert auf den Bedingungen, die wir hier schaffen, und den Erfahrungen, die sie hier machen.

You seem to have a very broad understanding of design and see it as more than just the task of finding an aesthetic form for a technical function.

In my view, design is a communicative and cultural process that culminates not just in a car but in a cultural object. I have developed this deeper understanding of design during my time at Ferrari.

If, as you say, design is a cultural process, is a Ferrari more than just a car?

A Ferrari is not just a car, it's an object of desire. We say that it's a dream, a dynamic sculpture. Something that goes far beyond a car. Maybe I'm not a typical car designer in this respect. I have always pursued a multidisciplinary approach, and I try to develop a much broader view of design, particularly automotive design.

Yet there are undeniable technical requirements that the design has to meet.

Of course. But we view the technical specifications or technical limitations as an opportunity for design, because there are limitations in all aspects of life. Limitations should inspire us to find new and unique solutions. We shift the boundaries of what is possible by transcending those boundaries time after time.

Sie scheinen ein sehr weites Verständnis von Design zu haben und sehen darin nicht nur die Aufgabe, eine ästhetische Form für eine technische Funktion zu finden.

Aus meiner Sicht ist Design ein kommunikativer und kultureller Prozess, an dessen Ende nicht einfach nur ein Auto, sondern ein Kulturobjekt steht. Während meiner Zeit bei Ferrari habe ich dieses tiefere Verständnis für Design entwickelt.

Wenn Design ein kultureller Prozess ist, wie Sie sagen: Ist dann ein Ferrari mehr als nur ein Auto?

Ein Ferrari ist nicht nur ein Auto, sondern ein Objekt der Begierde. Es ist ein Traum, wie wir zu sagen pflegen, eine dynamische Skulptur. Das geht weit über ein Auto hinaus. Vielleicht bin ich in dieser Hinsicht auch kein typischer Autodesigner. Ich habe schon immer einen multidisziplinären Ansatz verfolgt und versuche, eine viel breitere Sichtweise auf das Design, insbesondere auf das Automobildesign zu entwickeln.

Und doch gibt es unweigerlich technische Anforderungen, die das Design erfüllen muss.

Natürlich. Wir betrachten die technischen Bedingungen oder technischen Einschränkungen aber als Chance für das Design, denn Einschränkungen sind überall vorhanden. Einschränkungen sollten unsere Fantasie anregen, um neue und einzigartige Lösungen zu finden. Wir verschieben die Grenzen des Möglichen, indem wir sie immer wieder überschreiten.

"The Ferrari brand is based on three elements: innovation, driving thrill and beauty."

"Die Marke Ferrari basiert auf drei Elementen: Innovation, Fahrleidenschaft und Schönheit."

Flavio Manzoni – Senior Vice-President for Design

One of our jury members, Ken Okuyama, always used to say: "I design the cars that I can't afford myself." You and your team design luxury objects. But many of your designers are very young. How is it possible to design luxury that one can potentially not enjoy oneself?

There are different types of enjoyment. The enjoyment of owning a Ferrari, but also the enjoyment of creating a Ferrari.

Is that just a clever dodge?

Not at all. Designing a Ferrari means being allowed to dream and follow an idea that becomes a design object for our customers. Achilles Castiglioni once summarised this feeling very nicely when he said that design is like a delayed conversation with a customer. So there is also always a conversation about the design objects and symbols that we as designers create.

Is there a typical Ferrari customer or a typical Ferrari driver?

We always say: "Different Ferrari for different Ferraristi."

Einer unserer Juroren, Ken Okuyama, pflegte immer zu sagen: „Ich gestalte die Autos, die ich mir selbst nicht leisten kann." Sie und Ihr Team gestalten Luxusobjekte. Aber viele Ihrer Designer sind sehr jung. Wie kann man Luxus gestalten, den man selbst vielleicht nicht ausleben kann?

Nun, es gibt durchaus unterschiedliche Freuden. Die Freude, einen Ferrari zu besitzen, aber auch die Freude, einen Ferrari zu gestalten.

Ist das ein geschicktes Ausweichmanöver?

Keinesfalls. Die Gestaltung eines Ferrari bedeutet, träumen zu dürfen und einer Idee folgen zu können, die für unsere Kunden zu einem Designobjekt wird. Achilles Castiglioni hat dieses Gefühl einmal sehr schön zusammengefasst, indem er sagte, dass Design so etwas wie eine zeitversetzte Konversation mit einem Kunden sei. Es gibt also immer auch eine Konversation über die Designobjekte und Symbole, die wir als Designer schaffen.

Gibt es denn den typischen Ferrari-Kunden oder den typischen Fahrer eines Ferrari?

Wir pflegen immer zu sagen: „Different Ferrari for different Ferraristi."

"Design is a communicative and cultural process."
„Design ist ein kommunikativer und kultureller Prozess."

Flavio Manzoni – Senior Vice-President for Design

That's a clever answer!

It's the truth. The Ferraristi of a GT are not the same as the Ferraristi who drive an XX. They are entirely different people. They also have a completely different idea of what innovation, driving thrill and beauty mean. But ultimately every Ferrari will meet or exceed the different expectations.

How can these different perceptions of the Ferraristi be summed up in a design philosophy?

There's a wonderful quote that is said to have come from Plato: "Beauty is the splendour of truth." That basically explains and describes Ferrari. I think it fits perfectly.

Thank you for talking to us, Mr. Manzoni, and congratulations on winning the title "Red Dot: Design Team of the Year".

Das ist natürlich eine clevere Antwort!

Es ist die Wahrheit. Die Ferraristi eines GT sind nicht identisch mit den Ferraristi, die einen XX fahren. Es sind völlig verschiedene Menschen. Sie haben auch eine völlig unterschiedliche Vorstellung von Innovation, Fahrleidenschaft und Schönheit. Aber am Ende wird jeder Ferrari die unterschiedlichen Erwartungen erfüllen oder übertreffen.

Wie lassen sich denn diese unterschiedlichen Wahrnehmungen der Ferraristi in einer Designphilosophie zusammenfassen?

Es gibt dieses wunderbare Zitat, das angeblich auf Platon zurückgeht: „Schönheit ist der Glanz der Wahrheit." Im Grunde erklärt und beschreibt es Ferrari. Ich denke, es passt perfekt.

Vielen Dank für das Gespräch, Herr Manzoni, und herzlichen Glückwunsch zur Auszeichnung „Red Dot: Design Team of the Year".

Red Dot: Best of the Best
The best designers of their category
Die besten Designer ihrer Kategorie

The designers of the Red Dot: Best of the Best
Only a few products in the Red Dot Design Award
receive the "Red Dot: Best of the Best" accolade.
In each category, the jury can assign this award to
products of outstanding design quality and innovative
achievement. Exploring new paths, these products are
all exemplary in their design and oriented towards the
future.

The following chapter introduces the people who have
received one of these prestigious awards. It features
the best designers and design teams of the year 2019
together with their products, revealing in interviews
and statements what drives these designers and what
design means to them.

Die Designer der Red Dot: Best of the Best
Nur sehr wenige Produkte im Red Dot Design Award
erhalten die Auszeichnung „Red Dot: Best of the
Best". Die Jury kann mit dieser Auszeichnung in jeder
Kategorie Design von außerordentlicher Qualität
und Innovationsleistung besonders hervorheben. In
jeder Hinsicht vorbildlich gestaltet, beschreiten diese
Produkte neue Wege und sind zukunftsweisend.

Das folgende Kapitel stellt die Menschen vor, die diese
besondere Auszeichnung erhalten haben. Es zeigt
die besten Designer und Designteams des Jahres 2019
zusammen mit ihren Produkten. In Interviews und
Statements wird deutlich, was diese Designer bewegt
und was ihnen Design bedeutet.

Sebastian Meinecke
Urwahn Engineering GmbH

"Design engineering to perfection."

Do you have a specific design approach for your work as a designer?
During the creation of our products, it is critically important not to see things with the eyes of a design junky, because we want to offer the user more than just emotional added value. That is why the staged approach of integrated design engineering is the key tool we rely on in our development process. It is founded on the axioms of design, ergonomics, function, quality and safety which form the basis of our Urwahn Bikes.

How do you define design quality?
Design is in the eye of the beholder. So, as far as I'm concerned there's no right or wrong. However, design quality is a deciding factor that can greatly influence creative interpretation and the emotional reaction of the viewer.

Liegt Ihrer Arbeit als Designer ein bestimmter Gestaltungsansatz zugrunde?
Bei der Konzeption unserer Produkte ist es von fundamentaler Bedeutung, sie nicht nur aus dem Blickwinkel eines Designjunkies zu betrachten, weil wir dem Nutzer mehr als einen emotionalen Mehrwert bieten möchten. Daher bildet das phasenorientierte Vorgehensmodell des Integrated Design Engineerings das zentrale Instrument unserer Entwicklung, dessen Axiome Design, Ergonomie, Funktion, Qualität und Sicherheit in der Gestalt unserer Urwahn Bikes begründet sind.

Wie definieren Sie Designqualität?
Design liegt zunächst im Auge des Betrachters, sodass für mich kein Richtig und kein Falsch existiert. Dennoch ist die Qualität des Designs ein entscheidender Faktor, der die gestalterische Interpretation und die emotionale Reaktion des Betrachters deutlich beeinflussen kann.

reddot award 2019
best of the best

Manufacturer
Urwahn Engineering GmbH,
Magdeburg, Germany

Stadtfuchs
Urban Bike

See page 78
Siehe Seite 78

Adrien Roose, Tanguy Goretti, Karim Slaoui
COWBOY

"You can't stop a Cowboy."

„Einen Cowboy kann man nicht aufhalten."

What was your goal when you designed your award-winning product?
Cowboys like us never settle for the status quo. We always look for ways to make great even better. So that's why we designed improvements into 2.0 version of our electric, connected bike, featuring a motor system that delivers power and speed when needed, without gears to shift or buttons to push. The result is like riding an electric bike with an intuitive transmission.

How do you define design quality?
Design quality is self-evident when your customers easily and fully experience an incredibly complex product and an un-prompted smile of pleasure or joy creeps across their face.

Welches Ziel verfolgten Sie bei der Gestaltung Ihres ausgezeichneten Produktes?
Cowboys wie wir geben sich nie mit dem Status quo zufrieden. Wir suchen immer nach Möglichkeiten, wie wir das Großartige noch besser machen können. Das ist der Grund, warum wir Verbesserungen für die 2.0-Version unseres elektrischen, vernetzten Fahrrads entwickelt haben. Es hat ein Motor-system, das die nötige Leistung und Ge-schwindigkeit bietet, ohne dass man Gänge verstellen oder Knöpfe drücken muss. Das Ergebnis fühlt sich so an, als fahre man ein elektrisches Rad mit intuitivem Getriebe.

Wie definieren Sie Designqualität?
Designqualität ist offensichtlich, wenn der Kunde ein höchst komplexes Produkt einfach und in seiner Gänze erlebt und ein spontanes Lächeln sein Gesicht überzieht.

reddot award 2019
best of the best

Manufacturer
COWBOY, Brussels, Belgium

COWBOY
E-Bike

See page 80
Siehe Seite 80

Flavio Manzoni
Ferrari Design

"Beauty is the splendour of truth."

„Schönheit ist der Glanz des Wahren."

Plato

What was your goal when you designed your award-winning product?
Right from the beginning of the project, the Ferrari Design team and I have been aware that we were going to create something very important, a car in which to concentrate both technical skills and aesthetic research. A true single-seater roadster, the Monza SP1 is recognisable by its singular asymmetrical structure, the "monolithic" profile of the bodywork and the purity of the design. Produced in a limited edition and equipped with a 12-cylinder engine, it's the first of a new "Icon" series that takes inspiration from the most evocative Ferraris of the Fifties to introduce and elaborate new technical and formal themes through a unique imaginative projection into the future. Conceived as an enduring badge, the design reaffirms the symbiotic man-machine relationship and transfers the emotional perceptions of racing cars into a car destined for road use.

Welches Ziel verfolgten Sie bei der Gestaltung Ihres ausgezeichneten Produktes?
Seit den Anfängen des Projektes sind das Ferrari Design Team und ich uns bewusst gewesen, dass wir dabei waren, etwas sehr Bedeutendes zu gestalten: ein Auto, in dem sich technische Fähigkeiten und ästhetische Erforschung konzentriert bündeln. Der Monza SP1 ist ein richtiger einsitziger Roadster und durch seine einzigartige, asymmetrische Struktur, das „monolithische" Profil der Karosserie und die Reinheit des Designs sofort erkennbar. In limitierter Auflage und mit 12-Zylinder-Motor ist er das erste Modell der neuen „Icon"-Serie, die von den eindrucksvollsten Ferraris der 50er Jahre inspiriert wird. Allerdings greift die Serie neue technische und formale Themen in einer besonders phantasievollen Projektion in die Zukunft auf und verfeinert sie. Als beständiges Emblem bekräftigt das Design wieder die symbiotische Mensch-Maschine-Beziehung und überträgt die emotionale Wahrnehmung eines Rennwagens auf ein Auto, das für die Straße bestimmt ist.

reddot award 2019
best of the best

Manufacturer
Ferrari S.p.A., Maranello (Modena), Italy

Ferrari Monza SP1
Sports Car
Sportwagen

See page 98
Siehe Seite 98

36

Yasutake Tsuchida
Mazda Motor Corporation

"Car as art."

Who or what inspires you?
Japanese aesthetics. Beauty through subtraction is the key principle for the design of Mazda3. Specifically, we eliminated lines to emphasise beautiful reflections on the body. It's more than just being minimalist. Making pure design requires great effort and refinement through trial and error, which we believe can only be created by human hands.

How do you define design quality?
Quality design is something that is not swayed by short-sighted trends but design that lasts over time.

How do you keep abreast of new developments?
Mazda does not chase trends, instead we face our own roots and pursue Japanese aesthetics. This is because we believe that beauty transcends times and borders.

Wer oder was inspiriert Sie?
Die japanische Ästhetik. Schönheit durch Subtraktion ist das Grundprinzip für die Gestaltung des Mazda3. Insbesondere haben wir Linien entfernt, um die schönen Reflexionen auf der Karosserie hervorzuheben. Das ist mehr als Minimalismus. Klares Design erfordert große Anstrengungen und Verfeinerungen mittels Versuch und Irrtum – eine Methode, die unserer Meinung nach nur von Menschen ausgeführt werden kann.

Wie definieren Sie Designqualität?
Qualitätsdesign ist etwas, das sich nicht von kurzfristigen Trends beeinflussen lässt, sondern die Zeit überdauert.

Wie bleiben Sie über aktuelle Entwicklungen auf dem Laufenden?
Mazda jagt keinen Trends hinterher. Stattdessen konzentrieren wir uns auf unsere Wurzeln und folgen der japanischen Ästhetik. Denn wir glauben, dass Schönheit über Zeiten und Grenzen hinweg wirkt.

reddot **award** 2019
best of the best

Manufacturer
Mazda Motor Corporation,
Hiroshima, Japan

Mazda3
Passenger Car
Personenkraftwagen

See page 102
Siehe Seite 102

Centro Stile Ducati

"Style, sophistication and performance."

„Stil, Raffinesse und Leistung."

What was your goal when you designed your award-winning product?
Our goal was to combine three completely different kinds of bike in order to deliver the bike that didn't yet exist: a sport naked bike, a superbike – Ducati's core product – and a cruiser. The outcome is a segment-defining bike that blends performance, comfort, confidence-inspiring ergonomics and a bold, unique and unmistakable design.

Who or what inspires you?
In the specific case of the Diavel 1260, the inspiration came from the world of American muscle cars, with their over-the-top and aggressive design; from superhero comics; from dystopian movies' imagery; and from hi-tech products, where technology becomes a key design element.

Welches Ziel verfolgten Sie bei der Gestaltung Ihres ausgezeichneten Produktes?
Unser Ziel war die Kombination von drei vollkommen verschiedenen Motorrädern, um ein nie vorher dagewesenes Motorrad zu entwickeln: eine sportliche Variante des Naked Bikes, ein Superbike – Ducatis Hauptprodukt – und einen Cruiser. Ergebnis ist ein branchenbestimmendes Motorrad, das Leistung, Komfort, vertrauenswürdige Ergonomie und eine gewagte, einzigartige und unverkennbare Gestaltung verbindet.

Wer oder was inspiriert Sie?
Im speziellen Fall des Diavel 1260 kam die Inspiration aus der Welt der amerikanischen Muscle-Cars mit ihren überzogenen und aggressiven Designs, von Comics über Superhelden, von der Bildsprache dystopischer Filme und von Hightech-Produkten, in denen die Technik ein wesentliches Designelement ist.

reddot award 2019
best of the best

Manufacturer
Ducati Motor Holding S.p.A., Bologna, Italy

Ducati Diavel 1260
Motorcycle
Motorrad

See page 110
Siehe Seite 110

Masahiro Yasuda – Yamaha Motor Co., Ltd.
Shogo Kinoshita – GK Dynamics Inc.

"Think simple, think positive."

„Einfach denken, positiv denken."

What was your goal when you designed your award-winning product?
We wanted to become pioneers of opening up new possibilities for mobility by taking on the challenge of creating a sport-focused entry in our line-up of LMWs (Leaning Multi-Wheeler), and thereby create new value and excitement.

How do you define design quality?
As beauty. This of course includes a design's form, but a quality design often has a beauty that can influence even a person's behaviour.

Where will your industry be in ten years?
The market for mobility, the mentality of customers, and the values they hold may drastically change in the future, but we believe the unique fun and excitement people can experience through mobility will remain unchanged.

Welches Ziel verfolgten Sie bei der Gestaltung Ihres ausgezeichneten Produktes?
Wir wollten Vorreiter in der Entdeckung neuer Möglichkeiten der Mobilität werden, indem wir uns der Herausforderung stellten, eine sportliche Ergänzung für unsere LMW-Familie (Leaning Multi-Wheeler) zu gestalten und so eine neue Wertigkeit und Begeisterung zu bieten.

Wie definieren Sie Designqualität?
Als Schönheit. Das beinhaltet selbstverständlich die Formgebung einer Gestaltung, doch zeigt Designqualität oft auch eine Ästhetik, die sogar das Verhalten von Menschen beeinflussen kann.

Wo wird Ihre Branche in zehn Jahren stehen?
Der Mobilitätsmarkt, die Denkweise von Kunden und die Werte, die sie haben, können in der Zukunft radikal anders sein. Doch glauben wir, dass die einmalige Freude und Begeisterung, die Mobilität Menschen bietet, unverändert bleiben wird.

reddot award 2019
best of the best

Manufacturer
Yamaha Motor Co., Ltd.,
Iwata City, Shizuoka Prefecture, Japan

NIKEN
Motorcycle
Motorrad

See page 112
Siehe Seite 112

Oep Schilling, Vincent Beekman, Sander Ejlenberg
Cabiner

"Connecting people with nature."

„Die Menschen mit der Natur verbinden."

What was your goal when you designed your award-winning product?
To enable people to experience natural wilderness in an adventurous and comfortable way. The off-grid cabin design fits into its natural surroundings and uses renewable natural materials. The idea is that visitors need to make an effort to create comfort. The interior should be simple and intuitive.

Do you have a specific design approach for your work as a designer?
Start with the basic human needs and keep it simple.

What is your personal vision for the future?
To look to the future we need to take cues from the past. Technologies change fast but basic human needs stay constant.

Welches Ziel verfolgten Sie bei der Gestaltung Ihres ausgezeichneten Produktes?
Wir wollten es Menschen ermöglichen, die natürliche Wildnis auf abenteuerliche und bequeme Weise zu erleben. Die Off-Grid-Hütte passt sich der natürlichen Umgebung an und wird aus erneuerbaren Materialien gebaut. Die Idee ist, dass sich Besucher bemühen müssen, Komfort zu erzeugen. Die Inneneinrichtung sollte schlicht und intuitiv sein.

Liegt Ihrer Arbeit als Designer ein bestimmter Gestaltungsansatz zugrunde?
Mit den menschlichen Grundbedürfnissen beginnen und dann das Ganze möglichst einfach halten.

Wie sieht Ihre persönliche Zukunftsvision aus?
Um in die Zukunft blicken zu können, müssen wir Signale aus der Vergangenheit beachten. Technologien wandeln sich schnell, doch menschliche Grundbedürfnisse bleiben unverändert.

reddot **award** 2019
best of the best

Manufacturer
Wikkelhouse, Amsterdam, Netherlands

Cabiner
Off-Grid Hiking Cabin
Off-Grid-Wanderhütte

See page 130
Siehe Seite 130

Philips Design
Signify Design Team

"A passion for the meaning of light."

„Eine Leidenschaft für die Bedeutung von Licht."

What was your goal when you designed your award-winning product?
Keen drivers want the best for their cars, so our aim was to offer them a step change in quality and efficiency over current lighting products. Performance was obviously the key factor, but we wanted to achieve that within an attractive, elegant design. Harnessing the latest technology was central to the process.

Who or what inspires you?
We're strong believers in the value of intuitive design that brings clear functional benefits while appealing to the eye. For us, there's beauty in technology.

Why did you become a designer?
For two reasons. Firstly, because there isn't a product or service out there that can't be improved by good design, and secondly, because we enjoy the challenge of exceeding expectations.

Welches Ziel verfolgten Sie bei der Gestaltung Ihres ausgezeichneten Produktes?
Leidenschaftliche Autofahrer wollen für ihre Autos das Beste. Unser Ziel war daher, ihnen eine deutlich verbesserte Qualität und Leistungsfähigkeit unserer aktuellen Beleuchtungsprodukte zu bieten. Leistung war natürlich ausschlaggebend, doch wollten wir sie mit einem ansprechenden, eleganten Design verbinden. Wesentlich für den Prozess war der Einsatz modernster Technologie.

Wer oder was inspiriert Sie?
Wir sind zutiefst vom Wert einer intuitiven Gestaltung überzeugt, die klare funktionale Vorteile bietet und gleichzeitig optisch ansprechend ist. Für uns hat Technologie etwas Schönes.

Warum sind Sie Designer geworden?
Aus zwei Gründen: erstens, weil es kein Produkt oder keine Dienstleistung gibt, die nicht durch gute Gestaltung verbessert werden kann, und zweitens, weil wir Spaß daran haben, Erwartungen zu übertreffen.

reddot award 2019
best of the best

Manufacturer
Lumileds, Suresnes, France

Philips X-tremeUltinon gen2 LED retrofit
LED Automotive Lighting
LED-Fahrzeugbeleuchtung

See page 136
Siehe Seite 136

Dr. Paolo Cattaneo
MOMODESIGN

"Redefining the urban standard."

„Den urbanen Standard neu definieren."

Do you have a specific design approach for your work as a designer?
The design studio approach is never focused only on the project itself but is based primarily on a global vision of the market. We constantly try to reinterpret the concept of style and urban life by designing objects that meet the needs of new market signals.

Who or what inspires you?
Man has always been at the centre of our thoughts, with his desires, his requirements and his urban lifestyle. The metropolitan cities that continuously change and create new trends are our inspiration. This is our starting point when developing new products enriched in design, style and practicality, aimed at satisfying customers' new requirements and new expectations.

Liegt Ihrer Arbeit als Designer ein bestimmter Gestaltungsansatz zugrunde?
Der Ansatz unseres Designstudios beschränkt sich nie nur auf das Projekt, sondern basiert in erster Linie auf einer globalen Vision des Marktes. Wir versuchen ständig, das Konzept von Stil und urbanem Leben neu zu interpretieren, indem wir Objekte gestalten, die auf die Anforderungen neuer Marktsignale eingehen.

Wer oder was inspiriert Sie?
Schon immer stand der Mensch mit seinen Wünschen, seinen Bedürfnissen und seinem urbanen Lebensstil im Mittelpunkt unserer Ideen. Metropolen, die einem ständigen Wandel unterliegen und neue Trends auslösen, bilden unsere Quelle der Inspiration. Das ist unser Ausgangspunkt für die Entwicklung neuer Produkte, die wir mit Design, Stil und Zweckmäßigkeit anreichern. So versuchen wir, neue Anforderungen und neue Erwartungen der Verbraucher zu befriedigen.

reddot award 2019
best of the best

Manufacturer
MOMODESIGN, Milan, Italy

MOMODESIGN AERO
Motorcycle Helmet
Motorradhelm

See page 152
Siehe Seite 152

Mark van Roon, Jasper den Dekker
REV'IT! Sport International B.V.

"Inspire to ride."

„Zum Fahren inspirieren."

What was your goal when you designed your award-winning product?
The REV'IT! Expedition H2O boots have been designed to marry optimum protection, unrivalled endurance and the highest degree of comfort on and off the bike. Most adventure boots sacrifice comfort to allow a higher degree of protection. But settling for compromises was not an option, so we set ourselves the challenge to combine CE requirements, ergonomic engineering, functional design and top-level components in a highly comfortable, protective and waterproof adventure boot.

How do you define design quality?
Good product design serves or even creates a need and therefore enables people to do or experience something they have never been able to do or experience before. The real added value is not in the product or in the integrated solution itself, but in what the product enables, inspires and encourages you to do.

Welches Ziel verfolgten Sie bei der Gestaltung Ihres ausgezeichneten Produktes?
Die Stiefel REV'IT! Expedition H2O wurden für optimalen Schutz, unvergleichliche Belastbarkeit und den höchsten Grad an Komfort neben oder auf dem Motorrad konzipiert. Viele Adventure-Stiefel opfern Bequemlichkeit, um mehr Schutz bieten zu können. Doch Kompromisse waren für uns keine Option. Wir wollten CE-Anforderungen, Ergonomie, funktionale Gestaltung und erstklassige Komponenten verbinden, um sehr bequeme, Schutz bietende und wasserfeste Adventure-Stiefel zu kreieren.

Wie definieren Sie Designqualität?
Gutes Produktdesign bedient oder schafft sogar ein Bedürfnis und erlaubt Menschen, etwas zu tun oder zu erleben, das sie nie zuvor tun oder erleben konnten. Der wahre Mehrwert liegt nicht im Produkt oder der integrierten Lösung, sondern darin, wie das Produkt jemanden zu etwas befähigt, inspiriert oder bestärkt.

reddot award 2019
best of the best

Manufacturer
REV'IT! Sport International B.V.,
Oss, Netherlands

Expedition H2O
Motorcycle Boots
Motorradstiefel

See page 154
Siehe Seite 154

Fiskars Finland Oy Ab

"All things, even the simplest, can be made easier and smarter."
„Alle Dinge, selbst die simpelsten, können einfacher und intelligenter
 gemacht werden."

What was your goal when you
designed your award-winning product?
High user experience and performance.

Who or what inspires you?
Nordic nature.

When are you at your most creative?
The invention of new technologies
enables us to stay creative.

What is your personal vision for the
future?
Making the everyday extraordinary.

What does winning the Red Dot:
Best of the Best mean to you?
It is an indication of good design quality.

Welches Ziel verfolgten Sie bei der
Gestaltung Ihres ausgezeichneten
Produktes?
Hohe Benutzerfreundlichkeit und Leistung.

Wer oder was inspiriert Sie?
Die nordische Natur.

Wann sind Sie besonders kreativ?
Die Erfindung neuer Technologien erlaubt
es uns, auch weiterhin kreativ zu bleiben.

Wie sieht Ihre persönliche Zukunftsvision aus?
Das Alltägliche außergewöhnlich zu machen.

Was bedeutet die Auszeichnung mit
dem Red Dot: Best of the Best für Sie?
Es ist ein Zeichen guter Designqualität.

reddot award 2019
best of the best

Manufacturer
Fiskars Finland Oy Ab, Helsinki, Finland

Fiskars Norden
Axes
Äxte

See page 176
Siehe Seite 176

Oliver Schweizer
Schweizer Design Consulting

"Strategy – Dialogue – Character."
„Strategie – Dialog – Charakter."

What was your goal when you designed your award-winning product?
Our team combines analytical with creative thinking. We approach the core of a product step by step in order to give it a strong character. The goal is to achieve that special moment which a well-designed product evokes from the very first instant.

Who or what inspires you?
Inspiration waits around every corner. You can find solutions to big problems in the smallest things. There is also freedom for creativity in structure and order. It is important to bear this in mind.

What is your personal vision for the future?
I would like to sharpen the awareness of companies for good design. That's what I'm working on in order to create contemporary and aesthetic products with character.

Welches Ziel verfolgten Sie bei der Gestaltung Ihres ausgezeichneten Produktes?
Unser Team kombiniert analytisches mit kreativem Denken. Wir nähern uns dabei Stück für Stück dem Kern eines Produktes, um einen starken Charakter zu gestalten. Ziel ist der spezielle Moment, den ein gut gestaltetes Produkt vom ersten Augenblick an hervorruft.

Wer oder was inspiriert Sie?
Inspiration lauert hinter jeder Ecke. Man kann in den kleinsten Dingen Lösungen für große Probleme finden. Auch in Struktur und Ordnung sind Spielräume für Kreativität verborgen. Wichtig ist, den Blick dafür nicht zu verlieren.

Wie sieht Ihre persönliche Zukunftsvision aus?
Es ist mir ein Anliegen, das Bewusstsein der Unternehmen für gutes Design zu schärfen. Daran arbeite ich, damit zeitgemäße und ästhetische Produkte mit Charakter entstehen.

reddot award 2019
best of the best

Manufacturer
Lampuga GmbH, Rastatt, Germany

Lampuga Air
Electric Surfboard
Elektro-Surfboard

See page 188
Siehe Seite 188

Kunihiko Tanaka
FUJIFILM Corporation

What was your goal when you designed your award-winning product?
To design a beautiful projector that stimulates creativity.

When are you at your most creative?
When relaxing and walking.

How do you define design quality?
Beautiful, easy to use, not broken.

How do you keep abreast of new developments?
Talk to the front-line users and experience the latest content.

Where will your industry be in ten years?
We think it will be more enjoyable by projecting images more freely and easily.

Welches Ziel verfolgten Sie bei der Gestaltung Ihres ausgezeichneten Produktes?
Einen schönen Projektor zu gestalten, der die Kreativität fördert.

Wann sind Sie besonders kreativ?
Wenn wir entspannt sind und beim Wandern.

Wie definieren Sie Designqualität?
Schön, einfach anzuwenden, nicht gebrochen.

Wie bleiben Sie über aktuelle Entwicklungen auf dem Laufenden?
Durch Gespräche mit den Endnutzern und die Erfahrung der neuesten Inhalte.

Wo wird Ihre Branche in zehn Jahren stehen?
Wir sind der Meinung, dass sie angenehmer sein wird, weil Bilder dann freier und leichter projiziert werden können.

reddot award 2019
best of the best

Manufacturer
FUJIFILM Corporation, Tokyo, Japan

FP-Z5000
Projector
Projektor

See page 206
Siehe Seite 206

Seonkyu Kim, Cheolwoong Shin, Minjae Lee, Hyunbyung Cha, Yunjoo Kim, Young Kyung Kim
LG Electronics Inc.

"Emptying and Filling."
„Leeren und Füllen."

Do you have a specific design approach for your work as a designer?
When designing a product, we first consider whether the design contains the concept and ease of use suitable for the purpose of the product. We think this is the most important function of the design. Another important criterion is how valid the proposed concept is for our daily life.

How do you define design quality?
There need not be perfection in a design. We should try hard every time to create a more convenient and reasonable design rather than thinking about producing a perfect design. There is a big difference in the purpose and usability of products that are produced in this way and those that do not go through such a process. A clear design philosophy is the first step towards improving the quality of the design.

Liegt Ihrer Arbeit als Designer ein bestimmter Gestaltungsansatz zugrunde?
Wenn wir ein Produkt gestalten, überlegen wir zuerst, ob die Gestaltung das Konzept und die Anwenderfreundlichkeit bietet, die für den Zweck des Produkts angemessen sind. Wir glauben, dass das die wichtigste Funktion der Gestaltung ist. Ein weiteres wichtiges Kriterium ist, wie wirksam das vorgeschlagene Konzept im täglichen Gebrauch ist.

Wie definieren Sie Designqualität?
Ein Design muss nicht unbedingt Perfektion bieten. Wir sollten jedes Mal bemüht sein, eine praktischere, angemessenere Gestaltung zu entwickeln, anstatt darüber nachzudenken, ob wir ein perfektes Design schaffen können. Es gibt einen großen Unterschied zwischen den Produkten, die diesem Ansatz folgen, und denen, die keinen solchen Prozess durchlaufen. Eine klare Designphilosophie ist der erste Schritt, um die Qualität des Designs zu verbessern.

reddot award 2019
best of the best

Manufacturer
LG Electronics Inc., Seoul, South Korea

LG Signature R9
OLED TV

See page 212
Siehe Seite 212

Stefan Hohn
Noto GmbH

"Enriching life with elaborate design solutions."

„Das Leben mit durchdachten Gestaltungslösungen bereichern."

What was your goal when you designed your award-winning product?
We wanted to make the features and possibilities of the smart home system visible and accessible at the push of a button.

When are you at your most creative?
Being creative for me is not an isolated thing. Working together with others and triggering each other's ideas can multiply output by far.

How do you define design quality?
Exceptional design quality is not solely focusing on solving a problem or reducing complexity for the users, it should also enrich their daily activities and interactions with the products.

Welches Ziel verfolgten Sie bei der Gestaltung Ihres ausgezeichneten Produktes?
Wir wollten die Funktionen und Möglichkeiten intelligenter Haustechnik sichtbar und mit einem Knopfdruck zugänglich machen.

Wann sind Sie besonders kreativ?
Für mich ist kreativ sein nicht etwas, das man isoliert betrachten kann. Die Zusammenarbeit mit anderen und das gegenseitige Auslösen von Ideen kann den Output um ein Vielfaches vergrößern.

Wie definieren Sie Designqualität?
Außergewöhnliche Designqualität bedeutet, sich nicht nur auf die Lösung eines Problems oder die Reduzierung von Komplexität für den Nutzer zu konzentrieren, sondern den alltäglichen Umgang mit den Produkten für ihn darüber hinaus zu einer Bereicherung zu machen.

reddot award 2019
best of the best

Manufacturer
Crestron Electronics, Inc.,
Rockleigh, New Jersey, USA

TSR-310
Remote Control
Fernbedienung

See page 222
Siehe Seite 222

Yujin Morisawa
Sony Corporation, Creative Center

"Act before thinking, with an unwavering spirit of inquiry and ability
 to get things done."
„Handle vor dem Nachdenken, mit einem unbeirrbaren Forschergeist und
 der Fähigkeit, Dinge zu bewegen."

What was your goal when you designed your award-winning product?
I aimed to create a shape that is stable yet lightweight enough to have a soft presence, while at the same time not sacrificing sound in order to deliver superior audio.

Do you have a specific design approach for your work as a designer?
Most important is to understand the attributes of what I'm going to be designing, the product's purpose and its design concepts, then to have a "dialogue" with the item itself to know what form it innately "wants" to have.

What is your personal vision for the future?
My goal is to one day no longer be referred to as a designer. I want to create the environment that I live in on my own, that includes building it, and become someone who passes on knowledge.

Welches Ziel verfolgten Sie bei der Gestaltung Ihres ausgezeichneten Produktes?
Ich wollte eine Form schaffen, die stabil und dennoch leicht genug ist, um eine sanfte Präsenz zu haben, die dabei nicht an Klang einbüßt und eine überragende Tonqualität bietet.

Liegt Ihrer Arbeit als Designer ein bestimmter Gestaltungsansatz zugrunde?
Mir ist es am wichtigsten, die Eigenschaften dessen, was ich gestalte, zu verstehen, den Sinn des Produktes und seine Entwurfskonzepte, um dann in „Dialog" mit dem Objekt selbst zu treten und mir darüber klar zu werden, welche Form es von Natur aus haben möchte.

Wie sieht Ihre persönliche Zukunftsvision aus?
Mein Ziel ist es, eines Tages nicht mehr als Designer bezeichnet zu werden. Ich möchte das Umfeld, in dem ich lebe, selbst gestalten und herstellen, und jemand werden, der Wissen weitergibt.

reddot award 2019
best of the best

Manufacturer
Sony Video & Sound Products Inc.,
Tokyo, Japan

Glass Sound Speaker LSPX-S2
Wireless Speaker
Kabelloser Lautsprecher

See page 236
Siehe Seite 236

Drew Walcott, Peter Michaelian, Lucas Saule, Vince Voron, Grayson Byrd, Cody Proksa
Dolby Laboratories

"We design simple and seamless experiences that incorporate cutting-edge audio and visual technologies."

„Wir gestalten einfache und nahtlose Erlebnisse, die modernste Audio- und visuelle Technologien enthalten."

Do you have a specific design approach for your work as a designer?
Before putting pencil to paper, it is important we align on core principles and on what we want our product to evoke in the end user. Design should capture the value proposition, to ensure there is a connective thread through all touchpoints.

Where will your industry be in ten years?
Technology and design are continuously becoming more symbiotic. Design and experience are influencing technology at its core – giving birth to products that seamlessly work their way into your life, versus adapting your life around products. Products in the home will become more integrated, both physically and in how we interact with them.

Liegt Ihrer Arbeit als Designer ein bestimmter Gestaltungsansatz zugrunde?
Bevor wir anfangen, etwas zu zeichnen, ist es wichtig, dass wir uns auf Grundsätzliches einigen und auf das, was unser Produkt beim Benutzer bezwecken soll. Design sollte ein Wertversprechen verkörpern, um sicherzustellen, dass es einen roten Faden durch alle wichtigen Punkte gibt.

Wo wird Ihre Branche in zehn Jahren stehen?
Technik und Design werden immer symbiotischer. Design und Erfahrung beeinflussen den Kern der Technologieentwicklung und führen zu Produkten, die sich nahtlos in das Leben einfügen, anstatt das Leben den Produkten anzupassen. Produkte für das Wohnumfeld werden sich stärker integrieren – sowohl physisch als auch in der Art, in der wir mit ihnen umgehen.

reddot award 2019
best of the best

Manufacturer
Dolby Laboratories, San Francisco, USA

Dolby Dimension™
Wireless Headphones
Kabellose Kopfhörer

See page 246
Siehe Seite 246

Robert Suchy, Veronika Suchy, Patrick Suchy
clearaudio electronic GmbH

"Take the best and make it better – then it is just about good enough."

„Nimm das Beste, mache es besser – dann ist es gerade gut genug."

What was your goal when you designed your award-winning product?
It was the logical consequence of the technically expedient use of materials, an ideal form language and audiophile performance. clearaudio is a byword for an ultimate sound experience. The fact that our concept active also looks good is due to the acoustics. We would never compromise performance for the sake of design.

Why did you become a designer?
Because we were unhappy with what we saw and heard. So often, we've heard sound technology architects complaining, but they have still not created a design that works. clearaudio has worked for years on linking sight, sound and touch.

How do you keep abreast of new developments?
Unique design doesn't follow any trends; it follows a logic that has a purpose.

Welches Ziel verfolgten Sie bei der Gestaltung Ihres ausgezeichneten Produktes?
Es ging um die logische Konsequenz aus technisch sinnvollem Materialeinsatz, idealer Formgebung und audiophiler Performance. clearaudio steht für das ultimative Hörerlebnis. Dass unser concept active am Ende noch gut aussieht – das ist der Akustik geschuldet. Wir würden niemals die Leistung dem Design opfern.

Warum sind Sie Designer geworden?
Sehen, hören, unzufrieden sein. Viel zu oft haben Sound-Technik-Architekten zwar geschimpft, aber kein Design erschaffen, das funktioniert hat. clearaudio hat jahrzehntelang daran gearbeitet, Auge, Ohr und Haptik miteinander zu verbinden.

Wie bleiben Sie über aktuelle Entwicklungen auf dem Laufenden?
Einzigartiges Design folgt keinen Trends, es folgt seiner sinnbestimmten Logik.

reddot award 2019
best of the best

Manufacturer
clearaudio electronic GmbH,
Erlangen, Germany

concept active
Turntable
Schallplattenspieler

See page 264
Siehe Seite 264

Pinakesh De, Mikiyasu Ishikura
Panasonic Corporation

"Functional forms."
„Funktionale Formen."

What was your goal when you designed your award-winning product?
We aimed to design a simple hand tool, focusing on visual and cognitive clarity. While proposing a unique vertical cutting blade, it was important to have an honest and understandable design which the users feel comfortable with, and enable them to explore different ways of holding and using the product.

How do you define design quality?
Clarity of intention, beautifully crafted.

When are you at your most creative?
Long walks and mindfulness to think of new ideas, and then being in a flow state to execute the ideas.

Welches Ziel verfolgten Sie bei der Gestaltung Ihres ausgezeichneten Produktes?
Wir wollten ein einfaches Handgerät mit dem Schwerpunkt auf optische und kognitive Klarheit gestalten. Bei der Einführung eines einzigartigen, vertikalen Schneidmessers war es uns wichtig, ein vertrauenswürdiges und leicht verständliches Design zu erzielen, das für Benutzer komfortabel ist und ihnen erlaubt, unterschiedliche Arten der Handhabung und Anwendung auszuprobieren.

Wie definieren Sie Designqualität?
Klarheit der Intention, wunderschön gefertigt.

Wann sind Sie besonders kreativ?
Auf langen Spaziergängen und durch Aufmerksamkeit kommen wir auf neue Ideen. Und dann, wenn man im Flow ist, um diese Ideen umzusetzen.

reddot award 2019
best of the best

Manufacturer
Panasonic Corporation, Kyoto, Japan

i-SHAPER ER-GK80
Body Trimmer

See page 276
Siehe Seite 276

Ryan Mario Yasin
Petit Pli

Do you have a specific design approach for your work as a designer?
Design is problem solving mixed with value creation. Petit Pli takes an inter-disciplinary approach to wearable design which uses human-centred design methodologies, by understanding and utilising human behaviour, sociology and engineering techniques.

When are you at your most creative?
My approach to tackling a problem stems from first building a high-resolution image of the challenge by researching as many different perspectives as possible. I believe that it's only when you have a holistic understanding of a particular state, that you're able to fully comprehend and predict how a design can impact that steady state.

Liegt Ihrer Arbeit als Designer ein bestimmter Gestaltungsansatz zugrunde?
Design ist Problembewältigung, verbunden mit Wertschöpfung. Petit Pli folgt einem interdisziplinären Ansatz für ein tragbares Design und setzt auf menschenbezogene Designmethoden, indem menschliches Verhalten, Soziologie und Verfahrenstechniken verstanden und angewendet werden.

Wann sind Sie besonders kreativ?
Wenn ich ein Problem angehe, mache ich mir erst ein genaues Bild, indem ich so viele unterschiedliche Perspektiven wie möglich untersuche. Ich bin der Meinung, dass man nur dann verstehen und vorhersagen kann, wie eine Gestaltung einen bestimmten Zustand beeinflusst, wenn man diesen Zustand ganzheitlich begriffen hat.

reddot **award 2019**
best of the best

Manufacturer
Petit Pli, London, United Kingdom

Petit Pli – Clothes That Grow
Children's Clothing
Kinderbekleidung

See page 304
Siehe Seite 304

Samsonite Design Team

"Avoid following too many guiding principles, maxims and mottos – as they restrict free thinking."

„Vermeide es, zu vielen Leitprinzipien, Grundsätzen und Mottos zu folgen – denn sie schränken das freie Denken ein."

What was your goal when you designed your award-winning product?
To bring together sustainable materials and processes with intuitive functionality to make a striking yet useful product.

Do you have a specific design approach for your work as a designer?
Consider all possible aspects of any given project or brief and then combine the rational and functional elements with a small dose of irrationality – that creates a spark and a difference.

Where will your industry be in ten years?
Concepts like the 4th industrial revolution and the realities of machine learning/artificial intelligence will change parts of the design industry totally. The notion of being a designer will be different.

Welches Ziel verfolgten Sie bei der Gestaltung Ihres ausgezeichneten Produktes?
Nachhaltige Materialien und Verfahren mit intuitiver Funktionalität zu verbinden, um ein auffälliges und doch nützliches Produkt zu schaffen.

Liegt Ihrer Arbeit als Designer ein bestimmter Gestaltungsansatz zugrunde?
Alle möglichen Aspekte eines Produktes oder Auftrags in Betracht zu ziehen und dann die rationalen und funktionalen Elemente mit einer kleinen Dosis Unvernunft zu kombinieren – das ergibt den Funken und macht den Unterschied aus.

Wo wird Ihre Branche in zehn Jahren stehen?
Konzepte wie die 4. industrielle Revolution und die Realität des maschinellen Lernens/der künstlichen Intelligenz werden Teile der Designbranche total verändern. Auch die Auffassung des Designberufs wird eine andere sein.

reddot award 2019
best of the best

Manufacturer
Samsonite NV, Oudenaarde, Belgium

Neoknit
Luggage Collection
Gepäckkollektion

See page 316
Siehe Seite 316

Roland Heiler, Christian Schwamkrug, Manuel Röck
Studio F. A. Porsche

"Form equals function."
„Form gleich Funktion."

Do you have a specific design approach for your work as a designer?
As far as we are concerned, function – and in the case of a watch that is primarily its readability – is of prime importance. At the same time, we work with reduced forms and a clear architecture. The result is an approach that, together with the use of the appropriate functional and authentic materials (titanium, leather), generally leads to long-lasting products.

How do you keep abreast of new developments?
As we work for customers all over the world, we are active in numerous cities around the globe. This gives us an insight into a wide spectrum of technologies and fields of activity. Often, we can present our customers with technical solutions that we have discovered in a totally different context.

Liegt Ihrer Arbeit als Designer ein bestimmter Gestaltungsansatz zugrunde?
Bei uns steht generell die Funktion – und bei einer Uhr vor allem die Ablesbarkeit – im Vordergrund. Gleichzeitig arbeiten wir mit reduzierten Formen und einer klaren Architektur. Zusammen mit funktionsgerechten und authentischen Materialien (Titan, Leder) ergibt sich dadurch eine Haltung, die in der Regel zu langlebigen Produkten führt.

Wie bleiben Sie über aktuelle Entwicklungen auf dem Laufenden?
Da wir für Kunden weltweit arbeiten, sind wir in vielen Metropolen der Welt aktiv und gewinnen Einblick in unterschiedlichste Technologien und Branchen. Nicht selten können wir unseren Kunden technische Lösungen präsentieren, die wir in einem völlig anderen Zusammenhang kennengelernt haben.

reddot **award 2019**
best of the best

Manufacturer
Porsche Design Timepieces AG,
Solothurn, Switzerland

Porsche Design 1919 Chronotimer Flyback
Brown & Leather
Wristwatch
Armbanduhr

See page 334
Siehe Seite 334

Saloni Kaushik
Titan Company Limited

"Let your thinking be complex and the design be simple."

„Lass dein Denken komplex sein und deine Gestaltung einfach."

What was your goal when you designed your award-winning product?
I wanted to create designs that are unique and aesthetically appealing while also being affordable for the consumer. Modern working women in India today don't have a lot of choices when it comes to lightweight contemporary jewellery, and I wanted to create products that would fill this market gap. My goal was to create innovative designs by leveraging manufacturing techniques through their unusual application, which resulted in beautiful pieces of ultra-lightweight jewellery.

Who or what inspires you?
For me it's my birthplace, the princely state of Rajasthan in India. As a kid, I would travel a lot with my dad to different palaces and forts. He would tell me stories about great kings and their kingdoms. My designs are an amalgamation of the rich cultural heritage of India combined with my acquired love of minimalism.

Welches Ziel verfolgten Sie bei der Gestaltung Ihres ausgezeichneten Produktes?
Ich wollte einzigartige und ansprechende Designs schaffen, die für den Konsumenten zugleich bezahlbar sind. Frauen, die heute in Indien berufstätig sind, haben keine große Auswahl an leichtem, zeitgemäßem Schmuck. Ich wollte Produkte machen, die diese Marktlücke schließen. Mein Ziel war, durch die ungewöhnliche Anwendung von Herstellungstechniken innovative Gestaltungen zu schaffen mit dem Ergebnis schöner, extrem leichter Schmuckstücke.

Wer oder was inspiriert Sie?
Mein Geburtsort, der königliche Staat Rajasthan in Indien. Als Kind habe ich mit meinem Vater viele verschiedene Paläste und Festungen besucht, was einen tiefen Eindruck bei mir hinterlassen hat. Meine Gestaltungen sind eine Verschmelzung von Indiens reichhaltiger kultureller Geschichte und meiner angeeigneten Liebe zum Minimalismus.

reddot award 2019
best of the best

Manufacturer
Titan Company Limited, India

Ultra-Lightweight Laser-Cut
Tube Jewellery
Jewellery Collection
Schmuckkollektion

See page 344
Siehe Seite 344

Bicycles
Fahrräder

Bags
City bikes
E-bikes
Electric scooters
Gear and gear shift
Helmets
Lighting
Mountain bikes
Road bikes

Antrieb und Schaltung
Beleuchtung
Cityräder
E-Bikes
Elektroroller
Helme
Mountainbikes
Rennräder
Taschen

Stadtfuchs
Urban Bike

Manufacturer
Urwahn Engineering GmbH,
Magdeburg, Germany

In-house design
Urwahn Engineering GmbH

Web
www.urwahnbikes.com

reddot **award** 2019
best of the best

Urban all-rounder

In the wake of new urban traffic scenarios, the bicycle has increasingly taken centre stage for the versatile possibilities it offers. Designed for unhindered use in the city, the Stadtfuchs ("city fox") is an "all-rounder and perfect associate to take on all obstacles of the urban jungle". The design of its steel frame has been adapted to the often rapidly changing conditions in urban traffic, blending ergonomics, functionality and safety into a unity. The result is a novel elastic rear suspension that enables the bike to dampen bumps, benefiting the user's riding comfort. The seamlessly integrated LED light system is powered by a self-contacting hub dynamo to adequately illuminate the way at night. Moreover, this bike also features a smart GPS tracking system that protects against theft and allows users to locate the bike at any time. Equipped with a low-maintenance belt drive and an 11-speed hub gear, the bike speeds up silently at a fast pace, while the hydraulic braking system ensures proper braking force. The Stadtfuchs is functionally well-thought-out with technically sophisticated details, such as an internal cable routing and an integrated seat clamp. Entirely developed and manufactured locally in Germany, the bike's steel frame embodies a further expression of environmentally friendly mobility.

Urbaner Alleskönner

Im Zuge neuer Verkehrsszenarien rückt das Fahrrad mit seinen Möglichkeiten immer mehr in den Vordergrund. Der Stadtfuchs wurde für den uneingeschränkten Stadteinsatz konzipiert und zeigt sich als „Alleskönner und perfekter Begleiter, um die Hürden des urbanen Dschungels zu meistern". Die Gestaltung seines Stahlrahmens wurde an die oftmals rasanten Bedingungen im Stadtverkehr angepasst, mit dem Ziel der Optimierung von Ergonomie, Funktion und Sicherheit. Das Resultat ist ein neuartiger Hinterbau, der das Hinterrad elastisch aufhängt und Fahrbahnunebenheiten zugunsten des Fahrkomforts kompensiert. Ein vollständig integriertes und autark gespeistes LED-Lichtsystem sorgt bei Dunkelheit für eine ausgesprochen helle Beleuchtung. Dieses Fahrrad verfügt darüber hinaus über ein smartes GPS-Trackingsystem, das vor Diebstahl schützt, da der Nutzer das Rad jederzeit orten kann. Ausgestattet mit einem wartungsarmen Zahnriemen und einer 11-Gang-Nabenschaltung, erfolgt der Vortrieb geräuschlos und temporeich, während die hydraulisch arbeitenden Scheibenbremsen kraftvoll verzögern. Der Stadtfuchs ist funktional durchdacht und weist technisch raffinierte Details auf, wie eine interne Zugverlegung und eine integrierte Sattelklemme. Sein komplett in Deutschland entwickelter Stahlrahmen wird auch lokal produziert – als weiterer Ausdruck einer umweltfreundlichen Mobilität.

Statement by the jury
The stylish design of this bike perfectly integrates all the elements one would expect from a high-quality urban bike. Its appealing proportions give it a timeless and at the same time very modern look. The innovative construction of the elastic rear-wheel suspension makes this bike safe and comfortable to ride. Its outstanding features including the smart GPS tracking system and integrated LED lighting truly enrich everyday life.

Begründung der Jury
Die stilvolle Gestaltung dieses Fahrrads integriert auf perfekte Weise all die Elemente, die man von einem hochwertigen Urban Bike erwartet. Mit seinen ansprechenden Proportionen wirkt es zeitlos und zugleich sehr modern. Die innovative Konstruktion des Hinterbaus mit elastischer Aufhängung des Hinterrads macht dieses Fahrrad komfortabel und sicher. Exzellente Features wie ein smartes GPS-Trackingsystem und eine integrierte LED-Beleuchtung bereichern den Alltag.

Designer portrait
See page 30
Siehe Seite 30

COWBOY
E-Bike

Manufacturer
COWBOY, Brussels, Belgium

Design
Propeller Design AB
(Markus Stridsberg, Jaan Selg),
Stockholm, Sweden

Web
www.cowboy.com
www.propeller.se

reddot award 2019
best of the best

Mobile adventures

E-bikes are gaining more and more in popularity, as they offer many advantages for individual mobility. COWBOY has been developed to meet the needs of the urban commuters, who want to get to their destination faster. This e-bike features a novel, intuitive motor system that delivers power and speed the moment they are really needed. Since there are no gears that need to be shifted or buttons to be pushed, the bike offers a high degree of agility. Weighing in at only 16 kg, it allows easy manoeuvring through urban terrain, supported by hydraulic brakes that give controlled stopping power. Unlike the traditional chain, the bike's belt drive is silent, clean, and maintenance-free, while the modern dashboard constantly provides the rider with live data for orientation. A high degree of safety is also guaranteed through the feature of integrated front and rear lights, with the rear light intensifying when braking to effectively warn other road users following behind. Moreover, the agile mobility of this e-bike also goes hand in hand with modern communication technology. The associated smartphone app, in combination with the integrated GPS navigation system, not only offers a digital on/off key, it also features a theft notification and a "Find my bike" function via GPS tracking. Last but not least, the battery solution also implies high convenience. The battery gives a range of up to 70 km and is removable for recharging it anywhere.

Abenteuer Mobilität

Das E-Bike gewinnt immer mehr an Popularität und bietet für die individuelle Mobilität viele Vorteile. COWBOY wurde mit Blick auf die Bedürfnisse urbaner Pendler entwickelt, die schneller an ihr Ziel gelangen wollen. Dieses E-Bike ist ausgestattet mit einem neuartigen, intuitiven Motorsystem, das die Leistung und Geschwindigkeit dann bereitstellt, wenn sie wirklich benötigt werden. Da keine Gänge geschaltet oder Tasten gedrückt werden müssen, bietet es viel Agilität. Mit nur 16 kg ist es sehr leicht und erlaubt ein wendiges Manövrieren durch die Stadt, wobei Hydraulikbremsen für die kontrollierte Bremskraft sorgen. Der Riemenantrieb läuft im Vergleich zur bekannten Kette ruhig, sauber und wartungsfrei. Das zeitgemäße Dashboard liefert dabei dem Fahrer konstant Live-Daten zur Orientierung. Dank der integrierten Front- und Rückleuchten ist ein hohes Maß an Sicherheit gewährleistet. Beim Bremsvorgang leuchtet das Rücklicht stärker und hat so eine Signalwirkung für andere Verkehrsteilnehmer. Die agile Mobilität dieses E-Bikes geht einher mit moderner Kommunikationstechnologie. Eine zugehörige Smartphone-App bietet in Kombination mit dem integrierten GPS-Navigationssystem unter anderem einen digitalen Ein/Aus-Schlüssel sowie per GPS-Tracking eine Diebstahlbenachrichtigung und die Funktion „Find my bike". Mit viel Komfort ist die Akkulösung verbunden. Der Akku ist abnehmbar, hat eine Reichweite von bis zu 70 km und kann überall aufgeladen werden.

Statement by the jury

The COWBOY e-bike fascinates with its clear and minimalist design. It embodies an intelligent reduction to the essentials and invites users to wanting to discover e-bikes as a means of transportation. The removable battery offers a high range and is uncomplicated in use. With its innovative engine system, this e-bike delivers an advanced approach towards mobility. The digital features accessible via app connectivity are also highly convenient.

Begründung der Jury

Das E-Bike COWBOY fasziniert mit seinem klaren und minimalistischen Design. Es verkörpert eine intelligente Reduktion auf das Wesentliche und macht Lust darauf, diese Art der Fortbewegung für sich zu entdecken. Unkompliziert im Gebrauch ist der herausnehmbare Akku mit einer hohen Reichweite. Mit seinem innovativen Motorsystem ermöglicht dieses E-Bike eine fortschrittliche Form der Mobilität. Sehr komfortabel sind auch die digitalen Funktionen via App-Anbindung.

Designer portrait
See page 32
Siehe Seite 32

DOTS WOODENBIKE
Wooden Bicycle
Holzfahrrad

Manufacturer
Dots Design Studio, Bangkok, Thailand
In-house design
Krit Phutpim
Web
www.dotsobject.com

The DOTS WOODENBIKE was inspired by the passion for travelling and years of experience in design. With wood as material, the bicycle achieves an unusual vintage-style appearance. Plywood has been researched for its range of applications, strength and grip; all components have been handcrafted. The function for daily use and stylish aesthetics are harmoniously combined with the woods oak, teak and walnut.

Die Gestaltung des DOTS WOODENBIKE ist von der Leidenschaft für Reisen und langjähriger Erfahrung im Design inspiriert. Sie gelangt mit dem Material Holz zu einer ungewöhnlichen Fahrradanmutung im Vintage-Stil. Sperrholz wurde dafür auf seine Anwendungsmöglichkeiten, auf Stärke und Griffigkeit hin untersucht; sämtliche Bestandteile wurden von Hand gefertigt. Die Funktion für den täglichen Gebrauch und eine stilvolle Ästhetik gehen mit den Hölzern Eiche, Teak und Walnuss eine harmonische Verbindung ein.

Statement by the jury
The DOTS WOODENBIKE impresses with its extraordinary appearance with wooden elements and shines both in terms of craftsmanship and aesthetics.

Begründung der Jury
Das DOTS WOODENBIKE fasziniert durch sein außergewöhnliches Erscheinungsbild mit Holzelementen und glänzt gleichermaßen in handwerklicher wie ästhetischer Hinsicht.

URBANIZED bike
Urban Bicycle
Stadtfahrrad

Manufacturer
Urbanized Bikes, Sofia, Bulgaria
In-house design
Web
www.urbanizedbikes.com

The city bike URBANIZED combines aesthetics with casual riding pleasure and style with comfort. Whether you ride it to work or to your next appointment – the bicycle presents itself with sophisticated accessories that fit perfectly into an active everyday life. With its minimalist appearance, elegant lines, leather details, a choice of trendy colours and solid rubber tyres, which make punctures a thing of the past, it is a real eyecatcher.

Statement by the jury
In the design of the URBANIZED city bike, elegance, simplicity and high-quality components merge to create a well-designed attraction and a functional means of transport.

Das Stadtfahrrad URBANIZED verbindet Ästhetik mit lässigem Fahrspaß und Stil mit Komfort. Ob man damit zur Arbeit fährt oder zur nächsten Verabredung – das Rad präsentiert sich mit durchdachten Accessoires, die sich sinnvoll in einen aktiven Alltag einfügen. Mit seinem minimalistischen Erscheinungsbild, eleganten Linien, Details aus Leder, einer Auswahl an Trendfarben und Vollgummireifen, die nicht platt werden können, ist es ein echter Hingucker.

Begründung der Jury
In der Gestaltung des Stadtrads URBANIZED verschmelzen Eleganz, Einfachheit und hochwertig verarbeitete Komponenten zu einem formschönen Blickfang und funktionalen Fortbewegungsmittel.

Coleen
E-Bike

Manufacturer
Coleen, Bayonne, France
In-house design
Audrey Lefort, Thibault Halm
Web
www.coleen-france.com

The Coleen e-bike has been devised for purists and lovers of beautiful things. With its minimalist design, it achieves an optimal power-to-weight ratio. Other special features include a French engine with an efficiency factor of 94 per cent, a belt drive system with a 7-speed gearbox and a special full-grain leather for saddle and handles. A high-resolution display with GPS navigation and tracking as well as a call and message alarm is integrated into the handlebar; fork and frame are made of carbon.

Statement by the jury
The Coleen e-bike not only attracts attention with its stylishly reduced design, but also impresses with its excellent material qualities.

Das E-Bike Coleen wurde für Puristen und Liebhaber schöner Dinge entworfen. Mit seinem minimalistischen Design erreicht es ein hervorragendes Leistungsgewicht. Besondere Merkmale sind zudem ein in Frankreich produzierter Motor mit einem Wirkungsgrad von 94 Prozent, ein Riemenantriebssystem mit 7-Gang-Getriebe und ein spezielles Vollnarbenleder für Sattel und Griffe. Ein hochauflösendes Display mit GPS-Navigation und -Tracking sowie Anruf- und Mitteilungsalarm ist in die Lenkstange integriert; Gabel und Rahmen bestehen aus Carbon.

Begründung der Jury
Das E-Bike Coleen zieht durch seine stilvoll reduzierte Formgebung nicht nur die Blicke auf sich, sondern beeindruckt auch mit außergewöhnlichen Materialqualitäten.

Canyon LUX CF
Cross Country Mountain Bike

Manufacturer
Canyon Bicycles GmbH, Koblenz, Germany
In-house design
Wanjo Koch, Sebastian Hahn
Web
www.canyon.com

The LUX CF professional bike was developed specifically for cross-country riding, where minimum weight and optimum stiffness are decisive parameters. The big challenges were a precisely working suspension technology and a device for 1.6 litres of liquid. The enormous lightness is reflected in the thin tubes and the dynamically designed junctions. Other special features are the 8.2-gram chain stay guard and the tool-free quick-release axle.

Statement by the jury
The LUX CF professional bike owes its agility to a development uncompromisingly geared towards lightness. This also results in an attractive, reduced appearance.

Das Profirad LUX CF wurde gezielt für Cross-Country entwickelt, wo geringst-mögliches Gewicht bei hoher Steifigkeit entscheidende Parameter sind. Die großen Herausforderungen waren eine präzise arbeitende Federungstechnik und eine Vorrichtung für 1,6 Liter Flüssigkeit. Die außergewöhnliche Leichtigkeit spiegelt sich in den dünnen Rohren und den dynamisch gestalteten Knotenpunkten wider. Weitere Besonderheiten sind der 8,2 Gramm leichte Kettenstrebenschutz sowie die werkzeuglos zu bedienende Steckachse.

Begründung der Jury
Das Profirad LUX CF verdankt seine Agilität einer vollkommen auf Leichtigkeit ausgerichteten Entwicklung. Daraus resultiert auch das einprägsame, reduzierte Erscheinungsbild.

Canyon STRIVE CF
Enduro Mountain Bike

Manufacturer
Canyon Bicycles GmbH, Koblenz, Germany
In-house design
Christopher Herd, Peter Kettenring
Web
www.canyon.com

The STRIVE CF used in the Enduro World Cup conveys high functional performance. Since quick recognition was also important, a striking split of the lettering was designed and implemented in the colour as well as in the curvature of the surface. With the newly developed Shapeshifter system, which is concealed and protected in the spring deflexion, the riding behaviour and spring travel of the mountain bike can be changed at the touch of a button while riding.

Statement by the jury
The race bike STRIVE CF impresses with its innovative technology with Shapeshifter function as well as with the aesthetics of its unusual lettering.

Das im Enduro-Worldcup zum Einsatz kommende STRIVE CF vermittelt eine hohe funktionale Performance. Da auch die schnelle Wiedererkennbarkeit wichtig war, wurde ein markanter Bruch des Schriftzugs entworfen und farblich wie in der Wölbung der Oberfläche umgesetzt. Mit dem neu entwickelten Shapeshifter-System, das versteckt und geschützt in der Federungsumlenkung sitzt, lassen sich Fahrverhalten und Federweg des Mountainbikes während der Fahrt per Knopfdruck verändern.

Begründung der Jury
Das Racebike STRIVE CF besticht gleichermaßen durch seine innovative Technik mit Shapeshifter-Funktion wie ästhetisch durch den ungewöhnlichen grafischen Schriftzug.

Razorblade 29 III SL
Mountain Bike

Manufacturer
Simplon Fahrrad GmbH, Hard, Austria
In-house design
Web
www.simplon.com

The Razorblade 29 III SL was developed with uncompromising propulsion for any ascent. Its low weight and enormous stiffness make it the ideal peak climber. As a new feature, the cables are integrated in the cockpit making the bicycle look particularly trim. Despite its racing character, the Razorblade offers high seating comfort. The steering stop on the underside of the head tube as well as the chain stay protector on the inside provide optimum frame protection.

Statement by the jury
With its neat, minimalist appearance, the Razorblade 29 III SL reflects the high standards of its design in terms of speed and lightness.

Das Razorblade 29 III SL wurde mit einem sehr leistungsfähigen Vortrieb für jegliche Steigungen entwickelt. Sein geringes Gewicht und die außergewöhnliche Steifigkeit machen es zum sportlichen Gipfelkletterer, und dank der neuen Kabelintegration im Cockpit wirkt es besonders aufgeräumt. Trotz des Renncharakters bietet das Razorblade hohen Sitzkomfort. Zuverlässigen Rahmenschutz gewährleisten der Lenkanschlag an der Unterseite des Steuerrohrs sowie der Kettenstrebenprotektor an der Innenseite.

Begründung der Jury
Mit seinem aufgeräumten, minimalistischen Erscheinungsbild spiegelt das Razorblade 29 III SL den hohen Anspruch seiner Gestaltung hinsichtlich Geschwindigkeit und Leichtigkeit wider.

PARALANE^2
E-Road Bike
E-Rennrad

Manufacturer
FOCUS Bikes, Stuttgart, Germany
In-house design
Web
www.focus-bikes.com

The light, agile PARALANE^2 provides support when needed, combining the advantages of a racing bike and an e-bike. The removable motor/battery unit is decoupled from the drive and only noticeable when it makes the ride easier. System integration and lightweight construction are the key features of F.I.T. carbon (FOCUS Integration Technology). As part of the unusual frame design, high-strength fibres are dimensioned to offer high stability and rigidity.

Statement by the jury
PARALANE^2 combines the agility and dynamism of a racing bike with the support of an engine to create an extremely successful example of an e-road bike.

Das leichte, wendige PARALANE^2 bietet, wenn nötig, Unterstützung durch einen Motor und vereint so die Vorteile von Rennrad und E-Bike. Die abnehmbare Motor-/Batterieeinheit ist vom Antrieb entkoppelt und erst dann spürbar, wenn sie die Fahrt erleichtert. Systemintegration und Leichtbau sind die Hauptmerkmale von F.I.T.-Carbon (FOCUS Integration Technology). Hochfeste Fasern als Bestandteil des ungewöhnlichen Rahmendesigns sind dabei so dimensioniert, dass sie hohe Stabilität und Steifigkeit bieten.

Begründung der Jury
Die Agilität und Dynamik eines Rennrads und die Unterstützung durch einen Motor verbinden sich im PARALANE^2 zu einem überaus gelungenen Beispiel eines E-Rennrads.

RERE
Racing Bicycle
Rennrad

Manufacturer
CHAPTER2, Auckland, New Zealand
In-house design
Design
Onfire Design, Auckland, New Zealand
Web
www.chapter2bikes.com
www.weareonfire.co.nz

The RERE racing bike was developed with the aim of combining uncompromising stiffness and aerodynamics in such a way that every pedal revolution is converted into propulsion. In order to appeal to the cyclist emotionally, the tube profile was given a differentiated graphic silhouette and shows recesses on the front and rear wheels. Highlights such as a rotatable seat post, an integrated fork crown or Direct-Mount brakes round off the aesthetics, combined with optimum aerodynamic values.

Statement by the jury
The design of the RERE road bike, which is designed for maximum speed, achieves an outstanding alliance of functional components with emotionally appealing elements.

Das Rennrad RERE wurde mit dem Ziel entwickelt, bestmögliche Steifigkeit und Aerodynamik so miteinander zu verknüpfen, dass jede Pedalumdrehung in Vortrieb umgesetzt wird. Um den Radfahrer auch emotional anzusprechen, erhielt das Rohrprofil eine differenzierte grafische Silhouette und zeigt etwa Aussparungen an Vorder- und Hinterrad. Ausstattungsdetails wie eine drehbare Sattelstütze, eine integrierte Gabelkrone und Direct-Mount-Bremsen runden die mit sehr guten aerodynamischen Werten kombinierte Ästhetik ab.

Begründung der Jury
Der auf Schnelligkeit ausgelegten Gestaltung des Rennrads RERE gelingt eine herausragende Verknüpfung funktionaler Komponenten mit emotional ansprechenden Elementen.

HIMO·H1
Electric Scooter
Elektroroller

Manufacturer
Shanghai Himo Electric Technology Co., Ltd., Shanghai, China
In-house design
Weiwei Zhao
Web
www.himo-tech.com

HIMO·H1 is a foldable electric scooter that was developed as a companion for short distances. Designed in the shape of an H, it displays a concise, minimalist design language. Its powerful lithium battery offers 20 km of endurance and, seamlessly welded, is hidden in the aluminium frame. The scooter therefore weighs only 13.8 kg. The built-in folding mechanism is operated by a button and folds the scooter in four steps to a small, easily transportable A3 format.

HIMO·H1 ist ein faltbarer Elektroroller, der als Begleiter für kurze Wege entwickelt wurde. In der Form eines H entworfen, weist er eine prägnante, minimalistische Formensprache auf. Seine leistungsstarke Lithiumbatterie bietet eine Reichweite von 20 km und wurde nahtlos geschweißt im Aluminiumrahmen verborgen. Der Roller wiegt deshalb nur 13,8 kg. Die eingebaute Faltmechanik wird mit einem Knopf betätigt, und das Fahrzeug kann in vier Schritten zu einem kleinen, gut transportierbaren A3-Format zusammengeklappt werden.

Statement by the jury
The electric scooter HIMO·H1 inspires by its compact size and its innovative folding mechanism. This makes it easy and quick to operate.

Begründung der Jury
Der Elektroroller HIMO·H1 begeistert mit seiner kompakten Größe und dem innovativen Faltmechanismus. Dadurch ist er einfach und schnell zu bedienen.

Mobike E-bike
E-Bike

Manufacturer
Mobike Bike Product Center, Shanghai, China
In-house design
Gao Shusan, Zhang Siyuan, Ye Haiwei, Ke Weijia,
Lin Jianjun, Lv Zhiming, Xu Yixin
Design
Springtime Design, Amsterdam, Netherlands
Web
www.mobike.com
www.springtime.nl

This e-bike represents an intelligent and easily accessible solution for longer distances and transports. Its stable and clear construction is an expression of its high-quality manufacturing, integrated technologies and the company's modern design language. The frame is made of an aluminium alloy and a replaceable plastic shell. With a rear motor, integrated front and rear lights, a relatively light weight of 25.5 kg and an app that collects and retrieves a wide range of data, the e-bike is extremely suitable for everyday use.

Dieses E-Bike stellt eine intelligente und leicht zugängliche Lösung für längere Strecken und Transporte dar. Seine stabile, klare Bauweise ist Ausdruck der hohen Qualität in der Fertigung, der integrierten Technologien und der modernen Designsprache des Unternehmens. Der Rahmen besteht aus einer Aluminiumlegierung und einer auswechselbaren Kunststoffschale. Mit Heckmotor, Front- und Rückleuchten, einem verhältnismäßig geringen Gewicht von 25,5 kg und einer App, die verschiedenste Daten sammelt und abrufbar macht, zeigt sich das E-Bike als überaus alltagstauglich.

Statement by the jury
The simple and compact design of the Mobike E-bike conveys safety and robustness. With many functional details, it also meets contemporary requirements.

Begründung der Jury
Die schlichte und kompakte Gestaltung des Mobike E-bike vermittelt Sicherheit und Robustheit. Mit vielen funktionalen Details wird es überdies heutigen Anforderungen gerecht.

RoadBit E-Bike
E-Bike

Manufacturer
Hangzhou Qingqi Science and
Technology Co., Ltd., Hangzhou, China
In-house design
Zhiwei Guan
Web
www.qingqikeji.com

The RoadBit e-bike has been designed for shared use by people travelling within a radius of 2 to 8 km. Environmentally friendly and efficient, it helps to reduce traffic jams. Its one-piece frame integrates most cables, which ensures that the e-bike is waterproof. The eye-catching triangular structure towards the rear wheel makes it particularly stiff and robust. The bike and battery are connected to a digital system and can be tracked around the clock.

Statement by the jury
At first glance, the RoadBit e-bike scores with its clear, stable appearance; at second glance, it also proves to be a smart and sophisticated sharing bike.

Das RoadBit E-Bike wurde für die gemeinsame Nutzung durch Personen entwickelt, die im Umkreis von 2 bis 8 km unterwegs sind. Umweltfreundlich und effizient, trägt es dazu bei, Verkehrsstaus zu reduzieren. Sein Rahmen wurde aus einem Stück gefertigt und integriert die meisten Kabel, sodass das E-Bike wasserdicht ist. Die auffällige Dreiecksstruktur zum Hinterrad hin macht es besonders steif und robust. Rad und Batterie sind an ein digitales System angeschlossen und können rund um die Uhr verfolgt werden.

Begründung der Jury
Auf den ersten Blick punktet das RoadBit E-Bike mit seiner klaren, stabilen Anmutung, auf den zweiten erweist es sich zudem als smartes und durchdachtes Sharing-Bike.

muli
Cargo Bike
Lastenfahrrad

Manufacturer
muli-cycles GmbH, Driedorf, Germany
In-house design
Jonas Gerhardt, Sören Gerhardt
Web
www.muli-cycles.de

muli is a compact cargo bicycle that is optimally adapted to the needs and challenges of everyday urban life. It has been designed to be as short as possible and is equipped with a folding basket. This makes it both an agile everyday bike that can be taken on the subway or carried upstairs and a powerful cargo bicycle with a basket that holds 100 litres and a payload of up to 70 kg. Up to two children can be transported with an extra child seat.

Statement by the jury
The design concept of the muli cargo bicycle was consistently geared towards high everyday suitability and resulted in an unusually slim appearance.

Bei muli handelt es sich um ein kompaktes Lastenfahrrad, das sehr gut an die Bedürfnisse und Herausforderungen des städtischen Alltags angepasst ist. Es wurde so kurz wie möglich gebaut und ist mit einem klappbaren Korb ausgestattet. Dadurch ist es zugleich wendiges Alltagsrad, das sich mit in die U-Bahn nehmen oder Treppen hochtragen lässt, und leistungsfähiges Lastenrad mit einem Korb, der 100 Liter fasst und bis 70 kg Zuladung erlaubt. Mit einem extra Kindersitz können bis zu zwei Kinder transportiert werden.

Begründung der Jury
Das Designkonzept des Lastenfahrrads muli wurde konsequent auf hohe Alltagstauglichkeit ausgerichtet und mündete gleichzeitig in einer ungewöhnlich schlanken Anmutung.

Burley CoHo XC
Single Wheel Bike Trailer
Einradanhänger

Manufacturer
Burley, Eugene, Oregon, USA
Design
DesignThink, Inc.,
Phoenixville, Pennsylvania, USA
Web
www.burley.com
www.designthinkstudios.com

Burley CoHo XC is a single-wheel cargo trailer that is particularly stable and well-built; it was designed for bicycle camping and longer touring. Together with the one-hand steering and a quick-release axle attachment, the tool-free one-hand lock permits quick and easy coupling and uncoupling of the trailer. The intelligently designed frame is flush with the top of the mudguard and provides a flat surface for securing large objects.

Statement by the jury
The Burley CoHo XC cargo trailer immediately catches the eye for its well-thought-out mechanical design and meticulous workmanship.

Burley CoHo XC ist ein Einradanhänger, der besonders stabil und gut verarbeitet ist und für Fahrradcamping und längere Touren konzipiert wurde. Die werkzeugfreie Einhandverriegelung samt Einhandlenkung und eine Steckachsenbefestigung ermöglichen ein schnelles und einfaches An- und Abkoppeln des Anhängers. Der intelligent gestaltete Rahmen ist mit der Oberseite des Schutzblechs bündig und bietet eine ebene Fläche zur Sicherung großer Gegenstände.

Begründung der Jury
Beim Einradanhänger Burley CoHo XC fallen die durchdachte Konzeption seiner Mechanik sowie die sorgfältige Verarbeitung sofort ins Auge.

Bosch Performance Line CX
Drive Unit
Antriebseinheit

Manufacturer
Robert Bosch GmbH, Bosch eBike Systems,
Reutlingen, Germany
In-house design
Design
KISKA GmbH, Anif-Salzburg, Austria
Web
www.bosch-ebike.com
www.kiska.com

The new Performance Line CX stands for power and off-road cycling pleasure. The drive unit is powerful and efficient, and at the same time 25 per cent lighter than the previous generation. This allows manufacturers to integrate the drive unit cleanly into the frame of e-mountain bikes and to realise agile geometries. The new drive unit concept ensures minimal resistance beyond 25 km/h or when the engine is switched off. The magnesium housing noticeably reduces the overall weight of the bicycle.

Statement by the jury
More power and efficiency combined with a slimmed-down design are the outstanding features of the new Performance Line CX agile drive unit.

Die neue Performance Line CX steht für Power und Fahrspaß im Gelände. Das Antriebssystem ist leistungsstark und effizient und dabei um 25 Prozent leichter als die vorige Generation. Da sich die Drive Unit formschlüssig in den Rahmen von E-Mountainbikes integriert, lassen sich agile Geometrien realisieren. Ein neues Getriebekonzept sorgt für minimalen Tretwiderstand jenseits von 25 km/h oder bei abgeschaltetem Motor. Das Gehäuse aus Magnesium reduziert das Gesamtgewicht des Rads spürbar.

Begründung der Jury
Mehr Leistungskraft und Effizienz bei gleichzeitig verschlankter Konstruktion sind die hervorstechenden Merkmale der neuen agilen Antriebseinheit Performance Line CX.

reTyre One
Modular Tyre System
Modulares Reifensystem

Manufacturer
reTyre, Technium AS, Trollåsen, Norway
In-house design
Olaf Brage Marvik
Web
www.retyre.co

reTyre is a patented modular tyre system consisting of a basic tyre with integrated zips and removable skins. This allows the tread to be changed without having to remove the tyre itself. Thus, the user can quickly and easily adapt the functionality of a tyre to his current route and achieve the optimum driving experience. The four skins have been carefully designed to meet different requirements.

Statement by the jury
Highly innovative and functional, reTyre One allows the wheel tread to be changed without having to change the tyre. This significantly increases the flexibility and riding pleasure.

reTyre ist ein patentiertes modulares Reifensystem, das aus einem Basisreifen mit integrierten Reißverschlüssen und abnehmbaren Laufflächen (Skins) besteht. Damit lässt sich das Profil wechseln, ohne dass der Reifen selbst entfernt werden muss. Der Benutzer kann die Funktionalität eines Reifens auf diese Weise schnell und einfach an seine aktuelle Strecke und das gewünschte Fahrerlebnis anpassen. Die vier Skins wurden sorgfältig für die unterschiedlichen Anforderungen entwickelt.

Begründung der Jury
Höchst innovativ und funktional lässt sich mit reTyre One das Radprofil verändern, ohne dass der Reifen gewechselt werden muss. Das erhöht die Flexibilität und den Fahrspaß beträchtlich.

Super Record 12×2 Speed Disc Brake
Groupset for Road Bike
Brems-/Schaltset für Rennräder

Manufacturer
Campagnolo S.r.l., Vicenza, Italy
In-house design
Nicola Sgreva
Web
www.campagnolo.com

The new Super Record 12×2 Speed Disc Brake is characterised by slim lines and a streamlined design that expresses emotion, performance and aerodynamics. It is introduced with an innovative rear derailleur developed with 3D embrace technology that ensures high chain traction even on the smallest sprockets. The 24 gears can be fully utilised with the double connecting rod front derailleur. The lever is ergonomically designed and enables easy operation. The track bearings are connected in pairs and ensure high rigidity of the chainset. In addition, the disc brake technology provides excellent braking performance and controllability.

Die neue Super Record 12×2 Speed Disc Brake ist durch schlanke Linien und ein stromlinienförmiges Design gekennzeichnet, das Emotion, Leistung und Aerodynamik zum Ausdruck bringt. Sie wird mit einem innovativen Schaltwerk eingeführt, das unter Anwendung der 3D-Embrace-Technologie entwickelt wurde und auch bei den kleinsten Ritzeln für hohe Kettentraktion sorgt. Dank Umwerfer mit doppeltem Pleuel können die 24 Gänge voll genutzt werden. Der Hebel ist ergonomisch gestaltet und einfach zu betätigen. Die Spurlager sind paarweise verbunden und sorgen für hohe Steifigkeit der Kettenradgarnitur. Die Scheibenbremsentechnologie stellt zudem eine hervorragende Bremsleistung und -dosierbarkeit sicher.

Statement by the jury
This brake and shift set combines high-performance, technically and creatively state-of-the-art components to form a first-class unit for professional sport.

Begründung der Jury
In diesem Brems- und Schaltset verbinden sich auf Hochleistung ausgerichtete, technisch wie gestalterisch hochmoderne Komponenten zu einer eindrucksvollen Einheit für den Profisport.

MAGICSHINE ALLTY 1000 DRL BICYCLE LIGHT
Bike Lamp with DRL
Fahrradlampe mit Tagfahrlicht

Manufacturer
Shenzhen Minjun Electronic Technology Co., Ltd.,
Shenzhen, China
In-house design
Web
www.magicshine.com

ALLTY 1000 embodies a new concept for a bicycle lamp that integrates an independent unit for a daytime running light (DRL). This considerably increases cycling safety in urban traffic, as cyclists are always clearly visible during the day as well. It is USB rechargeable with battery indication, and has a waterproof rate of IPX7, which enables it to withstand extreme weather conditions. The lamp is easily mounted on a helmet or any handlebar with mounting rings.

ALLTY 1000 präsentiert ein neues Konzept einer Fahrradlampe mit integriertem, unabhängigen Tagfahrlicht (DRL – Daytime Running Light). Die Kombination erhöht die Sicherheit beim Radfahren maßgeblich, denn der Fahrer ist auch am Tag stets gut erkennbar. Das schlanke, nach IPX7 wassergeschützte Gehäuse mit integriertem Lithium-Ionen-Akku und USB-Ladeanschluss wird über den Druckschalter mit Ladestandanzeige betätigt. Die Montage am Helm oder der Stange erfolgt einfach und schnell mithilfe der beiliegenden Befestigungsringe.

Statement by the jury
The ALLTY 1000 bicycle lamp scores with its built-in daytime running light, which increases the cyclist's safety and impresses with its reduced look.

Begründung der Jury
Die Fahrradlampe ALLTY 1000 punktet mit dem eingebauten Tagfahrlicht, das die Sicherheit des Radfahrers erhöht, und vor allem auch mit einem reduziert gestalteten Look.

Burner Brake
Rear Light
Rücklicht

Manufacturer
Beryl, London, United Kingdom
In-house design
Daniel Barnes, Luke Gray
Design
GEO Product Creation,
Cheshire, United Kingdom
Web
www.beryl.cc
www.geo.co.uk

Burner Brake is an innovative bicycle rear light with different light patterns for better road safety. By combining the braking algorithm with LED technology, other road users can follow the cyclist's movements. If the integrated software, which is based on the machine learning technology, registers rapid braking, 24 LEDs with 200 lumens reliably warn the following traffic.

Statement by the jury
The design of the intelligent Burner Brake bicycle rear light combines a technically ingenious mechanism with a high level of safety to create an excellent innovation.

Burner Brake ist ein innovatives Fahrradrücklicht, das mit verschiedenen Leuchtmustern für eine bessere Sicherheit im Straßenverkehr aufwartet. Durch die Kombination des Bremsalgorithmus mit LED-Technologie können andere Verkehrsteilnehmer die Bewegungen des Radfahrers nachvollziehen. Registriert die mithilfe der Machine-Learning-Technologie konfigurierte, integrierte Software schnelles Abbremsen, warnen 24 LEDs mit 200 Lumen zuverlässig den nachfolgenden Verkehr.

Begründung der Jury
In der Gestaltung des intelligenten Fahrradrücklichts Burner Brake fügen sich ein technisch ausgeklügelter Mechanismus und hohe Sicherheit zu einer bestechenden Innovation.

Pixel 2-in-1 Light
Multi-function LED light
LED-Multifunktionsleuchte

Manufacturer
Beryl, London, United Kingdom
In-house design
Daniel Barnes, Marcus Kane
Design
Mettle Studio,
London, United Kingdom
Web
www.beryl.cc
www.mettle-studio.com

Pixel is a versatile luminaire for cyclists or runners. As tail light, it shines red and as head light white. With its special clip, it can be attached to bikes, helmets, bags or clothes. The product is waterproof and, at 18 grams, a real lightweight. Thanks to the protected LED technology, you can switch between tail light and head light at the touch of a button, to either continuous light or "heartbeat" blinking mode for extra high visibility.

Statement by the jury
Practical, compact and multifunctional – the robust Pixel light proves to be a real safety all-rounder on the bike or for joggers.

Pixel ist eine vielseitig einsetzbare Leuchte für Fahrradfahrer oder Läufer und leuchtet rot als Rücklicht und weiß als Vorderlicht. Mit ihrem speziellen Clip lässt sie sich an Bikes, Helmen, Taschen oder Kleidungsstücken befestigen. Das Produkt ist wasserfest und mit 18 Gramm ein Leichtgewicht. Dank der urheberrechtlich geschützten LED-Technologie kann man per Knopfdruck zwischen Rücklicht und Vorderlicht jeweils in die Leuchtmodi Dauerlicht oder „Herzschlag"-Blinkmodus für besonders hohe Sichtbarkeit wechseln.

Begründung der Jury
Praktisch, kompakt und multifunktional – damit erweist sich die robuste Leuchte Pixel als echter Allrounder für die Sicherheit auf dem Fahrrad oder beim Joggen.

Park & Diamond Helmet
Bicycle Helmet
Fahrradhelm

Manufacturer
Park & Diamond, New York, USA
In-house design
David Hall, Jordan Klein
Web
www.park-and-diamond.com

The protective Park & Diamond helmet looks like a stylish baseball cap, adapts to the wearer's head and folds to the size of a water bottle for transport. It has been developed with patented protective materials that are particularly efficient and stable when absorbing and dissipating energy. The outer cover can be exchanged to suit the wearer's personal taste, the inner cover can be removed to be washed.

Statement by the jury
In addition to its practical handling, the Park & Diamond bicycle helmet impresses with its functional and safe design as well as its trendy look.

Der schützende Helm Park & Diamond sieht wie eine stylische Baseballkappe aus, passt sich dem Kopf des Trägers an und lässt sich zum Transportieren auf die Größe einer Wasserflasche zusammenfalten. Es wurden patentierte Schutzmaterialien verarbeitet, die beim Aufnehmen und Ableiten von Energie besonders effizient und stabil sind. Der äußere Bezug lässt sich austauschen und ganz auf den persönlichen Geschmack des Trägers abstimmen, der innere kann zur Reinigung abgenommen werden.

Begründung der Jury
Neben seiner praktischen Handhabung besticht der Fahrradhelm Park & Diamond mit einer funktionalen und sicheren Bauweise sowie seinem trendigen Look.

MOUNTAINBIKE BACKPACK
Backpack
Rucksack

Manufacturer
OUTENTIC, Munich, Germany
In-house design
Christine Overbeck
Web
www.outentic.com

The focus of this innovative backpack is on the Bike Module and modularity. It offers 8 litres of filling capacity as a basis, complemented by the water-repellent Casual Module with 15 litres that comes in handy for longer tours, for example. The 4-point connection allows additional modules to be added in no time at all; the bike can be attached to the Bike Module so that it can be carried on the back. The respective device consists of an aluminium frame for a load of up to 25 kg and offers a secure hold.

Statement by the jury
This backpack convinces with its high modularity and its flexible application possibilities. Its outstanding advantage is that bicycles can also be carried with it.

Der Fokus dieses innovativen Rucksacks liegt auf dem Bike Module und der Modularität. Als Basis bietet er 8 Liter Füllvermögen, ergänzt um das wasserabweisende Casual Module mit 15 Litern etwa für längere Touren. Über die 4-Punkt-Anbindung lassen sich im Handumdrehen zusätzliche Module ergänzen; das Rad wird im Bike Module so eingehängt, dass es sich auf dem Rücken tragen lässt und die Hände frei sind. Die Vorrichtung dafür besteht aus einem Aluminiumrahmen, der bis 25 kg belastbar ist und sicheren Halt bietet.

Begründung der Jury
Dieser Rucksack überzeugt durch hohe Modularität und seine flexiblen Einsatzmöglichkeiten. Dass sich mit ihm auch Fahrräder tragen lassen, ist sein hervorstechendes Plus.

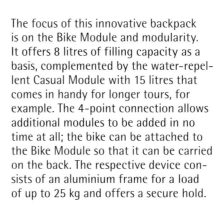

Norco Belford City Bag
Bicycle and City Bag
Fahrrad- und Citytasche

Manufacturer
ASISTA Teile fürs Rad GmbH & Co. KG,
Leutkirch, Germany
Design
Paula-D Design (Martina Stauber),
Amtzell, Germany
Web
www.norco-bags.de
www.paula-d.de

The distinctive silhouette of the Norco Belford bicycle and city bag with its elegant, feminine design forges a bridge between functionality and urban chic. The robust, water-repellent nylon material with its textile look ensures a long service life and high functionality. With self-explanatory Vario hooks, the bag can be attached to all standard bicycle racks. Suitable for various occasions, it incorporates an active, modern lifestyle.

Statement by the jury
The bicycle and city bag is as practical and functional as it is chic and stylish. It thus fully meets the demands of an urban lifestyle.

Die markante Silhouette der Fahrrad- und Citytasche Norco Belford mit ihrem eleganten, feminin anmutenden Design schlägt eine Brücke zwischen Funktionalität und urbanem Chic. Das robuste, wasserabweisende Nylonmaterial mit textiler Optik sorgt für eine lange Lebensdauer und einen hohen Gebrauchswert. Mittels selbsterklärender Vario-Haken lässt sich die Tasche an allen gängigen Fahrradgepäckträgern befestigen. Für verschiedene Gelegenheiten geeignet, ist sie Ausdruck eines aktiven, modernen Lebensstils.

Begründung der Jury
Diese Fahrrad- und Citytasche zeigt sich als ebenso praktisch und funktional wie schick und stilvoll. Damit wird sie den Ansprüchen eines urbanen Lifestyles vollauf gerecht.

Norco Portree
Rucksack Bag
Bicycle and City Bag
Fahrrad- und Citytasche

Manufacturer
ASISTA Teile fürs Rad GmbH & Co. KG,
Leutkirch, Germany
Design
Paula-D Design (Martina Stauber),
Amtzell, Germany
Web
www.norco-bags.de
www.paula-d.de

The Portree backpack bag combines an elegant design with sophisticated functionality. Made of robust, water-repellent nylon material, it has been tailored to the flowing use between the office, everyday life and leisure. It can be attached to standard bicycle racks by means of Vario hooks and, thanks to an integrated strap, serve as a practical backpack. A padded notebook compartment is included for professional use.

Statement by the jury
The design of the backpack bag impresses with a concept and design that skilfully combine fashionable lifestyle with environmentally conscious urban mobility.

Die Rucksacktasche Portree verbindet eine elegante Formensprache mit durchdachter Funktionalität. Aus robustem, wasserabweisendem Nylonmaterial hergestellt, wurde sie auf den fließenden Einsatz zwischen Büro, Alltag und Freizeit abgestimmt. Mittels Vario-Haken lässt sie sich an den gängigen Fahrradgepäckträgern befestigen und dank der integrierten Schultergurte auch als praktischer Rucksack verwenden. Für die berufliche Nutzung ist ein gepolstertes Notebook-Fach vorgesehen.

Begründung der Jury
Die Gestaltung der Rucksacktasche beeindruckt aufgrund einer Konzeption und Ausführung, die gekonnt schicken Lifestyle mit umweltbewusster urbaner Mobilität verknüpft.

Norco Kilmore
Commuter Bag
Bicycle and City Bag
Fahrrad- und Citytasche

Manufacturer
ASISTA Teile fürs Rad GmbH & Co. KG,
Leutkirch, Germany
Design
Paula-D Design (Martina Stauber),
Amtzell, Germany
Web
www.norco-bags.de
www.paula-d.de

The Kilmore bag is the ideal companion for modern urban mobility by bike. It is suitable for the city, work or shopping and stands out due to its simple exterior with a textile, waterproof surface material. An innovative manufacturing process using ultrasound technology joins two pieces of fabric together in a waterproof manner so that the bag combines lifestyle and design with elaborate manufacturing and functionality.

Statement by the jury
Practical handling, durable material combinations and a clear, stylish aesthetics – these are the outstanding features of this bag designed for modern locomotion.

Wer heutzutage in der Stadt gern das Rad als Fortbewegungsmittel nutzt, kann auf die Tasche Kilmore als zuverlässigen Begleiter setzen. Sie eignet sich für die City, den Weg zur Arbeit oder zum Einkaufen und fällt aufgrund ihres schlichten Äußeren mit textilem, wasserdichtem Oberflächenmaterial auf. In einem innovativen Fertigungsverfahren mit Ultraschalltechnik werden zwei Gewebestücke wasserdicht miteinander verbunden, sodass die Tasche Lifestyle und Design mit durchdachter Fertigung und Funktionalität kombiniert.

Begründung der Jury
Praktische Handhabung, langlebige Materialkombinationen und eine klare, stilvolle Ästhetik – damit ragt die für die heutigen Anforderungen an Mobilität entworfene Tasche besonders heraus.

Vehicles
Fahrzeuge

Accessories	Automobiltechnik
Aeroplane interior fittings	Busse
Agricultural machines	Caravans
Automobile technology	Elektrofahrzeuge
Buses	Fahrzeugbeleuchtungen
Caravans	Fahrzeug-Inneneinrichtung
Combined cars	Felgen
Compact cars	Flugzeug-Inneneinrichtung
Components	Gabelstapler
Electric vehicles	Kombifahrzeuge
Forklift trucks	Kompaktwagen
Fully integrated motorhomes	Komponenten
Mopeds	Landwirtschaftliche Maschinen
Motorbikes	Motorräder
Porch & cartop tents	Motorroller
Quads	Quads
Sports cars	Sportwagen
SUV / Off-road vehicles	Straßenbahnen
Tiny houses	SUV/Geländewagen
Train interior	Tiny Houses
Trams	Vollintegrierte Wohnmobile
Vehicle interior fittings	Vor- und Dachzelte
Vehicle lighting systems	Wassermotorräder
Water scooters	Zubehör
Wheel rims	Zuginterieur

Ferrari Monza SP1
Sports Car
Sportwagen

Manufacturer
Ferrari S.p.A.,
Maranello (Modena), Italy

In-house design
Ferrari Design (Flavio Manzoni)

Web
www.ferrari.com

reddot award 2019
best of the best

Ambassador of tradition and future

Ferrari can look back on a long tradition of successful sports car races, such as the Italian Mille Miglia, but it was not until later that the company began to also build cars for the road. Based on the V12 engine, the Ferrari Monza SP1 is a limited-edition special series that is also available as a two-seat model (Monza SP2). The first in the new "Icona" segment of special models, the design of the Monza SP1 draws inspiration from the most evocative Ferraris of the 1950s. It combines state-of-the-art technology with the maxim of pure design. Conceived as a single-seat road car, it impresses with an architecture that is based on a monolithic form with an aerodynamic wing profile. The complete absence of a roof and windscreen gave the Ferrari Design team, lead by Flavio Manzoni, the freedom to create captivating proportions that otherwise would not have been possible on a traditional spider. As a result, this Ferrari boasts an outstanding feel of speed that is otherwise only experienced by Formula 1 drivers. This driving experience is also derived from the concept of a cockpit that seems to be carved from the car's very volume to wrap around the driver. An innovative and patented "virtual wind - shield" deviates the airflow to deliver an impressive "en plein air" driving pleasure and comfort. Despite its roots, coherent with the Ferrari tradition, the Monza SP1 represents a new enticing projection into the future.

Botschafter von Tradition und Zukunft

Das Unternehmen Ferrari blickt auf eine lange Tradition in Sportwagenrennen wie der italienischen Mille Miglia zurück, begann jedoch erst später, Autos für die Straße zu bauen. Der Ferrari Monza SP1 ist eine auf einem V12-Motor basierende, limitierte Sonderserie, die auch in einer zweisitzigen Version (Monza SP2) erhältlich ist. Als das erste Modell in dem neuen "Icona" genannten Segment von Sondermodellen lehnt sich seine Gestaltung an die legendären Ferraris der 1950er Jahre an. Sie vereint modernste Technologie mit der Maxime der puren Form. Der Monza SP1 wurde als Einsitzer konzipiert und beeindruckt durch eine Architektur, die auf einer monolithischen Form mit aerodynamischem Flügelprofil basiert. Das vollständige Fehlen eines Daches und einer Windschutzscheibe gab dem Ferrari Design Team, angeführt durch Flavio Manzoni, die Freiheit für eindrucksvolle Proportionen, die bei einem herkömmlichen Spider nicht möglich gewesen wären. Als Ergebnis vermittelt dieser Ferrari dem Fahrer ein intensives Gefühl von Geschwindigkeit, wie es ansonsten nur Formel-1-Piloten kennen. Dieses Fahrerlebnis beruht auch auf dem Konzept eines Cockpits, das in das Volumen des den Fahrer umhüllenden Wagens eingeschnitten zu sein scheint. Die innovative, patentierte "virtuelle Windschutzscheibe" lenkt dabei den Luftstrom ab, um den Eindruck eines Fahrkomforts und Fahrspaßes "en plein air" zu gewährleisten. Trotz seiner mit der Ferrari-Tradition in Einklang stehenden Herkunft stellt der Monza SP1 so eine neue verführerische Projektion in die Zukunft dar.

Statement by the jury

Fuelled by the maxims of classic sports car design, the Ferrari Monza SP1 has achieved the perfect reduction to the essentials. Based on the Ferrari models of the 1950s, it establishes a novel expressive design vocabulary. Particularly impressive are the beautiful proportions and the quality of the finishes. Captivating with excellent design details such as the sloping waistline, the car establishes an intense relationship with the driver.

Begründung der Jury

Die Maximen klassischen Sportwagendesigns verinnerlichend, gelingt mit dem Ferrari Monza SP1 die perfekte Reduktion auf das Wesentliche. Ausgehend von den Ferrari-Modellen der 1950er Jahre, etabliert er eine neue expressive Formensprache. Er begeistert dabei insbesondere mit seinen schönen Proportionen und der Qualität seiner Oberflächen. Durch exzellent gemeisterte Details wie die abfallende Gürtellinie baut er ein intensives Verhältnis zum Fahrer auf.

Designer portrait
See page 34
Siehe Seite 34

Ferrari 488 Pista
Sports Car
Sportwagen

Manufacturer
Ferrari S.p.A., Maranello (Modena), Italy
In-house design
Ferrari Design (Flavio Manzoni)
Web
www.ferrari.com

The Ferrari 488 Pista's weight saving solutions, its powerful engine and vehicle dynamics boast a particular proximity to racing cars of the brand. Among the Formula 1 adaptations are the front S-Duct and the 488 GTE-inspired front diffusers, which create strong suction for increased downforce. The sporty concept of the front is echoed on the back: while the dolphin-tail rear spoiler signals lightness and efficiency, the rear volumes add a sense of the vehicle's power.

Die gewichtseinsparenden Lösungen, der Motor und die Fahrdynamik des Ferrari 488 Pista zeigen eine große Nähe zu den Rennwagen der Marke. Zu den Formel-1-Adaptionen gehören der frontale S-Duct ebenso wie vom 488 GTE inspirierte Diffusoren zur Erhöhung des Extraktions- und Lastgenerierungsvermögens. Das sportliche Konzept der Front spiegelt sich rückseitig: Während die „Schwalbenschwanz"-Heckflosse Leichtigkeit und Effizienz signalisiert, bringt der voluminöse Heckflügel die Kraft des Fahrzeugs zum Ausdruck.

Statement by the jury
The Ferrari 488 Pista fascinates with high performance and with a dynamic design idiom that communicates driving pleasure in a sensuous manner.

Begründung der Jury
Der Ferrari 488 Pista fasziniert durch Höchstleistung und eine dynamische Formensprache, die Fahrspaß sinnlich und direkt kommuniziert.

Ferrari SP38
Sports Car
Sportwagen

Manufacturer
Ferrari S.p.A., Maranello (Modena), Italy
In-house design
Ferrari Design (Flavio Manzoni)
Web
www.ferrari.com

This unique car, which can be driven both on road and on track, is based on the 488 GTB and inspired by the legendary F40. The model features clearly drawn-in flanks, running from the low beltline on the door to the rear wheelarch. Thus, the design reinforces the importance of the rear volume, while at the same time maintaining the airflow to the intercoolers. Three transversal slats slash across the engine cover to evacuate heat. The bodywork is coated with a newly conceived three-layer metallic red.

Dieser sowohl rennstrecken- als auch straßentaugliche Sportwagen ist ein Unikat auf Basis des 488 GTB, das vom legendären F40 inspiriert ist. Von der niedrigen Gürtellinie der Tür bis zum Heck zeigen sich im Profil deutlich eingezogene Flanken. Damit wird die Masse hinten optisch betont und gleichzeitig der Luftstrom zu den Ladeluftkühlern begünstigt. An der Motorhaube leiten drei markante Querlamellen die Wärme ab. Die Karosserie ist dreilagig in einem eigens entwickelten Metallicrot lackiert.

Statement by the jury
With its aesthetically curved silhouette and innovative detail solutions, the special edition car visualises an outstanding passion for racing.

Begründung der Jury
Mit ästhetisch geschwungener Silhouette und innovativen Detaillösungen visualisiert das Einzelstück eine herausragende Leidenschaft für den Rennsport.

Mazda3
Passenger Car
Personenkraftwagen

Manufacturer
Mazda Motor Corporation,
Hiroshima, Japan

In-house design
Yasutake Tsuchida

Web
www.mazda.com

reddot **award** 2019
best of the best

The essence of simplicity

Traditional Japanese aesthetics are infused by detailed rules on how to interpret the simplest of things and occurrences surrounding us. The new Mazda3 embodies a further development of the company's "Kodo" design philosophy, which embodies the essence of Japanese aesthetics. Accordingly, the car features a reduced body, which creates a powerful expression of vitality based on the interplay of light, shades and reflections. Conveying the notions of vitality and power, the cabin and body appear as a single solid mass. The "less is more" philosophy underlying the overall design is also continued in the interior. The cockpit showcases a horizontal and symmetric layout that centres on the driver, offering an optimum of user comfort. The ergonomically designed seat keeps the driver's pelvis upright to support natural posture and reduce fatigue. Furthermore, the newly interpreted vehicle platform is complemented by an optimised vehicle handling. It provides a direct response when accelerating, turning and braking, while the new chassis and body dampen input from the road before it reaches the body. In addition, the Mazda3 comes with highly advanced i-Activsense safety technology and efficient Skyactiv power trains. As an option, it can also be equipped with an innovative Skyactiv-X engine, a groundbreaking petrol engine that delivers the fuel efficiency of a diesel.

Die Essenz der Einfachheit

Die traditionelle japanische Ästhetik impliziert ausführliche Regeln, wie die einfachen Dinge und Vorkommnisse in der Umwelt zu interpretieren sind. Der aktuelle Mazda3 steht für die Weiterentwicklung der von dieser Ästhetik abgeleiteten Designsprache „Kodo". Er ist entsprechend mit einer reduzierten Karosserie gestaltet, die durch den Wechsel von Licht, Schatten und Reflexionen einen lebendigen Eindruck entstehen lässt. Die Attribute Kraft und Vitalität vermittelnd, zeigt er optisch vom Heck aus eine Verschmelzung von Fahrkabine und Karosserie. Die dem gesamten Design zugrunde liegende „Weniger ist mehr"-Philosophie wird auch im Interieur weitergeführt. Eine symmetrische sowie horizontale Anordnung des Cockpits rückt den Fahrer ins Zentrum und bietet ihm optimalen Bedienkomfort. Der ergonomisch durchdachte Fahrersitz hält das Becken des Fahrers aufrecht, um die natürliche Haltung zu unterstützen und Ermüdung vorzubeugen. Mit der neu interpretierten Fahrzeugplattform geht zudem ein optimiertes Fahrzeughandling einher. Es ermöglicht ein direktes Ansprechverhalten beim Beschleunigen, Wenden und Bremsen, während Vibrationen und Geräusche im Innenraum reduziert wurden. Der Mazda3 verfügt über die hochentwickelte i-Activsense-Sicherheitstechnologie und einen effizienten Skyactiv-Motor. Optional kann er mit einem innovativen Skyactiv-X-Motor ausgestattet werden, einem bahnbrechenden Benzinmotor mit Kompressionszündung, der die Kraftstoffeffizienz eines Diesels bietet.

Statement by the jury

With its purist, elegant design, the Mazda3 conveys a strong sense of sporty driving pleasure. The car impresses with its well-proportioned chassis. Integrating all the elements needed for an ecologically sound vehicle, it showcases beautiful details and a high-quality finish. Modelled on classic design principles, the interior is clear in structure and of exquisite quality. The car invites drivers to focus on the driving experience and simply enjoy it.

Begründung der Jury

Mit seiner puristischen, eleganten Gestaltung vermittelt der Mazda3 das Gefühl von Sportlichkeit. Er beeindruckt durch seinen wohlproportionierten Aufbau. Alle Elemente für ein ökologisches Fahrzeug integrierend, zeigt er schöne Details und ein hochwertiges Finish. Das an klassischen Designprinzipien orientierte Interieur ist übersichtlich und von exquisiter Qualität. Der Fahrer kann sich ganz auf sein Fahrerlebnis konzentrieren und es genießen.

Designer portrait
See page 36
Siehe Seite 36

Kia ProCeed
Passenger Car
Personenkraftwagen

Manufacturer
Kia Motors Corporation,
Seoul, South Korea
In-house design
Kia Design Center Europe
Web
www.kia.com

This compact shooting brake is the sportiest member of the Ceed family. The ProCeed embodies youthful dynamics by design, merging sleek, elegant lines with the versatility of a five-door body. The contours of the vehicle are marked by the low-slung roofline, which clearly drops off towards the strong shoulders and flows into the distinctive tailgate. Despite its elongated silhouette, the car offers a generous, family-friendly interior.

Dieser kompakte Shooting Brake ist das sportlichste Mitglied der Ceed-Familie. Das Design des ProCeed betont jugendliche Dynamik und verbindet schnittig-elegante Formen mit der Variabilität eines Fünftürers. Die Konturen des Fahrzeugs werden von der niedrigen Dachlinie geprägt, die zur kräftigen Schulterpartie hin deutlich abfällt und schließlich im markanten Heck mündet. Trotz seiner lang gestreckten Silhouette bietet der Wagen einen großzügigen, familienfreundlichen Innenraum.

Statement by the jury
The appearance of the Kia ProCeed demonstrates vigorous elegance, combined with the practical benefits of a five-door vehicle.

Begründung der Jury
Das Erscheinungsbild des Kia ProCeed zeigt kraftvolle Eleganz, verbunden mit den praktischen Vorzügen eines Fünftürers.

Kia Ceed Sportswagon
Passenger Car
Personenkraftwagen

Manufacturer
Kia Motors Corporation,
Seoul, South Korea
In-house design
Kia Design Center Europe
Web
www.kia.com

The Ceed Sportswagon showcases a dynamic look with cab-backward pro-portions, complemented by an extended bonnet and an assertive horizontal belt-line. The sweeping roof of the estate car drops down smoothly to the extended rear overhang. With its capacity of 625 litres, the loadbay is generous, sup-plemented by practical storage compart-ments in the boot floor. A low boot lip and remotely-actuated split rear seats further contribute to the convenience of the estate car.

Statement by the jury
With its flowing silhouette, the Kia Ceed Sportswagon exudes a confident and stylish look. It also impresses with a gen-erous trunk capacity.

Eine nach hinten gerückte Fahrgastzelle kennzeichnet das dynamische Erscheinungs-bild des Ceed Sportswagon, ergänzt durch eine längere Motorhaube und eine ausge-prägte Schulterlinie. Das Dach fällt fließend zum vergrößerten Hecküberhang ab. Mit 625 Litern bietet der Kofferraum viel Lade-volumen, dazu kommen praktische Ablage-fächer im Boden. Zur Alltagstauglichkeit des Kombis tragen auch seine niedrige Lade-kante sowie eine per Hebel vom Kofferraum aus umklappbare, geteilte Rücksitzbank bei.

Begründung der Jury
Durch seine harmonische Silhouette wirkt der Kia Ceed Sportswagon selbstbewusst und stilvoll. Er besticht zudem mit einem großzügigen Kofferraumvolumen.

Kia Ceed
Passenger Car
Personenkraftwagen

Manufacturer
Kia Motors Corporation,
Seoul, South Korea
In-house design
Kia Design Center Europe
Web
www.kia.com

In response to fierce competition in the compact class, the Ceed is longer, lower and wider than its predecessors. The advanced chassis lays the foundation for the rakish forms of the hatchback. Its extended bonnet, cab-backward stance, assertive horizontal beltline and longer rear overhang all work harmoniously together to lend the five-door vehicle an athletic appearance. This visual distinc-tiveness is further underlined by an un-adorned and well-balanced profile.

Statement by the jury
The sporty appearance of the Kia Ceed is defined by elegant lines and features that have been specifically tailored to road suitability.

Als Antwort auf den harten Wettbewerb in der Kompaktklasse zeigt sich der Ceed län-ger, flacher und breiter als seine Vorgänger. Das fortschrittliche Chassis bildet die Basis für den schnittigen Auftritt des Schräghecks: Eine Kombination aus längerer Motorhaube, weiter hinten positionierter Fahrgastzelle, markanter Schulterlinie und größerem Heck-überhang macht den Fünftürer zu einer athletischen Erscheinung. Betont wird das Format durch ein schnörkelloses, ausgewo-genes Profil.

Begründung der Jury
Eine elegante Linienführung und eine Aus-stattung, die klar auf Straßentauglichkeit setzt, prägen die sportive Erscheinung des Kia Ceed.

ŠKODA SCALA
Passenger Car
Personenkraftwagen

Manufacturer
ŠKODA AUTO a.s., Mladá Boleslav, Czech Republic
In-house design
Web
www.skoda-auto.com

The ŠKODA SCALA is a spacious hatchback which embodies the motto "smart understatement". Defined contours and dynamic elements lend the compact car a highly emotive appearance, complemented by distinctive details like block lettering at the rear, which replaces a logo. The name, which means "stairs" or "ladder" in Latin, insinuates that a new stage of development has been attained with this vehicle. Accordingly, the SCALA also features modern connectivity solutions, integrating the smartphone on board.

Der ŠKODA SCALA ist ein geräumiges Schrägheck, das die Devise „smartes Understatement" verkörpert. Herausgearbeitete Konturen und dynamische Elemente verschaffen dem Kompaktwagen einen emotionsbetonten Auftritt; hinzu kommen prägnante Details wie Blockschrift statt Logo am Heck. Der Name stammt aus dem Lateinischen, bedeutet „Treppe" oder „Leiter" und unterstreicht, dass mit diesem Fahrzeug eine neue Entwicklungsstufe erreicht wird. Dementsprechend bietet der SCALA auch zeitgemäße Konnektivitätslösungen, die das Smartphone an Bord einbinden.

Statement by the jury
Thanks to its expressive appearance, the ŠKODA SCALA exudes self-confidence in a relaxed way. The interior convinces with user-friendly technology.

Begründung der Jury
Durch sein ausdrucksstarkes Äußeres wirkt der ŠKODA SCALA auf gelassene Weise selbstbewusst. Die Innenausstattung überzeugt mit anwenderfreundlicher Technik.

Wey VV7
Passenger Car
Personenkraftwagen

Manufacturer
Great Wall Motor Company Limited,
Baoding, China
In-house design
Web
www.gwm-global.com

The VV7 is the first production vehicle in the manufacturer's premium segment. Curved lines visually extend the silhouette of the SUV, and the exhaust system adopts a sporty look. Leather seats create a comfortable feel on the inside. Technical highlights of the model include an advanced driver assistance system and an electronic mirror that provides a better view of traffic. Features like adaptive cruise control and autonomous emergency braking contribute to safe driving.

Statement by the jury
The Wey VV7 scores with an attractive overall concept that unites modern technology with a dynamic appearance.

Der VV7 ist das erste Serienfahrzeug in der Premiumsparte des Herstellers. Geschwungene Linien verlängern optisch die Silhouette des SUV, die Auspuffanlage ist sportlich gestaltet, im Inneren sorgen Ledersitze für gehobenen Komfort. An technischen Highlights bietet das Modell u. a. ein Fahrerassistenzsystem und einen elektronischen Innenspiegel, der einen besseren Überblick über den Verkehr ermöglicht. Zum sicheren Fahren tragen ein Abstandsregeltempomat und ein Notbremsassistent bei.

Begründung der Jury
Der Wey VV7 punktet mit einer attraktiven Gesamtkonzeption, die moderne Technik und ein dynamisches Erscheinungsbild vereint.

Peugeot 508 SW
Passenger Car
Personenkraftwagen

Manufacturer
Groupe PSA, Peugeot Deutschland GmbH,
Cologne, Germany
In-house design
Gilles Vidal
Web
www.peugeot.de

The Peugeot 508 SW comes with a distinctive front, showcasing narrow headlights, while the body displays a sleek silhouette with frameless doors. The luggage compartment has a volume of up to 1,780 litres. In addition to a digital instrument panel and a compact steering wheel, the cockpit offers a HD touchscreen. The latter allows access to various features, including radio and air conditioning or, in certain models, real-time navigation and smartphone apps. The car is equipped with numerous driver-assistance systems.

Statement by the jury
The spacious estate car impresses with remarkably elegant, dynamic looks, further enhanced by contemporary features.

Der Peugeot 508 SW zeichnet sich durch eine markante Front mit schmalen Scheinwerfern aus; die Karosserie zeigt eine schlanke Silhouette mit rahmenlosen Türen. Der Kofferraum hat ein Volumen von bis zu 1.780 Litern. Neben einem digitalen Kombiinstrument und kompakten Lenkrad findet sich ein HD-Touchscreen im Cockpit, der u. a. Zugriff auf Radio und Klimaanlage erlaubt, in einigen Versionen auch auf Echtzeitnavigation und eigene Smartphone-Apps. Der Wagen ist mit zahlreichen Fahrerassistenzsystemen ausgestattet.

Begründung der Jury
Der geräumige Kombi präsentiert sich in einer ausgesprochen eleganten, dynamischen Form, verbunden mit einer zeitgemäßen Ausstattung.

Hyundai Palisade
Passenger Car
Personenkraftwagen

Manufacturer
Hyundai Motor Company, Seoul, South Korea
In-house design
Hyundai Design Center (Luc Donckerwolke)
Web
www.hyundai.com/worldwide

The Palisade was designed as flagship SUV that embodies robust sportiness. A cascade grille with vertically arranged headlights characterises the front of the stout vehicle. The sides are dominated by expansive wheel arches, while the rear lights pick up on the vertical theme of the front. The interior can accommodate up to eight people on three rows of seats. Together with the airiness of the interior, the elongated lines promise a relaxed driving experience, featuring soft seats upholstered in nappa leather depending on the configuration.

Der als Vorzeige-SUV entworfene Palisade verkörpert robuste Sportlichkeit. Ein Kaskaden-Kühlergrill mit vertikal angeordneten Scheinwerfern prägt die Front des stabilen Fahrzeugs. Seitlich dominieren ausladende Radhäuser, während die Rückleuchten das vertikale Thema von vorn wieder aufnehmen. Im Innenraum finden auf drei Sitzreihen bis zu acht Personen Platz. Die gestreckten Linien und die Luftigkeit des Interieurs versprechen im Zusammenspiel mit weichen, je nach Ausstattungsvariante mit Nappaleder bezogenen Sitzen ein entspanntes Fahrerlebnis.

Statement by the jury
The spacious eight-seater appeals with a concise, autonomous design language. The stylish interior promotes enhanced driving comfort.

Begründung der Jury
Der geräumige Achtsitzer gefällt mit seiner prägnanten und eigenständigen Formensprache. Die stilvolle Innenausstattung sorgt für besonderen Fahrkomfort.

Ducati Diavel 1260
Motorcycle
Motorrad

Manufacturer
Ducati Motor Holding S.p.A.,
Bologna, Italy

In-house design
Centro Stile Ducati

Web
www.ducati.com

Powerful interpretation

Since long-distance rides require more from a motorcycle than just fast sprinting capabilities, the choice of a motorcycle is also subject to individual expectations regarding the bike's comfort and sportiness. With the aim of delivering maximum riding pleasure, the design of the Ducati Diavel 1260 motorcycle combines the performance of a maxi-naked bike with the ergonomics and the comfort of a muscle cruiser. It thus embodies a merger of the dynamic and aggressive riding position on a maxi-naked bike with the relaxed, more stretched posture on a cruiser. The result is a reinterpretation of performance and comfort that delivers riding pleasure for both cornering and travelling comfortably with company. The Diavel 1260 also impresses with its bold design appearance. The huge mass at the front and the extra-large 240-mm rear tyre make it look aggressive and muscular – an impression that is strongly counterbalanced by the bike's sharp and agile tail. Overall, the bike exudes a sleek and visually dynamic appearance, which is also due to the perfect integration of the Ducati trademark trellis frame, as well as high-quality finishes and other extremely carefully designed details that enhance its elegant appeal. Featuring a 159-hp Testastretta DVT 1262 engine, the motorcycle boasts high power and delivers effective acceleration for sporty rides and cornering.

Kraftvoll interpretiert

Da das Fahren weiter Strecken andere Anforderungen stellt als etwa das schnelle Sprinten, wird die Wahl eines Motorrads von individuellen Vorstellungen hinsichtlich seines Komforts und der Sportlichkeit bestimmt. Mit der Zielsetzung eines Höchstmaßes an Fahrspaß vereint die Gestaltung des Motorrads Ducati Diavel 1260 die Performance eines Maxi-Naked-Bikes mit dem Komfort und der Ergonomie eines Muscle-Cruisers. Es verkörpert die Mitte zwischen der dynamisch-aggressiven Fahrposition des ersteren und der entspannten, gestreckteren Haltung auf einer Cruiser-Maschine. Das Ergebnis ist eine Kombination aus Leistung und Komfort, womit der Fahrer sowohl das Kurvenfahren wie auch das komfortable Reisen in Gesellschaft genießen kann. Das Diavel 1260 beeindruckt mit einem charaktervollen Auftritt. Seine massig geformte Front sowie die Ausstattung mit einem besonders großen 240-mm-Hinterrad lassen es aggressiv und muskulös erscheinen. Dieser Eindruck wird ausgleichend konterkariert durch eine scharf geschnittene und agil anmutende Heckpartie. Insgesamt wirkt dieses Motorrad auch durch die schlüssige Integration seines Ducati-Gitterrohrrahmens visuell schlank und dynamisch. Eleganz verleihen ihm zusätzlich die überaus sorgfältige Detailgestaltung sowie ein hochwertiges Finish. Auf der Grundlage der Ausstattung mit einem 159 PS starken Testastretta DVT 1262-Motor ist es sehr leistungsfähig und ermöglicht eine effektive Beschleunigung für eine sportliche Kurvenfahrt.

Statement by the jury

The Ducati Diavel 1260 motorcycle has been designed to perfection in every detail. It impresses above all with an appearance exuding power and dynamics. Based on highly developed ergonomics, it offers an exceptionally comfortable riding posture. Its powerful engine delivers outstanding acceleration, which goes hand in hand with a very good roadholding property. It has thus managed to establish itself successful in the segment of traditional motorcycles.

Begründung der Jury

Das Motorrad Ducati Diavel 1260 wurde bis in jedes Detail perfekt durchgestaltet. Dabei beeindruckt es vor allem mit seiner kraftvollen Anmutung und Dynamik. Auf der Basis einer hochentwickelten Ergonomie bietet es eine außerordentlich komfortable Sitzhaltung. Sein leistungsfähiger Motor ermöglicht eine enorme Beschleunigung, die mit einer sehr guten Straßenlage einhergeht. Es kann sich somit erfolgreich im Segment der traditionellen Motorräder etablieren.

Designer portrait
See page 38
Siehe Seite 38

NIKEN
Motorcycle
Motorrad

Manufacturer
Yamaha Motor Co., Ltd.,
Iwata City,
Shizuoka Prefecture, Japan

In-house design
Masahiro Yasuda

Design
GK Dynamics Inc.
(Shogo Kinoshita), Tokyo, Japan

Web
http://global.yamaha-motor.com
www.gk-design.co.jp/dynamics

reddot award 2019
best of the best

Pushing boundaries

For motorcyclists, some roads can easily pose a challenge that also needs to be mastered physically. Here, the NIKEN motorcycle offers an innovative approach towards form and functionality. Featuring a three-wheel design and tiltable front wheels, this multi-wheeler can lean into turns like a motorcycle. Responding effortlessly, the wheels deliver very good grip and a feeling of stability on the road. Powered by a liquid-cooled in-line three-cylinder engine with a capacity of 847 cc and equipped with innovative LMW (Leaning Multi-Wheel) technology, this motorcycle can easily adapt to changing ride environments. This helps to inspire front-end confidence when cornering. The combination of LMW technology and a powerful high-torque engine not only delivers excellent performance for spirited, sporty riding on various road surfaces, it also allows for elegant carving of corners on twisty roads. Optimised weight distribution is ensured by the motorcycle's lightweight hybrid chassis. And taking advantage of a front suspension that pairs the 15" front wheels with dual-tube inverted forks mounted to the outside of the wheels, the body design visually accentuates the machine's sporty performance even further. The NIKEN thus offers even seasoned riders a whole new motorcycling experience.

Design für die Herausforderung

Für Motorradfahrer ist die befahrene Strecke oft auch eine Herausforderung, die sie körperlich meistern müssen. Das Motorrad NIKEN bietet dafür eine innovative Form und Funktionalität. Gestaltet mit einer 3-Rad-Konstruktion und neigbaren Vorderrädern, liegt es als Multi-Wheeler perfekt auf der Straße. Es reagiert sofort und weist eine sehr gute Bodenhaftung und das Gefühl von Stabilität auch bei starken Kurvenverläufen auf. Angetrieben wird es von einem flüssigkeitsgekühlten 3-Zylinder-Reihenmotor mit einem Hubraum von 847 ccm. Durch die Ausstattung mit der innovativen LMW-Technologie (Leaning Multi-Wheel) kann sich dieses Motorrad leicht sich verändernden Fahrumgebungen anpassen. Der Fahrer entwickelt deshalb bei seinen Kurvenfahrten rasch Vertrauen in die Maschine. Diese Technologie bietet im Zusammenspiel mit der starken Motorleistung und einem hohen Drehmoment eine hervorragende Performance für sportliches Fahren auf unterschiedlichen Straßenbelägen. Ermöglicht wird zudem auf kurvenreichen Straßen ein elegantes Schneiden der Kurven. Das leichte Hybrid-Chassis des Motorrads gewährleistet dabei eine optimierte Gewichtsverteilung. Mit dem Konzept einer Vorderradaufhängung, bei der die 15"-Vorderräder mit Zweirohr-Upside-Down-Federgabeln an der Außenseite der Räder kombiniert werden, betont die Karosseriegestaltung die sportliche Leistung der Maschine. Auf diese Weise ermöglicht sie selbst erfahrenen Fahrern ein neues Motorraderlebnis.

Statement by the jury

The futuristic and sporty style of the NIKEN motorcycle attracts high attention. The daring, unusual design of this three-wheel motorcycle is based on the principle of tiltable front wheels and embodies an impressive realisation of a strong concept. As a multi-wheeler it delivers a feeling of stability, functionality and high riding pleasure. Featuring a powerful three-cylinder engine, the motorcycle can easily master a wide variety of road surfaces and conditions.

Begründung der Jury

Mit seiner sportiv-futuristischen Formensprache zieht das Motorrad NIKEN die Aufmerksamkeit auf sich. Das Ungewöhnliche wagend, verwirklicht das Design dieses 3-Rad-Motorrads mit dem Prinzip neigbarer Vorderräder ein starkes Konzept, das beeindruckend umgesetzt wurde. Als Multi-Wheeler bietet es viel Fahrspaß, Funktionalität und gefühlte Stabilität. Mit seinem leistungsfähigen 3-Zylinder-Motor kann es sich leicht unterschiedlichsten Straßenverhältnissen anpassen.

Designer portrait
See page 40
Siehe Seite 40

CAKE Kalk
Electric Motorcycle
Elektromotorrad

Manufacturer
CAKE Zero Emission AB,
Stockholm, Sweden
In-house design
Stefan Ytterborn, David Gonzalez,
Marcus Carlsson
Web
www.ridecake.com

Kalk is intended for off-road use and features components specially developed for this purpose. Weighing only 67 kg, the electric motorcycle comes with an engine within a frame made of screwed aluminium profiles, at a position where conventionally powered bikes have the gearbox. From the cockpit, three riding modes can be selected without a clutch or shifting. Thanks to its digital presets, beginners and professionals can easily ride the bike at their own level.

Statement by the jury
This minimalist electric motorcycle convinces with an innovative concept and promises emission-free riding fun.

Kalk ist für das Fahren im Gelände gedacht und bietet eigens zu diesem Zweck entwickelte Bauteile. Der Motor des nur 67 kg schweren Elektromotorrads steckt in einem Rahmen aus verschraubten Aluminiumprofilen und sitzt an einer Stelle, wo konventionell angetriebene Bikes das Getriebe haben. Vom Cockpit aus sind ohne Kuppeln oder Schalten drei Drive-Modi abrufbar. Dank der digitalen Voreinstellung können Anfänger wie Profis das Motorrad auf ihrem Niveau fahren.

Begründung der Jury
Das minimalistische Elektromotorrad überzeugt mit einem innovativen Konzept und verspricht abgasfreien Fahrspaß.

Ujet
Electric Scooter
Elektroroller

Manufacturer
Ujet, Foetz, Luxembourg
Design
Leo Burnett-Laeufer
(Andreas Läufer), Berlin, Germany
Ujet (Patrick David), Ulm, Germany
BUSSE Design+Engineering
(Valerian Knaub, Felix Timm),
Elchingen, Germany
Web
www.ujet.com

The Ujet electric scooter offers a networked driving experience by giving easy access to GPS navigation, music streaming and telephony. Via a dedicated mobile app, the scooter can be locked or unlocked, tracked and monitored in terms of performance. Thanks to the sculpture-like frame, which can be folded, the two-wheeler also enables space-saving parking. Its battery can be recharged in a normal socket. Furthermore, the vehicle features orbital wheels.

Statement by the jury
With its integrated connectivity, this e-scooter skilfully uses modern technology. The innovative design of the frame creates a strong visual presence.

Der Elektroroller Ujet bietet ein vernetztes Fahrerlebnis, zu dem die bequeme Nutzung von GPS-Navigation, Musik-Streaming und Telefonie gehört. Über die zugehörige Smartphone-App lässt sich der Roller freischalten oder blockieren, lokalisieren und hinsichtlich seiner Leistung überwachen. Dank des skulpturartig geformten, klappbaren Rahmens erlaubt das Zweirad platzsparendes Parken. Die Akkus können an einer normalen Steckdose aufgeladen werden. Außerdem verfügt das Fahrzeug über Orbitalräder.

Begründung der Jury
Der vernetzte E-Roller nutzt gekonnt moderne Technologien. Durch die einfallsreiche Rahmengestaltung hat das Modell eine starke visuelle Präsenz.

Torrot Velocipedo
Electric Vehicle
Elektrofahrzeug

Manufacturer
Torrot Electric Europa S.A., Girona, Spain
In-house design
Design
Mormedi S.A., Madrid, Spain
Web
www.torrot.com
www.mormedi.com

The Velocipedo is a three-wheeled electric vehicle designed to combine the safety of a car with the flexibility of a motorcycle. In the standard version, the vehicle comes as a two-seater with a full roof, allowing it to be operated without a helmet. The one-seat cargo version, in contrast, offers space for a 210-litre topcase and requires helmet use. The exterior of both versions is distinguished by flowing lines that blend organically into the light, sleek bodywork.

Statement by the jury
The Torrot Velocipedo is a comfort-oriented vehicle and inspires with a particularly beautiful execution.

Das Velocipedo ist ein Elektrofahrzeug mit drei Rädern, das die Sicherheit eines Autos mit der Flexibilität eines Motorrades vereinen soll. In der Standardversion ist das Gefährt ein Zweisitzer und komplett überdacht, sodass es ohne Helm gefahren werden kann. Bei der Cargo-Variante mit einem Sitz und Platz für ein 210-Liter-Topcase besteht dagegen Helmpflicht. Das Exterieur beider Versionen ist von fließenden Linien gekennzeichnet, die sich organisch in die leichte, schnittige Karosserie einfügen.

Begründung der Jury
Das Torrot Velocipedo ist ein komfortorientiertes Fahrzeug und begeistert mit einer besonders schönen Ausführung.

Microlino
Microcar
Kabinenroller

Manufacturer
Microlino AG, Küsnacht, Switzerland
In-house design
Design
Marco Brunori, Bern, Switzerland
Web
www.microlino-car.com

The Microlino is perfectly suited to use as a city car. With a length of 2.4 metres, the electric vehicle offers perpendicular parking, while the front entrance makes it easy to exit onto the sidewalk. Other features include a full-length seat bench for two adults, a distinctive combination of headlights and side mirrors, and back wheels that are partly hidden by the bodywork. Thanks to its reduced weight, the compact "bubble car" consumes significantly less energy than other electric cars. Moreover, only about 40 per cent of the parts used in a conventional car are needed for its production.

Der Microlino eignet sich bestens als Elektrofahrzeug für die Stadt: Mit 2,4 Metern Länge lässt er sich quer einparken, und über die Fronttür gelingt der direkte Ausstieg auf den Gehweg. Weitere Features sind die durchgehende Sitzbank für zwei Personen, eine markante Kombination von Scheinwerfern und Seitenspiegeln und teils unter der Karosserie versteckte Hinterräder. Wegen ihres niedrigen Gewichts verbraucht die kompakte „Knutschkugel" deutlich weniger Energie als andere Elektroautos. Darüber hinaus werden für die Produktion nur etwa 40 Prozent der Teile eines herkömmlichen Autos benötigt.

Statement by the jury
The Microlino meets the mobility needs of the future in an environmentally friendly manner and impresses with its modernised retro look.

Begründung der Jury
Der Microlino wird den Mobilitätsanforderungen der Zukunft umweltfreundlich gerecht und beeindruckt mit seinem modernisierten Retro-Look.

Can-Am Maverick XRS Max
Side-by-Side Vehicle
Side-by-Side-Fahrzeug

Manufacturer
BRP Inc., Valcourt, Québec, Canada
In-house design
Web
www.brp.com

As a result of a different design approach, this vehicle features a dramatically lowered centre of gravity and increased suspension. The architecture has been extended to accommodate four passengers. Furthermore, the Rotax in-line triple engine has been turbo-charged to ensure efficient dynamics. Its 172 hp gives the side-by-side vehicle the ability to accelerate from 0 to 100 km/h in less than 5 seconds. The dynamics of the X3 model enable it to handle any terrain at high speeds.

Statement by the jury
The powerful, aggressive exterior of the Maverick XRS Max is in perfect harmony with the vehicle's off-road capabilities.

Als Ergebnis eines neuen Designansatzes hat dieses Gefährt einen betont niedrigen Schwerpunkt und eine verbesserte Federung. Die Fahrzeugarchitektur wurde erweitert, sodass vier Passagiere im Wagen Platz finden. Ein Dreizylinder-Rotax-Motor mit Turbolader sorgt für effiziente Dynamik: 172 PS ermöglichen es dem Side-by-Side-Fahrzeug, in weniger als 5 Sekunden von 0 auf 100 km/h zu beschleunigen. Die Dynamik des X3-Modells ermöglicht es, unwegsames Gelände auch bei hohen Geschwindigkeiten zu bewältigen.

Begründung der Jury
Beim Maverick XRS Max steht das kraftstrotzende Äußere in einem stimmigen Verhältnis zur Einsatztauglichkeit des Fahrzeugs.

Can-Am Maverick Sport Max
Side-by-Side Vehicle
Side-by-Side-Fahrzeug

Manufacturer
BRP Inc., Valcourt, Québec, Canada
In-house design
Web
www.brp.com

The Maverick Sport Max has a spacious cockpit for four occupants that includes four ergonomically constructed seats, additional footrests and grab bars for the passengers. Despite its generous interior, the side-by-side has a short wheelbase and is thus able to navigate even narrow paths and tight trails. With more than 100 patented accessories, the vehicle can be customised for any adventure. It is powered by an efficient 100 hp Rotax engine.

Statement by the jury
Spaciousness, stability and clever details characterise the Maverick Sport Max, which enables four people to have a shared off-road experience.

Der Maverick Sport Max verfügt über ein großzügiges Cockpit für vier Insassen, das vier ergonomisch konstruierte Sitze, zusätzliche Fußstützen und Haltegriffe für die Passagiere enthält. Trotz des geräumigen Innenraums hat das Side-by-Side-Fahrzeug einen kurzen Radstand und bleibt dadurch auch auf engen Pfaden manövrierfähig. Mit mehr als 100 patentierten Zubehörteilen kann das Gefährt für jedes Abenteuer individuell ausgestattet werden. Angetrieben wird es von einem 100 PS starken Rotax-Motor.

Begründung der Jury
Geräumigkeit, Stabilität und ausgeklügelte Details kennzeichnen den Maverick Sport Max, der vier Leuten ein gemeinsames Offroad-Erlebnis ermöglicht.

LinQ Premium Soft Bag
Off-Road Cargo Bag
Offroad Cargo Tasche

Manufacturer
BRP Inc., Valcourt, Québec, Canada
In-house design
Web
www.brp.com

The LinQ Premium Soft Bag has been tailored for off-road use and for mounting on Can-Am Maverick off-road vehicle. With a storage capacity of 65 litres, the soft cargo bag offers plenty of space to safely store equipment and food. Practical dividers serve to clearly organise the contents of the bag, while the three-part cover allows flexible access. The semi-hard shell design is robust and waterproof, complemented by a rubber seal that prevents dust from entering. The LinQ system makes this bag quickly attachable to the vehicle and safely remain in position.

Statement by the jury
A robust and sturdy impression is conveyed by this cargo bags. Thanks to a sophisticated, needs-oriented design, it also convinces in terms of functionality.

The LinQ Premium Soft Tasche ist auf den Einsatz im Gelände zugeschnitten und für das Anbringen auf Can-Am Maverick Offroad-Fahrzeugen konstruiert. Mit einem Stauraum von 65 Litern bietet die weiche Packtasche ausreichend Platz, um Ausrüstung und Proviant sicher unterzubringen. Praktische Trennelemente organisieren den Tascheninhalt übersichtlich, der dreiteilige Deckel ermöglicht einen variablen Zugriff. Die Halbhartschalenausführung ist robust und wasserfest, eine Gummidichtung verhindert, dass Staub eindringt. Das LinQ-System ermöglicht eine schnelle Befestigung und sichere Positionierung der Tasche am Fahrzeug.

Begründung der Jury
Einen stabilen und robusten Eindruck vermitteln diese Packtaschen, die dank ihrer ausgefeilten, bedarfsgerechten Konstruktion auch in funktionaler Hinsicht punkten.

Can-Am Ryker
Three-Wheeler

Manufacturer
BRP Inc., Valcourt, Québec, Canada
In-house design
Web
www.brp.com

This on-road rear-wheel drive vehicle embodies a distinctive mix of car and motorcycle. Thanks to the low seating position, the rider has more control over the three-wheeler. The Ryker offers special adjustable ergonomic features, allowing the foot pegs, brake and handlebars to be adjusted without tools and adapted to the rider's build or their preferred riding style. The accessories include various switch-out panels as well as accessories that can be easily replaced if required.

Dieses Onroad-Fahrzeug mit Hinterradantrieb stellt eine besondere Mischung aus Auto und Motorrad dar. Dank der niedrigen Sitzposition hat der Fahrer mehr Kontrolle über das Dreirad, das zudem besondere ergonomische Modifikationsmöglichkeiten bietet: Fußrasten, Bremse und Lenker können ohne Werkzeug eingestellt und an die Statur des Fahrers oder seinen bevorzugten Fahrstil angepasst werden. Als Zubehör stehen diverse Bedienfelder und Accessoires zur Verfügung, die bei Bedarf leicht eingewechselt werden können.

Statement by the jury
The Can-Am Ryker appeals with a bold frame design and innovative features that meet the special needs of the driver.

Begründung der Jury
Der Can-Am Ryker gefällt mit einer kühnen Rahmengestaltung und kommt den Bedürfnissen des Fahrers durch seine innovative Ausstattung entgegen.

Lynx Radien-X Platform
Snowmobile
Schneemobil

Manufacturer
BRP Inc., Valcourt, Québec, Canada
In-house design
Web
www.brp.com

The Radien-X snowmobile platform has been developed to meet with the extreme conditions of the far north, not only when driving on trails but also in deep snow. An ergonomically optimised riding position relieves the strain on the driver, enabling longer rides. In addition, the low-vibration four-stroke engine is fuel-efficient and ensures reliable drive performance. The exposed frame is equipped with robust, finely tuned body parts and a modern suspension.

Die Motorschlittenplattform Radien-X wurde entwickelt, um den extremen Bedingungen des hohen Nordens beim Fahren auf Wegen wie im Tiefschnee gerecht zu werden. Durch eine ergonomisch optimierte Lenkposition wird der Benutzer bei längeren Fahrten entlastet. Zudem sorgt der vibrationsarme, kraftstoffsparende Viertaktmotor für zuverlässigen Antrieb. Der freiliegende Rahmen ist mit robusten, fein aufeinander abgestimmten Karosserieteilen und einer modernen Aufhängung ausgestattet.

Statement by the jury
The Lynx Radien-X Platform convinces with high-tech efficiency and riding comfort. Both aspects contribute significantly to the usability of a snowmobile.

Begründung der Jury
Die Lynx Radien-X Platform überzeugt mit Hightech-Effizienz und Fahrkomfort. Beide Aspekte tragen spürbar zur Einsatztauglichkeit eines Schneemobils bei.

Sea-Doo RXT-X
Jetboat
Jetboot

Manufacturer
BRP Inc., Valcourt, Québec, Canada
In-house design
Web
www.brp.com

The narrow racing seat of the RXT-X and angled footwell wedges ensure a secure hold for the driver even at high speeds or in rough water. A wide hull with a low centre of gravity lends the boat stability. The back seat can be taken off and used for sunbathing or picnicking on land, offering even more space on the generously designed rear platform. The front storage features 102 litres of space and is directly accessible from the seat bench.

Statement by the jury
The RXT-X personal watercraft impresses with numerous amenities that increase riding pleasure, in particular with an ergonomically optimised seat.

Beim RXT-X sichern eine schmale Rennsitzbank und angewinkelte Keile im Fußraum die Position des Fahrenden – ein Vorteil bei hohen Geschwindigkeiten oder starkem Wellengang. Ein breiter Rumpf mit niedrigem Schwerpunkt macht das Boot stabil. Der Rücksitz lässt sich abnehmen und zum Sonnenbaden oder Picknicken an Land nutzen – auf der ausladenden hinteren Plattform entsteht dann noch mehr Platz. Das vordere Aufbewahrungsfach hat 102 Liter Volumen und ist von der Sitzbank aus direkt zugänglich.

Begründung der Jury
Das Wasserfahrzeug RXT-X beeindruckt mit zahlreichen Features, die den Fahrspaß erhöhen, insbesondere mit einer ergonomisch optimierten Sitzbank.

Sea-Doo FISH PRO
Jetboat
Jetboot

Manufacturer
BRP Inc., Valcourt, Québec, Canada
In-house design
Web
www.brp.com

The FISH PRO personal watercraft has been specially developed for angling, allowing users to explore fishing grounds that are normally reserved for larger boats. Its features include a navigation system and a fish finder. The ergonomically shaped seat facilitates movement on the boat; paired with bevelled foot wedges, the fisherman is well-positioned to tackle any fish. The extended stern offers a removable cooler with rod holders. Colour accents on the hull highlight important functions of the boat.

Statement by the jury
This jetboat is characterised by user-oriented equipment. Its sportive qualities are expressed through a powerful appearance.

Das Wasserfahrzeug FISH PRO wurde speziell für den Angelsport entwickelt: Mit ihm lassen sich auch Fischgründe ansteuern, die sonst größeren Booten vorbehalten sind. Ein Navigations- und Fischsuchgerät gehört zur Ausrüstung. Die ergonomisch geformte Sitzbank erleichtert es, sich auf dem Boot zu bewegen, während schräge Fußstützen für Stabilität beim Angeln sorgen. Auf dem verlängerten Heck befindet sich u. a. ein abnehmbarer Kühler mit Rutenhalterung. Farbige Akzente am Rumpf markieren wichtige Funktionen des Bootes.

Begründung der Jury
Eine benutzerorientierte Ausstattung zeichnet dieses Jetboot aus. Es bringt seine sportlichen Qualitäten in kraftvoller Form zum Ausdruck.

Lampuga Air
Electric Surfboard
Elektro-Surfboard

Manufacturer
Lampuga GmbH, Rastatt, Germany
Design
Schweizer Design Consulting (Oliver Schweizer,
Robin Ritter, Patrick Senfter, Farouk Zemni),
Stuttgart, Germany
Web
www.lampuga.com
www.schweizer.design

You can also find this product
on page 161 and 188.
Dieses Produkt finden Sie auch
auf Seite 161 und 188.

Equipped with a 10 kW (14 hp) engine,
the electrically driven surfboard
Lampuga Air offers emission-free mobility and a driving experience independent
of wind and waves, since it glides over
water at a speed of up to 50 km/h. It is
steered by weight transfer, while the
speed is regulated by a handheld remote
control. The board consists of an inflatable and foldable hull that surrounds
a power unit with the technical components. Thanks to the modular plug-and-
play system, the board can be assembled or disassembled in five minutes,
and it allows easy transportation.

Mit seinem 10 kW (14 PS) starken Motor
bietet das elektrisch betriebene Surfboard
Lampuga Air emissionsfreie Mobilität
und Fahrspaß unabhängig von Wind und
Wellen. Dabei gleitet es mit bis zu 50 km/h
über das Wasser. Die Steuerung erfolgt
über Gewichtsverlagerung, während die
Geschwindigkeit mittels Fernbedienung
geregelt wird. Das Surfboard hat einen aufblasbaren und faltbaren Rumpf, der eine
Antriebseinheit mit den technischen Komponenten umgibt. Dank des modularen
Plug-and-Play-Systems lässt sich das Board
in fünf Minuten auf- oder abbauen und
leicht transportieren.

Statement by the jury
Lampuga Air is an electric board that
meets the requirements of modern users
with its functionality and elegant
appearance.

Begründung der Jury
Lampuga Air ist ein Elektro-Board, das mit
seiner Funktionalität und seinem eleganten
Erscheinungsbild den Anforderungen
moderner Nutzer gerecht wird.

OMEGA V
Gondola Lift Cabin
Seilbahnkabine

Manufacturer
CWA Constructions SA/Corp.,
Olten, Switzerland

In-house design
CWA Constructions SA/Corp.

Web
www.cwa.ch

reddot award 2019
best of the best

Floating in elegance

Floating over landscapes, sights and other places of interest in a gondola lift cabin is always a special experience of its own. Reinterpreting the shape of a gondola lift cabin, the OMEGA V impresses with a purist design that is carried through into each detail. Its clear aesthetics is based on a three-dimensionally shaped roof design that merges the suspension and cabin to form an impressive unified whole. The design of the underfloor adds to the cabin's minimalist look, while the seamlessly integrated drainage and ventilation openings contribute to its optimised aerodynamics. The maximised glazing opens up a fantastic view onto the surroundings and makes the cabin appear as a light, minimalist means of transport. The ergonomically shaped individual seats are connected through precisely fitted links. All seat cover versions were developed to reference the purist overall design. The continuous, homogeneous ceiling effectively absorbs noise and further enhances the harmonious overall impression of the cabin interior. All surfaces on the inside and outside are even and smooth, with fasteners barely visible. The cabin has been developed for different uses, comprising skiing and summer tourism as well as urban transport. With its coherently implemented modular design, it allows adaptation to different requirements and offers a high degree of customisation.

Schwebende Eleganz

Mit einer Seilbahnkabine über Landschaften oder Sehenswürdigkeiten zu schweben, ist stets ein besonderes Erlebnis. Die Form einer Gondelkabine neu interpretierend, besticht die OMEGA V durch ein puristisches Design, das sich bis in die Details fortsetzt. Ihre klare Ästhetik basiert auf einer dreidimensionalen Dachkonstruktion, die die Elemente Aufhängung und Kabine zu einem eindrucksvollen Ganzen verschmelzen lässt. Die Gestaltung des Unterbodens unterstreicht die schlichte Optik, wobei nahtlos integrierte Entwässerungs- und Belüftungsöffnungen zu einer optimalen Aerodynamik beitragen. Die maximierte Verglasung sorgt für einen ausgezeichneten Blick auf die Umgebung und lässt die Kabine als leichtes, minimalistisches Transportmittel erscheinen. Die ergonomisch geformten Einzelsitze sind über passgenaue Elemente miteinander verbunden. Alle Sitzbezugsvarianten wurden in Anlehnung an das puristische Gesamtdesign entwickelt. Die durchgehende, homogene Decke unterstreicht den harmonischen Gesamteindruck des Innenraumes und absorbiert gleichzeitig wirkungsvoll Geräusche. Die Oberflächen auf der Innen- und Außenseite sind gleichmäßig und bündig, wobei die Befestigungselemente kaum sichtbar sind. Diese Kabine wurde für verschiedene Anwendungen konzipiert, wie den Ski- und Sommertourismus oder den Stadtverkehr. Ihr schlüssiger modularer Aufbau ermöglicht die Anpassung an unterschiedlichste Anforderungen und bietet einen hohen Individualisierungsgrad.

Statement by the jury

The OMEGA V gondola lift cabin impresses with its plain and purist form. Its generous glass construction, which lets light come in from all sides, gives cabin users the feeling as if riding in a floating crystal bowl. Nothing interferes with the visual experience. The elegant, high-quality cabin interior impresses with its noise-absorbing ceiling as well as the sporty appearance of the passenger seats.

Begründung der Jury

Die OMEGA V Seilbahnkabine besticht durch ihre schlichte und puristische Form. Ihre großzügige Glaskonstruktion mit einem Lichteinfall von allen Seiten vermittelt den Insassen das Gefühl, sich in einer schwebenden Kristallschale zu befinden. Nichts beeinträchtigt das visuelle Erleben. Das hochwertige und elegante Interieur überzeugt gestalterisch vor allem durch seinen schallabsorbierenden Dachhimmel und die sportive Anmutung der Sitze.

RECARO BL3710
Economy Class Seat
Economy-Class-Sitz

Manufacturer
RECARO Aircraft Seating,
Schwäbisch Hall, Germany
In-house design
André Gärtner, Christoph Schürg,
Oliver Forgatsch
Web
www.recaro-as.com

Weighing in at less than 10 kg, the BL3710 is a lightweight seat for short- and medium-haul flights. The modular system provides airlines with considerable freedom when it comes to seating configurations. The individual seat is ergonomically tailored to the needs of passengers. In particular, a six-way adjustable headrest with neck support allows passengers to lean back comfortably. The backrest features a tablet holder with an optimised viewing angle. Since it is mounted in a space-saving way, passengers can use their tablet even when the tray table is folded down.

Mit weniger als 10 kg Gewicht ist der BL3710 ein Leichtbausitz für Kurz- und Mittelstreckenflüge. Das modulare System lässt den Fluggesellschaften viel Freiheit bei der Sitzkonfiguration. Der Einzelsitz ist ergonomisch auf die Bedürfnisse der Passagiere abgestimmt, insbesondere trägt eine sechsfach verstellbare Kopfstütze mit Nackenunterstützung dazu bei, dass man sich bequem zurücklehnen kann. An der Rückenlehne befindet sich ein Tablet-Halter mit optimiertem Sichtwinkel. Da die Halterung platzsparend angebracht ist, können die Fluggäste ihre Tablets parallel zum ausgeklappten Tisch nutzen.

Statement by the jury
The BL3710 seat exemplifies how efficient construction can succeed in offering airline passengers an excellent level of comfort.

Begründung der Jury
Der BL3710 führt beispielhaft vor Augen, wie Fluggästen bei effizienter Bauweise ein hervorragender Komfort geboten werden kann.

T3 Coupé
Tram
Straßenbahn

Manufacturer
Prague Public Transit Co., Inc.,
Prague, Czech Republic
Design
anna maresova designers (Anna Marešová),
Prague, Czech Republic
Web
www.dpp.cz
www.annamaresova.com
Honourable Mention

This elegantly styled tram has been conceived for sightseeing tours in Prague. The design is based on the chassis of the legendary Tatra T3 tram, a Czech export hit in the 1960s. The mini bar in the passenger compartment is reminiscent of a 1950s ticket counter, while the arched window front is inspired by historical urban buses. The glazed rear part of the vehicle can be opened, allowing passengers to enjoy an open-air ride when the weather is fine.

Diese edel gestylte Straßenbahn wurde für Stadtrundfahrten in Prag konzipiert. Das Design baut auf dem Chassis der legendären Tram Tatra T3 auf, einem Exportschlager der Tschechoslowakei in den 1960er-Jahren. Die Minibar im Fahrgastraum ähnelt einem Ticketschalter der 1950er-Jahre, während die gewölbte Fensterfront von historischen Bussen inspiriert ist. Der hintere, verglaste Teil des Fahrzeugs kann geöffnet werden, sodass die Passagiere die Fahrt bei schönem Wetter unter freiem Himmel genießen können.

Statement by the jury
In designing the T3 Coupé, historic components were integrated into a modern context in a highly successful manner.

Begründung der Jury
Bei der Gestaltung der T3 Coupé wurden historische Komponenten auf ausgesprochen gelungene Weise in einen modernen Zusammenhang integriert.

The new S7
Die neue S7
Commuter Train
S-Bahn

Manufacturer
Stadler Rail AG, Bussnang, Switzerland
Design
RBS, Worblaufen, Switzerland
Tricon AG, Kirchentellinsfurt, Germany
Web
www.stadlerrail.com
www.rbs.ch
www.tricon-design.de

On this commuter train, the even distribution of doors with low-floor access improves the passenger flow. The interior provides ample space for passengers with strollers, luggage or wheelchairs. Illuminated grab poles set colourful accents, while simultaneously indicating the correct doors for disembarking and the closing of doors for enhanced safety. Dark carpeting and dark seat covers, together with indirect LED lighting, provide a comfortable atmosphere in the passenger compartment.

Statement by the jury
While the aesthetically balanced interior scores with its elegance, the functions of the S7 have been precisely tailored to passenger needs.

Bei dieser S-Bahn verbessern gleichmäßig verteilte Türen mit Niederflureinstieg den Fahrgastfluss. Im Innenraum finden Reisende, die mit Kinderwagen, Gepäck oder im Rollstuhl unterwegs sind, reichlich Platz. Beleuchtete Haltestangen setzen farbige Akzente; zugleich zeigen sie die Freigabe sowie das Schließen der Türen an, um die Sicherheit der Mitfahrenden zu erhöhen. Dunkler Teppichboden und dunkle Sitzbezüge sorgen zusammen mit indirekter LED-Beleuchtung für eine behagliche Atmosphäre.

Begründung der Jury
Während das geschmackvoll abgestimmte Ambiente durch Eleganz punktet, sind die Funktionen der S7 präzise auf die Bedürfnisse der Fahrgäste zugeschnitten.

Russian Railways Second-Class Night Train
Train Coach Interior
Zug-Interieur

Manufacturer
Vagonremmash, Moscow, Russia
Design
Ippiart Studio (Dmitry Nazarov, Reyhaneh Fathollah Nouri), Moscow, Russia
Web
www.vagonremmash.ru
www.ippiart.com

This modular interior system for overnight trains fits all standard railway carriages of the train operator. The features include individual lighting at the seat, 220 volt outlets and USB sockets, as well as tables with cup holders and storage options for personal belongings. Partitions and curtains ensure the privacy of passengers despite the cost-effective, open-plan layout. The service area offers vending machines, water dispensers and showers in the washrooms.

Statement by the jury
The train interior convinces with a contemporary appearance, complemented by many conveniences that make travelling enjoyable for passengers.

Dieses modulare Nachtzug-Interieur passt zu allen gängigen Wagen des Zugbetreibers. Zur Ausstattung gehören individuelle Beleuchtung am Platz, 220-Volt-Steckdosen sowie USB-Anschlüsse, Tische mit Getränkehaltern und Aufbewahrungsmöglichkeiten für persönliche Gegenstände. Durch Trennwände und Vorhänge wird die Privatsphäre der Passagiere trotz kostengünstiger Großraumaufteilung gewahrt. Der Servicebereich bietet neben Verkaufsautomaten auch Wasserspender. In den Waschräumen stehen Duschen bereit.

Begründung der Jury
Die Innenausstattung überzeugt mit einem modernen Erscheinungsbild und bietet viele Annehmlichkeiten, die den Reisenden die Zugfahrt erleichtern.

MAN Lion's City
City Bus
Stadtomnibus

Manufacturer
MAN Truck & Bus SE, Munich, Germany
In-house design
Thorsten Bergmaier-Trede, Matthias Böttcher,
Achim Burmeister, Sven Gaedtke, Lena Kliewer,
Martina Kögler, Prof. Andrea Lipp, Moritz Menacher,
Holger Rix, Steffen Schuster, Michael Streicher,
Stephan Schönherr, Holger Koos
Web
www.mantruckandbus.com
www.neoplan-bus.com

The MAN Lion's City is the base of a bus family with selectable diesel, gas, hybrid or electric power train. Thanks to the use of new technologies, the vehicle weighs 800 kg less than its predecessor. The completely segmented exterior with large glass surfaces improves service friendliness and can be painted offline. Inside, the bus appears generous and bright thanks to indirect LED lighting, coordinated colours and materials. All of the partitions and handrails are wall-mounted for easy cleaning. The drivers benefit from an ergonomically and attractively designed workplace.

Der MAN Lion's City ist das Basisfahrzeug einer Busfamilie mit wählbarem Diesel-, Gas-, Hybrid- oder E-Antrieb. Dank neuer Technologien wiegt der Bus 800 kg weniger als sein Vorgänger. Das komplett segmentierte Exterieur mit großen Glasflächen verbessert die Servicefreundlichkeit und ist offline lackierbar. Der Innenraum wirkt durch indirekte LED-Beleuchtung, abgestimmte Farben und Materialien großzügig und hell; Trennwände und Haltestangen sind reinigungsfreundlich ausschließlich an der Wand montiert. Die Fahrer profitieren von einem ergonomisch und attraktiv gestalteten Arbeitsplatz.

Statement by the jury
The city bus is characterised by a stylish appearance with flowing shapes. With its state-of-the-art equipment, it meets the requirements of passengers.

Begründung der Jury
Ein stilvolles Erscheinungsbild mit fließenden Formen kennzeichnet diesen Stadtbus, der den Fahrgastanforderungen mit einer modernen Ausstattung gerecht wird.

Volvo 9900
Coach
Reisebus

Manufacturer
Volvo Bus Corporation, Gothenburg, Sweden
In-house design
Dan Frykholm
Web
www.volvobuses.com

As the manufacturer's flaghip, this coach showcases a premium travel experience. Thanks to the angled window lines and the sloping floor, all passengers have an unobstructed view towards the outside. The driver's station offers both intuitive access to the controls and great visibility, allowing drivers to fully concentrate on their tasks. The design of the exterior places strong emphasis on fuel efficiency and generous luggage capacity, but also on safety aspects such as stability at higher speeds.

Als Flaggschiff des Herstellers wartet dieser Bus mit einem erstklassigen Reiseerlebnis auf. Dank der geneigten Fensterlinie und des abfallenden Bodenniveaus haben alle Passagiere uneingeschränkte Sicht nach draußen. Der Arbeitsplatz des Fahrers bietet sowohl intuitiv bedienbare Elemente als auch sehr gute Sicht, sodass die fahrende Person sich ganz auf ihre Aufgabe konzentrieren kann. Bei der Gestaltung des Exterieurs wurde Wert auf Kraftstoffeffizienz und großen Stauraum gelegt, aber auch auf Sicherheitsaspekte wie die Stabilität bei höheren Geschwindigkeiten.

Statement by the jury
With its distinctive window layout and rounded front, the Volvo 9900 exudes self-confidence and a strong sense of elegance, while the interior is characterised by cosiness.

Begründung der Jury
Mit markantem Fensterlayout und abgerundeter Front wirkt der Volvo 9900 selbstbewusst und elegant, während das Interieur von gepflegter Wohnlichkeit geprägt ist.

Cabiner
Off-Grid Hiking Cabin
Off-Grid-Wanderhütte

Manufacturer
Wikkelhouse,
Amsterdam, Netherlands

In-house design
Oep Schilling, Rick Buchter

Design
Sander Ejlenberg,
Vincent Beekman,
Amsterdam, Netherlands

Web
www.wikkelhouse.com
www.cabiner.com

reddot award 2019
best of the best

Sustained recreation

Exploring nature and landscapes is a strong tourism trend, as well as spending the nights in unusual places. The off-grid Cabiner hiking cabins offer an inspiring new approach towards overnight stays. Following the idea of a fully self-sustained circular design, the cabins use cardboard as their main building material. They are based on a groundbreaking construction technique that involves an innovative rotating mould tool to generate the house-shaped structure. The structure consists of a total of 24 layers that are bonded together using environmentally friendly glue. The result is a robust sandwich structure with optimal insulation properties. Moreover, the processed cardboard also has a delightful aesthetic appeal and possesses exceptional constructive strength. The cabins are placed in Dutch national parks and are only accessible by foot for nature lovers who want to enjoy a night in the wilderness. The interiors are designed to offer visitors a comfortable stay with access to clean drinking water, a hot shower and a non-odorous flushing toilet. With the aim of ensuring efficient energy consumption, the system runs on a photovoltaic cell and a manually operated water pump. Thus, the ground water is filtered and pressurised. Heating is achieved with a wood-fired stove, while an innovative exchanger serves to heat the water and ensures that there is no temperature overflow and no legionella risk.

Nachhaltige Erholung

Das Erkunden von Natur und Landschaft liegt im Trend, ebenso wie die Übernachtung an außergewöhnlichen Orten. Die Cabiner-Hütten bieten hier eine inspirierend neue Aufenthaltsmöglichkeit. Unter der Maxime eines Handelns in gänzlich geschlossenen, nachhaltigen Kreisläufen sind sie hauptsächlich aus dem Material Karton gestaltet. Grundlage dafür ist eine wegweisende Konstruktionstechnik, bei der ein innovatives rotierendes, die hausförmige Struktur erzeugendes Formwerkzeug zum Einsatz kommt. Dabei werden 24 verschiedene Schichten mittels eines umweltfreundlichen Klebstoffs miteinander verbunden. Das Ergebnis ist eine robuste Sandwichstruktur, die zudem optimale Dämmeigenschaften aufweist. Die Verarbeitung des Materials Karton führt zu einer reizvollen Ästhetik und außergewöhnlichen konstruktiven Festigkeit. Die Hütten befinden sich in niederländischen Nationalparks und sind nur zu Fuß erreichbar für Naturliebhaber, die eine Nacht in der Wildnis verbringen wollen. Ihr Innenraum bietet den Besuchern einen komfortablen Aufenthalt mit Zugang zu sauberem Trinkwasser, einer heißen Dusche und einer geruchsfreien Spültoilette. Um einen effizienten Energieverbrauch zu gewährleisten, verfügt das System über eine Solarzelle und eine von Hand betriebene Wasserpumpe. Das Grundwasser wird dabei gefiltert und unter Druck gesetzt. Geheizt wird mit einem Holzofen, ein innovativer Wärmetauscher erhitzt das Wasser und verhindert gleichzeitig eine Temperaturüberschreitung und die Gefahr von Legionellen.

Statement by the jury

Following a modern minimalist approach, these hiking cabins make impressive use of cardboard as a sustainable material for creating a robust and aesthetically appealing construction. The design consistency of both the exterior and the interior is highly noteworthy. Moreover, the Cabiner hiking cabins are also extremely efficient in terms of temperature and climate regulation for comfortable overnight stays. They blend into their natural surroundings and are environmentally neutral.

Begründung der Jury

Einem modernen minimalistischen Ansatz folgend, wird mit den Cabiner-Hütten das nachhaltige Material Karton eindrucksvoll für eine stabile und ästhetische Konstruktion genutzt. Bemerkenswert ist die Konsistenz der Gestaltung im Exterieur wie im Interieur. Diese ansprechenden Übernachtungsorte für Wanderer sind zudem überaus effizient in ihrer Temperatur- und Klimaregulierung. Sie fügen sich in die natürliche Umgebung ein und verhalten sich vollständig umweltneutral.

Designer portrait
See page 42
Siehe Seite 42

X-Cover
Rooftop Tent
Dachzelt

Manufacturer
iKamper, Paju, South Korea
In-house design
Soon Park
Web
www.ikamper.com
Honourable Mention

X-Cover is a patent-pending rooftop tent. Thanks to its sophisticated construction, the need for a bulky PVC cover – obligatory for many traditional models – is eliminated. Mounted on the car roof, X-Cover is conveniently transported, unfolds within just a few minutes and transforms into a generous sleeping space. Optional crossbars can be added for practical storage of equipment.

Statement by the jury
X-Cover impresses with its user-oriented functionality. This rooftop tent is not only easy to handle but also enthrals with a generous amount of space.

X-Cover ist ein zum Patent angemeldetes Dachzelt, das dank seiner ausgeklügelten Konstruktion auf die sperrige, bei vielen Modellen obligatorische PVC-Abdeckung verzichten kann. Auf dem Autodach montiert, lässt sich X-Cover praktisch transportieren, innerhalb weniger Minuten aufklappen und in einen großzügigen Schlafplatz verwandeln. Bei Bedarf können Querstangen zur praktischen Aufbewahrung der Ausrüstung ergänzt werden.

Begründung der Jury
X-Cover beeindruckt mit nutzerorientierter Funktionalität. Das Dachzelt ist komfortabel zu handhaben und punktet zudem mit einem großzügigen Platzangebot.

ERIBA Touring 820
Caravan

Manufacturer
Hymer GmbH & Co. KG,
Bad Waldsee, Germany
In-house design
Web
www.hymer.com
www.eriba.com

The silver metal panels and an overtly self-reliant design lend the ERIBA Touring 820 caravan a futuristic appearance. The interior is characterised by distinctively shaped furniture that is reminiscent of modern yacht design. The 180-degree Panorama Lounge at the front boasts an all-round view, as well as excellent seating comfort thanks to extra-high backrests. The ERIBA Smart Home control system is integrated as standard and can be controlled via a digital control panel or an app.

Statement by the jury
The ERIBA Touring 820 caravan fascinates with a sophisticated, high-quality design, as well as the comfortable and aesthetic interior furnishings.

Seine Verkleidung aus silbernem Glattblech und die prägnante, eigenständige Formgebung verleihen dem Caravan ERIBA Touring 820 ein futuristisches Erscheinungsbild. Der Innenraum zeichnet sich durch markant gestaltete Möbel aus, die an den modernen Yachtbau erinnern. Die 180-Grad-Panorama-Lounge im Bug bietet einen Rundumblick und dank extra hoher Lehnen ausgezeichneten Sitzkomfort. Serienmäßig integriert ist das ERIBA-Smart-Home-System, das sich über ein digitales Bedienpanel und per App steuern lässt.

Begründung der Jury
Der Caravan ERIBA Touring 820 besticht mit seiner hochwertigen, designorientierten Gestaltung sowie der komfortablen und ästhetischen Innenausstattung.

Hymermobil B-Class
ModernComfort I 580
Integrated Motorhome
Integriertes Reisemobil

Manufacturer
Hymer GmbH & Co. KG,
Bad Waldsee, Germany
In-house design
Design
Studio SYN, Rüsselsheim, Germany
Web
www.hymer.com
www.studio-syn.de

The Hymermobil B-Class ModernComfort I 580 combines the chassis cowl of the Mercedes Sprinter with the HYMER SLC chassis to create an independent, elegant and sporty design. A special eye-catcher is the glossy black radiator grille, which, together with the LED fog lights, blends harmoniously into the front design. Various assistance systems, including Active Distance Control, Crosswind Assist and Active Brake Assist, ensure an enhanced degree of safety.

Statement by the jury
This motorhome convinces with a dynamic exterior design marked by sporty proportions. The design of the interior is exceedingly generous and comfortable.

Das Hymermobil B-Klasse ModernComfort I 580 verbindet den Triebkopf des Mercedes Sprinter mit dem SLC-Chassis von HYMER zu einem eigenständigen, sportiv-eleganten Design. Besonderer Blickfang ist der schwarz glänzende Kühlergrill, der sich ebenso wie die LED-Nebelscheinwerfer harmonisch in die Gestaltung der Front einfügt. Unterschiedliche Assistenzsysteme wie der aktive Abstandsassistent oder ein Seitenwind- und Bremsassistent sorgen für ein hohes Maß an Sicherheit.

Begründung der Jury
Dieses Reisemobil überzeugt mit einem dynamischen, von sportlichen Proportionen geprägten Exterieurdesign. Die Innenraumgestaltung ist ausgesprochen großzügig und komfortabel.

AMAZONE ZG-TS 10001
Fertiliser Spreader
Düngerstreuer

Manufacturer
AMAZONEN-Werke,
H. Dreyer GmbH & Co. KG,
Hasbergen-Gaste, Germany
In-house design
Heinke Nienstermann
Web
www.amazone.de

This large-area fertiliser spreader features automatic spreader monitoring, which ensures that the exact amount of required fertiliser is delivered. Precise tracking with a steerable axle minimises damage to plants and soil during field passes. The hopper of the farm machine, which rises towards the rear, has a high load capacity. The all-round cover offers integrated storage compartments for tools and accessories, even giving users the possibility to wash their hands.

Statement by the jury
The ZG-TS 10001 impresses with sophisticated fertilisation technology, combined with a dynamic outer appearance that communicates readiness for work.

Dieser Großflächenstreuer bietet eine automatische Streuüberwachung und -regelung, die dafür sorgt, dass der Dünger passgenau ausgebracht wird. Mit seiner lenkbaren Achse fährt der Streuer spurtreu und minimiert Schäden an Pflanzen und Boden. Der nach hinten ansteigende Behälter der Landmaschine hat ein großes Fassungsvermögen. In der umlaufenden Verkleidung sind Transportfächer für Werkzeug und Zubehör integriert. Hier haben die Nutzer sogar die Möglichkeit, sich die Hände zu waschen.

Begründung der Jury
Der ZG-TS 10001 besticht durch ausgereifte Düngetechnik, verbunden mit einer dynamischen äußeren Form, die Einsatzbereitschaft ausdrückt.

AGRIFAC Condor Endurance II
Agricultural Sprayer
Landwirtschaftliches Sprühfahrzeug

Manufacturer
Agrifac Machinery BV,
Steenwijk, Netherlands
Design
Vanderveer Designers,
Geldermalsen, Netherlands
Web
www.agrifac.com
www.vanderveerdesigners.nl

The nozzles of this agricultural machine are individually controlled by sensors, cameras and artificial intelligence, enabling the precise spraying of plants. The fuel tanks between the wheels and the spray tank positioned at the centre of the machine are cast from a lightweight plastic material. The side elements and front cover are also moulded from high-impact plastic. The comparatively low overall weight of the sprayer facilitates high capacity.

Statement by the jury
The future-oriented technology of the Condor Endurance II goes hand in hand with a precisely executed, dynamic design.

Die Düsen dieser Landmaschine werden durch Sensoren, Kameras und künstliche Intelligenz gesteuert, sodass die Pflanzen passgenau besprüht werden können. Zwischen den Rädern befinden sich die Kraftstofftanks, die ebenso wie der mittig platzierte Spritzbehälter Gussformen aus einem leichten Kunststoffmaterial sind. Seitenelemente und Frontabdeckung bestehen ebenfalls aus schlagfestem Kunststoff. Das vergleichsweise geringe Gewicht des Sprühfahrzeugs ermöglicht ein großes Fassungsvermögen.

Begründung der Jury
Zukunftsorientierte Technik steht bei der Condor Endurance II im Einklang mit einem präzise ausgeführten, dynamischen Design.

CLG4180D
Motor Grader
Straßenhobel

Manufacturer
Guangxi Liugong Machinery Co., Ltd., Liuzhou, China
In-house design
Gary Edmund Major, Richard John Killgren, Edward Lee Wagner
Web
www.liugong.com

The cab of this motor grader is characterised by a five-pillar structure featuring a special single C-pillar, which allows a 320-degree field of view. The hood is made of lightweight, impact-resistant composite and can be raised at an angle of 50 degrees for improved service access. Looking over the hood, the driver can see the entire rear end of the machine, while the exhaust and pre-cleaner are aligned with the C-pillar to fall into the natural blind spot behind the driver's head. The shape of the blade carrier and the narrow A-pillars have also been configured to improve the visibility to the front.

Das Führerhaus dieses Straßenhobels zeichnet sich durch eine Fünf-Säulen-Struktur mit spezieller einzelner C-Säule aus, die ein Sichtfeld von 320 Grad ermöglicht. Die Motorhaube besteht aus leichtem, stoßfestem Verbundstoff; für eine einfachere Wartung lässt sie sich in einem Winkel von 50 Grad anheben. Über die Haube hinweg kann der Fahrer das gesamte hintere Maschinenende sehen, während Auspuff und Abgasfilter in einer Linie mit der C-Säule hinter ihm im toten Winkel liegen. Die Formen des Klingenträgers und der schmalen A-Säulen sind ebenfalls so ausgelegt, dass sie die Sicht nach vorn verbessern.

Statement by the jury
The CLG4180D grader offers a well-balanced mix of clean lines, functional materials and user-friendly features.

Begründung der Jury
Der Grader CLG4180D bietet eine ausgewogene Mischung aus klaren Linien, funktionellen Materialien und bedienerfreundlichen Eigenschaften.

Cat® EP14–20A(C)NT range
Electric Counterbalance Lift Trucks
Elektro-Gegengewichtsstapler

Manufacturer
Rocla Oy, Järvenpää, Finland
In-house design
Web
www.rocla.com
www.catlifttruck.com

This electric forklift range comes with 360-degree steering, which keeps the load particularly stable due to smooth but fast flowing turns. Its responsive drive system reacts to speed, steering and pedal movements, ensuring well-controlled handling and manoeuvring. In addition, the range is equipped with load-sensing hydraulics and features such as curve control and hill-hold. The customised functions and options of these Cat 48V models offer improved operator ergonomics and help to reduce fatigue.

Diese Elektro-Gabelstaplerreihe zeichnet sich durch ihre 360-Grad-Lenkung aus, die Lasten mit gleichmäßigen, aber schnellen Drehbewegungen besonders gut stabilisiert. Das Responsive-Drive-System passt die Leistung an die Geschwindigkeit der Pedalbetätigung an, sodass Aktionen leicht gesteuert werden können. Zudem ist die Reihe mit automatischer Lastenerkennung ausgestattet und wartet mit Features wie Kurvensteuerung und Berganfahrhilfe auf. Die maßgeschneiderten Funktionen und Optionen der Cat-48V-Modelle bieten eine verbesserte Ergonomie und lassen den Bediener weniger schnell ermüden.

Statement by the jury
The EP14–20A(C)NT range convinces with its advanced forklift technology and great adaptability, which simplifies the working process.

Begründung der Jury
Die Reihe EP14–20A(C)NT überzeugt mit fortschrittlicher Gabelstaplertechnik und großer Anpassungsfähigkeit, die den Arbeitsablauf im Betrieb vereinfacht.

Philips X-tremeUltinon gen2 LED retrofit
LED Automotive Lighting
LED-Fahrzeugbeleuchtung

Manufacturer
Lumileds, Suresnes, France

Design
Signify Design Team,
Shanghai, China
Philips Design,
Eindhoven, Netherlands

Web
www.philips.com

reddot award 2019
best of the best

Innovative performance
Until very recently, only new car owners could enjoy the LED aesthetics and performance. Thanks to new developments, passionate drivers can upgrade their existing bulbs to LED retrofit bulbs which offer similar style and performance. Fitted with exclusive OEM Altilon SMD LEDs, the Philips X-tremeUltinon gen2 LED delivers cool white light and excellent beam pattern. Presenting itself with sophisticated functionality and wide compatibility, this system allows easy and straightforward retrofitting of many cars that are not equipped with LED lighting yet. The modular design allows individual configurations for a wide variety of different models. The elegant and compact design of this LED lighting ensures easy, self-explanatory installation. The highly compact LEDs provide an accurate beam pattern and effective light output. The electromagnetic interference shielding complies with automotive industry standards for electromagnetic interference. The LED's patented heat management and the use of high-quality aluminium in a one-piece design both ensure a constant and durable high road illumination. The headlight bulbs feature an optimised colour tone and produce an intense, neutral white light beam for more road safety and driving comfort, especially at night. The Philips X-tremeUltinon gen2 LED allows safe driving without disturbing oncoming traffic or other road users.

Innovative Leistungsfähigkeit
Bis vor kurzem konnten lediglich die Besitzer von Neuwagen die Ästhetik und Leistung der LED-Technologie genießen. Dank neuer Entwicklungen, können passionierte Fahrer bestehende Leuchten mit LED-Lampen nachrüsten, die eine vergleichbare Stilistik und Performance aufweisen. Ausgestattet mit den exklusiven OEM-LEDs Altilon SMD, bietet die Philips X-tremeUltinon gen2 LED ein kühles weißes Licht und eine ausgezeichnete Lichtverteilung. Mit ihrer durchdachten Funktionalität und hohen Kompatibilität erlaubt sie ein unkompliziertes Nachrüsten. Die modulare Gestaltung ermöglicht individuelle Konfigurationen für die jeweiligen Fahrzeuge. Die elegante und kompakte Gestaltung dieser LED-Beleuchtung gewährleistet eine einfache, selbsterklärende Montage. Die sehr kompakten LEDs verfügen über eine präzise Lichtverteilung und effektive Lichtleistung. Sie sind zudem elektromagnetisch störsicher und konform zu Automobil-Industriestandards bei elektromagnetischen Interferenzen. Das patentierte Wärmemanagement und die hochwertige Fertigung aus einem einzigen Stück Aluminium sorgen für eine konstant und dauerhaft hohe Fahrbahnausleuchtung. Die Scheinwerferlampen arbeiten mit einer optimierten Lichtfarbe und erzeugen einen intensiven, neutralweißen Lichtstrahl für mehr Sicherheit und Fahrkomfort, gerade auch bei Nacht. Die Philips X-tremeUltinon gen2 LED erlaubt ein sicheres Fahren, ohne den entgegenkommenden Verkehr oder andere Verkehrsteilnehmer zu stören.

Statement by the jury
The Philips X-tremeUltinon gen2 LED possesses an excellent quality that speaks for itself. This product range not only realises the idea of easily retrofitting traditional car headlights, it also impresses with a highly consistent design. Every detail has been executed to very high standards and in a user-oriented way. Particularly outstanding in this design, which unites all elements in a coherent manner, is the perfectly solved thermal management design.

Begründung der Jury
Die Philips X-tremeUltinon gen2 LED zeigt eine hervorragende Qualität, die für sich selbst spricht. Die mit diesem Sortiment verwirklichte Idee des problemlosen Ersetzens traditioneller Fahrzeugbeleuchtung beeindruckt durch ihre gestalterische Konsequenz. Jedes Detail wurde dabei ausgesprochen hochwertig und nutzerorientiert ausgeführt. Bei dem alle Elemente schlüssig zusammenführenden Design fällt insbesondere das Wärmemanagement auf, das perfekt gelöst wurde.

Designer portrait
See page 44
Siehe Seite 44

ROADTIGER
Truck Driver Seat
Lkw-Fahrersitz

Manufacturer
GRAMMER AG, Amberg, Germany
In-house design
Richard Ott, Sandra Brombacher
Design
Carter Design Innovation Network (Raymond Carter),
Marina del Rey, California, USA
Tim Payne, Columbus, Ohio, USA
Web
www.grammer.com

The design objective of the ROADTIGER was to ensure an ergonomic and comfortable driving experience. This truck driver seat features a cleverly designed suspension system as well as flexible seat and height adjustment with memory function. Moreover, the three-point seat belt allows for individual adjustments. Two-stage seat heating and a headrest, which is integrated in the backrest, provide extra comfort. The modern design and the high-quality fabric and leather covers enhance the appearance of the driver cab.

Ein ergonomisches und komfortables Fahrerlebnis zu gewährleisten, war das Gestaltungsziel des ROADTIGER. Der Lkw-Fahrersitz verfügt über ein ausgeklügeltes Federungssystem sowie eine flexible Sitz- und Höheneinstellung mit Memory-Funktion. Auch der 3-Punkt-Gurt lässt sich individuell einrichten. Für besonderen Komfort sorgt die zweistufige Sitzheizung sowie die in die Lehne integrierte Kopfstütze. Die moderne Formgebung sowie die hochwertigen Stoff- und Lederbezüge werten das Fahrerhaus optisch auf.

Statement by the jury
The ROADTIGER truck driver seat is characterised by an ergonomically and aesthetically sophisticated design that also convinces in terms of functionality.

Begründung der Jury
Eine ergonomisch und ästhetisch durchdachte Gestaltung zeichnet den Lkw-Fahrersitz ROADTIGER aus, der auch in funktionaler Hinsicht zu überzeugen weiß.

Ventus S1 evo3
Car Tyre
Autoreifen

Manufacturer
Hankook Tire, Seoul, South Korea
In-house design
Seungkoo Kang, Seungju Kwak
Web
www.hankooktire.com

The design of the Ventus S1 evo3 car tyre focuses on improving driving performance and reducing noise emissions. The asymmetrical profile has been designed for high stability – on both wet and dry roads. The distinctive interlocking outer grooves of the tyre prevent aquaplaning on slick surfaces, providing a secure wet grip.

Statement by the jury
Ventus S1 evo3 features a sophisticated tread design that imparts reliability and offers improved road grip.

Bei der Gestaltung des Autoreifens Ventus S1 evo3 standen die Verbesserung der Fahrleistung sowie die Verringerung der Geräuschemission im Mittelpunkt. Das asymmetrische Profil ist auf hohe Festigkeit ausgelegt – auf nassen sowie trockenen Straßen gleichermaßen. Die markanten Außenrillen des Reifens greifen ineinander, um Aquaplaning auf glatten Oberflächen zu vermeiden und einen sicheren Nassgriff zu ermöglichen.

Begründung der Jury
Ventus S1 evo3 begeistert mit einem ausgeklügelten Profildesign, das Zuverlässigkeit vermittelt und eine verbesserte Straßenhaftung bietet.

Evoluzion F60
Car Tyre
Autoreifen

Manufacturer
Federal Corporation, Taoyuan City, Taiwan
In-house design
Web
www.federaltire.com

This sophisticated tyre tread has been developed for high-performance cars. Its design is reminiscent of claws. The distinctive pattern gives the tyre a dynamic, assertive look, while also ensuring a firm grip on wet roads. Circumferential tread grooves also guarantee precise handling at high speeds. Thanks to the silica-infused material, the Evoluzion F60 gains extra stability and convinces with extended durability.

Statement by the jury
The characteristic tread design of the Evoluzion F60 tyre leads to improved functionality and a safer driving experience – even at high speeds.

Dieses ausgefeilte Reifenprofil wurde für leistungsstarke Autos entwickelt. Seine Gestaltung erinnert an Klauen. Das prägnante Muster verleiht dem Reifen eine dynamische, selbstbewusste Optik und sorgt zugleich für festen Halt auf nassen Straßen. Umlaufende Profilrillen gewährleisten diesen auch bei hoher Geschwindigkeit. Dank des mit Silicagel angereicherten Materials erhält Evoluzion F60 zusätzliche Stabilität und überzeugt mit längerer Haltbarkeit.

Begründung der Jury
Die charakteristische Profilgestaltung des Reifens Evoluzion F60 führt zu verbesserter Funktionalität und zu einem sicheren Fahrgefühl – selbst bei hohen Geschwindigkeiten.

Yokohama
GEOLANDAR X-MT
Tyre for Off-Road Vehicles
Reifen für Geländefahrzeuge

Manufacturer
The Yokohama Rubber Co., Ltd.,
Tokyo, Japan
In-house design
Masayuki Nemoto
Design
nagahama design (Masayuki Fushimi),
Tokyo, Japan
Web
www.y-yokohama.com
www.nagahamadesign.com

This tyre is conceived for off-road vehicles and pickups. Its distinctive, powerful tread design is reminiscent of rocks and offers high traction on smooth, wet and even rocky roads. Its side block structure protects the tyre from damage. At the same time, it provides additional biting edges for better grip in extreme road conditions. The material used resists cutting and chipping.

Statement by the jury
GEOLANDAR X-MT has been optimised for off-road use. With its distinctive tread design, this tyre ensures stability and secure grip even in extreme conditions.

Dieser Reifen ist für Geländewagen und Pick-ups konzipiert. Sein markantes, kraftvolles Profildesign erinnert an Felsgestein und bietet auch auf steinigen, nassen und glatten Strecken eine hohe Traktion. Seine seitliche Blockstruktur schützt den Reifen vor Beschädigungen und bietet zugleich zusätzliche Greifkanten für besseren Halt bei extremen Straßenbedingungen. Das verwendete Material ist widerstandsfähig gegen Schnitte und Splitter.

Begründung der Jury
GEOLANDAR X-MT ist für den Offroad-Einsatz optimiert. Mit seinem prägnanten Profildesign bietet der Reifen auch unter extremen Bedingungen Stabilität und sicheren Halt.

70mai Dash Cam Pro
Dashcam

Manufacturer
70mai Co., Ltd., Shanghai, China
In-house design
Qing Xu
Web
www.70mai.com

The objective in the development of the 70mai Dash Cam Pro was to foster well-thought-out human-computer interaction. Features of the device, which is mounted at the height of the rear-view mirror, include an assistance system with an integrated real-time alert. It notifies the driver before the car veers off the road or runs the risk of colliding with another car. The camera is rotatable and produces clear and vivid images at a resolution of 5 MP.

Statement by the jury
The 70mai Dash Cam Pro consistently places the user centre stage. Both the design and handling of this car camera are highly user-friendly.

Das Ziel bei der Entwicklung der 70mai Dash Cam Pro war eine durchdachte Mensch-Computer-Interaktion. Zu den Funktionen des auf Höhe des Rückspiegels zu montierenden Gerätes gehört ein Assistenzsystem, das auch eine Alarmfunktion beinhaltet. Diese warnt den Fahrer, wenn das Auto von der Bahn abweicht oder Gefahr läuft, mit einem anderen Wagen zu kollidieren. Die Kamera ist drehbar und erzeugt mit ihrer 5-MP-Auflösung klare und lebendige Bilder.

Begründung der Jury
Die 70mai Dash Cam Pro stellt den Nutzer konsequent in den Mittelpunkt. Sowohl die Gestaltung als auch die Handhabung der Dashcam sind sehr anwenderfreundlich umgesetzt.

70mai Dash Cam
Dashcam

Manufacturer
70mai Co., Ltd., Shanghai, China
In-house design
Qing Xu
Web
www.70mai.com

With its minimalist design marked by flowing lines and a compact form, the 70mai camera fits into any car interior. It allows space-saving installation and guarantees a consistently clear view of the street. The camera produces images and videos at a resolution of 2,592 x 1,600 pixels. Voice control, parking monitoring and a collision alarm are integrated in the device, rounding off the functional scope.

Statement by the jury
An elegant, compact design, high functionality and user-friendly handling distinguish the 70mai Dash Cam.

Mit ihrer minimalistischen, von fließenden Linien geprägten Gestaltung und ihrer kompakten Form passt die Kamera in jedes Autointerieur. Sie lässt sich platzsparend anbringen und gewährleistet eine durchgängig freie Sicht auf die Straße. Bilder und Videos werden in einer Auflösung von 2.592 x 1.600 Pixeln aufgenommen. Eine Sprachsteuerung, eine Parküberwachung sowie ein Kollisionsalarm sind im Gerät integriert und runden den Funktionsumfang ab.

Begründung der Jury
Eine elegante, kompakte Gestaltung, hohe Funktionalität und benutzerfreundliche Handhabung zeichnen die 70mai Dash Cam aus.

CM51
Dashcam

Manufacturer
China Mobile IOT Company Limited,
Chongqing, China
In-house design
Pengfei Huang
Web
iot.10086.cn

The CM51 is a voice-controlled dashboard camera. Its sleek display is aligned parallel to the driver and, thanks to its rounded edges, projects an elegant look. The lens can be moved 15 degrees in all directions, greatly reducing the blind spot. Photos and videos are automatically saved and uploaded to the cloud in the event of unusual vibrations while driving.

Statement by the jury
A functionally sophisticated dashcam, the CM51 captivates with a discreetly designed, timeless housing.

Die CM51 ist eine sprachgesteuerte Dashcam. Ihr schlankes Display erhält durch seine abgerundeten Kanten eine elegante Anmutung und ist parallel zum Fahrer ausgerichtet. Das Objektiv lässt sich um 15 Grad in alle Richtungen bewegen, wodurch der tote Winkel stark reduziert wird. Fotos und Videos werden automatisch gespeichert und können – im Falle ungewöhnlicher Erschütterungen während der Fahrt – in die Cloud geladen werden.

Begründung der Jury
Die CM51 besticht als funktional durchdachte Dashcam mit dezent gestaltetem, zeitlos wirkendem Gehäuse.

Roav Bolt
Smart Car Charger
Intelligentes Autoladegerät

Manufacturer
Shenzhen Oceanwing Smart
Innovation Co., Ltd., Shenzhen, China
In-house design
Xiaoyu Niu, Sangmin Yu, Tong Li, Xuefeng Bai
Web
www.anker.com

Roav Bolt is a car charger with integrated Google Assistant and Bluetooth functionality that connects wirelessly to any car or smartphone. It employs voice control, which allows the driver to easily make phone calls or select navigation destinations. The extremely slim charger with its purist design is powered via the cigarette lighter and equipped with two USB ports.

Statement by the jury
Roav Bolt scores with a simple design that contributes to the overall premium appearance of this user-oriented car charger.

Roav Bolt ist ein Autoladegerät mit integriertem Google Assistant und Bluetooth-Funktion, über die es sich drahtlos mit jedem Auto und Smartphone verbinden lässt. Per Sprachsteuerung können so unkompliziert Anrufe getätigt oder Navigationsziele ausgewählt werden. Das sehr schlank gehaltene, puristisch gestaltete Ladegerät verfügt über zwei USB-Anschlüsse und wird über den Zigarettenanzünder mit Strom versorgt.

Begründung der Jury
Roav Bolt punktet mit einer schlichten Gestaltung, die zu dem hochwertigen Gesamteindruck des anwenderorientierten Autoladegerätes beiträgt.

Mini Car Charger
USB Car Charger
USB-Autoladegerät

Manufacturer
Shenzhen Renqing Excellent
Investment Co., Ltd., Shenzhen, China
In-house design
Zhuoxi Lin, Yanjuan Wu
Web
www.rockphone.hk

This mini car charger fits flush into the cigarette lighter and features two USB ports that offer the ability to charge multiple devices simultaneously. The main focus of the design was placed on an elegant appearance, achieved by the combination of natural leather and a silver-coloured zinc alloy. The slim leather strap also serves a function: pulling out the charger safely and quickly if required.

Statement by the jury
The mini car charger is very well thought out in terms of functionality and captivates with a timeless appearance that harmoniously integrates into car interiors.

Dieses Mini-Autoladegerät fügt sich bündig in den Zigarettenanzünder ein und bietet mit gleich zwei USB-Ports die Möglichkeit, mehrere Geräte parallel zu laden. Hauptaugenmerk der Gestaltung war ein stilvolles Erscheinungsbild, das durch die Kombination aus natürlichem Leder und silberner Zinklegierung erreicht wird. Das schmale Lederband ist zugleich funktional: An ihm lässt sich das Ladegerät bei Bedarf sicher und schnell herausziehen.

Begründung der Jury
Das Mini-Autoladegerät ist funktional sehr durchdacht und beeindruckt zudem mit einem zeitlosen Erscheinungsbild, das sich harmonisch in den Fahrzeuginnenraum integriert.

Tmall Genie Amap Autobox
Smart Voice Assistant
Intelligentes Assistenzsystem

Manufacturer
Amap Information Technology Co., Ltd.,
Beijing, China
Design
Zhejiang Tmall Technology Co., Ltd.
(Jianye Li, Zhichao Xue), Hangzhou, China
Web
www.autonavi.com
www.alibabagroup.com

Tmall Genie Amap Autobox is a voice-controlled, intelligent navigation and entertainment system that connects to selected vehicle models via USB. The cylindrical aluminium housing with its slim design boasts a highly modern look that lends a consistent form to the high-tech technology inside. The smart voice assistant filters noise from the environment, ensuring accurate voice recognition and precise control of all functions.

Die Autobox Tmall Genie Amap ist ein sprachgesteuertes, intelligentes Navigations- und Unterhaltungssystem, das mithilfe eines USB-Kabels in ausgewählten Fahrzeugtypen angeschlossen werden kann. Das schlanke, zylindrische Gehäuse aus Aluminium wirkt sehr modern und gibt der Hightechtechnologie im Inneren eine stimmige Form. Das intelligente Assistenzsystem filtert Störgeräusche aus der Umgebung und sorgt auf diese Weise für eine gute Spracherkennung und präzise Steuerung der Funktionen.

Statement by the jury
Tmall Genie Amap Autobox is a harmoniously designed voice assistant that impresses with innovative technology and user-friendly features.

Begründung der Jury
Tmall Genie Amap Autobox ist ein ausgewogen gestaltetes Assistenzsystem, das mit innovativer Technologie und benutzerfreundlichen Funktionen zu beeindrucken weiß.

T20
Car Refrigerator
Autokühlschrank

Manufacturer
Guangdong Indel B Enterprise Co., Ltd.,
Zhongshan, China
In-house design
Yu Xie
Web
www.indelb.cn

This car refrigerator keeps food, drinks, medicines and cosmetics reliably cold when travelling. The T20 is either powered via the cigarette lighter or by batteries. The desired storage temperature can be set individually for each compartment, allowing the contents to be frozen down to -18 degrees Celsius. The dark control element in the lid is easy to handle and sets a visually effective accent against the white lacquered surface.

Statement by the jury
The T20 successfully combines elegance and practicality, providing an aesthetically pleasing solution for the safe and cool transportation of food and medicines.

Der Autokühlschrank hält Lebensmittel, Getränke, Medikamente und Kosmetika auf Reisen zuverlässig kalt. T20 kann über den Zigarettenanzünder mit Energie versorgt oder über Batterien betrieben werden. Für jedes Fach lassen sich individuelle Lagertemperaturen einstellen, die je nach Inhalt bis auf -18 Grad runtergeregelt werden können. Das dunkle Bedienelement im Deckel ist leicht zu handhaben und setzt in der weiß lackierten Oberfläche optisch wirkungsvolle Akzente.

Begründung der Jury
T20 kombiniert Eleganz und Praktikabilität auf gelungene Weise und bietet eine ästhetisch ansprechende Lösung, um Lebensmittel und Medikamente sicher und kühl zu transportieren.

Thule Vector
Rooftop Cargo Box
Dachbox

Manufacturer
Thule Group AB, Malmö, Sweden
In-house design
Web
www.thule.com

With sporty lines and concise proportions, the Thule Vector rooftop box complements any vehicle design in a very stylish manner. Particularly eye-catching features are a dynamic, forward-leaning front and the smooth, seamless connection between lid and base. The rooftop box can be easily loaded from both sides; if required, an LED light built into the lid provides illumination even in the dark. To protect the contents, the inside of the box is lined with felt.

Statement by the jury
Thule Vector impresses with a self-reliant, sophisticated design. The matte and dark surfaces exude an elegant appeal.

Mit sportlichen Linien und prägnanten Proportionen ergänzt die Dachbox Thule Vector jedes Fahrzeugdesign sehr stilvoll. Besonders ins Auge fallen die glatte, nahtlose Verbindung zwischen Korpus und Deckel sowie die dynamisch nach vorne geneigte Front. Die Dachbox kann bequem von beiden Seiten beladen werden, ein im Deckel eingebautes LED-Licht sorgt auch bei Dunkelheit für eine bedarfsgerechte Ausleuchtung. Zum Schutz des Inhalts ist das Innere der Box mit Filz ausgelegt.

Begründung der Jury
Thule Vector beeindruckt mit einer eigenständigen, raffinierten Formgebung. Die matt und dunkel gehaltenen Oberflächen wirken elegant.

19RCS Corsa Corta
Brake Master Cylinder
Hauptbremszylinder

Manufacturer
Brembo S.p.A., Curno (Bergamo), Italy
In-house design
Web
www.brembo.com

The sporty styling of the 19RCS Corsa Corta brake master cylinder is specifically tailored to the dynamic design of sports motorcycles. Its anodised surface makes the cylinder housing durable and ensures that all integrated components run smoothly. A newly developed technology allows individual adjustments to the braking process. The easy-to-reach selector on the top of the cylinder lets the rider choose between the different responsiveness settings of "Normal", "Sport" and "Race", enabling the bite point of the brake to be tailored.

Statement by the jury
The 19RCS Corsa Corta brake master cylinder convinces with innovative, user-oriented technology that promotes an individual riding experience.

Die sportliche Formgebung des Hauptbremszylinders 19RCS Corsa Corta ist gezielt auf das dynamische Design von Sportmotorrädern abgestimmt. Seine eloxierte Oberfläche macht den Zylinder langlebig und die integrierten Komponenten leichtgängig. Eine neu entwickelte Technologie ermöglicht die individuelle Einstellung des Bremsvorgangs. Über den leicht zu erreichenden Wahlschalter an der Oberseite können die Einstellungen „Normal", „Sport" und „Race" gewählt und der Eingriffspunkt der Bremse angepasst werden.

Begründung der Jury
Der Hauptbremszylinder 19RCS Corsa Corta überzeugt mit einer innovativen, nutzerorientierten Technologie, die ein individuelles Fahrerlebnis ermöglicht.

Akrapovič Evolution Line (Titanium) for the BMW S 1000 RR
Akrapovič Evolution Line (Titan) für die BMW S 1000 RR
Exhaust System
Abgasanlage

Manufacturer
Akrapovič d.d., Ivančna Gorica, Slovenia
In-house design
Web
www.akrapovic.com

This exhaust system was developed especially for the BMW S 1000 RR motorcycle. The aim was to increase the performance of the engine, while at the same time reducing the weight of the machine. To achieve this, the system, which weighs only 4.1 kg, uses lightweight titanium alloys and a handcrafted carbon-fibre end cap, which also lend the system its distinctive appearance. The shape of the exhaust system continues the expressive lines of the machine and coherently blends into the sporty design of the motorcycle.

Diese Abgasanlage wurde speziell für das BMW-Motorrad S 1000 RR entwickelt. Ziel war es, die Leistungsfähigkeit des Motors zu erhöhen und gleichzeitig das Gewicht der Maschine zu reduzieren. Daher wurden für das nur 4,1 kg wiegende System leichte Titanlegierungen und eine handgefertigte Endkappe aus Karbon verwendet, die der Anlage zudem ihr charakteristisches Erscheinungsbild verleihen. In ihrer Formgebung greift die Abgasanlage die ausdrucksstarke Linienführung der Maschine auf und fügt sich stimmig in das sportive Design des Motorrads ein.

Statement by the jury
This exhaust system demonstrates high production quality. Its sophisticated design melds with the overall appearance of the motorcycle, while also setting aesthetic accents.

Begründung der Jury
Diese Abgasanlage zeugt von hochwertiger Fertigungsqualität. Ihre raffinierte Gestaltung fügt sich in das Gesamtbild des Motorrads ein und setzt zugleich ästhetische Akzente.

NG800
Automotive IoT Gateway
IoT-Gateway für Fahrzeuge

Manufacturer
NetModule AG, Bern, Switzerland
In-house design
Benjamin Amsler, René Straub
Design
BrandSystem GmbH (Christoph Marti, Pascal Schnell),
Basel, Switzerland
Web
www.netmodule.com
www.brandsystem.ch

NG800 is an IoT gateway to connect vehicles to wireless networks. With its technical and visual implementation, the device sets ecological and aesthetic standards in a field that otherwise caters mostly for functionality only. Visualising the flow of power and data in the device, the slim groove structure on the upper side embodies the main design element. Highly functional, it serves as reinforcement in order to generate the necessary contact pressure for the seal.

NG800 ist ein Internet-of-Things-Gateway, das Fahrzeuge mit dem Funknetzwerk verbindet. In seiner technischen und visuellen Umsetzung bringt das Gerät ästhetische sowie ökologische Ansprüche in ein Umfeld, in dem oftmals die Funktion im Vordergrund steht. Wichtiges Gestaltungselement ist die schlanke Rippenstruktur auf der Oberseite, die Kraft und Datenflüsse im Gerät visualisiert. Sie ist gleichzeitig hochfunktional und dient als Verstärkung, um den notwendigen Anpressdruck der Dichtung zu erzeugen.

Statement by the jury
In this IoT gateway, form and function engage in convincing symbiosis. The NG800 thus also aims to set aesthetic accents in a technical environment.

Begründung der Jury
Form und Funktion gehen bei dem IoT-Gateway eine überzeugende Symbiose ein. Damit setzt NG800 in einem technischen Umfeld auch ästhetische Akzente.

NIO Power Swap
Battery Swap Station
Batteriewechselstation

Manufacturer
NIO GmbH, Munich, Germany
In-house design
Kris Tomasson
Web
www.nio.com

The battery swap station NIO Power Swap is part of a comprehensive power supply system for electric vehicles. The modular and compact station can be accommodated on only three parking spaces and blends seamlessly into urban environments with its straightforward, modern design. The exterior catches the eye with a balanced combination of delicate lines and fine light impulses, exuding a sense of calmness and reliability.

Die Batteriewechselstation NIO Power Swap ist Teil eines umfassenden Stromversorgungssystems für Elektrofahrzeuge. Die modular und kompakt gestaltete Station beansprucht nur drei Stellplätze und fügt sich mit ihrem geradlinigen, modernen Design nahtlos in das urbane Umfeld ein. Bei der Betrachtung des Exteriors fällt die ausgewogene Kombination feiner Linien und leichter Lichtimpulse ins Auge, die Ruhe und Zuverlässigkeit ausstrahlt.

Statement by the jury
The NIO Power Swap impresses with a clear design concept that unites pioneering technologies, modern functionality and high user-friendliness.

Begründung der Jury
NIO Power Swap begeistert mit einem klaren Gestaltungskonzept, das zukunftsweisende Technologien, moderne Funktionalität und hohe Benutzerfreundlichkeit vereint.

EVBox Level 2 Business Charger
Charging Station for Electric Vehicles
Ladestation für Elektrofahrzeuge

Manufacturer
EVBox, Amsterdam, Netherlands
Design
VanBerlo, Eindhoven, Netherlands
Web
www.evbox.com
www.vanberlo.nl

EVBox Level 2 was designed to simplify electric vehicle charging and to make it accessible to all users. The charging station has a contemporary yet simple design that fits seamlessly into its environment. The 8" touchscreen display interface and visually guiding lighting elements make it intuitive to operate. Its cleverly designed cable management system protects the 5.5 metre charging cables from damage and also provides wheelchair users with access to the charging station.

EVBox Level 2 wurde entwickelt, um das Laden von Elektrofahrzeugen zu vereinfachen und allen Nutzern zu ermöglichen. Die Ladestation zeigt ein zeitgemäßes und einfaches Design, das sich nahtlos in seine Umgebung einfügt. Das 8"-Touchdisplay und visuell geführte Beleuchtungselemente unterstützen die intuitive Bedienung. Das ausgeklügelte Kabelmanagementsystem schützt die 5,50 Meter langen Ladekabel vor Beschädigungen und ermöglicht auch Rollstuhlfahrern einen barrierefreien Zugang zur Ladestation.

Statement by the jury
EVBox Level 2 convinces with a clear design language and operator-friendly functions, which enable fast, intuitive handling for any user.

Begründung der Jury
EVBox Level 2 überzeugt mit klarer Formensprache und bedienfreundlichen Funktionen, die jedem Anwender eine schnelle, intuitive Handhabung ermöglichen.

W1 Pro
Charging Station for Electric Vehicles
Ladestation für Elektroautos

Manufacturer
Wirelane GmbH, Munich, Germany
Design
IDEO (Nicki Schäfer), Munich, Germany
Web
www.wirelane.com
www.ideo.com

W1 Pro is a charging station for electric vehicles. The smart charge point is incorporated in the sleek polycarbonate housing. An LED display with an intuitive user interface offers clear guidance throughout the entire charging process. Various features are integrated in the charging station, including remote charge point management and over-the-air software updates, as well as QR code and barcode scanning. The convenient plug-and-play installation concept ensures safe and easy maintenance.

Statement by the jury
The W1 Pro charging station combines a wide range of functionality in a compact device that impresses with a minimalist, timeless appearance.

W1 Pro ist eine Ladestation für Elektroautos. Der intelligente Ladepunkt ist in ein schlankes Polycarbonatgehäuse eingearbeitet. Ein LED-Display mit intuitiver Benutzeroberfläche führt übersichtlich durch den gesamten Ladevorgang. Funktionalitäten wie Fernsteuerung des Ladepunktes und Over-the-Air-Software-Updates sowie QR-Code und Barcode-Scanning sind in der Ladestation integriert. Ein praktisches Plug-and-Play-Installationskonzept ermöglicht eine sichere und einfache Wartung.

Begründung der Jury
Die Ladestation W1 Pro führt vielfältige Funktionalitäten in einem kompakten Gerät zusammen, das mit seinem minimalistischen, zeitlosen Erscheinungsbild überzeugt.

Wallbox Copper
Charging Station for Electric Vehicles
Ladestation für Elektrofahrzeuge

Manufacturer
Wall Box Chargers S.L., Barcelona, Spain
In-house design
Design
ESNE – University of Design, Innovation and Technology, Madrid, Spain
Web
www.wallbox.com
www.esne.es

Wallbox Copper is an intelligent charging station for electric vehicles, whose clear, reduced language of form lends it a timeless appearance. The handling is straightforward: the device uses facial recognition and also Sense technology, which enables easy interaction with the charging station through simple gestures. The operation is further simplified by the myWallbox app, which allows for convenient adjustments of power output and continuous monitoring of energy consumption.

Statement by the jury
Wallbox Copper has emerged as a compelling combination of innovative technology, modern design and user-friendly handling.

Wallbox Copper ist ein intelligentes Ladegerät für Elektrofahrzeuge, dem seine klare, reduzierte Formensprache eine zeitlose Anmutung verleiht. Die Handhabung ist unkompliziert: Das Gerät arbeitet mit Gesichtserkennung sowie einer Sense-Technologie, die über simple Gesten eine einfache Interaktion mit der Ladestation erlaubt. Vereinfacht wird die Bedienung zudem durch die myWallbox-App. Diese ermöglicht die bequeme Einstellung der Leistung sowie die kontinuierliche Überprüfung des Energieverbrauchs.

Begründung der Jury
Wallbox Copper schafft eine überzeugende Einheit aus innovativer Technologie, modernem Design und anwenderfreundlicher Handhabung.

Sports and outdoor
Sport und Outdoor

Clasp knives and hunting knives	Fitnessgeräte
Equestrian sports	Fitnesszubehör
Fitness devices	Funktionsbekleidung
Fitness equipment	Golf und Golfzubehör
Flasks and bottles	Outdoorausrüstung
Functional clothing	Reitsport
Golf and golf accessories	Sportbekleidung
Outdoor equipment	Sportschuhe
Sports clothing	Taschen- und Jagdmesser
Sports shoes	Trendsport und Zubehör
Trend sports and equipment	Trinkflaschen
Water sports and equipment	Wassersport und Zubehör
Winter sports and equipment	Wintersport und Zubehör

MOMODESIGN AERO
Motorcycle Helmet
Motorradhelm

Manufacturer
MOMODESIGN, Milan, Italy

In-house design
Klaus Fiorino, Paolo Cattaneo
(Managing Director)

Web
www.momodesign.com

reddot **award** 2019
best of the best

The aesthetics of functionality

A motorcycle helmet serves not only to protect the rider, it also defines both the riding experience and the aesthetics of motorcycling. The design of the AERO jet helmet realises the goal of introducing a new generation of helmets in that it seeks to exceed established principles and combines innovative design with high functionality. This helmet possesses outstanding aerodynamic properties and showcases a clear and distinctive design language, which is based on a novel approach towards integrating the visor in the overall shape. The wide visor has been realised flush with the shell and requires no external attachment. The classic external visor movement has thus been eliminated and replaced by a new, patented internal movement. The visor is therefore highly comfortable to wear and easy to operate with a gentle movement. In addition, the visor features a special coating that effectively prevents both scratches and fogging. The integrative shape not only gives riders outstandingly clear visibility, it also reduces outside noise while riding. Moreover, the helmet offers an intelligent ventilation system with smart control that always ensures a good climate under the helmet and which can be adjusted by means of an app on the smartphone. Thanks to this intelligent ventilation system, the motorcyclist can maintain the attention while riding, especially in the urban environment, even when air flow is not sufficient. This way the helmet becomes an "active" element to increase comfort and safety.

Die Ästhetik der Funktionalität

Ein Motorradhelm schützt den Fahrer nicht nur, er definiert auch dessen Fahrgefühl und die Ästhetik des Motorradfahrens. Die Gestaltung des Jethelms AERO verwirklicht die Zielsetzung einer neuen Generation von Helmen, die Prinzipien überschreiten und innovatives Design mit hoher Funktionalität vereinen will. Dieser Helm verfügt über hervorragende aerodynamische Eigenschaften und zeigt eine klare und markante Formensprache, die auf einer neuartigen Integration des Visiers in die Gesamtform beruht. Das breite Visier wurde bündig mit der Schale entworfen und erfordert keine äußere Befestigung. Die klassische Visiermechanik an der Außenseite wurde entfernt, und dafür eine neue an der Innenseite entwickelt und patentiert. Das Visier lässt sich deshalb überaus komfortabel und mit einer sanften Bewegung bedienen. Es ist außerdem mit einer speziellen Beschichtung versehen, die ein Beschlagen und Verkratzen wirkungsvoll verhindert. Die integrative Form ermöglicht den Fahrern nicht nur eine ausgezeichnete und klare Sicht, sondern reduziert auch die Außengeräusche während der Fahrt. Darüber hinaus verfügt der Helm über ein Ventilationssystem mit intelligenter Steuerung, das stets für ein gutes Klima unter dem Helm sorgt und mittels App über das Smartphone eingestellt werden kann. Dank dieses intelligenten Systems kann der Fahrer seine Aufmerksamkeit stets aufrechterhalten, insbesondere in städtischen Umgebungen und wenn die Luftzufuhr unzureichend ist. Auf diese Weise trägt der Helm als „aktives" Element zur Erhöhung von Komfort und Sicherheit bei.

Statement by the jury

The AERO motorcycle helmet has emerged as an example of excellently integrated design elements, resulting in its expressive shape that inspires a high level of confidence in terms of functionality and reliability. This aerodynamic helmet achieves a high degree of wearing comfort and rider safety thanks to the innovative integration of the visor without conventional external attachment. It offers riders an outstanding all-round vision, as well as the benefits of a sophisticated smart ventilation system.

Begründung der Jury

Bei dem Motorradhelm AERO wurden alle Elemente gestalterisch exzellent umgesetzt, wobei eine aussagekräftige Form entstand, die ein hohes Vertrauen in seine Funktionalität und Zuverlässigkeit erweckt. Dieser aerodynamische Helm erreicht durch die innovative Integration des Visiers ohne klassische äußere Befestigung ein großes Maß an Komfort und Sicherheit. Er bietet dem Fahrer eine umfassende Rundumsicht und die Vorteile eines ausgereiften intelligenten Belüftungssystems.

Designer portrait
See page 46
Siehe Seite 46

Expedition H2O
Motorcycle Boots
Motorradstiefel

Manufacturer
REV'IT! Sport International B.V.,
Oss, Netherlands

In-house design
Mark van Roon,
Jasper den Dekker

Web
www.revitsport.com

reddot **award** 2019
best of the best

Design to extremes

Off-road motorcycling is defined by extreme conditions that place high demands on both man and materials. Off-road riders are exposed directly to the elements, with their feet and legs becoming dirty from splashing mud and water. Against this backdrop, the Expedition H2O motorcycle boots have been engineered with innovative properties for optimum off-road performance. They are 100 per cent waterproof, offer outstanding wearing comfort and are extremely user-friendly. Moreover, based on an innovative Dynamic Support Frame (DSF), their design combines the aspect of protection with a high degree of endurance. The sophisticated concept prevents the overstretching of tendons and muscles, while ensuring the necessary freedom of movement around the ankle area. The boots consist of three key protection components forming the calf support structure, the heel cup and a stability frame. The calf is supported by the use of the Boa closure system, which guarantees a perfect fit and the necessary firm tension with the simple twist of a dial. The heel cup provides protection to the ankle and is connected to the calf support at the ankle pivot points. Lastly, the stability frame allows the hydratex|Sphere waterproofing construction to be directly laminated to the outer shell of the boot and provides stiffness to the sole. This considerably helps reduce fatigue when standing on the foot pegs.

Design für die Extreme

Im Offroad-Motorradsport herrschen extreme Bedingungen, die hohe Anforderungen an Mensch und Material stellen. Die Fahrer sind direkt den Elementen ausgesetzt, Füße und Beine werden schmutzig von hochspritzendem Matsch oder Wasser. Die Motorradstiefel Expedition H2O wurden vor diesem Hintergrund entwickelt und dank innovativer Eigenschaften für das Offroad-Fahren optimiert. Sie sind 100-prozentig wasserdicht, bieten einen hervorragenden Tragekomfort und sind ausgesprochen nutzerfreundlich. Auf der Basis des innovativen Dynamic Support Frame (DSF) vereint ihre Gestaltung den Aspekt der Sicherheit zudem mit einem hohen Maß an Belastbarkeit. Das durchdachte Konzept verhindert die Überstreckung von Sehnen und Muskeln und gewährleistet die notwendige Bewegungsfreiheit des Fußgelenks. Gebildet wird es aus den drei Komponenten Wadenunterstützung, Fersenkappe und einem stabilisierenden Rahmen. Die Wadenunterstützung bieten diese Stiefel dank der Ausstattung mit dem Boa-Verschlusssystem, welches durch einfaches Drehen eines Knopfes einen festen und perfekten Sitz garantiert. Die Fersenkappe schützt den Knöchel und stellt am Fußgelenk die Verbindung zum Wadenschutz her. Der Stabilitätsrahmen schließlich ermöglicht es, eine hydratex|Sphere-Membran direkt außen auf den Stiefel zu laminieren und dadurch der Sohle Steifigkeit zu verleihen. Das verringert die Ermüdung, wenn der Fahrer in den Fußrasten stehend fährt.

Statement by the jury

The Expedition H2O motorcycle boots embody a perfect merger of form and function. They are made of high-quality materials, which make them durable, and fully waterproof thanks to a hydratex|Sphere membrane. Based on the innovative Dynamic Support Frame (DSF) concept, they guarantee maximum safety, comfort and accuracy of fit, covering the three protection components of calf support, heel cup and stability frame.

Begründung der Jury

Bei den Motorradstiefeln Expedition H2O vereinen sich auf perfekte Weise Form und Funktion. Sie sind durch die Ausstattung mit einer hydratex|Sphere-Membran komplett wasserdicht und aus hochwertigen Materialien gefertigt, was sie zudem langlebig macht. Basierend auf dem innovativen Konzept des Dynamic Support Frame (DSF) garantieren sie durch die drei Komponenten Wadenunterstützung, Fersenkappe und Stabilitätsrahmen ein Höchstmaß an Sicherheit, Komfort und Passgenauigkeit.

Designer portrait
See page 48
Siehe Seite 48

GP-EVO.R
Glove for Motor Cycling
Motorradhandschuh

Manufacturer
RS TAICHI Inc., Osaka, Japan
In-house design
Shigeo Kawakami
Web
www.rs-taichi.com

GP-EVO.R is a motorcycle glove with modern safety functions. Inspired by the traditional Japanese warrior armour called "ō-yoroi", the hard, resin-formed protector was applied to the otherwise soft glove in 3D printing, thus ensuring ergonomic functionality. In the event of a fall, the protector reduces the frictional resistance against the road surface; it also lessens the impact energy and prevents hand injuries. The combination of natural leather and elastic aramid fibre makes the glove comfortable and offers freedom of movement.

GP-EVO.R ist ein Motorradhandschuh mit modernen Sicherheitsfunktionen. Von der traditionellen, Õyoroi genannten japanischen Kriegerrüstung inspiriert, wurde der harte, aus Harz geformte Protektor im 3D-Druck auf den sonst weichen Handschuh aufgebracht, um ergonomische Funktionalität zu gewährleisten. Im Falle eines Sturzes verringert der Protektor den Reibungswiderstand gegen die Straßenoberfläche sowie die Aufprallenergie und verhindert Handverletzungen. Die Kombination aus Naturleder und einer elastischen Aramidfaser macht den Handschuh bequem und bietet Bewegungsfreiheit.

Statement by the jury
The motorcycle glove GP-EVO.R captivates with the complex processing of its different high-quality materials, which provide for optimal protection.

Begründung der Jury
Der Motorradhandschuh GP-EVO.R besticht durch die aufwendige Verarbeitung seiner verschiedenen hochwertigen Materialien, die für sehr guten Schutz sorgen.

Soundshield
Winter Sports Helmet with Headphones
Wintersporthelm mit Funkkopfhörern

Manufacturer
UNIT 1 Gear, Inc., Wilmington, Delaware, USA
In-house design
Javier Bertani, Juan García Mansilla, Joaquín Vincent, Marcos Gervasoni
Web
www.unit1gear.com

Soundshield is a winter sports helmet with detachable wireless headphones. They are seamlessly integrated into one combo and can be used both together and apart. The helmet houses the QUAD-4LOCK docking system which quickly but firmly connects both elements. Its sports-specific interface can even be used with gloves on and largely contributes to an incomparable user experience.

Statement by the jury
The design of Soundshield represents an impressive innovation: it enriches the world of winter sports by combining helmet and headphones into a sensational unit.

Soundshield ist ein Wintersporthelm mit abnehmbaren Funkkopfhörern. Sie sind nahtlos in eine Kombination integriert und können sowohl zusammen als auch getrennt verwendet werden. Der Helm enthält das Dockingsystem QUAD4LOCK, das beide Elemente schnell, aber fest miteinander verbindet. Seine sportspezifische Schnittstelle kann sogar mit Handschuhen bedient werden und trägt wesentlich zu einem unvergleichlichen Benutzererlebnis bei.

Begründung der Jury
Der Gestaltung von Soundshield gelingt eine eindrucksvolle Innovation: Sie bereichert die Welt des Wintersports durch die Verbindung von Helm und Kopfhörer zu einer aufsehenerregenden Einheit.

Rottefella MOVE™ Switch
Cross-Country Binding System
Langlaufski-Bindung

Manufacturer
Rottefella AS, Klokkarstua, Norway
In-house design
Magnus Anderssen, Thomas Holm
Web
www.rottefella.com

Rottefella MOVE Switch is a user-friendly binding system for cross-country skis. The skier can adjust the weight distribution to achieve a better grip and glide in changing snow conditions. The Rottefella MOVE Switch is intuitive and easy to use. By turning the self-explanatory red knob clockwise, the binding is moved forwards, counterclockwise it is shifted to the rear. With different adapters, both new and old skis can be upgraded.

Statement by the jury
The outstanding advantage of the Rottefella MOVE Switch ski binding is that it can be handled intuitively and adjusted individually – promising excellent performance in the snow.

Rottefella MOVE Switch ist ein nutzerfreundliches Bindungssystem für Langlaufski. Der Skifahrer kann damit die Gewichtsverteilung anpassen, um bei sich ändernden Schneeverhältnissen einen stärkeren Grip zu erreichen und besser zu gleiten. Rottefella MOVE Switch ist intuitiv und leicht zu bedienen. Durch Drehen des selbsterklärenden roten Knopfes im Uhrzeigersinn wird die Bindung vorwärts, entgegen dem Uhrzeigersinn nach hinten verschoben. Mit verschiedenen Adaptern lassen sich neue wie alte Ski upgraden.

Begründung der Jury
Das herausragende Plus der Skibindung Rottefella MOVE Switch ist, dass sie sich intuitiv handhaben und individuell einstellen lässt – und so hohe Performance im Schnee verspricht.

ARKTIS GTX
Mountaineering Glove
Bergsporthandschuh

Manufacturer
ESKA Lederhandschuhfabrik Ges. m. b. H. & Co. KG, Thalheim bei Wels, Austria
In-house design
Adelheid Pürstinger, Regina Loos
Web
www.eska.at

ARKTIS GTX is a changeable mountaineering glove for tourers, ice climbers or mountaineers. Its combination of fist and finger glove allows a quick change from a thin waterproof inner glove to a warm mitten with magnetically fixable fist and thumb caps and makes it just as useful for ascents as for mountaintops or descents into the valley. Even in icy cold, it provides warm hands, unlimited dexterity and best grip.

Statement by the jury
The ARKTIS GTX mountaineering glove impresses with its thoughtful design of two functions in one glove and thus offers the optimal solution for any activity in the mountains.

ARKTIS GTX ist ein wandelbarer Sporthandschuh für Tourengeher, Eiskletterer oder Bergsportler. Als Kombination aus Faust- und Fingerhandschuh ermöglicht er den schnellen Wechsel vom dünnen, wasserdichten Innenhandschuh zum warmen Fäustling mit magnetisch fixierbarer Faust- und Daumenkappe und ist ebenso zweckmäßig für Aufstiege wie für den Gipfel oder die Abfahrt ins Tal. Auch in eisiger Kälte hält er die Hände bei uneingeschränkter Fingerfertigkeit und bestem Griff warm.

Begründung der Jury
Der Bergsporthandschuh ARKTIS GTX beeindruckt durch seine überlegte Gestaltung zweier Funktionen in einem Handschuh. Damit ist er für das Gebirge wie geschaffen.

Armis Polo Helmet
Polo Helmet
Polohelm

Manufacturer
Charles Owen, Wrexham, Wales, United Kingdom
Design
Armis Sport Limited (Robin Spicer),
Towcester, Northamptonshire, United Kingdom
Web
www.charlesowen.com
www.armispolo.com

With its fresh design language, the Armis polo helmet showcases the technology inside. In form and materials, it draws on the classic style and was developed according to the British standard PAS 015, which ensures the same quality of each helmet produced. The shell is fitted with an EPS foam liner, while the integrated patented MIPS technology (Multi-directional Impact Protection System) mimics the brain's own protection system by adding a low-friction layer between head and helmet. Thus, the helmet absorbs more strain and offers better protection.

Der Polohelm Armis verleiht mit seiner dynamischen Formensprache der Technologie in seinem Inneren Ausdruck. In Form und Material knüpft er an den klassischen Stil an und wurde dem britischen Standard PAS 015 gemäß entwickelt. Dies stellt sicher, dass alle produzierten Helme die gleiche Qualität aufweisen. Die Außenhülle ist mit EPS-Schaumstoff gefüttert, während die patentierte MIPS-Technologie (Multi-directional Impact Protection System) mit der zusätzlichen reibungsarmen Schicht zwischen Kopf und Helm das Schutzsystem des Gehirns nachahmt. Der Helm nimmt dadurch mehr Belastung auf und bietet höheren Schutz.

Statement by the jury
Hardly noticeable from the outside, the Armis polo helmet integrates progressive technology skilfully in its shell, scoring with outstanding protection and better material quality.

Begründung der Jury
Von außen kaum wahrnehmbar integriert der Polohelm Armis fortschrittliche Technologie geschickt in seiner Schale und punktet so mit richtungsweisendem Schutz und erhöhter Materialqualität.

BICONIC
Golf Trolley
Golftrolley

Manufacturer
TiCad GmbH & Co. KG, Altenstadt, Germany
In-house design
Björn Hillesheim
Web
www.biconic.eu

The BICONIC golf trolley catches the eye with its innovative, conically shaped rear wheels, which also inspired its name. Its negative camber, together with its ergonomic grip and low weight, makes the golf cart suitable for off-road use and ensures stable, reliable driving across the course. Special aluminium profiles and high-strength turned and milled parts, which are also made of aluminium, contribute to a skilful combination of robustness, balance and quality. Sophisticated operating features predestine the trolley especially for younger golfers.

Der Golftrolley BICONIC fällt durch seine innovativen, konisch geformten Hinterräder ins Auge, die auch zu seinem Namen inspirierten. Ihr negativer Radsturz macht den Golfwagen zusammen mit dem ergonomischen Griff und dem geringen Gewicht offroad-tauglich und sorgt für ein stabiles, zuverlässiges Fahrverhalten im Gelände. Ergänzt durch spezielle Aluminiumprofile und hochfeste Dreh- und Fräseile, die ebenfalls aus Aluminium sind, entsteht eine konsequente Verbindung aus Robustheit, Balance und Qualität. Ausgeklügelte Bedienungsmerkmale prädestinieren den Trolley besonders für jüngere Golfer.

Statement by the jury
The design of the golf trolley impresses with an elaborate approach, which not only focuses on its important off-road capability, but also on weight and stability.

Begründung der Jury
Die Gestaltung des Golftrolleys begeistert mit ihrem durchdachten Ansatz, der neben der wichtigen Geländetauglichkeit auch Gewicht und Stabilität im Blick hat.

MYSTIC LEN10 Majestic X
Waist Harness for Kitesurfing
Hüfttrapez zum Kitesurfen

Manufacturer
North Actionsports BV, Mystic Boarding, Katwijk, Netherlands
In-house design
Max Blom, Edwin Schaap
Web
www.mysticboarding.com

The development of the MYSTIC LEN10 Majestic X waist harness aimed at a new level of support, comfort and a first-class finish. The harness surrounds the patented Bionic Core Frame a semi-rigid carbon back-support plate with a very stiff middle section. It prevents the harness from jamming the upper body while reducing the pressure on the back. At the same time, it allows rotation for maximum freedom of movement.

Bei der Entwicklung des Hüfttrapezes MYSTIC LEN10 Majestic X standen ein neues Unterstützungsniveau, Komfort und ein hochklassiges Finish im Vordergrund. Das Trapez umgibt den patentierten Bionic Core Frame – eine halbsteife Rückenstützplatte aus Carbon, die im Mittelteil sehr fest ist. Sie verhindert, dass der Oberkörper von dem Trapez gequetscht wird, und verringert den Druck auf den Rücken. Gleichzeitig lässt sie Drehungen zu, um größtmögliche Bewegungsfreiheit zu gewähren.

Statement by the jury
The MYSTIC LEN10 Majestic X waist harness masters the balancing act of providing optimum protection and support without restricting the kiter's mobility.

Begründung der Jury
Das Hüfttrapez MYSTIC LEN10 Majestic X meistert den Spagat, bestmöglichen Schutz und Halt zu bieten, ohne dabei die Beweglichkeit des Kiters einzuschränken.

Lampuga Air
Electric Surfboard
Elektro-Surfboard

Manufacturer
Lampuga GmbH, Rastatt, Germany
Design
Schweizer Design Consulting (Oliver Schweizer,
Robin Ritter, Patrick Senfter, Farouk Zemni),
Stuttgart, Germany
Web
www.lampuga.com
www.schweizer.design

You can also find this product
on page 120 and 188.
Dieses Produkt finden Sie auch
auf Seite 120 und 188.

The electrically powered surfboard Lampuga Air offers emission-free mobility on water and particular driving pleasure independent of wind and waves. With a 10 kW (14 hp) electric motor, it glides over water at a speed of up to 50 km/h. The Air consists of an inflatable and foldable hull that surrounds the Powerbox, which holds the board's technical components. Thanks to the modular plug-and-play system, the board is assembled and dis-assembled in five minutes and can easily be transported. It is steered by weight transfer, and the speed is regulated by a handheld remote control.

Das elektrisch betriebene Surfboard Lampuga Air bietet emissionsfreie Mobilität auf dem Wasser und besonderen Fahrspaß unabhängig von Wind und Wellen. Mit einem 10 kW (14 PS) starken Elektromotor gleitet es mit bis zu 50 km/h über das Wasser. Ein aufblas- und faltbarer Rumpf umgibt die formgebende Powerbox, die alle technischen Komponenten des Boards enthält. Dank des modularen Plug-and-Play-Systems ist das Surfboard in fünf Minuten auf- und abgebaut und lässt sich leicht transportieren. Die Steuerung erfolgt über Gewichtsverlagerung, während die Geschwindigkeit mittels Fernbedienung reguliert wird.

Statement by the jury
The design of the surfboard Lampuga Air inspires with its innovative electric drive. This makes water sports more varied and attractive in a new way.

Begründung der Jury
Das Surfboard Lampuga Air begeistert durch den innovativen elektrischen Antrieb. Der Wassersport wird dadurch abwechslungsreicher und auf neue Weise attraktiv.

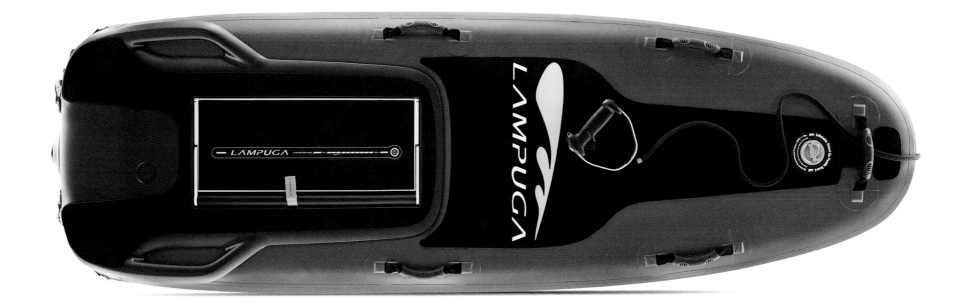

Awake RÄVIK
Electric Surfboard
Elektrisches Surfbrett

Manufacturer
Ride Awake AB, Limhamn, Sweden
In-house design
Brendon Vermillion, Philip Werner,
Jesper Randrup, Jordan Spack, Benjamin Alexander
Web
www.awakeboards.com

Awake RÄVIK is a high-quality electric surfboard. Regardless of waves or weather conditions, it offers riders optimal torque and exciting surfing experiences at high speeds without the harmful emissions of gas-powered jetboards. It is designed to offer first-class appeal to the fast-growing market. RÄVIK's wireless throttle delivers precise control and expresses the command of a high-performance vehicle in appearance and function.

Awake RÄVIK ist ein hochwertiges, elektrisch betriebenes Surfboard. Unabhängig von Wellen oder Wetterbedingungen bietet es ein optimales Drehmoment und aufregende Surferlebnisse bei hohen Geschwindigkeiten ohne die schädlichen Emissionen gasbetriebener Jetboards. Es wurde entwickelt, um dem schnell wachsenden Markt eine erstklassige Attraktion zu bieten. RÄVIKs kabelloser Griff erlaubt präzises Steuern und steht in Aussehen und Funktion für die Beherrschung eines Hochleistungsfahrzeugs.

Statement by the jury
The electric surfboard Awake RÄVIK inspires with its innovative drive. It makes surfing in any water a special pleasure.

Begründung der Jury
Das elektrische Surfbrett Awake RÄVIK begeistert mit seinem innovativen Antrieb und macht Surfen in jedem Gewässer zu einem besonderen Vergnügen.

LeFeet S1
Diver Propulsion Vehicle
Taucherantriebsfahrzeug

Manufacturer
Shenzhen Lefeet Innovation
Technology Co., Ltd., Shenzhen, China
In-house design
Lefeet Innovation Design Team
Web
www.lefeet.com
Honourable Mention

LeFeet S1 is a diver propulsion vehicle
that can make activities in and under
water easier, more effortless and, above
all, more exciting. Thanks to its compact
size, the DPV water scooter offers an
ideal way of gliding through the water.
Its modular design provides important
additional functions. It is available with
one or two handles and can also be attached to a paddle board, kayak or other
watercraft as an underwater motor.

Statement by the jury
The LeFeet S1 diving scooter attracts
attention with its remarkable configuration. It is versatile and offers great fun
in the water.

LeFeet S1 ist ein Taucherantriebsfahrzeug,
das Aktivitäten im und unter Wasser einfacher, müheloser und vor allem spannender
machen kann. In kompakter Größe bietet
der DPV-Wasserscooter eine unkonven-
tionelle Möglichkeit, durch das Wasser zu
gleiten. Sein modularer Aufbau stellt wichtige Zusatzfunktionen bereit. So ist er mit
einem oder zwei Griffen erhältlich und
kann auch als Unterwassermotor an einem
Paddelbrett, einem Kajak oder einem anderen Wasserfahrzeug befestigt werden.

Begründung der Jury
Der Tauchscooter LeFeet S1 macht durch
seine bemerkenswerte Konzeption auf sich
aufmerksam. Er ist vielseitig verwendbar
und bietet großes Vergnügen im Wasser.

Swii Power Float Board
Float Board
Schwimmbrett

Manufacturer
Tianjin Deepfar Ocean Technology,
Tianjin, China
In-house design
Chunjiang Tian, Prof. Jiancang Wei
Web
www.sublue.com

The Swii Power Float Board combines
malleable EVA materials with hard plastic
and consists of buoyancy materials, a
waterproof power supply system, a mobile
battery and a Hall switch. The board helps
non-swimmers to overcome their fear
of the water and become safe swimmers.
Easy to use and with excellent buoyancy,
it is easy to hold and glide on the water
with it. The lithium battery is quickly
rechargeable.

Statement by the jury
The electric Swii Power Floating Board is
skilfully designed to be easy to handle
and to offer a safe swimming experience
for non-swimmers.

Das Swii Power Float Board verbindet
verformbare EVA-Materialien mit hartem
Kunststoff und besteht aus Auftriebs-
materialien, einem wasserdichten Strom-
versorgungssystem, einem mobilen Akku
und einem Hall-Schalter. Das Board hilft
Nichtschwimmern, ihre Angst vor dem
Wasser zu überwinden und zu sicheren
Schwimmern zu werden. Dank einfacher
Bedienbarkeit und hervorragendem Auf-
trieb kann man es leicht halten und damit
auf dem Wasser gleiten. Die Lithiumbatterie ist schnell wiederaufladbar.

Begründung der Jury
Das elektrische Schwimmbrett Swii Power
Float Board ist gekonnt so konzipiert, dass
es einfach zu handhaben ist und Nichtschwimmern ein sicheres Schwimmerlebnis
verschafft.

Tonal Strength Training System
Fitness Machine
Krafttrainingsgerät

Manufacturer
Tonal, San Francisco, USA
Design
Whipsaw Inc. (Dan Harden, Cole Derby,
Ari Turgel, Elliot Ortiz, Zack Stephanchick),
San Jose, USA
Web
www.tonal.com
www.whipsaw.com

TONAL is a new strength training system for home or office. It uses an electromagnetic machine controlled by smart software and machine learning to provide even, dynamically changing resistive force. The two arms of the thin, wall-mounted system pivot out from their vertical rails and can be moved in all directions to accommodate every workout ranging from standing lat pull downs to squats to lateral chest flys. The sensors controlling the resistance respond automatically.

TONAL ist ein neues Krafttrainingsgerät für zu Hause oder das Büro. Es arbeitet auf Basis einer elektromagnetischen Maschine, die durch intelligente Software und maschinelles Lernen gesteuert wird und eine gleichmäßige, dynamisch wechselnde Widerstandskraft bereitstellt. Die beiden Arme des flachen, an der Wand hängenden Geräts schwenken aus ihren vertikalen Schienen aus und lassen sich nach allen Seiten bewegen, um das Training zu ermöglichen – angefangen vom Latziehen im Stehen über Kniebeugen bis hin zu seitlichen Brustflys. Die den Widerstand steuernden Sensoren reagieren automatisch.

Statement by the jury
With TONAL you can do a comprehensive strength training at home. The electromagnetically functioning system also looks stylish on the wall.

Begründung der Jury
Mit TONAL lässt sich ein umfassendes Krafttraining bequem zu Hause absolvieren. Das elektromagnetisch funktionierende Gerät sieht an der Wand zudem elegant aus.

Peloton Tread
Treadmill
Laufband

Manufacturer
Peloton Interactive, Inc., New York, USA
In-house design
Jason Poure, Mark Kruse, Nigel Alcorn
Web
www.onepeloton.com

The Peloton Tread stands out due to its sturdy carbon-steel frame and was specially developed for demanding workouts and full-body training with on-screen instructions. It features a shock-absorbing slat belt and a 32" HD touch screen that can be intuitively controlled and individually adjusted with innovative speed and incline knobs. With a mix of cardio and strength training, every fitness and performance level from beginners to professional athletes can be trained in the comfort of your own home, with the help of certified instructors on the screen if required.

Das Laufband Peloton Tread fällt durch seinen stabilen Rahmen aus Kohlenstoffstahl auf und wurde eigens für anspruchsvolle Workouts und Ganzkörpertraining mit Bildschirmunterstützung entwickelt. Es verfügt über einen stoßdämpfenden Lamellengurt und einen 32"-HD-Touchscreen, der sich intuitiv steuern und mit innovativen Geschwindigkeits- und Neigungsknöpfen individuell einstellen lässt. Mit einem Mix aus Cardio- und Krafttraining lässt sich somit jedes Fitness- und Leistungsniveau vom Anfänger bis zum Profisportler trainieren, und zwar bequem von zu Hause aus, bei Bedarf mithilfe zertifizierter Trainer live am Bildschirm.

Statement by the jury
The design of the Peloton Tread merges state-of-the-art technologies and an ergonomic construction to form an exclusive training device for the home.

Begründung der Jury
Im Design des Laufbands Peloton Tread verschmelzen neue Technologien und eine ergonomische Bauweise zu einem exklusiven Trainingsgerät für zu Hause.

WalkingPad A1
Treadmill
Laufband

Manufacturer
Kingsmith, Beijing, China
In-house design
Prof. Qing Chen, Xingwei Peng
Design
Xiaomi Inc., Beijing, China
Web
www.kingsmith.com.cn
www.mi.com

WalkingPad A1 is a treadmill for exercising at home with a maximum speed of 6 km/h, which is equivalent to a fast walk. Lightweight, small and smartly designed, it has a small pack size and is easy to store. Its timeless appearance allows it to be integrated harmoniously into its surroundings. It has a patented folding mechanism in the middle of the running surface and is made of an aluminium alloy that makes the floor firm and solid.

Statement by the jury
The treadmill WalkingPad A1 convinces with a design that has been specifically designed for training at home. It is easy to use and quickly stowed away.

WalkingPad A1 ist ein Laufband, mit dem man zu Hause trainieren kann und dessen Höchstgeschwindigkeit von 6 km/h einem schnellen Spaziergang entspricht. Leicht, klein und intelligent gestaltet, lässt es sich dank seines geringen Packmaßes gut lagern und aufgrund seines zeitlosen Designs harmonisch in Wohnräume integrieren. Es verfügt über einen patentierten Klappmechanismus in der Mitte der Lauffläche und besteht aus einer Aluminiumlegierung, die den Boden fest und solide macht.

Begründung der Jury
Das Laufband WalkingPad A1 überzeugt durch eine Gestaltung, die gezielt auf das Training zu Hause ausgerichtet wurde. Es ist leicht zu bedienen und rasch verstaut.

Kingsmith T1
Treadmill
Laufband

Manufacturer
Kingsmith, Beijing, China
In-house design
Prof. Qing Chen, Xingwei Peng
Web
www.kingsmith.com.cn

The treadmill T1 has a suspended running board furnished with a special, elastic running surface as shock-absorbing medium. With an increased spring rate, it offers sufficient flexibility. The weight is cushioned when hitting the treadmill, and noise is effectively reduced so that a pleasant running feeling is created. The easily collapsible device has a gradient of 4 per cent and thus comes close to running on the road.

Statement by the jury
The T1 treadmill impresses with its well-devised running board, which ensures ideal cushioning and offers an authentic running experience.

Das Laufband T1 verfügt über ein aufgehängtes Trittbrett, das eine spezielle, elastische Lauffläche als stoßdämpfendes Medium verwendet. Mit einer erhöhten Federungsrate bietet es ausreichend Flexibilität. Das Gewicht des Sportlers wird beim Aufkommen abgefedert und Geräusche werden effektiv reduziert, was ein angenehmes Laufgefühl entstehen lässt. Das einfach zusammenklappbare Gerät hat eine Steigung von vier Prozent, sodass man beim Training dem Laufen auf der Straße nahekommt.

Begründung der Jury
Das Laufband T1 besticht durch sein durchdacht konzipiertes Laufbrett, das für sehr gutes Abfedern sorgt und zugleich ein authentisches Lauferlebnis bietet.

AUGLETICS Eight Style
Rowing Machine
Rudergerät

Manufacturer
AUGLETICS GmbH,
Königs Wusterhausen, Germany
In-house design
Web
www.augletics.de
Honourable Mention

The AUGLETICS Eight Style ergometer is clad in a chic oak wall and can be optimally connected. It is almost noiseless as the resistance is generated by an eddy current brake. With a Virtual Coach, every stroke can be analysed in real time and the user's technique can be continuously improved. The integrated touch display ensures simple operation. The ergometer can be stowed away in two easy steps and, folded up, fits in any corner.

Statement by the jury
The AUGLETICS Eight Style rowing ergometer attracts attention with its stylish use of oak wood. The range of functions allows effective training at a high level.

Das Ergometer AUGLETICS Eight Style ist in ein schickes Eichengewand gekleidet und sehr gut vernetzbar. Es ist nahezu geräuschlos, da der Widerstand mittels Wirbelstrombremse erzeugt wird. Über einen Virtual Coach lässt sich jeder Ruderschlag in Echtzeit analysieren und die Technik des Benutzers immer weiter verbessern. Die einfache Bedienung erfolgt über das integrierte Touchdisplay. Mit zwei Handgriffen kann das Gerät verstaut werden und passt zusammengeklappt in jede Ecke.

Begründung der Jury
Das Ruderergometer AUGLETICS Eight Style fällt durch den geschmackvollen Einsatz von Eichenholz ins Auge. Sein Funktionsumfang erlaubt wirksames Training auf hohem Niveau.

Wonder Core Genius
Fitness Equipment
Fitnessgeräte

Manufacturer
Bodyorbit Co., Ltd., Taichung, Taiwan
In-house design
Web
www.bodyorbit.com

Wonder Core Genius are several fitness machines in one, including a smart app trainer. To meet the different demands of a comprehensive workout, it can be transformed into ten different applications without any tool in seconds, including a skipping rope, a hand gripper, a mode for push-ups, for squats and for full-body exercises. The individual components can be compactly stowed in the compartments of the device cassette. The app contains over 100 training videos for the individual muscle groups.

Wonder Core Genius sind mehrere Fitnessgeräte in einem, inklusive eines intelligenten App-Trainers. Um den unterschiedlichen Anforderungen an ein umfassendes Work-out gerecht zu werden, lässt sich Wonder Core Genius in wenigen Sekunden ganz ohne Werkzeug in zehn verschiedene Anwendungen umwandeln und bietet zum Beispiel ein Springseil, einen Handmuskeltrainer, einen Push-up-, einen Kniebeugen- und einen Ganzkörperübungsmodus. Alle Komponenten lassen sich kompakt in den Fächern der Gerätekassette verstauen. Die App enthält über 100 Trainingsvideos für die einzelnen Muskelgruppen.

Statement by the jury
With its multitude of different elements, the well-thought-out equipment set plus app meets the demands of contemporary fitness training to a high degree.

Begründung der Jury
Mit seiner Vielzahl verschiedener Elemente erfüllt das durchdacht konzipierte Geräteset plus App die Ansprüche an ein zeitgemäßes Fitnesstraining in hohem Maße.

Peloton Bootcamp Weights
Dumbell
Hantel

Manufacturer
Peloton Interactive, Inc., New York, USA
In-house design
Jason Poure, James Connors,
Lee Hendrickson
Web
www.onepeloton.com

The Peloton Bootcamp Weights are an ergonomically shaped pair of cast iron dumbbells with polyurethane coated ends. They are characterised by a clear, reduced design and stand out due to their striking transition from square weight plates to circular handle. Whenever and wherever you are, they offer the opportunity for strength and endurance training.

Statement by the jury
The Peloton Bootcamp Weights impress due to their classic simple design. Easy to handle, they are easy to train with anywhere.

Die Peloton Bootcamp Weights sind ein ergonomisch geformtes Paar Hanteln, die aus Gusseisen hergestellt und an den Enden mit Polyurethan beschichtet werden. Sie sind durch eine klare, reduzierte Gestaltung gekennzeichnet und fallen durch ihren fließenden Übergang vom Quadrat der Gewichtsscheiben zur runden Stange auf. Wann immer und wo immer man gerade ist, bieten sie die Möglichkeit zum Kraft- und Ausdauertraining.

Begründung der Jury
Die Peloton Bootcamp Weights imponieren durch ihre klassische, schlichte Gestaltung. Da sie einfach zu handhaben sind, lässt sich mit ihnen überall unkompliziert trainieren.

Taurus SelectaBell
Dumbbell
Hantel

Manufacturer
Sport-Tiedje GmbH, Schleswig, Germany
In-house design
Web
www.sport-tiedje.com

Taurus SelectaBell is a practical dumbbell, which combines several single dumbbells in only one. This saves space and makes dumbbell training comfortable and easy, as the weights can be changed in no time. The adjustment pin is pulled out and engaged again at the desired weight. The remaining weight plates remain in the stable receptacle in which the dumbbells are safely stored. Five weight gradations are available: 4.5, 9, 13.5, 18 and 22.5 kg.

Statement by the jury
Practical, compact and uncomplicated – these performance features make the Taurus SelectaBell dumbbell excellently suited for comfortable strength training at home.

Taurus SelectaBell ist eine praktische Kompakthantel, die mehrere Einzelhanteln in nur einer Hantel vereint. Das spart Platz und macht das Hanteltraining komfortabel und einfach, da sich die Gewichte im Nu wechseln lassen. Dazu wird der Verstellstift herausgezogen und beim gewünschten Gewicht wieder eingerastet. Die übrigen Gewichtsscheiben bleiben in der stabilen Aufnahmeschale zurück, in der die Hanteln sicher aufbewahrt sind. Es sind fünf Gewichtsabstufungen von 4,5, 9, 13,5, 18 und 22,5 kg erhältlich.

Begründung der Jury
Praktisch, kompakt und unkompliziert – mit diesen Leistungsmerkmalen empfiehlt sich die Hantel Tauraus SelectaBell als hervorragend geeignet für ein bequemes Krafttraining zu Hause.

Power & Go
Wireless Charging Armband
Sportarmband

Manufacturer
Guangzhou NOME Brand Management
Limited, Guangzhou, China
In-house design
Hao Chen, Bin Guo, Yingxin Gao
Design
Designest Industrial Design Co., Ltd.
(Bi Zhao, Congpo Sun, Peng Zhou),
Guangzhou, China
Web
www.nome.com

Power & Go is a stylish sports bracelet that integrates a wireless charging function. The battery capacity of 2,400 mAh allows at least one full charge of the usual smartphones. Thanks to the separation of the coil from the power bank, the package retains a thin profile for optimal comfort and stability when running. High-quality microfibre makes the strap breathable, water-resistant and easy to set. Reflective stripes increase safety.

Statement by the jury
The sports bracelet Power & Go surprises with its high functionality: It provides a full battery on the go and is easy to handle thanks to high-quality materials.

Power & Go ist ein stilvolles Sportarmband, das eine drahtlose Ladefunktion aufweist. Die Batteriekapazität von 2.400 mAh ermöglicht es, ein übliches Smartphone mindestens einmal vollständig aufzuladen. Durch die Trennung von Spule und Powerbank bleibt das Paket flach, was für besonderen Komfort und Stabilität beim Laufen sorgt. Hochwertige Mikrofaser macht das Band atmungsaktiv, wasserfest und einfach in der Einstellung. Reflektierende Streifen erhöhen die Sicherheit.

Begründung der Jury
Das Sportarmband Power & Go überrascht mit seiner hohen Funktionalität: Es sorgt für einen vollen Akku unterwegs und ist dank hochwertiger Materialien bequem zu handhaben.

Polar Vantage V
GPS Multisport Watch
Multisport-Uhr mit GPS

Manufacturer
Polar Electro Oy, Kempele, Finland
In-house design
Lauri Lumme
Web
www.polar.com

Polar Vantage V integrates advanced sports technology into a sleek, durable design and introduces the heart rate monitor Precision Prime and Polar's new running performance. The waterproof, GPS-enabled watch is equipped with innovative Smart Coaching features such as Training Load Pro and Recovery Pro as well as a new coach interface and has a permanently activated colour touch screen display. It offers a battery life of up to 40 hours.

Statement by the jury
The Polar Vantage V multisport watch impresses with an enormous, highly functional range of features and also has a stylish look.

Polar Vantage V integriert moderne Sporttechnologie in ein schlankes, langlebiges Design und führt den Herzfrequenzmesser Precision Prime und die neue Laufleistung von Polar ein. Die wasserdichte, GPS-fähige Uhr ist mit innovativen Smart Coaching-Funktionen wie Training Load Pro und Recovery Pro sowie einer neuen Coach-Schnittstelle ausgestattet und verfügt über ein ständig aktiviertes Farb-Touchscreen-Display. Sie bietet eine Akkulaufzeit von bis zu 40 Stunden.

Begründung der Jury
Die Multisport-Uhr Polar Vantage V überzeugt durch einen enormen, hochfunktionalen Leistungsumfang und zeigt darüber hinaus einen stilvollen Look.

Peloton Circuit Runners
Sneaker

Manufacturer
Peloton Interactive, Inc., New York, USA
In-house design
Jason Poure, Tom Cortese, Mark Eggert
Web
www.onepeloton.com

The Peloton Circuit Runners were specially developed for circuit training. They are equipped with a robust heel cap for good stability and a breathable mesh upper, which provides the necessary flexibility for this training. The laminated forefoot reinforcement provides stability across all equipment. The soft EVA midsole and rubber outsole round off the outstanding support for high sporting performance.

Statement by the jury
The design of these sneakers succeeds in meeting versatile circuit training expertly with materials that provide stability and flexibility at the same time.

Die Peloton Circuit Runners wurden eigens für Zirkeltraining entwickelt. Sie sind mit einer robusten Fersenkappe für gute Stabilität sowie einem atmungsaktiven Mesh-Obermaterial ausgestattet, das für dieses Training die nötige Flexibilität gewährt. Die laminierte Vorderfußverstärkung bietet über sämtliche Geräte hinweg Halt. Die Soft-EVA-Zwischensohle und die Außensohle aus Gummi runden die hervorragende Unterstützung bei hohen sportlichen Leistungen ab.

Begründung der Jury
Der Gestaltung dieser Sneakers gelingt es, der Vielseitigkeit von Zirkeltraining gekonnt mit Materialien zu begegnen, die für Stabilität und zugleich Flexibilität sorgen.

ECCO GOLF S-LITE
Golf Shoe
Golfschuh

Manufacturer
ECCO Golf, Tønder, Denmark
In-house design
Andrzej Bikowski
Web
www.ecco.com

The S-LITE golf shoe combines comfort, style and innovative technology to provide an ultra-light feel. The upper is made of micro-perforated Ecco yak leather and lined with soft fabric, which ensures durability and a breathable feel while playing. More than 100 moulded traction bars on the flexible E-DTS LITE outsole offer excellent grip for improved stability with every swing. The FLUIDFORM Direct Comfort technology ensures a finely tuned balance between cushioning and rebound.

Statement by the jury
Using the latest technology, the golf shoe has been skilfully designed to be light and comfortable to wear while ensuring a high level of stability.

Im Golfschuh S-LITE verbinden sich Komfort, Stil und innovative Technologien und ermöglichen ein besonders leichtes Tragegefühl. Das Obermaterial besteht aus mikroperforiertem Ecco-Yak-Leder und ist mit weichem Textil gefüttert, was sowohl Strapazierfähigkeit als auch Atmungsaktivität beim Spiel gewährleistet. Für eine hohe Stabilität bei jedem Schwung bieten mehr als 100 geformte „traction bars" (Zugstangen) auf der flexiblen E-DTS-LITE-Außensohle einen hervorragenden Halt. Die FLUIDFORM-Direct-Comfort-Technologie sorgt für ein fein abgestimmtes Verhältnis zwischen Dämpfung und Federung.

Begründung der Jury
Mit hochmodernen Technologien wurde der Golfschuh gekonnt so gestaltet, dass er sich leicht und komfortabel tragen lässt und gleichzeitig eine hohe Stabilität gewährleistet.

SphereWind 4.0 Run Jacket
Running Jacket
Laufjacke

Manufacturer
X-Technology Swiss R&D AG,
Wollerau, Switzerland
In-house design
Web
www.x-technology.com

The SphereWind 4.0 Run Jacket with patented ThermoSyphon technology supports natural thermodynamics in sweat management and improves the thermoregulation. The sleeves have been made more ergonomic: they do without under-arm seams, have been preset as running sleeves and boast new cuffs that also support ventilation and are very comfortable. A newly developed, weatherproof air outlet on the neck allows excess warm air to escape without draughts.

Statement by the jury
With its ergonomic design and ideal thermodynamics, the SphereWind 4.0 Run Jacket meets the high demands of modern functional clothing.

Die Laufjacke SphereWind 4.0 Run Jacket mit patentierter ThermoSyphon-Technologie unterstützt die natürliche Thermodynamik beim Schweißmanagement und verbessert die Thermoregulation. Die Ärmel wurden besonders ergonomisch gestaltet: Sie weisen keine Achselnähte auf, sind als Laufärmel voreingestellt und haben neue Manschetten, die die Belüftung ebenfalls unterstützen und sehr bequem sind. An einem neu entwickelten, wetterfesten Luftauslass am Hals kann überschüssige warme Luft entweichen, ohne dass es zu Zugluft kommt.

Begründung der Jury
Mit ihrem auf Ergonomie und bestmögliche Thermodynamik ausgerichteten Design wird SphereWind 4.0 Run Jacket den hohen Ansprüchen an moderne Funktionskleidung gerecht.

EFFEKTOR 4.0 Bike Bib
Shorts Padded
Bike Bib Shorts
Fahrradträgerhose

Manufacturer
X-Technology Swiss R&D AG,
Wollerau, Switzerland
In-house design
Web
www.x-technology.com

The EFFEKTOR 4.0 Bike Bib Shorts Padded stand out due to their Partialkompression technology. It improves temperature management by exerting pressure on the skin not over the entire surface but via bars. This maintains the cooling function of the sweat and the athlete saves strength. The neuro-response effect ensures that the muscles work faster and increases the performance potential. The anatomically shaped Endurance4000FX Bike Pad, which relieves pressure-sensitive blood vessels and nerves, offers optimum seating comfort.

Statement by the jury
The EFFEKTOR 4.0 Bike Bib Shorts Padded impress with their ingenious combination of innovative technologies and materials, which specifically increase the athlete's performance.

Die Fahrradträgerhose EFFEKTOR 4.0 Bike Bib Shorts Padded sticht durch ihre Partialkompressionstechnologie hervor. Sie verbessert das Temperaturmanagement, indem der Druck auf die Haut nicht flächig, sondern über Stege ausgeübt wird. Dadurch bleibt die Kühlfunktion des Schweißes erhalten, und der Sportler spart Kraft. Der Neuro-Response-Effekt sorgt dafür, dass die Muskeln schneller arbeiten und das Leistungspotenzial erhöht wird. Hohen Sitzkomfort bietet das anatomisch geformte Endurance-4000FX Bike Pad, das druckempfindliche Blutgefäße und Nerven entlastet.

Begründung der Jury
Die Fahrradträgerhose EFFEKTOR 4.0 Bike Bib Shorts Padded beeindruckt durch ihre ausgeklügelte Verbindung innovativer Technologien und Materialien, die die Leistung des Sportlers gezielt erhöhen.

THE TRICK® 4.0 Run Shirt
Running Shirt
Laufshirt

Manufacturer
X-Technology Swiss R&D AG, Wollerau, Switzerland
In-house design
Web
www.x-technology.com

THE TRICK 4.0 Run Shirt activates the body's thermoregulation earlier than previous ones and thus increases the performance in two ways. It prevents physical overheating and acts like a turbo for the other technologies that support the sweat management of the shirt. This holds especially true for the new 3D knit ThermoSyphon, which regulates the temperature on the outside and the sweat on the inside. A complex system of tunnels and channels with increased thread count per mm increases the evaporation area and improves stability even during movement.

Das Laufshirt THE TRICK 4.0 Run Shirt aktiviert die Thermoregulation des Körpers früher als die Vorgängermodelle und erhöht die Leistungsfähigkeit dadurch in zweifacher Hinsicht. Es verhindert die Überhitzung des Körpers und wirkt wie ein Turbo für die anderen Technologien, die das Schweißmanagement des Shirts unterstützen. Das gilt besonders für das neue 3D-Gestrick ThermoSyphon, das die Temperatur auf der Außenseite und den Schweiß auf der Innenseite reguliert. Ein komplexes System aus Tunneln und Kanälen mit hoher Fadenzahl pro mm vergrößert die Verdampfungsfläche und verbessert auch bei Bewegung die Stabilität.

Statement by the jury
The state-of-the-art technology and workmanship of THE TRICK 4.0 Run Shirt merge into a maturely functional and performance-enhancing product.

Begründung der Jury
Beim Laufshirt THE TRICK 4.0 Run Shirt verschmelzen aktuelle Technologie und Verarbeitung zu einem ausgereift funktionalen und leistungssteigernden Produkt.

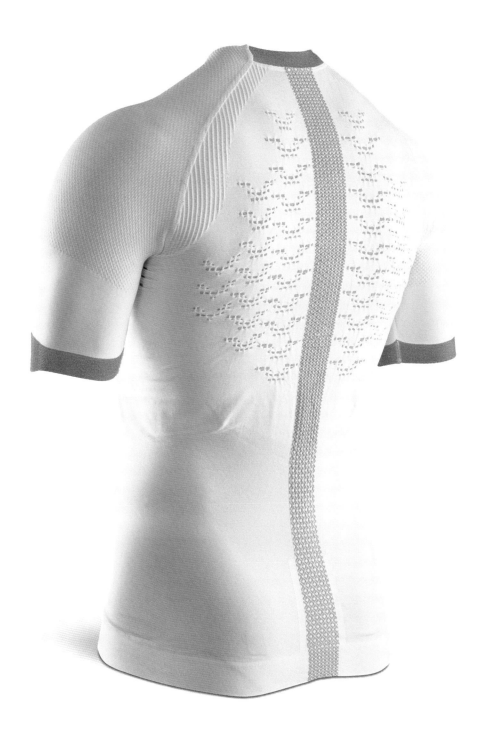

The North Face FUTURELIGHT™ Summit Series L5 Light Jacket
Jacket
Jacke

Manufacturer
VF Corporation, The North Face, Stabio, Switzerland
In-house design
Web
www.vfc.com
www.thenorthface.com

The Summit Series L5 Light Jacket is made of FUTURELIGHT, a new material which is manufactured using nanospinning on the basis of sustainable processes. It is currently one of the most technically advanced materials in terms of breathability and waterproofness. The new process also allows weight, stretch, durability, texture and construction – knitted or woven – to be adapted to the activity or environment to produce responsible garments.

Statement by the jury
The Summit Series L5 Light Jacket impresses with the outstanding properties of its innovative material, making it an exemplary example of sustainability.

Das Summit Series L5 Light Jacket besteht aus FUTURELIGHT, einem neuen Material, das mittels Nanospinning auf Basis nachhaltiger Prozesse hergestellt wird. Es ist eines der derzeit technisch höchstentwickelten Materialien in Bezug auf Atmungsaktivität und Wasserdichtigkeit. Dank des neuen Verfahrens lassen sich auch Gewicht, Dehnung, Haltbarkeit, Textur und Machart – gestrickt oder gewebt – an die Aktivität oder die Umgebung anpassen und so Kleidungsstücke verantwortungsbewusst fertigen.

Begründung der Jury
Das Summit Series L5 Light Jacket beeindruckt durch die herausragenden Eigenschaften seines innovativen Materials. Die Jacke wird so auch zu einem vorbildlichen Beispiel für Nachhaltigkeit.

60L Alpha Coat
Hunting Jacket
Jagdjacke

Manufacturer
HILLMAN, Boca Raton, USA
VIOMODA, Plovdiv, Bulgaria
In-house design
Web
www.hillmanhunting.com
www.viomoda.at

The 60L Alpha Coat has been specifically designed to stay dry in extreme weather conditions and to meet the needs of professional hunters and outdoor enthusiasts. It has been manufactured using Maul Guard technology from one of the world's strongest fibres, which can even protect against the attack of an animal. With every detail and element being thoughtfully and carefully assembled, the jacket offers excellent functionality and high comfort.

Statement by the jury
The 60L Alpha Coat, designed for hunting, is characterised by extremely robust and protective materials. The workmanship also meets the highest demands.

Die Jagdjacke 60L Alpha Coat wurde gezielt so konzipiert, dass sie auch unter extremen Wetterbedingungen trocken bleibt und den Anforderungen professioneller Jäger und Outdoor-Aktivisten genügt. Sie wurde unter Einsatz der Maul-Guard-Technologie aus einer der stärksten Fasern überhaupt hergestellt, die selbst vor dem Angriff eines Tieres schützen kann. Mit ihren durchdachten und sorgfältig zusammengefügten Elementen und Details bietet die Jacke hervorragende Funktionalität und hohen Komfort.

Begründung der Jury
Der für die Jagd konzipierte 60L Alpha Coat zeichnet sich durch äußerst robuste und schützende Materialien aus. Auch die Verarbeitung genügt höchsten Ansprüchen.

ATLAS
Sailing Trousers
Segelhose

Manufacturer
Sandiline d.o.o., Koper, Slovenia
In-house design
Sandi Ljutić
Web
www.sandiline.com

Sailing trousers must be top-performing and comfortable in every movement. With light stretchy materials on the sides of the torso, the lower leg and the shoulders, a product has been created that always adapts optimally to the body. It ensures both a tight fit and stretchability when sitting or in action. ATLAS moves, works and "breathes" with you. The power mesh net in the upper back and shoulder areas is as highly breathable as the wind- and waterproof material on the front of the torso.

Statement by the jury
The ATLAS sailing trousers succeed in offering comfort and high functionality at the same time. Their materials have been expertly matched and finished.

Segelhosen müssen bei jeder Bewegung leistungsstark und bequem sein. Mit leichten dehnbaren Materialien an den Seiten des Rumpfs, im Bereich der Unterschenkel und Schultern ist ein Produkt entstanden, das sich stets sehr gut dem Körper anpasst. Es gewährt einen engen Sitz und zugleich Dehnbarkeit beim Sitzen oder in Aktion. ATLAS bewegt sich, arbeitet und „atmet" mit. Das Powermesh-Netz im oberen Rücken- und Schulterbereich ist ebenso äußerst atmungsaktiv wie das wind- und wasserundurchlässige Material an der Vorderseite des Rumpfs.

Begründung der Jury
Der Segelhose ATLAS gelingt es, gleichzeitig Komfort und hohe Funktionalität zu bieten. Ihre Materialien wurden hervorragend aufeinander abgestimmt und verarbeitet.

Dachstein Iceland GTX
Outdoor Shoe
Outdoor-Schuh

Manufacturer
Dachstein Outdoor & Lifestyle GmbH, Salzburg, Austria
In-house design
Web
www.dachsteinschuhe.com

The DS Iceland GTX is a multifunctional outdoor shoe for cold and wet conditions. The membrane with the GORE-TEX Invisible Fit technology is laminated directly onto the gaiter, protects the feet, is absolutely waterproof and breathable. It eliminates wrinkles, reduces pressure points and dries quickly. The supporting mesh inner bootie features speed lacing on the inside of the shoe for a precise fit. The Vibram Fuga outsole ensures good grip on all terrain surfaces.

Der DS Iceland GTX ist ein multifunktionaler Outdoor-Schuh für kalte und nasse Witterungsbedingungen. Die Membran mit der GORE-TEX Invisible Fit Technologie ist direkt auf die Gamasche laminiert, schützt die Füße, ist wasserdicht und atmungsaktiv. Sie beseitigt Falten, reduziert Druckpunkte und trocknet schnell. Der stützende Mesh-Innenschuh ist an der Innenseite des Schuhs mit einer Speed-Schnürung ausgestattet, die eine präzise Passform bietet. Die Vibram Fuga Außensohle gewährleistet guten Grip auf allen Oberflächen im Gelände.

Statement by the jury
The DS IcelandGTX convinces with a design concept that focuses equally on functionality and aesthetics. Suitable for any outdoor adventure, it also looks good.

Begründung der Jury
Der DS Iceland GTX überzeugt mit einem gleichermaßen auf Funktionalität und Ästhetik fokussierten Gestaltungskonzept. Er ist für jedes Outdoor-Abenteuer geeignet und sieht auch gut aus.

Fiskars Norden
Axes
Äxte

Manufacturer
Fiskars Finland Oy Ab,
Helsinki, Finland

In-house design
Fiskars Finland Oy Ab

Web
www.fiskars.com
www.fiskarsgroup.com

reddot **award** 2019
best of the best

Pure performance

Axes are among mankind's oldest tools and generally display a very clear and pure aesthetics. The design of the axes of the Norden series embodies Finnish company Fiskars' long heritage of axe craftsmanship, a tradition that dates back to the 17th century. An important objective in their design was to solve the typical problems of axes with wooden shafts, whose handles wear over time and become fragile. Therefore, the handles are made of hickory wood and the innovative FiberComp material, which lend them a high-quality appearance and excellent safety in use. It makes the handles virtually unbreakable, while at the same time offering a natural look and feel of fine-crafted wood. This goes hand in hand with an innovative over-moulded head-shaft connection that keeps the head securely locked to the shaft. Ergonomically, the axes rest very well in the hand also due to their perfect weight distribution, which allows working with them for a long time without fatigue. For high efficiency, they also feature blades with advanced geometry and extremely sharp cutting edges. Thanks to a special coating, the blades do not get stuck in the wood. These axes provide an outstanding performance and are very easy to handle. The axe range consists of smaller models which are suitable for camping, as well as universal and splitting axes with handles from 40 cm to 48 cm.

Pure Performance

Die Axt ist eines der ältesten Werkzeuge der Menschheit, dem eine sehr klare und pure Ästhetik innewohnt. Die Gestaltung der Äxte der Norden-Serie verkörpert die bis in das 17. Jahrhundert zurückreichende Tradition des finnischen Unternehmens Fiskars in der Axtherstellung. Eine wichtige Zielsetzung dabei war, die typischen Probleme von Äxten mit Holzschäften zu lösen, deren Griffe mit der Zeit verschleißen und brüchig werden. Deshalb wird der Griff aus Hickoryholz und dem innovativen FiberComp-Material gefertigt, was für eine hochwertige Anmutung und ausgezeichnete Sicherheit beim Schlagen sorgt. Der Griff ist dadurch nahezu unzerstörbar, und es bleibt dennoch die natürliche Anmutung und Haptik des Holzes erhalten. Dies geht einher mit einer innovativen Verbindung von Schaft und Axtkopf, die diese fest und äußerst sicher zusammenfügt. Die Äxte liegen ergonomisch ausgesprochen gut in der Hand, ihr Gewicht ist perfekt austariert, weshalb man mit ihnen lange Zeit ohne Ermüdungserscheinungen arbeiten kann. Für eine hohe Effektivität verfügen sie zudem über eine verbesserte Klingengeometrie mit extrem scharfer Schneidkante. Dank einer speziellen Beschichtung bleibt die Klinge nicht im Holz stecken. Diese Äxte bieten eine sehr gute Performance, und es lässt sich leicht mit ihnen umgehen. Die Serie umfasst kleine Ausführungen für das Camping sowie Universal- und Spaltäxte mit einer Grifflänge von 40 bis 48 cm.

Statement by the jury

The axes of the Norden series harmoniously combine the aesthetics of these traditional tools with the highly functional properties of the special FiberComp material. The handles made of premium hickory wood thus deliver both durability and a special feel. The high quality of these axes is visible at first glance. The axes rest perfectly in the hand, offering excellent performance and maximum safety thanks to the innovative connection between shaft and axe head.

Begründung der Jury

Stimmig vereint sich bei den Äxten der Norden-Serie die Ästhetik des traditionellen Werkzeugs mit den hochfunktionalen Eigenschaften des speziellen FiberComp-Materials. Der Griff aus hochwertigem Hickoryholz erhält dadurch eine besondere Haptik und Langlebigkeit. Die hohe Qualität ist auf den ersten Blick sichtbar. Diese Äxte liegen perfekt in der Hand, bieten eine ausgezeichnete Performance und durch die innovative Verbindung von Schaft und Axtkopf auch ein Höchstmaß an Sicherheit.

Designer portrait
See page 50
Siehe Seite 50

COMBAR
Heavy Duty Multi-Tool
Multifunktionswerkzeug

Manufacturer
Aclim8, Nofit, Israel
Design
Prime Total Product Design, Tel Aviv, Israel
Web
www.aclim8.com
www.prime-do.com

COMBAR is a powerful multifunctional tool developed on the basis of extensive field research. It is suitable for the most diverse adventures in nature and combines the five essential elements: knife, saw, hammer, axe and spade in one tool. It is lightweight, beautifully designed and at the same time made of durable, high-quality materials. Technically mature and ergonomically designed, it offers high functionality and great pleasure in its versatile use in the field.

COMBAR ist ein leistungsfähiges Multifunktionswerkzeug, das auf Basis umfangreicher Feldstudien entwickelt wurde. Es eignet sich für die verschiedensten Abenteuer in der Natur und kombiniert die fünf wesentlichen Elemente Messer, Säge, Hammer, Axt und Spaten in einem Werkzeug. Es ist leicht, schön gestaltet und gleichzeitig aus langlebigen, hochwertigen Materialien gefertigt. Technisch ausgereift und ergonomisch gestaltet, bietet es neben hoher Funktionalität großes Vergnügen bei seinem vielseitigen Einsatz im Gelände.

Statement by the jury
The design of the multifunctional tool COMBAR combines sophisticated ideas for sensible use in nature with optimum handling.

Begründung der Jury
In der Gestaltung des Multifunktionswerkzeugs COMBAR verbinden sich ausgereifte Ideen zum sinnvollen Gebrauch in der Natur mit hervorragender Handhabung.

Walther Reign
Compressed-Air Rifle
Pressluftgewehr

Manufacturer
UMAREX GmbH & Co. KG, Arnsberg, Germany
In-house design
Seunghan Kang
Web
www.umarex.com

The compressed-air rifle Walther Reign stands out from the competition by its short bullpup construction and impresses with its low weight of only 2.6 kg. Thanks to sophisticated technology, it hits the target precisely. The rifle, made of high-strength aluminium and furnished with a premium black surface, adapts to the body with its ergonomic shape when it raised to the shoulder. The tensioning lever can be operated comfortably and intuitively by both right-handed and left-handed users – for both, the appropriate version is available.

Das Pressluftgewehr Walther Reign hebt sich durch seine kurze Bullpup-Bauweise von der Konkurrenz ab und beeindruckt durch sein geringes Gewicht von nur 2,6 kg. Dank ausgereifter Technik trifft es präzise. Beim Anlegen passt sich das aus hochfestem Aluminium und mit edler schwarzer Oberfläche gefertigte Gewehr mit seiner ergonomischen Form an den Körper an. Der Spannhebel lässt sich bequem und intuitiv sowohl von Rechts- als auch Linkshändern bedienen – für beide steht die jeweils passende Ausführung zur Verfügung.

Statement by the jury
The Walther Reign combines a superior scope of performance with a construction and finish that have been precisely matched to ergonomic use.

Begründung der Jury
Beim Walther Reign paart sich ein überlegener Leistungsumfang mit einer Konstruktion und Ausführung, die präzise auf den ergonomischen Gebrauch abgestimmt wurden.

Hunter Pro Alox
Swiss Army Knife
Schweizer Taschenmesser

Manufacturer
Victorinox AG, Ibach (Schwyz), Switzerland
In-house design
Web
www.victorinox.com

Hunter Pro Alox is an elegant, modern and sleek everyday carry. It combines a striking design with a robust blade, which makes it the ideal crossover for all out-door and urban activities. It is equipped with ribbed Alox scales that give the knife a non-slip, multidimensional finish. The lanyard hole integrated in the spring, the curved clip, which can be attached to practically any garment, and a paracord pendant round off the sophis-ticated design.

Statement by the jury
The pocket knife Hunter Pro Alox con-vinces as a multifunctional tool. Its powerful appearance is also due to its high-quality materials.

Das Hunter Pro Alox ist ein eleganter, moderner und schlanker Alltagsbegleiter. Es kombiniert ein markantes Design mit einer robusten Klinge und ist der ideale Allrounder für sämtliche Outdoor- und Großstadt-aktivitäten. Das Messer ist mit gerippten Alox-Schalen ausgestattet, die ihm ein grif-figes, multidimensionales Finish verleihen. Die in die Feder integrierte Befestigungsöse, der gebogene Clip, der sich an so gut wie jedem Kleidungsstück anbringen lässt, und ein Paracord-Anhänger runden das raffinierte Design ab.

Begründung der Jury
Das Taschenmesser Hunter Pro Alox überzeugt als multifunktionales Tool. Sein kraftvolles Erscheinungsbild verdankt es auch seiner hochwertigen Materialqualität.

Stacking
Thermal Container Set
Stapelbares
Thermobehälterset

Manufacturer
Tupperware (China) Co., Ltd.,
Guangzhou, China
Design
Tupperware Worldwide Product
Innovation Team,
Tupperware General Services N.V.,
Aalst, Belgium
Web
www.tupperwarebrands.com

With the Stacking Thermal Container Set you can easily transport hot and cold food when you are on the move. Thanks to the different sizes of its elements, meals can be optimally portioned for the day. The containers can be firmly con-nected to each other by means of the practical swivel joint on their base and lid and conveniently carried along. The temperature is maintained by the double wall insulation made of stainless steel in combination with the tightly closing insulating lid.

Statement by the jury
The well-conceived Stacking Thermal Container Set fascinates with its highly practical use for the transport of hot or cold meals.

Mit diesem stapelbaren Thermobehälterset kann man warmes wie kaltes Essen einfach transportieren, wenn man unterwegs ist. Dank der verschiedenen Größen seiner Teile können die Mahlzeiten für den Tag nach Wunsch portioniert werden. Die Behälter lassen sich mithilfe der praktischen Dreh-verbindung an Boden und Deckel fest miteinander verbinden und bequem mit-nehmen. Die Temperatur wird durch die doppelte Wandisolierung aus Edelstahl in Kombination mit dem dicht schließenden Isolierdeckel gehalten.

Begründung der Jury
Durchdacht konzipiert, begeistert das stapelbare Thermobehälterset mit seinem hohen praktischen Nutzwert für den Transport warmer oder kalter Mahlzeiten.

Skotti
Gas Grill
Gasgrill

Manufacturer
Vennskap, Christian Battel,
Meerbusch, Germany
Design
Daniel Brunner, Meerbusch, Germany
Web
www.skotti-grill.eu

The Skotti gas grill is not only portable but also collapsible and the ideal companion for outdoor activities in the forest, on the beach or on tours by bike or motorbike. It weighs just under 3 kg including carrying bag, fits flat in any hiking backpack and can be assembled in a few moments without tools. A grilled meal can be enjoyed with minimal effort, while barbecuing is absolutely safe. The eight parts of the appliance are made of high-quality stainless steel and are easy to clean.

Statement by the jury
The Skotti gas grill ensures highly practical, simple and safe handling and scores with an attractive appearance.

Der Gasgrill Skotti ist nicht nur tragbar, sondern auch zerlegbar und bei Outdoor-Aktivitäten im Wald, am Strand oder auf Touren mit Rad oder Motorrad ein origineller Begleiter. Er wiegt samt Transporttasche nur knapp 3 kg, passt flach in jeden Wanderrucksack und ist in wenigen Augenblicken ohne Werkzeug zusammengesteckt. Mit minimalem Aufwand lässt sich eine gegrillte Mahlzeit genießen, wobei beim Grillen stets Sicherheit gewährleistet ist. Die acht Teile des Geräts sind aus hochwertigem Edelstahl gefertigt und einfach zu reinigen.

Begründung der Jury
Der Gasgrill Skotti zeichnet sich durch eine überaus praktische, einfache und sichere Handhabung aus und punktet mit einem ansprechenden Erscheinungsbild.

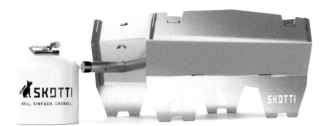

Drumi
Washing Machine
Waschmaschine

Manufacturer
Yirego Corp., Toronto, Canada
In-house design
Design
Yige Technology (Shenzhen) Co., Ltd.,
Shenzhen, China
Web
www.yirego.com

Drumi is a weather-proof and impact-resistant foot-powered washing machine. Its ergonomic pedal allows to wash up to 2 kg of laundry in 5 to 10 minutes at up to 600 revolutions and spin-dry it in 30 seconds. The patent-pending drum is made of compound curved stainless steel and can be removed. The machine requires no electricity or installation and can be stored in a small space thanks to its compact design. The carrying handle, which acts as a safety lock when turned back, makes it easy to move Drumi around.

Statement by the jury
The Drumi foot-powered washing machine impresses with its successful combination of mobility and sustainability and is an ideal solution for travelling.

Drumi ist eine wetter- und stoßfeste Waschmaschine mit Fußantrieb. Mit dem ergonomischen Pedal lassen sich in 5 bis 10 Minuten bis zu 2 kg Wäsche bei bis zu 600 Umdrehungen waschen und in 30 Sekunden trocken schleudern. Die zum Patent angemeldete Trommel aus gebogenem Verbunddedelstahl lässt sich herausnehmen. Der Betrieb der Maschine erfordert weder Strom noch Installation, und das Gerät kann dank seines kompakten Designs auf kleinem Raum untergebracht werden. Mit dem Tragegriff, der nach hinten gedreht als Sicherheitsschloss fungiert, lässt sich Drumi mühelos bewegen.

Begründung der Jury
Die Waschmaschine Drumi mit Fußantrieb beeindruckt durch ihre gelungene Kombination von Mobilität und Nachhaltigkeit und stellt eine sehr praktikable Lösung für unterwegs dar.

EcoFlow RIVER
Portable Power Station
Mobile Stromversorgung

Manufacturer
Ecoflow, Shenzhen, China
In-house design
Web
www.ecoflow.com

EcoFlow RIVER provides a portable, efficient and reliable power supply. The unit is lightweight yet powerful. It can be charged with solar energy and has an intelligent battery management system that is easy to use. It replaces dangerous fuel generators and is suitable for extended camping trips, disaster preparedness or living off the power grid. Medical equipment can also be powered on the go.

Statement by the jury
EcoFlow RIVER captivates with its high functionality, with which the device provides a reliable power supply wherever the user is.

EcoFlow RIVER bietet eine tragbare, effiziente und zuverlässige Stromversorgung. Das Gerät ist leicht und dennoch leistungsstark. Es kann über Solarenergie aufgeladen werden und verfügt über ein intelligentes Batteriemanagementsystem, das einfach zu bedienen ist. Es ersetzt gefährliche Kraftstoffgeneratoren und eignet sich für längere Campingaufenthalte, zur Vorsorge für den Katastrophenfall oder für ein vom Stromnetz unabhängiges Leben. Auch medizinische Geräte können damit unterwegs mit Strom versorgt werden.

Begründung der Jury
EcoFlow RIVER besticht durch die hohe Funktionalität, mit der das Gerät eine zuverlässige Stromversorgung bereitstellt, wo auch immer der Benutzer gerade ist.

Dometic PLB40
Portable Power Pack
Tragbarer Akku

Manufacturer
Dometic, Solna, Sweden
In-house design
Samuele Meda, Jens Nybacka,
Mikael Thelin, Kristoffer Olsson
Web
www.dometic.com

Dometic PLB40 is a portable power pack equipped with lithium iron phosphate cells. Although it is particularly compact and light-weight, it ensures high levels of mobile power. The sturdy outdoor design with an ergonomically shaped stainless-steel carrying handle makes the battery easy to transport and use in a variety of environments from simple camping to extensive expeditions. The battery can be charged via 12 V socket, solar panel or AC house power.

Dometic PLB40 ist eine tragbare, mit Lithium-Eisenphosphat-Zellen arbeitende Batterie, die bei hoher Leistung zugleich besonders kompakt und leicht ist. Die robuste, für den Außenbereich geeignete Konstruktion mit ergonomisch geformtem Tragegriff aus Edelstahl macht den Akku bequem transportabel und in verschiedenen Umgebungen, vom einfachen Camping bis zu aufwendigen Expeditionen, verwendbar. Die Batterie kann über 12-V-Steckdose, Solarpaneel oder Wechselspannungsnetz aufgeladen werden.

Statement by the jury
The design of the compact Dometic PLB40 battery reflects the performance and stability that characterise this well-thought-out mobile device.

Begründung der Jury
In der Gestaltung des kompakten Akkus Dometic PLB40 spiegeln sich die Leistungsfähigkeit und Stabilität wider, die das schlüssig konzipierte mobile Gerät kennzeichnen.

iMuto Power Station S5
Portable Solar Power Station
Mobile Stromversorgung

Manufacturer
iMuto Limited, Hong Kong
In-house design
Design
Shenzhen Tianbaotong Technology Co., Ltd. (Ray Lee),
Shenzhen, China
Shenzhen DBK Electronics Co., Ltd. (Chuang Wu Zhang, Terry Zeng),
Shenzhen, China
Web
www.imuto.com
www.dbk.com.hk

iMuto Power Station S5 is a solar-powered lithium-ion battery with high power (260 W) and capacity (50,000 mAh). With its simple design and rounded edges, it blends harmoniously into its surroundings and is easy to carry on a practical handle. Made of robust, stainless metal, it is particularly sturdy and can be used both indoors and outdoors. Its technology such as the clearly arranged display, various connections or a luminaire are arranged around the centre.

iMuto Power Station S5 ist ein solarbetriebener Lithium-Ionen-Akku mit hoher Leistung (260 W) und Kapazität (50.000 mAh). Durch seine schlichte Gestaltung mit abgerundeten Kanten integriert er sich harmonisch in die Umgebung und lässt sich an einem praktischen Griff gut mitführen. Besonders stabil aus robustem, rostfreiem Metall hergestellt, kann er drinnen wie draußen verwendet werden. Die Technik, wie das übersichtlich gestaltete Display, verschiedene Anschlüsse oder eine Leuchte, sind in der Mitte umlaufend angeordnet.

Statement by the jury
The design of this device for mobile energy supply is convincing due to its compact, stable housing and its functionally well-thought-out design.

Begründung der Jury
Die Gestaltung dieses Geräts zur mobilen Stromversorgung überzeugt durch ein kompaktes, stabiles Gehäuse und einen funktional durchdachten Aufbau.

Helinox Bench One
Portable Camping Bench
Tragbare Campingbank

Manufacturer
Helinox Inc., Incheon, South Korea
In-house design
Young Whan Lah
Web
www.helinox.com

Bench One was developed in partnership with DAC, a global leader in tent poles. Leveraging their understanding of cutting-edge technology in aluminium performance, the product was designed for maximum strength with minimum weight: it safely holds 145 kg and weighs 2,100 grams. Made from highly durable materials that can withstand the rigours of outdoor conditions, it easily accommodates two people or may be used as a side table. The seat surface of Bench One is firm and gets its tension through a cantilever locking system that also attaches the legs to the horizontal seat poles. Assembly is intuitive, fast and easy.

Bench One wurde mit DAC, einem bei Zeltstangen weltweit führenden Unternehmen, als Partner entwickelt. Basierend auf dessen Kenntnis der fortschrittlichsten Technologie im Bereich Aluminium, wurde eine durch maximale Tragkraft bei minimalem Gewicht gekennzeichnete Lösung gefunden: Bench One trägt problemlos 145 kg und wiegt nur 2.100 Gramm. Aus sehr langlebigem Material gefertigt, das widrigen Bedingungen im Freien standhält, bietet das Produkt eine Sitzgelegenheit für zwei Personen oder kann als Beistelltisch dienen. Die Sitzfläche ist hart und erhält durch ein Kragarm-Verriegelungssystem, mit dem auch die Beine an den waagrechten Sitzstangen befestigt werden, ihre Spannung. Der Aufbau gestaltet sich intuitiv, schnell und einfach.

Statement by the jury
Bench One impresses with the versatility of its use as well as its light yet stable construction. This makes it ideal for use in open terrain.

Begründung der Jury
Bench One beeindruckt durch die Vielseitigkeit seiner Nutzung sowie die leichte, zugleich stabile Machart. Damit wird die Konstruktion den Anforderungen im Gelände gezielt gerecht.

Ultralight Folded Hammock Stand
Cot
Feldbett

Manufacturer
KingCamp Outdoor Products Co., Ltd.,
Beijing, China
In-house design
Guo Qing Xu
Web
www.kingcamp.com.cn

This cot is characterised by an advanced construction concept with a foldable frame. With its small packing volume of 82 × 16 × 16 cm, including hammock stand, the cot can be stowed quickly in a bag and has a particularly light total weight of only 6.5 kg thanks to its aluminium frame. The lying surface is supported by a horizontal steel frame, which ensures high stability. The bed is easy to assemble in a few seconds and is equipped with a pillow for added comfort.

Statement by the jury
The cot is characterised by comfort and a small pack size with low weight and thus exactly meets the demands placed on outdoor equipment.

Dieses Feldbett ist durch ein fortschrittliches Konstruktionskonzept mit klappbarem Rahmen gekennzeichnet. Es ist schnell in einer Tasche verstaubar und beansprucht wenig Platz dank seines Packmaßes inkl. Gestell von 82 × 16 × 16 cm. Aufgrund des Gestells aus Aluminium hat es ein besonders geringes Gesamtgewicht von lediglich 6,5 kg. Die Liegefläche wird von einem horizontalen Stahlrahmen getragen, der hohe Stabilität gewährleistet. Das Bett lässt sich in wenigen Sekunden einfach aufbauen und ist mit einem Kopfkissen für zusätzlichen Komfort ausgestattet.

Begründung der Jury
Dieses Feldbett zeichnet sich durch Komfort und ein kleines Packmaß mit geringem Gewicht aus und entspricht so genau den Ansprüchen, die an Outdoor-Ausrüstung gestellt werden.

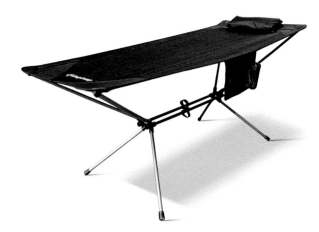

Umbrella
Regenschirm

Manufacturer
Hau Ya Co., Ltd., Taoyuan City, Taiwan
In-house design
Web
https://24h.pchome.com.tw/store/DXAB15

The umbrella stands out due to its different-coloured covers on the inside and outside as well as its handle, whose curve points in two directions. The reason for this is its twofold function: it not only protects against rain but can also be turned inside out after use so that the raindrops collect inside instead of running down the outside. Thus, the umbrella can be carried into the bathroom, for example, without leaving any traces. The innovative pressure technology for adjustment is integrated above the handle.

Statement by the jury
The umbrella draws attention with its original innovation that it both protects against rain and can collect the wet drops in its inverted shape.

Dieser Regenschirm fällt durch die verschiedenfarbigen Bezüge innen und außen sowie seinen Griff auf, dessen Rundung in zwei Richtungen weist. Grund ist die zweifache Funktion: Der Schirm schützt nicht nur ganz klassisch vor Regen, er lässt sich zudem nach Gebrauch wenden, sodass die Regentropfen nicht außen herunterlaufen, sondern sich im Inneren sammeln. Ohne Spuren zu hinterlassen, kann der Schirm so etwa ins Badezimmer getragen werden. Die innovative Drucktechnologie zum Einstellen ist über dem Griff integriert.

Begründung der Jury
Der Regenschirm macht durch die originelle Innovation auf sich aufmerksam, dass er gleichzeitig vor Regen schützt und die nassen Tropfen in seiner gewendeten Form auch sammeln kann.

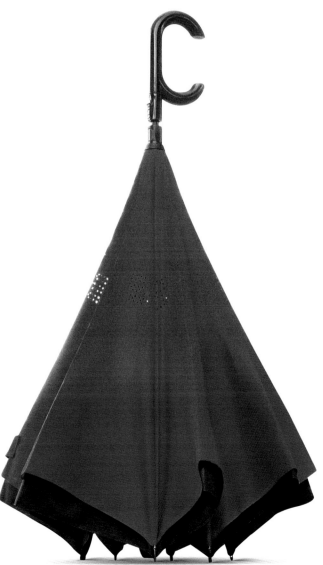

Leisure and games
Freizeit und Spiel

Musical equipment	Haustierbedarf
Musical instruments	Musik-Equipment
Pet supplies	Musikinstrumente
Sex toys	Sextoys
Skateboards	Skateboards
Toys	Spielzeuge

Lampuga Air
Electric Surfboard
Elektro-Surfboard

Manufacturer
Lampuga GmbH,
Rastatt, Germany

Design
Schweizer Design Consulting
(Oliver Schweizer, Robin Ritter,
Patrick Senfter, Farouk Zemni),
Stuttgart, Germany

Web
www.lampuga.com
www.schweizer.design

reddot award 2019
best of the best

Perfect lifestyle

Originating from the beaches of Hawaii, surfboards have become part of a lifestyle all around the globe today. The Lampuga Air reinterprets the classical surfboard and enables emission-free mobility on water through an integrated electric jet drive. The dynamic-looking board embodies high ergonomic and technical requirements in an aesthetically pleasing design. Powered by a 10 kW (14 hp) electric motor, the board glides across the water surface at a speed of up to 50 km/h. The board consists of a shape-defining Powerbox containing the board's technical components and an inflatable and foldable hull. Its design has been perfectly shaped for providing an agile surfing experience. Designed according to modular plug-and-play principles, the board fits into most car trunks and therefore allows for easy transportation. It can be assembled or disassembled in five minutes and ensures simple handling and low maintenance. The board is manoeuvered using weight transfer and features a stabilising tether, enabling surfing for the unexperienced. The acceleration is controlled using the hand-held remote control, which connects to the board via Bluetooth. The board is powered by a powerful, removable lithium-ion battery that is externally charged. To ensure a continued riding experience, the concept also includes an additional removable battery.

Ein formvollendetes Lebensgefühl

Der ursprünglich einmal von den Stränden Hawaiis und den dortigen Einwohnern stammende Surfsport steht in unserer Zeit für ein globales Lebensgefühl. Das Lampuga Air interpretiert das Surfboard neu und erlaubt dank eines integrierten elektrischen Antriebs emissionsfreie Mobilität auf dem Wasser. Bei dem dynamisch anmutenden Board vereinen sich die hohen ergonomischen und technischen Anforderungen in einem ästhetisch-zweckmäßigen Design. Angetrieben durch einen 10 kW (14 PS) starken Elektromotor, gleitet es mit bis zu 50 km/h über das Wasser. Es besteht aus der formgebenden Powerbox, die die technischen Komponenten enthält, und einem sie umgebenden aufblasbaren Luftschlauch. Der Rumpf und die Powerbox sind perfekt auf agiles Fahren ausgelegt. Da das Lampuga Air als modular aufgebautes Plug-and-Play-System gestaltet wurde, lässt es sich gut im Kofferraum transportieren. Es kann in fünf Minuten auf- und abgebaut werden und gewährleistet eine unkomplizierte Handhabung und Wartung. Die Steuerung erfolgt über Gewichtsverlagerung, während ein stabiles Halteseil den Gebrauch des Boards auch für Surf-Laien vereinfacht. Die Geschwindigkeit wird mittels einer Bluetooth-Fernbedienung am Haltegriff reguliert. Das Lampuga Air ist ausgestattet mit einem leistungsfähigen, herausnehmbaren Lithium-Ionen-Akku, der extern aufgeladen wird. Damit der Surfspaß ohne große Unterbrechung weitergehen kann, umfasst das Konzept ein Wechselakkusystem, das den einfachen Austausch des Akkus erlaubt.

Statement by the jury

With its innovative design, the Lampuga Air surfboard enables a new kind of surfing experience, independent of wind and waves. Driven by a powerful electric motor, it offers environmentally responsible operation without emissions. It is easy to transport and features a dynamic shape that is perfectly balanced on the water. In a comfortable manner, it is easy to control by simply shifting one's weight.

Begründung der Jury

Mit seiner innovativen Gestaltung ermöglicht das Surfboard Lampuga Air eine neue Art von Surferfahrung, unabhängig von Wind und Wellen. Angetrieben durch einen leistungsfähigen Elektromotor, bietet es einen ökologisch verantwortungsvollen Betrieb ohne Emissionen. Es ist leicht zu transportieren und liegt mit seiner dynamischen Form perfekt ausbalanciert auf dem Wasser. Auf komfortable Weise lässt es sich einfach per Gewichtsverlagerung steuern.

Designer portrait
See page 52
Siehe Seite 52

You can also find this product on page 120 and 161.
Dieses Produkt finden Sie auch auf Seite 120 und 161.

SPECTRA X
Sharable Electric Skateboard
Elektrisches Sharing-Skateboard

Manufacturer
Walnut Technology Limited, Shenzhen, China
In-house design
Jianghao Luo, Chinyun Yang
Web
www.walnutt.com

The model concept brought to the market by the electric skateboard SPECTRA X is committed to the idea of the joint use of resources and products. Focused on person-to-person sharing (P2P sharing), owners of a skateboard lease the right of use of their possession to interested parties. The sharing function available via the eBoard Go app is also scalable for other devices. The skateboard thus supports environmentally friendly mobility.

Das Sharing-Modell, das mit dem elektrischen Skateboard SPECTRA X auf den Markt kommt, ist der Idee der gemeinsamen Nutzung von Ressourcen und Produkten verpflichtet. Es beruht auf dem Prinzip des Teilens von Person zu Person (P2P-Sharing), das heißt, der Eigentümer des Skateboards vermietet es an Interessierte. Die über die eBoard-Go-App verfügbare Freigabefunktion ist auch für andere Geräte skalierbar. Damit trägt das Skateboard zu einer umweltfreundlichen Mobilität bei.

Statement by the jury
The electric skateboard SPECTRA X inspires with its innovative function of enabling sharing with a lot of driving fun by means of an app.

Begründung der Jury
Das elektrische Skateboard SPECTRA X begeistert mit seiner innovativen Funktion, mittels Sharing-App eine gemeinsame Nutzung mit viel Fahrspaß zu ermöglichen.

Doblocks
Educational Toy
Pädagogisches Spielzeug

Manufacturer
Shenzhen Science Technology Co., Ltd.,
Shenzhen, China
In-house design
Liangqiu Liu
Design
Shenzhen Qifang Design Studio
(Jiyong Wang, Jie Chen), Shenzhen, China
Web
www.sciencerboclub.com
Honourable Mention

Doblocks is an Arduino-based open source hardware platform for novice programmers. It contains 15 different colour and function modules that can be combined on the main module as desired, each with a magnetic connection. Users can easily write portable applications according to the combination in the Arduino IDE. In addition, the Bluetooth module can communicate with the app, making Internet of Things applications easier.

Statement by the jury
The hardware platform Doblocks stands out due to its simple handling and the multitude of its functions. This makes programming easy to learn.

Doblocks ist eine auf Arduino basierende Open-Source-Hardwareplattform für Programmieranfänger. Sie enthält 15 verschiedene Farb- und Funktionsmodule, die jeweils mit Magnetanschluss auf dem Hauptmodul beliebig kombiniert werden können. Benutzer können entsprechend der Kombination problemlos tragbare Anwendungen in Arduino IDE schreiben. Außerdem kann das Bluetooth-Modul mit der App kommunizieren, wodurch Internet-of-Things-Anwendungen einfacher werden.

Begründung der Jury
Die Hardwareplattform Doblocks sticht aufgrund ihrer einfachen Bedienbarkeit und der Vielzahl ihrer Funktionen hervor. Dadurch lässt sich Programmieren sehr leicht erlernen.

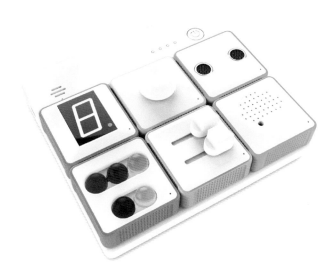

Harrel
Model Car Race Track
Spielzeug-Autorennbahn

Manufacturer
Harrel GmbH & Co., Solingen, Germany
In-house design
Harald Dannert
Web
www.harrel-rs.com

Harrel is a model car race track that can be used with all known slot cars to a scale of 1:32 and 1:24. Commercially available power supply units can be connected for control. The module is a complex assembly based on a high-quality wood composite. The surface is asphalt grey lacquer with quartz sand for the right grip. The connection segments and plastic components consist of high-performance polyamide and are screwed together as a module. A thick copper line connects the connections and supplies the visible conductors with electricity. The different modules can be easily plugged together to form an individual track of up to eight tracks next to each other.

Statement by the jury
Harrel convinces with its high connectivity for a multitude of racing car models. The module is also a piece of very high workmanship.

Harrel ist eine Spielzeug-Autorennbahn, die sich mit allen bekannten Slot Cars im Maßstab 1:32 und 1:24 nutzen lässt. Handelsübliche Netzgeräte können zur Steuerung angeschlossen werden. Das Modul ist eine komplexe Baugruppe auf Basis eines hochwertigen Holzwerkstoffs. Der Belag besteht aus asphaltgrauem Lack mit Quarzsand für den richtigen Grip. Die Anschlusssegmente und Kunststoffbauteile sind aus Hochleistungspolyamid gefertigt und werden als Baugruppe miteinander verschraubt. Eine dicke Kupferleitung verbindet die Anschlüsse und versorgt die sichtbaren Stromleiter mit Elektrizität. Die unterschiedlichen Module lassen sich leicht zusammenstecken und bilden so eine individuelle Strecke von bis zu acht Spuren nebeneinander.

Begründung der Jury
Harrel überzeugt durch seine hohe Anschlussfähigkeit für eine Vielzahl von Rennwagenmodellen. Das Modul ist zudem sehr hochwertig gearbeitet.

pidan Cat Surfing Tunnel
Katzentunnel

Manufacturer
Danke Co.,Ltd. (Pan Biwei), China
In-house design
Web
www.pidan.com

The pidan cat surfing tunnel is a modular piece of furniture that offers cats a soft and playful space. The main component is a two-layer felt structure that can serve as a floor mat. If required, the upper felt pad can be curved and fixed to form a tunnel structure. Each unit can be used individually or combined with others to give the cats a playground of different sizes and shapes. Brushes or adhesive rollers will help to keep the cat tunnel clean.

Beim Katzentunnel pidan handelt es sich um ein modulares Möbel, das Katzen einen weichen und verspielten Raum bietet. Hauptbestandteil ist eine zweilagige Struktur aus Filz, die als Bodenmatte eingesetzt werden kann. Das obere Filzpad kann auch gewölbt und so fixiert werden, dass sich ein Tunnel bildet. Jede Einheit kann einzeln genutzt oder mit anderen kombiniert werden, um für die Katzen Spielplätze unterschiedlicher Größe und Form aufzubauen. Um den Katzentunnel sauber zu halten, können Bürsten oder Fusselrollen verwendet werden.

Statement by the jury
The pidan cat tunnel impresses with its simple construction and pleasantly materials. Individually combinable, it also offers a lot of variety.

Begründung der Jury
Der Katzentunnel pidan besticht durch seine einfache Konstruktion und angenehme Materialien. Individuell kombinierbar, bietet er außerdem viel Abwechslung.

Oliver
Pet Bed
Haustierbett

Manufacturer
Werewoof, Sonderlust Ltd., London, United Kingdom
In-house design
Tong Xue, Jamie Baldock, Chiara Delucca, Marlon Bent
Web
www.werewoof.co.uk

Oliver is a pet bed padded with a very comfortable memory foam mattress. The mattress is sized to fit exactly into the handcrafted oak or American walnut frame that surrounds it. It can be handled effortlessly and is particularly easy to care for. Its simply removable cover is machine washable and available in various colours and patterns. The user thus has the choice to select a modern pet bed according to his taste.

Oliver ist ein Haustierbett, das mit einer sehr bequemen Matratze aus Memory-Schaum gepolstert ist. Die Matratze ist so bemessen, dass sie exakt in den hand-geformten Rahmen aus Eichenholz oder amerikanischem Nussbaum passt, der sie umschließt. Sie lässt sich mühelos hand-haben und ist besonders pflegeleicht. Ihr einfach zu entfernender Bezug ist maschi-nenwaschbar und in verschiedenen Farben wie Mustern erhältlich. Der Benutzer hat so die Wahl, das moderne Haustierbett ganz nach seinem Geschmack auszusuchen.

Statement by the jury
The design of the pet bed Oliver convinces with a minimalistic, high-quality appearance as well as an extremely user-friendly handling.

Begründung der Jury
Die Gestaltung des Haustierbetts Oliver überzeugt mit einem minimalistischen, hochwertigen Erscheinungsbild sowie einer überaus benutzerfreundlichen Handhabung.

A SPACE
Pet House
Haustierkorb

Manufacturer
JnY Archistudio, Seoul, South Korea
In-house design
Seungwon Jeon, Yunji Yi
Web
www.smallspace.co.kr

Pets also need a place to shelter them. The design of A SPACE allows the animal to comfortably lie or sit. The entrance is tilted by 33 degrees so that the pet may either make eye contact with the owner and have a good view of the room or cuddle backwards into the darker corner. The circular shape prevents the animal from hitting itself. The house is easy to assemble, wash and roll up for travel.

Statement by the jury
The A SPACE pet house stands out with its elaborate construction, which is highly practical to handle and offers comfort to the animal.

Auch Haustiere benötigen einen Ort, der ihnen Zuflucht gibt. A SPACE ist so konzipiert, dass das Tier bequem liegen oder sitzen kann. Dank der Neigung des Eingangs um 33 Grad ist es ihm möglich, entweder Augenkontakt mit dem Besitzer aufzunehmen und den Raum gut zu überblicken oder sich nach hinten in die dunklere Ecke zu kuscheln. Die Kreisform verhindert, dass sich das Tier stößt. Der Korb lässt sich leicht zusammenbauen, waschen und etwa zum Verreisen aufrollen.

Begründung der Jury
Der Haustierkorb A SPACE ragt aufgrund seiner durchdachten Konstruktion heraus, die sich äußerst praktisch handhaben lässt und dem Tier Komfort bietet.

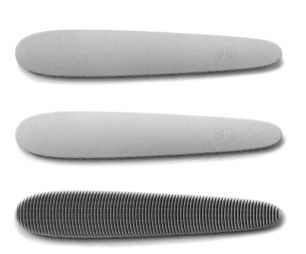

CAT GROOMER
Grooming Brush
Tierbürste

Manufacturer
Wataoka Co., Ltd., Kure, Japan
Design
GK Kyoto Inc. (Aiko Yokoyama, Natsumi Sakamoto), Kyoto, Japan
Web
www.wataoka.co.jp
www.gk-kyoto.com

CAT GROOMER is a pet brush that allows cats and their owners to share a playful moment. It is made with the special resin moulding technique of the file manufacturer Wataoka and also shows a shape similar to the file. Its special comb teeth have a fine texture and high precision. The overall design is as simple as it is elegant. Thanks to its compact size, it lies well in the hand.

Statement by the jury
The CAT GROOMER animal brush scores with its simple ergonomic design, which makes it extremely practical and pleasant to use.

CAT GROOMER ist eine Bürste für Haustiere, mit der Katzen und ihre Halter einen gemeinsamen spielerischen Moment erleben können. Sie wurde mit der besonderen Harzformtechnik des Feilenherstellers Wataoka gefertigt und zeigt auch eine der Feile ähnliche Formgebung. Ihre speziellen Kammzähne weisen eine feine Textur und hohe Präzision auf. Das Gesamtdesign ist schlicht und elegant zugleich, und die Bürste liegt durch die kompakte Größe gut in der Hand.

Begründung der Jury
Die Tierbürste CAT GROOMER punktet ihrer einfachen ergonomischen Gestaltung wegen, die sie sehr praktikabel und angenehm im Gebrauch macht.

JULIUS-K9® IDC®Longwalk
Dog Harness
Hundegeschirr

Manufacturer
K9-Sport Ltd, Szigetszentmiklós, Hungary
In-house design
Gyula Sebö
Web
www.julius-k9.com

The JULIUS-K9 dog harness has been configured to be particularly easy on the joints. The dog's sternum is held by an ergonomically designed, arching element. It converges with a well-padded saddle part on the back, which adjusts to the form of the animal and has a sporty appearance. Various colours emphasise the practical handle. Flexible elements have been installed in three places, which respond to even the smallest movements.

Statement by the jury
The design of the JULIUS-K9 dog harness impresses with its organic shape, which adapts itself optimally to the body thanks to specific reinforcements.

Das Hundegeschirr JULIUS-K9 wurde so gestaltet, dass es besonders gelenkschonend ist. Das Brustbein des Hundes wird von einem ergonomisch entworfenen, bogenförmig anliegenden Element gehalten. Auf dem Rücken läuft es mit dem gut gepolsterten Sattelteil zusammen, das sich der Form des Tieres angleicht und eine sportliche Anmutung hat. Verschiedene Farben heben den praktischen Griff hervor. An drei Stellen wurden flexible Elemente eingebaut, die selbst den kleinsten Bewegungen nachgeben.

Begründung der Jury
Die Gestaltung des Hundegeschirrs JULIUS-K9 beeindruckt durch ihre organische Formgebung, die sich dank spezifischer Verstärkungen dem Körper genau anpasst.

VARRAM Pet Fitness Robot
Pet Fitness Robot
Fitnessroboter für Haustiere

Manufacturer
VARRAM SYSTEM Co., Ltd.,
Daejeon, South Korea
In-house design
Kyungnam Kim, Byungjo Suh
Web
www.varram.com

Pets are often left alone at home for long periods of time. The VARRAM Pet Fitness Robot is an entertaining and engaging robot toy that can help pets with separation anxiety, depression, lethargy, obesity and other health-related issues. The robot engages pets through a five-stimulus AI with treat reward system. Furthermore, the Pet Fitness Robot can drive around while avoiding obstacles, toss treats, and through big data it can adjust individually to the pet.

Haustiere werden oft für längere Zeit zu Hause gelassen. Der VARRAM Pet Fitness Robot ist ein unterhaltsames und ansprechendes Spielzeug, das Haustiere bei Trennungsangst, Depression, Lethargie, Fettleibigkeit und anderen gesundheitlichen Problemen unterstützen kann. Der Roboter regt Haustiere über KI mit fünf Stimuli samt Belohnungssystem an. Darüber hinaus kann der Pet Fitness Robot herumfahren, Hindernissen ausweichen, Leckereien werfen und sich mittels Big Data individuell an das Haustier anpassen.

Statement by the jury
The VARRAM Pet Fitness Robot attracts attention through its functionality that is based on artificial intelligence, with which it can entertain and train animals.

Begründung der Jury
Der VARRAM Pet Fitness Robot macht durch seine mit künstlicher Intelligenz ausgestattete Funktionalität auf sich aufmerksam, womit er Tiere unterhalten und trainieren kann.

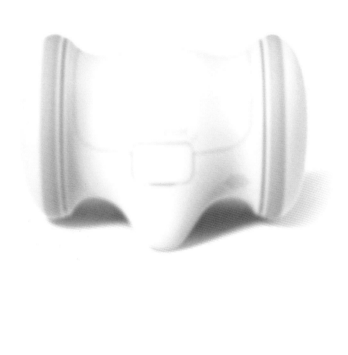

BENDABLE STRAP-ON
Sex Toy

Manufacturer
LOVELY PLANET, Gémenos, France
In-house design
Nicolas Busnel
Design
Idéact (Laurent Passini), Aubagne, France
Web
www.lovely-planet-distribution.com
www.ideact.fr

High quality and an ergonomic design are the special characteristics of the brand strap-on-me. The BENDABLE STRAP-ON is made of soft-touch silicone, which makes it very flexible and gives it a silken touch. It easily adapts to individual anatomy. In addition, the soft material stands out thanks to a pleasant feel. Available in four different sizes, the sex toy is equipped with BENDABLE technology – a position memory for optimum comfort during use. The triple stimulation in particular ensures pleasure according to personal preferences.

Hohe Qualität und ein ergonomisches Design zeichnen die Marke strap-on-me aus. Der BENDABLE STRAP-ON besteht aus Soft-Touch-Silikon, was ihn sehr flexibel macht und ihm einen seidigen Touch verleiht. Er passt sich leicht der individuellen Anatomie an. Darüber hinaus zeichnet sich das weiche Material durch eine angenehme Haptik aus. Das Sexspielzeug ist in vier verschiedenen Größen erhältlich und mit der BENDABLE-Technologie ausgestattet – einem Positionsspeicher für optimalen Komfort beim Gebrauch. Insbesondere die dreifache Stimulation sorgt für Vergnügen nach persönlichen Vorlieben.

Statement by the jury
The sex toy STRAP-ON catches the eye due to its organic form and ergonomics, which splendidly supports its handling.

Begründung der Jury
Das Sexspielzeug STRAP-ON fällt aufgrund seiner organischen Formgebung und einer Ergonomie ins Auge, die die Handhabung ausgezeichnet unterstützt.

TENGA SPINNER
Masturbator

Manufacturer
TENGA Co., Ltd., Tokyo, Japan
In-house design
Kai Tsuyama
Web
www.tenga-global.com

The SPINNER integrates a new technology that offers functional advantages. A coil embedded in the elastomer cover gives it its unmistakable appearance and widens when inserted. During use, contraction and expansion of the coil alternate, creating an automatic rotation. Three different versions of the nobby textures inside are available. They have been fine-tuned to optimise the airflow from inside upon insertion. After washing, the product, whose fresh, unusual design is intended to give a positive feeling, can be dried in the packaging.

Der SPINNER arbeitet mit einer neuen Technik, die funktionale Vorzüge bietet. In die Elastomerhülle ist eine Spule eingebettet, die ihm sein unverwechselbares Äußeres verleiht und sich beim Einführen weitet. Während des Gebrauchs zieht sich die Spule zusammen und dehnt sich aus, wodurch eine automatische Drehbewegung entsteht. Von den genoppten Texturen im Inneren gibt es drei unterschiedliche Varianten. Sie wurden fein abgestimmt, um den Luftstrom beim Einführen im Inneren zu optimieren. Nach der Reinigung kann das Produkt, dessen einprägsames, ungewöhnliches Design ein positives Gefühl wecken soll, in der Verpackung trocknen.

Statement by the jury
Its interesting design with the structures visible on the inside makes SPINNER an eye-catcher. In addition, it is easy to operate.

Begründung der Jury
Seine interessante Formgebung mit den im Inneren zu sehenden Strukturen macht SPINNER zu einem Blickfang und in der Bedienung gut handhabbar.

Cuddly Bird
Vibrator

Manufacturer
Courage & Wisdom, Shenzhen Youxing Technology Co., Ltd.,
Shenzhen, China
Design
inDare Design Strategy Limited (Qinglang Chen, Fengming Chen,
Yujie Chen, Shaolong Chen, Siting Lin, Huahui Lin),
Shenzhen, China
Web
www.couragewisdom.com
www.in-dare.com

Cuddly Bird combines the two functions clitoris massager and vibrator in one compact size. The intimate toy was developed to attract newcomers by reducing threshold anxiety. Therefore, it has been designed to have an appealing and cuddly appearance with a soft silicone surface for a pleasant feel. Both the suction and vibration functions are adjustable in four strengths from subtle to rhythmic pulsation.

Cuddly Bird vereint die beiden Funktionen Klitorismassagestab und Vibrator in einer kompakten Größe. Das Intimspielzeug wurde entwickelt, um die Schwellenangst zu verringern und auch Neulinge dafür zu gewinnen. Daher wurde es so gestaltet, dass es ein ansprechendes und „knuffiges" Erscheinungsbild hat und mit seiner weichen Silikonoberfläche eine angenehme Haptik bietet. Sowohl die Saug- als auch die Vibrationsfunktion ist in vier Stärken von subtilem bis zu rhythmischem Pulsieren variierbar.

Statement by the jury
With its both handy and subtle design, the vibrator Cuddly Bird immediately catches the eye. Functionally, it scores with versatile settings.

Begründung der Jury
Mit seinem handlichen und zugleich feinsinnigen Design springt der Vibrator Cuddly Bird sofort ins Auge. Funktional punktet er mit vielseitigen Einstellungen.

GEWA G9 WORKSTATION
Sound Module
Soundmodul

Manufacturer
GEWA music GmbH, Adorf, Germany
Design
8quadrat-design, Coburg, Germany
Web
www.gewamusic.com
www.8quadrat-design.de

The module G9 of the GEWA drum work station combines digital USB/PC interface, recording tool, patch bay, mixer, e-drum brain, touch panel, MP3 player and multi-effect device all in one. It is operated via a 10" touch display and four rotary knobs on the left side. With a 128 GB memory, it can store a variety of sounds. An additional 4 GB flash memory provides instant access to the presets. HD triggering allows the position of each beat to be detected with millimetre accuracy, while 3D full dynamic samples provide the sound.

In einem Gerät vereint das Modul G9 der GEWA-Drum-Workstation digitale USB-/PC-Schnittstelle, Aufnahme-Tool, Patch-Bay, Mixer, E-Drum Brain, Touchpanel, MP3-Player und Multieffektgerät. Bedient wird es über ein 10"-Touchdisplay und vier Drehregler an der linken Seite. Mit einer Kapazität von 128 GB kann es eine Vielzahl von Sounds speichern, und ein zusätzlicher 4-GB-Flash-Speicher bietet sofortigen Zugriff auf die Presets. Mittels HD-Triggering kann die Position der einzelnen Schläge millimetergenau erkannt werden; für die Klangerzeugung sorgen 3D-Full-Dynamic-Samples.

Statement by the jury
The easy-to-use G9 impresses with a range of features that is second to none. Numerous functions offer versatile music and gaming experiences.

Begründung der Jury
Das leicht zu bedienende G9 fasziniert mit einem Leistungsumfang, der seinesgleichen sucht. Zahlreiche Funktionen ermöglichen vielseitige Musik- und Spielerlebnisse.

GEWA G9 PRO L6
Digital Drum
Digitales Schlagzeug

Manufacturer
GEWA music GmbH, Adorf, Germany
Design
8quadrat-design, Coburg, Germany
Web
www.gewamusic.com
www.8quadrat-design.de

The GEWA G9 PRO L6 combines electronic sound generation with the visual appearance and feel of an acoustic drum set. When designing the sound generation, every kind of signal processing of a sound studio was taken as a reference and made accessible via an intuitive 10" touch display. This provides the musician with a drum set with several hundred sounds as well as the possibility to individually adapt them to his needs. The various drum surfaces offer a choice between a modern and a classic mode.

Das GEWA G9 PRO L6 verbindet elektronische Klangerzeugung mit dem optischen Erscheinungsbild und Spielgefühl eines akustischen Schlagzeugs. Bei der Konzeption der Klangerzeugung wurden alle Möglichkeiten der Signalverarbeitung eines Tonstudios als Referenz angenommen und über ein intuitiv zu bedienendes 10"-Touchdisplay zugänglich gemacht. So steht dem Musiker ein Schlagzeug mit mehreren hundert Klängen sowie die Möglichkeit zur Verfügung, diese seinen Bedürfnissen individuell anzupassen. Bei den verschiedenen Schlagflächen kann er zwischen modern und klassisch wählen.

Statement by the jury
With its enormous spectrum of sound generation, the GEWA G9 PRO L6 digital drum set offers a musician almost unlimited possibilities – a first-class performance range that convinces.

Begründung der Jury
Mit dem erstaunlichen Spektrum der Klangerzeugung sind einem Musiker am digitalen Schlagzeug GEWA G9 PRO L6 kaum Grenzen gesetzt – ein eindrucksvoller Leistungsumfang, der überzeugt.

Clavinova CSP Series
Digital Piano

Manufacturer
Yamaha Corporation, Hamamatsu, Japan
In-house design
Mami Sato, Piotr Stolarski
Web
www.yamaha.com

The digital pianos of the Clavinova CSP Series are linked to the dedicated app that lets you intuitively control all functions and play your favourite songs effortlessly. When a song is selected on a smart device, it automatically creates the piano accompaniment scores. In addition, the Stream Lights moving towards each key indicate which notes to play and when to play them. The Clavinova CSP Series also features a high-quality keyboard, speaker system and a broad range of sounds. Users can enjoy superb performance with the touch and feel of an acoustic grand. Without electronic buttons, they look like classic pianos and are available in black, polished ebony and white.

Die digitalen Klaviere der Clavinova CSP-Serie sind mit der spezifischen App verbunden, mit der sich alle Funktionen intuitiv steuern und Lieblingssongs mühelos abspielen lassen. Wenn ein Song auf einem intelligenten Gerät ausgewählt wird, werden automatisch die Noten für die Klavierbegleitung erstellt. Zusätzlich zeigen die Stream Lights an, die sich zu den einzelnen Tasten bewegen, welche Noten wann gespielt werden sollen. Die Pianoserie verfügt außerdem über eine hochwertige Tastatur, ein Lautsprechersystem und eine breite Palette an Sounds. Benutzer kommen in den Genuss hervorragender Leistung sowie den Kontakt und das Gefühl eines akustischen Flügels. Ohne elektronische Knöpfe wirken die Pianos wie klassische Klaviere und sind in Schwarz, poliertem Ebenholz und Weiß erhältlich.

Statement by the jury
The innovative lights indicating the keys to be hit are as outstanding as the automatic creation of scores. The stylish digital pianos increase the joy of playing the piano considerably.

Begründung der Jury
Die innovativen Lichtpunkte, die die anzuschlagenden Tasten anzeigen, sind so herausragend wie die automatische Erstellung von Noten. Damit steigern die stilvollen Digitalpianos die Freude am Klavierspielen erheblich.

ROLAND LX series
Digital Piano

Manufacturer
Roland Corporation,
Hamamatsu, Shizuoka, Japan
In-house design
Design
GBO Innovation Makers,
Antwerp, Belgium
Web
www.roland.com
www.gbo.eu

Roland's LX700 series comprises a range of instruments that are beautiful and inviting to play, each with outstanding performance and the latest technology in terms of sound, user interface and design. The special C-shaped front panel, which offers natural sound projection and controls directly in line of sight, is one of the features that reflect the piano's distinctive, timeless appearance with harmonious lines.

Statement by the jury
The new digital pianos of the LX700 series impress with a design concept that skilfully combines presence and aesthetics with high performance.

Die LX700-Serie von Roland umfasst eine Reihe von Instrumenten, die schön sind und zum Spielen einladen mit jeweils herausragender Leistung und moderner Technik in Bezug auf Klang, Benutzeroberfläche und Design. Das markante, zeitlose Erscheinungsbild mit harmonischer Linienführung macht sich etwa in der speziellen C-förmigen Blende der Frontplatte bemerkbar, die eine natürliche Klangprojektion und Steuerelemente direkt im Sichtfeld bietet.

Begründung der Jury
Die neuen Digitalpianos der LX700-Serie bestechen durch ein Designkonzept, das Präsenz und Ästhetik gekonnt mit hoher Performance verknüpft.

Digital Wireless MI Series
Instrument Pedal Wireless System
Drahtloses Pedalsystem für Instrumente

Manufacturer
MIPRO Electronics Co., Ltd.,
Chiayi City, Taiwan
In-house design
Web
www.mipro.com.tw
Honourable Mention

The easy-to-use wireless musical instrument system MIPRO allows musicians to move freely on stage during the performance. The large LCD screen and bright LED displays make programmed pre-settings clearly visible and turn complex operations into user-friendly functions with simple pedal switch steps. The robust metal construction and the ergonomic pedal are designed for durability.

Statement by the jury
The MIPRO instrument system convinces with its functional performance in a compact size and numerous pre-settings that facilitate performance on stage.

Das einfach zu bedienende kabellose Musikinstrumentensystem MIPRO ermöglicht es Musikern, sich während des Auftritts auf der Bühne frei zu bewegen. Der große LCD-Bildschirm und die hellen LED-Anzeigen machen die programmierten Voreinstellungen klar erkennbar und komplexe Bedienvorgänge zu benutzerfreundlichen Funktionen mit einfachen Fußschaltern. Die robuste Metallkonstruktion und das ergonomische Pedal sind auf Langlebigkeit ausgelegt.

Begründung der Jury
Das Instrumentensystem MIPRO überzeugt mit seiner funktionalen Leistung in kompakter Größe und zahlreichen Voreinstellungen, die den Auftritt erleichtern.

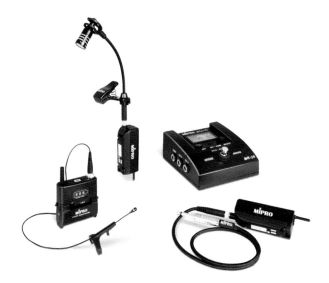

ICE CREAM
Intelligent Microphone
Intelligentes Mikrofon

Manufacturer
Shenzhen 21g Product Design Co., Ltd.,
Shenzhen, China
In-house design
Hongzhi Zhang, Haiping Zheng
Web
www.design21g.com

The intelligent microphone ICE CREAM is a new solution for karaoke, music sharing and outdoor activities. With its integrated stand speaker and microphone, you can sing anywhere and share music with friends. The various functions have been implemented in just a few buttons, so that the slim shape of the microphone radiates simple elegance and is very easy to hold. The charging interface is hidden on the bottom.

Statement by the jury
The ICE CREAM microphone fascinates with its elaborate design, which combines intuitive user-friendliness with sophisticated functional features.

Das intelligente Mikrofon ICE CREAM stellt eine neue Lösung für Karaoke, das Teilen von Musik und Outdoor-Aktivitäten dar. Mit integriertem Standlautsprecher und Mikrofon kann man damit überall singen und Musik mit Freunden teilen. Die verschiedenen Funktionen wurden in nur wenige Tasten implementiert, sodass das Mikrofon mit seiner schlanken Form schlichte Eleganz ausstrahlt und sich sehr gut halten lässt. Die Ladeschnittstelle verbirgt sich an der Unterseite.

Begründung der Jury
Das Mikrofon ICE CREAM begeistert mit seiner durchdachten Gestaltung, die intuitive Bedienfreundlichkeit mit einer anspruchsvollen Funktionsausstattung verknüpft.

Entertainment
Entertainment

Entertainment

Amplifiers	Abspielgeräte
Antenna	Antennen
Audio accessories	Audiozubehör
Bluetooth speakers	Beamer
E-readers	Bluetooth-Boxen
Headphones	E-Reader
Hi-fi systems	Fernbedienungen
Home cinema	Heimkinosysteme
MP3 / MP4 players	Hi-Fi-Systeme
Players	Kopfhörer
Projectors	MP3-/MP4-Player
Receivers	Receiver
Record players	Schallplattenspieler
Remote controls	Soundsysteme
Sound systems	Streaming Clients
Streaming clients	TV
TV accessories	TV-Wandhalterungen
TV wall mounts	TV-Zubehör
TVs	Verstärker

FP-Z5000
Projector
Projektor

Manufacturer
FUJIFILM Corporation,
Tokyo, Japan

In-house design
Kunihiko Tanaka

Web
www.fujifilm.com
http://design.fujifilm.com

reddot award 2019
best of the best

Aesthetic flexibility

Just as the laterna magica had been a further development of earlier ideas in the 17th century, the evolution of modern projection equipment, too, has undergone a long and exciting history of many improvements and advancements ever since its invention. Against this backdrop, the FP-Z5000 (FUJIFILM Projector Z5000) impresses with its two-axis, rotatable lens design. Instead of being fixedly installed within the device, as is the case with common projectors, the lens of this projector can be adjusted to face up or down, to the front or the rear, as well as to the left and right to project images in any desired direction – onto a wall, a screen, onto the ceiling or the floor, depending on the situation and location. In addition, it also allows easy switching between vertical and horizontal display. Since for so doing, the device itself does not need to be moved, it offers a very high degree of flexibility. With its high-performance, ultra-short-throw FUJINON lens, the device is capable of projecting bright and clear images on a 100" screen from a distance of only 75 cm. The easy-to-use projector features a compact body design with smooth, rounded corners that lend it an elegant appearance. Due to its sophisticated technical and aesthetic properties, this projector is particularly suitable for large-screen digital signage or spatial design projections at museums.

Ästhetische Flexibilität

So wie die bereits im 17. Jahrhundert bekannte Laterna magica eine Weiterentwicklung früherer Ideen war, hat die Evolution der Technologie und Form von Projektionsgeräten seitdem eine lange und spannende Geschichte durchlaufen. Der FP-Z5000 (FUJIFILM Projektor Z5000) beeindruckt durch die Gestaltung mit einem zweiachsigen, drehbaren Objektiv. Statt wie bei den üblichen Projektoren innerhalb des Gerätes fixiert, kann das Objektiv nach oben oder unten, nach vorn oder hinten, nach links oder rechts ausgerichtet werden, um Bilder in jede gewünschte Richtung zu projizieren – je nach Situation und Örtlichkeit an eine Wand, eine Leinwand, an die Decke oder auch auf den Boden. Darüber hinaus besteht die Möglichkeit, unkompliziert zwischen vertikaler und horizontaler Darstellung zu wechseln. Dies bietet ein hohes Maß an Flexibilität, da das Gerät selbst dafür nicht bewegt werden muss. Mit dem leistungsstarken Ultra-Short-Throw-Objektiv FUJINON können dabei aus einer Entfernung von nur 75 cm helle und klare Bilder auf eine 100" große Leinwand projiziert werden. Der leicht zu bedienende Projektor ist zudem kompakt gestaltet, wobei seine weich abgerundeten Ecken ihm Eleganz verleihen. Aufgrund seiner technischen und ästhetischen Eigenschaften eignet er sich deshalb auch besonders für großformatige digitale Beschilderungen oder für raumgestaltende Projektionen in Museen.

Statement by the jury

The clear, purist design of this projector embodies a unity in both form and function. Its sophisticated technology is integrated into a stylish device that also impresses with its compact dimensions. Thanks to the innovative two-axial rotatable lens, the projector provides a high degree of flexibility for a wide variety of applications. It delivers cleverly thought-out functionality and an intuitive approach towards its operation.

Begründung der Jury

Das klare, puristische Design dieses Projektors vereint stimmig Form und Funktion. Seine ausgereifte Technologie ist in ein stilvolles Gerät integriert, das auch durch seine kompakten Maße beeindruckt. Dank des innovativen zweiachsigen, drehbaren Objektivs weist der Projektor eine hohe Flexibilität mit vielfältigen Einsatzmöglichkeiten auf. Er bietet eine klug durchdachte Funktionalität und eine intuitive Art der Bedienung.

Designer portrait
See page 54
Siehe Seite 54

Nebula Capsule II
Portable Projector
Tragbarer Beamer

Manufacturer
Shenzhen Oceanwing Smart
Innovation Co., Ltd., Shenzhen, China
In-house design
Shuai Ma, Weizhi Sun, Xuefeng Bai
Web
www.anker.com

The Nebula Capsule II is a compact mini projector with Android TV 9.0 offering more than 3,600 native apps. Thanks to its new DLP chip, this device with 200 lumens projects HD images with a maximum diagonal of 100" onto a wall. A new autofocus technology ensures that the picture is optimally focused in less than a second. The cylindrically shaped device includes a 360-degree speaker emitting sound in all directions, thus filling the entire environment with sound.

Statement by the jury
This projector inspires with its very handy cylindrical shape. It can be easily taken along and delivers HD images in any given place.

Nebula Capsule II ist ein kompakter Mini-Beamer mit Android TV 9.0, das mehr als 3.600 native Apps bietet. Dank seines neuen DLP-Chips projiziert der Beamer mit 200 Lumen HD-Bilder mit einer maximalen Diagonalen von 100" an die Wand. Dabei sorgt eine neuartige Autofokus-Technologie dafür, dass das Bild in weniger als einer Sekunde scharf gestellt wird. Das zylindrisch gestaltete Gerät besitzt einen 360-Grad-Lautsprecher, der den Klang in alle Richtungen abstrahlt und so die ganze Umgebung beschallt.

Begründung der Jury
Der Beamer begeistert mit seiner überaus handlichen Zylinderform. Er ist leicht überallhin mitzunehmen und bringt HD-Bilder an jeden Ort.

Nebula Prizm Series
Projectors
Beamer

Manufacturer
Shenzhen Oceanwing Smart
Innovation Co., Ltd., Shenzhen, China
In-house design
Xiaoyu Niu, Sangmin Yu, Kebi Ding,
Weizhi Sun, Xuefeng Bai
Web
www.anker.com

The Nebula Prizm series offers LCD projectors with full HD and a native resolution of 1,080 pixels for projections up to a size of 120". It includes Android TV 9.0 with access to more than 3,600 apps. Sound is provided by two built-in 5 watt speakers coated with fabric, creating vivid stereo sound. This optical machine is fully closed and thus well protected from dust and dirt.

Statement by the jury
With comprehensive equipment, these projectors convince through their appealing design. Moreover, the combination with fabric gives the devices a homely note.

Die Nebula-Prizm-Serie bietet Full-HD-LCD-Beamer mit einer nativen Auflösung von 1.080 Pixeln für Projektionen bis zu 120". Mit an Bord ist zudem Android-TV 9.0 mit Zugriff auf mehr als 3.600 Apps. Für den Klang sorgen zwei eingebaute 5-Watt-Lautsprecher, die mit Stoff bespannt sind, wodurch sich ein lebendiger Stereoklang entfalten kann. Die optische Maschine ist vollständig geschlossen und dadurch vor Staub und Schmutz gut geschützt.

Begründung der Jury
Die umfassend ausgestatteten Beamer überzeugen mit ihrer ansprechenden Formgebung. Zudem gibt ihnen die Kombination mit Stoff eine wohnliche Note.

H1
Laser Projector
Laser-Beamer

Manufacturer
TCL Corporation, Shenzhen, China
In-house design
TCL Industrial Design Center
Web
www.tcl.com

The laser projector offers the user images in 4K quality with outstanding sound. The latter is emphasised by a cylindrically shaped speaker covered with fabric contrasting in colour. The housing itself highlights the inner ventilation system – with three internal fans and a cooler – through circumferential cooling fins, also contrasting in colour. This enables the user to easily grasp the functionality of the projector.

Statement by the jury
The design concept of the H1 laser projector with clearly distinguishable functional areas is implemented in an exemplary manner.

Der Laser-Beamer bietet dem Benutzer Bilder in 4K-Qualität mit einem ausgezeichneten Klang. Der Klang wird durch einen zylinderförmigen Lautsprecher hervorgehoben, der mit einem farblich zum Gehäuse kontrastierenden Gewebe überzogen ist. Das Gehäuse wiederum betont das innenliegende Belüftungssystem mit drei internen Lüftern und einem Kühler durch umlaufende, ebenfalls farblich abgesetzte Kühllamellen. Dadurch kann der Benutzer die Funktionalität des Beamers leicht erfassen.

Begründung der Jury
Das gestalterische Konzept mit klar unterscheidbaren funktionalen Bereichen ist beim Laser-Beamer H1 vorbildlich umgesetzt.

LG HU85L
4K UST Projector
4K-Ultra-Kurzdistanz-Beamer

Manufacturer
LG Electronics Inc., Seoul, South Korea
In-house design
Yoonyoung Cho, Eunbong Lee, Seongyeong Park
Web
www.lg.com

The HU85L is a 4K sound laser UST projector with 3,000 lumens capable of projecting 4K images and delivering sound in cinema quality. With its minimalist form, the projector blends well into stylish interiors. The design of the vertical vent grille is plain as well. It offers a large ventilation capacity with little noise emission. The speakers at the front are covered with woven wool fabric, protecting the device from dirt and setting a homely accent.

Statement by the jury
This projector convinces with its purist design. It focuses on function and ensures that the device fits with different home accessories.

HU85L ist ein 4K-Sound-Laser-UST-Beamer mit 3.000 Lumen, der Bilder in 4K projiziert und Sound in Kinoqualität liefert. Mit seiner minimalistischen Formgebung fügt der Beamer sich gut in ein stilvolles Interieur ein. Das vertikale Lüftungsgitter an der Seite ist ebenso schlicht gehalten und bietet ein großes Lüftungsvolumen bei einer geringen Geräuschentwicklung. Die Lautsprecher an der Vorderseite sind mit gewebtem Wollstoff überzogen, der das Gerät vor Staub schützt und einen wohnlichen Akzent setzt.

Begründung der Jury
Der Beamer überzeugt durch seine puristische Gestaltung. Sie stellt die Funktion in den Vordergrund und sorgt dafür, dass das Gerät zu unterschiedlichen Einrichtungen passt.

Jixin J1 Miniature Projector
Mini-Beamer

Manufacturer
Shenzhen Jixin Technology Co., Ltd., Shenzhen, China
Design
Shenzhen VENZO Design Co., Ltd. (Alexander Wang, Yaodong Zhao), Shenzhen, China
Web
www.ji-xitech.com
www.venzodesign.com.cn

The Jixin J1 is a portable projector with integrated intelligent hardware and a rechargeable battery designed for low power consumption. Thanks to the compact dimensions, it is easily transported and thus highly suitable for projecting images from a mobile source, for instance a smartphone. Movies and files can be displayed using a special soft light to prevent eye fatigue resulting from long viewing sessions.

Statement by the jury
This mini projector convinces with its good equipment and pleasingly slim format with which it easily slides into any bag.

Jixin J1 ist ein tragbarer Beamer mit integrierter intelligenter Hardware und einem Akku, der für einen geringen Stromverbrauch ausgelegt ist. Dank seiner kompakten Maße ist er einfach zu transportieren, wodurch er sich besonders gut dafür eignet, Bilder von einer mobilen Quelle wie z. B. einem Smartphone wiederzugeben. Filme und Dateien lassen sich mit einem speziellen weichen Licht darstellen, was verhindert, dass die Augen bei langen Sitzungen übermäßig beansprucht werden.

Begründung der Jury
Der Mini-Beamer überzeugt mit seiner guten Ausstattung und dem angenehm schlanken Format, mit dem er problemlos in jede Tasche gleitet.

Mijia LED
Smart Projector
Intelligenter Beamer

Manufacturer
Xiaomi Inc., Beijing, China
In-house design
Web
www.mi.com

With a resolution of 1,920 x 1,080 pixels, the minimalist Mijia projector is suitable for display of large-format images full of detail. The RGBB colour system (red, green, blue, blue) with an LED light source increases brightness by 10 per cent and brings about an impressive cinematic experience. The dust-tight housing protects the lens and the optical engine. Room-filling sound is produced by an integrated resonance chamber, a long sound induction tube and a hi-fi speaker.

Statement by the jury
The rounded edges lend this projector a congenial appearance, allowing it to blend seamlessly into the room like a home accessory.

Mit einer Auflösung von 1.920 x 1.080 Pixeln eignet sich der minimalistisch gestaltete Beamer Mijia für die Darstellung großformatiger, detailreicher Bilder. Das RGBB-Farbsystem (rot, grün, blau, blau) mit LED-Lichtquelle erhöht die Helligkeit um 10 Prozent und bietet ein beeindruckendes Heimkinoerlebnis. Das staubdichte Gehäuse schützt die Linse und den optischen Motor. Für einen raumfüllenden Klang sorgen ein integrierter Resonanzraum, eine lange Schallinduktionsröhre und ein Hi-Fi-Lautsprecher.

Begründung der Jury
Die gerundeten Kanten verleihen dem Beamer eine überaus sympathische Anmutung, dank derer er sich wie ein Wohnaccessoire in den Raum einfügt.

Xgimi Play
Projector
Beamer

Manufacturer
Chengdu XGIMI Technology Co., Ltd., Chengdu, China
In-house design
Prof. Shi Xiao, Yaxun Xia
Web
www.xgimi.com

The Xgimi Play is a compact projector for showing images with a size of 80 to 150". It is equipped with Harman Kardon speakers and a rechargeable battery, so that it delivers good sound and is suitable for mobile use. Its design pursues the approach of combining function and appearance in such a way that it harmonises well with any environment. Accordingly, design elements are used prudently and sparingly, exemplified by the ventilation slots that upgrade the cylindrical case as an eye-catcher.

Statement by the jury
The projector is a beautiful entertainment device enabling any room to be turned into a home cinema in an uncomplicated way.

Xgimi Play ist ein kompakter Beamer, der Bilder zwischen 80 und 150" projiziert. Er ist mit Harman-Kardon-Lautsprechern und einem Akku ausgestattet, sodass er einen guten Klang liefert und auch unterwegs eingesetzt werden kann. Seine Gestaltung folgt dem Ansatz, Funktion und Erscheinung so miteinander zu verbinden, dass er sich in jede Umgebung gut einfügt. Entsprechend sind gestalterische Elemente überlegt und sparsam eingesetzt, so z. B. die Lüftungsschlitze, die das zylindrische Gehäuse als Hingucker aufwerten.

Begründung der Jury
Der Beamer ist ein formschönes Entertainmentgerät, mit dem sich jeder Raum unkompliziert in ein Heimkino verwandeln lässt.

Xgimi Play X
Projector
Beamer

Manufacturer
Chengdu XGIMI Technology Co., Ltd., Chengdu, China
In-house design
Prof. Shi Xiao, Tao Luo
Web
www.xgimi.com

The Xgimi Play X is an intelligent projector delivering high-resolution images and impressive sound. With a projection size between 80 and 150" and a built-in Harman Kardon speaker, it is capable of quickly producing a cinematic atmosphere, especially in smaller spaces. Equipped with a rechargeable battery as well, it allows movies to be viewed anywhere. Its form and the metal case with grid structure are reminiscent of a speaker, highlighting the strong sound quality of the device.

Statement by the jury
With its compact design and rectangular shape, the projector requires only little floor space and is thus outstandingly suited to smaller rooms.

Der intelligente Beamer Xgimi Play X liefert hochauflösende Bilder und einen beeindruckenden Klang. Mit einer Projektionsgröße zwischen 80 und 150" und einem eingebauten Harman-Kardon-Lautsprecher schafft er besonders in kleineren Räumen schnell Kinoatmosphäre. Da er außerdem mit einem Akku ausgestattet ist, ermöglicht er das Betrachten von Filmen an jedem Ort. Seine Form und das Metallgehäuse mit einer Gitterstruktur erinnern an einen Lautsprecher, was auf die gute Klangqualität verweist.

Begründung der Jury
Der kompakt gestaltete Beamer benötigt dank seiner Quaderform nur wenig Stellfläche und eignet sich daher auch hervorragend für kleine Räume.

EV-100, EV-105
Projector
Beamer

Manufacturer
Seiko Epson Corporation,
Azumino City, Nagano Prefecture, Japan
In-house design
Web
www.epson.jp

This projector is used in exhibition spaces or shopping centres when lighting scenarios or videos are to be presented. With its reduced design, it is inconspicuous and, due to its cylindrical shape, appears rather as a spotlight when mounted to the ceiling. Particular emphasis was placed on a seamless appearance, which is achieved by concealing all connectors and cables as well as the ventilation slots.

Der Beamer kommt in Ausstellungsräumen oder Einkaufszentren zum Einsatz, wenn Beleuchtungsszenarien oder Videos präsentiert werden sollen. Mit seiner reduzierten Formgebung fällt er nicht auf und wirkt bei der Deckenmontage mit seiner zylindrischen Gestalt eher wie ein Lichtstrahler. Besondere Aufmerksamkeit wurde auch auf eine nahtlose Erscheinung gelegt, die erzielt wird, indem sämtliche Buchsen oder Kabel ebenso verborgen sind wie die Belüftungsschlitze.

Statement by the jury
With its cylindrical shape and seamless design, this cleverly designed beamer is optimally suited to inconspicuous use in any room or building.

Begründung der Jury
Dieser clever konzipierte Beamer ist durch seine Zylinderform und sein nahtloses Design bestens für den unauffälligen Einsatz in jedem Raum oder Gebäude geeignet.

LG Signature R9
OLED TV

Manufacturer
LG Electronics Inc.,
Seoul, South Korea

In-house design
Seonkyu Kim, Cheolwoong Shin,
Minjae Lee, Hyunbyung Cha,
Yunjoo Kim, Young Kyung Kim

Web
www.lg.com

reddot award 2019
best of the best

New freedom

Dedicated to lending ever-advancing technology an adequate form, the OLED television has undergone a remarkable evolutionary development since its debut. Against this backdrop, the new design of the LG Signature R9 opens up exciting new paths. This television adopts the innovative, multifunctional concept of a foldable, on-demand screen. Consistently integrated into the housing, it can be rolled out easily for use and rolled up again when not in use. This gives users a new kind of freedom, offering significantly more possibilities in placing and thus integrating a TV into a given interior. When the screen is rolled up, the unit turns into a piece of furniture or accessory that serves as a high sound quality audio player. The refined rectangular geometric design of the TV frame has been carefully honed. Since the frame and stand are made of real metal, the device is extremely stable and reveals a highly aesthetic silhouette in almost any space. The Kvadrat fabric applied onto the front speaker conveys a warm and emotionalising look and feel, while the self-explanatory cable management function is highly practical. Complementing the ultra-high resolution of the screen, the LG Signature R9 features a powerful 100-watt 4.2-channel sound system for realistic sound field experiences. It thus allows image and sound to be enjoyed at the highest level.

Neue Freiheit

Um der sich stetig erneuernden Technik eine adäquate Form zu geben, hat auch der OLED-Fernseher seit seinem ersten Erscheinen eine bemerkenswerte evolutionäre Entwicklung durchlaufen. Die Gestaltung des LG Signature R9 beschreitet hier spannende neue Wege. Dieses Fernsehgerät folgt dem innovativen, multifunktionalen Konzept eines faltbaren, bei Bedarf aktivierbaren Bildschirms. Sehr schlüssig in das Gehäuse integriert, lässt dieser sich komfortabel auf- und wieder einrollen. Dem Nutzer bietet sich so eine neue Art von Freiheit dank deutlich mehr Möglichkeiten, einen Fernseher in das Interieur zu integrieren. Mit eingerolltem Bildschirm wird das Gerät zu einem schönen Möbelstück und Accessoire, das als leistungsfähiger Audio-Player dient. Die edle, an einem Rechteck orientierte Gehäusegeometrie wurde sorgfältig angepasst. Da Rahmen und Ständer aus Echtmetall gefertigt sind, zeigt das Gerät im Raum eine sehr ästhetische Silhouette und ist zugleich ausgesprochen standsicher. Die Gestaltung des Front-Lautsprechers mit Kvadrat-Textilgewebe hat auf Betrachter dabei einen emotionalisierenden Effekt. Besonders praktikabel ist auch das gelungene selbsterklärende Kabelmanagement. Passend zur hochauflösenden Bildschirmqualität bietet der LG Signature R9 außerdem ein realitätsnahes akustisches Erleben mittels eines 4.2-Kanal-Sound-Systems mit 100 Watt Leistung. Bild und Sound können so auf höchstem Niveau genossen werden.

Statement by the jury

The LG Signature R9 OLED TV opens up new usage scenarios. Its high-resolution screen can be easily rolled out and up again as needed, which allows the device to be placed almost anywhere in a given room. Also, the brand-typical details of the LG Signature series have been skilfully implemented here in a well-proportioned and balanced design. Highly aesthetic and functional, this TV embodies a perfect merger of technology and design.

Begründung der Jury

Mit dem OLED-Fernseher LG Signature R9 eröffnen sich neue Szenarien des Einsatzes. Sein hochauflösender Bildschirm lässt sich komfortabel nach Bedarf auf- und einrollen, weshalb sich das Gerät beliebig im Raum platzieren lässt. Die markentypischen Details der LG Signature-Serie wurden hier gekonnt umgesetzt in einer wohlproportionierten und ausgewogenen Gestaltung. Funktional und hochästhetisch, verkörpert dieses Fernsehgerät die perfekte Kombination aus Technologie und Design.

Designer portrait
See page 56
Siehe Seite 56

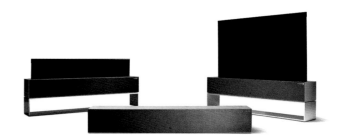

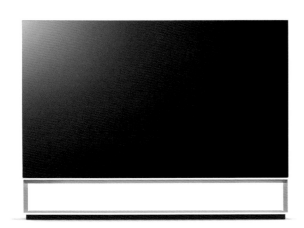

LG Signature Z9
8K OLED TV

Manufacturer
LG Electronics Inc., Seoul, South Korea
In-house design
Taeho Kim, Jeongrok Lee
Web
www.lg.com

With its 8K panel, the Signature Z9 OLED TV delivers razor-sharp images. The 88" display size makes the viewers feel as if they were completely immersed in the scene. A contributing factor is the bezel-less design, as nothing distracts from the screen. The metal back creates the impression of a single sheet of glass and harmonises optimally with the slim silhouette of the unit. The metal stand with integrated cable management underscores its quality.

Statement by the jury
This television excites with its oversized, very slim screen which promises an excellent cinematic experience and also convinces with regard to design.

Der OLED-Fernseher Signature Z9 liefert mit seinem 8K-Panel scharfe Bilder. Da der Bildschirm mit 88" sehr groß ist, erhält der Betrachter das Gefühl, ganz in das Geschehen eintauchen zu können. Dazu trägt auch das rahmenlose Design bei, denn nichts lenkt vom Bildschirm ab. Die Rückseite aus Metall erweckt den Eindruck einer einzelnen Glasscheibe und harmoniert bestens mit der schmalen Silhouette des Geräts. Der Bodenständer aus Metall mit integriertem Kabelmanagement unterstreicht seine Qualität.

Begründung der Jury
Der Fernseher begeistert mit seinem übergroßen, sehr schlanken Bildschirm, der ein ausgezeichnetes Kinoerlebnis verspricht und auch in gestalterischer Hinsicht überzeugt.

LG E9
OLED TV

Manufacturer
LG Electronics Inc., Seoul, South Korea
In-house design
Yuonui Chong, Jaeneung Jung, Byunglok Jeon, Jongchul Kim
Web
www.lg.com

With this TV, all elements around the screen have been removed to ensure a perfectly immersive cinematic experience. The screen itself floats on top of a sheet of glass that simultaneously functions as a base and fosters the appearance of a seamless front. The rear support conceals the cables connecting the screen and the system. The floating impression is augmented by a mirror-like coating of the support, which reflects the surrounding environment.

Statement by the jury
The concept of a floating image is realised in a convincing way by well-thought-out details. This lends the television an appearance of comfortable lightness.

Bei diesem Fernseher wurden alle Elemente rund um den Bildschirm entfernt, um das perfekte Eintauchen in die Filmwelt zu gewährleisten. Der Bildschirm selbst schwebt auf einer Glasscheibe, die gleichzeitig als Ständer fungiert und die Vorderseite nahtlos erscheinen lässt. Die hintere Stütze verbirgt die Kabel, die Bildschirm und System verbinden. Der schwebende Eindruck wird dadurch verstärkt, dass die Stütze mit einer spiegelnden Beschichtung versehen ist, die das Umfeld reflektiert.

Begründung der Jury
Die Vorstellung eines schwebenden Bildes wird durch überlegte Details überzeugend realisiert. Dies verleiht dem Fernseher eine angenehme Leichtigkeit.

LG C9
OLED TV

Manufacturer
LG Electronics Inc., Seoul, South Korea
In-house design
Byunglok Jeon, Jaeneung Jung
Web
www.lg.com

This OLED TV combines pure metal with a very slim display, producing natural light and brilliant colours. The refined, minimalist form harmonises well with different environments and thus blends easily with any ambience. The slim metal stand reflects the sound and elevates it to a quality reminiscent of a concert hall. The cables may be concealed by the cover so that the tidy overall appearance is maintained.

Statement by the jury
The OLED TV C9 stands out with a seamless design that integrates into any space and keeps the viewer's attention trained on the TV picture.

Der OLED-Fernseher kombiniert reines Metall mit einem sehr dünnen Display, das natürliches Licht und brillante Farben erzeugt. Die raffinierte, minimalistische Form harmoniert gut mit unterschiedlichen Umgebungen und fügt sich daher in jedes Ambiente ein. Der schmale Standfuß aus Metall reflektiert den Klang und hebt ihn auf eine Qualität, wie sie in einem Konzertsaal anzutreffen ist. Die Kabel lassen sich durch die Abdeckung verbergen, damit das aufgeräumte Gesamtbild erhalten bleibt.

Begründung der Jury
Der OLED-Fernseher C9 besticht durch seine nahtlose Formgebung, die sich in jeden Raum integriert und die Aufmerksamkeit auf dem Fernsehbild belässt.

LG SM8500
UHD TV

Manufacturer
LG Electronics Inc., Seoul, South Korea
In-house design
Hyoungwon Kim, Yoonsoo Kim, Yonghun Jang
Web
www.lg.com

The development of this medium-segment UHD TV is based on the simple geometric concept of a single curve, which emphasises its slim silhouette. The overall round shape in conjunction with the slender display fosters a clean and tidy appearance that places the screen centre stage. The semicircular stand is invitingly opened towards the front and offers stable support, directing the gaze of the user to the screen.

Statement by the jury
This slim TV with its reserved design is optimally suited for use in combination with existing consumer electronics.

Die Entwicklung dieses im mittleren Segment angesiedelten UHD-Fernsehgeräts beruht auf dem einfachen geometrischen Konzept einer Kurve, womit seine schlanke Silhouette betont wird. Die insgesamt runde Form im Zusammenspiel mit dem schlichten Display ergibt ein sauberes Erscheinungsbild, das den Bildschirm in den Mittelpunkt stellt. Der einladend nach vorne geöffnete halbkreisförmige Standfuß bietet einen stabilen Halt und lenkt den Fokus des Benutzers auf den Bildschirm.

Begründung der Jury
Der schlanke Fernseher ist dank seiner zurückgenommenen Formgebung bestens dazu geeignet, gemeinsam mit vorhandener Unterhaltungselektronik genutzt zu werden.

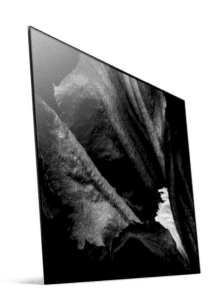

BRAVIA A9F Series
4K OLED TVs

Manufacturer
Sony Visual Products Inc., Tokyo, Japan
Design
Sony Corporation, Creative Center
(Yusuke Tsujita), Tokyo, Japan
Web
www.sonyvisual.co.jp
www.sony.net/design

The BRAVIA A9F OLED TVs combine excellent image quality with impressive sound directly emitted from the screen. This is done using Acoustic Surface Audio+ technology which produces sound through screen vibrations. In this way, audio and visual are both emitted from a single source. The overall design appears just as homogeneous, as the screen is supported by a stand with integrated speaker at the backside, so that no additional element is required for the sound.

Statement by the jury
The televisions impress with their well-conceived design, integrating significant functions into the construction in an innovative way.

Die OLED-Fernseher BRAVIA A9F kombinieren eine exzellente Bildqualität mit einem beeindruckenden Klang, der direkt vom Bildschirm ausgeht. Dies gelingt über die Technologie Acoustic Surface Audio+, die Töne durch Bildschirmvibrationen erzeugt. So kommen Klang und Bild aus einer Quelle. Ebenso homogen zeigt sich die Gestaltung, denn der Bildschirm wird an der Rückseite durch einen Ständer mit integriertem Lautsprecher gestützt, sodass kein zusätzliches Element für den Klang benötigt wird.

Begründung der Jury
Die Fernseher begeistern mit ihrer durchdachten Gestaltung, die wichtige Funktionen in innovativer Weise in die Konstruktion integriert.

BRAVIA Z9G Series
8K LCD TVs

Manufacturer
Sony Visual Products Inc., Tokyo, Japan
Design
Sony Corporation, Creative Center
(Hiroaki Yokota), Tokyo, Japan
Web
www.sonyvisual.co.jp
www.sony.net/design

These 8K LCD TVs are characterised by a design where every detail carries a functional aspect. As such, the speakers located at the top and bottom of the screen are combined with the bezel, while the aluminium front panel gives off heat to cool the system. This results in a reliable dissipation of the heat produced by processing high volumes of data. The patterning on the back also serves a purpose as it improves the rigidity of the housing.

Statement by the jury
The high-grade televisions convince with their meticulous design and carefully integrated functions.

Bei diesen 8K-LCD-Fernsehern ist jedes Detail funktionstragend. So werden die Lautsprecher, die sich oben und unten am Bildschirmrand befinden, mit der Blende kombiniert, während die Frontblende aus Aluminium Wärme abgibt, um das System zu kühlen, indem die Hitze, die bei der Verarbeitung der hohen Datenmengen entsteht, zuverlässig abgeleitet wird. Auch das Muster an der Rückseite erfüllt seinen Zweck, denn es erhöht die Steifigkeit des Gehäuses.

Begründung der Jury
Die hochwertigen Fernseher überzeugen mit ihrer überaus durchdachten Formgebung und sorgfältig integrierten Funktionen.

Philips 854 OLED TV

Manufacturer
TPV Technology Group, MMD,
New Taipei City, Taiwan
Design
TPV Technology Design Team,
Amsterdam, Netherlands
Web
www.tpvholdings.com

The Philips 854 OLED TV conveys its high picture performance through a well-thought-out use of high-grade materials. The OLED display rests on a sleek, polished T-shaped aluminum stand that keeps it at a distance from the surface and allows the screen to swivel. This clever arrangement increases user-friendliness and helps to ensure that the three-sided Ambilight is fully visible.

Statement by the jury
The Philips 854 OLED TV scores with its purist design which expresses outstanding quality.

Der OLED-Fernseher Philips 854 vermittelt seine hohe Bildqualität durch die überlegte Verwendung hochwertiger Materialien. Der OLED-Bildschirm ruht auf einem schlanken, polierten Aluminiumständer in T-Form, der ihn auf Abstand zur Oberfläche hält und es gestattet, den Bildschirm zu schwenken. Diese raffinierte Anordnung erhöht zum einen die Benutzerfreundlichkeit und trägt zum anderen dazu bei, dass das an drei Seiten befindliche Ambilight vollständig sichtbar ist.

Begründung der Jury
Der OLED-Fernseher Philips 854 punktet mit seiner puristischen Formgebung, die seine besondere Qualität zum Ausdruck bringt.

Philips 934 OLED TV

Manufacturer
TPV Technology Group, MMD,
New Taipei City, Taiwan
Design
TPV Technology Design Team,
Amsterdam, Netherlands
Web
www.tpvholdings.com

The design of the Philips 934 OLED TV aims to convey both award-winning picture quality and first-class audio reproduction. This is implemented through a Bowers & Wilkins soundbar stand utilising a bespoke Kvadrat fabric designed by Philips TV to enhance modern homes and tuned by Bowers & Wilkins for sound performance. The space between the TV and stand allows the Ambilight to visually float the TV above the soundbar.

Statement by the jury
This television impresses with its purist charisma. The excellent equipment rounds off the overall picture.

Das Design des OLED-Fernsehers Philips 934 zielt darauf ab, neben einer preisgekrönten Bildqualität eine hochwertige Audiowiedergabe zu vermitteln. Umgesetzt wird dies durch einen Soundbarstandfuß von Bowers & Wilkins, der mit maßgeschneidertem, von Philips TV entwickeltem Akustikgewebe von Kvadrat bezogen ist, das moderne Wohnräume aufwertet und zudem auf die Klangleistung von Bowers & Wilkins abgestimmt ist. Durch den Abstand zwischen Fernsehgerät und Standfuß lässt das Ambilight das Fernsehgerät visuell über der Soundbar schweben.

Begründung der Jury
Der Fernseher beeindruckt durch seine puristische Ausstrahlung. Hinzu kommt eine exzellente Ausstattung, die das Gesamtbild abrundet.

C7 TV

Manufacturer
TCL Corporation, Shenzhen, China
In-house design
TCL Industrial Design Center
Web
www.tcl.com

The C7 4K TV is characterised by a slightly curved display framed by a fine aluminium bezel. The premium aesthetic look is complemented by a back cover made of stainless steel. Situated at the front of the TV is a soundbar with acoustic fabric coating, which is part of the stand and emits clear, voluminous sound. Cables and connections are concealed, creating a seamless look.

Statement by the jury
The relocation of the speaker to the soundbar in the stand is a very clever solution. It provides sound for a comprehensive cinematic experience.

Der 4K-Fernseher C7 zeichnet sich durch einen leicht gekrümmten Bildschirm aus, der von einer feinen Aluminiumblende eingefasst ist. Die wertige Ästhetik wird durch die Rückseite aus Edelstahl vervollständigt. An der Vorderseite des Fernsehers befindet sich eine Soundbar mit einem Überzug aus Akustikstoff, die Teil des Standfußes ist und einen klaren, voluminösen Klang abstrahlt. Kabel und Anschlüsse sind zugunsten einer nahtlosen Erscheinung verborgen.

Begründung der Jury
Ausgesprochen gut gelöst ist die Auslagerung des Lautsprechers in Form einer Soundbar in den Standfuß. Sie liefert den Klang für ein umfassendes Kinoerlebnis.

Waterfall
OLED TV

Manufacturer
Skyworth, Shenzhen, China
In-house design
Mingming Wang, Liyuan Peng,
Yunbing Zhong, Chen Tang,
Zhiyong Chen
Web
www.skyworth.com

The design of the Waterfall OLED TV was inspired by the Iguazu Falls, known as the widest waterfalls on the planet. This role model finds its expression in the speaker rail, which is not, as usual, located below the screen but above it. Extending from this rail, the screen seems to flow down the wall like a waterfall. In addition, this arrangement contributes to better sound propagation in the room.

Statement by the jury
With its unusual design approach of locating the speaker rail above the screen, the TV offers new mounting options.

Als Inspiration für die Gestaltung des OLED-Fernsehers Waterfall dienten die Iguazu-Wasserfälle, die breitesten Wasserfälle der Welt. Dieses Vorbild findet seinen Ausdruck in der Lautsprecherleiste, die nicht wie üblich am unteren Rand des Bildschirms angebracht ist, sondern am oberen. Ausgehend von dieser Leiste scheint sich der Bildschirm wie ein Wasserfall an der Wand nach unten zu bewegen. Darüber hinaus trägt diese Anordnung dazu bei, dass sich der Klang besser im Raum ausbreiten kann.

Begründung der Jury
Der Fernseher bietet durch die ungewöhnliche Gestaltung mit einer oben angebrachten Lautsprecherleiste neue Möglichkeiten bei der Montage.

S9A
OLED TV

Manufacturer
Skyworth, Shenzhen, China
In-house design
Xingkang Liu, Liyuan Peng,
Mingming Wang, Shuxiao Wei,
Junting Liu, Zhiyong Chen
Web
www.skyworth.com

The S9A OLED TV offers the viewer a balanced sight from all sides, as each design detail was carried out in a careful way. The television does not have a stand; instead, the display is held in position by a support featuring a minimalist design, similar to an easel. With a slight backward tilt, the TV is positioned at an optimum viewing angle and allows users to completely immerse themselves in the action.

Statement by the jury
With its purist design, this television embodies an unmistakable language of form that integrates into living areas like a piece of art.

Der OLED-Fernseher S9A bietet dem Betrachter von allen Seiten eine ausgewogene Ansicht, da jedes gestalterische Detail sorgfältig ausgeführt wurde. Einen Standfuß besitzt der Fernseher nicht, stattdessen wird das Display durch eine minimalistisch ausgeführte Stütze wie eine Staffelei in Position gehalten. Durch diese Neigung steht der Fernseher in einem optimalen Blickwinkel und gestattet es dem Benutzer, ganz in das Geschehen einzutauchen.

Begründung der Jury
Der puristisch gestaltete Fernseher zeigt eine unverwechselbare Formensprache und fügt sich wie ein Kunstwerk in den Wohnbereich ein.

Q70 AI Smart TV

Manufacturer
Skyworth, Shenzhen, China
In-house design
Qiang Li, Changquan Wu, Yihao Zhang,
Chen Tang, Lixing Chen, Shuxiao Wei,
Zhiyong Chen
Web
www.skyworth.com

The ultra-high-resolution picture of the
Q70 AI Smart TV is the result of dual-cell
technology. It comprises, firstly, the
4K display panel and, secondly, a layer of
2K glass located under the panel and
controlling pixel illumination. The result
is a brilliant picture rich in details and
without smear effects. The outstanding
visual quality is paired with Dolby Atmos
sound. The design of the TV is characterised by curved glass seamlessly joining at
the panel.

Statement by the jury
This television stands out with its exquisite aesthetics. It spotlights the excellent
picture quality and lends the unit its
own character.

Das ultrahochauflösende Bild des
Q70 AI Smart TV ist Resultat der Dual-Cell-
Technologie. Sie umfasst zum einen das
4K-Anzeigefeld und zum anderen eine
Schicht aus 2K-Glas, die sich unter dem
Panel befindet und die Ausleuchtung
der Pixel steuert. Das Ergebnis ist ein sehr
detailreiches, brillantes Bild ohne Schmier-
effekte. Gepaart ist das ausgezeichnete
Bild mit Dolby-Atmos-Sound. Gestalterisch
prägt den Fernseher ein Ständer aus gebogenem Glas, der sich übergangslos an
das Panel anschließt.

Begründung der Jury
Der Fernseher besticht durch seine ausgesuchte Ästhetik. Sie verweist auf das
ausgezeichnete Bild und verleiht ihm einen
eigenen Charakter.

Screen TV
OLED TV

Manufacturer
Skyworth, Shenzhen, China
In-house design
Jie He, Liyuan Peng,
Shangping Chen, Mingming Wang,
Shuxiao Wei, Zhiyong Chen
Web
www.skyworth.com
Honourable Mention

The design of the Screen TV is inspired
by a paravent screen, a traditional
Chinese piece of furniture. The OLED TV
can be combined with folding elements
and used like a room partition, for instance to conceal certain areas or to re-
divide spaces in a room. A sound system
consisting of array speakers is situated
on both sides of the ensemble, offering
an intense sound experience.

Statement by the jury
The Screen TV reflects a successful symbiosis of state-of-the-art consumer electronics and a versatile piece of furniture.

Die Formgebung des Screen TVs ist von
einem Paravent, einem traditionellen
chinesischen Möbelstück, inspiriert. Der
OLED-Fernseher lässt sich mit Klappelemen-
ten kombinieren und kann in dieser Anordnung wie ein Raumteiler eingesetzt werden, um z. B. Bereiche zu kaschieren oder
den Raum neu aufzuteilen. An beiden Seiten
des Ensembles befindet sich ein aus Array-
Lautsprechern bestehendes Soundsystem,
das ein intensives Klangerlebnis bietet.

Begründung der Jury
Der Screen TV ist eine gelungene Symbiose
aus moderner Unterhaltungselektronik und
einem vielseitigen Möbelstück.

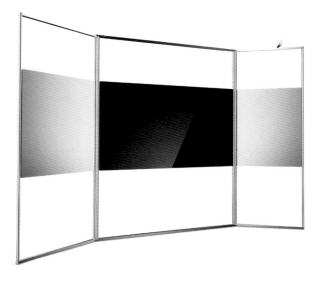

K600 TV
Keyboard
Tastatur

Manufacturer
Logitech, Lausanne, Switzerland
In-house design
Web
www.logitech.com

The K600 TV is a versatile all-in-one keyboard enabling the multiple functions of smart TVs. The familiar key layout facilitates comfortable text input as well as precise menu and cursor control, easily allowing you to navigate through menus or select websites. A feature of the keyboard is a large touchpad and a D-Pad significantly simplifying cursor control. As the keys are nearly silent when pressed, the television experience remains undisturbed.

K600 TV ist eine vielseitige All-in-one-Tastatur, mit der sich die vielfältigen Funktionen von Smart-TVs nutzen lassen. Das vertraute Tastenlayout vereinfacht die komfortable Texteingabe und präzise Menü- und Cursorsteuerung, um leicht durch Menüs zu navigieren oder Websites anzuwählen. Als Merkmal besitzt die Tastatur ein großes Touchpad sowie ein D-Pad, das die Steuerung des Cursors wesentlich vereinfacht. Da sich die Tasten nahezu geräuschlos betätigen lassen, bleibt das Fernseherlebnis ungestört.

Statement by the jury
The K600 TV keyboard excites with its ease of use, allowing the user to exhaust all functions of his smart TV.

Begründung der Jury
Die Tastatur K600 TV begeistert mit ihrem Bedienkomfort, der es dem Benutzer gestattet, sämtliche Funktionen seines Smart-TVs auszuschöpfen.

WM6681 Flux Wall Mount
TV-Wandhalterung

Manufacturer
Universal Electronics, Enschede, Netherlands
Design
D'Andrea & Evers Design (Luigi D'Andrea, Huub Mulhof),
Enter, Netherlands
Web
www.oneforall.com
www.de-design.nl

This wall mount was developed to enable the user to move the attached TV in a smooth but controlled way. It is equipped with four cast metal arms in which the cables can be concealed. Situated at the centre of the arms is a gas spring to guide all movements. When moving the TV towards the preferred position, the gas spring gives the user a complete feeling of control. As all touch points have scratch-resistant padding, both TV and wall are protected from damage. The two-colour mount is visually discreet and fits to any wall.

Diese Wandhalterung wurde entwickelt, um einen daran befestigten Fernseher sanft, aber kontrolliert bewegen zu können. Sie ist mit vier gegossenen Metallarmen ausgestattet, in denen sich die Kabel verstecken lassen. In der Mitte der Arme sitzt eine Gasfeder, die alle Bewegungen lenkt. Wird der Fernseher in die bevorzugte Position bewegt, gibt die Gasfeder das volle Gefühl der Kontrolle. Da alle Berührungspunkte kratzfest gepolstert sind, ist sowohl der Fernseher als auch die Wand vor Beschädigungen geschützt. Die zweifarbig ausgeführte Halterung ist optisch unauffällig und passt zu jeder Wand.

Statement by the jury
Thanks to the gas spring, a television can be easily brought into the position desired. In addition, the wall mount stands out with well-conceived details like the cable routing and padding.

Begründung der Jury
Dank der Gasfeder lässt sich ein Fernseher bequem in die gewünschte Position bringen. Zudem gefällt die Wandhalterung mit durchdachten Details wie der Kabelführung und Polsterung.

TSR-310
Remote Control
Fernbedienung

Manufacturer
Crestron Electronics, Inc.,
Rockleigh, New Jersey, USA

Design
Noto GmbH (Stefan Hohn),
Hürth, Germany

Web
www.crestron.com
www.noto.design

reddot **award** 2019
best of the best

Intuitive interaction

Since there are highly diverse processes involved in intelligent home automation, the systems for controlling heating, lighting and the safety technology also undergo constant improvements. The design of the TSR-310 remote control provides an aesthetically and functionally convincing solution for the interaction of users with the complex technology. Equipped with a touchscreen, it promotes uncomplicated control of home automation systems. The precision-crafted and perfectly weighted design follows the objective of optimising the functionality of the predecessor model. The rugged, self-contained construction of the remote has achieved durability and a high-quality appeal. Also impressive are its outstanding ergonomics, complemented by a finely tuned feedback when operating the buttons. Wrapped in a satiny smooth surface, the easy-grip housing of the remote control rests pleasantly in the hand. Features such as voice control, buttons that can be engraved according to custom requirements and the possibility of creating user profiles offer a high level of convenience. The TSR-310 is completely customisable and fully programmable. In use, it offers simple adjustment of the audio volume, easy flipping through channels, browsing the media library and operating the included pan/tilt camera. With just one device, everyone within a home can easily access their favourite entertainment, from TV channels and videos to games and music, at a single push of a button.

Intuitive Interaktion

Da die Vorgänge im Rahmen einer intelligenten Hausautomation sehr vielfältig sind, werden auch die Systeme für die Steuerung von Heizung, Beleuchtung und Sicherheitstechnik stetig verbessert. Die Gestaltung der Fernbedienung TSR-310 findet eine ästhetisch wie funktional überzeugende Lösung für die Interaktion des Nutzers mit der komplexen Technologie. Mit einem Touchscreen ausgestattet, dient sie der unkomplizierten Steuerung des Home-Automation-Systems. Ihre präzise und ausgewogene Gestaltung folgt der Zielsetzung, die Funktionalität des Vorgängermodells zu optimieren. Die robuste, in sich schlüssige Konstruktion macht diese Fernbedienung hochwertig und langlebig. Beeindruckend ist zudem die ausgezeichnete Ergonomie in Kombination mit einem fein abgestimmten Feedback bei der Bedienung der Tasten. Samtig anmutende Oberflächen lassen die Fernbedienung griffsicher und geschmeidig in der Hand liegen. Durch Features wie Voice-Control, nach Kundenwunsch gravierbare Tasten und die Möglichkeit der Erstellung von Nutzerprofilen bietet sie einen hohen Komfort. Die TSR-310 ist dabei vollständig individualisier- und programmierbar. Im Einsatz erlaubt sie das einfache Regeln der Audio-Lautstärke, das Wechseln des TV-Kanals, das Stöbern durch die Mediathek oder auch die Justierung einer Kamera. Mit nur einem Gerät kann jeder Bewohner eines Haushalts seine favorisierte Quelle, wie TV-Kanal, Spiele oder Musik, über einen einzelnen Klick erreichen.

Statement by the jury

Featuring a remarkably innovative interface, this remote control skilfully places user experience centre stage. The touchscreen and a well-thought-out button operation make the TSR-310 intuitive and self-explanatory to use. The remote control rests perfectly balanced in the hand and fascinates with its satiny smooth surface. Completely customisable and fully programmable, it easily and optimally adapts to user needs and requirements.

Begründung der Jury

Mit einem bemerkenswert innovativen Interface wird bei dieser Fernbedienung das Nutzererleben gekonnt in den Mittelpunkt gerückt. Mit Touchscreen und einer durchdachten Tastenbedienung ist die TSR-310 im Gebrauch sehr klar und selbsterklärend. Die Fernbedienung liegt perfekt ausbalanciert in der Hand und fasziniert mit ihrer samtweichen Oberfläche. Durch ihre vollständige Individualisier- und Programmierbarkeit passt sie sich den Nutzerbedürfnissen optimal an.

Designer portrait
See page 58
Siehe Seite 58

Caster
Remote Control
Fernbedienung

Manufacturer
Tech4home, São João da Madeira, Portugal
In-house design
Mariana Couto, Tiago Correia
Web
www.tech4home.pt

The Caster remote control was designed for use with Telefonica's Movistar and TV service. Important control elements are the centrally arranged D-pad area and the strikingly placed symbol for the integrated voice command function that lets the user interact with Aura, Movistar's virtual assistant. On the reverse side of the remote control, a soft coating provides additional comfort and a good grip, which enables particularly secure handling. The most frequently used buttons on the remote control light up when the device is picked up in a dimly lit room.

Die Caster-Fernbedienung wurde für die Nutzung des Telefonica Movistar- und TV-Dienstes entwickelt. Wichtige Kontroll-elemente sind der zentral angeordnete D-Pad-Bereich und das auffällig platzierte Symbol für die integrierte Voice-Command-Funktion, die den Benutzer mit Aura, dem virtuellen Assistenten von Movistar, inter-agieren lässt. Auf der Rückseite der Fernbe-dienung sorgt eine weiche Beschichtung für zusätzlichen Komfort und einen guten Grip, was ein besonders sicheres Handling ermöglicht. Die am häufigsten verwendeten Tasten der Fernbedienung leuchten, wenn das Gerät in einem eher dunklen Raum in die Hand genommen wird.

Statement by the jury
The Caster remote control is excellently tailored to the user's needs and de-mands. Its range of functions and ergo-nomic features also contribute to its high calibre.

Begründung der Jury
Die Fernbedienung Caster präsentiert sich als hervorragend an die Bedürfnisse des Benutzers angepasst. Auch Funktions-umfang und Ergonomie bieten ein hohes Niveau.

r157.7 androidtv remote control
Fernbedienung

Manufacturer
ruwido austria gmbh, Neumarkt, Austria
Design
zeug Design GmbH, Salzburg, Austria
Web
www.ruwido.com
www.zeug.at

Characteristic for the product language of the r157.7 remote control is that the entire top part features the same geometry. The slightly curved appearance of the matte-eroded, pre-stressed surface is consistently continued in the button curvature. The central navigation cursor consists of black chrome with polished chamfer and is flush with the most frequently used function buttons. The integrated voice transmission function simplifies the search for content.

Statement by the jury
The r157.7 remote control is a visually appealing and functionally sophisticated input device offering outstanding operating convenience.

Charakteristisch für die Produktsprache der r157.7 ist, dass das gesamte Oberteil über die gleiche Geometrie verfügt, da sich das leicht gewölbte Erscheinungsbild der matt erodierten Oberfläche in der Tastenkrümmung fortsetzt. Der zentrale Navigations-Cursor besteht aus Schwarzchrom mit polierter Fase und ist gehäusebündig von den am häufigsten verwendeten Funktionstasten umgeben. Die integrierte Sprach-übertragung erleichtert Nutzern die Suche nach Inhalten.

Begründung der Jury
Die Fernbedienung r157.7 ist ein visuell ansprechendes und funktional ausgereiftes Eingabegerät, das einen ausgezeichneten Bedienkomfort liefert.

consistent design r407
IPTV Set-Top Box and Remote Control
IPTV-Receiver und Fernbedienung

Manufacturer
ruwido austria gmbh, Neumarkt, Austria
Design
zeug Design GmbH, Salzburg, Austria
Web
www.ruwido.com
www.zeug.at

The straightforward product architecture of the Android TV remote control is oriented to user-friendliness and determined by levelled buttons and a clearly raised central navigational ring. An aligned set-top box was designed that is scalable depending on the technology integrated. A subtle glow underscores the floating impression of its downward-levelled, highly polished surface. Both units correlate in terms of design and materiality.

Statement by the jury
This shapely duo excites with its outstanding workmanship and perfectly coordinated design.

Die geradlinige Produktarchitektur der Android-TV-Fernbedienung ist auf Benutzer-freundlichkeit ausgerichtet und wird durch nivellierte Tasten sowie einen deutlich abgesetzten Cursor-Ring bestimmt. Dazu wurde ein passender Receiver entwickelt, der je nach integrierter Technologie skalierbar ist. Ein subtiles Leuchten unterstreicht den schwebenden Eindruck der nach unten hin abgesetzten Hochglanzoberfläche. Beide Geräte entsprechen sich in Formgebung und Materialität.

Begründung der Jury
Das formschöne Duo begeistert durch seine ausgezeichnete Verarbeitung und die perfekt aufeinander abgestimmte Gestaltung.

HR-310
Remote Control
Fernbedienung

Manufacturer
Crestron Electronics, Inc., Rockleigh, New Jersey, USA
Design
Noto GmbH (Stefan Hohn), Hürth, Germany
Web
www.crestron.com
www.noto.design

The HR-310 remote control stands out due to features like ergonomic design, finely tuned button feedback, voice control, user profiles and custom engravable buttons. Due to its velvet-like surfaces, it rests safely and smoothly in the hand. With its backlit buttons, the remote control can also be used in dark environments. In the upper area, nine buttons are located that may be customised and assigned to favoured playback sources or used for lighting control. The lower part of the remote holds at the user's disposal everything that is required for enjoying multimedia content.

Die Fernbedienung HR-310 zeichnet sich durch Merkmale wie ein ergonomisches Design, ein fein abgestimmtes Tasten-Feedback, Voice-Control, Nutzerprofile und nach Kundenwunsch gravierbare Tasten aus. Mit ihren samtartigen Oberflächen liegt sie sicher und geschmeidig in der Hand. Da die Tasten hinterleuchtet sind, kann die Fernbedienung auch in dunklen Umgebungen verwendet werden. Im oberen Bereich befinden sich neun Tasten, die mit favorisierten Wiedergabequellen oder einer Lichtsteuerung belegt werden können. Der darunter liegende Tastaturbereich hält alles bereit, was zum Genießen von Multimediainhalten benötigt wird.

Statement by the jury
The HR-310 remote control impresses with an ergonomic design consistently oriented to the user. It is thus a valuable addition to the consumer electronics already in the home.

Begründung der Jury
Die Fernbedienung HR-310 begeistert mit ihrer konsequent am Nutzer orientierten ergonomischen Formgebung und ist damit eine wertvolle Ergänzung zu vorhandener Unterhaltungselektronik.

Gome Smart TV Remote (86GM5399U)
Fernbedienung

Manufacturer
Gome Intelligent Technology Co., Ltd., Beijing, China
In-house design
Anqi Wang
Web
www.gomesmart.com

User-friendliness, ergonomics and aesthetics are the central ideas in the design of this remote control. The buttons are arranged in such a way that the most frequently used functions are easily accessible. The buttons can be told apart thanks to their different forms and surfaces, enabling easy identification even without looking. With the oval cylindrical shape and recess for the index finger on the backside, the device rests comfortably in the hand and can be operated with ease.

Statement by the jury
This remote control stands out with its ergonomic design, which makes its use a pleasure and also guarantees a relaxing TV viewing experience.

Benutzerfreundlichkeit, Ergonomie und Ästhetik sind die zentralen Ideen bei der Gestaltung dieser Fernbedienung. Die Tasten sind so angeordnet, dass die am häufigsten verwendeten Funktionen bequem zu erreichen sind. Unterscheiden lassen sich die Tasten durch ihre verschiedenen Formen und Oberflächen, wodurch sie auch ohne hinzusehen gut identifiziert werden können. Mit der ovalen Zylinderform und der Einbuchtung an der Rückseite für den Zeigefinger liegt das Gerät gut in der Hand und kann leicht bedient werden.

Begründung der Jury
Die Fernbedienung besticht mit ihrer ergonomischen Gestaltung, welche die Verwendung zum Vergnügen macht und ein entspanntes Fernseherlebnis garantiert.

Universal Remote Control
Universalfernbedienung

Manufacturer
Tuya Inc., Hangzhou, China
In-house design
Yugen Zhong
Web
www.tuya.com

This universal remote control is based on an advanced Wi-Fi module with low energy consumption and is compatible with common infrared household appliances. With its round pebble shape, it rests well in the hand and ensures 360-degree signal coverage, even when held for an extended period to enjoy the smooth haptics of the device. As the remote control is capable of learning, it adapts to the user's habits and can thus be integrated seamlessly into the Smart Home.

Statement by the jury
With its unconventional shape, this universal remote control appears like a timeless piece of jewellery, thus enriching any modern interior.

Diese Universalfernbedienung fußt auf einem fortschrittlichen Wi-Fi-Modul mit einem niedrigen Energieverbrauch und ist mit gängigen Infrarot-Haushaltsgeräten kompatibel. Mit ihrer runden Kieselsteinform liegt sie gut in der Hand und bietet selbst dann eine 360-Grad-Signalabdeckung, wenn der Benutzer sie länger in der Hand hält, um die glatte Form zu erfühlen. Da die Fernbedienung lernfähig ist, passt sie sich an die Gewohnheiten des Anwenders an und kann so nahtlos in das Smart Home integriert werden.

Begründung der Jury
Mit ihrer eigenwilligen Form mutet die Universalfernbedienung wie ein zeitloses Schmuckstück an und bereichert damit jedes moderne Interieur.

Sonata 1
Soundbar and Receiver
Soundbar und Empfänger

Manufacturer
TechniSat Digital GmbH, Daun, Germany
In-house design
Web
www.technisat.com

The Sonata 1 combines elegant design with advanced technology. The system consists of a soundbar and a UHD receiver united in a 4.5 mm thick, black anodised aluminium case with a finely perforated speaker grille. Its clear, oblong shape naturally follows the lines of the TV and thus blends naturally into the living environment. The soft edges create a flowing design, giving the soundbar visual lightness, despite its 6 kg weight.

Statement by the jury
The soundbar impressively integrates multiple functions in a form that superbly harmonises with modern consumer electronics.

Sonata 1 kombiniert ein elegantes Design mit fortschrittlicher Technik. Das System besteht aus einer Soundbar und einem UHD-Receiver, vereint in einem Gehäuse aus 4,5 mm dickem, schwarz eloxiertem Aluminium mit einem fein gelochten Lautsprechergitter. Seine klare, längliche Form folgt wie selbstverständlich den Linien des Fernsehers und fügt sich so natürlich in die Wohnlandschaft ein. Die weichen Kanten sorgen für ein fließendes Design, das der Soundbar trotz ihres Gewichts von 6 kg eine optische Leichtigkeit verleiht.

Begründung der Jury
Die Soundbar integriert in beeindruckender Weise vielfältige Funktionen in einer Form, die hervorragend mit vorhandener Unterhaltungselektronik harmoniert.

BR-O8
Bluetooth Transmitter and Receiver
Bluetooth-Sender und -Empfänger

Manufacturer
Shenzhen Aukey E-Business Co., Ltd., Shenzhen, China
In-house design
Yang Wang
Web
www.aukey.com

The unobtrusively designed BR-O8 Bluetooth adapter expands wired audio devices to include wireless functionality, for instance to stream music from a smartphone to speakers or headphones. Support for Bluetooth 5 and aptX ensures a solid wireless signal with extended range for optimum sound quality without delay. The easy-to-use touch display shows the current connection status and always keeps the user up to date.

Statement by the jury
This handy adapter offers high utility value, as it ensures that even older multimedia devices can be controlled via Bluetooth.

Der unaufdringlich gestaltete Bluetooth-Adapter BR-O8 erweitert kabelgebundene Audiogeräte mit Wireless-Funktionalität, um z. B. Musik vom Smartphone auf Lautsprecher oder Kopfhörer zu streamen. Die Unterstützung für Bluetooth 5 und aptX gewährleistet ein stabiles Funksignal mit erweiterter Reichweite für optimale Klangqualität ohne Verzögerung. Das einfach zu bedienende Touchdisplay zeigt den aktuellen Verbindungsstatus an und hält den Anwender stets auf dem Laufenden.

Begründung der Jury
Der handliche Adapter bietet einen hohen Nutzwert, denn er sorgt dafür, dass sich auch ältere Multimediageräte per Bluetooth ansteuern lassen.

Wireless HDMI Video Transmitter and Receiver
Kabelloser HDMI-Video-Sender und -Empfänger

Manufacturer
Shenzhen Aukey E-Business Co., Ltd., Shenzhen, China
In-house design
Minmin Zhang
Web
www.aukey.com

This user-friendly transmission system streams HDMI content wirelessly from a computer or other source device via Bluetooth to an HDMI screen over a distance of up to 15 metres. The transmitter and receiver units are very compact and thus adaptable to any environment. The design is characterised by discreet elegance so that they fit well with already existing presentation and multimedia devices.

Statement by the jury
The discreet design of the transmitter/receiver system with rounded lines conveys easy handling and facilitates access to the product.

Dieses benutzerfreundliche Übertragungssystem streamt drahtlos HDMI-Inhalte von einem Computer oder einem anderen Quellgerät über Bluetooth an einen HDMI-Bildschirm in einer Entfernung von bis zu 15 Metern. Sender- und Empfängereinheit sind sehr kompakt und lassen sich problemlos in jedem Raum aufstellen. Die Formgebung ist von einer zurückhaltenden Eleganz geprägt, sodass sie gut zu schon vorhandenen Präsentations- und Multimediageräten passen.

Begründung der Jury
Die dezente Gestaltung des Sender-/Empfängersystems mit gerundeten Linien vermittelt eine einfache Handhabung und erleichtert den Zugang zum Produkt.

Beam
Soundbar

Manufacturer
Sonos Europe, Munich, Germany
In-house design
Web
www.sonos.com

The Beam is a compact soundbar with a precious, timeless design that turns entertainment into an experience for the entire family. It delivers impressive sound for all audio content such as series, films, music, radio plays, podcasts and games. Thanks to the integrated Amazon Alexa speech assistant, it is effortlessly controlled by voice, but alternatively also by the Sonos app, the apps of partners such as Spotify and Audible or simply by touching the speaker directly. The soundbar supports AirPlay 2 and, like all Sonos speakers, is easily integrable into a Sonos sound system.

Beam ist eine kompakte Soundbar in edlem, zeitlosem Design, die Entertainment für die gesamte Familie zum Erlebnis macht. Sie gibt sämtliche Audioinhalte wie Serien, Filme, Musik, Hörspiele, Podcasts und Games mit einem beeindruckenden Klang wieder. Dank integrierter Amazon-Alexa-Sprachassistenz lässt sie sich bequem mit der Stimme steuern, wahlweise aber auch mit der Sonos-App, den Apps von Partnern wie Spotify und Audible oder ganz einfach per Berührung direkt am Gerät. Die Soundbar unterstützt AirPlay 2 und lässt sich wie alle Sonos-Lautsprecher problemlos in ein Sonos-Soundsystem integrieren.

Statement by the jury
The Beam is a soundbar with a monolithic presence. It complements up-to-date home entertainment devices in an outstanding way and upgrades the multimedia experience.

Begründung der Jury
Beam ist eine Soundbar mit monolithischer Präsenz. Sie ergänzt hervorragend aktuelle Home-Entertainment-Geräte und wertet das Multimedia-Erlebnis auf.

AI Remote Control Hub
Fernbedienung und Hub

Manufacturer
LG Uplus, Seoul, South Korea
In-house design
Seoyeon Lee
Web
www.uplus.co.kr

The AI Remote Control Hub is a remote control and hub for the Internet of Things. It enables numerous devices to be controlled via voice or app, such as TVs, set-top boxes or air conditioners. The plain round shape was chosen deliberately so that the hub may be placed and used anywhere in the house or apartment in an uncomplicated way. It is made of cost-effective ABS material, making it affordable for everyone.

Statement by the jury
The handy device blends smoothly into any interior and offers comfortable functions for managing the networked home.

Der AI Remote Control Hub ist Fernbedienung und Hub für das Internet der Dinge. Sowohl per Sprache als auch per App lassen sich damit zahlreiche Geräte wie Fernseher, Set-Top-Box oder Klimaanlage steuern. Die einfache runde Form wurde bewusst gewählt, damit der Hub überall in Haus oder Wohnung platziert und unkompliziert verwendet werden kann. Hergestellt ist er aus kostengünstigem ABS-Material, wodurch er für jedermann erschwinglich ist.

Begründung der Jury
Das handliche Gerät fügt sich unauffällig in jedes Interieur ein und bietet komfortable Funktionen, um das vernetzte Zuhause zu managen.

MeBox
Set-Top Box

Manufacturer
ZTE Corporation, Shenzhen, China
In-house design
Zhang Qian
Web
www.zte.com.cn

The MeBox is an Android-based set-top box for the home, which can serve as networked-attached and cloud storage. It also supports 4K video streaming and offers a large number of TV programs. Media content can be retrieved and applications managed via an app. The design places value on a congenial appearance with flowing forms, so as to harmonise the MeBox with the home environment.

Statement by the jury
The MeBox plays skilfully with geometric figures without appearing obtrusive. In this way, it is ideally suitable for use in private areas.

Die MeBox ist eine auf Android basierende Set-Top-Box für den Heimbereich, die als Netzwerk- wie auch als Cloudspeicher dient. Sie unterstützt darüber hinaus das Streamen von 4K-Videos und bietet zahlreiche Fernsehprogramme. Über eine App können Medien auch per Fernzugriff abgerufen und Anwendungen verwaltet werden. Damit die MeBox gut in ein häusliches Umfeld passt, wurde bei der Gestaltung Wert auf eine freundliche Anmutung mit fließenden Formen gelegt.

Begründung der Jury
Die MeBox spielt gekonnt mit geometrischen Figuren, ohne aufdringlich zu wirken. So eignet sie sich ideal für den Einsatz im Privatbereich.

SV9494 Ball Antenna
Indoor Antenna
Innenantenne

Manufacturer
Universal Electronics, Enschede, Netherlands
Design
D'Andrea & Evers Design (Luigi D'Andrea, Huub Mulhof),
Enter, Netherlands
Web
www.oneforall.com
www.de-design.nl

This indoor antenna for reception of DVB T/DVB T2 programs is tuned by simply rotating the top. The discreet light ring indicates the signal strength so that the user can easily determine the optimal orientation: the better the signal, the more light becomes visible. During operation of the antenna, the automatic gain control balances out variations in signal strength so that the television picture is always at its optimum. To prevent interference in reception, the antenna is shielded against mobile radio signals.

Die Innenantenne für den Empfang von DVB-T/DVB-T2-Programmen wird durch einfaches Drehen der Oberseite ausgerichtet. Dabei zeigt der diskrete Lichtring die Signalstärke an, sodass der Benutzer leicht die optimale Ausrichtung bestimmen kann: Je besser das Signal ist, desto mehr Licht wird sichtbar. Während des Betriebes der Antenne gleicht die automatische Verstärkungsregelung Signalschwankungen aus, damit das Fernsehbild jederzeit optimal ist. Um Störungen beim Empfang zu vermeiden, ist die Antenne gegen Mobilfunksignale abgeschirmt.

Statement by the jury
Operating and orienting the SV9494 Ball Antenna is child's play. It convinces with its futuristic design, turning it into an artful object in living spaces.

Begründung der Jury
Die SV9494 Ball Antenna ist kinderleicht auszurichten und überzeugt mit ihrer futuristischen Gestaltung, die sie zu einem kunstvollen Objekt in Wohnräumen werden lässt.

Google Chromecast
Streaming Media Player

Manufacturer
Google LLC, Mountain View, California, USA
In-house design
Web
https://store.google.com

The Chromecast equips a TV with the Google Assistant so that content from compatible mobile devices can be casted and navigated by voice. Thanks to its minimalist design, the media player requires almost no space. Its appealing form with soft edges provides a pleasant tactile feel in the hands for an agreeable user experience. It is available in different colours so that it may be found more easily behind or next to the television.

Chromecast stattet einen Fernseher mit dem Google Assistant aus, sodass sich Inhalte von kompatiblen Mobilgeräten übertragen lassen und mit der Stimme navigiert werden kann. Der Media-Player benötigt dank seiner minimalistischen Gestaltung so gut wie keinen Platz. Seine ansprechende Form mit weichen Kanten macht ihn zum Handschmeichler, der eine angenehme Nutzererfahrung verspricht. Erhältlich ist er in unterschiedlichen Farben, damit er sich hinter oder neben dem Fernseher leichter finden lässt.

Statement by the jury
The Google Chromecast is an excellent example of a design approach focusing on the principle "reduction to the essentials".

Begründung der Jury
Google Chromecast ist ein hervorragendes Beispiel für einen Gestaltungsansatz, der das Prinzip „Reduktion auf das Wesentliche" in den Mittelpunkt stellt.

Clova Desk
Smart Display
Intelligentes Display

Manufacturer
NAVER Corp., Seongnam, South Korea
LINE Corp., Tokyo, Japan
In-house design
NAVER Corp., Seongnam, South Korea
Web
www.navercorp.com

The Clova Desk is an intelligent desktop device with a 7" wide screen and a 20 watt output speaker. Its front is tilted by seven degrees so that the display remains easy to see regardless of how far away the user may be. The angles are characterised by a soft curvature that reduces the overall size of the display and improves the viewing experience. The housing is made of reinforced polycarbonate material with a matte UV-SF coating finish, giving the device an appealing gloss when exposed to light. The Clova Desk includes a rechargeable battery and is thus also suited for mobile use.

Clova Desk ist ein intelligentes Gerät für den Schreibtisch mit einem 7"-Breitbildschirm und einem 20-Watt-Ausgangslautsprecher. Seine Vorderseite ist um sieben Grad geneigt, sodass unabhängig davon, wie weit der Benutzer entfernt ist, das Display gut erkannt wird. Die Winkel sind von einer sanften Krümmung gekennzeichnet, die zum einen die Gesamtgröße des Displays verringert und zum anderen das Seherlebnis angenehmer macht. Für das Gehäuse wurde verstärktes Polycarbonat mit einer matten UV-SF-Beschichtung verwendet, die dem Gerät unter Lichteinfall einen ansprechenden Glanz verleiht. Clova Desk verfügt über einen Akku und kann auch mobil eingesetzt werden.

Statement by the jury
The Clova Desk is excellently tailored to users' needs as its design is appealing with regard to both ergonomics and optics.

Begründung der Jury
Clova Desk orientiert sich ausgesprochen gut an den Bedürfnissen der Benutzer, denn es ist gleichermaßen ergonomisch wie auch optisch ansprechend gestaltet.

Suning AI
Smart Alarm Clock
Intelligente Weckuhr

Manufacturer
Suning Intelligent Terminal Co., Ltd.,
Nanjing, China
In-house design
Huiren La, Lei Zhang, Bing Jiang, Wei Liu
Web
www.suning.com

Intelligent voice broadcasts, a TFT display and a physical button control are integrated in this smart alarm clock. The combination of ABS and linen provides this device with its characteristic features. By means of an app it can be controlled by gestures and voice; the screen can be activated and it is even possible to control other devices in the bedroom. In addition, the smart alarm clock makes useful information available, for example a weather report, news or a lexicon; apart from these, over 20 million audio books and programmes, 10 million radio stations and over 800,000 children's programmes.

Statement by the jury
The Suning AI Smart Alarm Clock surprises with its many useful, additional services and pleases with its elegant appearance.

Intelligente Stimmübertragung, ein TFT-Display sowie physische Tastenkontrolle sind in dieser smarten Weckuhr integriert. Die Kombination von ABS und Leinen verleiht dem Gerät eine charakteristische Anmutung. Mittels App wird es durch Gesten und Sprache steuerbar, der Bildschirm lässt sich aktivieren und es ist sogar möglich, andere Einrichtungen im Schlafzimmer zu steuern. Zudem stellt die smarte Weckuhr nützliche Informationen bereit wie etwa einen Wetterbericht, Nachrichten oder ein Lexikon, außerdem über 20 Millionen Hörbücher und Programme, zehn Millionen Radiosender und über 800.000 Angebote für Kinder.

Begründung der Jury
Die Suning AI Smart Alarm Clock überrascht mit vielen nützlichen zusätzlichen Diensten und gefällt mit ihrem eleganten Erscheinungsbild.

Smart Clock
Intelligente Uhr

Manufacturer
Lenovo, Morrisville, North Carolina, USA
In-house design
Web
www.lenovo.com

The Smart Clock features intelligent functions such as the Google Assistant, which answers questions and executes instructions. The device with its 4" display delivers information clearly, plays music, podcasts and audio books and can control the Smart Home via voice command. The back of the clock is coated with fabric and thus fits particularly well in the bedroom to be used as a radio alarm clock. A USB port for charging a smartphone complements the equipment.

Statement by the jury
Inspired by a traditional radio alarm clock, the Smart Clock scores with contemporary features that significantly facilitate everyday life in the Smart Home.

Die Smart Clock besitzt intelligente Funktionen wie den Google Assistant, der Fragen beantwortet und Anweisungen ausführt. Das Gerät mit 4"-Display stellt Informationen übersichtlich dar, gibt Musik, Podcasts und Hörbücher wieder und steuert das Smart Home per Spracheingabe. Die Rückseite der Uhr ist mit Stoff überzogen, wodurch sie besonders gut ins Schlafzimmer passt, um sie als Radiowecker zu verwenden. Eine USB-Schnittstelle zum Aufladen eines Smartphones vervollständigt die Ausstattung.

Begründung der Jury
Angelehnt an einen traditionellen Radiowecker punktet die Smart Clock mit zeitgemäßen Merkmalen, die den Alltag im Smart Home wesentlich erleichtern.

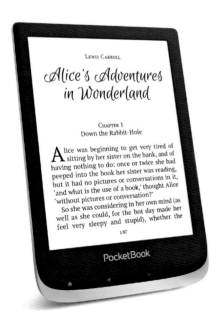

PocketBook Touch
Lux 4 (627), PocketBook
Touch HD 3 (632)
E-Readers

Manufacturer
PocketBook International SA,
Lugano, Switzerland
In-house design
Alexander Morokko
Web
www.pocketbook-int.com

These e-readers were designed for avid readers who seize every opportunity to enjoy books. Comfortable mechanical buttons and a pleasant soft touch surface ensure enjoyable handling. The devices are equipped with an eye-friendly e-ink display of the latest generation. They support 17 book formats without need for conversion and also four graphic formats. Moreover, the e-readers include Wi-Fi and a special function for switching into sleep mode quickly.

Statement by the jury
The e-readers captivate with their compact format and state-of-the-art equipment, offering everything that mobile readers expect today.

Für begeisterte Leser, die jede Gelegenheit nutzen, um Bücher zu genießen, wurden diese E-Reader entwickelt. Komfortable mechanische Tasten und eine Soft-Touch-Oberfläche sorgen für ein angenehmes Handling. Die mit einem augenfreundlichen E-Ink-Display der neuesten Generation ausgestatteten Geräte unterstützen 17 Buchformate ohne Konvertierung sowie vier Grafikformate. Weiterhin verfügen die E-Reader über Wi-Fi und eine besondere Funktion, mit der sie schnell in den Sleep-Modus versetzt werden können.

Begründung der Jury
Die E-Reader bestechen mit ihrem kompakten Format und der zeitgemäßen Ausstattung, die alles bietet, was der mobile Leser von heute erwartet.

Boox Blue
Musical Instrument Accessory
Zubehör für Musikinstrumente

Manufacturer
Onyx International Inc., Guangzhou, China
In-house design
Yuting Dan, Yukai Liu, Lingang Yin
Web
www.boox.com

Boox Blue is a remote control pedal in the form of piano keys that allows musicians to operate an e-reader with their feet. When the pedal is pressed, the page on the Bluetooth-connected e-reader is turned. This is convenient when playing from written scores as the musician need not manually turn the page but rather can continue the performance fluently. This is of particular advantage in ensembles as the interplay can take place in an undisturbed way. The pedal presents itself in a piano key design, which is a successful allusion to the music and also considerably simplifies the operation of the device.

Boox Blue ist ein Fernbedienungspedal in der Form von Klaviertasten, mit dem Musiker einen E-Reader mit dem Fuß bedienen können. Wird das Pedal betätigt, wird die Seite auf dem per Bluetooth verbundenen E-Reader umgeblättert. Dies ist beim Spielen vom Blatt angenehm, denn der Musiker muss nicht von Hand umblättern, sondern kann sein Spiel fließend fortsetzen. Besonders in Ensembles ist dies von Vorteil, da das Zusammenspiel störungsfrei ablaufen kann. Das Pedal zeigt sich im Pianotasten-Design, was zum einen eine gelungene Anspielung an die Musik darstellt, zum anderen die Bedienung wesentlich vereinfacht.

Statement by the jury
Not only is the Boox Blue very helpful in playing music, but it is also an appealing design solution that optimally fits into an artistic environment.

Begründung der Jury
Boox Blue ist nicht nur überaus hilfreich beim Musizieren, sondern auch eine gestalterisch ansprechende Lösung, die ideal in ein künstlerisches Umfeld passt.

Glass Sound Speaker LSPX-S2
Wireless Speaker
Kabelloser Lautsprecher

Manufacturer
Sony Video & Sound
Products Inc., Tokyo, Japan

Design
Sony Corporation,
Creative Center (Yujin Morisawa,
Manabu Fujiki), Tokyo, Japan

Web
www.sony-videosound.co.jp
www.sony.net/design

reddot award 2019
best of the best

Fascinating symbiosis

The Italian pianist and composer Ferruccio Busoni once described music as an ever-present "part of the vibrating universe". The Glass Sound Speaker LSPX-S2 is an innovative system of light and music that fuses advanced technology and design. The design of this second-generation speaker has realised a minimised size while maintaining a stable centre of gravity by housing the inner elements as low in the configuration as possible. The tweeter's small-diameter cylinder and the zinc die-cast housing helped minimise the size of the neck and thus bring the up-facing full-range speaker and tweeter into optimal aural harmony. The result is a speaker of clear and organic appearance, which may even be placed in the middle of a dining table. The light body with upward-beaming LED, which is characteristic of this speaker, delivers high luminosity and features an innovatively shaped lens reflector unit that diffuses the reflection to illuminate the entire surrounding area. The light emanates indirectly and does not blind users. The Glass Sound Speaker LSPX-S2 thus embodies a fascinating, multifunctional light object in symbiosis with a highly powerful audio speaker. This allows music to be experienced in a novel, sensual way.

Faszinierende Symbiose

Der italienische Pianist und Komponist Ferruccio Busoni bezeichnete Musik einst als einen „Teil des schwingenden Weltalls", der stets präsent sei. Der Glass Sound Speaker LSPX-S2 stellt ein innovatives System aus Licht und Musik dar, bei dem hochentwickelte Technologie und Design miteinander verschmelzen. Die Gestaltung dieses Lautsprechers in der zweiten Generation realisiert ein minimiertes Volumen und einen stabilen Schwerpunkt dadurch, dass die inneren Elemente so niedrig wie möglich in die Struktur integriert werden. Der Zylinder des Hochtonlautsprechers mit seinem geringen Durchmesser und das Zink-Druckgussgehäuse sorgen für die minimierte Größe, wodurch der nach oben gerichtete Breitbandlautsprecher und der Hochtöner in einer optimalen akustischen Ausgewogenheit stehen. Das Ergebnis ist ein organisch und klar anmutender Lautsprecher, der auch gut auf einem Esstisch stehen kann. Der für diesen Lautsprecher charakteristische Lichtkörper mit einer nach oben abstrahlenden LED weist eine hohe Leuchtkraft auf und verfügt über eine innovativ geformte Linsen-Reflektor-Einheit, die das Licht streut und die gesamte Umgebung erhellt. Die Beleuchtung erfolgt indirekt und blendet deshalb nicht. Der Glass Sound Speaker LSPX-S2 verkörpert so ein faszinierendes, multifunktionales Lichtobjekt in Symbiose mit einem sehr leistungsfähigen Lautsprecher. Musik kann auf neue und sinnliche Weise erfahren werden.

Statement by the jury

The LSPX-S2, the second generation of the Glass Sound Speaker, combines in an outstandingly harmonious way aesthetics and functionality with a unique visual and acoustic experience. Noteworthy is the integration of sophisticated technology into a well-proportioned housing of nostalgic appeal. Reminiscent of a candle in operation, it embodies the emergence of a new kind of speaker. Light and sound merge into a captivating convergence of seeing and hearing.

Begründung der Jury

Der Glass Sound Speaker LSPX-S2 kombiniert auch in der zweiten Generation überaus stimmig Ästhetik und Funktionalität mit einem besonderen akustischen und visuellen Erleben. Bemerkenswert ist der Einsatz hochentwickelter Technologie in einem nostalgisch anmutenden, wohlproportionierten Gehäuse. Im Betrieb an eine Kerze erinnernd, wurde hier eine neue Art von Lautsprecher kreiert. Licht und Klang verschmelzen zu einem bestechenden Mix aus Hören und Sehen.

Designer portrait
See page 60
Siehe Seite 60

Tmall Genie CC
Smart Speaker
Intelligenter Lautsprecher

Manufacturer
Zhejiang Tmall Technology Co., Ltd.,
Hangzhou, China
In-house design
Hao Chen, Zhao Liu
Web
www.alibabagroup.com

The Tmall Genie CC is a smart speaker with voice assistant offering the option of visual interaction. Thanks to the 7" IPS display, the user cannot only hear but also see the answer, simplifying operation and expanding usage scenarios. The carefully designed surfaces and contours give the speaker pleasant haptics, inviting the user to pick it up to watch videos, listen to music or engage in video chats. The speaker includes a rechargeable battery so that it is well suited to mobile use.

Der Tmall Genie CC ist ein intelligenter Lautsprecher mit Sprachassistent, der die Möglichkeit zur visuellen Interaktion bietet. Dank des 7"-IPS-Displays kann der Benutzer die Antwort nicht nur hören, sondern auch sehen, wodurch die Bedienung einfacher wird und sich die Nutzungsszenarien erweitern. Die sorgfältig gestalteten Oberflächen und Konturen verleihen dem Lautsprecher eine angenehme Haptik, sodass man ihn gerne in die Hand nimmt, um Videos zu betrachten, Musik zu hören oder per Video-Chat zu kommunizieren. Auch ein Akku ist integriert, sodass der Lautsprecher unterwegs verwendet werden kann.

Statement by the jury
The Tmall Genie CC scores with its coherent, congenial design. It harmonises with different interiors and references uncomplicated handling.

Begründung der Jury
Tmall Genie CC punktet mit seiner schlüssigen, sympathischen Formgebung. Sie harmoniert mit verschiedenen Interieurs und verweist auf eine unkomplizierte Handhabung.

Connect
Smart Speaker with Display
Intelligenter Lautsprecher mit Display

Manufacturer
Cleer, Inc., San Diego, USA
In-house design
Web
www.cleer.us

The Connect is a smart speaker with an 8" colour display, equipped with a two-way speaker and DSP for room-filling sound. With a sliding stand at the back, it can be tilted from 25 to 75 degrees for versatile use. Additional features are Bluetooth, a camera with sliding shutter and two omnidirectional far-field microphones ensuring precise speech interaction. Also, an app is available for controlling the speaker.

Statement by the jury
The speaker convinces with its clever stand, which not only facilitates different tilting angles but also provides a striking contrast to the flat display.

Connect ist ein intelligenter Lautsprecher mit 8"-Farbdisplay, der mit einem 2-Wege-Lautsprecher und DSP für raumfüllenden Klang ausgestattet ist. Er lässt sich mit seinem verschiebbaren Ständer an der Rückseite von 25 bis 75 Grad neigen, wodurch er vielfältig eingesetzt werden kann. Zu seinen Merkmalen zählen weiterhin Bluetooth, eine Kamera mit Schieber sowie zwei omnidirektionale Fernfeldmikrofone, die die präzise Sprachinteraktion gewährleisten. Darüber hinaus steht eine App zur Steuerung zur Verfügung.

Begründung der Jury
Der Lautsprecher überzeugt durch den überaus pfiffigen Ständer, der nicht nur verschiedene Neigungen ermöglicht, sondern auch einen reizvollen Kontrast zum flachen Display bietet.

Google Home Hub
Smart Display
Intelligentes Display

Manufacturer
Google LLC, Mountain View, California, USA
In-house design
Web
https://store.google.com

The Google Home Hub is as thin as a tablet or flatscreen TV and is covered in fabric like a piece of furniture. It includes two sound field microphones, thus enabling playback of music or intuitive control of the Smart Home via voice control. In addition, all information is shown on the screen. Its design is discreet and compact so that it can be set up anywhere in the house or flat. If the display is not in use, then it shows photos just like a picture frame.

Statement by the jury
The smart display captivates with its discreet design, low space requirements and comprehensive functionality.

Google Home Hub ist so dünn wie ein Tablet oder Flachbildfernseher und wie ein Möbel mit Stoff überzogen. Er besitzt zwei Feldmikrofone, ermöglicht also die Wiedergabe von Musik oder die intuitive Steuerung des Smart Homes per Spracheingabe und zeigt zusätzlich alle Informationen auf dem Display an. Seine Formgebung ist dezent und kompakt, sodass er sich überall im Haus oder in der Wohnung aufstellen lässt. Wird der Hub nicht verwendet, zeigt er wie ein Bilderrahmen Fotos an.

Begründung der Jury
Das intelligente Display punktet durch seine zurückhaltende Gestaltung, den geringen Platzbedarf und die umfassenden Funktionen.

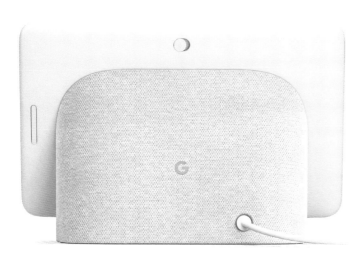

Smart Tab
Tablet and Smart Dock
Tablet und Dockingstation

Manufacturer
Lenovo, Morrisville, North Carolina, USA
In-house design
Web
www.lenovo.com

The Smart Tab is a 10.1" Android tablet that turns into an intelligent display as soon as it is placed in the smart dock. It is then expanded with the Alexa voice assistant in order to, on demand, play music or movies, answer questions, receive news or display the calendar. In addition, thanks to the integrated far-field microphones, it provides the option of controlling the Smart Home. The speakers ensconced in the smart dock ensure that the sound is distributed well throughout the room.

Statement by the jury
The tablet and smart dock complement each other in an excellent way and turn the tablet into a multifunctional control centre in a modern home.

Das Smart Tab ist ein 10,1"-Android-Tablet, das sich in ein intelligentes Display verwandelt, sobald es im Smart Dock platziert wird. Es wird dann mit dem Sprachassistenten Alexa erweitert und spielt auf Zuruf Musik oder Filme ab, beantwortet Fragen, empfängt Nachrichten oder stellt den Kalender dar. Zusätzlich bietet es dank der Fernfeldmikrofone die Möglichkeit, das Smart Home zu steuern. Die im Smart Dock integrierten Lautsprecher sorgen dafür, dass sich der Klang gut im Raum verteilt.

Begründung der Jury
Tablet und Smart Dock ergänzen sich auf hervorragende Weise und machen das Tablet zu einer multifunktionalen Schaltzentrale in einem modernen Zuhause.

Roku TV Wireless Speakers
Kabellose Lautsprecher

Manufacturer
Roku, Los Gatos, California, USA
Design
Bould Design, San Mateo, California, USA
Web
www.roku.com
www.bould.com

This wireless speaker system is designed for use with a Roku TV and shows an overall appearance which is characterized by a low-key functional elegance. It automatically connects to the television and produces room-filling stereo sound. Additionally, the speakers can also stream music from services like Pandora or from a Bluetooth-enabled device. The minimalist form of the speakers is wrapped in a custom-designed fabric and capped with a recessed silicone cap that holds the remote control.

Statement by the jury
Thanks to their balanced design, the speakers harmonise with a Roku TV in an outstanding way. They also impress with an appealing contrast of different materials.

Dieses kabellose Lautsprechersystem ist für die Verwendung mit einem Roku-Fernsehgerät konzipiert und zeigt eine Gesamterscheinung, die von einer unauffälligen, funktionalen Eleganz geprägt ist. Es verbindet sich automatisch mit dem Fernseher und erzeugt einen raumfüllenden Stereoton. Darüber hinaus können die Lautsprecher auch Musik von Diensten wie Pandora oder einem Bluetooth-fähigen Gerät streamen. Die minimalistisch geformten Lautsprecher sind mit einem speziell angefertigten Stoff umwickelt und mit einer versenkten Silikonkappe versehen, auf die die Fernbedienung Platz findet.

Begründung der Jury
Dank ihrer ausgewogenen Gestaltung harmonieren die Lautsprecher hervorragend mit einem Roku-Fernseher. Zudem punkten sie mit dem reizvollen Gegensatz unterschiedlicher Materialien.

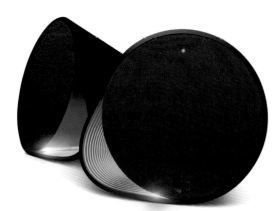

G560
Gaming Speakers
Gaming-Lautsprecher

Manufacturer
Logitech, Lausanne, Switzerland
In-house design
Web
www.logitechg.com

Powered by Lightsync technology, the G560 gaming speakers synchronise brilliant RGB lighting and powerful audio in real time to match on-screen gameplay action. The lighting responds to the rhythm of the sound and creates corresponding light effects. The light and animation effects with around 16.8 million colours are customisable in four illumination zones. Thanks to the integrated Easy-Switch technology, up to four devices may be connected at the same time.

Statement by the jury
The G560 gaming speakers are superbly suited to enriching the user's multimedia experience, whether gaming or listening to music.

Die G560-Gaming-Lautsprecher synchronisieren dank der Lightsync-Technologie eine brillante, auf das Spielgeschehen am Bildschirm angepasste RGB-Beleuchtung sowie einen leistungsstarken Klang in Echtzeit. Die Beleuchtung reagiert dann im Rhythmus der Töne und erzeugt daran angepasste Lichteffekte. Die Licht- und Animationseffekte mit rund 16,8 Millionen Farben in vier Beleuchtungszonen lassen sich personalisieren. Dank der integrierten Easy-Switch-Technologie können bis zu vier Geräte gleichzeitig angeschlossen werden.

Begründung der Jury
Die Gaming-Lautsprecher G560 sind hervorragend dazu geeignet, das multimediale Nutzererlebnis, sei es beim Spielen oder Musikhören, zu bereichern.

Ultimate Ears Megaboom 3, Boom 3
Bluetooth Speakers
Bluetooth-Lautsprecher

Manufacturer
Logitech, Lausanne, Switzerland
In-house design
Design
NONOBJECT,
Portola Valley, California, USA
Web
www.ultimateears.com

The Megaboom 3 and Boom 3 Bluetooth speakers deliver balanced 360-degree sound with deep bass and include convenient one-touch control. They are water-repellent and drop-proof as well. The speakers are coated with a durable and weatherproof acoustic fabric. They are available in appealing colours that display a particular visual appeal when exposed to light, as the fabric is woven from two different-coloured threads, giving the textile surface its shimmering structure.

Statement by the jury
These speakers excite with their robust workmanship and refined woven fabric cover, lending them an attractive appearance.

Einen ausgewogenen 360-Grad-Sound, tiefe Bässe und eine komfortable One-Touch-Steuerung bieten die Bluetooth-Lautsprecher Megaboom 3 und Boom 3. Zusätzlich sind sie wasserabweisend und verkraften auch Stürze. Ummantelt sind die Lautsprecher von einem Akustikgewebe, das überaus widerstandsfähig und wetterfest ist. Erhältlich sind sie in ansprechenden Farben, die bei Lichteinfall einen besonderen Reiz entfalten. Der Stoff ist nämlich aus zwei verschiedenfarbigen Fäden gewebt, wodurch das Gewebe eine schillernde Struktur erhält.

Begründung der Jury
Die Lautsprecher begeistern mit ihrer robusten Verarbeitung und dem raffiniert gewebten Stoffbezug, der ihnen eine attraktive Ausstrahlung verleiht.

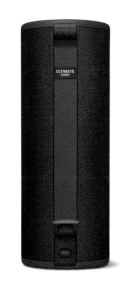

SYMFONISK
Wi-Fi Speaker
Wi-Fi-Lautsprecher

Manufacturer
IKEA of Sweden AB,
Älmhult, Sweden
In-house design
Andreas Fredriksson,
Mikael Warnhammar
Web
www.ikea.com

The SYMFONISK Wi-Fi book-shelf speaker delivers excellent sound and can be used, thanks to its rectangular shape, as a wall rack when mounted horizontally. It carries a weight of up to 3 kg and may thus serve as shelf for books or decorative items. With its plain design and discreet colours, the speaker blends well with different interiors. It is controlled via the Sonos app, can be grouped together and also supports multiroom mode.

Statement by the jury
SYMFONISK convinces with its inventive design, giving it expanded functionality and turning it into a useful item of interior furnishing.

Der Bücherregal-Wi-Fi-Lautsprecher SYMFONISK bietet einen ausgezeichneten Klang und lässt sich dank seiner schlichten Quaderform wie ein Wandregal verwenden, wenn er horizontal montiert wird. Er trägt bis zu 3 kg und eignet sich damit für die Ablage von beispielsweise Büchern oder Dekoartikeln. Dank seiner zurückhaltenden Formgebung und der dezenten Farben fügt er sich gut in verschiedene Interieurs ein. Der Lautsprecher wird mit der Sonos-App gesteuert, kann zu Gruppen zusammengefasst werden und unterstützt den Multiroom-Modus.

Begründung der Jury
SYMFONISK überzeugt mit seiner durchdachten Formgebung. Sie verleiht ihm eine erweiterte Funktionalität und macht ihn zum nützlichen Einrichtungsgegenstand.

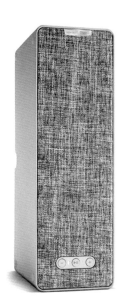

Wood
Bluetooth Speakers
Bluetooth-Lautsprecher

Manufacturer
belaDESIGN, Hangzhou, China
In-house design
Zhang Fei, Chen Zuo, Bi Shun, Tang Jia
Design
Hangzhou Teague Technology Co., Ltd.
(Shi Hong, Cui Yangbin), Hangzhou, China
Web
www.beladesign.cn

The Bluetooth speakers feature simple rectangular shapes with rounded surfaces, increasing the size of the resonance bodies. Each speaker is made from a single piece of wood, so that the wood grain is continuous for a seamless housing design. To produce a better, fuller sound, the holes are precision cut with a laser. The switches are made of wood as well, so that the overall appearance remains coherent.

Statement by the jury
The Bluetooth speakers score with their clean and tidy workmanship, highlighting wood as a natural raw material.

Die Bluetooth-Lautsprecher besitzen einfache rechteckige Formen mit gewölbten Oberflächen, die die Resonanzkörper vergrößern. Ein Lautsprecher wird jeweils aus einem Stück Holz hergestellt, sodass die Holzmaserung durchgehend ist und das Gehäuse nahtlos erscheint. Die Löcher wurden zugunsten eines besseren Klangs präzise mit einem Laser gefräst. Auch die Schalter wurden aus Holz gefertigt, damit das einheitliche Gesamtbild erhalten bleibt.

Begründung der Jury
Die Bluetooth-Lautsprecher punkten mit ihrer sauberen Verarbeitung, durch die der natürliche Werkstoff Holz gekonnt in Szene gesetzt wird.

JBL JR Pop
Bluetooth Portable Speaker
Tragbarer Bluetooth-
Lautsprecher

Manufacturer
Harman International,
Northridge, California, USA
In-house design
Hyojin Kim
Web
www.harman.com

The JBL JR Pop Bluetooth speaker is designed specifically for children and therefore is small enough to fit in their small hands. It features durable materials and a waterproof design according to the IPX7 standard. The device is also equipped with a strap to snap it to a backpack. It comes in a variety of vibrant colour combinations and a multi-colour lighting mode that is activated when music is playing. The rechargeable battery supplies power for up to five hours of playtime.

Statement by the jury
The JBL JR Pop excites with its playful design and practical fastening strap. It is thus optimally tailored to a young target group.

Der Bluetooth-Lautsprecher JBL JR Pop wurde speziell für Kinder entwickelt und ist daher klein genug, um in ihre kleinen Hände zu passen. Er ist aus haltbaren Materialien gefertigt und besitzt ein wasserfestes Design gemäß IPX7-Standard. Das Gerät ist außerdem mit einem Riemen ausgestattet, um es an einem Rucksack zu befestigen. Es ist in verschiedenen lebendigen Farbkombinationen und mit mehrfarbigen Lichtmotiven erhältlich, die aktiviert werden, wenn Musik abgespielt wird. Der Akku liefert Strom für bis zu fünf Stunden Spielzeit.

Begründung der Jury
Der JBL JR Pop begeistert mit seiner verspielten Formgebung und der praktischen Befestigungsschlaufe. Damit ist er hervorragend auf eine junge Zielgruppe abgestimmt.

PartyBox 100,
PartyBox 300
Speakers
Lautsprecher

Manufacturer
Harman International,
Northridge, California, USA
In-house design
Web
www.harman.com

The PartyBoxes 100 and 300 were designed to fill parties with sound, be it a small gathering at home or a larger celebration. The speakers are equipped with LEDs that light up in the rhythm of the music. They have a rechargeable battery, and the PartyBox 300 additionally includes a 12 volt DC input for the cigarette lighter socket in vehicles. A guitar or microphone can also be connected and amplified by the speaker, and it is possible to interconnect multiple devices.

Statement by the jury
The PartyBoxes are ideal for spontaneous use and, with their integrated LED lighting, create an atmosphere of illumination.

Die Lautsprecher PartyBox 100 und 300 wurden entwickelt, um Partys mit Musik zu beschallen, sei es eine kleinere Party zu Hause oder eine Feier im größeren Rahmen. Die Boxen sind mit LEDs ausgestattet, die im Rhythmus der Musik leuchten. Sie besitzen einen Akku, die PartyBox 300 verfügt darüber hinaus über einen 12-Volt-Eingang für den Zigarettenanzünder im Auto. Auch eine Gitarre oder ein Mikrofon lassen sich anschließen, um Sound über den Lautsprecher auszugeben. Mehrere Geräte können zudem zusammengeschaltet werden.

Begründung der Jury
Die PartyBoxen sind ideal für den spontanen Einsatz geeignet und sorgen mit ihrer integrierten LED-Beleuchtung für Stimmung.

PartyBox 1000
Bluetooth Speaker
Bluetooth-Lautsprecher

Manufacturer
Harman International,
Northridge, California, USA
In-house design
Web
www.harman.com

With an audio output power of 1,100 watts, a 12" subwoofer and two 7" mid-range speakers, the PartyBox 1000 produces rich sound. It also includes full panel lighting with a stroboscope light and a DJ launch pad for control of music playback. Three modes of light shows are already preset so that the party can start without lengthy technical preparations. Part of the equipment is an armband offering the option of controlling the lighting with gestures.

Statement by the jury
The high-performance speaker is truly multitalented, enabling the intuitive control of music playback and light effects.

Mit einer Ausgangsleistung von 1.100 Watt, einem 12"-Subwoofer und zwei 7"-Mitteltönern produziert die PartyBox 1000 einen satten Sound. Sie besitzt zudem ein Beleuchtungsfeld mit Stroboskoplicht und ein DJ-Launchpad für die Kontrolle der Musikwiedergabe. Drei Lichtshows sind bereits voreingestellt, damit die Party ohne große technische Vorbereitung starten kann. Zum Lautsprecher gehört auch ein Armband, das die Möglichkeit bietet, die Beleuchtung mit Gesten zu steuern.

Begründung der Jury
Der leistungsfähige Lautsprecher ist ein wahres Multitalent, mit dem sich Musikwiedergabe und Lichteffekte intuitiv steuern lassen.

JBL Flip 5
Portable Bluetooth Speaker
Tragbarer Bluetooth-
Lautsprecher

Manufacturer
Harman International,
Northridge, California, USA
In-house design
Hyojin Kim
Web
www.harman.com

The JBL Flip 5 offers amazing sound, is waterproof according to the IPX7 standard and enables wireless Bluetooth streaming. The speaker can be placed horizontally or vertically thus finding the required space everywhere. To enjoy stereo sound, two speakers can be paired, and multiple speakers may be linked for even greater sound volume. The built-in rechargeable battery guarantees operating time of up to 12 hours. The speaker is available in 11 vivid colours.

Statement by the jury
Thanks to its versatility and robust workmanship, the JBL Flip 5 is an ideal speaker for all kinds of recreational activities.

JBL Flip 5 bietet leistungsstarken Sound, ist wasserfest nach IPX7-Standard und ermöglicht das kabellose Streaming per Bluetooth. Aufstellen lässt sich der Lautsprecher horizontal oder vertikal und findet daher überall den benötigten Platz. Um Stereoklang genießen zu können, lassen sich zwei Lautsprecher koppeln, für ein größeres Klangvolumen können auch mehrere Geräte verbunden werden. Rund zwölf Stunden Betriebszeit sind mit dem integrierten Akku möglich, der Lautsprecher ist in elf lebendigen Farben erhältlich.

Begründung der Jury
Dank seiner Vielseitigkeit und robusten Ausführung ist der JBL Flip 5 ein idealer Lautsprecher für alle Arten von Freizeitaktivitäten.

JBL Charge 4
Portable Bluetooth Speaker
Tragbarer Bluetooth-
Lautsprecher

Manufacturer
Harman International,
Northridge, California, USA
In-house design
Dario Distefano
Web
www.harman.com

The JBL Charge 4 portable Bluetooth speaker delivers powerful sound with strong bass and is equipped with a newly developed transducer. As it is covered with industrial fabrics and waterproof according to the IPX7 standard it is very robust and durable. An additional feature of the speaker is its powerbank which delivers 20 hours of playtime and charges smartphones and tablets.

Statement by the jury
The JBL Charge 4 shows a consistent design that reflects its rich sound and also underlines the durability of the housing.

Der tragbare Bluetooth-Lautsprecher JBL Charge 4 bietet einen kraftvollen Sound und ist mit einem neu entwickelten Wandler ausgestattet. Da er mit Industriegewebe bezogen und nach IPX7-Standard wasserfest ist, ist er äußerst widerstandsfähig und haltbar. Eine weitere Funktion des Lautsprechers ist seine Powerbank, die Energie für bis zu 20 Stunden Spielzeit liefert sowie Smartphones und Tablets aufladen kann.

Begründung der Jury
Der JBL Charge 4 zeigt eine konsistente Formgebung: Sie verweist auf seinen satten Klang und unterstreicht zudem die Widerstandsfähigkeit des Gehäuses.

Harman Kardon Esquire Mini 2
Portable Bluetooth Speaker
Tragbarer Bluetooth-
Lautsprecher

Manufacturer
Harman International,
Northridge, California, USA
In-house design
Gianni Teruzzi
Web
www.harman.com

With its thin speaker drivers and specially tuned acoustics, the ultra-slim Harman Kardon Esquire Mini 2 Bluetooth speaker delivers high-fidelity sound. Moreover, it features a conferencing system with noise cancellation for crystal clear conference calls on the go. The speaker supports up to ten hours of playtime and comes with a built-in powerbank to charge other mobile devices. Thanks to its practical stand on the back, it can also be positioned upright.

Statement by the jury
The Bluetooth speaker pleases with its slim, reduced design. It is not only extremely handy, but also well suited to the business field.

Mit seinen dünnen Lautsprechertreibern und der speziell abgestimmten Akustik liefert der sehr schlanke Bluetooth-Lautsprecher Harman Kardon Esquire Mini 2 Sound in Hi-Fi-Qualität. Darüber hinaus besitzt er ein Konferenzsystem mit Geräuschunterdrückung, mit dem unterwegs Konferenzgespräche klar und deutlich geführt werden können. Der Lautsprecher unterstützt bis zu zehn Stunden Spielzeit und verfügt über eine integrierte Powerbank, um andere mobile Geräte aufzuladen. Dank seines praktischen Ständers an der Rückseite kann er zudem aufrecht positioniert werden.

Begründung der Jury
Der Bluetooth-Lautsprecher gefällt mit seiner schlanken, reduzierten Gestaltung. Damit ist er nicht nur äußerst handlich, sondern auch im Business-Bereich gut einzusetzen.

Clova Friends mini
Smart Speakers
Intelligente Lautsprecher

Manufacturer
NAVER Corp., Seongnam, South Korea
LINE Corp., Tokyo, Japan
In-house design
NAVER Corp., Seongnam, South Korea
Web
www.navercorp.com

The Clova Friends mini speakers are equipped with the Clova language assistant and are capable of streaming music, reading fairy tales or sending messages. They are AI-enabled, which means that they can learn to adapt to the user's wishes and demands with increased use. The speakers are designed as applied famous characters, which makes them suitable for use in children's rooms and considerably facilitates personal interaction with the device. In addition, an individual character is assigned to each figure so that the user can choose his or her favourite.

Die Lautsprecher Clova Friends mini sind mit dem Sprachassistenten Clova ausgestattet und können Musik streamen, Märchen vorlesen oder Nachrichten senden. Sie sind KI-fähig, lernen also mit zunehmender Benutzung, sich auf die Wünsche des Anwenders einzustellen. Gestaltet sind die Lautsprecher als bekannte Charaktere, wodurch sie sich auch für die Verwendung im Kinderzimmer eignen und die persönliche Interaktion mit dem Gerät erheblich erleichtert wird. Darüber hinaus ist jeder Figur ein eigener Charakter zugeordnet, sodass der Benutzer seinen Favoriten wählen kann.

Statement by the jury
With their playful shaping, the Clova Friends mini have a very likeable appearance, thus simplifying access for younger and older users.

Begründung der Jury
Mit ihrer verspielten Formgebung wirken die Clova Friends mini überaus sympathisch. Dadurch erleichtern sie den Zugang für jüngere und ältere Benutzer.

Dolby Dimension™
Wireless Headphones
Kabellose Kopfhörer

Manufacturer
Dolby Laboratories,
San Francisco, USA

In-house design
Dolby Laboratories

Design
nonobject,
Portola Valley, California, USA

Web
www.dolby.com
www.nonobject.com

reddot award 2019
best of the best

Mediators of worlds
Listening with headphones allows to be immersed in entertainment. But sometimes it is necessary to stay in touch with the surroundings. Dolby Dimension headphones are equipped with the innovative Dolby LifeMix technology that offers individual control over how much users hear of their surroundings, from a perfect blend of their entertainment and life around them to shutting out the world with active noise cancellation. The Cinematic Sound delivers an incredible sound experience thanks to advanced digital signal processing that significantly enhances the sound of content. For convenience, Source Buttons on the headset can be easily paired with three different Bluetooth devices, allowing users to connect to their entertainment at the touch of a button. A secure, custom-curved headband maximises comfort over long periods of time, and the ear cups are fully wrapped in a durable synthetic leather, progressively getting softer before seamlessly blending into the custom-formed ear pads. The perforated cores of the ear cups hint at the headphones' ability to let sound in while housing the omnidirectional microphones for Dolby LifeMix. To ensure the headphones are always charged and within easy reach, the intuitive Power Base charging station is included in the package.

Mittler der Welten
Das Hören über Kopfhörer ermöglicht ein tiefes Eintauchen in die Entertainment-Welt, wobei man jedoch manchmal auch in Kontakt mit seiner Umgebung bleiben muss. Die Dolby Dimension-Kopfhörer sind ausgestattet mit der innovativen Dolby LifeMix-Technologie, die dem Nutzer eine individuelle Kontrolle darüber erlaubt, welchen Anteil an Umgebungsgeräuschen er hören will, von einer perfekten Kombination aus Entertainment und Außenwelt bis hin zu einer kompletten Geräuschunterdrückung. Die Cinematic Sound-Technologie bietet dabei ein außergewöhnliches akustisches Erlebnis dank einer hochentwickelten digitalen Signalverarbeitung, die den Klang erheblich verbessert. Source-Tasten am Headset können komfortabel mit drei verschiedenen Bluetooth-Geräten gekoppelt werden, was per einfachem Tastendruck ein schnelles Zugreifen auf die gewünschte Programmquelle ermöglicht. Die Gestaltung mit einem sicheren, individuell anpassbaren Bügel maximiert den Tragekomfort auch über lange Zeit, während die Ohrmuscheln von strapazierfähigem Kunstleder umgeben sind und immer weicher werden, bevor sie nahtlos in die individuell geformten Ohrpolster übergehen. Die perforierten Kerngehäuse der Ohrmuscheln verweisen auf die Maxime der Transparenz und beherbergen die omnidirektionalen Mikrofone für Dolby LifeMix. Als unkomplizierte Ladestation sorgt die im Lieferumfang enthaltene Power Base dafür, dass diese Kopfhörer stets geladen und immer in Reichweite bleiben.

Statement by the jury
The attractively designed Dolby Dimension Bluetooth headphones deliver a special kind of listening experience. They are equipped with powerful, high-quality Cinematic Sound technology and the innovative Dolby LifeMix technology, which allows users to adjust the degree of external noise cancellation as needed. In keeping with their high-quality design, the individually adjustable headphones are also highly comfortable to wear.

Begründung der Jury
Die attraktiv gestalteten Bluetooth-Kopfhörer Dolby Dimension kreieren eine besondere Art von Hörerlebnis. Ausgestattet sind sie mit der leistungsfähigen Cinematic Sound-Technologie für hohe Audioqualität und der innovativen Dolby LifeMix-Technologie, die es ermöglicht, den Grad der Unterdrückung äußerer Geräusche je nach Bedarf anzupassen. Die individuell einstellbaren Kopfhörer sind dabei im Einklang mit ihrer hochwertigen Ausführung ergonomisch sehr komfortabel.

Designer portrait
See page 62
Siehe Seite 62

BOOM by MIIEGO
Bluetooth Headphones
Bluetooth-Kopfhörer

Manufacturer
MIIEGO, Padborg, Denmark
In-house design
Christian Jeppesen
Web
www.miiego.com

The Bluetooth headphones BOOM by MIIEGO are appropriate for workouts and everyday use. The interchangeable earpads are an important feature: for relaxed music listening, the user can pick earpads made of soft PU leather; for workouts or other activities, the variant with breathable, washable mesh fabric may be chosen. The user is able to pick from a range of different colours and patterns to match his or her individual style.

Statement by the jury
The concept of interchangeable earpads is very clever as it allows the wearer to use the headphones in different scenarios.

Sowohl für den Sport als auch für den normalen Alltag ist der Bluetooth-Kopfhörer BOOM by MIIEGO geeignet. Wichtiges Merkmal sind die austauschbaren Ohrpolster: Für das entspannte Musikhören greift der Anwender zu Ohrpolstern aus weichem PU-Leder, bei Aktivitäten oder beim Sport wählt er die Variante aus atmungsaktivem, waschbarem Mesh-Gewebe. Hier steht ihm eine Palette von unterschiedlichen Farben und Mustern zur Verfügung, um dem individuellen Stil gerecht zu werden.

Begründung der Jury
Überaus durchdacht ist das Konzept der auswechselbaren Ohrpolster, denn es gestattet dem Benutzer, den Kopfhörer in unterschiedlichen Szenarien einzusetzen.

MPOW Bluetooth Headset

Manufacturer
Shenzhen Qianhai Patuoxun Network & Technology Co., Ltd., Shenzhen, China
In-house design
Chino Hu
Web
www.qxptx.com

This Bluetooth-enabled headset is equipped with select 40 mm drivers and HAC chips delivering clear and balanced sound. The earcups with generously designed cushions provide a precise fit around the ear and reliably shield the user from outside noise, enabling undisturbed enjoyment of music. Control buttons are located directly at the earcup and are activated by gentle touch. The lightweight headset can be folded up and stowed away in a little bag for transport.

Statement by the jury
With regard to equipment, carrying comfort and handling, this Bluetooth headset embodies a balanced overall package for music lovers.

Der Bluetooth-fähige Kopfhörer ist mit ausgewählten 40-mm-Treibern und HAC-Chips ausgestattet, die für einen klaren und ausgewogenen Klang sorgen. Die Ohrmuscheln mit großzügigen Polstern schließen sich passgenau um das Ohr und schirmen den Benutzer zuverlässig von Außengeräuschen ab. Damit ermöglichen sie den ungestörten Musikgenuss. Steuerungstasten befinden sich direkt an der Ohrmuschel und werden durch sanftes Berühren aktiviert. Der leichte Kopfhörer kann für den Transport gefaltet und in einer kleinen Tasche verstaut werden.

Begründung der Jury
Hinsichtlich Ausstattung, Tragekomfort und Handhabung zeigt sich das Bluetooth-Headset als ausgewogenes Gesamtpaket für Musikliebhaber.

ThinkPad X1
Noise-Cancelling Headphones
Kopfhörer mit Geräuschunterdrückung

Manufacturer
Lenovo, Morrisville, North Carolina, USA
In-house design
Web
www.lenovo.com

In order to deflect ambient noise, the ThinkPad X1 headphones employ a combination of active and electronic noise cancellation. The active variant is suitable for undisturbed music enjoyment, while the electronic variant is used during communication. The headphones are equipped with 40 mm drivers, Bluetooth 5.0 and a USB C port for use as a wired version with a laptop. For transport, the headphones may be folded flat.

Statement by the jury
The ThinkPad X1 headphones stand out with their sophisticated noise-cancellation functionality, offering the appropriate solution in any situation. This turns the headphones into a real all-rounder.

Um Umgebungsgeräusche abzuschirmen, setzt der Kopfhörer ThinkPad X1 auf die Kombination von aktiver und elektronischer Geräuschunterdrückung. Die aktive Variante eignet sich für den ungestörten Musikgenuss, während die elektronische Variante bei Gesprächen zum Einsatz kommt. Der Kopfhörer ist mit 40-mm-Treibern, Bluetooth 5.0 und USB C ausgestattet, kann also auch kabelgebunden mit einem Laptop verwendet werden. Für den Transport lässt er sich flach zusammenlegen.

Begründung der Jury
Der Kopfhörer ThinkPad X1 besticht durch seine ausgefeilte Geräuschunterdrückung, die in jeder Situation die passende Lösung bietet. Damit ist der Kopfhörer ein echter Allrounder.

SC 135/165 USB
Headsets

Manufacturer
Sennheiser Communications A/S,
Ballerup, Denmark
Design
Brennwald Design
(Chang-Chin Hwang, Jörg Brennwald),
Kiel, Germany
Øystein Helle Husby, Oslo, Norway
Web
www.senncom.com
www.brennwald-design.de
www.oysteinhusby.com

With the SC 135/165 USB headset series, users can comfortably conduct phone calls and listen to music to relax. The microphone boom, which is concealed in rest position, turns the SC 165 USB into high-grade stereo headphones during breaks in communication. Combined with a robust, elegant design are enhanced wearing comfort and practical features, such as foldable earcups or call control integrated into the cable. The ergonomic design enables fatigue-free work or restful listening for many hours.

Statement by the jury
Thanks to its clever shaping, this versatile headset series is an excellent choice for both communication and listening to music.

Mit der Headset-Serie SC 135/165 USB lässt sich sowohl komfortabel telefonieren als auch entspannt Musik hören. Der Mikrofonarm ist beim SC 165 USB in Ruhestellung versteckt und verwandelt das Headset in Kommunikationspausen in einen hochwertigen Stereokopfhörer. Der verbesserte Tragekomfort und praktische Features wie klappbare Ohrmuscheln und eine im Kabel integrierte Anrufsteuerung sind mit einem robusten, eleganten Design vereint. Die ergonomische Gestaltung ermöglicht das ermüdungsfreie Arbeiten oder entspannte Hören über viele Stunden.

Begründung der Jury
Dank seiner cleveren Formgebung ist die wandlungsfähige Headset-Serie sowohl für die Kommunikation als auch zum Musikhören eine ausgezeichnete Wahl.

HP Omen Mindframe
Gaming Headset

Manufacturer
HP Inc., Palo Alto, California, USA
In-house design
HP Design Team
Web
www.hp.com

Gamers are often confronted with the problem of headsets tending to overheat the area around the ears during longer gaming sessions. The Omen Mindframe headset provides a remedy, as it is equipped with an active cooling function that dissipates heat from the ears outwards. It also features a microphone with noise cancellation, a self-adjusting headband and 7.1 DTS surround sound for immersive gaming. The design places value on an integral exterior appearance, concealing individual components.

Statement by the jury
Thanks to its active cooling function, the Omen Mindframe is ideally suited for gamers. The headset also impresses with its coherent design.

Gamer sehen sich häufig mit dem Problem konfrontiert, dass Headsets im Bereich der Ohren zu Überwärmung führen. Omen Mindframe schafft Abhilfe, denn es ist mit einer aktiven Kühlung ausgestattet, die die Wärme von der Ohrmuschel nach außen ableitet. Zudem besitzt es ein Mikrofon mit Geräuschunterdrückung, einen sich selbst anpassenden Kopfbügel und 7.1-DTS-Surround-Sound für immersives Gaming. Bei der Gestaltung wurde Wert auf ein ganzheitliches Äußeres gelegt, bei dem einzelne Teile verborgen sind.

Begründung der Jury
Dank seiner aktiven Kühlung ist Omen Mindframe ideal für Gamer geeignet. Darüber hinaus punktet das Headset mit seiner schlüssigen Gestaltung.

Alienware AW988
Wireless Gaming Headset
Kabelloses Gaming-Headset

Manufacturer
Dell, Round Rock, Texas, USA
In-house design
Dell Experience Design Group
Web
www.dell.com
www.delledgdesign.com

The Alienware AW988 wireless gaming headset offers 7.1 surround sound for immersive gaming and crystal-clear communication. It is made of robust, lightweight materials that guarantee comfortable wearing. In particular, the soft earpads made of moisture-wicking material are very comfortable and enable intensive gaming over many hours. Thanks to adjustable, rotatable and extendable components, the headset can be tailored precisely to individual needs.

Statement by the jury
This headset stands out with its excellent wearing comfort, which is, particularly for gamers, often the significant feature in selecting a product.

Das kabellose Gaming Headset Alienware AW988 bietet 7.1-Surround-Sound für immersives Spielen und eine kristallklare Kommunikation. Hergestellt ist es aus robusten, leichten Materialien, die für ein gutes Tragegefühl sorgen. Besonders die weichen Ohrpolster aus feuchtigkeitsableitendem Material sind überaus komfortabel und ermöglichen stundenlanges Spielen. Darüber hinaus lässt sich das Headset dank verstellbarer, drehbarer und ausziehbarer Komponenten individuell anpassen.

Begründung der Jury
Das Headset besticht durch den ausgezeichneten Tragekomfort, der gerade für Gamer oft das entscheidende Merkmal für die Wahl eines Produktes ist.

G Pro Gaming Headset

Manufacturer
Logitech, Lausanne, Switzerland
In-house design
Web
www.logitechg.com

The G Pro gaming headset is lightweight and robust. Thanks to the premium leatherette ear pads, it is also comfortable to wear during long gaming sessions. It accommodates Pro-G drivers for high quality audio and a professional condenser microphone for crystal clear communication. The headset connects through detachable cables and controls. Since exterior noise is shielded well and even the finest sound details are audible, gamers can hear and locate approaching enemies early on, which offers strategic advantages during gaming.

Statement by the jury
The gaming headset convinces with its comprehensive equipment optimally suited to the needs and requirements of professional gamers.

Das Gaming-Headset G Pro ist leicht, robust und dank der hochwertigen Ohrpolster aus Kunstleder auch bei langen Spiele-Sessions komfortabel. Es verfügt über Pro-G-Treiber für eine erstklassige Audioqualität und ein professionelles Kondensatormikrofon sorgt für kristallklare Kommunikation. Die Verbindung erfolgt über abnehmbare Kabel und Steuerungen. Da Außengeräusche gut abgeschirmt werden und auch feinste Klangdetails hörbar sind, können Spieler herannahende Gegner frühzeitig lokalisieren, was beim Gaming strategische Vorteile bietet.

Begründung der Jury
Das Gaming-Headset überzeugt mit seiner umfassenden Ausstattung, die bestens an die Anforderungen von professionellen Spielern angepasst ist.

Arctis 9X, 9P
Gaming Headsets

Manufacturer
SteelSeries, Frederiksberg, Denmark
In-house design
Rasmus Christian Madsen, Tino Soelberg
Design
Swift Creatives, Aarhus, Denmark
Web
www.steelseries.com
www.swiftcreatives.com

The Arctis 9X and 9P gaming headsets are tailored to console gamers. Each model features the convenience of native wireless for Xbox and PlayStation, providing gamers with latency-free and high-quality audio. The headsets also come with an additional Bluetooth connection so that they can be used wirelessly, everywhere. Moreover, a retractable noise-cancelling microphone and custom-engineered sound drivers lend a crystal-clear quality to hearing in-game sounds and talking with teammates.

Statement by the jury
With these premium headsets, console players can enjoy comfortable wireless communication, which considerably enhances the gaming fun.

Die Gaming-Headsets Arctis 9X und 9P sind auf Konsolenspieler zugeschnitten. Jedes Modell liefert den Komfort einer nativen kabellosen Verbindung für die Xbox und PlayStation und bietet Spielern eine verzögerungsfreie und hochwertige Audioqualität. Die Headsets sind außerdem mit einer zusätzlichen Bluetooth-Verbindung ausgestattet, sodass sie überall kabellos verwendet werden können. Zudem sorgen ein einziehbares Mikrofon mit Geräuschunterdrückung und speziell entwickelte Soundtreiber für eine kristallklare Qualität beim Gaming-Sound und beim Gespräch mit Teamkollegen.

Begründung der Jury
Mit diesen erstklassigen Headsets kommen auch Konsolenspieler in den Genuss einer bequemen kabellosen Kommunikation, wodurch der Spielspaß merklich gesteigert wird.

Arctis Pro Series
(GameDac & Wireless)
Gaming Headsets

Manufacturer
SteelSeries, Frederiksberg, Denmark
In-house design
Rasmus Christian Madsen, Tino Soelberg
Design
Swift Creatives, Aarhus, Denmark
Web
www.steelseries.com
www.swiftcreatives.com

In connection with the D/A converter and the amplifier, the Arctis Pro series delivers hi-fi sound for gaming and ensures that the gamer can hear high-resolution, 24-bit audio signals with no downsampling. The headsets are equipped with reliable dual-wireless technology, speaker drivers capable of 40,000 hertz and a ClearCast microphone guaranteeing crystal-clear communication. With the ski goggle headband and fabric earpads, they also have comfortable wearing properties.

Statement by the jury
The headsets of the Arctis Pro series deliver first-class sound and enable the gamer to become completely immersed in the action.

Die Arctis-Pro-Serie liefert in Verbindung mit dem D/A-Wandler und dem Verstärker Hi-Fi-Klang für Spiele und stellt sicher, dass der Gamer hochauflösende 24-Bit-Audiosignale ohne Downsampling hören kann. Die Headsets sind mit der zuverlässigen Dual-Wireless-Technologie, 40.000-Hertz-fähigen-Lautsprechertreibern und einem ClearCast-Mikrofon ausgestattet, das die klare Kommunikation gewährleistet. Darüber hinaus bieten sie mit dem Skibrillenkopfband und Ohrpolstern aus Stoff angenehme Trageeigenschaften.

Begründung der Jury
Einen erstklassigen Klang liefern die Headsets der Arctis-Pro-Serie und verschaffen dem Gamer dadurch die Möglichkeit, vollständig in das Geschehen einzutauchen.

Live650BTNC
Headphones
Kopfhörer

Manufacturer
Harman International,
Northridge, California, USA
In-house design
Web
www.harman.com

Thanks to active noise cancellation, the Live650BTNC headphones permit undisturbed musical enjoyment. The rechargeable battery powers the headphones for up to 30 hours, or 20 hours in Bluetooth mode with active noise cancellation. If the battery runs low, they can also be used with a cable. The touch buttons are located at the earcup and enable access to Google Assistant and Alexa, for instance to retrieve up-to-date information. Music playback is also easily controlled via these buttons.

Statement by the jury
The Live650BTNC headphones convince with their coherent, state-of-the-art range of function. In addition, they score with their comfortable usability.

Dank aktiver Geräuschunterdrückung gestattet es der Kopfhörer Live650BTNC, Musik ungestört zu genießen. Der Akku liefert Energie für 30 Stunden bzw. 20 Stunden im Bluetooth-Betrieb mit Geräuschunterdrückung. Geht die Energie zur Neige, kann die Musikübertragung auch per Kabel erfolgen. Die Touch-Bedientasten befinden sich am Ohrstück und bieten Zugriff auf Google Assistant und Alexa, um z. B. aktuelle Informationen abzurufen. Auch die Musikwiedergabe wird bequem über diese Tasten gesteuert.

Begründung der Jury
Der Kopfhörer Live650BTNC überzeugt mit seinem stimmigen, zeitgemäßen Funktionsumfang. Darüber hinaus punktet er mit der komfortablen Bedienbarkeit.

Live400BT
Headphones
Kopfhörer

Manufacturer
Harman International,
Northridge, California, USA
In-house design
Web
www.harman.com

The Live400BT headphones are equipped with 40 mm drivers and deliver powerful sound with enhanced bass. The equipment includes the language assistants Alexa and Google Assistant, which can be activated, just like the music control, by lightly tapping the earcup. Owing to integrated TalkThru technology, conversations may be held without removing the headphones. One battery charge powers them for up to 24 hours, or they can be connected by cable to the source player.

Statement by the jury
Thanks to the rechargeable battery and cable, the Live400BT is always ready to use and thus an excellent choice for music lovers who are frequently on the go.

Der Kopfhörer Live400BT ist mit 40-mm-Treibern ausgestattet und bietet einen kraftvollen Klang mit verstärktem Bass. Zur Ausstattung gehören die Sprachassistenten Alexa und Google Assistant, die ebenso wie die Musiksteuerung mit einem leichten Tippen auf die Ohrmuschel aktiviert werden. Auch Gespräche lassen sich dank integrierter TalkThru-Technologie führen, ohne den Kopfhörer abzunehmen. Eine Akkuladung reicht für bis zu 24 Stunden, alternativ kann der Kopfhörer per Kabel an das Zuspielgerät angeschlossen werden.

Begründung der Jury
Dank Akku und Kabel ist der Live400BT immer einsatzbereit und daher für Musikliebhaber, die häufig unterwegs sind, eine ausgezeichnete Wahl.

WH-1000XM3
Wireless Headphones
Kabelloser Kopfhörer

Manufacturer
Sony Video & Sound Products Inc.,
Tokyo, Japan
Design
Sony Corporation, Creative Center
(Taku Yaegashi), Tokyo, Japan
Web
www.sony-videosound.co.jp
www.sony.net/design

The WH-1000XM3 wireless headphones use a specially developed HD noise-cancelling processor for sophisticated noise suppression. This function is automatically adjusted according to what the user does at any given time. In addition, when the quick-attention mode is activated, users can listen to their immediate environment without having to take off the headphones. The overall design of the headphones, in particular the housing design and the earpads, is also tailored to optimum noise suppression.

Statement by the jury
The WH-1000XM3 headphones constitute a perfect combination of form and function. The result is a technically sophisticated, visually attractive product.

Der Kopfhörer WH-1000XM3 nutzt einen speziell entwickelten HD-Noise-Cancelling-Prozessor für eine ausgefeilte Geräuschunterdrückung. Diese wird automatisch angepasst, je nachdem, was der Benutzer gerade tut. Darüber hinaus können Benutzer im Quick-Attention-Modus ihre Umgebung hören, ohne den Kopfhörer abzunehmen. Auch die Gestaltung des Kopfhörers, insbesondere die Gehäusekonstruktion und die Ohrpolster, ist auf eine optimale Geräuschunterdrückung abgestimmt.

Begründung der Jury
Form und Funktion gehen beim Kopfhörer WH-1000XM3 eine perfekte Verbindung ein. Das Ergebnis ist ein technisch ausgereiftes, visuell attraktives Produkt.

TOUCHit
Wireless Headphones
Kabelloser Kopfhörer

Manufacturer
SACKit ApS, Aalborg, Denmark
Design
Whynot Design & Innovation,
Venice, Italy
Web
www.sackit.eu
www.whynot-design.com

TOUCHit are wireless headphones with a plain design and active noise cancellation. They combine premium materials like metal, leather and fabric to create a product representing the taste and lifestyle of modern people. All details come together to enable a generally pleasant experience for the wearer. Contributing to this in particular are the earpads with two cushions, as the special design enhances the sound and also the wearing comfort.

Statement by the jury
Material selection, workmanship and design are impressive highlights of the TOUCHit wireless headphones and lend emphasis to their quality.

TOUCHit ist ein schlicht gestalteter, kabelloser Kopfhörer mit aktiver Geräuschunterdrückung. Er kombiniert wertige Materialien wie Metall, Leder und Stoff zu einem Produkt, das den Geschmack und Lebensstil moderner Menschen repräsentiert. Alle Details fügen sich zusammen zu einer rundum angenehmen Erfahrung für den Benutzer. Besonders die Ohrpolster mit zwei Kissen tragen hierzu bei, denn das spezielle Design verbessert sowohl den Klang als auch den Tragekomfort.

Begründung der Jury
Materialwahl, Verarbeitung und Formgebung setzen den kabellosen Kopfhörer TOUCHit eindrucksvoll in Szene und unterstreichen seine Qualität.

Enduro 100
Bluetooth Headphones
Bluetooth-Kopfhörer

Manufacturer
Cleer, Inc., San Diego, USA
In-house design
Web
www.cleer.us

The outstanding feature of the Enduro 100 headphones is their long operating time of 100 hours with a single battery charge. Thanks to Bluetooth 5.0 with ACC and aptX, the headphones guarantee excellent multimedia performance. Phone calls are initiated and received via the built-in microphone. For transport, the headphones can be folded up and stowed away in the included travel case. They are available in innovative colours, such as champagne and gun metallic.

Statement by the jury
The headphones excite with their extremely long operating time, liberating music lovers from the need for a power supply on longer trips.

Herausragendes Merkmal des Kopfhörers Enduro 100 ist seine lange Betriebszeit von 100 Stunden mit einer einzigen Akkuladung. Dank Bluetooth 5.0 mit ACC und aptX liefert er darüber hinaus eine ausgezeichnete Multimedia-Performance. Anrufe lassen sich über das eingebaute Mikrofon annehmen und tätigen. Zum Transport kann der Kopfhörer zusammengefaltet und im mitgelieferten Etui verstaut werden. Erhältlich ist er in innovativen Farben, darunter Champagner und Gun Metallic.

Begründung der Jury
Der Kopfhörer begeistert mit seiner äußerst langen Einsatzzeit, die den Musikfreund auch auf längeren Touren von einer Stromversorgung unabhängig macht.

Halo
Smart Wireless Neck Speaker
Intelligenter kabelloser
Nackenlautsprecher

Manufacturer
Cleer, Inc., San Diego, USA
In-house design
Web
www.cleer.us

The Halo wireless speaker is worn around the neck and produces a personal sound bubble for its user. This allows the wearer to enjoy music while also being able to perceive the environment at the same time. As both speakers feature a magnetic clasp, the device can be attached to a bag or backpack. Part of the equipment is the Google Assistant, providing information at the push of a button. The integrated rechargeable battery with its quick-charge function supplies power for up to 12 hours of listening enjoyment.

Statement by the jury
The Halo delights with its clever design, which not only turns it into a fashionable accessory but also offers high utility value.

Der kabellose Lautsprecher Halo wird um den Nacken gelegt und erzeugt eine persönliche Klangblase für seinen Benutzer. Dadurch lässt sich Musik erleben, während gleichzeitig die Umgebung wahrgenommen werden kann. Da die beiden Lautsprecher magnetisch sind, kann das Gerät an einer Tasche oder einem Rucksack befestigt werden. Zur Ausstattung zählt auch der Google Assistant, der Informationen auf Knopfdruck liefert. Bis zu zwölf Stunden Hörvergnügen ermöglicht der integrierte Akku mit Schnellladefunktion.

Begründung der Jury
Halo begeistert durch seine pfiffige Gestaltung, die ihn nicht nur zu einem modischen Accessoire macht, sondern auch einen hohen Nutzen liefert.

My Theater
Neck Speaker
Nackenlautsprecher

Manufacturer
EM-Tech Co., Ltd., Anyang, South Korea
In-house design
Byoungjin Kim
Web
www.em-tech.co.kr

The My Theater neck speaker is equipped with Bluetooth and offers users the option of enjoying a high-quality sound experience without losing the ability to perceive the environment at the same time. The speakers tilt towards the ears in order to prevent other people close by from being disturbed or annoyed by the sound. Moreover, this arrangement is meant to minimise stress on the eardrums.

Statement by the jury
My Theater convinces with its slender design and cleverly arranged speakers. Modern music aficionados can thus enjoy their favourite songs in a natural way.

Der Nackenbügel-Lautsprecher My Theater ist mit Bluetooth ausgestattet und bietet Benutzern die Möglichkeit, ein qualitativ hochwertiges Klangerlebnis zu genießen und gleichzeitig die Umgebung wahrzunehmen. Die Lautsprecher neigen sich in Richtung der Ohren, um zu verhindern, dass Personen in der Nähe durch den Sound belästigt werden. Zudem soll durch diese Anordnung die Belastung für das Trommelfell minimiert werden.

Begründung der Jury
My Theater überzeugt mit seinem schlanken Design und den clever ausgerichteten Lautsprechern. So kann der Musikfreund seine Lieblingssongs auf natürliche Weise genießen.

AKG N200NC Wireless
Wireless Earbuds
Kabelloser In-Ear-Kopfhörer

Manufacturer
Harman International,
Northridge, California, USA
In-house design
Web
www.harman.com

The lightweight earbuds AKG N200NC Wireless combine high-grade metal and rubber materials in a featherlight package. They offer ten hours of playback using Bluetooth and also produce excellent sound via the specially designed aux-in port. This port is a practical feature when travelling, as the user can comfortably connect to the existing entertainment system in the train or plane. The dual-mic function enables clearly audible phone calls even in loud environments.

Statement by the jury
With their clever, reserved design, the earbuds AKG N200NC Wireless offer convincing features. They harmonise with any clothing style and fit into any environment.

Der leichte In-Ear-Kopfhörer AKG N200NC Wireless vereint hochwertiges Metall und Gummi in einem federleichten Paket. Er bietet eine zehnstündige Wiedergabe per Bluetooth und erzeugt auch über den speziell gestalteten AUX-Eingang einen ausgezeichneten Klang. Dieser Anschluss ist auf Reisen praktisch, denn der Benutzer kann sich bequem mit dem Unterhaltungssystem in Bahn oder Flugzeug verbinden. Die Dual-Mikrofon-Funktion ermöglicht klare Telefongespräche auch in lauten Umgebungen.

Begründung der Jury
Der AKG N200NC Wireless weiß mit seiner durchdachten, zurückhaltenden Formgebung zu überzeugen. Er passt zu jedem Kleidungsstil und lässt sich in jeder Umgebung einsetzen.

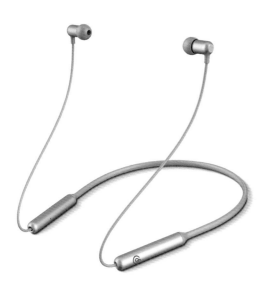

ME02B Plus
Bluetooth Earbuds
Bluetooth In-Ear-Kopfhörer

Manufacturer
Hangzhou NetEase Yanxuan Trading Co., Ltd.,
Hangzhou, China
In-house design
Wentao Liang, Yang Ju
Web
www.163.com

The intelligent Bluetooth neckband earbuds ME02B Plus feature a weight of merely 22 grams. As the neckband is sheathed in silicone, it offers a comfortable fit even over longer periods of use. Part of the neckband and the earbuds are coated with anodised aluminium, giving the product a high-grade appearance. Integrated into the earphones is the option to bookmark favourite songs from the app NetEase Cloud Music, which is popular in China, so as to enjoy one's favourite music on the go at any time.

Statement by the jury
ME02B Plus captivates with a discreet, coherent design, which is not only timeless but also harmonises well with different clothing styles.

ME02B Plus ist ein intelligenter Bluetooth-Nackenbügelkopfhörer mit einem Gewicht von nur 22 Gramm. Da das Nackenband mit Silikon ummantelt ist, bietet es auch bei langer Nutzung ein angenehmes Tragegefühl. Ein Teil des Nackenbandes und die Ohrhörer sind mit eloxiertem Aluminium beschichtet, was dem Produkt eine hochwertige Anmutung verleiht. Integriert ist die Möglichkeit, in der in China populären App NetEase Cloud Music ausgewählte Songs als Lesezeichen zu setzen, um unterwegs jederzeit seine Lieblingsmusik genießen zu können.

Begründung der Jury
ME02B Plus besticht durch seine zurückhaltende, schlüssige Gestaltung, die nicht nur zeitlos ist, sondern auch gut mit unterschiedlichen Kleidungsstilen harmoniert.

Google Pixel USB-C Earbuds
In-Ear-Kopfhörer

Manufacturer
Google LLC,
Mountain View, California, USA
In-house design
Web
https://store.google.com

The Pixel USB-C earbuds are optimised for use with the Pixel 3 smartphone. They are comfortable to wear, offer outstanding sound and, thanks to the integrated remote control, are also convenient to use. As the Google Assistant is also on board, the user can retrieve information through voice control, enter notes and start conversations in up to 40 different languages using the Google Translate function. With their adjustable anchor loops, the earbuds guarantee a secure fit in the ear. In addition, the semi-enclosed housing will let ambient sound pass through.

Statement by the jury
The Google Pixel USB-C earbuds display a coherent design; it is characterised by state-of-the-art features and offers excellent usability.

Der Pixel USB-C-Kopfhörer ist für die Verwendung mit dem Smartphone Pixel 3 optimiert. Er ist bequem zu tragen, bietet einen ausgezeichneten Klang und lässt sich dank der integrierten Fernbedienung auch bequem bedienen. Da der Google Assistant ebenfalls mit an Bord ist, kann der Benutzer auch per Sprache Informationen abrufen, Notizen eingeben oder mit Google Translate Konversationen in bis zu 40 verschiedenen Sprachen starten. Die Ohrstöpsel mit ihren verstellbaren Schlaufen sitzen sicher im Ohr. Darüber hinaus lässt das halb geschlossene Gehäuse auch Umgebungsgeräusche durch.

Begründung der Jury
Der Kopfhörer Google Pixel USB-C ist schlüssig gestaltet, zeichnet sich durch zeitgemäße Merkmale aus und bietet eine gute Bedienbarkeit.

GLIDiC Sound Air WS-5100
Bluetooth Earbuds
Bluetooth-In-Ear-Kopfhörer

Manufacturer
SoftBank Commerce & Service Corp.,
Tokyo, Japan
In-house design
Takahiro Nakamichi
Web
www.cas.softbank.jp

The GLIDiC Sound Air WS-5100 Bluetooth earbuds with neckband harmonise well with both everyday clothing and business attire thanks to their elegant form. The rechargeable battery includes a quick-charge function so that the earbuds can be fully charged in less than ten minutes. When in continuous operation, they are powered for up to 5.5 hours. When not in use, the earbuds may be simply folded up and stowed away in a small bag.

Statement by the jury
With their unobtrusive design, the Bluetooth earphones convince in any situation as a perfect companion, be it in everyday life or on a business trip.

Der GLIDiC Sound Air WS-5100 ist ein Bluetooth-In-Ear-Kopfhörer mit Nackenband, der dank seiner eleganten Form sowohl zur Alltagskleidung getragen werden kann als auch gut mit einem Business-Outfit harmoniert. Der Akku verfügt über eine Schnellladefunktion und kann in weniger als zehn Minuten vollständig geladen werden. Im Dauerbetrieb reicht die Energie dann für 5,5 Stunden. Bei Nichtgebrauch kann der Kopfhörer einfach zusammengeklappt und in einer kleinen Tasche verstaut werden.

Begründung der Jury
Mit seiner unaufdringlichen Formgebung überzeugt der Bluetooth-Kopfhörer in jeder Situation als perfekter Begleiter, sei es im Alltag oder auf Geschäftsreise.

OnePlus Bullet Wireless
Wireless Earbuds
Kabelloser In-Ear-Kopfhörer

Manufacturer
OnePlus Technology, Shenzhen, China
In-house design
Web
www.oneplus.com

The design of the OnePlus Bullet Wireless earbuds is inspired by horns, which lends emphasis to their clear sound quality. The earbuds are equipped with magnetic switches enabling music playback to be controlled: when the earbuds are fitted together, music playback stops; when they are released, music playback continues. The round neckband with its skin-friendly surface can be worn comfortably, and with their additional loop, the earbuds fit securely in the ear.

Statement by the jury
The earbuds OnePlus Bullet Wireless score with their functional, well-conceived design and good wearing properties.

Eine von Hörnern inspirierte Gestaltung kennzeichnet den In-Ear-Kopfhörer OnePlus Bullet Wireless, was seine klare Klangqualität unterstreicht. Der Kopfhörer ist mit magnetischen Ohrhörern ausgestattet, mit denen die Musikwiedergabe gesteuert werden kann: Werden die Ohrhörer zusammengesteckt, stoppt die Musikwiedergabe, werden sie gelöst, wird die Musikwiedergabe fortgesetzt. Der runde Nackenbügel mit der hautfreundlichen Oberfläche lässt sich angenehm tragen; zudem sitzen die Ohrstöpsel dank ihrer zusätzlichen Schlaufe sicher im Ohr.

Begründung der Jury
Der In-Ear-Kopfhörer OnePlus Bullet Wireless punktet mit seiner funktionalen, durchdachten Gestaltung und seinen guten Trageeigenschaften.

AKG N200AWireless
Wireless Earbuds
Kabelloser In-Ear-Kopfhörer

Manufacturer
Harman International,
Northridge, California, USA
In-house design
Web
www.harman.com

The AKG N200AWireless earbuds deliver clear, warm bass without overpowering, instead giving the user a comfortable listening experience. Particular value is placed on an optimum fit for athletes, reflected in the rounded housing and ergonomically shaped earhooks. In addition, the headphones are sweat- and waterproof, so that they can also be used in rainy weather. The equipment includes a quick-charge function, a microphone and a remote control.

Statement by the jury
The meticulously processed wireless earbuds inspire with their anatomic fit and with functions that are superbly tailored to athletes.

Der Kopfhörer AKG N200AWireless bietet eine klare, warme Basswiedergabe, die nicht überfordert und dem Endverbraucher ein angenehmes Hörerlebnis verschafft. Besonderer Wert wird auf eine für Sportler optimale Passform gelegt, was sich im abgerundeten Gehäuse und den ergonomisch geformten Ohrhaken widerspiegelt. Zusätzlich ist der Kopfhörer schweiß- und wasserdicht, sodass er auch bei Regen getragen werden kann. Zur weiteren Ausstattung zählen Schnellladefunktion, Mikrofon und Fernbedienung.

Begründung der Jury
Der sorgfältig verarbeitete kabellose In-Ear-Kopfhörer begeistert mit seiner anatomischen Passform und den hervorragend auf Sportler abgestimmten Funktionen.

A801
Wireless Earbuds
Kabelloser In-Ear-Kopfhörer

Manufacturer
Cannice, Shenzhen, China
In-house design
Web
www.cannice.com

With separate earbuds, the A801 offers unlimited freedom when listening to music and conducting phone calls. Bluetooth 5.0 guarantees a stable connection between the earbuds and a source player; in addition, ambient noise is filtered out to optimise call quality. Phone calls, music or information provided by the integrated Siri voice assistant is controlled or retrieved by tapping the left earbud. A single battery charge powers the earbuds for around six hours of runtime, which can be extended thanks to the charging box.

Statement by the jury
These earbuds score with their comprehensive state-of-the-art equipment and reduced, custom-tailored design allowing for inconspicuous wearing.

Mit den getrennten Ohrhörern bietet der A801 uneingeschränkte Freiheit beim Musikhören und Telefonieren. Bluetooth 5.0 garantiert eine stabile Verbindung zwischen Kopfhörer und Zuspielgerät, zudem werden Umgebungsgeräusche unterdrückt, um die Anrufqualität zu optimieren. Anrufe, Musik oder Informationen vom integrierten Sprachassistenten Siri werden durch Tippen auf den linken Ohrhörer gesteuert bzw. abgerufen. Eine Akkuladung bietet rund sechs Stunden Spielzeit, die dank der Ladebox problemlos verlängert werden kann.

Begründung der Jury
Der Kopfhörer punktet mit seiner umfassenden zeitgemäßen Ausstattung und dem passgenauen reduzierten Design, das das unauffällige Tragen erlaubt.

TRACK Air
Wireless Earbuds
Kabelloser In-Ear-Kopfhörer

Manufacturer
Libratone, Copenhagen, Denmark
Design
Swift Creatives, Aarhus, Denmark
Web
www.libratone.com
www.swiftcreatives.com

The TRACK Air wireless earbuds feature noise-isolating functionality. They deliver clear sound and also enable phone calls in excellent voice quality. The extremely lightweight earbuds fit comfortably in the ear and can thus be worn over longer periods of time. One battery charge suffices for eight hours of operating time; when the earphones are placed in the charging box, this time can be extended for another 32 hours. The earbuds are available in black, white and pink.

Statement by the jury
The TRACK Air stands out with its sophisticated equipment and feather-light design, promising carefree music enjoyment in any situation.

TRACK Air ist ein kabelloser In-Ear-Kopfhörer mit Geräuschisolierung. Er bietet einen klaren Sound und gestattet ebenso Telefongespräche in ausgezeichneter Sprachqualität. Die äußerst leichten Ohrhörer sitzen bequem im Ohr und lassen sich daher über längere Zeiträume gut tragen. Eine Akkuladung reicht für acht Stunden, werden die Ohrhörer in die Ladebox gelegt, können sie für weitere 32 Stunden aufgeladen werden. Der Kopfhörer ist in Schwarz, Weiß und Rosa erhältlich.

Begründung der Jury
TRACK Air besticht mit seiner durchdachten Ausstattung und dem federleichten Design, das unbeschwerten Musikgenuss in jeder Situation verspricht.

Tarah Pro
Wireless Earbuds
Kabelloser In-Ear-Kopfhörer

Manufacturer
Logitech, Lausanne, Switzerland
In-house design
Design
MNML, Chicago, Illinois, USA
Web
www.jaybirdsport.com

The Tarah Pro wireless earbuds were designed for endurance athletes and adventurers requiring a durable, robust and weatherproof product that also offers a high degree of wearing comfort. For this purpose, the earbuds feature smooth, easily interchangeable ear tips and rotatable in-ear components that can be worn above or below the ears. Another practical feature is the automatic standby function that is activated as soon as the magnetic earbuds connect with each other.

Statement by the jury
The functionality and equipment of the Tarah Pro are excellently tailored to the requirements of active music lovers, making it a reliable companion in any kind of weather.

Der kabellose Kopfhörer Tarah Pro wurde für Ausdauersportler und Abenteurer entwickelt, die ein langlebiges, robustes und wetterfestes Produkt benötigen, das überdies einen hohen Tragekomfort bietet. Zu diesem Zweck besitzt der Kopfhörer glatte, leicht austauschbare Ohreinsätze und drehbare In-Ear-Komponenten, die sich über oder unter den Ohren tragen lassen. Praktisch ist auch die automatische Stand-by-Funktion, die aktiviert wird, sobald die magnetischen Ohrhörer zusammengesteckt werden.

Begründung der Jury
Funktionen und Ausstattung des Tarah Pro sind hervorragend auf die Bedürfnisse von aktiven Musikliebhabern abgestimmt, dies macht ihn bei jedem Wetter zu einem zuverlässigen Begleiter.

TicPods Free 2
Wireless Earbuds
Kabelloser In-Ear-Kopfhörer

Manufacturer
Mobvoi US LLC, San Francisco, USA
In-house design
Yu Chen
Web
www.mobvoi.com

The TicPods Free 2 wireless earbuds are equipped with up-to-date technologies, such as intuitive touch control elements, in order to activate important functions by tapping the housing lightly. This enables the user to control volume, take and end phone calls, activate the voice assistant or navigate directly through music. As the earphones are equipped with a six-axis sensor, they can determine, in combination with the GPS information from the coupled smartphone, where the user is located at any time.

Statement by the jury
These lightweight earbuds convince with their well-conceived range of function. They offer high operating comfort without the need for cumbersome handling of the smartphone.

Der kabellose In-Ear-Kopfhörer TicPods Free 2 ist mit aktuellen Technologien ausgestattet, darunter intuitive Touch-Bedienelemente, um wichtige Funktionen durch einfaches Tippen auf das Gehäuse zu aktivieren. So lässt sich z. B. die Lautstärke regeln, telefonieren, der Sprachassistent anschalten oder durch die Musik navigieren. Da der Kopfhörer mit einem 6-Achsen-Sensor ausgestattet ist, kann er in Kombination mit den GPS-Informationen vom gekoppelten Smartphone erkennen, wo sich der Benutzer gerade befindet.

Begründung der Jury
Das Leichtgewicht überzeugt mit seinem durchdachten Funktionsumfang und bietet einen hohen Bedienkomfort, der das umständliche Hantieren mit dem Smartphone überflüssig macht.

TRACK Air+
Wireless Earbuds
Kabelloser In-Ear-Kopfhörer

Manufacturer
Libratone, Copenhagen, Denmark
Design
Swift Creatives, Aarhus, Denmark
Web
www.libratone.com
www.swiftcreatives.com

The TRACK Air+ wireless earbuds are equipped with four-step noise cancellation. They can be adjusted automatically and manually, enabling users to exactly determine the extent to which they wish to listen to ambient sound. The earbuds are splash-proof and sweat-resistant, making them particularly suitable for athletes. They are safely stored in a compact charging case which supplies power for up to 24 hours of runtime.

Statement by the jury
With its sophisticated noise cancellation functionality, the TRACK Air+ earbuds are ideal for athletes when it comes to working out safely.

Mit einer vierstufigen Geräuschunterdrückung ist der kabellose In-Ear-Kopfhörer TRACK Air+ ausgestattet. Sie lässt sich automatisch und manuell anpassen, damit der Anwender genau einstellen kann, welches Maß an Umgebungsgeräuschen er wahrnehmen möchte. Die Ohrhörer sind spritzwassergeschützt und schweißresistent und somit besonders für Sportler geeignet. Im kompakten Ladeetui werden die Ohrhörer sicher verstaut und gleichzeitig mit Energie für bis zu 24 Stunden Spielzeit aufgeladen.

Begründung der Jury
Mit der ausgefeilten Geräuschunterdrückung bietet der Kopfhörer TRACK Air+ gerade für Sportler eine sinnvolle Funktion, die die Sicherheit beim Training erhöht.

Ally Plus
Wireless Earbuds
Kabelloser In-Ear-Kopfhörer

Manufacturer
Cleer, Inc., San Diego, USA
In-house design
Web
www.cleer.us

The Ally Plus are robust, IPX5 splash-resistant earbuds offering up to ten hours of music playback, with an additional 20 hours in connection with the charging case. They were designed for use with voice control and are equipped with noise reduction functionality, thus enhancing communication in particularly loud environments. Phone calls can be made or received using either one or both ear tips. When the earbuds are taken off, music playback stops automatically.

Statement by the jury
The Ally Plus scores with its excellent operability and carefully considered functions. It thus proves to be a good choice for active users in any situation.

Ally Plus ist ein robuster, nach IPX5 spritzwassergeschützter Kopfhörer, der bis zu zehn Stunden Wiedergabe plus 20 weitere Stunden in Verbindung mit der Ladebox bietet. Er wurde für die Verwendung mit Sprachsteuerung konzipiert und ist mit einer Geräuschreduzierung ausgestattet, die die Kommunikation besonders in lauten Umgebungen verbessert. Anrufe werden wahlweise mit einem Ohrhörer oder mit beiden Ohrhörern entgegengenommen. Wird der Kopfhörer abgenommen, stoppt die Musik automatisch.

Begründung der Jury
Ally Plus punktet mit seiner ausgezeichneten Bedienbarkeit und den durchdachten Funktionen. Damit erweist er sich in jeder Situation als gute Wahl für aktive Benutzer.

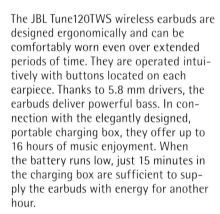

JBL Tune120TWS
Wireless Earbuds
Kabelloser In-Ear-Kopfhörer

Manufacturer
Harman International,
Northridge, California, USA
In-house design
Web
www.harman.com

The JBL Tune120TWS wireless earbuds are designed ergonomically and can be comfortably worn even over extended periods of time. They are operated intuitively with buttons located on each earpiece. Thanks to 5.8 mm drivers, the earbuds deliver powerful bass. In connection with the elegantly designed, portable charging box, they offer up to 16 hours of music enjoyment. When the battery runs low, just 15 minutes in the charging box are sufficient to supply the earbuds with energy for another hour.

Statement by the jury
The shape of the earbuds and the charging box is optimally coordinated, enabling comfortable use and a convenient user experience.

Der kabellose In-Ear-Kopfhörer JBL Tune120TWS ist ergonomisch gestaltet und kann über längere Zeit angenehm getragen werden. Bedient wird er intuitiv mit Tasten, die sich an jedem Ohrhörer befinden. Dank eines 5,8-mm-Treibers liefert der Kopfhörer kraftvolle Bässe. In Verbindung mit der elegant gestalteten, tragbaren Ladebox bietet er 16 Stunden Musikgenuss. Geht der Akku zur Neige, genügen 15 Minuten in der Ladebox, um die Ohrhörer mit Energie für eine zusätzliche Stunde zu versorgen.

Begründung der Jury
Die Form von Ohrhörern und Ladebox ist optimal aufeinander abgestimmt, was eine komfortable Anwendung und angenehme Benutzererfahrung ermöglicht.

JBL Endurance Peak
Wireless Earbuds
Kabelloser In-Ear-Kopfhörer

Manufacturer
Harman International,
Northridge, California, USA
In-house design
Web
www.harman.com

One full battery charge of the Endurance Peak suffices for 28 hours of wireless operation. Thanks to a quick-charge function, ten minutes of charging will power the earbuds for another hour. As soon as the user starts wearing the earbuds, they automatically turn on; when removed, they are turned off. With a flexible hook placed around the ears, they provide a very secure fit during a workout. In addition, they are resistant to water and sweat. The earbuds are operated by directly touching the earpiece.

Statement by the jury
With their sporty design, secure fit in the ear and long battery runtime, the Endurance Peak offers everything demanded by active music lovers today.

Eine Akkuladung des Endurance Peak reicht für 28 Stunden kabellosen Betrieb aus. Die Schnellladefunktion versorgt die Ohrhörer nach einer zehnminütigen Aufladung noch eine Stunde lang mit Strom. Werden sie angelegt, schalten sie sich automatisch ein, werden sie aus dem Ohr genommen, schalten sie sich aus. Mit ihrem flexiblen Haken, der um das Ohr gelegt wird, sitzen sie beim Sport überaus sicher. Darüber hinaus sind sie wasser- und schweißresistent. Die Bedienung erfolgt per Touch direkt am Ohrhörer.

Begründung der Jury
Mit seinem sporttauglichen Design, dem sicheren Sitz im Ohr und der langen Akkulaufzeit bietet der Endurance Peak alles, wonach aktive Musikliebhaber heute verlangen.

UA True Wireless Flash
Wireless Earbuds
Kabelloser In-Ear-Kopfhörer

Manufacturer
Harman International,
Northridge, California, USA
In-house design
Web
www.harman.com

The UA True Wireless Flash earbuds are water- and sweat-resistant and thus ideally suited to use during athletic exercise. The flexible hooks on each earcup guarantee a secure fit even during high-activity sports. A special feature is the TalkThru technology, enabling communication with the workout partner by lowering the music volume and amplifying speech signals. The headphones also allow ambient sound to pass through, so that the user is safe and sound when on the go.

Statement by the jury
With their sophisticated technical equipment and ergonomic design, the UA True Wireless Flash is optimally adapted to an active lifestyle.

Der Kopfhörer UA True Wireless Flash ist wasser- und schweißresistent und damit ideal für die Verwendung beim Sport geeignet. Die flexiblen Haken an jedem Ohrhörer garantieren den sicheren Sitz auch bei bewegungsintensivem Training. Eine Besonderheit ist die TalkThru-Technologie, die es gestattet, mit dem Trainingspartner zu kommunizieren, indem die Musik gedrosselt und die Sprache verstärkt wird. Umgebungsgeräusche werden ebenfalls durchgelassen, damit der Anwender sicherer unterwegs sein kann.

Begründung der Jury
Mit seiner ausgefeilten technischen Ausstattung und der ergonomischen Gestaltung ist der UA True Wireless Flash optimal an einen aktiven Lebensstil angepasst.

JBL Reflect Flow
Wireless Earbuds
Kabelloser In-Ear-Kopfhörer

Manufacturer
Harman International,
Northridge, California, USA
In-house design
Web
www.harman.com

The JBL Reflect Flow wireless earbuds are specially tailored to athletic activities. They do completely without cables, are water- and sweat-resistant and offer ten hours of playtime with an additional 20 hours if the charging case is used. When an athlete wants to listen to music during a workout while perceiving the immediate surroundings simultaneously, the Ambient Aware function comes to good use. The ergonomically designed ear tips with hook provide a comfortable and secure fit even during vigorous workout sessions.

Statement by the jury
The JBL Reflect Flow is tailored to an athletic lifestyle down to the last detail, from their weatherproof design all the way to the vivid colouring.

Der JBL Reflect Flow ist speziell auf sportliche Aktivitäten ausgelegt. Der Kopfhörer kommt ganz ohne Kabel aus, ist wasser- und schweißresistent und bietet zehn Stunden Spielzeit mit 20 zusätzlichen Stunden, wenn die Ladebox verwendet wird. Möchte der Sportler beim Training Musik hören und gleichzeitig die Umgebung wahrnehmen, steht die Ambient-Aware-Funktion zur Verfügung. Die ergonomisch gestalteten Ohrstöpsel mit Ohrhaken sitzen auch bei bewegungsintensiven Workouts sicher und bequem im Ohr.

Begründung der Jury
Der JBL Reflect Flow ist bis ins Detail an einen sportlichen Lebensstil angepasst, angefangen beim wetterfesten Design bis hin zur frischen Farbgebung.

WF-SP900
Wireless Headphones
Kabelloser Kopfhörer

Manufacturer
Sony Video & Sound Products Inc.,
Tokyo, Japan
Design
Sony Corporation, Creative Center
(So Morimoto), Tokyo, Japan
Web
www.sony-videosound.co.jp
www.sony.net/design

As the WF-SP900 headphones are water- and dustproof according to the IP65/IP68 standards, and even include internal memory, music can be enjoyed anywhere – be it in the water, while exercising or on the go. They do completely without cables for free, undisturbed movement and thus also eliminate cable noise, which would otherwise impair the hearing pleasure. The headphones also feature an ambient sound mode, allowing the user to listen to the immediate environment, voices and music in a well-balanced mix.

Statement by the jury
With the wireless, waterproof design and internal memory, these headphones offer the highest possible degree of independence when listening to music.

Da die Ohrhörer WF-SP900 nach IP65/IP68-Schutzart wasser- und staubdicht sind und zusätzlich über einen internen Speicher verfügen, lässt sich Musik überall genießen – sei es im Wasser, beim Sport oder unterwegs. Sie kommen vollständig ohne Kabel aus, stören also nicht bei der Bewegung und erzeugen auch keine Kabelgeräusche, die den Hörgenuss beeinträchtigen. Der Ambient-Sound-Modus gestattet es dem Benutzer, Umgebungsgeräusche, Stimmen und Musik in einer ausgewogenen Mischung zu hören.

Begründung der Jury
Mit dem kabellosen, wasserfesten Design und dem internen Speicher bietet der Kopfhörer das größtmögliche Maß an Unabhängigkeit beim Musikhören.

GLIDiC Sound Air TW-7000
Wireless Earbuds
Kabelloser In-Ear-Kopfhörer

Manufacturer
SoftBank Commerce & Service Corp.,
Tokyo, Japan
In-house design
Koshi Odaira
Web
www.cas.softbank.jp

With the GLIDiC Sound Air TW-7000 wireless earbuds, users can listen to music and take phone calls anytime and anywhere. The design of the earbuds is elegant and, with their ergonomic shape, adapts to ears of any size. The development was strongly focused on a user-friendly design. A visual accent is set by the high-gloss surface of the earbuds, making them appear almost like a piece of jewellery when worn in the ear. They are complemented by a compact charging case that fits into any bag.

Statement by the jury
These earbuds allow for carefree music enjoyment without irritating cables. In addition, they stand out with their clever, user-oriented design.

Mit den kabellosen Ohrhörern GLIDiC Sound Air TW-7000 können Benutzer jederzeit und überall Musik hören und telefonieren. Die Ohrhörer sind elegant und ergonomisch gestaltet und passen sich jeder Ohrgröße an. Darüber hinaus wurde bei der Entwicklung viel Wert auf ein benutzerfreundliches Design gelegt. Einen visuellen Akzent setzt die glänzende Oberfläche der Ohrhörer, wodurch sie im Ohr fast wie ein Schmuckstück wirken. Ergänzt werden sie durch ein kompaktes Ladeetui, das in jeder Tasche Platz findet.

Begründung der Jury
Die Ohrhörer ermöglichen einen unbeschwerten Musikgenuss ohne störende Kabel und bestechen zusätzlich mit ihrem durchdachten, anwenderorientierten Design.

CL2 Planar
Wireless Earbuds
Kabelloser In-Ear-Kopfhörer

Manufacturer
RHA Technologies,
Glasgow, United Kingdom
In-house design
Kyle Hutchison
Web
www.rha-audio.com

CL2 Planar uses a novel planar magnetic driver to produce accurate audio, available in both wired and wireless configurations. Thanks to this innovative technology, it is a pioneer in the field of closed back in-ear headphones. It was developed using high-quality materials and advanced manufacturing processes, taking inspiration from the aerospace and fine jewellery industries. The durable and aesthetically pleasing zirconium dioxide used to create the durable housings protects the intricate driver.

Statement by the jury
The CL2 Planar wireless earbuds render an exceptionally high-grade impression. This holds true for the housing with its striking design and for the technical equipment as well.

Der CL2 Planar verwendet für die Erzeugung präziser Audiosignale einen neuartigen planaren magnetischen Treiber, der in kabelgebundenen und kabellosen Konfigurationen eingesetzt werden kann. Dank dieser innovativen Technologie ist er ein Vorreiter im Bereich der geschlossenen In-Ear-Kopfhörer. Entwickelt wurde er unter Verwendung hochwertiger Materialien und fortschrittlicher Herstellungsverfahren mit Inspiration aus der Luftfahrt und Schmuckindustrie. Das robuste und ästhetisch ansprechende Zirconiumdioxid, aus dem die haltbaren Gehäuse hergestellt werden, schützt den komplexen Treiber.

Begründung der Jury
Ausgesprochen hochwertig präsentiert sich der kabellose In-Ear-Kopfhörer CL2 Planar. Dies gilt sowohl für das markant gestaltete Gehäuse als auch für die technische Ausstattung.

T3
Wireless Earbuds
Kabelloser In-Ear-Kopfhörer

Manufacturer
Shenzhen Mees Tech Co., Ltd.,
Shenzhen, China
In-house design
Ave Huang
Web
www.meestech.com

The T3 are Bluetooth earbuds that provide a stable connection with a compatible source device, thanks to their integrated antenna. When the battery is fully charged, the user can listen to music for up to seven hours. The stereo earphones are operated via buttons responding to just a slight touch. In this way, music lovers need not exert pressure on the headphones, nor are they disturbed by sounds produced by pushing a button.

Statement by the jury
The T3 Bluetooth earbuds are optimally suited to daily use. They offer all the important functions, are lightweight and simple to operate.

T3 ist ein Kopfhörer mit Bluetooth, der dank seiner integrierten Antenne eine stabile Verbindung mit einem kompatiblen Quellgerät bietet. Ist der Akku vollständig geladen, kann der Nutzer bis zu sieben Stunden lang Musik hören. Bedient wird der Stereokopfhörer über Touch-Tasten, die schon bei einer sanften Berührung reagieren. Dadurch muss der Musikfreund keinen Druck auf den Ohrhörer ausüben und wird auch nicht durch Geräusche, die beim Drücken einer Taste entstehen würden, gestört.

Begründung der Jury
Für den täglichen Einsatz ist der Bluetooth-Kopfhörer T3 bestens geeignet. Er bietet alle wichtigen Funktionen, ist leicht und lässt sich einfach bedienen.

F2
Wireless Earbuds
Kabelloser In-Ear-Kopfhörer

Manufacturer
Shenzhen Mees Tech Co., Ltd.,
Shenzhen, China
In-house design
Ave Huang
Web
www.meestech.com

The F2 wireless earbuds are equipped with Bluetooth 5.0, weigh only 4.5 grams each and are watertight. They connect automatically to a smartphone and, thanks to their patented antenna design, provide a stable connection for music enjoyment without skips or drops. The nano coating and special structure of the earphones render them watertight according to the IPX7 standard, so that they may be easily worn during exercise.

Statement by the jury
The F2 earbuds stand out with their extremely low weight. Another highlight is the good implementation of wireless connectivity, guaranteeing stable pairing.

Der mit Bluetooth 5.0 ausgestattete kabellose Kopfhörer F2 ist wasserdicht und wiegt je Ohrstöpsel nur 4,5 Gramm. Mit einem Smartphone koppelt er sich automatisch und bietet dann dank seiner patentierten Gestaltung mit Antenne eine stabile Verbindung für einen Musikgenuss ohne Aussetzer oder Sprünge. Die Nanobeschichtung und besondere Struktur der Ohrhörer machen den Kopfhörer nach IPX7-Standard wasserdicht, sodass er auch beim Sport problemlos getragen werden kann.

Begründung der Jury
Der In-Ear-Kopfhörer F2 besticht durch sein überaus geringes Gewicht. Hervorzuheben ist auch die gute Umsetzung der Wireless-Konnektivität, die ein stabiles Pairing gewährleistet.

MW07
True Wireless Earphones
Kabelloser In-Ear-Kopfhörer

Manufacturer
Master & Dynamic, New York, USA
In-house design
Web
www.masterdynamic.com

The MW07 true wireless earphones are characterised by high-grade materials assembled in an innovative construction process. With the 10 mm beryllium drivers, they deliver an extraordinary acoustic experience with warm sound. When the earbuds are taken out, proximity sensors on each unit register this, and music playback is paused. Five silicone ear tips and two fit wing sizes offer tailored comfort, thus eliminating the drumming effect experienced when walking with earphones. An elegant stainless-steel charging case also serves to accommodate the earbuds.

Der kabellose In-Ear-Kopfhörer MW07 zeichnet sich durch hochwertige Materialien aus, die in einem innovativen Konstruktionsprozess in Form gebracht wurden. Er bietet dank seiner 10-mm-Beryllium-Treiber eine außergewöhnliche Akustik mit einem warmen Klang. Wird der Kopfhörer abgenommen, registrieren dies Näherungssensoren an jedem Ohrhörer, und die Musikwiedergabe pausiert. Fünf Ohreinsätze aus Silikon und zwei passende Flügelgrößen sorgen für einen maßgeschneiderten Sitz, der den Trommeleffekt beim Gehen mit Ohrhörern eliminiert. Verstaut werden die Ohrhörer in einem eleganten Ladegehäuse aus Edelstahl.

Statement by the jury
The MW07 earbuds render an elegant and premium impression, complemented by high wearing comfort and well-conceived functions like proximity sensors.

Begründung der Jury
Elegant und hochwertig präsentiert sich der In-Ear-Kopfhörer MW07. Dazu gesellen sich ein hoher Tragekomfort und durchdachte Funktionen wie z. B. der Näherungssensor.

Nokia True Wireless Earbuds
Kabelloser In-Ear-Kopfhörer

Manufacturer
HMD, Espoo, Finland
In-house design
Chien-Hsin Huang, Chun-Kai Huang
Web
www.hmdglobal.com

The True Wireless Earbuds combine high comfort with a slim design. With a weight of just five grams and its slim charging case, the earbuds require little space in the bag and are optimally suited to mobile use. The aluminium charging case offers solid protection and serves as a rechargeable battery, capable of completely charging the earbuds three times over. It is effortlessly opened with the push-to-open mechanism. The charging status of the earbuds can be easily read on the LED indicator lights.

Statement by the jury
The combination of a multifunctional charging case with ultra-lightweight earphones is very smart. Music can be comfortably enjoyed on the go for a longer period of time.

Die True Wireless Earbuds verbinden hohen Komfort mit einem schlanken Design. Die nur fünf Gramm leichten Ohrhörer und das schmale Ladeetui benötigen wenig Platz in der Tasche und sind bestens für die Mitnahme geeignet. Das Ladeetui aus Aluminium bietet einen soliden Schutz und dient als Akku, um die Ohrhörer dreimal vollständig aufzuladen. Geöffnet wird es mühelos mit dem Push-to-open-Mechanismus. Der Ladezustand der Ohrhörer lässt sich an den LED-Leuchten leicht ablesen.

Begründung der Jury
Überaus pfiffig ist die Kombination eines multifunktionalen Ladeetuis mit ultraleichten Ohrhörern. Damit lässt sich Musik unterwegs lange und bequem genießen.

BOLT BT 700
True Wireless Earbuds
Kabelloser In-Ear-Kopfhörer

Manufacturer
Phiaton Corporation, Seoul, South Korea
In-house design
Web
www.phiaton.com

The BOLT BT 700 wireless earbuds are IPX4 sweat- and water-resistant and feature balanced armature drivers for a rich, detailed sound. The compact charging speaker case can charge the earphones up to three times for a total of 20 hours of playtime, while its quick charge feature allows for one hour of music playing from just a 15-minute charge. Touch-sensitive buttons in the earbuds allow for music and call control, and access to Siri and Google Assistant. Plus, two mics on each earbud deliver crystal-clear phone quality and audio transparency to hear one's surroundings.

Statement by the jury
The BOLT BT 700 earbuds include comprehensive equipment, deliver first-class sound and also convince with the practical charging case.

Der kabellose In-Ear-Kopfhörer BOLT BT 700 ist nach IPX4-Standard schweiß- und spritzwassergeschützt und verfügt über symmetrische Ankertreiber für einen satten, detaillierten Sound. Das kompakte Ladeetui kann die Ohrhörer bis zu dreimal aufladen, was einer Gesamtspielzeit von 20 Stunden entspricht, während die Schnellladefunktion eine Stunde Musikwiedergabe nach nur 15 Minuten Ladezeit ermöglicht. Berührungsempfindliche Tasten an den Ohrhörern gestatten die Musik- und Anrufsteuerung sowie den Zugriff auf Siri und Google Assistant. Zwei Mikrofone an jedem Ohrhörer sorgen für kristallklare Telefonqualität und Audiotransparenz, um die Umgebung zu hören.

Begründung der Jury
Der Kopfhörer BOLT BT 700 ist umfassend ausgestattet, liefert einen erstklassigen Sound und überzeugt ebenfalls durch die praktische Ladebox.

concept active
Turntable
Schallplattenspieler

Manufacturer
clearaudio electronic GmbH,
Erlangen, Germany

In-house design
Patrick Suchy

Web
www.clearaudio.de

reddot award 2019
best of the best

Symbiotic integration

For many music lovers, listening to vinyl records is still a listening experience unrivalled by any later technology. The concept active turntable presents itself as a fully featured, all-in-one system. Following the principle of "ready to play", this turntable integrates all technical elements needed for playback and listening. The integrated phono preamp and additional headphone output allow analogue playback and volume control directly on the turntable without having to add additional equipment. In addition to the headphone output, the turntable also features an RCA socket at the rear of the deck for plugging the turntable into a separate amplifier, as is otherwise standard, in order to listen to the music via external loudspeakers. The integrated preamp can also be switched off completely in order to send the signal directly to an external phono preamplifier. The also integrated headphone amplifier with excellent audio quality is suitable for all high-quality, dynamic headphones as well as active speakers. The concept active is available with either the frictionless, magnetic bearing concept tonearm or the direct-wired Satisfy Kardan Aluminium tonearm. This is rounded off by the option of a high-quality moving magnet or moving coil cartridge. The concept active is fully factory-set and ready to play on delivery, with all key parameters from tracking force to anti-skating being fine-tuned in the manufacturing process.

Symbiotisch integriert

Für viele Musikliebhaber ist das Hören von Musik mit dem Plattenspieler nach wie vor ein unvergleichliches Hörerlebnis. Der concept active wird dem als All-in-one-System in hohem Maße gerecht. Dieser Plattenspieler vereint im Sinne eines „ready to play"-Konzepts alle technischen Komponenten für das Abspielen und das Hören. Der integrierte Phonovorverstärker mit zusätzlichem Kopfhörerausgang ermöglicht die analoge Musikwiedergabe und Lautstärkeregulierung direkt am Laufwerk ohne weiteres benötigtes elektronisches Equipment. Anstelle des Kopfhörerausgangs können auch die Cinchbuchsen auf der Rückseite des Laufwerks verwendet werden, um wie gewohnt über einen separaten Verstärker und Lautsprecher Musik zu hören. Der integrierte Vorverstärker ist zudem komplett abschaltbar, um das Signal auch direkt an einen externen Phonovorverstärker übermitteln zu können. Der ebenfalls integrierte, in seiner Tonqualität exzellente Kopfhörerverstärker ist für alle hochwertigen, dynamischen Kopfhörer und Aktiv-Lautsprecher geeignet. Erhältlich ist der concept active entweder mit dem innovativen, reibungsfreien magnetgelagerten concept-Tonarm oder dem kardanisch gelagerten Satisfy Kardan Aluminium-Tonarm. Abgerundet wird dies wahlweise durch einen hochwertigen Moving-Magnet- oder Moving-Coil-Tonabnehmer. Der concept active ist werksseitig komplett eingestellt und spielbereit. Die Auflagekraft des Tonabnehmers und das Antiskating sind ebenso bereits einjustiert.

Statement by the jury

The fascinating purism of the concept active turntable is characterised by the consistent use of a smooth, rounded stylistic idiom. In a successful balance between simplicity and complexity, its design integrates all necessary elements for sophisticated music listening experiences. Thus, this innovative system embodies a beautiful device of premium-quality analogue technology in an otherwise digital age.

Begründung der Jury

Der faszinierende Purismus des Schallplattenspielers concept active ist geprägt durch den konsequenten Einsatz einer weichen, runden Formensprache. In einer gelungenen Balance zwischen Einfachheit und Komplexität integriert seine Gestaltung alle notwendigen Elemente für den gehobenen Hörgenuss. Das innovative System verkörpert so ein schönes Stück analoger Technik auf höchstem Niveau im digitalen Zeitalter.

Designer portrait
See page 64
Siehe Seite 64

Amp
Amplifier
Verstärker

Manufacturer
Sonos, Santa Barbara, USA
In-house design
Web
www.sonos.com

The new Sonos Amp is a versatile high-performance amplifier that supplies wired speakers with sound from virtually any source. It supports Apple AirPlay 2 as well as more than 70 streaming services and includes an HDMI ARC connector for the television. The amplifier fits into standard AV racks used by retailers. Via the integrated HDMI and line-in connectors, it is easy to connect TVs, turntables, CD changers and other audio components to the amplifier and thus to integrate them into the Sonos system.

Der neue Sonos Amp ist ein leistungsstarker und vielseitig einsetzbarer Verstärker, der kabelgebundene Lautsprecher mit Sound aus nahezu jeder Quelle versorgt. Er unterstützt Apple AirPlay 2 sowie mehr als 70 Streamingdienste und verfügt über einen HDMI-ARC-Anschluss für den Fernseher. Der Verstärker passt in Standard-AV-Racks, die von Fachhändlern verwendet werden. Über die integrierten HDMI- und Line-In-Anschlüsse können Fernseher, Plattenspieler, CD-Wechsler und andere Audiokomponenten einfach mit dem Verstärker verbunden und in das Sonos-System eingebunden werden.

Statement by the jury
With its functional diversity, this amplifier convinces all along the line. A highlight is its comprehensive connectivity enabling the easy networking of multimedia devices.

Begründung der Jury
Mit seiner Funktionsvielfalt weiß der Verstärker Amp auf ganzer Linie zu überzeugen. Hervorzuheben ist seine umfassende Konnektivität, die die einfache Vernetzung von Multimediageräten ermöglicht.

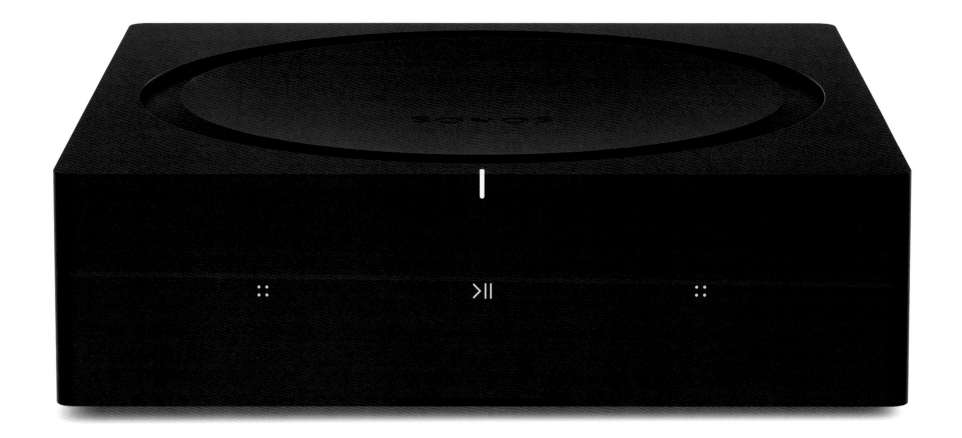

Roku Touch
Remote Control
Fernbedienung

Manufacturer
Roku, Los Gatos, California, USA
Design
Bould Design, San Mateo, California, USA
Web
www.roku.com
www.bould.com

The Touch tabletop remote is an accessory for the Roku TV Wireless Speakers. The button layout is self-explanatory and optimised for intuitive input. This is combined with a sculpted yet minimalist design that finds expression in the characteristic Roku "squircular" shape. The keypad of the remote, formed in silicone, has a pleasing silky feel and the buttons provide a gratifying haptic experience.

Statement by the jury
The Touch convinces with its congenial appearance and clearly arranged operating panel. This facilitates access to the product considerably.

Die Touch-Tischfernbedienung ist ein Zubehör für die kabellosen Roku-TV-Lautsprecher. Das Tastenlayout ist selbsterklärend und für eine intuitive Eingabe optimiert. Dies wird kombiniert mit einem skulpturalen, aber minimalistischen Design, das sich in der charakteristischen Roku-Form „Squircular" ausdrückt. Die aus Silikon geformte Tastatur der Fernbedienung fühlt sich angenehm seidig an und die Tasten sorgen für ein erfreuliches haptisches Erlebnis.

Begründung der Jury
Touch überzeugt mit seiner freundlichen Anmutung und dem übersichtlichen Bedienpanel. Dies erleichtert den Zugang zum Produkt erheblich.

Whooshi
Hi-Fi Bluetooth Amplifier
Hi-Fi-Bluetooth-Verstärker

Manufacturer
Infomir SA, Geneva, Switzerland
In-house design
Ivan Shmatko
Web
www.whooshi.me

The Whooshi hi-fi amplifier equips wired headphones with Bluetooth, thus enabling wireless high-quality transmission from a smartphone, tablet or laptop. Alternatively, it can be used as an amplifier for a laptop audio system. Thanks to a 300 mAh rechargeable battery, it enables more than eight hours of operating time. The slim device with its recessed grips rests comfortably in the hand and, with a practical clip, is easily attached to clothing.

Statement by the jury
The organic form of this Bluetooth amplifier is highly visually appealing and also facilitates comfortable handling on the go.

Der Hi-Fi-Verstärker Whooshi stattet einen kabelgebundenen Kopfhörer mit Bluetooth aus und ermöglicht damit die kabellose Übertragung von Musik in hoher Qualität von jedem Smartphone, Tablet oder Laptop. Alternativ kann er auch als Verstärker am Laptop eingesetzt werden. Dank seines 300-mAh-Akkus erlaubt er eine Wiedergabe von mehr als acht Stunden. Das schlanke Gerät liegt mit seinen Griffmulden gut in der Hand und lässt sich mit einem praktischen Clip auch an der Kleidung befestigen.

Begründung der Jury
Die organische Form des Bluetooth-Verstärkers ist visuell äußert ansprechend und gestattet besonders unterwegs eine angenehme Handhabung.

nuPro X
Active Hi-Fi Speakers
Hi-Fi-Aktivlautsprecher

Manufacturer
Nubert electronic GmbH,
Schwäbisch Gmünd, Germany
In-house design
Design
whiteID GmbH & Co. KG (Andreas Hess),
Schorndorf, Germany
Web
www.nubert.de
www.white-id.com

The nuPro X series consists of speakers with an elegant design, outstanding sound quality and intuitive operability. With a flawless matte-lacquered surface and the characteristic corner radii of the housing, they are an unobtrusive yet accentuated eye-catcher that harmoniously blends with modern living and working environments. The series includes the two compact models nuPro X-3000 and nuPro X-4000 for desktop or shelf use, as well as the nuPro X-6000 floor-standing speaker delivering up to 800 watts and the premium model nuPro X-8000 with a subwoofer and peak power of up to 1,120 watts.

Die Serie nuPro X umfasst elegant gestaltete Lautsprecher mit einer ausgezeichneten Klangqualität und intuitiver Bedienbarkeit. Mit ihrer makellosen Schleiflack-Oberfläche und den charakteristischen Eckradien des Korpus sind sie ein unaufdringlicher und dennoch akzentuierter Blickfang, der sich in moderne Wohn- und Arbeitsumgebungen integriert. Zur Serie gehören die beiden kompakten Modelle nuPro X-3000 und nuPro X-4000, die sich für den Einsatz am Schreibtisch oder in einem Regal empfehlen. Hinzu kommen die Standbox nuPro X-6000 mit einer Leistung von bis zu 800 Watt sowie das Topmodell nuPro X-8000 mit Subwoofer und einer Leistung von bis zu 1.120 Watt.

Statement by the jury
The speaker series impresses with its unmistakable design that catches the eye, while still harmonising very well with any interior.

Begründung der Jury
Die Lautsprecherserie beeindruckt durch ihre unverwechselbare Gestaltung, die einerseits die Blicke auf sich zieht, andererseits aber auch hervorragend mit jedem Interieur harmoniert.

JBL Tower X
Marine Speakers
Bootslautsprecher

Manufacturer
Harman International,
Northridge, California, USA
In-house design
Amin Einakian
Web
www.harman.com

The JBL Tower X is a speaker system in maritime design optimised for use on boats. The speakers feature 360-degree rotational brackets and RGB lighting. Woofers and tweeters are optimised for outstanding bass reproduction and real-istic sound. They are slightly angled in the housing, thus projecting the sound over the stern of the boat. This reduces smearing effects due to water reflections, enabling the boater to enjoy excellent sound.

Statement by the jury
The marine speakers impress with their well-conceived technical equipment, providing optimum sound in a demanding environment.

Der JBL Tower X ist ein für den Einsatz auf Booten optimiertes Lautsprechersystem in maritimem Design. Es verfügt über 360-Grad-Drehhalterungen und RGB-Beleuchtung. Tiefton- und Hochtonlautsprecher sind für eine hervorragende Basswiedergabe und einen realistischen Klang optimiert. Sie sind im Gehäuse leicht geneigt, was den Schall über das Heck des Bootes lenkt, wodurch Verschmierungseffekte aufgrund von Wasserreflexionen verringert werden und der Bootsfahrer einen exzellenten Klang genießen kann.

Begründung der Jury
Die Bootslautsprecher beeindrucken mit ihrer durchdachten technischen Ausstattung, die in einem anspruchsvollen Umfeld für einen optimalen Klang sorgt.

Revel PerformaBe Series
Speaker Series
Lautsprecher-Serie

Manufacturer
Harman International,
Northridge, California, USA
In-house design
Jason Gokavi
Web
www.harman.com

The Revel PerformaBe series was designed to redefine performance expectations. The core component of these models is a 1" beryllium tweeter driven by massive 85 mm dual ceramic magnets. This results in higher efficiency, an enhanced dynamic range, reduced distortion and a better performance than achieved through aluminium or titanium tweeters. The low-frequency and mid-range transducers made of ceramics also offer sound rich in details for an outstanding audio performance across the entire frequency range.

Statement by the jury
Thanks to sophisticated, innovative technology and premium components, the Revel PerformaBe speaker series is a highlight for demanding music lovers.

Die Serie Revel PerformaBe wurde entwickelt, um die Erwartungen an Leistung neu zu definieren. Das Herzstück der Modelle ist ein 1"-Beryllium-Hochtöner, der von massiven 85-mm-Doppelkeramikmagneten angetrieben wird. Er liefert eine höhere Effizienz, einen verbesserten Dynamikbereich, eine geringere Verzerrung und eine bessere Leistung als Hochtöner aus Aluminium oder Titan. Die Tief- und Mitteltöner aus Keramik bieten ebenfalls einen detailreichen Klang, sodass über alle Bereiche Sound in hervorragender Qualität zu hören ist.

Begründung der Jury
Dank ausgefeilter, innovativer Technik und hochwertiger Komponenten ist die Lautsprecherserie Revel PerformaBe ein Highlight für anspruchsvolle Musikliebhaber.

Infinity Kappa Marine
Marine Speakers
Bootslautsprecher

Manufacturer
Harman International,
Northridge, California, USA
In-house design
Tomas Deluna
Web
www.harman.com

The Infinity Kappa Marine is equipped with woofer, mid-range and tweeter motors that are sealed and splashproof. The unconventionally shaped construction made of polypropylene and polycarbonate is resistant to UV rays and salt spray, rendering the speakers ideal for a maritime environment. Another highlight is the RGB LED lighting using seven colours and shining an elegant light on the surrounding environment.

Statement by the jury
The Infinity Kappa Marine inspires with its unmistakeable shape reminiscent of a boat steering wheel, thus perfectly harmonising with ship furnishings.

Im Infinity Kappa Marine befinden sich je ein versiegelter, spritzwassergeschützter Woofer, Mitteltöner und Hochtönermotoren. Die eigenwillig geformte Konstruktion aus Polypropylen und Polycarbonat ist außerdem UV- und salzwasserbeständig, wodurch sich der Lautsprecher ideal für eine maritime Umgebung eignet. Erwähnenswert ist zudem die RGB-LED-Beleuchtung, die sieben Farben einsetzt und ein elegantes Licht auf die Umgebung wirft.

Begründung der Jury
Infinity Kappa Marine begeistert mit seiner eigenständigen Formgebung, die an ein Steuerrad erinnert und dadurch ausgezeichnet zu einer Schiffsmöblierung passt.

Studioart A100
Room Speaker
Lautsprecher

Manufacturer
Revox Deutschland GmbH,
Villingen-Schwenningen, Germany
In-house design
Web
www.studioart-revox.com

The Studioart A100 Room Speaker offers excellent sound quality and is capable of processing high-resolution audio files of up to 25 bits and 192 kHz. The compact active speaker with integrated bass reflex technology has a height of merely 22.2 cm, thus requiring hardly any space. It is operated either per app or via the touchscreen that also offers access to the music source files. Thanks to wireless connection and Wi-Fi connectivity, it can be wirelessly linked to other Studioart speakers. A rechargeable battery is integrated for mobile use.

Statement by the jury
The slim, plain design of the speaker blends optimally with any modern interior and has the advantage of emanating room-filling sound.

Der Studioart A100 Room Speaker bietet eine ausgezeichnete Klangqualität und verarbeitet hochauflösende Audiodateien bis zu 25 Bit und 192 kHz. Der kompakte Aktivlautsprecher mit integrierter Bass-reflextechnologie ist lediglich 22,2 cm groß und benötigt daher nur wenig Platz. Bedient wird er wahlweise per App oder über den Touchscreen, der ebenfalls den Zugang zu den Musikquellen bietet. Dank Funk und Wi-Fi kann er mit anderen Studioart-Lautsprechern verbunden werden. Für den mobilen Einsatz ist ein Akku integriert.

Begründung der Jury
Die schlanke, schlichte Gestalt des Lautsprechers passt hervorragend in ein modernes Interieur und hat den Vorteil, dass der Sound raumfüllend abgestrahlt wird.

LG AJ7
Audio System

Manufacturer
LG Electronics Inc., Seoul, South Korea
In-house design
Sangho Lee, Sooyoung Park
Web
www.lg.com

The AJ7 audio system blends into a home interior just like a piece of furniture. The basic idea of the design concept is "honesty and simplicity", manifesting in straight lines and plain elements. This approach results in a piece of furniture reminiscent of a small cabinet or side table. The homely appearance is underscored by the use of high-grade walnut wood, by largely dispensing with artificial materials and by atmospheric lighting at the bottom.

Statement by the jury
This audio system stands out with its coherent design, skilfully combining the two worlds of furniture and consumer electronics.

Das Audio-System AJ7 fügt sich wie ein Möbelstück in die Inneneinrichtung ein. Der Grundgedanke des Designkonzepts ist „Ehrlichkeit und Einfachheit", was sich in geraden Linien und einfachen Elementen manifestiert, die sich zu einem Möbelstück formieren, das an einen kleinen Schrank oder Beistelltisch erinnert. Unterstrichen wird die wohnliche Anmutung durch die Verwendung von hochwertigem Walnussholz, den weitgehenden Verzicht auf künstliche Materialien und eine stimmungsvolle Beleuchtung am unteren Rand.

Begründung der Jury
Das Audio-System besticht durch seine schlüssige Gestaltung, die die beiden Welten Möbel und Unterhaltungselektronik gekonnt miteinander verbindet.

MEDION LIFE P64934
Micro Audio System

Manufacturer
Medion AG, Essen, Germany
In-house design
Medion Design Team
Web
www.medion.com

The Medion Life P64934 micro audio system is characterised by a vertical cuboid design which places all control functions at the top in an ergonomically sensible way. A clear design language visualises the functions and operating elements. In addition, with the vertical alignment, the display is positioned at the centre of the speaker front for a clear view. With its built-in DAB+ technology, the audio system is capable of receiving radio stations in brilliant sound quality. The USB port allows for the playing of one's own music through a USB flash drive. This clear structure of the functional components presents the Medion ID Style.

Statement by the jury
The coherent and distinct design highlights the relevant functions of the audio system, making its operation child's play.

Das Micro-Audiosystem Medion Life P64934 ist durch einen vertikalen, quaderförmigen Aufbau gekennzeichnet, bei dem alle Steuerungsfunktionen ergonomisch sinnvoll auf der Oberseite liegen. Dabei visualisiert eine klare Formensprache die Funktionen und Bedienelemente. Zudem positioniert sich das Display in der vertikalen Ausrichtung gut sichtbar in der Mitte der Lautsprecherfront. Das Audiosystem empfängt Radiosender dank DAB+-Technologie in brillanter Klangqualität. Zusätzlich ermöglicht ein USB-Eingang das Einspielen von persönlicher Musik per USB-Stick. Diese klare Gliederung der Funktionsbestandteile präsentiert den Medion ID-Style.

Begründung der Jury
Die schlüssige und definierte Gestaltung hebt die relevanten Funktionen des Audiosystems hervor und macht die Bedienung zum Kinderspiel.

SC-C50
Wireless Speaker System
Kabelloses Lautsprechersystem

Manufacturer
Panasonic Corporation, Kyoto, Japan
In-house design
Tomohiro Yasuda
Web
www.panasonic.com
www.panasonic.net/design

The SC-C50 wireless speaker system is particularly suitable for music lovers who use streaming services. A special feature of the system is that the sound processing is adapted to the place where the speaker system is set up. There are three preset modes: free-standing, close to a wall and near a corner. The speaker is capable of automatically calibrating additional set-up variants for optimum sound generation. The case made of aluminium and reinforced resin has a special shape which minimises unwanted resonance.

Statement by the jury
With its sculptural design, the speaker system appears like a piece of art and conveys its strong sound properties in an impressive way.

Besonders für Musikliebhaber, die Streaming-Dienste nutzen, ist der kabellose Lautsprecher SC-C50 geeignet. Seine Besonderheit ist, dass er die Schallverarbeitung an den Ort anpasst, an dem er aufgestellt wird. Drei Modi sind voreingestellt: frei, wandnah und ecknah. Weitere Varianten misst der Lautsprecher automatisch ein, um den optimalen Klang zu generieren. Das Gehäuse aus Aluminium und verstärktem Harz ist speziell geformt, wodurch Resonanzen minimiert werden.

Begründung der Jury
Mit seiner skulpturalen Formgebung erscheint das Lautsprechersystem wie ein Kunstwerk und vermittelt eindrucksvoll seine guten Klangeigenschaften.

LG SL9
Soundbar

Manufacturer
LG Electronics Inc., Seoul, South Korea
In-house design
Junki Kim, Sungyong Park
Web
www.lg.com

With its plain, straight-line design, the SL9 soundbar harmonises well with any state-of-the-art TV, preferably 55" devices. It is optimised for placement on a piece of TV furniture or for wall mounting. The sound in Dolby Atmos quality is emitted from the top surface, and the cables are arranged in such a way that they don't create disturbances with any of the two set-up versions. When the television is not in use, the buttons of the soundbar are concealed. As soon as the TV is turned on, the buttons become visible again.

Statement by the jury
The SL9 soundbar excites with its minimalist design and refined details such as the clever cable management and the concealable operating buttons.

Mit ihrem schnörkellosen, geradlinigen Design passt die Soundbar SL9 gut zu jedem aktuellen Fernseher, vorzugsweise zu 55"-Geräten. Sie ist optimiert für die Platzierung auf einem TV-Möbel oder die Montage an der Wand. Dafür wird der Klang in Dolby-Atmos-Qualität von der Oberseite abgestrahlt und auch die Kabel sind so angeordnet, dass sie bei beiden Aufbauvarianten nicht stören. Wird der Fernseher nicht verwendet, werden die Tasten der Soundbar ausgeblendet. Sobald er eingeschaltet wird, sind die Tasten wieder beleuchtet.

Begründung der Jury
Die Soundbar SL9 begeistert mit ihrer minimalistischen Formgebung und raffinierten Details wie dem guten Kabelmanagement und den ausblendbaren Bedientasten.

SC-HTB200
Soundbar

Manufacturer
Panasonic Corporation, Kyoto, Japan
In-house design
Gakuto Takahashi
Web
www.panasonic.com
www.panasonic.net/design

The SC-HTB200 soundbar shows a compact, elegant design, enabling it to be placed virtually anywhere, such as under the television or on a narrow piece of TV furniture. Its trapezoidal shape reduces unwanted resonance and enhances the rigidity of the enclosure. This makes the soundbar capable of producing powerful, dynamic sound despite its compact dimensions. The surfaces are characterised by fabrics and textures in pursuit of a design that, on the one hand, harmonises with living room furnishings and, on the other, integrates well with modern TVs.

Statement by the jury
The soundbar stands out with its flowing language of form, prudentially designed surfaces and comprehensive technical equipment.

Die Soundbar SC-HTB200 zeigt eine kompakte, elegante Formgebung, dank derer sie sich überall aufstellen lässt, sei es unter dem Fernseher oder auf einem schmalen TV-Möbel. Ihre trapezförmige Gestalt reduziert unerwünschte Resonanzen und verbessert die Steifigkeit des Gehäuses. Dies führt dazu, dass die Soundbar trotz ihrer kompakten Maße einen kraftvollen, dynamischen Sound produziert. Die Oberflächen sind von Stoffen und Texturen geprägt, um ein Design anzustreben, das einerseits mit der Möblierung im Wohnraum harmoniert und andererseits gut zu modernen Fernsehgeräten passt.

Begründung der Jury
Die Soundbar gefällt mit ihrer fließenden Formensprache, den überlegt gestalteten Oberflächen und einer umfassenden technischen Ausstattung.

DMP-Z1
Digital Music Player

Manufacturer
Sony Video & Sound Products Inc.,
Tokyo, Japan
Design
Sony Corporation, Creative Center
(Takashi Sogabe), Tokyo, Japan
Web
www.sony-videosound.co.jp
www.sony.net/design

The DMP-Z1, a digital music player with a built-in analogue amplifier, reduces signal deterioration and noise caused by cable connections. It is operated with direct current, which is stable and relatively silent. The chassis of the player is fashioned from aluminium, which not only provides high rigidity but also minimises unnecessary resonance and distortion. The large, analogue volume controls with gold plating are another significant feature, underscoring the premium appearance of the player.

Statement by the jury
This digital music player convinces with technical equipment that is carefully considered down to the last detail. It promises sound quality at the highest level.

Der DMP-Z1, ein digitaler Musikplayer mit eingebautem Analogverstärker, reduziert die Signalverschlechterung und das Rauschen bei Kabelverbindungen und arbeitet darüber hinaus mit Gleichstrom, der stabil und geräuscharm ist. Das Gehäuse des Players besteht aus Aluminium, das nicht nur eine hohe Steifigkeit bietet, sondern auch unnötige Resonanzen und Verzerrungen minimiert. Wichtiges Merkmal sind zudem große, analoge Lautstärkeregler mit Goldbeschichtung, die die wertige Anmutung unterstreichen.

Begründung der Jury
Der digitale Musikplayer überzeugt durch seine durchdachte technische Ausstattung bis ins Detail. Sie verspricht Klangqualität auf höchstem Niveau.

R-100
Sound Amplifier
Tonverstärker

Manufacturer
EM-Tech Co., Ltd.,
Anyang, South Korea
In-house design
Sunghyun Heo
Web
www.em-tech.co.kr

The R-100 sound amplifier is designed for people with hearing impairment. It transmits audio signals from a source connected via Bluetooth, for instance from headsets or speakers, so that the user can listen to incoming sound without irritating ambient noise. The compact device is attached to clothing with a clip so that the sound is emitted in close proximity to the user. The advantages of the device play out in particular in the context of conferences and lectures.

Statement by the jury
The R-100 sound amplifier presents itself as a useful tool. At the same time, it impresses with its inconspicuous design and practical fastening clip.

Der Tonverstärker R-100 ist für Menschen mit Hörbeeinträchtigung konzipiert. Er überträgt Audiosignale, die von einer per Bluetooth verbundenen Quelle eingespielt werden, z. B. von Headsets oder Lautsprechern, damit der Anwender sie ohne störende Umgebungsgeräusche hören kann. Das kompakte Gerät wird mit einem Clip an der Kleidung befestigt, sodass der Ton in unmittelbarer Nähe des Anwenders ausgegeben wird. Besonders im Rahmen von Konferenzen und Vorträgen spielt das Gerät seine Vorteile aus.

Begründung der Jury
Als nützliches Hilfsmittel präsentiert sich der Tonverstärker R-100. Zugleich punktet er mit seinem unauffälligen Design und dem praktischen Befestigungsclip.

RS201
Hi-Fi Media Player

Manufacturer
CITECH, ROSE,
Seoul, South Korea
In-house design
Mi-Jung Jung, Yu-Jin Ahn
Web
www.hifirose.com

A particular feature of the RS201 hi-fi media player is its 8.8" touch display, which may be operated intuitively so that users can easily select different sound sources and comfortably access the network server as well. The player supports almost all methods of playback, such as the DLNA-based wired and wireless network system, Bluetooth, AirPlay, DIAL, podcast and Internet radio. The player includes numerous interface ports, including AUX, USB and optical input.

Statement by the jury
This media player captivates with its self-explanatory graphical user interface, which makes the entire diversity of multimedia content child's play.

Besonderes Merkmal des Hi-Fi-Media-Players RS201 ist sein 8,8"-Touch-Display, das sich intuitiv bedienen lässt, sodass Benutzer unterschiedliche Tonquellen leicht anwählen und auch auf den Netzwerkserver bequem zugreifen können. Der Player unterstützt fast alle Wiedergabemethoden, wie das DLNA-basierte kabelgebundene und kabellose Netzwerksystem, Bluetooth, AirPlay, DIAL, Podcast und Internetradio. Auch zahlreiche Schnittstellen sind mit an Bord, darunter AUX, USB und ein optischer Eingang.

Begründung der Jury
Der Media-Player besticht durch seine selbsterklärende grafische Benutzeroberfläche, dank derer die ganze Vielfalt multimedialer Inhalte kinderleicht genutzt werden kann.

A&norma SR15
Portable Audio Player
Tragbarer Audioplayer

Manufacturer
Iriver, Seoul, South Korea
In-house design
Baekjin Seong, Jisun Kim
Design
Metal Sound Design (Kukil Yu),
Seoul, South Korea
Web
www.iriver.com
www.ilmsd.com

The design of the A&norma SR15 portable audio player is characterised by two rectangles at an oblique angle, symbolising the freedom of music and the sound vibrations floating in the air. In addition, this housing shape enables the user to hold the device without needing to turn the wrist, while still making it possible to view the display as a whole. Moreover, the lateral volume wheel allows for one-hand operation.

Statement by the jury
The striking design is an unmistakable feature of the A&norma SR15 audio player, which also contributes to comfortable handling.

Die Formgebung des tragbaren Audioplayers A&norma SR15 ist von zwei sich schräg überlagernden Rechtecken geprägt, die die Freiheit der Musik und in der Luft schwebende Schwingungen symbolisieren. Darüber hinaus trägt diese Gehäuseform dazu bei, dass der Benutzer das Gerät halten kann, ohne das Handgelenk zu verdrehen, und das Display dennoch komplett frei bleibt. Zusätzlich gestattet das Laustärkerädchen am Rand die Bedienung mit einer Hand.

Begründung der Jury
Das markante Design macht den Audioplayer A&norma SR15 unverwechselbar und trägt zudem dazu bei, dass er sich bequem handhaben lässt.

A&ultima SP1000M
Portable Audio Player
Tragbarer Audioplayer

Manufacturer
Iriver, Seoul, South Korea
In-house design
Baekjin Seong, Jisun Kim
Design
Metal Sound Design (Kukil Yu),
Seoul, South Korea
Web
www.iriver.com
www.ilmsd.com

The A&ultima SP1000M is a hi-fi audio player in mini format. Its lightweight aluminium body displays a high degree of rigidity. The asymmetrical design, with bevelled lateral parts, produces ever-changing reflections when exposed to light, creating the impression of sound bouncing off. The crown wheel lends the device an analogue touch and enables direct and immediate control of the music playback.

Statement by the jury
Striking design, control items with retro charm and striking body colouring foster a sensuous experience when operating this high-grade audio player.

Beim A&ultima SP1000M handelt es sich um einen Hi-Fi-Audioplayer im Miniformat. Das Gehäuse besteht aus Aluminium, das leicht ist und eine gute Steifigkeit bietet. Seine asymmetrische Gestaltung mit den gefasten Gehäuseseiten reflektiert das Licht immer wieder neu, wodurch der Eindruck eines abprallenden Tons vermittelt wird. Das Kronenrad verleiht dem sorgfältig verarbeiteten Gerät einen analogen Touch und gestattet die unmittelbare Steuerung der Musikwiedergabe.

Begründung der Jury
Die markante Formgebung, die Steuerung mit Retrocharme und die aparte Gehäusefarbe machen die Bedienung des hochwertigen Audioplayers zu einem sinnlichen Erlebnis.

Cosmetic tools	Glätteisen
Hair straighteners	Haartrockner
Hairdryers	Hygieneartikel
Hygiene articles	Kosmetiktools
Manicure and pedicure devices	Maniküre- und Pediküregeräte
Massage devices	Massagegeräte
Oral hygiene devices	Mund- und Zahnpflege
Shaving and hair removal devices	Rasierer und Haarentfernung
Ultrasonic devices	Ultraschallgeräte

Spas and personal care
Wellness und Personal Care

i-SHAPER ER-GK80
Body Trimmer

Manufacturer
Panasonic Corporation,
Kyoto, Japan

In-house design
Pinakesh De, Mikiyasu Ishikura

Web
www.panasonic.com
www.panasonic.net/design

reddot award 2019
best of the best

Attractive partner

In the ever-refining understanding of beauty and aesthetics, the treatment of body hair too has come to play an ever more important role. The ER-GK80 body trimmer has been optimised for hair removal in various areas of the male body. This beard and hair trimmer exudes an expressive elegance based on its I-shaped design that lends it a distinctive and iconic appearance. Its functional construction with vertically arranged blades offers high cutting performance and safety. Thus, the device adapts very well to the body contours and with gentle pressure slides gently over the skin for improved trimming results even in sensitive skin areas. To enhance safety and protect against cuts, the tips of the blades have been rounded. The ER-GK80 is perfectly balanced and rests ergonomically in the hands. Its user comfort is further enhanced through the use of haptically pleasing materials. Another important aspect is that the unit is fully waterproof and can therefore be easily and safely used in the shower. Since the handle is made of a non-slip rubber, it rests safely in the hand even when wet. In addition, the device comes with an outstandingly convenient and self-explanatory attachment that serves to set the hair length simply by turning a dial. The device is thus suitable for a wide variety of users and their individual needs.

Attraktiver Partner

Bei dem sich stetig wandelnden Verständnis von Ästhetik und Schönheit spielt auch der Umgang mit der Körperbehaarung eine immer wichtigere Rolle. Der Body-Trimmer ER-GK80 wurde für die Haarentfernung an den verschiedenen Bereichen des männlichen Körpers optimiert. Dieser Bart- und Haarschneider zeigt eine ausdrucksvolle Eleganz, wobei ein I-förmiges Design ihm eine ikonische Erscheinung verleiht. Er bietet eine hohe Leistung und Sicherheit durch die funktionale Gestaltung mit vertikal angeordneten Klingen. Das Gerät kann sich dadurch sehr gut anpassen und gleitet mit sanftem Druck und verbesserter Schneidfähigkeit auch über empfindliche Stellen der Haut. Um die Sicherheit vor Schnittverletzungen zu erhöhen, wurden die Spitzen der Klingen abgerundet geformt. Der ER-GK80 liegt dabei perfekt austariert und sehr ergonomisch in der Hand des Nutzers. Der Einsatz haptisch angenehmer Materialien erhöht den Komfort. Ein wichtiger Aspekt ist zudem, dass das Gerät vollständig wasserdicht ist und deshalb problemlos unter der Dusche verwendet werden kann. Da der Griff aus einem rutschfesten Gummi besteht, liegt er auch im nassen Zustand sicher in der Hand. Ausgesprochen komfortabel ist außerdem ein funktionaler Aufsatz, der selbsterklärend die Wahl der Haarlänge durch einfaches Drehen eines Einstellrads ermöglicht. Das Gerät eignet sich so für vielfältige Bedürfnisse und unterschiedlichste Nutzer.

Statement by the jury

With its I-shaped design, the ER-GK80 body trimmer looks highly appealing, almost graceful. It is suitable for all body areas thanks to the innovative vertical arrangement of the blades, delivering outstandingly precise trimming results. The distinctive quality of this beard and hair trimmer is also reflected in the device's sophisticated ergonomics. Resting very well in the hand, the non-slip rubber handle makes it safe and comfortable to use even under the shower.

Begründung der Jury

Mit seinem I-förmigen Design wirkt der Body-Trimmer ER-GK80 sehr ansprechend und grazil. Durch die innovative vertikale Anordnung der Klingen werden alle Körperbereiche erfasst und äußerst präzise Schneidergebnisse erzielt. Die ausgesuchte Qualität dieses Bart- und Haarschneiders zeigt sich darüber hinaus in seiner durchdachten Ergonomie. Er liegt sehr gut in der Hand und lässt sich mit seinem gummierten Griff auch unter der Dusche sicher und bequem benutzen.

Designer portrait
See page 66
Siehe Seite 66

i-SHAPER
Beard Trimmer
Bartschneider

Manufacturer
Panasonic Corporation, Kyoto, Japan
In-house design
Pinakesh De, Mikiyasu Ishikura
Web
www.panasonic.com
www.panasonic.net/design

The design of the i-SHAPER rests on a classic razor and is suitable for different beard stylings. With the i-shape and vertical blade, beard tips and edges can be seen more easily and treated with particular precision. Rounded shaving heads treat the skin with care. The beard length desired can be preset in 0.5 mm increments. A waterproof construction prevents clogging with beard hairs.

Statement by the jury
The i-SHAPER supports daily beard care reliably and swiftly. The clear, straightforward design underlines the masculine character.

Die Gestaltung des i-SHAPER lehnt sich am klassischen Rasiermesser an und eignet sich für verschiedene Bartstylings. Bartränder werden durch die i-Form und eine vertikale Klinge leichter gesehen und können mit besonderer Präzision bearbeitet werden. Abgerundete Scherköpfe schonen die Haut. Die gewünschte Bartlänge wird in Abständen von 0,5 mm voreingestellt. Verstopfungen mit Barthaaren werden durch eine wasserfeste Konstruktion vermieden.

Begründung der Jury
Der i-SHAPER unterstützt zuverlässig und schnell die tägliche Bartpflege. Das klare, schnörkellose Design unterstreicht den maskulinen Charakter.

Series 5000
Beard Trimmer
Bartschneider

Manufacturer
Philips, Eindhoven, Netherlands
In-house design
Philips Design
Web
www.philips.com

The Series 5000 balances easy functionality with comfortable handling. It features a detail trimmer, and adjustable long and short combs for a more precise trim result. Body highlights indicate the specifically correct handling to the user. The use of rubberised surfaces – including the zoom wheel – as well as metallic elements with matte surfaces provide attractive accents and indicate the robustness of the device. The slim shell is waterproof for quick cleaning.

Statement by the jury
A high degree of functionality and comfortable handling characterise the well-conceived design of the Series 5000.

Bei der Series 5000 sind einfache Funktionalität und komfortable Bedienung aufeinander abgestimmt. Sie beinhaltet einen Präzisionstrimmer sowie verstellbare lange und kurze Kammaufsätze für besonders präzise Ergebnisse. Hervorhebungen am Gehäuse weisen dem Nutzer den Weg zur speziell richtigen Handhabung. Der Einsatz von gummierten Flächen – einschließlich des Zoomrads – und Metallelementen mit matten Oberflächen setzt reizvolle Akzente und weist auf die Robustheit des Geräts hin. Das schlanke Gehäuse ist wasserdicht und somit schnell zu reinigen.

Begründung der Jury
Eine hohe Funktionalität sowie eine komfortable Handhabung charakterisieren die gut durchdachte Gestaltung der Series 5000.

Quattro Vintage
Razor
Rasierer

Manufacturer
Wilkinson Sword GmbH, Solingen, Germany
Design
GENERATIONDESIGN GmbH,
Wuppertal, Germany
Web
www.wilkinson.de
www.generationdesign.de

The Quattro Vintage razor meets the contemporary need for natural materials in the bathroom. It makes use of a traditional style giving it the appearance of an individual manufactured product. The high-grade handle is optically and haptically reminiscent of a piece of wood. It is manufactured using the plastic injection moulding process, yet it is possible to combine different front and back parts as well as different print templates. This allows for up to 256 individual manufacturing configurations.

Statement by the jury
The design of the Quattro Vintage razor stands out with its clever use of materials and aesthetics mirroring the modern zeitgeist.

Der Quattro Vintage kommt dem zeitgemäßen Bedürfnis nach natürlichen Materialien auch im Badezimmer entgegen. Der Rasierer bedient sich einer traditionellen Formensprache, die ihm die Anmutung eines individuellen Manufakturprodukts verleiht. Das hochwertige Griffstück erinnert optisch und in seiner Haptik an Holz. Obwohl im Kunststoffspritzguss-Verfahren hergestellt, lassen sich unterschiedliche Vorder- und Rückteile kombinieren sowie verschiedene Druckvorlagen anwenden. Das ermöglicht eine Herstellung in bis zu 256 individuellen Konfigurationen.

Begründung der Jury
Die Gestaltung des Rasierers Quattro Vintage besticht mit einem geschickten Materialeinsatz und einer Ästhetik, die den modernen Zeitgeist widerspiegelt.

BodyGroom Series 7000
Body Groomer
Körperrasierer

Manufacturer
Philips, Eindhoven, Netherlands
In-house design
Philips Design
Web
www.philips.com

The body groomers of the 7000 series offer a two-sided waterproof system consisting of trimmer and shaver. Both elements have each their own control panel with clearly communicated functions. The design placed particular focus on the special ergonomic requirements. A combination of matted and strongly rubberised surfaces with strong patterning provides a particularly safe grip under the shower. With the pivoting shaving head, all body areas are easily reachable.

Statement by the jury
Thanks to the well-conceived design of the BodyGroom Series 7000, fast and efficient cutting and trimming is possible with just one device.

Die Körperrasierer der Serie 7000 bieten ein zweiseitiges wasserfestes System aus Trimmer und Rasierer. Beide Elemente haben ein jeweils eigenes Bedienfeld mit klar kommunizierten Funktionen. Gestalterisch liegt besonderes Augenmerk auf den speziellen ergonomischen Erfordernissen: Eine Kombination aus mattierten und stark gummierten Oberflächen mit kräftiger Musterung sorgt für einen besonders sicheren Griff unter der Dusche. Durch den beweglichen Scherkopf sind alle Körperregionen gut erreichbar.

Begründung der Jury
Dank der durchdachten Gestaltung der BodyGroom Series 7000 gelingen schnelles und effizientes Schneiden und Trimmen mit nur einem Gerät.

S9000 Prestige
Shaver
Rasierapparat

Manufacturer
Philips, Eindhoven, Netherlands
In-house design
Philips Design
Web
www.philips.com

The rotating shaving heads of the S9000 Prestige are constructed in such a way that they are capable of even shaving a seven-day beard. The design of the shaver is inspired by luxury-class watches and cars. A wireless charging pad charges the device automatically after placing it upon it, keeping it fully operational at all times. All operating elements are precisely processed and consist of high-grade materials.

Statement by the jury
The S9000 Prestige shaver exudes expressive aesthetics and amazes with its high-performance properties capable of meeting the cutting demands of different beard lengths.

Die rotierenden Scherköpfe des S9000 Prestige sind so ausgearbeitet, dass sie sogar einen Sieben-Tage-Bart rasieren können. Die Gestaltung des Rasierapparats ist von Uhren und Autos der Luxusklasse inspiriert. Ein kabelloses Ladepad lädt das Gerät automatisch nach jedem Ablegen und hält es damit stets vollständig einsatzbereit. Sämtliche Bedienelemente sind präzise gefertigt und bestehen aus hochwertigem Material.

Begründung der Jury
Der Rasierapparat S9000 Prestige verströmt eine ausdrucksstarke Ästhetik und verblüfft durch eine Leistungsstärke, die verschiedenen Bartlängen gerecht wird.

6000 Series
Shaver
Rasierapparat

Manufacturer
Philips, Eindhoven, Netherlands
In-house design
Philips Design
Web
www.philips.com

The shaver offers men who previously used manual blades a particularly skin-friendly solution. The design of the device is reminiscent of wet shaving elements; as such, the user interface is only visible when required. In addition, a strong focus is placed on a safe handle. Material and surface texture communicate to the user the skin-friendly properties of the shaver. Metallic surfaces create a high-quality appearance.

Statement by the jury
The use of forms of the 6000 Series creates confidence and thus facilitates the transition from wet to electric shave.

Der Rasierapparat bietet Männern, die zuvor manuell rasierten, eine besonders hautschonende Lösung. Die Gestaltung des Gerätes erinnert an Elemente der Nassrasur, so wird etwa die Benutzerschnittstelle nur bei Bedarf sichtbar. Ein starker Fokus liegt zudem auf der Betonung eines sicheren Griffs, Material und Oberflächenbeschaffenheit kommunizieren dem Nutzer die hautfreundlichen Eigenschaften des Rasierers. Metallische Oberflächen sorgen für eine hochwertige Anmutung.

Begründung der Jury
Die Formensprache der 6000 Series schafft Vertrauen und erleichtert so den Umstieg von der Nass- auf die moderne Elektrorasur.

HN1
Nose Hair Trimmer
Nasenhaartrimmer

Manufacturer
Huanxing Technology (Hangzhou) Co., Ltd.,
Hangzhou, China
Design
Chang Jin, Hangzhou, China
Web
www.handx.com.cn

The waterproof HN1 nose hair trimmer is controlled by a discreetly placed button at the bottom. This results in a uniform and seamless appearance of the handle. A rugged aluminium surface and small diameter give the device a refined impression. At the same time, this shape supports easy handling and invites the user to take the trimmer along for mobile use. The small and smooth head portion treats the nasal walls with care.

Statement by the jury
With its well-conceived design, the HN1 nose hair trimmer is a refined accessory at home as well as during travel.

Der wasserfeste Nasenhaartrimmer HN1 wird über eine dezent angebrachte Taste an der Unterseite gesteuert. Dadurch fällt der Griffteil einheitlich und nahtlos aus. Eine raue Aluminiumoberfläche und ein geringer Durchmesser verleihen dem Gerät eine edle Anmutung. Zugleich unterstützt diese Gestaltung die einfache Handhabe und lädt dazu ein, das Gerät unterwegs mitzunehmen. Der glatte und klein konstruierte Kopfteil schont die Nasenwände.

Begründung der Jury
Seine wohldurchdachte Gestaltung macht den Nasenhaartrimmer HN1 zu Hause wie auch auf Reisen zu einem edlen Accessoire.

Silk Expert Pro 5
IPL Hair Removal Device
IPL-Haarentfernungsgerät

Manufacturer
Procter & Gamble Service GmbH,
Kronberg im Taunus, Germany
Design
Braun Design Team,
Kronberg im Taunus, Germany
Web
www.braun.com

Thanks to fast light pulses at a high energy level, the Silk Expert Pro 5 glides over the skin continuously. The SensoAdapt function adjusts the intensity of light automatically. Via three additional modes, users can adjust this intensity according to personal preferences. An additional precision head supports the use in smaller areas as well. The tapered, angled handle enables multiple grip positions for precise handling in all body regions. The large activation button is always easily accessible.

Statement by the jury
Thanks to sophisticated technology, the Silk Expert Pro 5 meets high demands with regard to safe and efficient hair removal.

Dank schneller Lichtimpulse auf hohem Energieniveau gleitet der Silk Expert Pro 5 kontinuierlich über die Haut. Die Senso-Adapt-Funktion passt die Lichtintensität automatisch an. Über drei ergänzende Modi können Nutzer diese darüber hinaus dem persönlichen Empfinden anpassen. Ein zusätzlicher Präzisionsaufsatz unterstützt die Anwendung auch in kleineren Bereichen. Das taillierte, abgewinkelte Handstück ermöglicht verschiedenste Griffpositionen für eine präzise Handhabung in allen Körperregionen. Die große Aktivierungstaste ist stets einfach zugänglich.

Begründung der Jury
Dank ausgefeilter Technologie wird der Silk Expert Pro 5 auch hohen Ansprüchen an eine sichere und effiziente Haarentfernung gerecht.

Kasho Chrome Series
Haircutting Scissors
Haarschneideschere

Manufacturer
KAI Corporation, Tokyo, Japan
In-house design
Jun Otsuka
Web
www.kai-group.com

Manufactured from high-grade Japanese stainless steel, the Kasho Chrome series is characterised by clear lines. Thanks to its ergonomic form and the traditional finger rests, it lies comfortably in the hand. The flat screw system enables a single-step adjustment of the required pressure. Applying the special "Ultimate Edge" technology, the semi-convex and hollow grinded scissor blades are carefully processed, honed and highly polished and thus guarantee a very good cutting edge retention and sharpness.

Statement by the jury
Thanks to a well-conceived design and manufacturing technology, the Kasho Chrome series proves to be a professional precision tool.

Klare Linien prägen die aus hochwertigem japanischem Edelstahl gefertigte Kasho Chrome Serie. Dank ihrer ergonomischen Form und der traditionellen Fingerauflage liegt die Haarschneideschere angenehm in der Hand. Das flache Schraubensystem ermöglicht ein stufenweises Einstellen der erforderlichen Spannung. Die mit der speziellen „Ultimate Edge"-Technologie semi-konvex und hohl geschliffenen Scherenblätter werden sorgfältig bearbeitet, abgezogen sowie feinpoliert und haben so eine sehr gute Schnitthaltigkeit und Schärfe.

Begründung der Jury
Dank einer wohldurchdachten Gestaltung und Fertigungstechnik erweist sich die Kasho Chrome Serie als professionelles Präzisionswerkzeug.

Joewell SPM Black
Haircutting Scissors
Haarschneideschere

Manufacturer
Tokosha Co., Ltd., Tokyo, Japan
In-house design
Web
www.joewell.co.jp

The haircutting scissors of the Joewell SPM Black series are conceived for professional use. The blades have been manufactured using a powder metallurgical process, resulting in a hardness 12 times that of regular metal. The handle shape conforms to the ergonomics of the hand in different styling techniques, and a protective silicone coating additionally helps to avoid fatigue symptoms. Using ion plating, the scissors are coated in black and are thus particularly abrasion-resistant.

Statement by the jury
The use of high-quality materials and good ergonomic properties characterise the design of the Joewell SPM Black haircutting scissors.

Die Haarschneideschere der Serie Joewell SPM Black ist für den professionellen Gebrauch konzipiert. Die Klingen sind in einem pulvermetallurgischen Verfahren hergestellt und somit bis zu zwölfmal härter als gewöhnliches Metall. Die Griffform kommt der Ergonomie der Hand bei verschiedenen Stylingtechniken sehr entgegen, eine Schutzschicht aus Silikon hilft zusätzlich, Ermüdungserscheinungen zu vermeiden. Die Schere ist mittels Ionenplattierung schwarz beschichtet und damit besonders abriebfest.

Begründung der Jury
Ein hochwertiger Materialeinsatz und gute ergonomische Eigenschaften charakterisieren die Gestaltung der Haarschneideschere Joewell SPM Black.

StraightCare Essential
Hair Straightener
Glätteisen

Manufacturer
Philips, Eindhoven, Netherlands
In-house design
Philips Design
Web
www.philips.com

In just 30 seconds, the innovative StraightCare Essential hair straightener has attained the operational heat required. The heated surface is particularly wide and colour-contrasted; in addition, it is highlighted by a shiny outer edge at the handle. A tapered design provides comfort and safety during handling. The inner handle revealed by a curved surface allows for viewing the intuitive user interface and keratin-infused heating plates.

In nur 30 Sekunden hat das innovative Glätteisen StraightCare Essential die notwendige Arbeitshitze erreicht. Die erhitzte Fläche ist besonders breit und farblich abgesetzt, zusätzlich wird sie durch eine glänzende Außenkante am Griff hervorgehoben. Eine sich verjüngende Formgebung sorgt für Komfort und Sicherheit bei der Handhabung. Eine geschwungene Oberseite gibt den Blick frei auf die innere Grifffläche mit einer intuitiv erfassbaren Benutzerschnittstelle sowie Heizflächen mit Keratinzusatz.

Statement by the jury
The StraightCare Essential hair straightener arouses enthusiasm with its harmonic design enabling particularly easy handling.

Begründung der Jury
Das Glätteisen StraightCare Essential begeistert mit einer harmonischen Gestaltung, die eine besonders einfache Handhabung ermöglicht.

SYLPH
Hairdryer
Haartrockner

Manufacturer
Shenzhen Wizevo Technology Co., Ltd.,
Shenzhen, China
In-house design
Web
www.wizevo.com

This hairdryer with the measurements 46 x 46 x 174 mm and a weight of merely 150 grams is particularly well suited for mobile use during travel. Airflow speed is infinitely variable, with five modes that are at the user's disposal. The nozzle is magnetically attached to the narrow, straight cut handle. A magnetic hanging fixture helps to save space. With the special airflow multiplication, the hair is dried particularly fast, and a temperature control function avoids the risk of overheating.

Statement by the jury
The SYLPH hairdryer convinces with its clever, clean design. Thanks to its compact dimensions, it also fits easily in any kind of luggage.

Dieser Haartrockner hat die Maße 46 x 46 x 174 mm und wiegt nur 150 Gramm, er eignet sich daher besonders gut für die Mitnahme auf Reisen. Die Fönstärke lässt sich stufenlos einstellen und es stehen fünf Modi zur Verfügung. Der Aufsatz hält magnetisch auf dem schmalen, gerade geschnittenen Griff. Eine ebenfalls magnetische Hängevorrichtung hilft, Platz zu sparen. Mit der speziellen Luftstromverstärkung wird das Haar besonders schnell getrocknet, eine Temperaturkontrolle schützt es vor Überhitzung.

Begründung der Jury
Der Haartrockner SYLPH überzeugt durch sein cleveres, geradliniges Design. Zudem passt er dank seiner kompakten Konstruktion in jedes Gepäck.

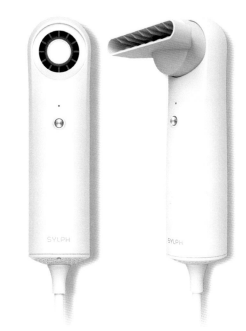

HL5
Hairdryer
Haartrockner

Manufacturer
Hangzhou Rosou Electronic
Technology Co., Ltd., Hangzhou, China
In-house design
Chang Jin
Web
https://zhibai.tmall.com

Nozzle and body of the HL5 hairdryer are attached to each other with an uncomplicated magnetic mechanism. The device offers three fan modes. A special ionising mode sprays the hair with an ultra-fine water mist. A hot wind mode dries the hair particularly fast, whereby the degree of heat is adapted to the existing room temperature. In cold wind mode, the hair is styled in a very gentle way. In this mode, the nozzle can also be detached without potential harm to the hands.

Statement by the jury
The HL5 hairdryer impresses with its user-friendly design and well-conceived functionality.

Düse und Körper des Haartrockners HL5 halten durch einen unkomplizierten Magnetmechanismus zusammen. Das Gerät bietet drei Fönstärken. Ein spezieller ionisierender Modus besprüht das Haar mit einem ultrafeinen Wassernebel. Ein heißes Gebläse trocknet das Haar besonders schnell, wobei der Hitzegrad der jeweiligen Raumtemperatur angepasst wird. Im kalten Gebläsemodus wird das Haar sehr schonend gestylt. Durch ihn kann auch die Düse ohne Gefahr für die Hände abgenommen werden.

Begründung der Jury
Der Haartrockner HL5 beeindruckt mit seiner nutzerfreundlichen Gestaltung und einer klug durchdachten Funktionalität.

SilenceDry
Hairdryer
Haartrockner

Manufacturer
Arçelik A.Ş., Istanbul, Turkey
In-house design
Doğaç Can Sağırosmanoğlu
Web
www.arcelik.com.tr
Honourable Mention

Thanks to an innovative vertical blower technology, this high-performance hairdryer is particularly silent. A combination of copper and plastic textures with different surfaces gives the SilenceDry a high-quality appearance. Another characteristic feature is the air intake positioned at the upper side. The dryer offers three temperature and two airflow settings. A cold setting stabilises the styled hair, an integrated ionic function provides additional suppleness.

Statement by the jury
With its particular silent operation and state-of-the-art design, the SilenceDry hairdryer is an outstandingly innovative product.

Dank einer innovativen vertikalen Gebläsetechnologie arbeitet dieser leistungsstarke Haartrockner besonders leise. Eine Kombination aus Kupfer- und Kunststofftexturen mit verschiedenen Oberflächen verleiht dem SilenceDry eine hochwertige Anmutung. Charakteristisch ist auch die an der Oberseite angebrachte Luftansaugung. Das Gerät bietet drei Temperatur- und zwei Luftstromstufen. Eine Kaltstufe stabilisiert das gestylte Haar, eine integrierte Ionic-Funktion sorgt für dessen Geschmeidigkeit.

Begründung der Jury
Mit einer besonders geräuscharmen Funktionsweise zeigt der zeitgemäß gestaltete Haartrockner SilenceDry Innovation.

TWINOX® M
Manicure, Pedicure and Facial Care Tools
Maniküre-, Pediküre- und Gesichtspflege-Instrumente

Manufacturer
ZWILLING Beauty Group GmbH, Düsseldorf, Germany
In-house design
Design
Kurz Kurz Design (Dorian Kurz), Solingen, Germany
Web
www.zwillingbeauty.com
www.kurz-kurz-design.de

The TWINOX M line adresses especially the modern man: the tools for hair, beard and nail care with increased grip width sit very well in the hand and show a high-quality matte black finish. The scratch-resistant PVD coating gives the stainless steel tools an improved cutting performance and durability. The two-piece case made of black neat's leather is equipped with a beard scissor and a comb. The versatile seven-piece case presents all instruments required for a comprehensive manicure, pedicure and facial hair grooming.

Die Linie TWINOX M spricht besonders den modernen Mann an: Die Instrumente für die Haar-, Bart- und Nagelpflege mit erweiterter Griffbreite liegen sehr gut in der Hand und zeigen ein hochwertiges matt-schwarzes Finish. Die kratzbeständige PVD-Beschichtung verleiht den Edelstahlinstrumenten eine erhöhte Schneidleistung und Langlebigkeit. Das zweiteilige Etui aus schwarzem Rindleder ist ausgestattet mit Bartschere und Kamm. Das vielseitige siebenteilige Etui bietet alle Produkte für eine umfangreiche Hand-, Fuß- und Gesichtshaarpflege.

Statement by the jury
The expressive design of the TWINOX M line attracts attention with its consistently masculine appearance.

Begründung der Jury
Die ausdrucksstarke Gestaltung der Linie TWINOX M zieht durch ein konsequent maskulines Erscheinungsbild die Aufmerksamkeit auf sich.

TWINOX® Gold Edition
Manicure and Pedicure Tools
Maniküre- und Pediküre-Instrumente

Manufacturer
ZWILLING Beauty Group GmbH, Düsseldorf, Germany
In-house design
Web
www.zwillingbeauty.com

The TWINOX Gold Edition captures the zeitgeist by an appearance of timeless elegance, high-quality material and luxury. The ergonomically well-shaped instruments are undergoing an extensive production process with a scratch-resistant PVD coating and thus ensure an enhanced cutting performance and durability. The traditional gold shade and a matte surface finish underline the noble impression of the instruments. Available within the TWINOX Gold Edition are single manicure instruments as well as valuable three- and five-piece cases made of blue neat's leather.

Mit der Anmutung von zeitloser Eleganz, hochwertigem Material und Luxus spricht die TWINOX Gold Edition den Zeitgeist an. Die ergonomisch wohlgeformten Instrumente wurden in einem aufwendigen Verfahren mit einer kratzbeständigen PVD-Beschichtung versehen und garantieren eine erhöhte Schneidleistung und Langlebigkeit. Der traditionelle Goldton und eine mattierende Oberfläche betonen den edlen Charakter der Instrumente. Erhältlich ist die TWINOX Gold Edition als praktische Einzelinstrumente wie auch in Form von hochwertigen drei- und fünfteiligen blauen Rindlederetuis.

Statement by the jury
The nail care set of the elegant TWINOX Gold Edition convinces with its excellent material properties.

Begründung der Jury
Das Nagelpflegeset der elegant anmutenden TWINOX Gold Edition überzeugt durch seine hervorragenden Materialeigenschaften.

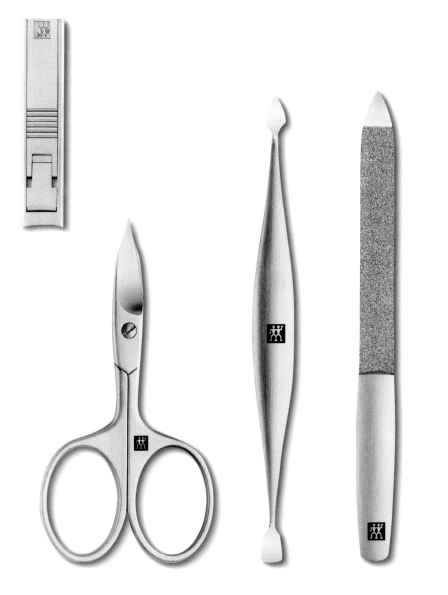

Clic
Toothbrush
Zahnbürste

Manufacturer
Procter & Gamble Service GmbH,
Kronberg im Taunus, Germany
Design
Oral Care Design Team,
Kronberg im Taunus, Germany
Web
www.oralb.com

The specially developed ClicFit connection
allows for periodic replacement of the
brush head while keeping the long-lasting
high-quality handle. The Clic toothbrush
shows an elegant and plain design, matte
black and chrome-coloured surfaces
give it a refined appearance. With a fine
balance of weights, the toothbrush lies
comfortably in the hand. Thanks to the
weight balance, it furthermore always
rests on its backside and keeps the brush
head upright. Attached to the magnetic
wall holder, the toothbrush renders a
virtually floating impression.

Statement by the jury
The design of the Clic toothbrush combines functionality with sustainable
handling of materials and an elegant appearance at a high level.

Die speziell entwickelte ClicFit-Verbindung
ermöglicht den regelmäßigen Austausch
der Aufsteckbürste bei dauerhafter Nutzung
des hochwertigen Handstücks. Die Zahnbürste Clic weist eine elegante und schlichte
Formsprache auf, mattschwarze und chrom-
farbene Oberflächen verleihen eine edle
Anmutung. Durch die ausgewogene Balance
liegt die Bürste angenehm in der Hand. Dank
der Gewichtsverteilung legt sie sich zudem
stets auf die Rückseite und hält den Bürstenkopf aufrecht. An dem magnetischen Wand-
halter angebracht, vermittelt die Zahnbürste
einen nahezu schwebenden Eindruck.

Begründung der Jury
Die Gestaltung der Zahnbürste Clic vereint
auf hohem Niveau Funktionalität mit einem
nachhaltigen Materialumgang und einem
eleganten Erscheinungsbild.

Pulsonic Slim Luxe
Sonic Toothbrush
Schallzahnbürste

Manufacturer
Procter & Gamble Service GmbH,
Kronberg im Taunus, Germany
Design
Oral Care Design Team,
Kronberg im Taunus, Germany
Web
www.oralb.com

The Pulsonic Slim Luxe sonic toothbrush is characterised by an elegant, modern design. Thanks to its accented slim form, it provides an ergonomic fit in the hand. This lightweight and compact sonic toothbrush can be comfortably used both at home and during travel. Its high-quality metallic finish harmonises with the minimalist shaping. For smooth and thorough cleaning, the brush head vibrates at a frequency of more than 31,000 oscillations per minute. For individual dental care, three different cleaning modes are at the user's disposal.

Statement by the jury
The Pulsonic Slim Line sonic toothbrush impresses with a convincing use of technology as well as with a refined minimalist appearance.

Die Schallzahnbürste Pulsonic Slim Luxe zeichnet sich durch ein elegantes, modernes Design aus. Dank ihrer betont schlanken Form liegt sie ergonomisch in der Hand. Diese leichte und kompakte Schallzahnbürste lässt sich sehr gut zuhause sowie auf Reisen verwenden. Ihre hochwertige Metallic-Lackierung harmoniert mit der minimalistischen Gestaltung. Der Bürstenkopf vibriert für eine gründliche und sanfte Reinigung mit über 31.000 Schwingungen pro Minute. Für eine individuelle Zahnpflege stehen drei verschiedene Putzmodi zur Verfügung.

Begründung der Jury
Die Schallzahnbürste Pulsonic Slim Line beeindruckt mit einem überzeugenden Technikeinsatz sowie mit einem minimalistisch edlen Aussehen.

ProtectiveClean
Electric Toothbrushes
Elektrische Zahnbürsten

Manufacturer
Philips, Eindhoven, Netherlands
In-house design
Philips Design
Web
www.philips.com

The modular constructed Protective-Clean electric toothbrush series offers a wide colour range, allowing the user an individual choice. Thanks to a slim body, the buttons are easily reached. A slightly asymmetric cut communicates intuitively the correct handling with one hand. A smart brush head and pressure sensor track brushing time as well as pressure and indicate when a top unit should be replaced. By doing without superfluous details, these electric toothbrushes are easily cleaned.

Statement by the jury
With a fresh colour design, the intuitively operated ProtectiveClean toothbrush series picks up a contemporary sense of style in a skilful manner.

Die modular aufgebaute Zahnbürsten-serie ProtectiveClean bietet eine breite Farb-palette und ermöglicht dem Nutzer indivi-duelle Auswahl. Die Tasten werden dank einem schmalen Körper einfach erreicht. Ein leicht asymmetrischer Schnitt kommu-niziert intuitiv die richtige Bedienung mit einer Hand. Ein intelligenter Bürstenkopf und ein Drucksensor verfolgen Putzdauer und Andruckstärke und zeigen an, wann ein Aufsatz ersetzt werden sollte. Durch den Verzicht auf überflüssige Details sind diese elektrischen Zahnbürsten einfach zu reinigen.

Begründung der Jury
Mit einer frischen Farbgestaltung greift die intuitiv bedienbare ProtectiveClean Zahnbürstenserie gekonnt zeitgemäßes Stilempfinden auf.

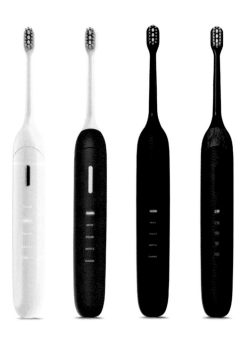

BOCALI
Sonic Toothbrush
Schallzahnbürste

Manufacturer
Shenzhen Baojia Battery Technology Co., Ltd., Shenzhen, China
In-house design
Design
MIPOW (Wai Yung Stanley Yeung), Shenzhen, China
Web
www.baojiabattery.com
www.mipow.com

The sonic toothbrush is offered in the four elegant versions Ceramic White, Matte Black, Chinoiserie and Athleisure. The magnetic levitation motor works with a highly efficient vibration frequency of up to 516 hertz in the four modes clean-ing, whitening, polishing and softening. The seamlessly integrated buttons and round body guarantee a comfortable grip and easy cleaning, yet they also give the toothbrush a very harmonic appear-ance.

Statement by the jury
With its selection of high-quality materials and refined look, the efficient BOCALI sonic toothbrush is an eye-catcher in any bathroom.

Die Schallzahnbürste wird in den vier edlen Ausführungen Ceramic White, Matte Black, Chinoiserie und Athleisure angeboten. Der magnetische Levitationsmotor arbeitet mit einer hocheffizienten Frequenzleistung von bis zu 516 Hertz in den vier Modi Clean, White, Polish und Gentle. Die nahtlos inte-grierten Tasten und der gerundete Körper sorgen dafür, dass die Zahnbürste ange-nehm gehalten und einfach gereinigt wer-den kann, verleihen ihr jedoch auch eine sehr harmonische Anmutung.

Begründung der Jury
Mit ihrem hochwertigen Materialeinsatz und ihrem edlen Aussehen ist die effiziente Schallzahnbürste BOCALI ein Blickfang in jedem Badezimmer.

EW 1511
Oral Irrigator
Munddusche

Manufacturer
Panasonic Corporation, Kyoto, Japan
In-house design
Ushio Bessho, Ryota Uchida
Web
www.panasonic.com
www.panasonic.net/design

This practical and rechargeable oral irri-gator enhances the user's health by ap-plying high-pressure water to flush out periodontal pockets and gaps between teeth while massaging the gums. Tiny air bubbles help to clean hard-to-reach spots thoroughly with special supersonic water jet technology. With its clear ap-pearance, the oral irrigator can be placed in such a way that it is always at hand. The compact ergonomic grip features a water tank with a capacity of 200 ml.

Statement by the jury
The design of the EW 15111 oral irrigator combines easy handling with professional functionality. It is also appealing due to its modern shaping.

Diese praktisch aufladbare Munddusche verbessert die Gesundheit des Nutzers, in-dem sie im Hochdruckverfahren Zahnfleisch-taschen und Lücken ausspült sowie das Zahnfleisch massiert. Winzige Luftblasen reinigen selbst schwer erreichbare Stellen gründlich mit einer speziellen Supersonic-Water-Jet-Technologie. In ihrem klaren Er-scheinungsbild lässt sich die Munddusche stets griffbereit platzieren. Der kompakte ergonomische Griff fasst 200 ml Wasser.

Begründung der Jury
Die Gestaltung der Munddusche EW 15111 verbindet eine einfache Handhabung mit professioneller Funktionalität. Zudem gefällt ihre moderne Formgebung.

Piuma
Toothbrush
Zahnbürste

Manufacturer
Piuma Care S.r.l., Noventa di Piave (Venezia), Italy
Design
Hangar Design Group, Mogliano Veneto (Treviso), Italy
Web
www.piumacare.com
www.hangardesigngroup.com

The design of the Piuma toothbrush focuses on straight lines and contrasting colours. Particularly lightweight materials originating from the medical industry give the brush high flexibility and stability at the same time. The handle is ergonomically well-conceived, and its surface finish ensures symptom-free hand movement during dental care. Discreet nubs for care of the tongue create an additional optical effect. A patented system inside the matted base, made of innovative material specifically designed for this application such as Gravi-Tech, indicates the age of the toothbrush.

Die Gestaltung der Zahnbürste Piuma setzt auf gerade Linienführung und Kontrastfarben. Besonders leichte aus der Medizintechnik stammende Materialien verleihen der Bürste hohe Flexibilität bei gleichzeitiger Stabilität. Der Griff ist ergonomisch durchdacht ausgeführt, auch seine Oberflächenbeschaffenheit sorgt für eine beschwerdefreie Handführung während der Zahnpflege. Dezente Noppen für die Zungenpflege sorgen für einen zusätzlichen optischen Effekt. Eine patentierte Einrichtung in der mattierten Basis aus innovativem Material wie etwa Gravi-Tech, das speziell für diese Anwendung entwickelt wurde, zeigt das Alter der Zahnbürste an.

Statement by the jury
With its state-of-the-art aesthetics, the Piuma toothbrush is an elegant accessory in the bathroom.

Begründung der Jury
Ihre zeitgemäße Ästhetik macht die Zahnbürste Piuma zu einem eleganten Accessoire im Badezimmer.

Tmall Genie QUEEN
Smart Make-up Mirror
Intelligenter Make-up-Spiegel

Manufacturer
Zhejiang Tmall Technology Co., Ltd., Hangzhou, China
In-house design
Guanghao Wu, Jianye Li
Web
www.alibabagroup.com

The Tmall Genie Queen is a combination of innovative lighting design and intelligent voice activation technology. The pre-installed AliGenie AI Assistant quickly and precisely registers the individual make-up routine of the user. The system is capable of automatically creating a skin profile and supporting the user in maintaining or enhancing the skin condition on a long-term basis. With regard to design, the device shows a classic geometric cut, a smooth, outwardly directed line management as well as an elegant juxtaposition of the colour hues pearl white and rose gold.

Der Tmall Genie Queen ist eine Kombination aus innovativem Lichtdesign und intelligenter Sprachaktivierungstechnologie. Der vorinstallierte AliGenie AI Assistant registriert die individuelle Make-up-Routine von Nutzern schnell und präzise. Automatisch kann das System ein Hautprofil erstellen und dabei unterstützen, den Hautzustand langfristig zu erhalten oder zu verbessern. In gestalterischer Hinsicht zeigt das Gerät einen klassischen geometrischen Schnitt, eine weiche nach außen gerichtete Linienführung sowie ein elegantes Nebeneinander der Farbtöne Perlweiß und Roségold.

Statement by the jury
Equipped with artificial intelligence, the elegantly designed Tmall Genie Queen make-up mirror stands out with its impressive functionality.

Begründung der Jury
Eine beeindruckende Funktionalität zeichnet den mit künstlicher Intelligenz ausgestatteten, elegant gestalteten Make-up-Spiegel Tmall Genie Queen aus.

AMIRO Mini
LED Make-up Mirror
LED-Make-up-Spiegel

Manufacturer
Shenzhen Accompany Tech Co., Ltd.,
Shenzhen, China
In-house design
Messizon Li, Neo Wang, Zhilong Cheng
Web
www.accompanytech.com

The 6.5" OLED table mirror adapts the technology of a smartphone screen backlight in an innovative manner. In this way, the Amiro Mini can be used indoors as well as outdoors and is capable of illuminating all portions of the face very well. A blue light filter protects the user's eyes. The design dispensed with any redundancies, resulting in a very reduced appearance based on the principles of Zen philosophy.

Statement by the jury
With the creative use of smartphone technology, the Amiro Mini meets the needs and requirements particularly of young female users in an impressive way.

Der 6,5"-OLED-Tischspiegel adaptiert auf innovative Weise die Technologie einer Smartphone-Hintergrundbeleuchtung. Dadurch kann der Amiro Mini in Innenräumen wie auch im Außenbereich verwendet werden und alle Gesichtspartien sehr gut ausleuchten. Ein Blaulichtfilter schützt das Augenlicht. In gestalterischer Hinsicht wird auf Redundanzen verzichtet, wodurch sich ein auf Grundsätzen der Zen-Philosophie beruhendes, sehr reduziertes Design ergibt.

Begründung der Jury
Mit dem kreativen Einsatz von Smartphone-Technologie erfüllt der Amiro Mini eindrucksvoll die Bedürfnisse insbesondere junger Nutzerinnen.

AMIRO Otree
LED Sensor Mirror
LED-Sensorspiegel

Manufacturer
Shenzhen Accompany Tech Co., Ltd.,
Shenzhen, China
In-house design
Messizon Li, Neo Wang
Web
www.accompanytech.com

The light of the Amiro Otree can be adjusted with an app, whether the user puts on make-up for a day at the office or a restaurant visit in the evening. Via a sensor, light intensity can be controlled without having to use the hands. In an innovative way, the 8" OLED table mirror adapts the technology of a smartphone screen backlight. With regard to its design in different vivid colours, it is inspired by a solar tree.

Statement by the Jury
With its modern appearance, the LED sensor mirror stands out in particular due to its innovative option of contact-free operation.

Mittels einer App wird das Licht des Amiro Otree angepasst, ob sich Nutzer nun für das Büro schminken oder etwa für einen abendlichen Restaurantbesuch. Mittels Sensor kann die Lichtstärke ohne Zuhilfenahme der Hände gesteuert werden. Auf innovative Weise adaptiert der 8"-OLED-Tischspiegel die Technologie einer Smartphone-Hintergrundbeleuchtung. In seiner Gestaltung, die in verschiedenen frischen Farbtönen ausgeführt ist, ist er einem Solarbaum nachempfunden.

Begründung der Jury
Der modern gestaltete LED-Sensorspiegel gefällt besonders durch die innovative Möglichkeit der berührungsfreien Bedienung.

The Magic Mirror
Make-up Mirror
Make-up-Spiegel

Manufacturer
MINISO Hong Kong Limited,
Guangzhou, China
In-house design
Cheng Feng Lin
Web
www.miniso.com

Base and mirror of the Magic Mirror are connected by a flexible hose, enabling individual adjustment according to the user's needs, yet also giving it a playful look. The mirror can also be scaled down in its dimensions and thus stowed away easily. With its special silica gel suction cups at the bottom, the mirror can be mounted to the wall without any residues.

Statement by the jury
The Magic Mirror _____
_____
can be varied in a playful way.

Standfuß und Spiegel des Magic Mirror sind durch eine flexible Schlauchleitung verbunden, wodurch er sich ganz nach Bedarf individuell justieren lässt, ihm aber auch ein verspieltes Aussehen verliehen werden kann. Das Gerät lässt sich so auch sehr klein dimensionieren und platzsparend verstauen. Durch spezielle Saugnäpfe aus Kieselsäuregel an der Unterseite kann der Spiegel auch rückstandsfrei an der Wand montiert werden.

Begründung der Jury
Der Magic Mirror besticht durch sein un-
_____
auf spielerische Weise variieren lässt.

YOYO
Make-up Mirror
Make-up-Spiegel

Manufacturer
Shenzhen Jianyuanda Science &
Technology Co., Ltd., Shenzhen, China
Design
inDare Design Strategy Limited
(Qinglang Chen, Fengming Chen,
Yujie Chen, Shaolong Chen),
Shenzhen, China
Web
www.jydmirror.com
www.in-dare.com

The YOYO can be used both as handheld mirror and mounted to the base. By use of a strong magnet, the grip snaps safely into place but can also be swivelled to the appropriate angle in the base. An LED ring consisting of 64 lamp beads provides full and clear illumination which appears soft for protection of the eyes. With just one intuitively operable button, whiteness and colour temperature are measured. A 2,000 mAh lithium battery supplies power for up to one week.

Statement by the jury
The YOYO make-up mirror attracts attention with its clever conceived functionality and easy operability.

YOYO lässt sich sowohl als Handspiegel als auch auf der Bodenstation montiert verwenden. Durch einen starken Magneten rastet der Griff sicher ein, lässt sich aber auch individuell in der Bodenstation in den passenden Winkel schwenken. Ein LED-Ring aus 64 Kugeln sorgt für eine satte und klare Beleuchtung, die zur Schonung der Augen zugleich weich wirkt. Mit nur einer intuitiv erfassbaren Taste werden Weißgehalt und Farbtemperatur gemessen. Eine 2.000-mAh-Lithiumbatterie sorgt bis zu eine Woche lang für Energie.

Begründung der Jury
Der Make-up-Spiegel YOYO zieht die Aufmerksamkeit mit einer clever durchdachten Funktionalität und einer einfachen Bedienbarkeit auf sich.

LG Pra.L
LED Skincare Set
LED-Hautpflegeset

Manufacturer
LG Electronics Inc., Seoul, South Korea
In-house design
Sanghoon Yoon, Sunha Park
Web
www.lg.com

The pearl coloured devices of the LG Pra.L LED skincare set harmonise well with the gold coloured, slightly shining inserts. The silicone and metal used for manufacture of the device is also applied in the medical field. The basic form of the utensils is slim and plain, the stable grips enable safe use. The form of the four different heads is completely geared towards the corresponding function. The associated LED mask is particularly lightweight and, with its glasses-like temples, can be worn comfortably just like a pair of glasses.

Statement by the jury
The Pra.L LED skincare set does well with a functionally coherent design. The harmonic colouration gives the set a refined appearance.

Die perlfarbenen Geräte des LED-Hautpflegesets LG Pra.L harmonieren gut mit den goldfarbenen, leicht glänzenden Einsätzen. Das verwendete Silikon und Metall kommt auch im medizinischen Bereich zum Einsatz. Die Grundform der Utensilien ist schlank und schlicht, die stabilen Griffe ermöglichen eine sichere Anwendung. Die vier unterschiedlichen Köpfe sind in ihrer Form ganz auf die jeweilige Funktion ausgerichtet. Die zugehörige LED-Maske ist besonders leicht und angenehm zu tragen, durch zwei seitliche Bügel wird sie wie eine Brille aufgesetzt.

Begründung der Jury
Das LED-Hautpflegeset Pra.L punktet mit einem funktional schlüssigen Design. Die harmonische Farbgebung sorgt für eine edle Anmutung.

AMIRO Cotton
Facial Cleansing Brush
Gesichtsreinigungsbürste

Manufacturer
Shenzhen Accompany Tech Co., Ltd.,
Shenzhen, China
In-house design
Messizon Li, Neo Wang, Zhilong Cheng
Web
www.accompanytech.com

This facial cleansing brush achieves a particularly smooth softness, comparable to that of very young skin, through a double silicone layer. The outer layer has shore hardness A, the inner layer shore hardness 00. This reduces the natural oscillation of the brush, avoids abrasions, and the brush can penetrate the pores more easily. The design in the shape of a cotton flower additionally highlights the soft character of the Amiro Cotton.

Statement by the jury
The Amiro Cotton gains merit with an imaginative shaping turning the facial cleansing brush into an appealing bathroom accessory.

Eine besonders sanfte Weichheit, vergleichbar mit jener ganz junger Haut, erreicht diese Gesichtsreinigungsbürste durch eine doppelte Silikonhülle, deren äußere Schicht eine Shore-A-Härte von 40 und deren innere eine Shore-A-Härte von 00 aufweist. Dadurch wird die Eigenschwingung der Bürste reduziert, das Entstehen von Schürfungen vermieden und die Bürste kann gut in die Poren vordringen. Die Gestaltung in Form einer Baumwollblüte hebt den weichen Charakter von Amiro Cotton zusätzlich hervor.

Begründung der Jury
Amiro Cotton punktet mit einer fantasievollen Formgebung, welche die Gesichtsreinigungsbürste zu einem ansprechenden Badezimmeraccessoire macht.

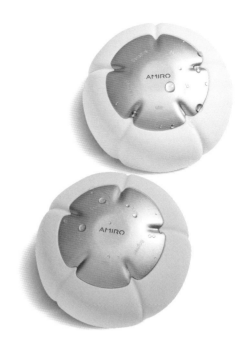

Facial Cleansing Brush
Gesichtsreinigungsbürste

Manufacturer
Shenzhen IMUB Intelligent Beauty Co., Ltd.,
Shenzhen, China
In-house design
Ma Zheng, Zhang Xinwei
Web
www.imub.com.cn

Utilising an efficient magnetic levitation acoustic motor, the brush part of this device swings at 28,800 times per minute. It features a five-gear adjustment and can thus be adapted to the needs of different skin types. An innovative mechanism ensures that the transfer of the vibration onto the hand is dampened. The Facial Cleansing Brush presents itself in a reduced, up-to-date design. Thanks to a wireless charging station, the device can be easily stowed away.

Statement by the jury
The Facial Cleansing Brush convinces with its easy operability. Another highlight is that it is capable of adapting to different skin types.

Mittels eines effizienten Magnetschwebemotors auf Akustikfrequenz bewegt sich der Bürstenteil dieses Geräts bis zu 28.800-mal pro Minute. Es lässt sich in fünf Einstellungen justieren und damit den Bedürfnissen verschiedener Hauttypen anpassen. Ein innovativer Mechanismus sorgt dafür, dass sich die Schwingung nur gedämpft auf die Hand überträgt. Äußerlich zeigt sich die Facial Cleansing Brush in einem zeitgemäß reduzierten Design. Dank einer kabellosen Ladestation kann das Gerät einfach verstaut werden.

Begründung der Jury
Die Facial Cleansing Brush überzeugt durch einfache Bedienbarkeit. Außerdem gefällt, dass sie sich verschiedenen Hauttypen anpasst.

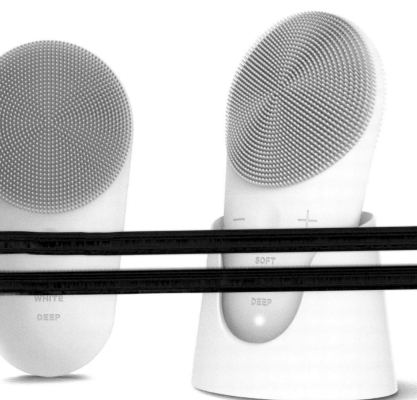

Facial Massager
Gesichtsmassagegerät

Manufacturer
RAVO Group, Dongguan, China
Design
Ningbo Moma Industrial Design Co., Ltd. (Huancan Yang, Min Liu), Ningbo, China
Web
www.ravogroup.com
www.designmoma.com

Thanks to a fine weight balance and high-quality surface finishes, the facial massager can easily be held and operated at any angle with the hand. A well-conceived flowing design gives the device a refined appearance and conforms to ergonomic requirements. The user can easily adapt the interchangeable massage heads according to skin type and individual need of skin tightening.

Dank präzise austariertem Gewicht und hochwertiger Oberflächenbeschaffenheit lässt sich das Gesichtsmassagegerät besonders gut mit der Hand in jedem gewünschten Winkel führen. Eine durchdachte fließende Gestaltung verleiht dem Gerät eine edle Anmutung und kommt der Ergonomie sehr entgegen. Die austauschbaren Massageköpfe kann die Nutzerin gemäß ihrem Hauttyp und individuellen Bedarf an Hautstraffung einfach anpassen.

Statement by the jury
The facial massage device communicates its beneficial, pleasant and stimulating effect with its streamlined, balanced design.

Begründung der Jury
Das Gesichtsmassagegerät kommuniziert mit einer stromlinienförmigen, ausgewogenen Gestaltung seinen wohltuenden und belebenden Effekt.

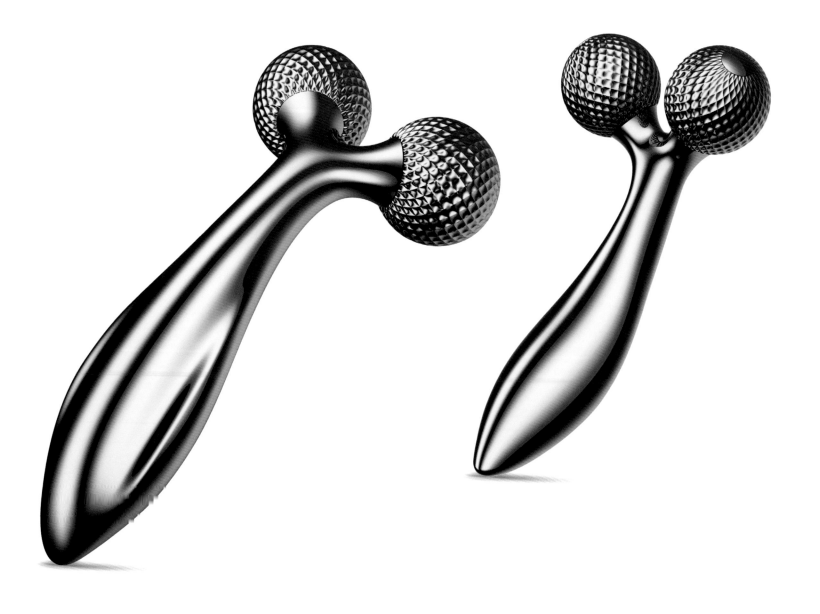

Facial Massager
Gesichtsmassagegerät

Manufacturer
RAVO Group, Dongguan, China
Design
Ningbo Moma Industrial Design Co., Ltd. (Huancan Yang, Min Liu), Ningbo, China
Web
www.ravogroup.com
www.designmoma.com

Two opposed arches, which overlap again at the end, form the handle of this facial massage device. Next to the very advantageous aesthetics created by this, this design also supports an ergonomical handling. The interchangeable massage heads show different surface finishes. They can easily be selected according to skin type and care needs.

Zwei gegenläufige Bögen, die einander am Ende wieder überschneiden, bilden den Handgriff dieses Gesichtsmassagegerätes. Neben der dadurch erzielten sehr vorteilhaften Ästhetik unterstützt diese Gestaltung eine ergonomische Bedienung. Eine unterschiedliche Oberflächenbeschaffenheit weisen die austauschbaren Massageköpfe auf. Je nach Hauttyp und Pflegebedarf kann zwischen ihnen einfach ausgewählt werden.

Statement by the jury
This facial massage device stands out with ergonomically impressive quality that also convinces with regard to functionality.

Begründung der Jury
Mit einer ergonomisch beeindruckenden Qualität punktet dieses Gesichtsmassagegerät, das auch in funktionaler Hinsicht überzeugt.

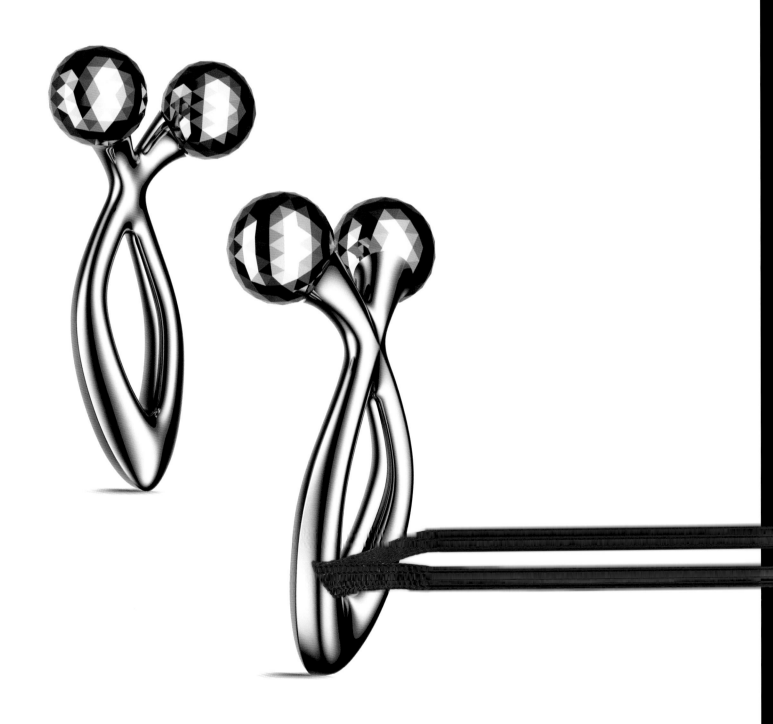

Nanoscale Microneedle
Skincare Device
Hautpflegegerät

Manufacturer
Shenzhen IMUB Intelligent Beauty Co., Ltd.,
Shenzhen, China
In-house design
Ma Zheng, Zhang Xinwei
Web
www.imub.com.cn

The skincare device pierces very fine channels into the skin and thus applies regenerating active ingredients particularly effectively. With a high-frequency piston movement, the nano microchip opens the skin to the stratum corneum; the dermis layer and subcutaneous nerves remain untouched. Subsequently, the active ingredient is inserted into the opened skin layer where it is ten to 20 times more effective than by just applying it directly onto the skin. Through the self-healing effect of the skin, the opened pores heal up again within 20 minutes. The compact device is easily operated.

Statement by the jury
Thanks to its sophisticated technology, the Nanoscale Microneedle skincare device works particularly gentle and efficient.

Das Hautpflegegerät sticht sehr feine Kanäle in die Haut und appliziert so regenerierende Wirkstoffe besonders effizient. Der Nano-Microchip öffnet in einer hochfrequenten Kolbenbewegung die Haut bis zur Hornschicht; Lederschicht und subkutane Nerven bleiben unberührt. Anschließend wird der Wirkstoff in die geöffnete Hautschicht eingeführt, wo er sich zehn- bis zwanzigmal effektiver auswirkt als bei einem Auftragen direkt auf der Haut. Durch den Selbstheilungseffekt der Haut schließen sich die geöffneten Poren nach 20 Minuten wieder. Das kompakte Gerät lässt sich einfach bedienen.

Begründung der Jury
Dank seiner ausgeklügelten Technologie arbeitet das Hautpflegegerät Nanoscale Microneedle besonders schonend und effizient.

Huawei AI Care
Skin Scanner
Hautscanner

Manufacturer
Huawei Device (Shenzhen) Co., Ltd.,
Shenzhen, China
In-house design
Web
www.huawei.com

This intelligent skin scanner works in combination with an app. After pulling off the protective capsule, it is pressed gently onto the face where it measures and records the skin condition. Based on its data analysis, it suggests the appropriate skincare advice to the user. The design of the Huawei AI Care follows the example of common cosmetic products for women and assists in a natural integration of the scanner into everyday life.

Statement by the jury
The Huawei AI Care stands out with its coherent design turning the skin scanner into a practical device for everyday beauty care.

Dieser intelligente Hautscanner funktioniert in Verbindung mit einer App. Nach Abzug der Schutzkapsel wird er sanft an das Gesicht gedrückt, wo er den Hautzustand misst und aufzeichnet und der Nutzerin aufgrund seiner Datenanalyse die geeignete Hautpflege vorschlägt. Gestaltet ist der Huawei AI Care nach dem Vorbild üblicher Kosmetikprodukte für Frauen, was unterstützt, dass sich seine Anwendung wie selbstverständlich in den Alltag integrieren lässt.

Begründung der Jury
Der Huawei AI Care besticht durch seine schlüssige Formgebung, die den Hautscanner zu einem praktischen Gerät für die tägliche Schönheitsroutine macht.

Skincare Device
Hautpflegegerät

Manufacturer
Ningbo Ruifu Industrial Group Co., Ltd.,
Ningbo, China
Design
Ningbo Moma Industrial Design Co., Ltd.
(Haohui Bao, Huancan Yang), Ningbo, China
Web
www.ravogroup.com
www.designmoma.com

Different skin types of different ages can be enhanced with this skincare device using colour photoelectric pulse technology, electronic muscle stimulation and LED light. The shape of the device is inspired by the silhouette of a whale. Flowing forms give the device a very elegant appearance and are also very advantageous with regard to handling. The seamlessly integrated buttons enable intuitive control.

Statement by the jury
The smooth, organic appearance of this skincare device inspires trust and animates the user to take advantage of it on a regular basis.

Verschiedene Hauttypen unterschiedlichen Alters können durch dieses Schönheitspflegegerät mittels photoelektrischer Farbimpulse, elektronischer Muskelstimulation und LED-Licht verbessert werden. Die Form des Geräts ist von der Silhouette eines Wales inspiriert. Fließende Formen lassen das Gerät sehr elegant wirken und haben zugleich einen sehr vorteilhaften Effekt auf die Handhabe. Die nahtlos integrierten Tasten ermöglichen eine intuitive Steuerung.

Begründung der Jury
Das schmeichelnde, organische Anmutung Design weckt Vertrauen und animiert zur regelmäßigen Nutzung dieses Hautpflegegerätes.

Clear Skin Microderm Tool
Microdermabrasion Tool
Gerät zur Mikrodermabrasion

Manufacturer
Tweezerman International LLC,
ZWILLING Beauty Group,
Port Washington, New York, USA
In-house design
Jillian Halbig
Web
www.tweezerman.com
Honourable Mention

This dermatologically tested device offers an easy way to perform microdermabrasion at home. The sleek and simple tool of glass and chrome is designed to go deeper into the skin. It removes the top layers of dead, dull skin cells to expose fresh, new skin underneath. A specially designed metal pattern inset into the glass provides the exfoliating effect. When applied with light pressure and moved in downward strokes on the face, the metal part gently abrades the top layer of skin on the forehead, cheek, nose and chin area.

Statement by the jury
With this tool and its intelligent combination of glass and metal, microdermabrasion can also be done at home in an impressive way.

Dieses dermatologisch getestete Gerät bietet einen einfachen Weg, um Mikrodermabrasion zuhause durchzuführen. Das geschmeidige und einfache Produkt aus Glas und Chrom ist konzipiert, um tiefer in die Haut einzudringen. Es entfernt die oberen Schichten aus abgestorbenen, matten Hautzellen und legt die darunterliegende frische, neue Haut frei. Ein speziell entwickelter Metalleinsatz, eingesetzt in das Glas, bewirkt den Peelingeffekt. Mit leichtem Druck angesetzt und in Abwärtsbewegungen über das Gesicht geführt, trägt das Metallteil die obere Hautschicht an Stirn, Wangen, Nase und Kinn sanft ab.

Begründung der Jury
Die Mikrodermabrasion gelingt mit dieser intelligenten Kombination aus Glas und Metall in beeindruckender Weise auch zuhause.

Moistick
Facial Steamer
Gesichtsbefeuchter

Manufacturer
Shenzhen Stylepie Lifestyle Co., Ltd.,
Shenzhen, China
In-house design
Web
www.stylepie.com

Applying ultrasonic technology, the Moistick provides the skin easily and quickly with moisture while on the go. It is particularly small, shaped like a lipstick and can thus be easily stowed away in a handbag. Through the use of polycarbonate, it was possible to create a particularly thin yet robust, straight-lined housing wall. Rechargeable lithium batteries power the facial steamer for up to one month with one full charge.

Statement by the jury
Thanks to a sophisticated style, the Moistick facial steamer has particularly small dimensions and can thus be easily taken along everywhere.

Mittels Ultraschall versorgt der Moistick die Gesichtshaut unterwegs einfach und schnell mit Feuchtigkeit. Er ist geformt wie ein Lippenstift und besonders klein und lässt sich somit einfach in einer Handtasche verstauen. Durch den Einsatz von Polykarbonat wurde eine besonders dünne und dennoch robuste, sehr geradlinig verlaufende Gehäusewand entwickelt. Wiederaufladbare Lithiumbatterien halten den Gesichtsbefeuchter bis zu einem Monat in Betrieb.

Begründung der Jury
Dank einer ausgeklügelten Gestaltung hat der Gesichtsbefeuchter Moistick besonders kleine Ausmaße und lässt sich so überallhin bequem mitnehmen.

FaceSpa
Facial Steamer
Gesichtsbefeuchter

Manufacturer
Shenzhen Baojia Battery Technology Co., Ltd.,
Shenzhen, China
In-house design
Design
MIPOW (Wai Yung Stanley Yeung),
Shenzhen, China
Web
www.baojiabattery.com
www.mipow.com

The FaceSpa electric facial steamer is compartmented in two chambers. The smaller upper tank suffices for one to two applications, the larger lower one is used for all-day facial care. After squeezing the cap twice to avoid unintentional release in the handbag, FaceSpa automatically sprays a refreshing water mist in the form of tiny nano-size water particles. The merely ten centimetres large device provides 90 applications when fully charged.

Statement by the jury
The user-friendly design of the FaceSpa facial steamer allows for skin refreshment at any time, thanks to its electronic spray mechanism.

Der elektrische Gesichtsbefeuchter FaceSpa ist in zwei Kammern unterteilt. Der kleinere obere Tank reicht aus für ein bis zwei Anwendungen, der untere für die Hautbefeuchtung über den gesamten Tag. Nach zweifachem Drücken der Kappe, um ein unbeabsichtigtes Auslösen in der Handtasche zu vermeiden, versprüht FaceSpa automatisch einen erfrischenden Wassernebel in Form winziger Wasserpartikel im Nanobereich. Voll aufgeladen funktioniert das nur zehn Zentimeter große Gerät für 90 Anwendungen.

Begründung der Jury
Die nutzerfreundliche Gestaltung des Gesichtsbefeuchters FaceSpa ermöglicht dank des elektronischen Sprühmechanismus jederzeit eine Hauterfrischung.

Flip Lip
Lip Gloss Applicator
Lipgloss-Applikator

Manufacturer
CTK Cosmetics Co., Ltd.,
Seongnam, South Korea
In-house design
Prof. Jaehui Lee, Prof. Justine Go
Web
www.ctkcosmetics.com

This one-hand applicator was developed so that it wouldn't be necessary to use both hands when applying lip gloss. Held in just one hand, the cap of the Flip Lip can be folded back with just one finger. By applying pressure on the lower part of the body, the lip gloss is squeezed out of the top piece. This part can be exchanged to adapt to different consistencies. The application succeeds without soiling the device with the content. Only one per cent of the lip gloss remains unused in the container.

Statement by the jury
With its well-conceived design, the Flip Lip proves to be a clever product solution for mobile lip care.

Damit die Zuhilfenahme beider Hände beim Auftragen von Lipgloss entfallen kann, wurde dieser einhändig bedienbare Applikator entwickelt. In einer Hand gehalten, lässt sich die Abdeckung des Flip Lip mit nur einem Finger zurückklappen. Durch Druck auf den Körper unterhalb wird der Lipgloss anschließend aus dem Aufsatz herausgedrückt. Dieser kann ausgetauscht werden, um unterschiedlichen Konsistenzen gerecht zu werden. Die Anwendung gelingt, ohne das Gerät mit dem Inhalt zu verschmutzen. Nur ein Prozent des Lipglosses verbleibt ungenutzt in dem Behälter.

Begründung der Jury
Mit einer wohldurchdachten Gestaltung erweist sich der Flip Lip als eine clevere Produktlösung für die Lippenpflege unterwegs.

stress releaZer
Relaxation Aid and
Breathing Trainer
Entspannungshilfe und
Atemtrainer

Manufacturer
Beurer GmbH, Ulm, Germany
Design
paul martin (Martin Paul Hoffmann),
Kaiserslautern, Germany
Web
www.beurer.com
www.paul-martin.net

The stress releaZer contains a vibration motor. When the user lays the device on the diaphragm, it facilitates access to relaxed breathing. To adapt the breathing training to the personal state of health in the best possible way, three cycles with different lengths are at the user's disposal. A switchable illuminated ring pulses at the configured breathing rhythm and acts as a mood light. Optionally, a heat function at the bottom can be activated for further relaxation.

Statement by the jury
Thanks to well-conceived functionality, the stress releaZer reduces states of exhaustion in a natural way and helps to achieve a relaxed breathing rhythm.

In den stress releaZer ist ein Vibrationsmotor eingebaut. Wird das Gerät auf das Zwerchfell gelegt, erleichtert es dem Nutzer den Zugang zu einer entspannten Atmung. Um das Atemtraining dem persönlichen Befinden bestmöglich anzupassen, stehen drei unterschiedlich lange Zyklen zur Auswahl. Ein zuschaltbarer Leuchtring pulsiert zusätzlich im eingestellten Atemrhythmus und fungiert als Stimmungslicht. Optional kann zur weiteren Entspannung eine Wärmefunktion an der Unterseite aktiviert werden.

Begründung der Jury
Dank gut durchdachter Funktionalität lindert der stress releaZer auf natürliche Art Erschöpfungszustände und verhilft zu einem entspannten Atemrhythmus.

Restool
Foot Massager
Gerät zur Fußmassage

Manufacturer
Hutech Industry Co., Ltd.,
Gimpo City, Gyeonggi Province, South Korea
In-house design
Cheol Hong Seo
Web
www.i-hutech.com

For a foot massage, the cover of the Restool is simply removed. Subsequently, the user puts his feet into two integrated reservoirs made of fabric. Via four intuitive buttons with LED lighting, he can now set, according to his needs, massage mode and degree of heat. After the massage, the cover is placed on top again. The Restool can then, due to its design as a piece of furniture, remain in the living room area and be used as footrest or stool with additional heating function. The homely appearance is enhanced by the use of wood, leather and textile.

Für eine Fußmassage wird die Abdeckung des Restool einfach abgenommen. Anschließend steckt der Nutzer seine Füße in zwei integrierte Reservoirs aus Stoff. Mittels vier intuitiv erfassbarer Tasten mit LED-Beleuchtung stellt er nun nach seinen Bedürfnissen Massageart und Wärmegrad ein. Nach der Massage wird die Abdeckung wieder aufgelegt, der Restool kann ob seiner Gestaltung als Möbelstück im Wohnbereich verbleiben und als Fuß- oder Sitzhocker, der zusätzlich beheizbar ist, genutzt werden. Die wohnliche Anmutung wird verstärkt durch die Verwendung von Holz, Leder und Textil.

Statement by the jury
With its sophisticated design, the Restool succeeds in impressively combining a shapely home accessory with a beneficial and pleasant massage device.

Begründung der Jury
Mit seiner ausgefeilten Gestaltung gelingt beim Restool eindrucksvoll die Vereinigung eines formschönen Wohnaccessoires mit einem wohltuenden Massagegerät.

Scalp 2
Massage Device
Massagegerät

Manufacturer
Shenzhen Breo Technology Co., Ltd., Shenzhen, China
In-house design
Fei Du, Wenxu Gan
Web
www.breo.com.cn
Honourable Mention

A head and body massage through the four fingers of Scalp 2 promotes blood circulation, has a stimulating effect, alleviates itching and provides relaxation in general. The four different attachments each offer other massage techniques and can be easily detached for cleaning and for interchanging. The curved device is waterproof and can thus be used in the bath, under the shower or in connection with massage oil or other personal care products.

Eine Massage von Kopf oder Körper durch die vier Finger von Scalp 2 fördert die Blutzirkulation, wirkt belebend, lindert Juckreiz und sorgt allgemein für Entspannung. Die vier verschiedenen Aufsätze, die jeweils andere Massagetechniken bieten, können zur Reinigung abgenommen und ausgetauscht werden. Das geschwungen geformte Gerät ist wasserfest und kann somit in der Badewanne, unter der Dusche oder in Verbindung mit Massageöl oder anderen Pflegeprodukten verwendet werden.

Statement by the jury
The Scalp 2 massage device pleases with its organic design and sophisticated functions promoting relaxation.

Begründung der Jury
Das Massagegerät Scalp 2 gefällt mit seiner organischen Formgebung und seinen ausgereiften, entspannungsfördernden Funktionen.

Hot Water Bag
Hot-Water Bottle
Wärmflasche

Manufacturer
Shenzhen Zhizhi Brand Incubation Co., Ltd.,
Shenzhen, China
In-house design
Web
www.jordanjudy.com

This hot-water bottle is filled with cold water which can be heated up within three minutes in the microwave oven. The very soft and easy-to-clean silicone is food-safe and thus also unobjectionably suited for use on babies. The knitted sleeve is offered with different patterns. It also keeps the water warm, is washable and does not need to be ironed. For a cooling effect, the water can be refrigerated.

Statement by the jury
The Hot Water Bag gains merit with its fast and practical functionality. The affectionate design conveys warmth in emotional terms as well.

Diese Wärmflasche wird mit kaltem Wasser befüllt, das sich innerhalb von drei Minuten in der Mikrowelle erhitzen lässt. Das sehr weiche und leicht zu reinigende Silikon ist lebensmittelecht und somit unbedenklich auch für eine Anwendung bei Babys geeignet. Der gestrickte Überzug wird in verschiedenen Mustern angeboten. Er hält das Wasser zusätzlich warm, ist waschbar und bügelfrei. Für einen abkühlenden Effekt kann das Wasser in der Flasche tiefgekühlt werden.

Begründung der Jury
Hot Water Bag punktet mit einer schnellen und praktischen Funktionsweise. Das liebevolle Design verbreitet auch in emotionaler Hinsicht Wärme.

U Shape Hot Water Bag
Hot-Water Bottle
Wärmflasche

Manufacturer
Shenzhen Zhizhi Brand Incubation Co., Ltd.,
Shenzhen, China
In-house design
Huide Luo
Web
www.jordanjudy.com

The U Shape Hot Water Bag is designed in such a way that it can be comfortably laid around the neck. The silicone sleeve is filled with water and heated up in the microwave oven for three minutes. The bag is then put into a knitted fabric sleeve. It also keeps the water at its temperature and produces comfortable haptics in the throat and neck area. With an additional knitted ribbon, the bottle is fixed in the chest area, and the user is able to move around freely.

Statement by the jury
Thanks to an innovative design, the U Shape Hot Water Bag adapts to the throat-neck area in a non-slip manner. In addition, it is quickly ready for use.

Die U Shape Hot Water Bag ist so konstruiert, dass sie bequem um den Hals gelegt werden kann. Der Silikonmantel wird mit Wasser befüllt und innerhalb von drei Minuten in der Mikrowelle erhitzt. Um diesen herum wird anschließend eine gestrickte Stoffumhüllung gegeben. Diese hält das Wasser zusätzlich auf Temperatur und erzeugt eine angenehme Haptik im Hals- und Nackenbereich. Mittels eines zusätzlichen gestrickten Bändchens wird die Flasche im Brustbereich fixiert und der Nutzer kann sich frei bewegen.

Begründung der Jury
Dank einer innovativen Formgebung passt sich die U Shape Hot Water Bag rutschsicher dem Hals-Nacken-Bereich an. Zudem ist sie schnell einsatzbereit.

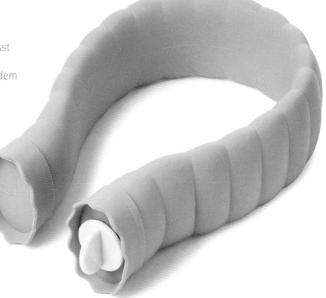

Backpacks	Aktentaschen
Briefcases	E-Zigaretten
Camera bags	Herrenmode
E-cigarettes	Kamerataschen
Glasses	Koffer
Men's wear	Korrekturbrillen
Parasols & umbrellas	Reisetaschen
Shoes	Rucksäcke
Smart accessories	Schuhe
Sports glasses	Smarte Accessoires
Suitcases	Sonnen- & Regenschirme
Sunglasses	Sonnenbrillen
Travelling bags	Sportbrillen
Trolleys	Trolleys
Underwear & lingerie	Unterwäsche & Dessous

Fashion, lifestyle and accessories
Mode, Lifestyle und Accessoires

Petit Pli – Clothes That Grow
Children's Clothing
Kinderbekleidung

Manufacturer
Petit Pli,
London, United Kingdom

In-house design
Petit Pli

Web
www.petitpli.com

reddot award 2019
best of the best

Perfectly adapted

Children grow very quickly, especially in the first two years of their life. Their rapid growth results in garments fitting and being used for short time periods. Petit Pli creates clothes that grow with children to bridge this period and reduce waste. These garments are both aesthetically beautiful and highly innovative. They are designed to grow with children aged nine months to four years, spanning seven discrete sizes. Thus, they serve as a continuous companion in a child's development. The "one size fits all" concept of Petit Pli is made possible because these garments are embedded with a patent-pending structure, allowing children unparalleled freedom of movement. Petit Pli suits are lightweight, rainproof and can easily be machine-washed. On account of children between nine months and four years playing and moving around a lot, these garments have a breathable rainproof coating. Because of the garments' special structure, it is amazing how they allow being pulled to the right size in two directions as needed. The clothes thus adapt to the current size of the child over a longer period, avoiding being either too big or too small. Petit Pli has been developed, above all, in response to a widespread throwaway culture as well as unethical practices synonymous with the fast fashion industry. Moreover, the aim of the design is to convey the value of longevity and innovation in clothing in the next generation – inspiring, instilling and planting the seed for slower consumption behaviours.

Perfekt angepasst

Besonders in ihren ersten zwei Lebensjahren wachsen Kinder sehr rasch. Als Ergebnis passt ihnen Kleidung immer nur für kurze Zeit. Petit Pli basiert auf der Idee mitwachsender Bekleidung, um diesen Zeitraum zu überbrücken und Abfall zu reduzieren. Die Kleidungsstücke sind ästhetisch schön und hochinnovativ, da sie über bis zu sieben verschiedene Kleidergrößen hinweg mit Kindern im Alter von neun Monaten bis zu vier Jahren mitwachsen. Sie werden somit zum stetigen Begleiter in deren Entwicklung. Das Konzept der „Einheitsgröße" von Petit Pli beruht auf dem besonderen, mit einer zum Patent angemeldeten Struktur versehenen Stoff, der Kindern eine unvergleichliche Bewegungsfreiheit bietet. Petit Pli-Kleidung ist sehr leicht, regenfest und kann in der Maschine gewaschen werden. Da sich Kinder in diesem Alter viel bewegen, sind die Kleidungsstücke mit einer wasserdichten, atmenden Beschichtung versehen. Verblüffend ist die Möglichkeit, diese Bekleidung aufgrund der speziellen Stoffstruktur nach Bedarf in zwei Richtungen auf die passende Größe ziehen zu können. Die Kleidungsstücke entsprechen damit jeweils der aktuellen Größe des Kindes und sind weder zu groß noch zu klein. Entwickelt wurde Petit Pli vor allem auch als Antwort auf die verbreitete Wegwerfmentalität unserer Zeit sowie unethische Praktiken in der Modeindustrie. Zielsetzung der Gestaltung war es zudem, bereits der künftigen Generation den Wert einer innovativen, langlebigen Bekleidung zu vermitteln – als Quelle, Inspiration und Grundlage eines entschleunigten Konsumverhaltens.

Statement by the jury

The fascinating concept of growing clothes offers parents of toddlers a highly functional and child-friendly alternative. Made from an innovative material, these smart and lightweight garments can adapt to the growth of children across seven different sizes. Moreover, they are comfortable to wear, breathable and easy to wash in machines. In the often little sustainable fashion industry, they embody an innovative product solution.

Begründung der Jury

Das faszinierende Konzept mitwachsender Kleidung gibt den Eltern von Kleinkindern eine funktionale und kindgerechte Alternative an die Hand. Gefertigt aus einem innovativen Material, können sich diese smarten und leichten Kleidungsstücke über sieben Kleidergrößen hinweg dem Wachstum anpassen. Sie sind dabei angenehm zu tragen, atmungsaktiv und problemlos in der Maschine waschbar. In der oft wenig nachhaltigen Modebranche stellen sie eine zukunftsweisende Produktlösung dar.

Designer portrait
See page 68
Siehe Seite 68

MAGZIP
Zip
Reißverschluss

Manufacturer
IDEAL FASTENER (Guangdong) Industries Ltd.,
Zhaoqing City, Guangdong Province, China
In-house design
Scott Lawrence Peters, David Whitney Lyndaker
Web
www.idealfastener.com
Honourable Mention

The characteristic of this zip fastener is the magnetic structure of the end piece, which even snaps firmly into place when it is operated with one hand. Little dexterity is required for opening and closing. No jamming or blocking – with this promise, the zip fastener meets the requirements of various user groups such as emergency personnel, police officers, hurried parents and children or people with physical challenges. MAGZIP is part of the standard equipment of well-known sport brands and is patented.

Das Kennzeichen dieses Reißverschlusses ist die magnetische Struktur seines Endteils, das auch dann fest einrastet, wenn es nur mit einer Hand bedient wird. Beim Auf- und Zumachen ist nur wenig Fingerfertigkeit erforderlich. Kein Verhaken oder Blockieren – mit diesem Versprechen kommt der Reißverschluss den Bedürfnissen so unterschiedlicher Nutzergruppen wie Rettungskräften, Polizisten, Kindern oder Menschen mit eingeschränkter Motorik entgegen. MAGZIP gehört zur Standardausstattung bekannter Sportmarken und ist patentgeschützt.

Statement by the jury
Thanks to the excellent idea of using a magnetic closure, MAGZIP is conspicuous and easy to handle.

Begründung der Jury
Dank der hervorragenden Idee, einen Magnetverschluss zu verwenden, fällt MAGZIP auf und ist leicht zu handhaben.

Memory Gel Grip Sports Bra
Sports Bra
Sport-BH

Manufacturer
Regina Miracle International (Holdings) Limited, Hong Kong
In-house design
Design
Le Ying Trading (Hong Kong) Limited, Hong Kong
Web
www.reginamiracleholdings.com
www.howherownwords.com

The memory gel band integrated into this sports bra stretches to over three times its original size when the wearer pulls the garment over her shoulders. After the bra has been put on, the band recovers to 94 percent of the original length, thus providing a secure hold in the lower breast area. The bra's breathable spacer pad has a cooling impact and comes with anti-odour Creora yarn to provide a supportive stretch effect. Strategically fitted band and cup sizes give the wearer a comfortable wearing experience.

Das in diesen Sport-BH integrierte Memory-Gelband dehnt sich auf mehr als dreifache Originallänge aus, wenn das Kleidungsstück angezogen wird. Anschließend schnurrt das Band auf 94 Prozent der Originalgröße zusammen und bietet dadurch viel Halt im Unterbrustbereich. Das atmungsaktive Futtermaterial hat kühlende Wirkung und ist mit geruchshemmendem Creora-Garn ausgestattet, das einen bequemen Sitz unterstützt. Die ergonomische Band- und Körbchendimensionierung sorgt für ein angenehmes Gefühl beim Tragen des BHs.

Statement by the jury
In the Memory Gel Grip Sports Bra, a purist style, state-of-the art material and a great fit complement each other to create a successful product solution.

Begründung der Jury
Beim Memory Gel Grip Sports Bra ergänzen sich klare Linien, atmungsaktives Funktionsmaterial und eine genaue Passform zu einer gelungenen Produktlösung.

Arctic Patrol 3-in-1 Jacket
Winter Jacket
Winterjacke

Manufacturer
Helly Hansen AS, Oslo, Norway
In-house design
Web
www.hellyhansen.com

The Arctic Patrol Jacket comprises down with a filling power of 600 cuin from responsible sources. A PFC-free impregnation is used to protect the outer shell. The jacket is waterproof, windproof and promises cosy warmth even at minus temperatures. If required, the down liner and the shell jacket can be easily separated and packed away. The icing on the cake is that the jacket is biologically decomposable – except for the rain shell and the zip-fasteners, which, however, are recyclable.

Statement by the jury
With its high-quality features, the Arctic Patrol Jacket sets standards in the classes of comfort, durability and sustainability.

Das Arctic Patrol Jacket enthält Daunen mit einer Bauschkraft von 600 cuin aus verantwortungsbewusster Produktion. Eine PFC-freie Imprägnierung schützt den Oberstoff. Die Jacke ist wasserdicht, winddicht und verspricht wohlige Wärme auch bei Minustemperaturen. Bei Bedarf lassen sich die Dauneneinlage und die Außenjacke leicht separieren und klein zusammenpacken. Als I-Tüpfelchen ist die Jacke biologisch abbaubar – bis auf die Außenjacke und die Reißverschlüsse, die jedoch recycelt werden können.

Begründung der Jury
Mit seiner hochwertigen Ausstattung setzt das Arctic Patrol Jacket Standards in puncto Komfort, Langlebigkeit und Nachhaltigkeit.

gripmore Socks
Upper Sneaker
Footwear
Schuhe

Manufacturer
gripmore Co., Ltd., Taipei City, Taiwan
In-house design
James Ho, Yeitai Qin, Ernie Tsai, Sylvia Shih
Design
Dongguan Jianghao Plastic Co., Ltd.
(Lanhai Lin, Wei Cui), Dongguan, China
Web
www.gripmore.net
www.gripmore.com

The upper part of these trainers is knitted using 3D technology, with the effect that little waste is produced and that the sock part features a seamless design. No glue is used except between sock and sole. By accurate seating and the elasticity of the sock, but also by a remarkably low weight, the shoe provides comfortable wear. The integrated closure system provides enhanced stability. The patent outer sole with giant undercut cleats cushions every step and gives the foot a firm hold.

Statement by the jury
The gripmore Socks Upper Sneaker impresses with clever details and a coherent look. The manufacture skilfully uses the advantages of new technologies.

Das Oberteil dieses Sneakers wird mit 3D-Technik gestrickt. Dadurch fällt nur wenig Abfall an, und das Sockenteil hat keine störenden Nähte. Eine Verklebung ist nur zwischen Socke und Sohle nötig. Komfortabel wird der Schuh durch seinen passgenauen Sitz und die Dehnbarkeit der Socke, aber auch durch ein geringes Gesamtgewicht. Ein integriertes Verschlusssystem erhöht die Stabilität. Die patentierte Außensohle mit hohen Stollen federt jeden Schritt ab und gibt dem Fuß besonderen Halt.

Begründung der Jury
Der gripmore Socks Upper Sneaker beeindruckt mit pfiffigen Details und einem stimmigen Gesamtbild. Bei der Herstellung wurden die Vorteile neuer Techniken klug genutzt.

bi × sole
Footwear
Schuhe

Manufacturer
FRONTIER Inc., Osaka, Japan
In-house design
Shinji Honda
Design
RISE.DESIGN (Takayuki Shimizu),
Osaka, Japan
Web
www.frontier-inc-web.com
www.rise-design11.com

These multifunctional sandals are characterised by a maximally reduced, urban style. The wearer has the choice of two different types: a closed form and an open variant with holes. The closed sole is recommended in rainy weather or use in the garden. Alternatively, the perforated sole assures pleasant foot ventilation on hot days and lets water drain off easily. Since they are made of EVA foam resin, the sandals are well-cushioned and extremely light.

Statement by the jury
A wide range of applications, an extraordinary low weight and a purist appearance – these are the special advantages of bi × sole.

Der Stil dieses vielseitigen Schuhs ist maximal reduziert und urban. Die Träger haben die Wahl zwischen zwei verschiedenen Sohlentypen: einer geschlossenen und einer offenen Variante mit Löchern. Während sich die geschlossene Sohle bei Regenwetter oder für den Gebrauch im Garten empfiehlt, bewirkt die perforierte Sohle an heißen Tagen eine angenehme Belüftung des Fußes und lässt Wasser einfach ablaufen. Da der Schuh aus EVA-Schaumharz besteht, ist er gut gepolstert und außerordentlich leicht.

Begründung der Jury
Breit gefächerte Einsatzmöglichkeiten, ein auffallend geringes Gewicht und ein puristisches Erscheinungsbild – das sind die besonderen Vorzüge von bi × sole.

XpreSole
Footwear
Schuhe

Manufacturer
CCILU International Inc., Taichung, Taiwan
In-house design
Steve Hsu, Wilson Hsu
Web
www.ccilu.com
Honourable Mention

Damp coffee grains release methane, a greenhouse gas that harms the earth's atmosphere more than CO_2. In order to address this issue, XpreSole uses spent coffee grounds combined with natural rubber as a midsole material. The recycled grounds provide softness for the sole, while also preventing perspiration and unpleasant smells. The pressure on the foot is evenly distributed by means of a responsive plantar design, which uses 114 elastic pillars in the outsole.

Statement by the jury
XpreSole skilfully implements the claim of offering a comfortable sandal which makes an ecological contribution by means of using recycled material.

Feuchter Kaffeesatz stößt Methan aus, ein Treibhausgas, das die Erdatmosphäre stärker schädigt als CO_2. Im Hinblick auf dieses Problem nutzt XpreSole gebrauchtes Kaffeepulver als Zwischensohlenmaterial. Mit Naturkautschuk kombiniert, sorgt das Recyclingmaterial für eine bequeme Weichheit der Zwischensohle. Die Kaffee-Einlage beugt außerdem Schweiß und schlechten Gerüchen vor. In der Außensohle des Schuhs sind 114 elastische Stützen eingebaut, die den Plantardruck gleichmäßig verteilen.

Begründung der Jury
Der Anspruch, eine bequeme Sandale anzubieten, die durch die Verwendung von Recyclingmaterial einen ökologischen Beitrag leistet, wird mit XpreSole gekonnt erfüllt.

P+US ZERO+A1
Eyewear
Brillenkollektion

Manufacturer
Plus Eyewear (Shenzhen) Limited,
Shenzhen, China
Design
Plus Eyewear Limited
(Sze Tung Wong, Jack Kam Pui Cheung),
Hong Kong
Web
www.pluseyewear.com

This collection was developed with the aim of irritating wearers with as little weight as possible. Consequently, the ZERO+A1 frame comes with a light and slim design. Since the frame consists of stainless steel, it is resistant and, despite its delicate structure, provides a secure hold. The hinge system does without screws or welded connections. All components are adjustable, allowing the glasses to be precisely fitted to the shapes of the face and of the head.

Statement by the jury
With a feather-light frame of unobtrusive elegance, the ZERO+A1 turns wearing glasses into a barely perceptible experience.

Diese Kollektion wurde mit dem Ziel entwickelt, Brillenträgern eine möglichst leichte Sehhilfe zu bieten. Entsprechend feingliedrig präsentiert sich das Gestell von ZERO+A1. Da die Brillenfassung aus Edelstahl besteht, ist sie stabil und gibt den Gläsern trotz des zarten Rahmens sicheren Halt. Das Scharniersystem kommt ohne Schrauben oder geschweißte Verbindungen aus. Alle Teile lassen sich einstellen, damit die Brille genau an die jeweilige Gesichts- und Kopfform angepasst werden kann.

Begründung der Jury
Mit einer federleichten Fassung von unaufdringlicher Eleganz macht die ZERO+A1 das Brillentragen zu einem kaum spürbaren Erlebnis.

MYKITA LITE ELGARD
Glasses
Brille

Manufacturer
MYKITA, Berlin, Germany
In-house design
Web
www.mykita.com

The ELGARD model of the MYKITA LITE collection conveys the impression of being a pure acetate pair of glasses. A closer look, however, reveals a filigree stainless steel construction that adds stability to the acetate front. The frame is manufactured using a multistep engineering process during which precision-milled acetate rings are mounted in the 0.6-mm-thin stainless steel frame of the front. Muted colours and discreet colour gradients emphasise the casual character of these navigator-style glasses.

Statement by the jury
ELGARD combines the advantages of an acetate and a metal frame. These well-proportioned glasses offer a high level of comfort.

Das Modell ELGARD aus der Kollektion MYKITA LITE erweckt den Eindruck, eine reine Acetatbrille zu sein. Bei genauerer Betrachtung zeigt sich jedoch eine filigrane Edelstahlkonstruktion, die der Acetatfront Stabilität verleiht. Das Gestell wird in einem mehrstufigen Verfahren gefertigt, bei dem präzise gefräste Acetatringe in einen 0,6 mm dünnen Edelstahlrahmen montiert werden. Gedeckte Farbtöne und dezente Farbverläufe unterstreichen den lässigen Charakter der Navigatorform.

Begründung der Jury
ELGARD vereint die Vorzüge einer Acetat- und einer Metallfassung. Ihrem Träger bietet die formvollendete Brille ein hohes Maß an Komfort.

Hyphen Sunglasses
Sunglasses Collection
Sonnenbrillenkollektion

Manufacturer
Hyphen Eyewear,
Cupertino, California, USA
In-house design
Hans Haenlein, Odin Cappello
Web
www.hyphen-eyewear.com
Honourable Mention

These sunglasses feature a conical hinge that rotates the temple arms into the back of the frame. When folded in, the glasses are remarkably slim, and the gently curved case easily slips into a pocket. The sunglasses also come with an elevated nose pad, which accommodates a lower nose bridge. The collection suits Africans or Asians particularly well, because the high-fitting eyewear harmoniously covers their eyebrows.

Statement by the jury
The Hyphen Sunglasses stand out by their particularly innovative construction, which is tailored to the needs of special user groups.

Diese Sonnenbrillen haben Scharniere, mit denen sich die Bügel parallel zur gewölbten Front einklappen lassen. Zusammengeklappt ist die Brille schmal, und das geschwungene Etui erleichtert die Mitnahme in der Tasche. Die Sonnenbrillen verfügen auch über einen erhöhten Nasensteg, der sich speziell für einen flachen Nasenrücken eignet. Die Kollektion steht Personen mit afrikanischen oder asiatischen Wurzeln besonders gut, weil die hoch sitzenden Brillen vorteilhaft ihre Augenbrauen bedecken.

Begründung der Jury
Die Hyphen Sunglasses zeichnen sich durch ihre besonders innovative Konstruktion aus, die auf eine bestimmte Gruppe von Brillenträgern zugeschnitten ist.

neubau Walter & Wassily
Sunglasses
Sonnenbrille

Manufacturer
Silhouette International, Linz, Austria
In-house design
Roland Keplinger
Web
www.silhouette-international.com

The partly 3D-printed edition Walter & Wassily is dedicated to the artists Walter Gropius and Wassily Kandinsky, commemorating the centenary of the Bauhaus school. A straight titanium wire and circular lenses characterise the geometric outline of the unisex piece. On the inside, the brand's logo is only visible from a certain angle. In line with the reduced graphic language of the frame, the colour range is limited to chrome or matte brass with black or black and white.

Statement by the jury
Walter & Wassily impresses with high-quality craftsmanship and an unusual appearance that approaches the qualities of a work of art.

Anlässlich des 100. Jahrestages der Bauhaus-Gründung ist die teilweise im 3D-Druck gefertigte Edition Walter & Wassily den Künstlern Walter Gropius und Wassily Kandinsky gewidmet. Ein gerader Titandraht und kreisrunde Gläser prägen die geometrischen Konturen des Unisex-Modells. Auf der Innenseite ist das Markenlogo nur aus einem bestimmten Blickwinkel zu erkennen. Im Einklang mit der reduzierten Formensprache ist das Farbprogramm auf Chrom oder mattes Messing mit Schwarz oder Schwarz-Weiß beschränkt.

Begründung der Jury
Walter & Wassily beeindruckt mit hochwertiger Verarbeitung und einer ausgefallenen Erscheinung, die an die Qualitäten eines künstlerischen Objektes heranreicht.

LINDBERG sun titanium
Sunglasses Collection
Sonnenbrillenkollektion

Manufacturer
LINDBERG, Aabyhøj, Denmark
In-house design
Web
www.lindberg.com

In these glasses, an ultra-thin acetate rim connects with a titanium frame. The distinctive material mix of the frame allows for a variety of colour combinations. See-through elements create interesting visual effects – such as the lenses seemingly floating in the oversized frames. In addition, various spectacle shapes ensure variety in the collection. The conspicuous sunglasses are geared towards lightness, flexibility and a customised hold. Each frame is compatible with prescription lenses.

Ein feiner Innenrand aus Acetat ist bei diesen Sonnenbrillen mit einem Titanrahmen verbunden. Der auffällige Materialmix des Gestells ermöglicht vielfältige Farbkombinationen. Darüber hinaus führen durchsichtige Elemente zu interessanten optischen Effekten – beispielsweise wirken die Brillengläser so, als ob sie in der großen Fassung schwebten. Daneben sorgen diverse Rahmenformen für Abwechslung in der Kollektion. Die auffälligen Sonnenbrillen sind auf Leichtigkeit, Flexibilität und einen maßgeschneiderten Sitz getrimmt. Alle Fassungen sind mit Korrektionsgläsern kompatibel.

Statement by the jury
Style confidence, low weight and good ergonomic values characterise these inventive sunglasses that catch the eye with their two frame components.

Begründung der Jury
Stilsicherheit, ein geringes Gewicht und gute Ergonomiewerte zeichnen diese originellen Brillen aus, die mit zwei Rahmenkomponenten zum Blickfang werden.

GENTLE DSM RX
Sunglasses
Sonnenbrille

Manufacturer
AD Global Co., Ltd., Tainan City, Taiwan
In-house design
Ray Chang
Web
www.adhoceyewear.com

The frame of the GENTLE DSM RX sunglasses unites three materials: metal, plastic and rubber. The curved design creates a wide and uninterrupted field of view. At the same time, this shape effectively protects the wearers' eyes from wind and glare. Comfortable positioning is aided by ergonomically optimised balance and adjustable nose pads. The casually styled model allows to replace lenses by a mere click. Ophthalmic lenses can be inserted as well as lenses without vision correction.

Der Rahmen der GENTLE DSM RX vereint drei Materialien: Metall, Kunststoff und Gummi. Die gerundete Kontur der Sonnenbrille schafft ein breites, irritationsfreies Sichtfeld. Zugleich schützt diese Form die Augen wirkungsvoll vor Wind und Lichteinfall. Der ergonomisch optimierte Schwerpunkt der Brille sorgt zusammen mit verstellbaren Nasenpads für einen bequemen Sitz. Per bloßem Klick lassen sich die Gläser des lässig gestylten Modells austauschen. Als Linsen sind Korrektionsgläser ebenso geeignet wie Gläser ohne Korrekturfunktion.

Statement by the jury
The GENTLE DSM RX convinces both with a trendy appearance and from a functional point of view, notably with its convenient mechanism for changing lenses.

Begründung der Jury
Die GENTLE DSM RX überzeugt sowohl mit einem trendigen Look als auch in funktioneller Hinsicht, insbesondere mit ihrem praktischen Wechselglasmechanismus.

Neoknit
Luggage Collection
Gepäckkollektion

Manufacturer
Samsonite NV,
Oudenaarde, Belgium

In-house design
Don Wilson

Web
www.samsonite.com

reddot award 2019
best of the best

Travelling ambassador

Luggage is a personal expression of individuality like apparel and shoes, and at the same time must comply with strict functional needs and requirements. The Neoknit collection of rolling luggage and bags has been created for increasingly demanding, eco-conscious users. In the manufacturing process, the primary material is a knitted, fully recycled polyester (RPET) yarn. The knitting process and subsequent final assembly is almost entirely automated and programmed to reduce waste as much as possible. The various models of the collection all feature individual patterns and motifs. Some of them recall traditional knitting, while others boast highly advanced 3D techniques. The overall appearance of each model is the result of an integrated design, development and refinement process which is aimed at combining the least wasteful production path with the highest possible functionality. The design of Neoknit explores the formal limits of traditional luggage, offering users guidance and orientation through partly transparent insights into the construction of this luggage. Thanks to its groundbreaking concept, this luggage collection turns into a travelling ambassador promoting sustainability.

Reisender Botschafter

Das persönliche Reisegepäck ist ebenso Ausdruck von Individualität wie Kleidung und Schuhe, und muss zugleich strikten funktionalen Bedürfnissen und Ansprüchen genügen. Die Neoknit-Kollektion von Rollkoffern und Taschen richtet sich an die wachsende Zielgruppe der umweltbewussten Reisenden. Bei der Herstellung ist das Ausgangsmaterial ein gewebtes, vollständig recyceltes Polyestergarn (RPET). Das Webverfahren und die Endproduktion laufen nahezu komplett automatisiert und so programmiert ab, dass möglichst wenig Material verbraucht wird. Die verschiedenen Modelle der Kollektion sind jeweils in unterschiedlichen Mustern und Motiven gestaltet. Manche erinnern an traditionelle Webmuster, während andere den Charakter von hochentwickelter 3D-Technologie zeigen. Das Erscheinungsbild jedes einzelnen Modells ist das Resultat eines integrativen Gestaltungs- sowie Entwicklungs- und Veredelungsprozesses, der in seiner Gesamtheit darauf abzielt, eine möglichst ressourcenschonende Produktion mit einem Höchstmaß an Funktionalität zu verbinden. Das Design von Neoknit lotet die formalen Grenzen traditionellen Gepäcks aus und bietet dem Nutzer durch eine teils transparente Konstruktion im Inneren Führung und Orientierung. Dank ihres wegweisenden Konzepts wird diese Gepäckkollektion auf Reisen selbst zu einem Botschafter der Nachhaltigkeit.

Statement by the jury

The design of Neoknit merges a strong sense of aesthetics and functionality with high environmental awareness. Using minimal material and a virtually circular production process, the luggage embodies a trendsetting solution. This luggage collection is beautiful to look at, of very high quality and outstandingly durable. It exudes a sporting appeal, practical and comfortable in use. Its well-thought-out details like the functional inside pockets are enthralling.

Begründung der Jury

Die Gestaltung von Neoknit vereint einen Sinn für Ästhetik und Funktionalität mit hohem Umweltbewusstsein. Ihre unter minimalem Materialeinsatz und in nahezu geschlossenen Kreisläufen erfolgende Produktion ist zukunftsweisend. Diese Gepäckkollektion ist schön anzusehen und qualitativ sehr hochwertig, was sie zudem langlebig macht. Sie wirkt sportiv, ist handlich und komfortabel. Praktische Details wie die funktionalen Innentaschen begeistern den Nutzer.

Designer portrait
See page 70
Siehe Seite 70

Zigo
Luggage Collection
Kofferkollektion

Manufacturer
Samsonite NV, Oudenaarde, Belgium
In-house design
Federica Mucci
Web
www.samsonite.com

The Zigo series consists of cabin cases and matching accessories. The collection stands out due to its distinctive mix of laminated mesh fabric, diamond-textured hard back shells and soft polyurethane trim. Extra large rollers are included in the trolleys, providing a comfortable strolling experience in uneven terrain. The big yet thin wheels are carefully integrated in the shell, taking up only little space inside. Made-to-measure protective caps and anchor fixing of straps add further useful accents.

Statement by the jury
The luggage collection combines fashionable refinement with features that offer commuters and travellers expert support.

Die Gepäckserie Zigo besteht aus Kabinenkoffern und passendem Zubehör. Ein prägnanter Mix aus laminiertem Netzgewebe, rautenförmig strukturierten Rückenschalen und weichem Polyurethan-Besatz kennzeichnet die Kollektion. Die Trolleys sind mit extragroßen Rollen ausgestattet, damit Reisende auf unebenem Terrain gut manövrieren können. Die großen, dabei aber dünnen Räder sind platzsparend in die Schale eingebettet. Maßgeschneiderte Schutzkappen und Schultergurte mit Ankerfixierung setzen weitere nützliche Akzente.

Begründung der Jury
Bei der Kofferkollektion verbindet sich modische Raffinesse mit einer Ausstattung, die Pendlern und Reisenden gekonnt Unterstützung bietet.

Beam Backpack
Solar Backpack
Solarrucksack

Manufacturer
Guangzhou Kingsons Leather Products Co., Ltd., Guangzhou, China
In-house design
Dengtai Tan, Fuchu Fu
Web
www.kingsons.com

The exterior of the Beam Backpack is furnished with thin-film solar cells. The flexible solar panels assure that the user can charge electronic devices such as smartphones, tablets or MP3 players while outdoors. Thanks to a patented USB adaptor system, it is not necessary to open the backpack for plugging in the charging cable. Inside, the partitioning includes a computer compartment and various pockets which allow fast access to objects of daily use.

Statement by the jury
The Beam Backpack offers a clear-cut, harmonious design and delights as an eco-friendly source of power which is tailored to the users' needs.

An der Außenseite des Beam Backpack befinden sich Dünnschicht-Solarzellen. Die flexiblen Solarmodule sorgen dafür, dass die Benutzer elektronische Geräte wie Smartphones, Tablets oder MP3-Player unterwegs jederzeit aufladen können. Dabei ist es dank eines patentierten USB-Adaptersystems nicht notwendig, den Rucksack zum Einstecken des Ladekabels zu öffnen. Das Rucksackinnere verfügt über ein Computerfach und diverse leicht zugängliche Taschen für Alltagsgegenstände.

Begründung der Jury
Äußerlich klar und harmonisch gestaltet, begeistert der Beam Backpack als umweltfreundliche Energiequelle, die auf die Nutzerbedürfnisse zugeschnitten ist.

Catalyst Waterproof
20L Backpack
Rucksack

Manufacturer
Catalyst Lifestyle, Hong Kong
In-house design
Joshua Wright
Web
www.catalystcase.com

This extra light backpack has a water pressure resistance of 10,000 mm and comes with taped waterproof seams. The backpack can be folded up small and stowed in its carrying pouch. A breast strap with whistle is attached to the breathable, quick-drying shoulder straps. A water bottle fits in the side pockets, while the roll-top closure helps to store bulky items. The tapered overall profile ensures that the load on the back is distributed evenly.

Statement by the jury
This backpack offers reliable outdoor support with an exceptionally low weight and small packing size.

Dieser extraleichte Rucksack hat eine Wassersäule von 10.000 mm und ist an den Nähten wasserdicht versiegelt. Der Rucksack lässt sich im zugehörigen Beutel klein gefaltet aufbewahren. Er hat atmungsaktive, schnell trocknende Schultergurte, an denen ein Brustriemen mit Pfeife befestigt ist. In die Seitentasche passt eine Trinkflasche, während der Rolltop-Verschluss hilft, sperrige Gegenstände zu verstauen. Durch das konisch zulaufende Rucksackprofil wird die Last auf dem Rücken gleichmäßig verteilt.

Begründung der Jury
Dieser Rucksack bietet verlässliche Outdoor-Unterstützung mit einem außergewöhnlich geringen Gewicht und kleinen Packmaß.

DAYFARER
Backpack
Rucksack

Manufacturer
MODERN DAYFARER, Cologne, Germany
In-house design
David Hundertmark
Web
www.moderndayfarer.com

The main idea behind the DAYFARER is to offer a backpack that allows a smooth transition from the world of work to sports activities. Accordingly, a ventilated shoe compartment at the bottom of the bag keeps trainers away from other belongings, while an upholstered laptop pocket ensures the transport of the work equipment. The spacious main compartment opens flat like a suitcase, shoulder straps and back are well cushioned. The backpack is made of ballistic nylon fabric with water-repelling external coating.

Hinter dem DAYFARER steht die Idee, einen Rucksack zu bieten, der einen reibungslosen Übergang von der Arbeitswelt zu sportlichen Aktivitäten ermöglicht. Dementsprechend hält ein Schuhfach an der Unterseite des Rucksacks Sportschuhe gut belüftet von anderen Gegenständen fern, während ein separates Laptopfach für den Transport des Arbeitsgerätes sorgt. Das geräumige Hauptfach öffnet sich flach wie ein Koffer; Rückseite und Schultergurte sind gut gepolstert. Gefertigt ist das Modell aus ballistischem Nylon mit wasserabweisender Außenbeschichtung.

Statement by the jury
An intelligent configuration makes this backpack easy to use. The allrounder also pleases with a sporty, sleek appearance.

Begründung der Jury
Eine intelligente Aufteilung macht die Handhabung dieses Rucksacks einfach. Der Allrounder gefällt zudem mit einem sportlich-schlanken Erscheinungsbild.

kofta SS18 IMAGO
Bag Collection
Taschenkollektion

Manufacturer
kofta, Kyiv, Ukraine
In-house design
Konstantin Kofta
Web
www.koftastudio.com
Honourable Mention

The kofta SS18 IMAGO series comprises a backpack which is shaped like a stag beetle along with 13 other leather accessories. Diversity and growth in nature are the overriding themes of the collection, whose motifs are implemented in a particularly lifelike and detailed way. The manufacture of the bags combines craftsmanship with high-tech: the production relies on 3D printing processes as well as on traditional moulding, pressing and painting of leather.

Statement by the jury
The creatively designed and well-coordinated components of the SS18 IMAGO collection make a powerful fashion statement.

Der Rucksack in Hirschkäferform bildet zusammen mit 13 anderen Lederaccessoires die Serie kofta SS18 IMAGO. Vielfalt der Natur und Wachstum zählen zu den übergreifenden Themen der Kollektion, deren Motive betont lebensecht und detailliert umgesetzt sind. Bei der Herstellung der Taschen trifft Handwerk auf Hightech: Moderne 3D-Druckverfahren kommen bei der Verarbeitung ebenso zum Einsatz wie traditionelles Prägen, Pressen und Bemalen des Leders.

Begründung der Jury
Die kreativ gestalteten und gut aufeinander abgestimmten Elemente der Kollektion SS18 IMAGO setzen ein kraftvolles modisches Statement.

VOCIER Avant Work Bag
Briefcase
Aktentasche

Manufacturer
VOCIER GmbH, Vienna, Austria
In-house design
Michael Kogelnik
Web
www.vocier.com

This briefcase has been specially conceived for businesswomen. The classic model is inspired by Yves Saint Laurent and his legendary trouser suit for women. The bag construction combines hard-shell sturdiness with the flexibility of a soft cover, while the interior is organised into three compartments, fitting a 13" laptop and various business documents. In order to secure the contents in an upright position, the briefcase opens up to a maximum angle of 45 degrees.

Statement by the jury
The Avant Work Bag scores with elegance and a self-confident look, combined with special user convenience.

Diese Aktentasche ist speziell für Geschäftsfrauen konzipiert. Inspiriert ist das klassische Modell von Yves Saint Laurent und dessen legendärem Hosenanzug für Frauen. Die Taschenkonstruktion verbindet die Robustheit von Hartschalengepäck mit der Flexibilität einer weichen Hülle, während das dreiteilige Fächersystem genug Platz für einen 13"-Laptop und diverse Arbeitsunterlagen bietet. Um den Inhalt in aufrechter Position zu sichern, öffnet sich die Tasche maximal bis zu einem Winkel von 45 Grad.

Begründung der Jury
Eleganz und eine selbstbewusste Ausstrahlung verbinden sich bei der Avant Work Bag mit einem besonderen Benutzerkomfort.

Manfrotto Pro Light Reloader Spin-55
Trolley
Rollkoffer

Manufacturer
Manfrotto, Vitec Imaging Solutions S.p.A., Cassola (Vicenza), Italy
In-house design
Michele Montemezzi
Web
www.manfrotto.com

The Pro Light Reloader Spin-55 is a photographic camera roller bag in carry-on size which includes an individually adjustable compartment system for safely transporting professional cameras and lenses. Since the inner compartments can be fully removed, the trolley can also be used as a normal travel suitcase. The external shell consists of sturdy yet light polycarbonate to provide full protection; four double spinner wheels ensure smooth rolling. From the front, travellers have quick access to the interior compartment.

Statement by the jury
The trolley is optimally designed for transporting heavy photographic gear. It is versatile in use and convinces with a harmonious form.

Der Pro Light Reloader Spin-55 ist ein Fotokamera-Trolley in Bordgepäckgröße, der ein individuell anpassbares Fächersystem enthält, um professionelle Kameras und Objektive sicher zu transportieren. Da sich die Inneneinteilung entnehmen lässt, kann der Trolley auch als normaler Reisekoffer verwendet werden. Die Außenschale aus robustem, leichtem Polycarbonat bietet umfassenden Schutz für das Gepäck; vier stabile Doppelrollen sorgen für Leichtgängigkeit. Von vorn haben Reisende schnellen Zugriff auf das Innenfach.

Begründung der Jury
Der Trolley ist optimal auf den Transport schwerer Fotoausrüstungen ausgerichtet. Er ist vielseitig einsetzbar und überzeugt mit einer ebenmäßigen Form.

OUMOS CONTAINER 92L
Luggage
Koffer

Manufacturer
OUMOS Travel, Caen, France
In-house design
Charles-Henry Regaud, Hung Shih Ming
Web
www.oumos.com

The shape of this suitcase is inspired by military airdrop boxes. The exterior is made of polycarbonate with a micro-structure finish, which counteracts scratches. The aluminium frame enhances impact resistance. The rectangular form of the case makes good use of the interior space, while 360-degree swivel rollers assure running ease. As an additional feature, a sachet in the interior exudes wisteria and peach blossom fragrances. The sachet also contains the natural mineral vermiculite, which eliminates unpleasant smells and has the effect of dehumidification in the luggage.

Das Erscheinungsbild dieses Koffers ist von Militärkisten inspiriert. Äußerlich besteht das Gepäckstück aus Polycarbonat mit einem Mikrostruktur-Finish, das Kratzern entgegenwirkt. Der Aluminiumrahmen erhöht die Stoßfestigkeit. Durch die rechteckige Kofferform wird der Innenraum gut ausgenutzt, während 360-Grad-Rollen für Beweglichkeit sorgen. Als kleines Extra verströmt ein Beutel im Kofferinneren Glyzinien- und Pfirsichblütenduft. Das Duftsäckchen enthält auch das natürliche Mineral Vermiculit, das unangenehme Gerüche neutralisiert und das Gepäck entfeuchtet.

Statement by the jury
The roomy OUMOS CONTAINER coherently embodies reliability and stability. Furthermore, the fragrance feature lends the case a luxurious touch.

Begründung der Jury
Der geräumige OUMOS CONTAINER verkörpert schlüssig Zuverlässigkeit und Stabilität. Zudem verleiht die Duftausstattung dem Koffer eine luxuriöse Note.

Millennial
Transparent Carry-On Luggage
Transparenter Kabinentrolley

Manufacturer
Traveler's Choice Travelware, Los Angeles, California, USA
In-house design
Joseph Chen
Web
www.travelerchoice.com

This trendy hand luggage effectively asserts both fashionable and functional claims. In the transparent trolley case, style-conscious travellers can show off their latest travel gear, while the built-in power bank allows on-the-go phone charging when travelling. A thin-walled yet sturdy hard shell of 100 per cent polycarbonate protects whatever items are packed in the carry-on case. Thanks to its high-quality Cyclone spherical wheel system, the spinner has good traction properties and is easy to move.

Dieses trendorientierte Handgepäckstück macht sowohl modische als auch funktionale Ansprüche geltend. Stilbewusste Reisende können in dem transparenten Trolley ihre neueste Reiseausrüstung präsentieren, während die eingebaute Powerbank die Möglichkeit bietet, das Smartphone unterwegs aufzuladen. Eine dünnwandige und dennoch robuste Hartschale aus 100 Prozent Polycarbonat schützt die im Koffer verstauten Gegenstände. Dank seines hochwertigen Cyclone-Kugelrollsystems hat der Trolley eine gute Bodenhaftung und ist leichtgängig.

Statement by the jury
With its transparent look and integrated charging function, the Millennial effectively sets itself apart from other luggage. It offers excellent manoeuvrability.

Begründung der Jury
Mit seinem durchsichtigen Look und der integrierten Ladefunktion hebt der Millennial sich effektvoll von anderem Gepäck ab. Er lässt sich sehr gut manövrieren.

Level 8 Aviator
Luggage
Koffer

Manufacturer
Chengdu Skywalker Technology Co., Ltd.,
Chengdu, China
Design
Smartisan Technology Co., Ltd.,
Beijing, China
Web
www.level8.com.cn
www.smartisan.com

The housing of this trolley consists of aluminium-magnesium alloy, a tough material which is often used for aircraft joints. The wheels are coated with wear-resistant rubber and feature double bearings. Consequently, the wheel design ensures flexible, quiet rotation, eliminating unnecessary vibration of the luggage. The telescope rod, which is adjustable to four heights, increases convenience. Further features are TSA locks and a storage capacity of 38 litres inside the case.

Statement by the jury
Low weight, no-frills functionality and advantageous material properties make the Level 8 Aviator a convincing piece of business luggage.

Das Gehäuse dieses Trolleys besteht aus einer Aluminium-Magnesium-Legierung, einem robusten Werkstoff, der oft für Flugzeugteile verwendet wird. Die Räder sind mit verschleißfestem Gummi überzogen und haben Doppelkugellager. So rollt der Koffer leise und ist sehr beweglich; unnötiges Vibrieren wird vermieden. Eine in vier Höhen arretierbare Teleskopstange erhöht den Bedienkomfort zusätzlich. Weitere Ausstattungsdetails sind TSA-Schlösser und ein Stauraum von 38 Litern im Kofferinneren.

Begründung der Jury
Der Level 8 Aviator überzeugt als Businessgepäck mit geringem Gewicht, schnörkelloser Funktionalität und vorteilhaften Materialeigenschaften.

Thule Revolve
Luggage Collection
Kofferkollektion

Manufacturer
Thule Group AB, Malmö, Sweden
In-house design
Web
www.thule.com

The lightweight Thule Revolve cases are made of impact-resistant polycarbonate and have oversize rear wheels in order to glide smoothly over the ground – no matter whether it is a carpet or cobblestones. The telescope handle effectively prevents the case from lurching. The case corners are additionally protected inside; on the outside, the rigid frame and reinforced front panel ensure extra robustness. The custom-fitted felt lining keeps contents in place and absorbs vibration during transport.

Statement by the jury
Thule Revolve merges well-considered functionality and modern form into a harmonious unity.

Die leichten Hartschalenkoffer der Serie Thule Revolve bestehen aus stoßfestem Polycarbonat und haben übergroße Hinterräder, damit sie gut über den Boden gleiten – egal, ob es sich um Teppich oder Kopfsteinpflaster handelt. Einem Schlingern des Koffers wirkt der stabile Teleskopgriff entgegen. Innen sind die Kofferecken zusätzlich geschützt, außen sorgt die verstärkte Vorderseite für Widerstandsfähigkeit. Das maßgeschneiderte Filzinnenfutter sichert das Gepäck und dämpft Vibrationen beim Transport.

Begründung der Jury
Bei Thule Revolve wurden durchdachte Funktionalität und eine moderne Formgebung harmonisch in Einklang gebracht.

TUPLUS Aluminum Alloy
Luggage
Koffer

Manufacturer
Shanghai Tuplus Travel Technology Co., Ltd.,
Shanghai, China
In-house design
Guohui Qian, Zhuo Zhou
Web
www.tuplus.com

The body of this case has been manufactured using aluminum alloy extruded with CNC bending. The front panel can be opened vertically, so that the user can comfortably remove items. The surrounding lines on the case serve the purpose of giving the body rigidity with the lowest possible weight. Furthermore, the linear contours support the hold of the screw fastening in the interior. The double bearing system of the wheels increases transport convenience by ensuring quiet and smooth running.

Statement by the jury
The TUPLUS Aluminum Alloy case convinces as a lightweight with useful details. Thanks to its distinctive lines, it presents itself as if made from one piece.

Der Korpus dieses Gepäckstücks wurde mit CNC-Technik aus einer Aluminiumlegierung gefertigt. Wenn der Koffer aufrecht steht, öffnet sich die Vorderklappe vertikal, sodass man bequem etwas entnehmen kann. Die umlaufenden Linien am Gehäuse dienen dem Zweck, den Koffer bei möglichst geringem Gewicht zu versteifen. Zudem stabilisieren die linearen Konturen die Verschraubung im Inneren. Die doppelte Lagerausführung der Räder erhöht durch leisen und leichtgängigen Lauf den Rollkomfort.

Begründung der Jury
Der Koffer TUPLUS Aluminum Alloy überzeugt als Leichtgewicht mit zweckmäßigen Details. Durch die markante Linienführung wirkt er wie aus einem Guss.

90FUN Puppy 1
Smart Suitcase
Smarter Koffer

Manufacturer
Runmi, Shanghai, China
In-house design
Difei Wu
Web
www.90fun.com.cn

The 90FUN Puppy 1 is furnished with intelligent technology that allows the suitcase to roll by itself and prevents it from tipping over. Thanks to its automatic adjustment system, the cabin trolley travels easily over uneven terrain. Multiple interactive assistant modes are offered, e.g. bi-directional (forward and reverse) following, ramp travel and braking. Users have the option of operating the case by remote control or setting up an auto-following mode within a five-metre range.

Statement by the jury
An extended range of functions make this trolley case a convenient companion. The futuristic exterior matches the innovative quality of the case.

Der 90FUN Puppy 1 ist mit intelligenter Technik ausgestattet, die den Koffer in die Lage versetzt, selbständig zu fahren, und ihn vor dem Umkippen bewahrt. Dank seines automatischen Anpassungssystems bewegt sich der Bordtrolley mühelos über unebenen Boden. Mehrere interaktive Modi stehen zur Verfügung, z. B. Vorwärts- und Rückwärtsgang, Rampenfahren und Bremsen. Die Nutzer haben die Wahl, den Koffer per Fernbedienung zu steuern oder einen Auto-Following-Modus im Fünf-Meter-Radius einzurichten.

Begründung der Jury
Ein erweiterter Funktionsumfang macht diesen Trolley zu einem komfortablen Begleiter. Das futuristische Äußere entspricht den innovativen Qualitäten des Koffers.

Mi Luggage with Front Bag
Koffer

Manufacturer
Runmi, Shanghai, China
In-house design
Yiran Qian, Bo Tian,
Qian Kang, Wei Song
Web
www.90fun.com.cn

At the airport, travellers regularly have to present items from their hand luggage, such as a laptop, travel documents or an umbrella. In this metallic shimmering case made of sturdy polycarbonate, personal belongings can be stowed in the upholstered front compartment and quickly be taken out when required, while the main compartment remains closed. TSA locks secure the valuables inside the luggage. A brake lever for the 360-degree rotating wheels ensures that the case does not roll away unintentionally – a practical function when travelling on public transport.

Bei Kontrollen müssen Flugreisende regelmäßig Gegenstände aus dem Handgepäck holen, etwa ihr Laptop, Reisedokumente oder einen Schirm. In diesem metallisch schimmernden Koffer aus robustem Polycarbonat können die persönlichen Habseligkeiten im gepolsterten Vorderfach verstaut werden und sind schnell greifbar, während das Hauptfach geschlossen bleibt. TSA-Schlösser sichern die Wertsachen im Gepäck. Ein Bremshebel für die um 360 Grad drehbaren Räder bewirkt, dass der Koffer nicht versehentlich wegrollt – eine praktische Funktion bei Fahrten in öffentlichen Verkehrsmitteln.

Statement by the jury
The case catches the eye with its elegant appearance and, in addition, offers a convenient solution for security checks.

Begründung der Jury
Der Koffer fällt mit seinem eleganten Erscheinungsbild ins Auge und wartet zudem mit einer durchdachten Lösung für Sicherheitschecks auf.

doppler zero,99
Mini Umbrella
Taschenschirm

Manufacturer
doppler, E. doppler & Co GmbH, Braunau-Ranshofen, Austria
In-house design
Margit Würflingsdobler
Web
www.dopplerschirme.com
www.doppler-regenschirme.com
www.my-zero99.com

This remarkably light mini umbrella weighs only 99 grams, somewhat less than a bar of chocolate. The covering consists of thin polyester material and is 90 cm in diameter. When folded, the umbrella has a length of only 21 cm, fitting easily into the inside of a jacket or into a handbag. Due to the use of high-quality carbon elements, it is a reliable companion in wind and weather and withstands inversion. The model comes with a telescopic aluminium pole in minimalist design. It is available in nine trendy colours as well as in black, navy and red.

Mit 99 Gramm wiegt dieser federleichte Schirm weniger als eine Tafel Schokolade. Das Schirmdach besteht aus dünnem Polyestergewebe und hat einen Durchmesser von 90 cm. Zusammengefaltet ist der Schirm nur 21 cm lang, sodass er problemlos in die Innentasche eines Sakkos oder in die Handtasche passt. Aufgrund der Verarbeitung mit hochwertigen Carbonelementen ist er ein verlässlicher Begleiter bei Wind und Wetter, der auch ein Umschlagen verträgt. Das Modell hat einen Alu-Teleskopstock mit minimalistischem Griffdesign und ist in neun Trendfarben sowie in Schwarz, Marine und Rot erhältlich.

Statement by the jury
The mini umbrella zero,99 delights with its exceptionally low weight and small package size. In addition, it has a fashionable appearance.

Begründung der Jury
Der Taschenschirm zero,99 begeistert mit einem außergewöhnlich geringen Gewicht und kleinem Packmaß. Zudem hat er eine modische Ausstrahlung.

FARE®-Precious
Golf Umbrella
Gästeschirm

Manufacturer
FARE – Guenther Fassbender GmbH, Remscheid, Germany
In-house design
Web
www.fare.de

This umbrella comes with a matte aluminium shaft in gold or copper, combined with a black or white covering. Special features, such as a snap button on the closing strap and matching metal tips, complete the overall classy appearance. By pressing the release button, an expansive cover opens. Thanks to its fibreglass frame, the umbrella is very stable. It can easily be closed again after flipping over because of strong gusts of wind. Soft touch material and black, shiny plastic meet at the ergonomically shaped handle.

Ein schwarzer oder weißer Bezug ist bei diesem Schirm mit einem matten Aluminiumstock in Gold oder Kupfer kombiniert. Details wie ein Druckknopf am Schließband und passende Metallspitzen runden das edle Gesamtbild ab. Durch Druck auf die Auslösetaste öffnet sich ein ausladendes Dach. Ein Fiberglasgestell macht den Schirm sehr stabil; nach Umschlagen durch zu starken Wind lässt er sich leicht wieder schließen. Am ergonomisch geformten Griff treffen mattes Soft-Touch-Material und schwarz glänzender Kunststoff aufeinander.

Statement by the jury
With its conspicuous refinements, the umbrella design sets standards in terms of usability and elegance.

Begründung der Jury
Das Design des auffällig veredelten Schirms setzt Maßstäbe im Bereich der Benutzerfreundlichkeit und Eleganz.

FARE®-FiligRain Only95
Mini Umbrella
Taschenschirm

Manufacturer
FARE – Guenther Fassbender GmbH, Remscheid, Germany
In-house design
Web
www.fare.de

The FiligRain Only95 weighs only 95 grams without sleeve. With 20.3 cm length, it fits into any jacket or common ladies' handbag. The basic material of the frame is aluminium. For the ribs, aluminium combined with carbon steel and fibreglass is used to improve wind resistance. In case the umbrella flips over, it can be closed with the safety slider and is immediately ready for use again. The covering consists of extra-light polyester and comes in almost all colours with high UV protection of factor 50+.

Der FiligRain Only95 wiegt ohne Futteral nur 95 Gramm und passt mit 20,3 cm Länge sowohl in ein Jackett als auch in eine gängige Handtasche. Das Gestell besteht aus Aluminium, bei den Schienen sorgt eine Kombination von Aluminium mit Carbonstahl und Fiberglas für Windfestigkeit. Falls der Schirm einmal umschlägt, kann er mit dem Sicherheitsschieber geschlossen werden und ist sofort wieder einsetzbar. Der Bezug besteht aus sehr leichtem Polyestermaterial, das in fast allen Farbtönen einen UV-Schutz von UPF 50+ bietet.

Statement by the jury
The maximally reduced and flexible umbrella effectively matches contemporary mobility, which increasingly requires a lightweight equipment.

Begründung der Jury
Der maximal reduzierte und flexible Schirm passt effektiv zum modernen Lebensstil, der es zusehends erfordert, mit leichtem Gepäck mobil zu sein.

VPOD and V-BANK
E-Cigarette and Charging Case
E-Zigarette und Ladeetui

Manufacturer
FOGWARE Technology (Shenzhen) Co., Ltd.,
Shenzhen, China
In-house design
Yuxiong Dong
Web
www.fogwaretech.com

The VPOD e-cigarette requires no complicated transfer of liquids or change of coil, as it can be easily handled with plug-in pods. As soon as the e-cigarette is put into the matching case, it charges automatically, while integrated safety features prevent overcharging, discharging or short circuits. The V-BANK provides about 48 hours of power and, with its folding lid, keeps the e-cigarette clean. It can also be used as a power bank for charging other electronic devices.

Statement by the jury
Easy handling characterises the e-cigarette as well as its charger. The set also convinces due to its appealing haptics and stylish appearance.

Bei der E-Zigarette VPOD ist kein komplizierter Liquid- oder Verdampferwechsel nötig, da sie mit praktischen Einsteckkapseln befüllt wird. Im zugehörigen Etui lädt sie sich automatisch auf, wobei integrierte Sicherheitsfunktionen ein Überladen, Entladen oder einen Kurzschluss verhindern. Die V-BANK liefert etwa 48 Stunden lang Strom und hält das innen liegende Zigarettenmundstück durch einen Klappdeckel sauber. Sie kann auch zum Aufladen anderer elektronischer Geräte genutzt werden.

Begründung der Jury
Einfache Bedienbarkeit zeichnet E-Zigarette wie Ladegerät aus. Zudem überzeugt das Set mit einem haptisch ansprechenden, stilvollen Erscheinungsbild.

Times Square
Digital Perfume Flacon
Digitaler Parfümflakon

Manufacturer
HEINZ-GLAS GmbH & Co. KGaA,
Kleintettau, Germany
In-house design
Jonas Rentsch, Thomas König
Web
www.heinz-glas.com

Times Square is a refillable perfume bottle with digital function which offers a 2.4" screen, an integrated loudspeaker and 128 MB of memory. Whenever the smart bottle is raised, it displays previously loaded photos or plays songs or videos. Among the enabled file formats are JPG, BMP, PNG and GIF as well as mp4, AVI, QuickTime or WMV. Using the USB port, consumers can also personalise the bottle, for example with a favourite saying.

Statement by the jury
The perfume flacon combines the classic material glass in an extraordinary way with high-tech and gains merit with highly emotional content.

Times Square ist ein wiederauffüllbarer Flakon mit digitaler Funktion, der über einen 2,4"-Display, einen integrierten Lautsprecher und 128 MB Speicherkapazität verfügt. Wenn der smarte Flakon angehoben wird, spielt er zuvor gewählte Fotos, Songs oder Videos ab. Zu den geeigneten Dateiformaten gehören JPG, BMP, PNG und GIF ebenso wie mp4, AVI, QuickTime oder WMV. Mittels USB-Anschluss können die Nutzer das Behältnis auch personalisieren, beispielsweise mit einem Lieblingsspruch.

Begründung der Jury
Der Parfümflakon kombiniert den klassischen Werkstoff Glas auf außergewöhnliche Weise mit Hightech und punktet mit einem hohen emotionalen Gehalt.

Flow by Plume Labs
Air Pollution Sensor
Luftverschmutzungssensor

Manufacturer
Plume Labs, Paris, France
In-house design
Alexis Boyer
Design
frog design, London, United Kingdom
Web
www.plumelabs.com
www.frogdesign.com

Flow is a personal air pollution sensor – a companion to explain what is in the air. The sensor and its connected app give a minute-by-minute breakdown of the pollutants the users are exposed to throughout their day by measuring real-time concentrations of NO_2, VOC, $PM_{2.5}$ and PM_{10}. Flow is designed to be a tool to connect, and a tool to empower. Users help crowdsource air pollution levels across their city, empowering others to breathe cleaner air and supporting healthier communities worldwide.

Flow ist ein persönlicher Luftverschmutzungssensor – ein Begleiter, der erklärt, was sich in der Luft befindet. Der Sensor und seine angeschlossene App geben einen minütlichen Überblick über die Schadstoffe, denen die Anwender tagsüber ausgesetzt sind, indem Echtzeitkonzentrationen von NO_2, VOC, $PM_{2.5}$ und PM_{10} gemessen werden. Flow ist als Tool zur Verbindung und zur Selbsthilfe konzipiert. Über Crowdsourcing dokumentieren die Nutzer die Luftverschmutzung in ihrer Stadt, unterstützen andere in ihrem Bestreben, bessere Luft zu atmen und setzen sich so weltweit für gesündere Lebensumstände ein.

Statement by the jury
To a great degree application-oriented and elegantly styled, Flow bridges the gap between personal and collective benefit.

Begründung der Jury
In hohem Maße anwendungsbezogen und formschön gestylt, schlägt Flow eine Brücke zwischen persönlichem und kollektivem Nutzen.

Luxury watches	Armbanduhren
Rings	Dreizeigeruhren
Skeleton watches	Luxusuhren
Three-hand watches	Ringe
Wall clocks	Skelettuhren
Wristwatches	Wanduhren

Watches and jewellery
Uhren und Schmuck

Porsche Design 1919 Chronotimer Flyback Brown & Leather
Wristwatch
Armbanduhr

Manufacturer
Porsche Design Timepieces AG,
Solothurn, Switzerland

In-house design
Studio F. A. Porsche,
Zell am See, Austria

Web
www.porsche-design.com

reddot award 2019
best of the best

Shape in time

Professor Ferdinand Alexander Porsche, founder of Porsche Design, expressed his ideas of consistent design through an innovative, understated design language. To this day, concepts are straightforward, purist, and uncompromisingly functional. This philosophy is particularly evident in the 1919 Collection. In order to display the time for intuitive reading from every angle, the radius of the dial is as large as possible. In addition, a notably slim titanium case was created with distinctive minute indices positioned at the outer edges of the dial, boldly foregoing the need for a tachymeter bezel. The well-balanced design lends this watch a high sense of visual lightness, which is further enhanced by the elegantly proportioned strap. As an expression of functionality-oriented creative design, the lugs are connected to the clasp over the entire surface to achieve a uniform force distribution and thus higher stability, durability and ergonomics. The colour scheme in a deep hue of brown lends the 1919 Chronotimer Flyback Brown & Leather a decidedly contemporary touch, without compromising its timeless-looking characteristics. The innovative wristwatch concept is rounded off by the first own developed Porsche Design Caliber Werk 01.200 movement, which is equipped with a technically sophisticated flyback function.

Form in der Zeit

Professor Ferdinand Alexander Porsche, der Gründer von Porsche Design, artikulierte sein Verständnis von schlüssiger Objektgestaltung in einer zurückgenommenen und innovativen Formensprache. Sie ist schnörkellos, reduziert, puristisch und fokussiert vor allem die Funktion. Eine Maxime, die insbesondere in der 1919 Collection zum Ausdruck kommt. Um dem Träger die Zeit aus jedem Blickwinkel heraus intuitiv anzeigen zu können, ist der Radius des Zifferblatts großflächig angelegt. Zusätzlich wurde das Gehäuse aus Titan besonders schmal konzipiert, die markante Minuterie am äußeren Rand positioniert und gestalterisch bewusst auf eine Tachymeterskala verzichtet. Das gut ausbalancierte Design verleiht dieser Uhr ein hohes Maß an Leichtigkeit, ihre Eleganz wird durch ein formschönes Armband noch verstärkt. Als Ausdruck der an der Funktionalität orientierten kreativen Gestaltung sind die Bandanstöße vollflächig an die Spange angebunden, um so durch eine gleichmäßige Kraftverteilung mehr Stabilität, Langlebigkeit und Ergonomie zu erreichen. Die Farbgebung in einem tiefen Braunton verleiht dem 1919 Chronotimer Flyback Brown & Leather eine betont zeitgemäße Note, ohne seine zugleich zeitlos anmutende Persönlichkeit zu beeinträchtigen. Abgerundet wird das innovative Uhrenkonzept durch das erste eigenständig entwickelte Porsche Design Kaliber Werk 01.200, welches mit einer technisch anspruchsvollen Flyback-Funktion ausgestattet ist.

Statement by the jury

This watch impressively embodies the intellectual inheritance of Ferdinand Alexander Porsche. The design incorporates a subtle and harmonious composition of materials, colours and surfaces, processed to the highest technical standards. The individual elements are perfectly related in their functionality. Also well designed in terms of ergonomics, the housing showcases a sense of lightness that is visually appealing and pleasant to the touch.

Begründung der Jury

Diese Uhr verkörpert eindrucksvoll das geistige Erbe von Ferdinand Alexander Porsche. Ihre Gestaltung ist eine harmonische und feinsinnige Komposition aus Materialien, Farben und Oberflächen bei höchster technischer Qualität. Die einzelnen Elemente stehen zueinander in perfekter Beziehung und Funktionalität. Das auch in seiner Ergonomie gut gestaltete Gehäuse zeigt dabei eine visuelle Leichtigkeit, die haptisch spürbar ist.

Designer portrait
See page 72
Siehe Seite 72

Flieger Verus 40
Wristwatch
Armbanduhr

Manufacturer
STOWA GmbH & Co. KG, Engelsbrand, Germany
In-house design
Jörg Schauer
Web
www.stowa.de

The modern sans-serif typography of the Flieger Verus 40 is reduced to hour, minute and second, further unnecessary or obtrusive printings on the dial have been omitted. Large, illuminating hands and numerals are optically the focus. The wristwatch contains a high-value mechanical movement, decoration and unnecessary complications are, however, renounced, therefore servicing and repair worldwide are quick and easy. The fine matte case can be restored easily, thus saving resources.

Die moderne serifenlose Typografie der Flieger Verus 40 reduziert sich auf Stunde, Minute und Sekunde, weitere überflüssige oder störende Bedruckungen auf dem Zifferblatt wurden weggelassen. Große, leuchtende Zeiger und Ziffern stehen optisch im Vordergrund. Die Armbanduhr umfasst ein hochwertiges mechanisches Uhrwerk, auf Verzierungen und überflüssige Komplikationen wird jedoch verzichtet, so gelingt die Wartung und Reparatur weltweit schnell und einfach. Das feinmattierte Gehäuse kann ressourcenschonend und einfach wieder wie neu aufgearbeitet werden.

Statement by the jury
With its innovative sustainability concept and the aesthetic reduction to essentials, the Flieger Verus 40 skilfully gets to the heart of the times.

Begründung der Jury
Mit ihrem innovativen Nachhaltigkeitskonzept und der ästhetischen Reduktion auf das Wesentliche trifft die Flieger Verus 40 gekonnt den Kern der Zeit.

Flying Regulator Night and Day
Wristwatch
Armbanduhr

Manufacturer
Chronoswiss AG, Lucerne, Switzerland
In-house design
Web
www.chronoswiss.com

The original model of this mechanical wristwatch was developed 30 years ago. The particular characteristic is that it shows a day and night display at nine o'clock which is designed in the form of a titanium dome. Thanks to the Super-LumiNova coating, the stars shine on the night side. The hands and index displays are easily readable at any time due to this illuminating material. At three o'clock, the date is shown in the form of a three-day display. A funnel-shaped scale at six o'clock opens a view to the seconds wheel. The watch dial construction contains 19 components altogether.

Das ursprüngliche Modell dieser mechanischen Armbanduhr wurde vor 30 Jahren entwickelt. Besondere Charakteristik zeigt sie mit einer Tag-/Nacht-Anzeige auf neun Uhr, die in Form einer Halbkugel aus Titan gestaltet ist. Dank Super-LumiNova-Beschichtung leuchten die Sterne auf der Nachtseite. Auch die Angaben auf Zeigern und Indexen werden durch dieses Leuchtmaterial einfach und jederzeit ablesbar. Auf drei Uhr befindet sich das Datum in Form einer Drei-Tages-Anzeige. Eine trichterförmige Skala auf sechs Uhr gibt den Blick frei auf das Sekundenrad. Insgesamt umfasst die Zifferblattkonstruktion 19 Teile.

Statement by the jury
The Flying Regulator Night and Day proves to be a worthy successor of an icon of watch-making art, which impresses through its precision and high-quality materials.

Begründung der Jury
Der Flying Regulator Night and Day erweist sich als würdiger Nachfolger einer Ikone der Uhrmacherkunst, der durch Präzision und hochwertige Materialien besticht.

AIKON Skeleton Manufacture
Wristwatch
Armbanduhr

Manufacturer
Maurice Lacroix SA, Saignelégier, Switzerland
In-house design
Web
www.mauricelacroix.com

The anthracite skeletonised model with a 45-mm case is made of stainless steel and has a satin finished surface. The struts between the recesses as well as the six riders of the bezel are polished. A glance behind the case which is coated in black PVD offers an open view of the manufacture calibre ML234. This is structured bridge for bridge through five concentric circles and appears from the centre of the spring barrel at one o'clock. All components of the manufactured movement are open and bead blasted, from the spring barrel to the flywheel.

Das anthrazitfarbene Skelettmodell mit 45-mm-Gehäuse besteht aus Edelstahl und hat satinierte Oberflächen. Die Streben zwischen den Aussparungen wie auch die sechs Reiter der Lünette sind poliert. Ein Blick hinter das Gehäuse mit schwarzer PVD-Beschichtung gewährt freie Sicht auf das Manufakturkaliber ML234. Dieses ist Brücke für Brücke durch fünf konzentrische Kreise strukturiert und kommt ausgehend von der Mitte des Federhauses bei ein Uhr zur Geltung. Alle Komponenten des Manufakturwerks, vom Federhaus bis hin zur Schwungmasse, sind durchbrochen und perlgestrahlt.

Statement by the jury
The AIKON Skeleton Manufacture draws visual attention to accuracy and engineering. Its design succeeds with a fascinating consensus of playfulness and technology.

Begründung der Jury
Die AIKON Skeleton Manufacture setzt Genauigkeit und Mechanik optisch in Szene. Ihrer Gestaltung gelingt ein faszinierender Konsens von Verspieltheit und Technik.

Dual Time Resonance
Wristwatch
Armbanduhr

Manufacturer
Armin Strom AG, Biel, Switzerland
In-house design
Claude Greisler
Web
www.arminstrom.com

The oval shaped case is the logical consequence of the two side-by-side instead of vertical configurations of the movements. The additional space allows for two spring housings per movement and a longer power reserve. Thus, the glass back enables a view of the four spring housings simultaneously winding up. The independent movements make it possible for the Dual Time Resonance to display two time zones or a timer or countdown setting. Furthermore, a power reserve indicator and a 24-hour indicator are located at six o'clock on the hand-guilloche dials.

Statement by the jury
The ingenious and well-considered design of the Dual Time Resonance offers a fascinating display of precision.

Das ovale Gehäuse ist die logische Konsequenz der zwei nebeneinander statt vertikal angeordneten Werke; es bietet zusätzlichen Platz für zwei Federhäuser pro Werk und eine längere Gangreserve. So werden durch den gläsernen Boden vier sich gleichzeitig aufziehende Federhäuser sichtbar. Die unabhängigen Werke ermöglichen es der Dual Time Resonance, zwei Zeitzonen anzuzeigen bzw. eine Timer- oder Countdown-Einstellung. Zudem finden sich Gangreserve- und 24-Stunden-Anzeige bei sechs Uhr auf den von Hand guillochierten Zifferblättern.

Begründung der Jury
Die raffiniert und durchdacht gestaltete Dual Time Resonance bietet ein faszinierendes Schauspiel an Präzision.

Backpage
Wristwatch
Armbanduhr

Manufacturer
Grossmann Uhren GmbH,
Glashütte, Germany
Design
Neodesis Sàrl, Le Locle, Switzerland
Web
www.grossmann-uhren.com
www.neodesis.ch

The mirror image calibre 107.0 makes the mechanism of the Backpage visible on the dial side. Through a large aperture, the characteristic movement details such as the Grossmann balance wheel, the hand-engraved balance cock or the ratchet wheel with three-band snailing can all be observed while on the wrist. The fully surrounding minute scale and an hour display from eleven to five o'clock serve as a framework for the moving calibre presentation. The imposed hour indexes and numerals in gold correspond to the colour of the case which is in rose gold. The lowered screwed ring of the small second hand displays the sophisticated bearing of the second hand shaft with a screwed gold chaton.

Statement by the jury
The Backpage discloses effective insights into the inner workings and conveys at the same time a soothing harmony.

Das gespiegelte Kaliber 107.0 macht die Mechanik der Backpage auf der Zifferblattseite sichtbar. Durch einen großen Ausschnitt können die charakteristischen Uhrwerkdetails wie die Grossmann'sche Unruh, der handgravierte Unruhkloben oder das Sperrrad mit dem dreifach gestuften Sonnenschliff am Handgelenk beobachtet werden. Als Rahmen für die bewegte Kaliberpräsentation dienen die voll umlaufende Minutenskala und eine Stundenanzeige von elf bis fünf Uhr. Die aufgesetzten Stundenindexe und -ziffern aus Gold korrespondieren mit der Farbe des Gehäuses in Roségold. Der tiefer eingedrehte Ring der kleinen Sekunde zeigt die anspruchsvolle Lagerung der Sekundenzeigerwelle mit einem verschraubten Goldchaton.

Begründung der Jury
Die Backpage eröffnet wirkungsvolle Einblicke in ihr Innenleben und vermittelt zugleich wohltuende Ausgeglichenheit.

Zeitgeist Automatik
Wristwatch
Armbanduhr

Manufacturer
Lilienthal Lifestyle GmbH, Berlin, Germany
In-house design
Jacques Colman, Lars Hofmann
Web
www.lilienthal.berlin

The Zeitgeist Automatik is accurately engineered, having a Swiss mechanical movement with decorated rotor, a screwed glass case back, details in Super-LumiNova and use of sapphire glass. The design reflects typical style elements of Berlin's urban character: for the dial, the typography of the Berlin street signs was used, the crown is set in the only 10 mm thick housing and is formed to resemble the iconic World Clock located in the public square of Alexanderplatz. The minutes are shown on the outside, the hours in the centre of the face.

Statement by the jury
The Zeitgeist Automatik convinces with the combination of exclusivity and sturdiness as well as a successful integration of Berlin style elements.

Die Zeitgeist Automatik ist hochwertig verarbeitet durch ein Schweizer Mechanikwerk mit dekoriertem Rotor, einen verschraubten Glasboden, Details in Super-LumiNova sowie den Einsatz von Saphirglas. Das Design greift typische Stilelemente aus dem Berliner Stadtbild auf: Für das Zifferblatt wurde die Typografie der Berliner Straßenschilder verwendet und die in das nur 10 mm hohe Gehäuse eingelassene Krone ist wie die ikonische Weltzeituhr am Alexanderplatz geformt. Die Minuten werden außen, die Stunden im Zentrum des Zifferblattes dargestellt.

Begründung der Jury
Die Zeitgeist Automatik überzeugt durch die Verbindung von Exklusivität und Robustheit sowie eine gelungene Integration Berliner Stilelemente.

Lunascope
Wristwatch
Armbanduhr

Manufacturer
MeisterSinger GmbH & Co. KG,
Münster, Germany
In-house design
Manfred Brassler
Web
www.meistersinger.de

The slim, stainless steel housing of the Lunascope encompasses a particularly large moon phase indicator, for which the upper half of the face was snappily cut out. Within it, the moon moves against a dark blue starry sky. Its generous dimensions allow recognition also of fine details of the realistically displayed moon surface. The moon phase indication does not require any adjustment for 128 years and operates thus with particular precision.

Statement by the jury
The Lunascope astronomical wristwatch fascinates due to its unusual precision and detailed depiction of the moon.

Das schlanke Edelstahlgehäuse der Lunascope rahmt eine besonders große Mondphasenanzeige, für die die obere Hälfte des Zifferblatts schwungvoll ausgeschnitten wurde. Darin bewegt sich der Mond vor einem dunkelblauen Sternenhimmel. Sein großzügiger Durchmesser lässt auch feine Details der realistisch wiedergegebenen Mondoberfläche erkennen. Die Mondphasenindikation benötigt erst nach 128 Jahren eine kleine Justierung und arbeitet damit besonders genau.

Begründung der Jury
Die astronomische Armbanduhr Lunascope fasziniert durch ihre außergewöhnliche Präzision und die detailgetreue Darstellung des Mondes.

EZM 12
Wristwatch
Armbanduhr

Manufacturer
Sinn Spezialuhren GmbH,
Frankfurt/Main, Germany
In-house design
Web
www.sinn.de

This wristwatch has been specially developed for emergency medical uses. The relevant windows of time for this profession such as the "Platinum Ten Minutes" and the "Golden Hour" can be monitored with the inner bezel. The outer bezel indicates the times for administering medication. The second hand is rotor-shaped and serves as a scale for monitoring the pulse in 15-second intervals. The timepiece has no sharp edges, so that gloves remain undamaged. Due to innovative mechanisms, the strap and rotary bezel can be easily removed for disinfection.

Statement by the jury
The dynamically sporty appearance of the EZM 12 is impressive. The special properties for emergency medicine are implemented with convincing functionality.

Diese Armbanduhr ist speziell auf die Bedürfnisse von Notfallmedizinern ausgerichtet. Für diesen Beruf relevante Zeitfenster wie die „Platinum Ten Minutes" und die „Golden Hour" können mit dem Innendrehring überwacht werden. Der Außendrehring gibt Applikationszeitpunkte für Medikamente an. Der rotorförmige Sekundenzeiger dient als Skala zur Überwachung der Pulsfrequenz im 15-Sekunden-Rhythmus. Der Zeitmesser weist keine scharfen Kanten auf, so bleiben Schutzhandschuhe intakt. Durch innovative Mechanismen lassen sich Armband und Drehring zur Desinfektion einfach abnehmen.

Begründung der Jury
Das dynamisch-sportive Auftreten des EZM 12 beeindruckt. Die speziellen Eigenschaften für die Notfallmedizin sind überzeugend funktional umgesetzt.

QLOCKTWO® 180 Creator's Edition
Silver & Gold
Wall Clock
Wanduhr

Manufacturer
QLOCKTWO Manufacture GmbH,
Marco Biegert und Andreas Funk,
Schwäbisch Gmünd, Germany
In-house design
Web
www.qlocktwo.com

On the 180 × 180 cm wall clock, time is represented with an innovative concept. On a matrix of 110 seemingly randomly arranged letters, the course of time is presented in five-minute steps. The four illuminated dots in the corners show the minutes exactly. The 12-carat white gold alloy of the front surface consists of equal parts of silver and gold. White gold leaves are applied by hand to the front in the manufactory and the surface is refined in a patination process. The oxidised silver part generates an irregular patina which is fixed after receiving the desired colour and provides each clock with an individual surface structure.

Auf der 180 × 180 cm großen Wanduhr wird die Zeit mit einem innovativen Konzept dargestellt. Auf einer Matrix aus 110 scheinbar willkürlich angeordneten Buchstaben wird der Zeitverlauf in Fünf-Minuten-Schritten präsentiert. Die vier Leuchtpunkte in den Ecken geben die Minuten genau wieder. Die 12-Karat-Weißgoldlegierung der Front besteht zu gleichen Teilen aus Silber und Gold. Weißgoldblätter werden in der Manufaktur von Hand auf die Front aufgebracht und die Oberfläche in einem aufwendigen Patinierungsprozess veredelt. Der oxidierende Silberanteil erzeugt eine unregelmäßige Patina, die nach Erhalt der gewünschten Farbgebung fixiert wird und jeder Uhr eine individuelle Oberflächen-struktur verleiht.

Statement by the jury
The innovative wall clock takes centre stage in the room without dominating it and makes reading the time an experience far beyond the literal sense of the word.

Begründung der Jury
Die innovative Wanduhr weiß den Raum zu bestimmen, ohne ihn zu dominieren, und macht Zeitanzeige weit über den eigentlichen Wortsinn hinaus erfahrbar.

Ultra-Lightweight Laser-Cut Tube Jewellery
Jewellery Collection
Schmuckkollektion

Manufacturer
Titan Company Limited, India

In-house design
Saloni Kaushik,
Pooja Kabra (Project Mentor)

Web
www.titancompany.in

reddot award 2019
best of the best

Intricate cutwork

Across all eras, gold jewellery has always borne
witness to both its place of origin and the artistry of
its time. Thus, craftsmanship and innovative technologies often enter into a symbiotic relationship. This
collection of neckwear, bangles and rings has been
created by using a special bending technique for tubes
with unusual cross sections like star, arch and lotus.
The thickness of the gold sheet used is as low as
0.2 mm, allowing for pieces of jewellery that are ultra-
lightweight and use less material. Their distinctive
appeal is in the further processing by using a precision
laser cutting machine to intricate patterns onto
the tubes. Establishing a new approach, familiar laser
cutting has here been applied to round and square
tubes with a width of only 2 to 2.5 mm. Even triangular cross sections can be processed to feature
cut-outs on both the sides with superior quality finish
and precision. The differentiation of these pieces
of jewellery is further enhanced by setting diamond-
studded units onto these sophisticated laser-cut
tubes. This staggeringly novel design concept in the
field of fine jewellery has also given birth to a sturdy
18-carat gold bangle. Made from round and square
tubes, this bangle features intricate cutwork that adds
to its beauty in gold with a weight of just four grams.

Filigrane Schnittkunst

Quer durch alle Epochen zeugt Goldschmuck stets von
der Kunstfertigkeit seiner Zeit und seines Entste-
hungsortes. Handwerk und innovative Technologien
gehen dabei oft eine symbiotische Beziehung ein. Die
Kollektion aus Halsschmuck, Armreifen und Ringen
entsteht durch den Einsatz einer speziellen Technik, bei
der Röhrchen mit lotus-, bogen- oder sternförmigen
Querschnitten gebogen werden. Die Dicke des verwendeten Goldbleches beträgt dabei nur 0,2 mm, weshalb die Schmuckstücke sehr leicht sind und weniger
Material benötigt wird. Ihr besonderer Reiz liegt
zudem in der weiteren Bearbeitung, da mittels einer
Laserschneidmaschine komplexe Muster in das Metall
geschnitten werden. Auf neuartige Weise kommt diese
Technik bei runden und eckigen Röhrchen mit einer
Breite von nur 2 bis 2,5 mm zur Anwendung. Selbst
auf dreieckigen Querschnitten können beidseitig Aus-
schnitte mit höchster Qualität und Präzision ausgeführt werden. Individualität erhalten diese Schmuckstücke außerdem dadurch, dass auf den so bearbeiteten
Röhrchen mit Diamanten besetzte Elemente platziert
werden. Durch dieses verblüffend neue Gestaltungs-
konzept im Bereich hochwertigen Schmucks entstand
so auch ein robuster 18-Karat-Gold-Armreif. Gefertigt
aus runden und eckigen Röhrchen, zeigt er eine ausgefeilte Schnittkunst, die seine Ästhetik in Gold bei
einem minimalen Gewicht von nur vier Gramm zusätzlich erhöht.

Statement by the jury

This jewellery collection impresses with a design that
subtly combines traditional craftsmanship with the
use of innovative technology. It showcases appealing
patterns cut by laser into tubes that have been bent
from extremely thin gold sheet. The result of a complex production process, these pieces of jewellery
amaze with pure manufacturing precision. Extremely
light and elegant, they are imbued by a captivating,
sensual expression.

Begründung der Jury

Diese Schmuckkollektion begeistert durch eine
Gestaltung, die auf feinsinnige Weise traditionelle
Handwerkskunst mit dem Einsatz innovativer
Technologie vereint. In aus äußerst dünnwandigem
Goldblech gebogenen Röhrchen werden per Laser
ornamentale Muster geschnitten. Die in einem
komplexen Prozess entstehenden Schmuckstücke
verblüffen durch die Präzision ihrer Ausführung.
Außerordentlich leicht und elegant, zeigen sie einen
bestechend sinnlichen Ausdruck.

Designer portrait
See page 74
Siehe Seite 74

Good Fortune Gourd
Jewellery Collection
Schmuck-Kollektion

Manufacturer
Beijing Forbidden City Culture Development Co., Ltd.,
Beijing, China
Design
Juan Juan Hu Jewellery Design (Juan Juan Hu),
Shanghai, China
Web
www.juanjuanhu.com
Honourable Mention

The Good Fortune Gourd jewellery collection consists of a necklace, ring and earrings. They are all ornamented with elements in the shape of a calabash, a traditional Chinese lucky emblem. It represents success and good harvest. A pearl is enclosed in the pendant of the bracelet which can be detached or worn attached. The earrings can be worn optionally only as pearl studs or included in the suspended calabash elements.

Die Schmuck-Kollektion Good Fortune Gourd setzt sich zusammen aus Halskette, Ring und Ohrringen. Sie sind jeweils mit Elementen in Form eines Flaschenkürbisses versehen, einem traditionellen chinesischen Glückssymbol. Es versinnbildlicht Erfolg und gute Ernte. In dem Anhänger der Halskette ist eine Perle eingeschlossen, die sich entnehmen und ebenfalls an der Kette befestigen lässt. Die Ohrringe lassen sich wahlweise nur als Perlenstecker oder inklusive des hängenden Kürbiselementes tragen.

Statement by the jury
The jewellery collection impresses with its jaunty aesthetics. It skilfully typifies parts of the Chinese teachings of good fortune.

Begründung der Jury
Die Schmuck-Kollektion beeindruckt in ihrer unbeschwerten Ästhetik. Gekonnt versinnbildlicht sie Teile der chinesischen Glückslehre.

PRISMA
Wedding Rings
Trauringe

Manufacturer
August Gerstner Ringfabrik GmbH & Co. KG,
Pforzheim, Germany
In-house design
Annelie Waldhier-Fröhling
Web
www.gerstner-trauringe.de

In the iridescent colour play of these wedding rings, nuances of various gold tones flow gently into one another. Light reflexion generates a silky impression on the surface. Each movement causes the light to reflect differently, imparting on the ring an organic and lively impression. Seven natural coloured diamonds, brilliantcut, colourfully matched to the particular golden shade are mounted throughout the whole width of one of both rings and provide the impression of a light band.

Bei dem irisierenden Farbenspiel dieser Trauringe fließen die Nuancen unterschiedlicher Goldtöne sanft ineinander. Die Reflexion des Lichts erzeugt einen seidigen Eindruck auf der Oberfläche. Bei jeder Bewegung wird das Licht anders reflektiert, was den Ringen eine organische und lebendige Anmutung verleiht. Sieben naturfarbene Diamanten im Brillantschliff, farblich genau auf die jeweilige Goldfarbe abgestimmt, sind über die gesamte Breite eines der beiden Ringe eingelassen und vermitteln den Eindruck eines Lichtbandes.

Statement by the jury
The PRISMA wedding rings are reserved in their form and provide euphoria and simultaneously accordance, due to their harmonious interplay of colour tones and finish.

Begründung der Jury
In der Form zurückhaltend, vermitteln die Trauringe PRISMA durch das harmonische Zusammenspiel von Farbtönen und Finish Euphorie und Einklang zugleich.

The jury 2019
International orientation and objectivity
Internationalität und Objektivität

The jurors of the Red Dot Award: Product Design
All members of the Red Dot Award: Product Design jury are appointed on the basis of independence and impartiality. They are independent designers, academics in design faculties, representatives of international design institutions, and design journalists.

The jury is international in its composition, which changes every year. These conditions assure a maximum of objectivity. The members of this year's jury are presented in alphabetical order on the following pages.

Die Juroren des Red Dot Award: Product Design
In die Jury des Red Dot Award: Product Design wird als Mitglied nur berufen, wer völlig unabhängig und unparteiisch ist. Dies sind selbständig arbeitende Designer, Hochschullehrer der Designfakultäten, Repräsentanten internationaler Designinstitutionen und Designfachjournalisten.

Die Jury ist international besetzt und wechselt in jedem Jahr ihre Zusammensetzung. Unter diesen Voraussetzungen ist ein Höchstmaß an Objektivität gewährleistet. Auf den folgenden Seiten werden die Jurymitglieder des diesjährigen Wettbewerbs in alphabetischer Reihenfolge vorgestellt.

David Andersen
Denmark
Dänemark

David Andersen, born in 1978, graduated from Glasgow School of Art and the Fashion Design Academy in 2003. Until 2014, he developed designs for ready-to-wear clothes, shoes, perfume, underwear and home wear and emerged as a fashion designer working as chief designer at Dreams by Isabell Kristensen as well as designing couture for the royal Danish family, celebrities, artists etc. under his own name. In 2007, he debuted his collection "David Andersen". He has received many awards and grants for his designs, e.g. a grant from the National Art Foundation. David Andersen is also known for his development of sustainable clothing with his collection, Zero Waste, and has received several awards for his work on ecology and sustainable productions. David Andersen has changed his job as Vice President for Design at Rosendahl Design Group and is now working for the fur giant, KC FUR in China, as Design Director. Furthermore, David Andersen is a guest lecturer at different schools and colleges.

David Andersen, 1978 geboren, studierte an der Glasgow School of Art und der Fashion Design Academy, wo er 2003 sein Examen machte. Bis 2014 fertigte er Entwürfe für Konfektionsware, Schuhe, Parfüm, Unterwäsche und Homewear. Daraus entwickelte sich eine Karriere als Modedesigner und er begann, bei Dreams von Isabell Kristensen als Chefdesigner zu arbeiten sowie unter seinem eigenen Namen Couture für die dänische Königsfamilie, Prominente, Künstler etc. zu entwerfen. Im Jahr 2007 stellte er erstmals seine eigene „David Andersen"-Kollektion vor. Für seine Entwürfe erhielt er bereits viele Auszeichnungen und Fördergelder, darunter ein Stipendium der National Art Foundation (Nationale Kunststiftung). David Andersen hat sich auch mit „Zero Waste", einer Kollektion nachhaltiger Kleidung, einen Namen gemacht, und mehrere Auszeichnungen für seine Arbeit im Bereich von Umwelt und nachhaltiger Produktion erhalten. David Andersen hat seine ehemalige Stelle als Vizepräsident für Design bei der Rosendahl Design Group aufgegeben und ist jetzt Design Director für den riesigen Pelzkonzern KC Fur in China. Darüber hinaus ist er Gastdozent an verschiedenen Schulen und Hochschulen.

01–02
Designs of David Andersen's
sustainable "Zero Waste" collection
Entwürfe aus David Andersens
nachhaltiger Kollektion „Zero Waste"

01

02

"The most important thing is to be true to oneself. Never compromise unless it is a necessity."

„Das Wichtigste ist, sich selbst treu zu bleiben. Niemals Kompromisse eingehen, es sei denn, es ist absolut notwendig."

What can people surprise you with in your role as fashion designer?
Most people think that being a fashion designer is glamour, red runner and lots of parties. The fashion industry is filled with glamour, but you have to create it yourself and that is hard work.

What, in your opinion, makes for good design?
Good design must be able to stand for itself and, at the same time, do something good for the person who will carry it. The design becomes interesting when there is a good story behind and through the choice of materials, shape and colour.

What, currently, stands out especially in the fashion industry?
An incredible amount is happening. In recent years, we have worked hard to create a more sustainable approach to the way we work with our clothing. In a short time, there has been tremendous development in sustainable fashion, which is incredibly interesting to be a part of, and to work every day to do better.

Womit können Menschen Sie in Ihrer Rolle als Modedesigner überraschen?
Die meisten Menschen glauben, dass das Leben eines Modedesigners aus Glamour, roten Teppichen und vielen Partys besteht. Die Modeindustrie ist voller Glamour, doch muss man ihn selbst schaffen und das erfordert harte Arbeit.

Was macht Ihrer Meinung nach gutes Design aus?
Gutes Design muss sowohl für sich alleine funktionieren als auch für denjenigen, der es trägt, etwas Gutes tun. Design wird interessant, wenn es im Hintergrund eine gute Story gibt – und auch durch die Wahl von Materialien, Form und Farbe.

Was ist gerade besonders auffallend in der Modeindustrie?
Es geschieht wahnsinnig viel. In den letzten Jahren haben wir hart gearbeitet, um einen nachhaltigeren Ansatz für unsere Arbeit in der Modebranche zu etablieren. In relativ kurzer Zeit hat es im Bereich nachhaltiger Mode eine enorme Entwicklung gegeben. Es ist sehr interessant, Teil davon zu sein und jeden Tag zu versuchen, besser zu werden.

Prof. Masayo Ave
Japan/Germany
Japan/Deutschland

Professor Masayo Ave is the founder of the design studio MasayoAve creation and SED.Lab, Sensory Experience Design Laboratory in Berlin. The Japanese designer merges culture and disciplines and brings to bear her expertise in her sensory-based innovative design works and also in the field of design education. A graduate in architecture from Hosei University in Japan, her design career began in Milan in the early 1990s. Taking a sensorial and imaginative approach to basic design principles, her focus on material exploration and experimental design development brought her critical fame and many international design awards. In the early 2000s, Masayo Ave also became involved in the field of design education and was appointed a professor at University of Arts in Berlin, the Estonian Academy of Arts and recently at Berlin International University of Applied Sciences. As a prominent designer-teacher, she has also been dedicating her career to developing a new design education programme for children and young people that encompasses sensory-based design experiences.

Professor Masayo Ave ist Gründerin des Designstudios MasayoAve creation und des SED.Lab, einem Labor für sensorische Designforschung in Berlin. Die japanische Designerin verschmilzt Kultur mit Wissenschaftsfächern und bringt ihre Fachkenntnisse in ihre innovativen, auf Sensorik basierenden Gestaltungsprojekte ein, ebenso wie auf dem Gebiet der Designausbildung. Nach einem Architekturabschluss an der Hosei University in Japan begann sie ihre Designkarriere in Mailand in den frühen 1990er Jahren. Maßgebende Designgrundlagen ging sie mit einem sensorischen und ideenreichen Konzept an. Ihre Ausrichtung auf Rohstoffforschung und experimentelle Designentwicklung hatte das Lob der Kritiker und viele internationale Designauszeichnungen zur Folge. In den frühen 2000er Jahren fing Masayo Ave an, sich auch mit der Designausbildung zu beschäftigen, und wurde zur Professorin an der Universität der Künste in Berlin sowie an der Estländischen Kunstakademie und unlängst an der Berlin International University of Applied Sciences ernannt. Als prominente Designerin und Lehrerin hat sie sich im Laufe ihrer Karriere für die Entwicklung eines neuen Designausbildungsprogramms für Kinder und Jugendliche eingesetzt, das auch auf Sensorik basierende Designerlebnisse beinhaltet.

01 GENESI
Table light with a cover made
from a washable open-cell
polyester and a body in chromed
steel, launched in her own collection "MasayoAve creation", 1998
Tischleuchte mit einem Lampen-
schirm aus waschbarem, offenpo-
rigem Polyester und einem Körper
aus verchromtem Stahl, erschienen
in ihrer eigenen Kollektion
„MasayoAve creation", 1998

01

"My advice for young designers
is to observe details of their
everyday living environment with
a scientific designer's eye. The
answer exists there and is waiting
to be discovered."

„Mein Ratschlag für junge Designer
ist, die Details des täglichen
Lebens mit einem wissenschaftlichen
Designerauge zu betrachten. Die
Antwort ist dort zu finden und war-
tet nur darauf, entdeckt zu werden."

How did you get into design?
By being imaginative and curious about the potential
of industrial materials in relation to lifestyle culture.

**What does the "MasayoAve creation" design studio
stand for?**
It is a cross-disciplinary platform where design projects
and sensory experiences interconnect.

**What, to date, has been the most exciting project
of your career?**
Each moment in the past projects was unforgettably
exciting, but I may say the newest sensory experience
design project which I am now working on is the most
exciting one.

Where do you find inspiration?
Learning the fundamentals of design is to get a
comprehensive understanding of one's own living environment through perceptive senses. The everyday
discoveries of tiny details in nature have inspired
me a lot.

Wie sind Sie zum Design gekommen?
Indem ich dem Potenzial für industrielle Materialien
in Bezug auf unsere Lebenskultur mit Phantasie und
Neugierde begegnet bin.

**Wofür steht das Designstudio „MasayoAve
creation"?**
Es ist eine interdisziplinäre Plattform, die Designprojekte
mit sensorischen Erlebnissen verbindet.

Was war Ihr bisher spannendstes Projekt?
Jeder Moment vergangener Projekte war unvergesslich
spannend, doch kann ich sagen, dass das neueste Design-
projekt für sensorische Erlebnisse, an dem ich gerade
arbeite, das spannendste ist.

Woher nehmen Sie Ihre Inspiration?
Wenn man die Grundlagen der Gestaltung lernt, erwirbt
man mithilfe seiner sinnlichen Wahrnehmung auch
ein grundlegendes Verständnis seines Lebensraums. Die
täglichen Entdeckungen kleinster Details in der Natur
haben mich sehr inspiriert.

Martin Beeh
Germany
Deutschland

Martin Beeh is a graduate in Industrial Design from the Darmstadt University of Applied Sciences in Germany and the ENSCI-Les Ateliers, Paris, and completed a postgraduate course in business administration. In 1995, he became design coordinator at Décathlon in Lille/France, in 1997 senior designer at Electrolux Industrial Design Center Nuremberg and Stockholm and furthermore became design manager at Electrolux Industrial Design Center Pordenone/Italy, in 2001. He is a laureate of several design awards as well as founder and director of the renowned student design competition "Electrolux Design Lab". In the year 2006, he became general manager of the German office of the material library Material ConneXion in Cologne. Three years later, he founded the design office beeh_innovation. Martin Beeh lectured at the Folkwang University of the Arts in Essen, the University of Applied Sciences Schwäbisch Gmünd and the University of Applied Sciences Hamm-Lippstadt and was professor for design management at the University of Applied Sciences Ostwestfalen-Lippe in Lemgo from 2012 to 2015. He has furthermore developed the conference format "materials.cologne" as a dialogue platform for materials, design and innovation.

Martin Beeh absolvierte ein Studium in Industriedesign an der Fachhochschule Darmstadt und an der ENSCI-Les Ateliers, Paris, sowie ein Aufbaustudium der Betriebswirtschaft. 1995 wurde er Designkoordinator bei Décathlon in Lille/Frankreich, 1997 Senior Designer im Electrolux Industrial Design Center Nürnberg und Stockholm sowie 2001 Design Manager im Electrolux Industrial Design Center Pordenone/Italien. Er ist Gewinner diverser Designpreise und gründete und leitete den renommierten Designwettbewerb für Studierende, das „Electrolux Design Lab". Im Jahr 2006 wurde er General Manager der deutschen Niederlassung der Materialbibliothek „Material ConneXion" in Köln. Drei Jahre später gründete Martin Beeh das Designbüro beeh_innovation. Martin Beeh hatte Lehraufträge an der Folkwang Universität der Künste in Essen, an der Hochschule für Gestaltung Schwäbisch Gmünd und an der Hochschule Hamm-Lippstadt und war von 2012 bis 2015 Professor für Designmanagement an der Hochschule Ostwestfalen-Lippe in Lemgo. Darüber hinaus entwickelte er das Konferenzformat „materials.cologne" als Plattform für den Dialog zwischen Material, Design und Innovation.

01
Key visual of the
materials.cologne –
the conference for
design and innovation 2019
Initiative and project
management: beeh_innovation
Design: Büro Freiheit
Keyvisual der
materials.cologne –
Die Konferenz für
Design und Innovation 2019
Initiative und Projektleitung:
beeh_innovation
Design: Büro Freiheit

01

"Good design is as little 'visual noise' as possible: if the product comes up with a convincing solution and is easy and intuitive to use."

„Gutes Design ist so wenig ‚weißes Rauschen' wie möglich: wenn das Produkt eine überzeugende Lösung bietet und einfach und intuitiv zu benutzen ist."

With what can a product surprise you?
As a designer, design manager and design juror I evaluate if a product gives an original, human, effective and sustainable solution to an identified problem. If the product is also nice to look at and to work with, it is a good product. To make it really a pleasant surprise, the product should have more benefits and functions then you might first think.

What inspires you?
I had the chance to intensively research the design process of Ray and Charles Eames. Curiosity, experiment, a strong purpose, profoundness, patience combined with a thinking from sketch to production to user, are part of a "total design process" – together with all crafts from others that we need to integrate to create value-adding products.

Which innovations will in future influence our everyday life?
Sustainability is first, smart digital integration second. We will use and share products, not own them.

Womit kann Sie ein Produkt überraschen?
Als Designer, Designmanager und Designjuror beurteile ich ein Produkt danach, ob es eine originelle, menschliche, wirksame und nachhaltige Lösung für ein bestimmtes Problem bietet. Wenn es auch noch gut aussieht und angenehm zu handhaben ist, ist es ein gutes Produkt. Eine wirklich positive Überraschung ist es, wenn es mehr Vorteile und Funktionalitäten bietet, als man zuerst denkt.

Was inspiriert Sie?
Ich habe die Chance gehabt, den Designprozess von Ray und Charles Eames intensiv zu erforschen. Neugierde, Experimentierfreude, Zielstrebigkeit, Tiefe und Geduld, verbunden mit einem Prozess, der von der Skizze über die Herstellung bis zum Verbraucher durchdacht ist, sind Teil eines „kompletten Designprozesses" – genauso wie das Handwerk aller Beteiligten, das wir in den Prozess einfließen lassen müssen, um ein Produkt mit Mehrwert zu schaffen.

Welche Innovationen werden künftig unseren Alltag prägen?
An erster Stelle Nachhaltigkeit, dann die intelligente digitale Integration. Wir werden Produkte gemeinsam benutzen, statt sie zu besitzen.

Gordon Bruce
USA

Gordon Bruce is the owner of Gordon Bruce Design LLC and has been a design consultant for 45 years working with many multinational corporations in Europe, Asia and the USA. He has worked on a wide range of products, interiors and vehicles – from aeroplanes to computers to medical equipment to furniture. From 1991 to 1994, Gordon Bruce was a consulting vice president for the Art Center College of Design's Kyoto programme and, from 1995 to 1999, chairman of Product Design for the Innovative Design Lab of Samsung (IDS) in Seoul, Korea. In 2003, he played a crucial role in helping to establish Porsche Design's North American office. For many years, he served as head design consultant for Lenovo's Innovative Design Center (IDC) in Beijing. He recently worked with Bühler, in Switzerland, and Huawei Technologies Co., Ltd., in China. Gordon Bruce is a visiting professor at several universities in the USA and China. He has been an author for Phaidon Press, London and has written for several international design magazines. He has several products in various permanent design collections such as with MoMA, in New York City. Gordon Bruce recently received Art Center College of Design's "Lifetime Achievement Award".

Gordon Bruce ist Inhaber der Gordon Bruce Design LLC und seit mittlerweile 45 Jahren als Designberater für zahlreiche multinationale Unternehmen in Europa, Asien und den USA tätig. Er arbeitete bereits an einer Reihe von Produkten, Inneneinrichtungen und Fahrzeugen – von Flugzeugen über Computer bis hin zu medizinischem Equipment und Möbeln. Von 1991 bis 1994 war Gordon Bruce beratender Vizepräsident des Kioto-Programms am Art Center College of Design sowie von 1995 bis 1999 Vorsitzender für Produktdesign beim Innovative Design Lab of Samsung (IDS) in Seoul, Korea. Im Jahr 2003 war er wesentlich daran beteiligt, das Büro von Porsche Design in Nordamerika zu errichten. Über viele Jahre war er leitender Designberater für Lenovos Innovative Design Center (IDC) in Beijing. In letzter Zeit arbeitete er für Bühler, Schweiz, und für Huawei Technologies Co., Ltd. in China. Gordon Bruce ist Gastprofessor an zahlreichen Universitäten in den USA und in China. Er war auch als Buchautor für Phaidon Press in London und als Verfasser von Artikeln für diverse internationale Designmagazine aktiv. Einige seiner Produkte werden in verschiedenen Dauerausstellungen gezeigt, unter anderem im MoMA in New York. Kürzlich erhielt Gordon Bruce vom Art Center College of Design den Lifetime Achievement Award.

01
Recreational High-Bypass
Turbofan Bi-Plane
Design concept for Industrial
Design Magazine, 1984
Freizeit-Hochbypass-Mantel-
stromtriebwerk-Doppeldecker
Designkonzept für Industrial
Design Magazine, 1984

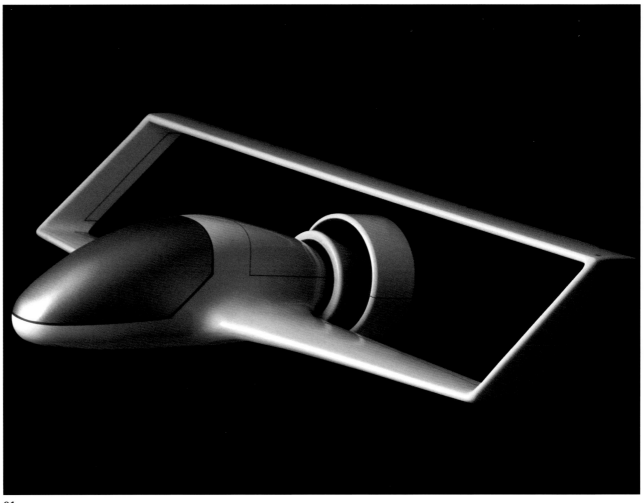

01

"Seeing design beyond professional practices, business strategies, and fashion statements, young designers need to advance their own heightened sense of design mindfulness, because design is a way of thinking about all one does in life."

„Junge Designer sollten bei Design an mehr als die berufliche Praxis, Geschäftsstrategien und Mode-statements denken und einen gestei-gerten Sinn für Designachtsamkeit entwickeln, da Design eine Geistes-haltung ist, mit der man alles betrachtet, was man im Leben tut."

To what do you attach particular importance when judging products?
The basis for my design judgement is similar to that of a three-legged stool where all supports need to be strong. The first leg is why is a design relevant? If this aspect is unique and pertinent to resolving problems, it brings credibility to the design idea. The second one concerns how the design conforms to the user. This gives credence to the design idea. The third leg is whether the product represents the true character of the designer or the company and embodies a design spirit, attitude and philosophy that gives it a distinctive quality.

What direction would you like product design to take in future?
There are many benefits to be gained from the products we use, as in the areas of health, safety, productivity or ecology. However, they can embody unanticipated hidden dangers as well. Just look at the downside of our civility due to the effects from smart phones and gaming upon minds and behaviour. So, future design professions need to eliminate any of the bad hidden within the good in our products.

Worauf legen Sie bei der Bewertung von Produkten besonderen Wert?
Die Basis für mein Designurteil ähnelt der Struktur eines dreibeinigen Hockers, bei dem alle drei Beine stark sein müssen. Das erste Bein ist, ob eine Gestaltung relevant ist. Wenn dieser Aspekt einzigartig und zweckdienlich ein Problem löst, ist die Designidee glaubwürdig. Das zweite Bein betrifft die Art, in der die Gestaltung auf den Nutzer eingeht. Das gibt der Designidee Überzeugungskraft. Das dritte Bein ist, ob das Produkt die wahre Natur des Designers oder des Unternehmens darstellt und den Geist, die Einstellung und die Philosophie des Designs verkörpert. Das gibt ihm eine unverkennbare Qualität.

Was wünschen Sie sich für die Zukunft des Produktdesigns?
Die Produkte, die wir benutzen, liefern uns viele Vorteile, so wie in den Bereichen Gesundheit, Sicherheit, Produkti-vität oder Ökologie. Allerdings können sie auch unerwar-tete Gefahren mit sich bringen. Nehmen Sie nur mal den Rückgang an Höflichkeit aufgrund des negativen Effekts, den Smartphones und Computerspiele auf unseren Ver-stand und unser Verhalten haben. Zukünftige Designbe-rufe werden daher all das Schlechte, das in dem Guten unserer Produkte versteckt ist, beseitigen müssen.

Gisbert L. Brunner
Germany
Deutschland

Gisbert L. Brunner, born in 1947, has been working on watches, pendulum clocks and other precision timepieces since 1964. During the quartz clock crisis of the 1970s, his love for the apparently dying-out mechanical timepieces grew. His passion as a hobby collector eventually led to the first newspaper articles in the early 1980s and later to the by now more than 20 books on the topic. Amongst others, Brunner works for magazines such as Chronos, Chronos Japan, Ganz Europa, Handelszeitung, Prestige, Terra Mater, GQ and ZEIT Magazin. He also shares his expertise on Focus Online. Together with a partner, he founded the Internet platform www.uhrenkosmos.com in 2018. After the successful Watch Book I (2015) and Watch Book II (2016), the teNeues publishing house published the Watch Book Rolex, written by Gisbert L. Brunner, in June 2017. The book has appeared in German, English and French and has already been reprinted several times due to high international demand.

Gisbert L. Brunner, Jahrgang 1947, beschäftigt sich seit 1964 mit Armbanduhren, Pendeluhren und anderen Präzisionszeitmessern. Während der Quarzuhren-Krise in den 1970er Jahren wuchs seine Liebe zu den anscheinend aussterbenden mechanischen Zeitmessern. Ein leidenschaftliches Sammelhobby führte ab den frühen 1980er Jahren zu ersten Zeitschriftenartikeln und inzwischen mehr als 20 Büchern über dieses Metier. Brunner ist u. a. für Magazine wie Chronos, Chronos Japan, Ganz Europa, Handelszeitung, Prestige, Terra Mater, GQ und ZEIT Magazin tätig. Darüber hinaus stellt er seine Expertise Focus Online zur Verfügung. 2018 gründete er zusammen mit einem Partner die Internet-Plattform www.uhrenkosmos.com. Nach den erfolgreichen Publikationen Watch Book I (2015) und Watch Book II (2016) publizierte der teNeues Verlag im Juni 2017 das wiederum von Gisbert L. Brunner verfasste Watch Book Rolex in den Sprachen Deutsch, Englisch und Französisch. Aufgrund der hohen internationalen Nachfrage musste es schon mehrfach nachgedruckt werden.

**01 THE WATCH BOOK –
COMPENDIUM**
Published by teNeues, 2019
Erschienen bei teNeues, 2019

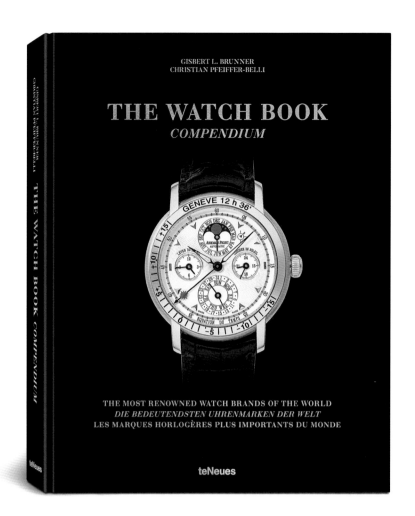

01

"The most exciting trends in the world of watches at the moment are coloured watch faces, smartwatches, bronze casings and a retro look."

„Die spannendsten Trends der Uhrenbranche sind aktuell farbige Zifferblätter, Smartwatches, Bronzegehäuse und Retrolook."

What does a watch have to offer in order to persuade you of its merits?
Naturally, it must look good, have a harmonious design and the correct signature as well as show real watch-making quality or be truly original.

Where will the watch industry be ten years from now?
That's something nobody can really predict with any certainty as the middle and long-term impact of smartwatches is not yet clear at the moment. But one thing is sure, the traditional mechanical watch will survive.

What is the hallmark of good design?
In good, considered design, it is almost inevitable that form follows function. It is not ostentatious, but appeals instead with a classical, more reserved appearance. Nevertheless, it attracts attention. A significant aspect, where applicable, is ease of use.

How do you proceed when evaluating products?
Step by step. Firstly by screening a watch, then by examining all aspects in detail as well as its tactile properties.

Was muss eine Uhr mitbringen, um Sie zu überzeugen?
Sie muss natürlich gut aussehen, ein stimmiges Design und die richtige Signatur besitzen sowie uhrmacherische Qualität vorweisen oder besonders originell sein.

Wo wird die Uhrenbranche in zehn Jahren stehen?
Das kann niemand mit letzter Sicherheit vorhersagen, weil die mittel- und langfristigen Auswirkungen der Smartwatch momentan noch nicht absehbar sind. Aber die gute alte Mechanik wird sicher überleben.

Was kennzeichnet gutes Design?
Bei gutem, durchdachtem Design folgt die Form beinahe zwangsläufig der Funktion. Es wirkt nicht vordergründig, sondern besticht durch klassischen, eher zurückhaltenden Auftritt. Trotzdem weckt es die Aufmerksamkeit des Betrachters. Ein maßgeblicher Aspekt ist, sofern gegeben, eine intuitive Bedienbarkeit.

Wie gehen Sie bei der Bewertung von Produkten vor?
Schrittweise. Erst Screening, dann Begutachtung der Uhr aus allen Perspektiven inklusive aller Details sowie Prüfung der Haptik.

Rüdiger Bucher
Germany
Deutschland

Rüdiger Bucher, born in 1967, graduated in political science from Philipps-Universität Marburg and completed the postgraduate study course "Interdisciplinary studies on France" in Freiburg, Germany. Since 1995, he has been in charge of "Scriptum. Die Zeitschrift für Schreibkultur" (Scriptum. The magazine for writing culture) at the Verlagsgruppe Ebner Ulm publishing house where he became editorial manager of Chronos, the leading German-language special interest magazine for wrist watches in 1999. As chief editor since 2005, he has positioned Chronos internationally with subsidiary magazines and licensed editions in China, Korea, Japan and Poland. At the same time, Rüdiger Bucher established a successful corporate publishing department for Chronos. Since 2014, he has been editorial director and, in addition to Chronos, is also in charge of the sister magazines "Uhren-Magazin" (Watch Magazine), "Klassik Uhren" (Classic Watches) and the New York-based "WatchTime". Rüdiger Bucher lectures as an expert for mechanical wrist watches and is a sought-after interview partner for various media.

Rüdiger Bucher, geboren 1967, absolvierte ein Studium in Politikwissenschaft an der Philipps-Universität Marburg und das Aufbaustudium „Interdisziplinäre Frankreich-Studien" in Freiburg. Ab 1995 betreute er beim Ebner Verlag Ulm fünf Jahre lang „Scriptum. Die Zeitschrift für Schreibkultur", bevor er im selben Verlag 1999 Redaktionsleiter von „Chronos", dem führenden deutschsprachigen Special-Interest-Magazin für Armbanduhren wurde. Ab 2005 Chefredakteur, hat sich Chronos seitdem mit Tochtermagazinen und Lizenzausgaben in China, Korea, Japan und Polen international aufgestellt. Gleichzeitig baute Rüdiger Bucher für Chronos einen erfolgreichen Corporate-Publishing-Bereich auf. Seit 2014 verantwortet er als Redaktionsdirektor neben Chronos auch die Schwestermagazine „Uhren-Magazin", „Klassik Uhren" sowie die in New York beheimatete „WatchTime". Als Experte für mechanische Armbanduhren hält Rüdiger Bucher Vorträge und ist ein gefragter Interviewpartner für verschiedene Medien.

01

"Good design should ensure that appearance and tactile properties evoke positive emotions and also reflect the unique characteristics of the brand."

„Gutes Design sollte optisch wie haptisch positive Emotionen hervor-rufen und zugleich die besonderen Eigenheiten der Marke verkörpern."

What fascinates you about watches?
The fact that they manage to show the time with a precision of 99.99 per cent – often completely by mechanical means. Also, that the technology and design history of major brands, which are often over 150 years old, is encapsulated in such a small space.

What three qualities must a watch have in order to persuade you of its merits?
It must evoke strong emotions, be instantly recognisable, and easy and fast to read.

Where will the watch industry be five years from now?
There will be increased digitalisation and online selling will be much more established. Brands will be even more important, and, at the same time, need to keep reinventing themselves.

How do you proceed when evaluating products?
I check whether the design is new and unique, if the proportions are correct and if it is pleasant to wear. I also establish whether the design gets across the idea behind the watch and its function.

Was begeistert Sie an Uhren?
Dass sie es – oft mit rein mechanischen Mitteln – schaffen, die Zeit mit einer Präzision von 99,99 Prozent anzuzeigen. Und dass sich auf so kleinem Raum die Technik- und Designgeschichte großer, oft 150 Jahre alter Marken widerspiegelt.

Welche drei Eigenschaften muss eine Uhr mitbringen, um Sie zu überzeugen?
Sie muss starke Gefühle evozieren, unverwechselbar sowie gut und schnell ablesbar sein.

Wo wird die Uhrenbranche in fünf Jahren stehen?
Sie wird noch mehr digitalisiert und der Onlinehandel deutlich stärker etabliert sein. Marken werden noch wichtiger und müssen sich gleichzeitig immer wieder neu erfinden.

Wie gehen Sie bei der Bewertung von Produkten vor?
Ich prüfe, ob das Design neu und einzigartig ist, ob die Proportionen der Uhr stimmen und wie es sich mit der Haptik verhält. Ich untersuche, ob und wie das Design die Idee, die hinter der Uhr und ihrer Funktion steht, zur Geltung bringt.

Prof. Jun Cai
China

Jun Cai is professor at the Academy of Arts & Design, and director of the Design Management Research Lab at Tsinghua University in Beijing. He is also external reviewer for the Aalto University and Design School of Hong Kong Polytechnic University. Professor Cai has focused on research for design strategy and design management since the 1990s. Through exploration of design-driven business innovation and user-centred design thinking by theoretical and practical research, he was a consultant for more than 60 projects for among others Motorola, Nokia, LG, Boeing, Lenovo, Coway, Fiyta and Aftershockz. Furthermore, he has published papers and publications on design research, design strategy and design management.

Jun Cai ist Professor an der Academy of Arts & Design sowie Direktor des Design Management Research Lab an der Tsinghua University in Beijing. Er ist zudem externer Referent der Aalto University und der Designschule der Polytechnic University in Hongkong. Bereits seit den 1990er Jahren konzentriert sich Professor Cai auf die Forschung in den Bereichen Designstrategie und Designmanagement. Aufgrund seiner Erforschung von design-orientierter Geschäftsinnovation und benutzerzentriertem Designdenken durch theoretische und praktische Forschung war er in mehr als 60 Projekten beratend tätig, unter anderem für Motorola, Nokia, LG, Boeing, Lenovo, Coway, Fiyta und Aftershockz. Außerdem hat er bereits Abhandlungen und Veröffentlichungen über Designforschung, Designstrategie und Designmanagement verfasst.

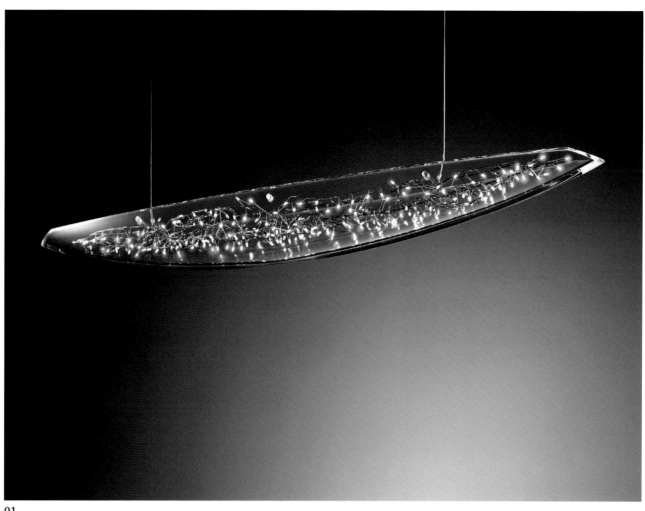

01

"The quality of design improves the core competence of a company from market differentiation to brand recognition."

„Die Designqualität verbessert die Kernkompetenz eines Unternehmens, angefangen bei der Marktdifferenzierung bis hin zum Markenbekanntheitsgrad."

You are a professor at the Academy of Arts & Design. What advice do you give your students for their future career?
Be creative and have space in your heart for love and empathy. Be sensitive to changes in nature and always concerned with environment. A designer should have the responsibility not only to bring the beauty to the world, but also to protect our home planet.

What do you find most enjoyable about your work as a jury member?
It is exciting to see the progress of design and to witness change. I am always inspired by the work of talented designers, by their creative innovation and unique imagination.

What does a product have to offer in order to surprise you?
An experience far beyond function and an external shape that touches me inside. A really good product can be a reliable partner that only emerges when you need it.

Sie sind Professor an der Academy of Arts & Design. Welchen Rat geben Sie Ihren Studenten für ihre zukünftige Karriere?
Seid kreativ und habt in euerm Herzen Platz für Liebe und Empathie. Nehmt die Veränderungen in der Natur mit Sensibilität wahr und kümmert euch um die Umwelt. Ein Designer hat nicht nur die Aufgabe, Schönes zur Welt zu bringen, sondern ist auch für den Schutz unseres Planeten verantwortlich.

Was macht Ihnen an Ihrer Arbeit als Juror am meisten Spaß?
Es ist aufregend, den Fortschritt und die Veränderung im Design beobachten zu können. Mich inspiriert immer wieder die Arbeit der talentierten Designer, ihre kreativen Neuerungen und einzigartige Phantasie.

Was muss ein Produkt mitbringen, um Sie zu überraschen?
Ein Erlebnis, das über die Funktion hinausgeht, und eine äußere Form, die mich im Innersten berührt. Ein wirklich gutes Produkt kann ein verlässlicher Partner sein, der nur dann erscheint, wenn er gebraucht wird.

Vivian Wai-kwan Cheng
Hong Kong
Hongkong

On leaving the Kee Hong Kong Design Institute after 19 years of educational service, Vivian Cheng founded "Vivian Design" in 2014 to provide consultancy services and promote her own art in jewellery and glass. She graduated with a BA in industrial design from the Hong Kong Polytechnic University and was awarded a special prize in the Young Designers of the Year award hosted by the Federation of Hong Kong Industries in 1987, and the Governor's Award for Industry: Consumer Product Design in 1989, after joining Lambda Industrial Limited as the head of the product design team. In 1995 she finished her master's degree and joined the Vocational Training Council, teaching product design, and later became responsible for, among others, establishing an international network with design-related organisations and schools. Vivian Cheng was the International Liaison Manager at the Hong Kong Design Institute (HKDI), member of the Board of Directors of the Hong Kong Design Centre (HKDC) from 2002 to 2004, and was board member of the World Design Organization (formerly Icsid) from 2013 to 2017. Furthermore, she has been a panel member for various adjudication boards of the government and various NGOs.

Nach 19 Jahren im Lehrbetrieb verließ Vivian Cheng 2014 das Hong Kong Design Institute und gründete „Vivian Design", um Beratungsdienste anzubieten und ihre eigene Schmuck- und Glaskunst weiterzuentwickeln. 1987 machte sie ihren BA in Industriedesign an der Hong Kong Polytechnic University. Im selben Jahr erhielt sie einen Sonderpreis im Wettbewerb „Young Designers of the Year", veranstaltet von der Federation of Hong Kong Industries, sowie 1989 den Governor's Award for Industry: Consumer Product Design, nachdem sie bei Lambda Industrial Limited als Leiterin des Produktdesign-Teams angefangen hatte. 1995 beendete sie ihren Masterstudiengang und wechselte zum Vocational Training Council, wo sie Produktdesign unterrichtete und später u. a. für den Aufbau eines internationalen Netzwerks mit Organisationen und Schulen im Designbereich verantwortlich war. Vivian Cheng war International Liaison Manager am Hong Kong Design Institute (HKDI), Vorstandsmitglied des Hong Kong Design Centre (HKDC) von 2002 bis 2004 sowie Gremiumsmitglied der World Design Organization (ehemals Icsid) von 2013 bis 2017. Außerdem war sie Mitglied verschiedener Bewertungsgremien der Regierung und vieler Nichtregierungsorganisationen.

01 FIRE
Casting in Shibuichi (metal alloy)
Shibuichi-Guss (Metalllegierung)

02 AIR
Casting in silver
Silberguss

01

02

"A piece of jewellery must have value in emotion and design values, besides being well produced, well crafted and perfect inside out."

„Ein Schmuckstück muss eine Wertigkeit an Emotionen und Designwerten ausdrücken und natürlich auch hervorragend gemacht, gut ausgearbeitet und rundum perfekt sein."

What trends have caught your attention in the fashion industry?
Its currently biggest challenge is making its products sustainable. How to retain the product values and make them last over time are the biggest difficulties the fashion industry is encountering.

What do you appreciate about the evaluation process at Red Dot?
The evaluation process is very fair and the jury is given full autonomy while judging the products. Design is well respected during the course of judging and if the jury should have any doubt at all, no decision will be made until all is cleared.

What experience has had a long-term impact on your career?
The design process is never a linear equation to find a solution, but a multi-directional and there are thousands of ways to reach the destination. As such, it makes me understand that there is always another way to create an answer.

Welche Trends können Sie in der Modebranche ausmachen?
Zurzeit liegt die größte Herausforderung für die Modebranche darin, die Produkte nachhaltig zu gestalten, ihre Produktwerte zu bewahren und sicherzustellen, dass sie sich langfristig bewähren. Das sind die größten Schwierigkeiten, die die Branche überwinden muss.

Was schätzen Sie am Evaluationsprozess bei Red Dot?
Der Evaluationsprozess ist sehr fair und die Jury hat während der Bewertung der Produkte vollkommene Freiheit. Design wird während der Jurierung sehr ernst genommen. Sollte ein Juror irgendeinen Zweifel haben, wird keine Entscheidung getroffen, bis nicht alle einverstanden sind.

Welche Erfahrung prägte Ihre Karriere nachhaltig?
Der Designprozess ist keine lineare Gleichung, mit der man eine Lösung findet, sondern ein Mehrwegprozess. Denn es gibt tausend verschiedene Wege, mit denen man ans Ziel kommen kann. Ich habe gelernt, dass es immer auch einen anderen Weg gibt, um eine Antwort zu finden.

Mårten Claesson
Sweden
Schweden

Mårten Claesson was born in Lidingö, Sweden, in 1970. After studying at the Vasa Technical College in Stockholm in the department of construction engineering and at the Parsons School of Design in New York in the departments of architecture and product design, he graduated in 1994 with an MFA degree from Konstfack, the University College of Arts, Crafts and Design in Stockholm. He is co-founder of the Swedish design partnership Claesson Koivisto Rune, which is multidisciplinary in the classic Scandinavian way and which pursues the practice of both architecture and design. Mårten Claesson is also a writer and lecturer in the field of architecture and design.

Mårten Claesson wurde 1970 in Lidingö, Schweden, geboren. Nachdem er am Vasa Technical College in Stockholm im Fachbereich Bautechnik und an der Parsons School of Design in New York im Fachbereich Architektur und Produktdesign studiert hatte, schloss er 1994 sein Studium mit einem MFA-Abschluss der Konstfack, der Universität für Kunst, Handwerk und Design in Stockholm, ab. Er ist Mitgründer der schwedischen Design-Sozietät „Claesson Koivisto Rune", die im klassisch-skandinavischen Sinne multidisziplinär in Architektur und Design arbeitet. Mårten Claesson ist darüber hinaus als Autor und Dozent tätig.

01

"Good teamwork is flat, without hierarchy. And with a work outcome that is greater than the sum of the individuals' capacity."

„Gute Teamarbeit ist flach, ohne Hierarchie. Und das Ergebnis der Arbeit ist stärker als die Summe der individuellen Fähigkeiten."

What does a product have to offer in order to persuade you of its merits?
The product should be designed in such a way that its use becomes self-explanatory, with sound and ecological materials, in an overall quality. But above all the design has to evoke a sense of beauty.

What will the house of the future look like?
At present, the individual expression is back but many times only as a kind of pick-your-style in the marketplace. I hope to see a more genuine architecture, focusing on the essentials: spatiality and honest materials.

In 2019, Bauhaus celebrates its 100th anniversary. To what extent has this school of design influenced your work?
I read the history of Bauhaus before attending design university. When I had studied for just one year, I travelled to Dessau (and stayed in one of the studio flats) together with my two new friends, today my partners Eero Koivisto and Ola Rune. So, I guess to call Bauhaus formative would be almost an understatement.

Was muss ein Produkt mitbringen, um Sie zu überzeugen?
Das Produkt sollte so gestaltet sein, dass seine Nutzung offensichtlich ist. Es sollte aus soliden, ökologischen Materialien bestehen und rundum von einer hohen Qualität sein. Vor allem aber sollte das Design eine Empfindung von Schönheit hervorrufen.

Wie sieht das Haus der Zukunft aus?
Zurzeit erlebt die individuelle Ausdrucksform ein Comeback, doch häufig nur als eine aus dem Marktangebot gewählte Stilrichtung. Ich hoffe, dass wir mehr authentische Architektur sehen werden, die ihr Augenmerk auf das Wesentliche richtet: Räumlichkeit und ehrliche Materialien.

Das Bauhaus feiert 2019 sein 100-Jahr-Jubiläum. Inwieweit hat die Designschule Ihre Arbeit beeinflusst?
Ich habe die Geschichte des Bauhauses gelesen, bevor ich an der Universität Design studierte. Nach dem ersten Studienjahr reiste ich zusammen mit zwei neuen Freunden nach Dessau (und wohnte mit ihnen in einer der 1-Zimmer-Wohnungen). Heute sind das meine Partner, Eero Koivisto und Ola Rune. Bauhaus als nachhaltig prägend zu bezeichnen, wäre daher wohl untertrieben.

Vincent Créance
France
Frankreich

After graduating from the Ecole Supérieure de Design Industriel, Vincent Créance began his career in 1985 at the Plan Créatif agency where he became design director in 1990 and developed numerous products for high-tech and consumer markets. In 1996, he joined Alcatel as Design Director for all phone activities on an international level. In 1999, he became Vice President Brand in charge of industrial design, user experience and communications for the Mobile Phones BU. In 2004, Vincent Créance advanced to the position of Design and Corporate Communications Director of the Franco-Chinese joint-venture TCL & Alcatel Mobile Phones. In 2006, he became president and CEO of MBD Design, one of the major design agencies in France, providing design solutions in transport design and product design. Then, in 2017 he created the Design Center of the Université Paris-Saclay, bringing together 14 famous French engineering schools and research institutes, with the mission to promote design in this new ecosystem. Créance is a member of the board of directors of APCI (Agency for the Promotion of Industrial Creation), and of ENSCI (National College of Industrial Creation), and a member of the Design Strategic Advisory Board for Paris Region and for Strate College.

Vincent Créance begann seine Laufbahn nach seinem Abschluss an der Ecole Supérieure de Design Industriel 1985 bei der Agentur Plan Créatif. Hier stieg er 1990 zum Design Director auf und entwickelte zahlreiche Produkte für den Hightech- und Verbrauchermarkt. 1996 ging er als Design Director für sämtliche Telefonaktivitäten auf internationaler Ebene zu Alcatel und wurde 1999 Vice President Brand, zuständig für Industriedesign, User Experience sowie die gesamte Kommunikation für den Geschäftsbereich „Mobile Phones". 2004 avancierte Vincent Créance zum Design and Corporate Communications Director des französisch-chinesischen Zusammenschlusses TCL & Alcatel Mobile Phones. 2006 wurde er Präsident und CEO von MBD Design, einer der wichtigsten Designagenturen in Frankreich, und entwickelte Designlösungen für Transport- und Produktdesign. Im Jahr 2017 gründete er das Centre de Design der Université Paris-Saclay und vereinte 14 berühmte französische Ingenieurschulen und Forschungsinstitute in dem Bestreben, Design in diesem neuen Ökosystem zu fördern. Créance ist Vorstandsmitglied von APCI (Agency for the Promotion of Industrial Creation) und von ENSCI (National College of Industrial Design) sowie Mitglied im wissenschaftlichen Designbeirat der Region Paris und des Strate College.

Tram for Reims Tramway, France
The Alstom tram shows five different joyful and bubbly colours. This one in yellow has a unique design for the city of Champagne, which subliminally evokes a champagne flute.
Straßenbahn für Reims Tramway, Frankreich
Die Alstom-Straßenbahn gibt es in fünf verschiedenen freudigen und lebendigen Farbtönen. Diese Bahn in Gelb trägt ein einzigartiges Design für die Stadt Champagne, das unterschwellig an eine Champagnerflöte erinnert.

01

"An accolade gives designers and brands the feeling of playing a significant role in the great adventure of product design."
„Eine Auszeichnung gibt Designern und Marken das Gefühl, in dem großen Abenteuer des Produktdesigns eine bedeutende Rolle zu spielen."

What typifies the evaluation process at Red Dot?
The jurors come from a wide mix of continents: more than a globalised international point of view, this offers a multicultural judgement. I also very much appreciate that the independence of us jurors is not just a phrase but a precious asset.

Does a well-designed product make elaborate communication design redundant?
A brand is like an opera bringing together singers, musicians, director, scenographer, etc. – each of them must serve the same dramaturgy in harmony. When all of them resonate together, it becomes magical. Design as one of the most important communication tools must be outstanding to hold its rank in the structure.

What can consumers expect from products today?
To improve our everyday life, while preserving our future. In other words, it mostly means useful, simple and attractive products, creating respectful jobs for people, and preserving our resources.

Was macht den Evaluierungsprozess bei Red Dot aus?
Die Juroren kommen von den verschiedensten Kontinenten. Zusätzlich zu einer globalisierten, internationalen Sichtweise bedeutet das ein multikulturelles Urteil. Ich schätze außerdem ungemein, dass unsere Unabhängigkeit als Juroren nicht nur eine Phrase, sondern ein kostbares Gut ist.

Macht ein gut gestaltetes Produkt ausgeklügeltes Kommunikationsdesign überflüssig?
Eine Marke ist wie eine Oper, die Sänger, Musiker, den Intendanten, den Szenografen usw. zusammenbringt – in Eintracht muss jeder von ihnen der gleichen Dramaturgie dienen. Wenn alle harmonieren, wird es magisch. Design als eines der wichtigsten Kommunikationsinstrumente muss hervorragend sein, um in der Struktur seine Stelle bewahren zu können.

Was darf ein Konsument heutzutage von Produkten erwarten?
Dass sie den Alltag verbessern und gleichzeitig die Zukunft bewahren. Mit anderen Worten meine ich damit hauptsächlich Produkte, die nützlich, einfach und attraktiv sind, wertschätzende Arbeitsplätze für Menschen schaffen und unsere Ressourcen schonen.

Martin Darbyshire
Great Britain
Großbritannien

Martin Darbyshire founded tangerine in 1989 and under his stewardship it has developed into a global strategic design consultancy that creates award-winning solutions for internationally recognised brands such as LG, Samsung, Hyundai, Toyota, Nikon, Huawei, Virgin Australia and Cepsa. Before founding tangerine, he worked for Moggridge Associates and then in San Francisco at ID TWO (now IDEO). A design leader on the international stage, Martin Darbyshire combines his work for tangerine with a worldwide programme of keynote speeches and activities promoting the importance of design. He has served as UKT&I Ambassador for the UK Creative Industries and two terms as a board member of the World Design Organization (formerly Icsid). He was also formerly a visiting professor at Central Saint Martins. Martin Darbyshire is a trustee of the UK Design Council and a juror at the Red Dot Award and Contemporary Good Design. Moreover, the UK Creative Industries Council recognised his global export success awarding him the CIC International Award 2016.

Martin Darbyshire gründete tangerine 1989. Unter seiner Leitung entwickelte sich das Büro zu einem globalen strategischen Designberatungsunternehmen, das preisgekrönte Lösungen für weltweit anerkannte Marken wie LG, Samsung, Hyundai, Toyota, Nikon, Huawei, Virgin Australia und Cepsa entwickelt. Zuvor arbeitete er für Moggridge Associates und dann in San Francisco bei ID TWO (heute IDEO). Als ein weltweit führender Designer verbindet Martin Darbyshire seine Arbeit für tangerine mit einem globalen Programm von Keynote-Referaten und -Aktivitäten, um den bedeutenden Beitrag von Design hervorzuheben. Martin Darbyshire war für das Ministerium für Handel und Investition des Vereinigten Königreichs Botschafter des Bereichs Kreativindustrie und für zwei Amtszeiten Gremiumsmitglied der World Design Organization (ehemals Icsid). Er war zudem Gastdozent an der Central Saint Martins. Martin Darbyshire ist Kurator des UK Design Council sowie Juror des Red Dot Awards und von Contemporary Good Design. Darüber hinaus wurde er für seinen weltweiten Exporterfolg vom UK Creative Industries Council mit dem CIC International Award 2016 ausgezeichnet.

01

"Good design needs to be groundbreaking, effective and appealing."
„Gutes Design muss bahnbrechend,
wirksam und ansprechend sein."

How do you proceed when evaluating products?
It's always a balance of physically experiencing something on the day and comparing it to one's present
experience of comparable things. Listening to the
points of view across the judges to reach a unified
viewpoint is also an important step.

With what can a designer surprise you?
Achieving something really new and meaningful in a
crowded market.

**Where do you expect the design industry to be ten
years from now?**
Better understood and more appreciated.

Which three qualities do you value in a customer?
Open-mindedness. Objectivity. Curiosity.

**Wie gehen Sie bei der Bewertung der Produkte
vor?**
Es ist immer ein Balanceakt zwischen der greifbaren
physischen Erfahrung eines Produkts an dem Tag und den
Erfahrungen, die man mit vergleichbaren Produkten
gesammelt hat. Ein weiterer wichtiger Schritt ist es, auch
die Meinungen der anderen Juroren zu erwägen, um
dann einen vereinten Standpunkt zu finden.

Womit kann ein Designer Sie überraschen?
Indem er in einem überfüllten Markt etwas wirklich
Neues und Sinnhaftes schafft.

Wo sehen Sie die Designbranche in zehn Jahren?
Besser verstanden und mehr geschätzt.

**Welche drei Eigenschaften schätzen Sie an einem
Kunden?**
Aufgeschlossenheit. Objektivität. Neugier.

Katrin de Louw
Germany
Deutschland

Katrin de Louw studied interior design at Detmold School for Architecture and Interior Design. Since 1997, she has been working as an independent interior designer and design manager in the furniture industry and for manufacturers of materials. In 2006, she instigated the "servicepoint A30" trend and event forum in East Westphalia, thereby setting up a nationally leading network of material manufacturers and suppliers to the furniture industry, that discusses innovative trends in furniture and interior design and provides information on topics that are of interest to the industry. Katrin de Louw's agency "TRENDFILTER – Designzukunft für Möbel und Materialien" (future of design of furniture and materials) advises global players from industry, trade and the retail sector including Abet Laminati, BASF, Continental Group, Europlac, Koelnmesse, SURTECO GROUP, Swiss Krono Group, Westag & Getalit and and Windmöller Flooring. She is recognised as the leading trend expert for furniture, interiors and materials in German-speaking countries. She also works as a freelance author and provides comprehensive design consulting services together with her team of interior, product and graphic designers as well as marketing professionals.

Katrin de Louw studierte Innenarchitektur an der Detmolder Schule für Architektur und Innenarchitektur. Seit 1997 ist sie als selbständige Innenarchitektin und Designmanagerin der Möbelindustrie und für Materialhersteller tätig. 2006 initiierte sie mit dem Trend- und Eventforum „servicepoint A30" in Ostwestfalen das bundesweit führende Netzwerk von Materialherstellern und Möbelzulieferern, das innovative Trends im Möbel- und Raumdesign diskutiert und über branchenrelevante Themen informiert. Mit ihrem Büro „TRENDFILTER – Designzukunft für Möbel und Materialien" berät Katrin de Louw Global Player aus Industrie, Handwerk und Handel, darunter Abet Laminati, BASF, Continental Group, Europlac, Koelnmesse, SURTECO GROUP, Swiss Krono Group, Westag & Getalit und Windmöller Flooring. Sie gilt als führende Trendexpertin für Möbel, Inneneinrichtungen und Materialien im deutschsprachigen Raum, ist freie Autorin und bietet zusammen mit ihrem Team aus Innenarchitekten, Produkt- und Grafikdesignern sowie Marketingexperten umfassendes Design Consulting an.

01
New works with new materials
in the spotlight: a branch of
the Swiss Krono Group on the
Kurfürstendamm in Berlin
Neues Arbeiten mit neuen Materialien im Fokus: die Dependance
der Swiss Krono Group am Berliner
Kurfürstendamm

01

"Materials transport emotions, because a virtual impulse cannot yet replace the experience of touch. Haptics are therefore increasingly important and will, in future, be a critical factor in the success of a product."

„Materialien sind emotionale Träger, denn haptische Erlebnisse sind mit virtuellen Impulsen noch nicht vergleichbar. Die Haptik wird also immer wichtiger und ist zukünftig mitentscheidend für den Erfolg eines Produkts."

What future innovations do you expect to see in materials and surfaces?

Particularly the combination of high-tech with sustainability will, in future, lead to ideas for new materials, their processing and uses. Waste products will also increasingly be seen as a source of raw materials. In general, more and more materials will become part of the cradle-to-cradle cycle.

Could you describe your typical day at TRENDFILTER?

Happy and varied. We have so many different projects related to materials and interior design that nothing is routine. Trend research and design consultation for national and international companies form an important part of that work, but we also carry out special exhibitions, industry events, workshops, presentations and publishing activities.

What material trends are noticeable in the furniture industry?

Aside from sustainable materials, there is a trend to use completely new materials. It is up to industry to explore fresh avenues not only in the choice of materials and their processing, but also in how they can be recycled in the future.

Welche Neuheiten erwarten Sie künftig im Bereich der Materialien und Oberflächen?

Insbesondere die Verknüpfung von Hightech und Nachhaltigkeit wird zukünftig neue Ideen für Materialien, deren Verarbeitung und Einsatzmöglichkeiten auf den Markt bringen. Auch Abfälle werden zunehmend als Rohstoffquelle wahrgenommen und generell gelangen Materialien stärker in den Cradle-to-Cradle-Kreislauf.

Wie sieht Ihr Alltag bei TRENDFILTER aus?

Fröhlich und bunt. Wir haben so viele unterschiedliche Projekte rund um das Thema „Material und Inneneinrichtung", dass nichts zur Gewohnheit wird. Dabei sind Trendrecherche und Design Consulting für nationale und internationale Unternehmen eine wichtige Säule. Aber auch Sonderschauen, Branchenevents, Workshops, Vorträge und Autorentätigkeiten gehören dazu.

Welche Materialtrends gibt es in der Möbelindustrie?

Neben dem Trend zu nachhaltigen Materialien gibt es den zu ganz neuen Materialien. Hier ist es an der Industrie, neue Wege zu gehen – sowohl bei der Materialwahl und deren Verarbeitung als auch dabei, wie Materialien zukünftig recycelt werden können.

Saskia Diez
Germany
Deutschland

After a stay in Paris in 1996, Saskia Diez began training in Germany as a goldsmith which she completed in 2000 as the local state winner. In 2001, she began studying industrial design, but at the same time worked for Christian Haas, where she designed lighting, china or paper products, as well as for Rosenthal and Konstantin Grcic. She started working under her own name in 2005 and, amongst others, designed trade fair stands for different companies before returning to jewellery work. In 2007/08, she set up her own label. Her aim was to explore the very notion of jewellery from invisible jewellery (perfume) to new ways of wearing jewellery, the use of new materials – also for handbags, sunglasses, nail varnish, etc. Saskia Diez works together with designers, companies, brands and artists including Arita Porzellan, e15, Pan and the Dreams, Uslu Airlines, Netaporter, Bevza, Kismet, Geza Schön, Mirko Borsche, Gym Yilmaz, Hermès, Viu, Stählemühle and the Julia Stoschek Collection.

Nach einem Aufenthalt in Paris 1996 begann Saskia Diez eine Ausbildung zur Goldschmiedin, die sie 2000 als Landessiegerin abschloss. 2001 nahm sie ein Studium in Industriedesign auf und arbeitete parallel bei Christian Haas, wo sie Leuchten, Geschirr oder Papeterie entwarf, bei Rosenthal und Konstantin Grcic. 2005 begann sie, unter eigenem Namen tätig zu werden, und entwarf unter anderem Messeauftritte für diverse Firmen, bevor sie zum Schmuck zurückkehrte und 2007/08 ihr eigenes Label gründete. Ihre Intention ist es, den Schmuckbegriff von unsichtbarem Schmuck (Parfum) über neue Arten, Schmuck zu tragen, bis hin zu neuen Materialien, auch für Taschen, Sonnenbrillen, Nagellack etc., auszuloten. Saskia Diez arbeitet mit Designern, Unternehmen, Marken und Künstlern zusammen, darunter Arita Porzellan, e15, Pan and the Dreams, Uslu Airlines, Netaporter, Bevza, Kismet, Geza Schön, Mirko Borsche, Gym Yilmaz, Hermès, Viu, Stählemühle sowie Julia Stoschek Collection.

01 Gold ME
Sunglasses, chained, 2016
These glasses come without edges or frame and were cut from a single piece of nylon. They were developed in cooperation with the glasses company VIU and made in Italy. The nylon makes them flexible, stable, lightweight and comfortable to wear. All metal parts of the shades have been gold-plated. The glasses themselves are lightly veiled with a gold dust finish.

Sonnenbrille mit Kette, 2016
Diese Brille hat keine Ränder und keinen Rahmen. Sie wurde aus einem einzigen Stück geschnitten, in Zusammenarbeit mit der Brillen-firma VIU entwickelt und in Italien hergestellt. Das Nylon-Material macht sie sehr flexibel, stabil, leicht und bequem zu tragen. Alle Metallteile der Brille sind vergoldet. Die Brillengläser wurden mit einem leichten Schleier aus Goldstaub versehen.

01

"What I find fascinating about jewellery is that it allows me to get very close to people. Jewellery is almost always charged with memories, life stories, love or even sorrow. It can be used to express a good deal, to strengthen oneself, adorn oneself, prepare oneself."

„An Schmuck fasziniert mich, dass ich Menschen damit sehr nahekomme. Schmuck ist fast immer aufgeladen mit Erinnerungen, Lebensgeschichten, Liebe oder auch Trauer. Mit Schmuck kann man sehr viel ausdrücken, sich stärken, schmücken, rüsten."

What jewellery do you personally like wearing?
I mostly wear a kind of "basic kit" for several months without a break: a pair of ear cuffs, rings, bracelets. Things, that I don't even take off when I go to bed. And depending on whether I am going out, how I feel, how decked out I want to be or on the occasion, I may add earrings or a necklace. I particularly like ear jewellery. It frames the face, is always visible, no matter how busy the party may be.

What distinguishes your design "signature"?
I always try to see things with a fresh pair of eyes, to extend the notion of jewellery and to push boundaries. So, it is always exciting to try out new materials or techniques. What is very important to me is that my jewellery must be wearable. It is more low-key than loud, but always distinct. I like working on a single idea, focusing on it and reducing it until I reach a point when the essence emerges.

With what can a designer surprise you?
With quirkiness, consistency, personality, intelligence.

Welchen Schmuck tragen Sie selbst gerne?
Meistens trage ich eine Art Grundausstattung mehrere Monate ununterbrochen: ein Paar Ear Cuffs, Ringe, Arm-reifen. Dinge, die ich dann auch zum Schlafen nicht mehr ablege. Und je nachdem, ob ich ausgehe, wie ich mich fühle, wie sehr ich geschmückt sein will oder was der Anlass ist, kommen dann noch Ohrringe oder eine Kette dazu. Ohrschmuck mag ich besonders gerne, er rahmt das Gesicht, ist immer sichtbar, egal, wie voll die Party ist.

Was kennzeichnet Ihre gestalterische Handschrift?
Ich versuche immer wieder, Dinge neu zu sehen, den Schmuckbegriff auszuweiten und Grenzen zu verschieben. So bleibt es für mich spannend, neue Materialien oder Techniken auszuprobieren. Sehr wichtig ist mir dabei: Mein Schmuck ist tragbar. Er ist eher leise als laut, aber immer klar. Ich arbeite gerne an einer einzelnen Idee, stelle sie in den Mittelpunkt und reduziere um sie herum so lange, bis sich deren Essenz herauskristallisiert.

Wie kann ein Designer Sie überraschen?
Mit Eigenheit, Schlüssigkeit, Persönlichkeit, Intelligenz.

Stefan Eckstein
Germany
Deutschland

Stefan Eckstein is the founder and CEO of ECKSTEIN DESIGN in Munich. The studio focuses on industrial, interaction and corporate industrial design. Stefan Eckstein studied industrial design at the Muthesius Academy of Fine Arts and Design in Kiel and ergonomics at the Anthropological Institute of the University of Kiel, Germany. Together with his design team, he has received many design awards in national and international competitions. Today, Stefan Eckstein is recognised as a renowned designer for industrial design. In line with his principle, "reduction to the essential leads to a better result", he has developed a user-driven approach to innovation, called "agile design development". It combines innovative concept- and development methods in a structured thought process. Stefan Eckstein has served on numerous international juries, has been a member of the Association of German Industrial Designers (VDID) for 25 years and was elected president of the Association in 2012. Under his management, the VDID CODEX was developed. Today, it serves as a model for the ethical values of the profession of industrial designers.

Stefan Eckstein ist Gründer und Geschäftsführer von ECKSTEIN DESIGN, einem Studio für Industriedesign, Interaction Design und Corporate Industrial Design in München. Er studierte Industrial Design an der Kieler Muthesius-Hochschule und Ergonomie am Anthropologischen Institut der Christian-Albrechts-Universität zu Kiel. Zusammen mit seinem Designteam erhielt er zahlreiche Auszeichnungen. Heute gehört Stefan Eckstein zu den renommierten Designern im Bereich des Industrial Designs. Gemäß seiner Philosophie „Reduzierung auf das Wesentliche führt zu einem besseren Ergebnis" entwickelte er eine nutzerorientierte Innovationsmethode, die „Agile Designentwicklung". In einem besonders strukturierten Denkprozess werden dabei innovative Konzept- und Entwicklungsphasen miteinander verbunden. Stefan Eckstein ist international als Juror tätig, seit über 25 Jahren Mitglied im Verband Deutscher Industrie Designer (VDID) und seit 2012 Präsident des Verbandes. Der VDID CODEX wurde unter seiner Leitung entwickelt und steht heute als Leitbild für die ethischen Werte des Berufsstandes.

01 METRAHIT IM XTRA
A digital multimeter is a technical hand-held measuring instrument used to monitor electrical devices in areas such as industry, communication technology, labs or outdoors. A special new feature is a replaceable battery pack which increases the operational readiness of the equipment through a reserve of charged batteries.
For GOSSEN METRAWATT, 2018.

Ein Digitalmultimeter ist ein technisches Handmessgerät für die Prüfung stromführender Geräte im professionellen Bereich wie Industrie, Kommunikationstechnik und Labor oder im Außenbereich. Besonderes Novum ist der wechselbare Akkupack, der die Einsatzbereitschaft des Geräts durch Vorhalten mehrerer geladener Akkus erhöht.
Für GOSSEN METRAWATT, 2018.

01

"Industrial design refers to the design of products, systems and an interactive product world. It makes sense of things and renders them efficient and understandable."

„Industriedesign ist die Gestaltung von Produkten, Systemen und der interaktiven Produktwelt. Es gibt den Dingen Sinn und macht sie effizient und verständlich."

Why does a back to basics approach lead to a better final result?
The term "reduction" has Latin origins. It comes from the verb "reducere" and means to lead back or bring back. In the context of the question it is today generally used to imply "limit to the essentials". This means the design focuses on usability, function and aesthetics. The clarity gained by this approach deliberately draws the attention of users to the essential features of a product or system and gives them a better designed product.

What is "agile design development"?
Agile design development is a user-oriented innovation method with a pared down structure. It links a structured iterative process to short concept and development phases in a team environment. The customer is always an important element of the design process. In this way, internal and external expertise are brought together.

Warum führt die Reduzierung auf das Wesentliche zu einem besseren Ergebnis?
Der Begriff „Reduktion" hat seinen Ursprung im Lateinischen. Er kommt von „reducere" und bedeutet „zurückführen". Im heutigen Gebrauch ist jedoch eher die Begrenzung auf das Wesentliche als Kernaussage gemeint. Auf diese Weise wird über die Gestaltung mehr Aufmerksamkeit auf Usability, Funktion und Ästhetik gerichtet. Durch die so gewonnene Überschaubarkeit wird der User auf das Wesentliche eines Produkts oder Systems gelenkt und bewusst geführt und bekommt so ein besser gestaltetes Produkt.

Was ist „Agile Designentwicklung"?
Agile Designentwicklung ist eine nutzenorientierte Innovationsmethode mit schlanker Struktur. Sie verbindet einen strukturierten Iterationsprozess mit kurzen Konzept- und Entwicklungsphasen im Team. Der Kunde ist dabei stets ein wichtiger Teil des Designprozesses, und so werden interne und externe Kompetenzen gebündelt.

Robin Edman
Sweden
Schweden

In 2017, Robin Edman founded the Robin Edman Innovation company and has since been working as an independent design consultant. He was previously, from 2001 onwards chief executive of SVID, the Swedish Industrial Design Foundation. After studying industrial design at Rhode Island School of Design, he joined AB Electrolux Global Design in 1981 and parallel to this started his own design consultancy. In 1989, Robin Edman joined Electrolux North America as vice president of Industrial Design for Frigidaire and in 1997, moved back to Stockholm as vice president of Electrolux Global Design. Throughout his entire career he has worked towards promoting a better understanding of users, their needs and the importance of design in society at large. His engagement in design-related activities is reflected in the numerous international jury appointments, speaking engagements, advisory council and board positions he has held. Robin Edman served on the board of the World Design Organization (formerly Icsid) from 2003 to 2007, the last term as treasurer. From 2015 to 2017, he has been the president of BEDA (Bureau of European Design Associations).

Robin Edman gründete 2017 das Unternehmen „Robin Edman Innovation" und ist seitdem selbständig als Designberater tätig. Zuvor war er seit 2001 Firmenchef der SVID, der Swedish Industrial Design Foundation. Nach einem Industriedesign-Studium an der Rhode Island School of Design kam er 1981 zu AB Electrolux Global Design und startete parallel seine eigene Unternehmensberatung für Design. 1989 wechselte Edman zu Electrolux North America als Vizepräsident für Industrial Design für Frigidaire und kehrte 1997 als Vizepräsident von Electrolux Global Design nach Stockholm zurück. Während seiner gesamten Karriere setzte er sich für ein besseres Verständnis für Nutzer und ihre Bedürfnisse ebenso ein wie für die Bedeutung von Design in der Gesellschaft insgesamt. Sein Engagement in designbezogenen Aktivitäten spiegelt sich in zahlreichen Jurierungsberufungen sowie in Rednerverpflichtungen und Positionen in Gremien sowie Beratungsausschüssen wider. Von 2003 bis 2007 war Robin Edman Mitglied im Vorstand der World Design Organization (ehemals Icsid), in der letzten Amtsperiode als Schatzmeister. Von 2015 bis 2017 war er Präsident von BEDA (Bureau of European Design Associations).

The company re:innovation
specialises in design-driven
innovation in supporting management in businesses and the
public sector to grow, become
more efficient and better serve
their customers. Presently
working with start-ups to multinationals.

Das Unternehmen re:innovation
ist auf gestaltungsorientierte
Innovation spezialisiert, die Füh-
rungskräfte von Unternehmen
und staatlichen Behörden dabei
unterstützt, zu expandieren,
wirtschaftlicher zu werden und
ihre Kunden besser zu versorgen.
Aktuell arbeitet re:innovation
sowohl mit Start-ups als auch
mit multinationalen Konzernen
zusammen.

re:innovation

01

"Design as a driver of societal and cultural change has the power to transform human behaviour and can radically change the way we perceive, execute and develop our products, services and systems."

„Design als Träger gesellschaftlichen und kulturellen Wandels hat die Kraft, menschliches Verhalten zu verändern, und verwandelt auch die Art, wie wir unsere Produkte, Dienstleistungen und Systeme sehen, erschaffen und entwickeln."

Please name three features of good design:
Good design consists of the integration of functional, emotional and social utilities. A product, service, process or strategy needs to include all three: the way it works, how do I feel about using it and what do other people say. Not until all three get together in a sustainable way, is it good design.

How important is user friendliness in a product?
Extremely important! Without a focus on the users and the way the products are perceived, used and dis-carded of, a product will never reach its full potential and achieve success.

To what extent do well designed products make our everyday life easier?
To a very high extent! A product that fulfils human desires and caters to the functional, emotional and societal needs will deliver at its best without hardly being noticed. The best designed products deliver way beyond expectations – in a way as if it was the most natural thing in the world.

Bitte nennen Sie drei Merkmale guten Designs:
Gutes Design besteht aus der Integration funktionaler, emotionaler und sozialer Leistungen. Ein Produkt – wie auch eine Dienstleistung, ein Prozess oder eine Strategie – muss alle drei einbeziehen: wie das Produkt funktioniert, wie ich mich fühle, wenn ich das Produkt verwende, und was andere Leute darüber sagen. Erst wenn alle drei nachhaltig im Einklang sind, ist es gutes Design.

Wie wichtig ist die Benutzerfreundlichkeit eines Produktes?
Extrem wichtig! Wenn Nutzer und die Art, in der Produkte gesehen, verwendet und entsorgt werden, nicht im Mittel-punkt stehen, wird ein Produkt nie sein ganzes Potenzial ausschöpfen und Erfolg erzielen.

Inwieweit erleichtern gut gestaltete Produkte unseren Alltag?
Enorm! Ein Produkt, das die Sehnsüchte von Menschen erfüllt und auf ihre funktionalen, emotionalen und sozialen Bedürfnisse eingeht, leistet sein Bestes, wenn es kaum bemerkt wird. Die am besten gestalteten Produkte liefern weit mehr als erwartet – fast so, als sei es das Natürlichste der Welt.

Prof. Lutz Fügener
Germany
Deutschland

Professor Lutz Fügener began his studies at the Technical University Dresden, where he completed a foundation course in mechanical engineering. He then transferred to the Burg Giebichenstein University of Art and Design in Halle/Saale, Germany, where he obtained a degree in industrial design in 1995. In the same year, he became junior partner of Fisch & Vogel Design in Berlin. Since then, the firm (today called "studioFT") has increasingly specialised in transportation design. Two years after joining the firm, Lutz Fügener became senior partner and co-owner. In 2000, he was appointed as Professor of Transportation Design/3D Design by Pforzheim University and there chairs the prestigious BA degree course in transportation design. Lutz Fügener is also active as an author and journalist for a number of different daily newspapers, weekly magazines and periodicals, as well as blogs in which he writes on mobility-related design topics.

Professor Lutz Fügener absolvierte ein Grundstudium in Maschinenbau an der Technischen Universität Dresden und nahm daraufhin ein Studium für Industrial Design an der Hochschule für Kunst und Design, Burg Giebichenstein, in Halle an der Saale auf. Sein Diplom machte er im Jahr 1995. Im selben Jahr wurde er Juniorpartner von Fisch & Vogel Design in Berlin. Seit dieser Zeit spezialisierte sich das Büro (heute „studioFT") mehr und mehr auf den Bereich „Transportation Design". Zwei Jahre nach seinem Einstieg wurde Lutz Fügener Seniorpartner und gleichberechtigter Mitinhaber des Büros. Im Jahr 2000 wurde er von der Hochschule Pforzheim auf eine Professur für Transportation Design/3D-Gestaltung berufen und ist Leiter des renommierten BA-Studiengangs für Fahrzeugdesign. Lutz Fügener ist als Autor und Journalist für verschiedene Tageszeitungen, Wochenmagazine, Periodika und Blogs tätig und schreibt über Themen des Designs im Zusammenhang mit Mobilität.

01 BEE
An autonomous vehicle for
Continental
Ein autonomes Fahrzeug für
Continental

01

"In the future, automotive designers must address a wider set of issues and focus more intensely on other areas in the design world where they can intersect such as User Experience Design (UX) and fields dominated by engineering."

„Fahrzeugdesigner müssen sich in Zukunft thematisch breiter aufstellen und Schnittstellen zu designinternen Bereichen wie User-Experience-Design (UX) sowie vom Ingenieurwesen bestimmten Feldern intensivieren."

With what can a car surprise you?
As cars are so complex, there are many different ways. The spectrum ranges from successful, aesthetic proportions to the outstanding design of form and material through to an obvious, functionally convincing overall concept.

What challenges will automotive designers have to deal with in future?
The attempted global commercialisation of cars is currently challenged by the increasingly heterogeneous development of the markets. While the impact of production, distribution and use of cars on the environment has led to tremendous pressure in Europe, the largest international market in the Far East is clamouring for larger vehicles such as SUVs. Another challenge is the automation of cars which is taking fundamentally different approaches in the USA, Europe and China. Predictions for future car purchase behaviour also pose a major challenge, not least for designers. New ways of using vehicles require different cars. Emotional aspects of driving are also under debate and are increasingly shifting to the topic of personal mobility.

Womit kann ein Auto Sie überraschen?
Dank seiner Komplexität auf sehr verschiedene Art und Weise. Das Spektrum reicht von gelungenen, ästhetischen Proportionen über eine hohe Gestaltungsqualität in Form und Material bis zum sinnfälligen, funktional überzeugenden Gesamtkonzept.

Welche Herausforderungen müssen Automobildesigner künftig meistern?
Gegen die möglichst weltweite Vermarktung von Automobilen steht derzeit eine zunehmend heterogene Entwicklung der Märkte. Während hierzulande der Druck in Bezug auf die Auswirkungen von Herstellung, Verteilung und Nutzung auf die Umwelt groß ist, verlangt der größte internationale Markt in Fernost eher voluminöse Automobile im SUV-Format. Dazu kommt die Automatisierung des Fahrens, die in USA, Europa und China grundlegend andere Ansätze zeigt. Auch Prognosen zum Verhalten künftiger Fahrzeugkäufer stellen nicht zuletzt Designer vor große Herausforderungen. Neue Nutzungskonzepte verlangen andere Fahrzeuge. Emotionale Aspekte des Fahrens stehen zur Debatte bzw. verlagern sich zunehmend in Bereiche der individuellen Mobilität.

Hideshi Hamaguchi
USA/Japan

Hideshi Hamaguchi graduated with a Bachelor of Science in chemical engineering from Kyoto University. Starting his career with Panasonic in Japan, Hamaguchi later became director of the New Business Planning Group at Panasonic Electric Works, Ltd. and then executive vice president of Panasonic Electric Works Laboratory of America, Inc. In 1993, he developed Japan's first corporate Intranet and also led the concept development for the first USB flash drive. Hideshi Hamaguchi has over 15 years of experience in defining strategies and decision-making, as well as in concept development for various industries and businesses. As Executive Fellow at Ziba Design and CEO at monogoto, he is today considered a leading mind in creative concept and strategy development on both sides of the Pacific and is involved in almost every project this renowned business consultancy takes on. For clients such as FedEx, Polycom and M-System he has led the development of several award-winning products.

Hideshi Hamaguchi graduierte als Bachelor of Science in Chemical Engineering an der Kyoto University. Seine Karriere begann er bei Panasonic in Japan, wo er später zum Direktor der New Business Planning Group von Panasonic Electric Works, Ltd. und zum Executive Vice President von Panasonic Electric Works Laboratory of America, Inc. aufstieg. 1993 entwickelte er Japans erstes Firmen-Intranet und übernahm zudem die Leitung der Konzeptentwicklung des ersten USB-Laufwerks. Hideshi Hamaguchi verfügt über mehr als 15 Jahre Erfahrung in der Konzeptentwicklung sowie Strategie- und Entscheidungsfindung in unterschiedlichen Industrien und Unternehmen. Als Executive Fellow bei Ziba Design und CEO bei monogoto wird er heute als führender Kopf in der kreativen Konzept- und Strategieentwicklung auf beiden Seiten des Pazifiks angesehen und ist in nahezu jedes Projekt der renommierten Unternehmensberatung involviert. Für Kunden wie FedEx, Polycom und M-System leitete er etliche ausgezeichnete Projekte.

01

"Innovation I would define as unprecedented, controversial, yet achievable."

„Ich würde Innovation als etwas noch nie Dagewesenes, Kontroverses, jedoch Erreichbares definieren."

What inspired you to create the USB stick?
Rather than the problem itself, I was inspired by the biases of professionals trying to solve the problem on effective data storage.

What was the most important moment of your career to date?
I feel like I am inspired by every single detail around me, every day. The sensitivity towards these perpetual inspirations took me here where I am today.

With what can a designer surprise you?
With a sense of unease which has been carefully designed for viewers to feel in an unexpected way.

What do you pay particular attention to when evaluating products?
I look for beautiful intentions behind each design.

Was inspirierte Sie zum USB-Stick?
Eher als das Problem an sich inspirierten mich die Vorurteile der Fachleute, die versuchten, das Problem der effektiven Datenspeicherung zu lösen.

Was war der bedeutendste Moment Ihrer bisherigen Karriere?
Ich habe den Eindruck, dass jedes noch so kleine Detail in meiner Umgebung mich inspiriert – jeden Tag. Die Sensibilität für diese ständigen Inspirationen hat mich dorthin gebracht, wo ich heute bin.

Womit kann ein Designer Sie überraschen?
Mit einem Gefühl der Unruhe, das vom Designer bewusst hervorgerufen wird, damit Betrachter das Produkt auf unerwartete Weise erleben.

Worauf achten Sie bei der Bewertung von Produkten?
Ich suche bei jedem Design nach den schönen Absichten, die hinter der Gestaltung stecken.

Prof. Renke He
China

Professor Renke He, born in 1958, studied civil engineering and architecture at Hunan University in China. From 1987 to 1988, he was a visiting scholar at the Industrial Design Department of the Royal Danish Academy of Fine Arts in Copenhagen and, from 1998 to 1999, at North Carolina State University's School of Design. Renke He is dean and professor of the School of Design at Hunan University and is also director of the Chinese Industrial Design Education Committee. Currently, he holds the position of vice chair of the China Industrial Design Association.

Professor Renke He wurde 1958 geboren und studierte an der Hunan University in China Bauingenieurwesen und Architektur. Von 1987 bis 1988 war er als Gastprofessor für Industrial Design an der Royal Danish Academy of Fine Arts in Kopenhagen tätig, und von 1998 bis 1999 hatte er eine Gastprofessur an der School of Design der North Carolina State University inne. Renke He ist Dekan und Professor an der Hunan University, School of Design, sowie Direktor des Chinese Industrial Design Education Committee. Er ist derzeit zudem stellvertretender Vorsitzender der China Industrial Design Association.

01
Scarf design with traditional
Dong minority brocade patterns
for the New Channel Design &
Social Innovation Programme.
Design: School of Design of
Hunan University, China.
Schaldesign mit traditionellen
Brokatmustern der Dong-Minder-
heit für das New Channel Design &
Social Innovation Programme.
Gestaltung: Designschule der
Hunan-Universität, China.

01

"For the young generation of designers global warming and sustainable development will be real challenges and responsibilities."

„Für die jüngere Designergeneration sind der Klimawandel und eine nachhaltige Entwicklung die wirklichen Herausforderungen und Aufgabenbereiche."

What qualities must a well-designed product have?
High functionality, a well-designed human-machine relationship, eco-friendliness and aesthetic attractiveness.

What do you pay particular attention to when evaluating products?
In our digital age, technology becomes more and more complicated in many product designs. Interactive design is the key issue when evaluating products. Good interactive design makes for a good user experience – the most important value of design.

What would the ideal design apprenticeship look like, in your opinion?
Learning by doing is a long tradition in the design profession. Practice makes perfect is still an important rule in design education. In my opinion, the ideal design apprenticeship is a platform or system which encourages students to join design teams in design studios or companies in order to practice real projects under the guidance of skilled designers.

Welche Qualitäten muss ein gut gestaltetes Produkt aufweisen?
Eine hohe Funktionalität, eine gut gestaltete Schnittstelle zwischen Mensch und Maschine, Umweltfreundlichkeit und ästhetischen Reiz.

Worauf legen Sie bei der Bewertung von Produkten besonderen Wert?
In unserem digitalen Zeitalter wird die Technik in vielen Produktdesigns immer komplizierter. Die interaktive Gestaltung ist bei der Bewertung von Produkten der zentrale Punkt. Eine gute interaktive Gestaltung führt zu einem guten Nutzererlebnis – der wichtigste Beitrag von Design.

Wie sähe die ideale Designlehre für Sie aus?
„Learning by Doing" hat in der Designbranche schon lange Tradition. Die wichtige Regel „Übung macht den Meister" gilt in der Designausbildung auch heute noch. Meiner Meinung nach ist die ideale Designlehre eine Plattform oder ein System, das Studenten anregt, Teil eines Designteams in einem Designstudio oder einem Unternehmen zu werden, damit sie wirkliche Projekte unter der Anleitung sachkundiger Designer ausführen können.

Prof.
Carlos Hinrichsen
Chile

Professor Carlos Hinrichsen graduated as an industrial designer in Chile in 1982 and earned his master's degree in engineering in Japan in 1991. Currently, he is Vice-Chancellor of Academic Affairs of INACAP Polytechnic and University, the largest in the country. At present, Chile is in transition from an efficiency-based towards an innovation-based economy where INACAP contributes with actions and initiatives to achieve this important aim for the country, mixing research, innovation, business, design and engineering spheres. From 2007 to 2009, Carlos Hinrichsen was president of the World Design Organization (formerly Icsid) and currently serves as senator within the organisation. In 2010, he was honoured with the distinction "Commander of the Order of the Lion of Finland". From 2014 to 2016, he was dean of the Faculty of Business, Engineering and Digital Arts at the Gabriela Mistral University in Santiago and from 2016 to 2017, he was the Senior Managing Coordinator of Engineering Design in the School of Engineering in the P. Universidad Católica de Chile. For more than three decades he has led interdisciplinary teams to enable corporations, educational and other institutions to gain leadership and competitive positioning.

Professor Carlos Hinrichsen machte 1982 seinen Abschluss in Industriedesign in Chile und erhielt 1991 seinen Master der Ingenieurwissenschaft in Japan. Aktuell ist er Rektor für Studienangelegenheiten an der INACAP Fachhochschule und Universität, der größten im Land. Zurzeit befindet sich Chile im Übergang von einer effizienzbasierten zu einer innovationsbasierten Wirtschaft, in der INACAP mit Maßnahmen und Initiativen dazu beiträgt, dieses wichtige Landesziel durch eine Mischung aus Forschung, Innovation, Handel, Design und Ingenieurwesen zu erreichen. Von 2007 bis 2009 war Carlos Hinrichsen Präsident der World Design Organization (ehemals Icsid) und dient heute als Senator innerhalb der Organisation. 2010 wurde er mit der Auszeichnung „Commander of the Order of the Lion of Finland" geehrt. Von 2014 bis 2016 war er Dekan der Fakultät für Handel, Ingenieurwesen und Digitale Künste an der Gabriela-Mistral-Universität in Santiago und von 2016 bis 2017 leitender geschäftsführender Koordinator für Engineering Design an der P. Universidad Católica de Chile. Seit mehr als drei Jahrzehnten leitet er interdisziplinäre Teams, um Unternehmen, Bildungsinstituten und anderen Organisationen zu helfen, eine marktführende und starke Wettbewerbsposition zu erlangen.

01

The INACAP Polytechnic and University is a learning ecosystem with technology-based study programmes, distributed in 26 campuses throughout Chile. In this scenario, the Fablab INACAP is part of the largest network of rapid prototyping labs in the country, promoting interdisciplinarity and active learning with a focus on innovation, entrepreneurship, applied research and development.

Die Universität INACAP ist ein lernendes Ökosystem mit technologiegestützten Studiengängen, die auf 26 Campus-Standorten in ganz Chile angeboten werden. In dieser Konstellation ist Fablab INACAP Teil des größten Netzwerks an Rapid-Prototyping-Laboratorien im Land und fördert Interdisziplinarität sowie aktives Lernen mit einem Schwerpunkt auf Innovation, Unternehmergeist, angewandter Forschung und Entwicklung.

01

"As a child, I realised that good design contributes to human beings' happiness, and over the years I confirmed that impression. Design also needs to be sustainable in its social, economic and environmental dimensions."

„Als Kind habe ich festgestellt, dass gutes Design zum Glücksgefühl der Menschen beitragen kann. Mit den Jahren hat sich dieser Eindruck bestätigt. Design muss allerdings ebenfalls aus sozialer, wirtschaftlicher und ökologischer Sicht nachhaltig sein."

What do you pay particular attention to when evaluating products?

I focus on the unique or particular way of responding to the needs and requirements of end users, as well as how this product responds to what we know today as a circular economy. Besides, I try to recognise the relationship between design and quality, and identify which of the products fit their purpose best.

What trends have you noticed in the design industry?

In a world where new technologies are modelling, transforming the industry, business and society in which we live every day, I see trends as an effort by design solutions at the level of products, services or experiences to capture value in these changing processes, and as a means of adding value for multiple users with new requirements and changing demands, who now expect an almost instantaneous response, due to the changes and speed of response generated by the impact of the digital transformation.

Worauf legen Sie bei der Bewertung von Produkten besonderen Wert?

Ich achte auf die einzigartige oder besondere Art und Weise, wie ein Produkt auf die Bedürfnisse und Anforderungen der Benutzer eingeht, und auf das, was wir heute als Kreislaufwirtschaft bezeichnen. Außerdem versuche ich, das Verhältnis von Gestaltung zu Qualität zu erkennen und zu erfassen, welche Produkte ihren Zweck am besten erfüllen.

Welche Trends können Sie in der Designbranche identifizieren?

In einer Welt, in der neue Technologien die Industrie, den Handel und die Gesellschaft, in der wir jeden Tag leben, formen und umwandeln, sehe ich Trends als einen Versuch an, aus diesen Änderungsprozessen mithilfe von Designlösungen in der Form von Produkten, Dienstleistungen und Erlebnissen Wert zu schöpfen. Sie bieten ebenfalls einen Mehrwert für eine Vielzahl von Nutzern mit neuen Anforderungen und wechselnden Bedürfnissen, die aufgrund der durch die digitale Transformation verursachten Veränderungen und Reaktionsgeschwindigkeit eine fast sofortige Reaktion erwarten.

387

Simon Husslein
Germany/Switzerland
Deutschland/Schweiz

Simon Husslein was born in Werneck, Germany, in 1976 and studied industrial design from 1995 to 2000 at Darmstadt University of Applied Sciences. From 2000 to 2005, he worked closely with his mentor and friend Hannes Wettstein at Wettstein's studio in Zurich. From 2005 to 2007, he completed a master's degree in Design Products at the London Royal College of Art. Subsequently, he led a number of projects in London and Shanghai and lectured at Shanghai's Tongji University. Between 2008 and 2014, he put his mark on a large number of projects at the Studio Hannes Wettstein in Zurich where he was creative director and member of the executive committee. In 2015, he founded the Atelier Simon Husslein. Simon Husslein develops products, furniture, installations and spatial design. Since 2017, he has been professor of interior architecture at Geneva School of Art and Design, HEAD – Geneva, Switzerland.

Simon Husslein, geboren 1976 in Werneck, Deutschland, studierte von 1995 bis 2000 Industrial Design an der Fachhochschule Darmstadt. Von 2000 bis 2005 arbeitete er eng mit seinem Mentor und Freund Hannes Wettstein in dessen Zürcher Studio zusammen. Von 2005 bis 2007 absolvierte er ein Masterstudium in Design Products am Royal College of Art in London. Danach betreute er eigene Projekte in London und Shanghai und unterrichtete an der Tongji University in Shanghai. Zwischen 2008 und 2014 prägte er als Creative Director und Mitglied der Geschäftsleitung eine Vielzahl der Projekte des Studios Hannes Wettstein in Zürich. 2015 gründete er das Atelier Simon Husslein. Simon Husslein entwickelt Produkte, Möbel, Installationen und Raumgestaltungen. Seit 2017 ist er Professor für Interior Architecture an der Geneva School of Art and Design, HEAD – Genf, Schweiz.

01 Minimatik
Wristwatch for NOMOS
Glashütte/SA Roland
Schwertner KG
Armbanduhr für NOMOS
Glashütte/SA Roland
Schwertner KG

01

"If good design is the result of a meticulous design process, then it stands a much better chance of maintaining its position in the market for a very long time."

„Gutes Design als Resultat eines sorgfältigen Designprozesses erhöht die Chance signifikant, dass sich ein Produkt überdurchschnittlich lange in seinem Marktumfeld behaupten kann."

What do you pay particular attention to when evaluating products?
A watch has many different features that must add up and make a whole. In the case of a new model, one of the questions that arises concerns the authenticity of the concept. In general, I pay a good deal of attention to the use of detailing. How has the transition between the strap and the body of the watch been managed? Does the design of the casing harmonise with the surface treatment? Do the various elements have a common design typology? Only when the design is consistent and well implemented in all aspects is it worth an award.

What distinguishes your design "signature"?
Precision, emotion and the pursuit of the archetype.

What matters when it comes to teamwork?
If the mix of personalities is right, the team can achieve great things.

Worauf legen Sie bei der Bewertung von Produkten besonderen Wert?
Bei einer Uhr gibt es sehr viele unterschiedliche Aspekte, die als Ganzes stimmen müssen. Bei einer Neukreation stellt sich beispielsweise die Frage der Authentizität des Entwurfs. Generell achte ich sehr auf den Umgang mit Details: Wie verläuft der Übergang zwischen Bandanschluss und Gehäuse? Wurde die Gehäusegestaltung mit der Veredelungstechnologie der Oberflächen schlüssig abgestimmt? Haben die verschiedenen Elemente eine gemeinsame Gestaltungstypologie? Nur wenn das Design auf allen Ebenen konsequent und gut umgesetzt wurde, verdient es eine Auszeichnung.

Was kennzeichnet Ihre gestalterische Handschrift?
Präzision, Emotionalität und die Suche nach dem Archetypus.

Worauf kommt es bei Teamarbeit an?
Wenn die Mischung aus Persönlichkeiten stimmt, kann im Team Großes erreicht werden.

Qiong Er Jiang
China

Qiong Er Jiang, founder of lifestyle brand SHANG XIA, is an internationally renowned designer. After many years studying in Europe, she brings a cosmopolitan approach and multi-cultural experience to her designs. As artistic director and CEO of SHANG XIA, she combines traditional crafts with contemporary design. Her works received wide acclaim and distinguished design awards at national and international level, being collected by world-class museums like British Museum, Musée Guimet and Musée des Arts Décoratifs. In 2011, Forbes named Qiong Er Jiang as one of the 25 most influential Chinese in "Global Fashion and Lifestyle". Furthermore, she was honoured several times in recognition of her contribution to the cultural exchange between China and France.

Qiong Er Jiang, Gründerin der Lifestyle-Marke SHANG XIA, ist eine international renommierte Designerin. Nachdem sie mehrere Jahre in Europa studiert hat, verfolgt sie bei ihren Entwürfen einen weltoffenen und multikulturellen Ansatz. Als Artistic Director und CEO von SHANG XIA kombiniert sie traditionelles Handwerk mit zeitgenössischem Design. Ihre Arbeiten haben sowohl auf nationaler als auch auf internationaler Ebene große Anerkennung und angesehene Auszeichnungen erhalten. Außerdem werden sie in Museen von Weltrang wie dem British Museum, dem Musée Guimet und dem Musée des Arts Décoratifs gesammelt. 2011 zählte Forbes Qiong Er Jiang zu den 25 einflussreichsten Chinesen im Bereich „Global Fashion und Lifestyle". Darüber hinaus wurde sie mehrere Male für ihren Beitrag zum kulturellen Austausch zwischen China und Frankreich geehrt.

01 GARDEN
Round Box in red Bo Luo lacquer
with gold inlay. The red and
gold lidded box is inspired by the
traditional Chinese Cuan Pan
vessel sets, signifying happiness
and completeness.
Runde Schachtel mit roter
Bo-Luo-Lackarbeit und goldenen
Intarsien. Die Schachtel mit dem
rot-goldenen Deckel wurde von
den traditionellen chinesischen
Cuan-Pan-Gefäße-Sets inspiriert
und symbolisiert Glück und
Vollkommenheit.

01

"My experience in Europe offered
me the chance to see my own
culture from another angle. The
opportunity to twist my views in
this unique way offered a positive
influence in the creations of my
designs."

„Meine Erfahrungen in Europa haben
mir erlaubt, meine eigene Kultur aus
einer anderen Perspektive zu sehen.
Diese Gelegenheit, meine Sichtweise
auf so eine einzigartige Weise um-
zustellen, hat sich positiv auf mein
gestalterisches Schaffen ausgewirkt."

What does a product have to offer in order to surprise you?
Emotion, emotion and emotion. Of course, the emotion can come from the material of the product,
craftsmanship, design concept, or cultural background
story. And it may even come from all of these things
combined!

What distinguishes your design "signature"?
My design encapsulates an encounter, or a dialogue,
between: tradition and modernity, craft and technology, functionality and emotion, past and future.
There is true emotion put into and captured through
my designs.

Why is the cultural exchange between different nations valuable?
From my understanding, though the nations are different, the culture is fundamentally the same: it's
about love and beauty. The cultural exchange can be
conveyed through expression and style to portray
"beauty", while feeling and understanding this allows
for deeper "emotion". The diversity of these trans-
lations enriches our lives and makes it meaningful.

Was muss ein Produkt mitbringen, um Sie zu überzeugen?
Emotion, Emotion und noch mal Emotion! Selbstverständlich kann diese Emotion von dem Material des
Produkts, seiner Handwerkskunst, dem Gestaltungskonzept oder dem kulturellen Hintergrund ausgehen. Es
kann sogar eine Verschmelzung aller dieser Quellen sein.

Was kennzeichnet Ihre gestalterische Handschrift?
Mein Design bringt eine Begegnung, einen Dialog zwi-
schen Tradition und Moderne, Handwerk und Technik,
Funktionalität und Gefühl, Vergangenheit und Zukunft
auf den Punkt. In meinen Gestaltungen steckt ehrliche
Emotion.

Warum ist der kulturelle Austausch zwischen verschiedenen Nationen wichtig?
Nach meiner Auffassung unterscheiden sich Nationen
zwar, doch ist die Kultur prinzipiell die gleiche: Es geht
immer um Liebe und Schönheit. Der kulturelle Austausch
kann durch eine Stilrichtung und eine Ausdrucksform,
die „Schönheit" darstellt, vermittelt werden. Wenn man
das versteht und spürt, ist das „emotionale Erlebnis"
stärker. Die Vielfalt dieser Interpretationen bereichert
unser Leben und gibt ihm Bedeutung.

Prof.
Cheng-Neng Kuan
Taiwan

In 1980, Professor Cheng-Neng Kuan earned a master's degree in Industrial Design (MID) from the Pratt Institute in New York. He is currently a chair professor and served as the vice president of Shih-Chien University, Taipei, Taiwan, from 2008 to 2017. With the aim of developing a more advanced design curriculum in Taiwan, he founded the Department of Industrial Design, in 1992. He served as department chair until 1999. Moreover, Cheng-Neng Kuan founded the School of Design in 1997 and had served as the dean from 1997 to 2004 and as the founding director of the Graduate Institute of Industrial Design from 1998 to 2007. He had also held the position of the 16th chairman of the board of China Industrial Designers Association (CIDA), Taiwan. His fields of expertise include design strategy and management as well as design theory and creation. Having published various books on design and over 180 research papers and articles, he is an active member of design juries in his home country and internationally. He is a consultant to major enterprises on product development and design strategy.

1980 erwarb Professor Cheng-Neng Kuan einen Masterabschluss in Industriedesign (MID) am Pratt Institute in New York. Derzeit ist er Lehrstuhl-Professor und war von 2008 bis 2017 Vizepräsident der Shih-Chien University in Taipeh, Taiwan. 1992 gründete er mit dem Ziel, einen erweiterten Designlehrplan zu entwickeln, das Department of Industrial Design in Taiwan. Bis 1999 war Cheng-Neng Kuan Vorsitzender des Instituts. Darüber hinaus gründete er 1997 die School of Design, deren Dekan er von 1997 bis 2004 war. Von 1998 bis 2007 war er Gründungsdirektor des Graduate Institute of Industrial Design. Zudem war er der 16. Vorstandsvorsitzende der China Industrial Designers Association (CIDA) in Taiwan. Seine Fachgebiete umfassen Designstrategie, -management, -theorie und -kreation. Neben der Veröffentlichung verschiedener Bücher über Design und von mehr als 180 Forschungsarbeiten und Artikeln ist er aktives Mitglied von Designjurys in seiner Heimat sowie auf internationaler Ebene. Zudem ist er als Berater für Großunternehmen im Bereich Produktentwicklung und Designstrategie tätig.

01 Plier
A piece of furniture for an open space, designed by Lin-Huei Hwang, can be transformed into a screen panel or bar table. This project was selected as a winner of Taiwan's Young Pin Design Award 2017.
Ein Möbelstück für ein Freigelände, von Lin-Huei Hwang gestaltet. Es kann als eine Leinwand oder als ein Bartisch verwendet werden. Dieses Projekt wurde zu einem Gewinner des Young Pin Design Award 2017 in Taiwan gekürt.

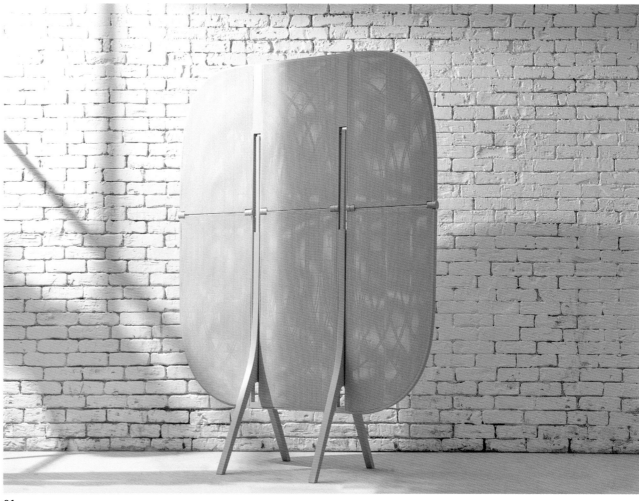

01

"Good design needs to bring inspiring emotional satisfaction right to the target users."
„Gutes Design muss seiner Zielgruppe direkte, inspirierende und emotionale Befriedigung bieten."

With what can a product surprise you?
A composition of concept and language that seems unfamiliar to me yet opens up a new design horizon.

How do you proceed when evaluating products?
By seeing and thinking if the first impression offers design reasons that convince me of its excellence.

What message would you like to give your students for their future career?
Keep exploring the messages of lifestyle changes, and use your design to give it a specific meaning.

What challenges will designers have to meet in future?
Facing unprecedented ecological crisis, we designers have to rethink the spirit of brands with regard to human welfare.

Womit kann ein Produkt Sie überraschen?
Mit einer Kombination aus Konzept und Formensprache, die mir unbekannt ist und mir einen neuen Designhorizont eröffnet.

Wie gehen Sie bei der Bewertung der Produkte vor?
Indem ich sehe und überlege, ob der erste Eindruck Gründe für das Design liefert, die mich von seiner Vortrefflichkeit überzeugen.

Welche Botschaft möchten Sie Ihren Studenten mit auf den Weg geben?
Weiterhin die Botschaften aufzuspüren, die aus den Veränderungen im Lebensstil hervorgehen, und ihren Gestaltungskonzepten eine bestimmte Bedeutung zu verleihen.

Welchen Herausforderungen müssen sich Designer künftig stellen?
In Anbetracht der beispiellosen ökologischen Krise müssen wir Designer den Sinn von Marken in Bezug auf das Gemeinwohl überdenken.

Steve Leung
Hong Kong
Hongkong

Born and bred in Hong Kong, Steve Leung is a leading international architect, interior and product designer. His works reflect the projects' unique characters with his contemporary touch, taking inspirations from Asian culture and arts. Honoured as the Winner of 19th Andrew Martin International Interior Designer of the Year Award, his projects have been credited with more than 130 international corporate and design awards. He established his own architectural and urban planning consultancy in 1987, later restructured into Steve Leung Architects Ltd. (SLA) and Steve Leung Designers Ltd. (SLD). In 2018, SLD Group was listed on the Main Board of the Hong Kong Stock Exchange. Headquartered in Hong Kong with five branches in Beijing, Shanghai, Guangzhou, Shenzhen and Tianjin and with 600 dedicated designers and professionals, the Group is one of the largest interior design practices in Asia. Steve Leung is enthusiastically engaged in the design industry as the current President of the International Federation of Interior Architects/Designers (IFI) and as one of the founders of "C-Foundation", committed in actively promoting the development of the design profession in Asia and worldwide.

Steve Leung, in Hongkong geboren und aufgewachsen, ist ein führender internationaler Architekt, Innenarchitekt und Produktdesigner. Seine Arbeit spiegelt die einzigartigen Eigenschaften der Projekte wider und gibt ihnen einen zeitgemäßen Schliff, der von fernöstlicher Kultur und Kunst inspiriert ist. Steve Leung ist Gewinner des 19. Andrew Martin International Interior of the Year Award und wurde fernerhin mit mehr als 130 weiteren internationalen Unternehmens- und Designauszeichnungen gekürt. Er gründete 1987 seine eigene Beratungsagentur für Architektur und Städtebau und strukturierte sie später in Steve Leung Architects Ltd. (SLA) und Steve Leung Designers Ltd. (SLD) um. 2018 wurde die SLD Group im Hauptsegment an der Hongkonger Börse notiert. Mit Hauptsitz in Hongkong und fünf Niederlassungen in Beijing, Shanghai, Guangzhou, Shenzhen und Tianjin sowie 600 engagierten Designern und Fachleuten ist die Gruppe eines der größten Innenarchitekturbüros in Asien. Steve Leung engagiert sich mit Begeisterung in der Designindustrie – als der derzeitige Präsident der International Federation of Interior Architects/Designers (IFI) und als einer der Gründer der „C-Foundation", die aktiv zur Förderung des Designberufs in Asien und weltweit beiträgt.

01 Fusital – H377 Series SL
Duemilasedici
The door handle collection in collaboration with Fusital is based on a contemporary minimalist design inspired by the bold geometry of Chinese traditional brass hardware and antique door lockset.

Die in Zusammenarbeit mit Fusital produzierte Türgriff-Kollektion basiert auf einem zeitgemäßen, minimalistischen Gestaltungs-konzept, das seine Inspiration in der auffallenden Geometrie traditio-neller chinesischer Messingwaren und antiker Türschlösser findet.

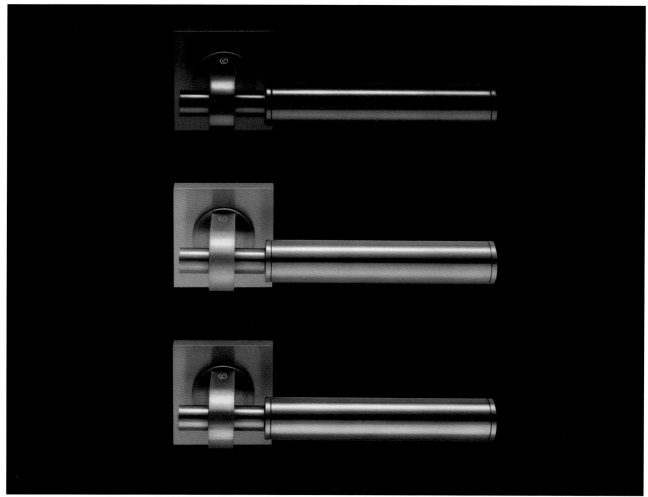

01

"I'm happy that by being a part of this jury, the passion and joy of creation can be passed on to many more designers, globally."

„Ich freue mich, dass ich als Mitglied der Jury die Gelegenheit habe, die Leidenschaft und die Freude am Gestalten an viele weitere Designer zu vermitteln, und das international."

What was the deciding moment of your career?
It was establishing my own studio at 30 and restruc-turing it to do both architecture and interior design in 1997. I started developing business in Mainland China three years after. It was a life changing moment and I'm thankful that it created interesting and rewarding chapters in the years after.

Are there noticeable differences between customers with different backgrounds?
Clients have different needs and preferences and are influenced by distinctive cultural and lifestyle fea-tures. But eventually design is about life, and life is about people, living and experience. In the end, origi-nal ideas that respond to people's fundamental needs functionally and more so psychologically will be the most sought-after designs, inspiring a positive change in daily life.

Was war der entscheidende Moment Ihrer Karriere?
Es war die Gründung meines eigenen Studios im Alter von 30 Jahren und dann in 1997 die Umstellung auf sowohl Architektur als auch Innenarchitektur. Drei Jahre später habe ich damit begonnen, das Geschäft in Festlandchina aufzubauen. Es war der Punkt, an dem sich mein Leben verändert hat, und ich bin dankbar dafür, dass es mir in den Jahren danach noch interessante und bereichernde Kapitel beschert hat.

Erkennen Sie Unterschiede zwischen Kunden verschiedener Herkunft?
Kunden haben unterschiedliche Bedürfnisse und Vorlieben und werden von ihren verschiedenen kulturellen Eigen-heiten und Lebensformen beeinflusst. Letztlich befasst sich Design aber mit dem Leben und im Leben geht es um Menschen – darum, wie sie leben, und um die Erlebnisse, die sie haben. Am Ende werden originelle Ideen, die funktional und besonders psychologisch auf die grund-legenden Bedürfnisse von Menschen eingehen, die begehrtesten Gestaltungen sein und einen positiven Wandel im Alltag bewirken.

Dr. Thomas Lockwood
USA

Dr. Thomas Lockwood is co-author of the books "Innovation by Design" (2017) and "The Handbook of Design Management" (2011) as well as author of "Design Thinking" (2009), "Corporate Creativity" (2009), and "Building Design Strategy" (2008). He received a PhD, an MPhil and an MBA in Design Management after a BA in Business and Design. Thomas Lockwood is recognised as a thought leader at integrating design and innovation practice into business, and building great design and UX organisations. In 2011, he formed Lockwood Resource, an international consulting and recruiting firm specialising in design and innovation leadership. Previously, he was president of the Design Management Institute (DMI) from 2005 to 2011, a visiting professor at Pratt University, and from 1996 to 2005 a corporate design director at Sun Microsystems and StorageTek, among others. He created high-tech skiwear for the US Olympic Nordic Ski Team, corporate design programmes for Fortune 500 organisations and internationally led conferences and workshops.

Dr. Thomas Lockwood ist Co-Autor der Bücher „Innovation by Design" (2017) und „The Handbook of Design Management" (2011) sowie Autor von „Design Thinking" (2009), „Corporate Creativity" (2009) und „Building Design Strategy" (2008). Nach einem Bachelorabschluss in Unternehmensdesign und Gestaltung machte er seinen MPhil und MBA und promovierte in Designmanagement. Thomas Lockwood gilt als ein Vordenker für die Integration von Design und Innovation in der Wirtschaft und für den Aufbau starker Design- und UX-Unternehmen. 2011 gründete er Lockwood Resource, eine internationale Beratungs- und Personalvermittlungsfirma, die sich auf Design und Innovationsführerschaft spezialisiert hat. Zuvor war er u. a. Präsident des Design Management Institute (DMI) von 2005 bis 2011, Gastprofessor an der Pratt University sowie von 1996 bis 2005 Corporate Design Director bei Sun Microsystems und StorageTek. Er entwickelte Hightech-Skibekleidung für das Olympic Nordic Ski Team der USA sowie Corporate-Design-Programme für Fortune-500-Unternehmen und leitete internationale Kongresse und Workshops.

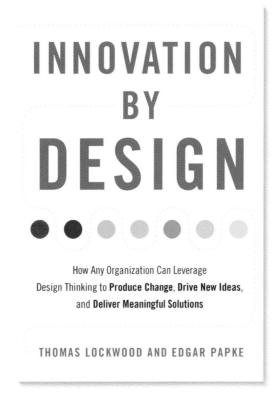

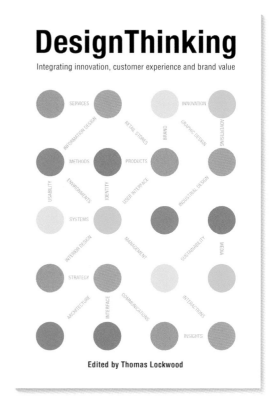

01

02

"Good design solves problems
perfectly."
„Gutes Design löst Probleme perfekt."

**In your opinion, what would the world look like
without innovation?**
It would probably look more like the animal kingdom.
It is impossible to know what animals think, but as an
outsider, I would imagine them to be more content,
more peaceful and more observant. Innovation is
what advances our societies.

**How can a company become an innovation leader
in its sector?**
By reaching beyond technology innovation and
embracing a strategy of open innovation. This requires
a shift in focus from sales and what a company can
make to a focus on what people actually need. The
path means embracing design thinking and human
centred design, in order to solve the right problems.

**What development could significantly improve our
world?**
An app to create world peace! Truly, if we all could all
just accept one another as we are, rather than impos-
ing our doctrines and individual agendas upon others.

**Wie sähe eine Welt ohne Innovation Ihrer Meinung
nach aus?**
Sie würde wahrscheinlich mehr dem Tierreich ähneln.
Es ist unmöglich zu wissen, was Tiere denken, doch als
Außenstehender stelle ich mir vor, dass sie zufriedener,
ruhiger und aufmerksamer sind. Innovation ist der Motor,
der unsere Gesellschaften vorantreibt.

**Wie wird man als Unternehmen zum
Innovationsführer seiner Branche?**
Indem man mehr als nur technische Innovation erzielt
und sich eine Strategie der offenen Innovation zu eigen
macht. Das erfordert eine Verlagerung des Schwerpunktes
weg vom Vertrieb und dem, was ein Unternehmen herstellen kann, hin zu dem, was Menschen wirklich brauchen.
Das erreicht man, wenn man auf Designdenken und
eine menschenorientierte Gestaltung umstellt, um so die
richtigen Probleme zu lösen.

**Welche Entwicklung könnte unsere Welt
maßgeblich verbessern?**
Eine App, die Weltfrieden schafft! Ehrlich, wenn wir einander nur alle akzeptieren könnten, so wie wir sind, anstatt
einander unsere Dogmen und persönlichen Einstellungen
aufzudrücken.

Wolfgang K. Meyer-Hayoz
Switzerland
Schweiz

Wolfgang K. Meyer-Hayoz studied mechanical engineering, visual communication and industrial design and graduated from the Stuttgart State Academy of Art and Design. After a number of years as an in-house designer in industry, he founded the Meyer-Hayoz Design Engineering Group in 1985. The multiple award-winning company works in the fields of medical engineering, biotechnology, life sciences as well as on the design of machines, robots and other appliances. The company also advises start-ups as well as multinationals in the areas of design strategy, industrial design, user-interface design, temporary architecture and communication design. From 1987 to 1993, Wolfgang K. Meyer-Hayoz was honorary president of the Swiss Design Association (SDA). He serves as jury member on international design panels and is a member of the Association of German Industrial Designers (VDID) and the Swiss Management Society (SMG). In addition, he is a member of the group of supporters for the Institute of Marketing at the University of St. Gallen and chairs change management and turnaround projects in the field of design strategy.

Wolfgang K. Meyer-Hayoz absolvierte Studien in Maschinenbau, Visueller Kommunikation sowie Industrial Design mit Abschluss an der Staatlichen Akademie der Bildenden Künste in Stuttgart. Nach Jahren als Inhouse-Designer in der Industrie gründete er 1985 die Meyer-Hayoz Design Engineering Group. Das vielfach international ausgezeichnete Unternehmen ist in Medizintechnik, Biotechnologie, Life Sciences sowie Maschinen-, Robotik- und Gerätedesign tätig und berät Start-up-Unternehmen ebenso wie Weltmarktführer in den Kompetenzbereichen Design Strategy, Industrial Design, User Interface Design, Temporary Architecture und Communication Design. Von 1987 bis 1993 führte Wolfgang K. Meyer-Hayoz ehrenamtlich als Präsident die Swiss Design Association (SDA). Er engagiert sich als Juror in internationalen Designgremien, ist Mitglied im Verband Deutscher Industrie Designer (VDID) und der Schweizerischen Management Gesellschaft (SMG) sowie aktives Mitglied im Förderkreis des Instituts für Marketing der Universität St. Gallen und moderiert Change-Management- und Turnaround-Projekte im designstrategischen Bereich.

01 Multitron
Incubation shaker for the reliable
and easy cultivation of micro-
organisms and cell cultures, for
Infors AG, Switzerland
Inkubationsschüttler für die
zuverlässige und komfortable
Kultivierung von Mikroorganismen
und Zellkulturen, für Infors AG,
Schweiz

02 ICM 710/PCM 710
Range of compact control
units for burglar alarms, for
Securiton AG, Switzerland
Kompakte Bediengeräteserie für
Einbruchmeldeanlagen, für
Securiton AG, Schweiz

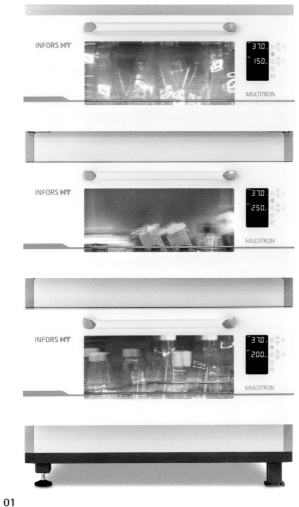

01

02

"It takes time, conviction and mutual esteem to develop a strategic direction for companies through design – our customers need to understand that design services cannot be produced quickly like in a pressure cooker."

„Die strategische Ausrichtung von Unternehmen durch gestalterische Arbeit benötigt Zeit, Überzeugung und stets die gegenseitige Wert-schätzung – unsere Kunden müssen also verstehen, dass Designleistun-gen nicht wie aus einem Schnell-kochtopf zu haben sind."

How do you keep reinventing yourself as a designer?
I have always been an inquisitive person. New materials, technologies, possibilities for the use of things and their application to new business models have always fascinated and motivated me to think a step further in the spirit of anticipation.

Where do you find the energy for your impressive commitment to your profession?
I am convinced that designers have a very fine and pronounced sense of intuition so that they notice changes and upheavals in society early on. The aware-ness and recognition of these changes gives us designers the unique opportunity to develop new solutions, first conceptually and later physically. For me, this process is a "source of energy".

What makes your work so exciting?
Every job is new and different. Every customer has their own specific requests and every company champions new values and value propositions in its own way. It never gets boring!

Wie erfinden Sie sich als Designer immer wieder neu?
Ich war schon immer ein sehr neugieriger Mensch. Neue Materialien, Technologien, Nutzungsmöglichkeiten und deren Anwendung für neue Geschäftsmodelle haben mich immer fasziniert und angespornt, noch einen Schritt weiter zu denken, im Sinne der Antizipation.

Woher schöpfen Sie die Energie für Ihr großes berufliches Engagement?
Ich bin überzeugt, dass Gestalter ein sehr feines und aus-geprägtes Gespür haben und daher Veränderungen und Umbrüche in unserer Gesellschaft früh wahrnehmen. Das Bewusstsein und Erkennen dieser Veränderungen gibt uns als Gestaltern gleichzeitig die einzigartige Chance, hieraus neue Lösungsansätze erst gedanklich und dann physisch zu entwickeln. Diesen Prozess empfinde ich als permanenten „Energiespender".

Was macht Ihren Beruf so spannend?
Jede Aufgabe ist neu und anders. Jeder Kunde hat seine spezifischen Wünsche und jedes Unternehmen vertritt auf seine Weise immer wieder neue Werte und Wertvor-stellungen. Langeweile kommt hierdurch nie auf!

Prof. Jure Miklavc
Slovenia
Slowenien

Professor Jure Miklavc graduated in industrial design from the Academy of Fine Arts in Ljubljana, Slovenia, and has nearly 20 years of experience in the field of design. He started his career working as a freelance designer, before founding his own design consultancy, Studio Miklavc. Studio Miklavc works in the fields of product design, visual communications and brand development and is a consultancy for a variety of clients from the industries of light design, electronic goods, user interfaces, transport design and medical equipment. Sports equipment designed by the studio has gained worldwide recognition. From 2013 onwards, the team has been working for the prestigious Italian motorbike manufacturer Bimota. Designs by Studio Miklavc have received many international awards and have been displayed in numerous exhibitions. Jure Miklavc has been involved in design education since 2005 and is currently a lecturer and head of industrial design at the Academy of Fine Arts and Design in Ljubljana.

Professor Jure Miklavc machte seinen Abschluss in Industrial Design an der Academy of Fine Arts and Design in Ljubljana, Slowenien, und verfügt über nahezu 20 Jahre Erfahrung im Designbereich. Er arbeitete zunächst als freiberuflicher Designer, bevor er sein eigenes Design-Beratungsunternehmen „Studio Miklavc" gründete. Studio Miklavc ist in den Bereichen Produktdesign, Visuelle Kommunikation und Markenentwicklung sowie in der Beratung zahlreicher Kunden der Branchen Lichtdesign, Elektronische Güter, Benutzeroberflächen, Transport-Design und Medizinisches Equipment tätig. Die von dem Studio gestalteten Sportausrüstungen erfahren weltweit Anerkennung. Seit 2013 arbeitet das Team für den angesehenen italienischen Motorradhersteller Bimota. Studio Miklavc erhielt bereits zahlreiche Auszeichnungen sowie Präsentationen in Ausstellungen. Seit 2005 ist Jure Miklavc in der Designlehre tätig und aktuell Dozent und Head of Industrial Design an der Academy of Fine Arts and Design in Ljubljana.

01

01 Carefoot
Integral project of building a brand, corporate identity, products and communication for children's shoes by Austrian company Alpvent. The solution incorporates a convenient size measuring system with an app.

Umfassendes Projekt für den Aufbau der Marke, Corporate Identity, Produkte und Kommunikation der Kinderschuhe der österreichischen Firma Alpvent. Die Lösung schließt ein praktisches App-basiertes Messsystem für Schuhgrößen ein.

"I hope that in ten years, product design will be more involved with the real solutions for environmental problems. Designers will also be more connected to the field of robotics and artificial intelligence."

„Ich hoffe, dass sich das Produktdesign in zehn Jahren mehr mit den wirklichen Lösungen für Umweltprobleme auseinandersetzt. Designer werden sich auch mehr mit dem Bereich der Robotertechnik und künstlichen Intelligenz befassen."

What constitutes good design?
Good design is usually a consequence of emotional intelligence and transforms technical innovation in a way that is understandable, pleasant and enjoyable for the user and is not invasive for the environment. Good design is also more than just a summary of different parameters – in the best scenarios it influences us in such a way that it changes the way in which we live to the positive.

What distinguishes your design "signature"?
My design signature is more about the process and approach rather than some typical formal language. I believe in design viewed in context. In that respect I would say that "empathy" is the focus of my work – towards users, environment, technology and identity.

What message would you like to give young designers for their future careers?
I would want to encourage them to be extra curious and sensitive to real needs and to the environment.

Was macht gutes Design aus?
Gutes Design ist generell das Ergebnis emotionaler Intelligenz und verwandelt technische Innovation derart, dass sie für den Nutzer verständlich, angenehm und erfreulich ist, ohne die Umwelt zu belasten. Gutes Design ist auch mehr als die Summe verschiedener Parameter. In den besten Fällen beeinflusst es uns dahingehend, dass es unser Leben positiv verändert.

Was kennzeichnet Ihre gestalterische Handschrift?
Meine gestalterische Handschrift findet sich eher in dem Prozess und Ansatz als in einer charakteristischen Formensprache wieder. Ich glaube an eine Gestaltung, die im Kontext betrachtet werden sollte. In dieser Hinsicht würde ich sagen, dass „Empathie" im Fokus meiner Arbeit steht – Empathie für Nutzer, die Umwelt, Technik und Identität.

Welche Botschaft möchten Sie jungen Designern mit auf den Weg geben?
Ich würde sie dazu ermutigen, besonders neugierig zu sein – und sensibel für echte Bedürfnisse und die Umwelt.

Adriana Monk
Switzerland
Schweiz

Adriana Monk studied product design at the Art Center College of Design in La Tour-de-Peilz, Switzerland, and graduated from Pasadena, USA, beginning her career at the BMW Group Designworks/USA. She subsequently established herself as the automotive industry's leading interior designer for luxury brands such as Rolls-Royce, Jaguar and Land Rover, before pursuing her passion for yachts. In 2008, she founded Monk Design in Switzerland. The agency's focus is on boat interiors, exclusive detailing and graphic design for performance yachts, for both private clients and boats produced in series. With a balanced sense of proportions and aesthetics, Adriana Monk produces new creative solutions. Her work has won several international awards including the World Superyacht Award, Red Dot, iF and the Eurobike Design Award. She is a guest lecturer at the Royal College of Art in London and at the International University of Monaco and also a jury member at competitions like the Design & Innovation Awards of Boat International.

Adriana Monk studierte Produktdesign am Art Center College of Design in La Tour-de-Peilz, Schweiz, und machte ihren Abschluss in Pasadena, USA, bevor sie ihre Karriere bei BMW Group Designworks/USA startete. Anschließend etablierte sie sich als führende Innenarchitektin der Automobilbranche für Luxusmarken wie Rolls-Royce, Jaguar und Land Rover, bevor sie ihrer Leidenschaft für Yachten nachging. 2008 gründete sie Monk Design in der Schweiz. Der Schwerpunkt liegt auf Boot-Interieurs, exklusiven Detailausführungen und Grafikdesign für Performance-Yachten, sowohl für Privatkunden als auch für Serienboote. Mit einem ausgewogenen Sinn für Proportionen und Ästhetik gelangt Adriana Monk zu neuen, kreativen Lösungen. Ihre Arbeit wurde mehrfach international ausgezeichnet, u. a. mit dem World Superyacht Award, Red Dot, iF und dem Eurobike Design Award. Sie ist als Gastdozentin am Royal College of Art in London und der International University of Monaco sowie als Jurorin z. B. des Design & Innovation Awards von Boat International tätig.

01 monk-e-shine lamp, model L1180
Low-voltage reading lamp specifically designed for yachts, produced by Palagi Marine Lights, Italy. The double rotation axis allows for a very wide range of light direction. Clean design with no visible fixings.
Speziell für den Bootsbau gestaltete Niedervolt-Leseleuchte, hergestellt von Palagi Marine Lights, Italien. Dank der 2-Achsen-Rotation ist die Beleuchtungsmöglichkeit sehr groß. Montage ohne sichtbare Schrauben.

01

"Honesty, purity and simplicity are words that resonate with my design discipline. I believe that a design will stand the test of time if it is not only functional but also aesthetically pleasing."

„Ehrlichkeit, Reinheit und Schlichtheit sind Worte, die mit meiner Auffassung von Gestaltung in Einklang stehen. Ich glaube, dass eine Gestaltung nur dann überdauert, wenn sie sowohl funktional als auch ästhetisch überzeugt."

To what do you attach particular importance when judging products?
Judging other people's work is an honour and a very demanding task. By reading the documentation I assess if the design brief has been respected, and whether the product is unique and innovative. By using and handling the products I look for beauty and function as well as quality and the intuitive operation of the product.

Why did you decide to leave the automotive industry and pursue your passion for yachts?
After ten years designing automotive interiors for various luxury brands, I wanted to challenge my creativity. Yachts have always fascinated me: sculptural forms that glide through water. I was awestruck when I first saw a 100-foot carbon-fibre hull. I then proceeded to study naval architecture and get my sailing licence before pursuing my dream: working for Wally Yachts was the stepping stone to leave the automotive industry and open my own design studio, following my passion for yachts.

Worauf legen Sie bei der Bewertung von Produkten besonderen Wert?
Das Werk anderer beurteilen zu dürfen, ist eine Ehre und eine sehr anspruchsvolle Aufgabe. Beim Lesen der Unterlagen bewerte ich, ob die Designvorgaben respektiert wurden und ob das Produkt einzigartig und innovativ ist. Beim Benutzen und Handhaben der Produkte achte ich auf Schönheit und Funktion sowie auf Qualität und die intuitive Bedienung des Produkts.

Warum haben Sie sich dazu entschieden, die Automobilbranche zu verlassen und Ihrer Leidenschaft für Yachten nachzugehen?
Nach zehn Jahren der Gestaltung von Innenräumen für Fahrzeuge verschiedener Luxusmarken wollte ich etwas für meine Kreativität tun. Yachten haben mich schon immer fasziniert: skulpturale Formen, die durch Wasser gleiten. Als ich das erste Mal einen 100-Fuß-Schiffsrumpf aus Kohlefaser sah, war ich sprachlos. Ich habe dann erst Schiffbau studiert und einen Segelschein gemacht, bevor ich meinen Traum verwirklichen konnte: Für Wally Yachts zu arbeiten, war das Sprungbrett für den Abschied aus der Automobilbranche und erlaubte mir, meiner Leidenschaft für Yachten zu folgen und mein eigenes Designstudio aufzubauen.

403

Prof. Dr. Ken Nah
Korea

Professor Dr. Ken Nah graduated with a Bachelor of Science in Industrial Engineering from Hanyang University, South Korea, in 1983. He deepened his interest in Human Factors/Ergonomics by earning a master's degree from Korea Advanced Institute for Science and Technology (KAIST) in 1985. He received a Ph.D. in Engineering Design from Tufts University, Boston, in 1996. Ken Nah is also a USA Certified Professional Ergonomist (CPE), for the first time as a Korean. He is currently a professor of Design at the International Design School for Advanced Studies (IDAS), Hongik University in Seoul as well as director of the Human Experience and Emotion Research (HE.ER) Lab. Since 2002 he has been the director of the International Design Trend Center (IDTC). Ken Nah was the director general of "World Design Capital Seoul 2010". Alongside his work as a professor, he is also the senior vice-president of the Korea Federation of Design Associations (KFDA) and the Korea Association of Industrial Designers (KAID). Ken Nah has been an advisor on design policy to several ministries of the Korean government since 2000.

Professor Dr. Ken Nah graduierte 1983 an der Hanyang University in Südkorea als Bachelor of Science in Industrial Engineering. Sein Interesse an Human Factors/Ergonomie vertiefte er 1985 mit einem Masterabschluss am Korea Advanced Institute for Science and Technology (KAIST). 1996 promovierte er im Bereich „Konstruktive Gestaltung" an der Tufts University in Boston. Darüber hinaus ist Ken Nah ein in den USA zertifizierter Ergonom (CPE). Derzeit ist er Professor für Design an der International Design School for Advanced Studies (IDAS) der Hongik University in Seoul sowie Direktor des „Human Experience and Emotion Research (HE.ER)"-Labors. Seit 2002 ist er zudem Leiter des International Design Trend Centers (IDTC). Ken Nah war Generaldirektor der „World Design Capital Seoul 2010". Neben seiner Lehrtätigkeit als Professor ist er Senior-Vizepräsident der Korea Federation of Design Associations (KFDA) und der Korea Association of Industrial Designers (KAID). Seit 2000 ist Ken Nah ferner als Berater in Designpolitik für verschiedene Ministerien der koreanischen Regierung tätig.

01

"One trend I have noticed in current design is a seamless assimilation of 'smartness' in products to achieve maximum ease and convenience for users."

„Ein Trend, der mir im aktuellen Design aufgefallen ist, ist die nahtlose Integration von ‚Intelligenz' in Produkte, um Nutzern maximalen Komfort und Anwenderfreundlichkeit zu bieten."

What constitutes an ergonomic product?
Ergonomics, or more appropriately, Human Factors, is defined as a human-centred design discipline seeking for an optimal solution for human users in their working and living environment. Therefore, a product design based on human factors should be easy, convenient, safe, and pleasant to use physically, physiologically, and psychologically and meet emotional wants as well.

How will the product design discipline develop over the ten years to come?
I guess the next ten years will be the most turbulent years for any discipline including design due to big data, AI and convergence. Design should quickly adapt the technology, especially for generative design and engineering analysis, not to mention marketing and business. In a nutshell, design as a discipline will at the same time become general on one hand and very specific on the other hand, which will make it the most challenging and exciting area.

Was macht ein ergonomisches Produkt aus?
Ergonomie oder besser gesagt die Arbeitswissenschaft wird als eine am Menschen orientierte Gestaltungsdisziplin definiert, die versucht, eine optimale Lösung für menschliche Nutzer in ihrem Arbeits- und Lebensumfeld zu entwickeln. Daher sollte ein Produktdesign, das auf Arbeitswissenschaft beruht, einfach, komfortabel, sicher und physisch, physiologisch und psychologisch angenehm zu benutzen sein. Gleichzeitig sollte es auch emotionale Bedürfnisse erfüllen.

Wie wird sich das Produktdesign in den kommenden zehn Jahren entwickeln?
Ich tippe darauf, dass die nächsten zehn Jahre die turbulentesten Jahre in jedem Sektor sein werden, auch in der Gestaltung; und das aufgrund von Big Data, KI und Konvergenz. Design sollte die neue Technologie schnell anwenden und anpassen, besonders für generatives Design und technische Analysen, mal ganz abgesehen von Marketing und der Geschäftswelt. Kurz und gut: Design als Disziplin wird auf der einen Seite sehr allgemein werden und auf der anderen sehr spezifisch, wodurch es zu dem spannendsten, aber auch anspruchsvollsten Sektor werden wird.

Alexander Neumeister
Germany/Brazil
Deutschland/Brasilien

Alexander Neumeister is a high-tech industrial designer, who lives both in Germany and Brazil. A graduate of the Ulm School of Design and a one-year scholarship student at the Tokyo University of Arts, he specialised in the fields of medicine, professional electronics and transportation. Among some of his best-known works are the "Transrapid" maglev trains, the German ICE trains, the Japanese Shinkansen "Nozomi 500", as well as numerous regional trains and subways for Japan, China and Brazil, and the C1 and C2 trains for the Munich underground. Aside from working on projects for large German companies, he was design consultant for Hitachi/Japan for 21 years. From 1983 to 1987, he was board member and later vice-president of the World Design Organization (formerly Icsid). In 1992, Alexander Neumeister and his team received the honorary title "Red Dot: Design Team of the Year". In 2011, he was awarded the design prize of the city of Munich and in 2015, he won the EU's "European Railway Award" in recognition of his contribution to railway design.

Alexander Neumeister arbeitet als Hightech-Industriedesigner und ist in Deutschland wie in Brasilien zu Hause. Als Absolvent der Hochschule für Gestaltung in Ulm und Stipendiat der Tokyo University of Arts für ein Jahr spezialisierte er sich auf die Bereiche Medizin, Professionelle Elektronik und Verkehr. Die Magnetschwebebahn „Transrapid", die deutschen ICE-Züge, der japanische Shinkansen „Nozomi 500", aber auch zahlreiche Regionalzüge und U-Bahnen in Japan, China und Brasilien sowie die U-Bahnen C1 und C2 für München zählen zu seinen bekanntesten Entwürfen. Neben Projekten für deutsche Großunternehmen war er 21 Jahre lang Designberater für Hitachi/Japan. Von 1983 bis 1987 war er Vorstandsmitglied und später Vizepräsident der World Design Organization (ehemals Icsid). 1992 wurden Alexander Neumeister und sein Team mit dem Ehrentitel „Red Dot: Design Team of the Year" ausgezeichnet. 2011 erhielt er den Designpreis der Landeshauptstadt München und 2015 den „European Railway Award" der EU für seine Leistungen auf dem Gebiet des Railway-Designs.

01

"In my opinion, good design is the successful combination of materials and function, but it also includes the ability to adapt to different environments and the exclusion of superfluous decorations."

„Gutes Design ist für mich die gelungene Kombination von Materialaufwand und Funktion. Aber auch der Verzicht auf unnötige Dekoration und die Fähigkeit, sich in Umgebungen einzuordnen."

You were responsible for the design of the ICE. What does it feel like to site in the flagship of the Deutsche Bahn?
I designed both the ICE concept train, as well as the ICE-3. My team and I created open seating areas for the design with compartments at the end of one of the carriages – with minimally greater distances between the seats in first class. The design work on the train began in 1996 and now, more than 20 years later, I still enjoy travelling in "my ICE-3". The interior has lost none of its elegance.

What would you still like to achieve professionally?
At over 75, I asked myself how many more trains I still want to design in order to be satisfied. I decided to hand my shares over to my partner and to leave N+P Industrial Design. In Germany, I still advise a former colleague, who works as a freelancer in Munich, and in Brazil I work for two companies in the electronics sector. I have never regretted the decision to step back a bit.

Sie waren für das Design des ICEs verantwortlich. Wie fühlt es sich an, in dem Flaggschiff der Deutschen Bahn zu sitzen?
Ich habe sowohl den ICE-Versuchszug wie auch den ICE-3 gestaltet. Für das Design haben mein Team und ich offene Sitzlandschaften geschaffen mit Abteilen am Ende eines Waggons – für die erste Klasse mit geringfügig größeren Sitzabständen. Das Design startete 1996 und nun, mehr als 20 Jahre danach, macht es mir immer noch Spaß, in „meinem ICE-3" zu reisen. Der Innenraum hat nichts von seiner Eleganz eingebüßt.

Was möchten Sie beruflich noch erreichen?
Mit über 75 Jahren stellte ich mir die Frage, wie viele Züge ich noch gestalten wollte, um zufrieden zu sein. Ich entschloss mich, meine Anteile an meine Partner abzu-geben und aus N+P Industrial Design auszusteigen. In Deutschland berate ich noch einen ehemaligen Mitarbeiter, der sich in München selbständig gemacht hat, und in Brasilien arbeite ich für zwei Unternehmen im Elektronik-bereich. Die Entscheidung, das alles zu reduzieren, habe ich nie bereut.

Ken Okuyama
Japan

Ken Kiyoyuki Okuyama, industrial designer and CEO of Ken Okuyama Design, was born in 1959 in Yamagata, Japan, and studied automobile design at the Art Center College of Design in Pasadena, California. He has worked as a chief designer for General Motors, as a senior designer for Porsche AG, and as design director for Pininfarina S.p.A., being responsible for the design of Ferrari Enzo, Maserati Quattroporte and many other automobiles. He is also known for many different product designs such as motorcycles, furniture, robots and architecture. Ken Okuyama Design was founded in 2007 and provides business consultancy services to numerous corporations. Ken Okuyama also produces cars, eyewear and interior products under his original brand. He is currently a visiting professor at several universities and also frequently publishes books.

Ken Kiyoyuki Okuyama, Industriedesigner und CEO von Ken Okuyama Design, wurde 1959 in Yamagata, Japan, geboren und studierte Automobildesign am Art Center College of Design in Pasadena, Kalifornien. Er war als Chief Designer bei General Motors, als Senior Designer bei der Porsche AG und als Design Director bei Pininfarina S.p.A. tätig und zeichnete verantwortlich für den Ferrari Enzo, den Maserati Quattroporte und viele weitere Automobile. Zudem ist er für viele unterschiedliche Produktgestaltungen wie Motorräder, Möbel, Roboter und Architektur bekannt. Ken Okuyama Design wurde 2007 als Beratungsunternehmen gegründet und arbeitet für zahlreiche Unternehmen. Ken Okuyama produziert unter seiner originären Marke auch Autos, Brillen und Inneneinrichtungsgegenstände. Derzeit lehrt er als Gastprofessor an verschiedenen Universitäten und publiziert zudem Bücher.

01

"I always seek, sketch and write way before the job comes in. My hands show me the way, like a fortune teller."

„Lange bevor der Auftrag kommt, bin ich ständig auf der Suche, skizziere und schreibe. Meine Hände weisen mir den Weg, genau wie bei einem Wahrsager."

What was the development process for the Ferrari Enzo like?
Single talent doesn't make a good car. It was a miracle to gather spirited geniuses like Luca Cordero di Montezemolo and Sergio Pininfarina and to be part of the team as a designer at the very end of the last century. It will never happen again.

What advice do you most frequently give to customers?
I am a "chef" for a good design. I put up a menu, customers come, we talk, and I give a lot more than they expected with a good surprise.

What do you like about your role as consultant?
Together with the top management, we define a future vision and solutions to get there, sharing confidentiality. For that reason, we only work with one company in each industry. It's like being a family.

Wie sah der Entwicklungsprozess des Ferrari Enzo aus?
Einzelne Talente machen kein gutes Auto. Es war ein Wunder Ende des letzten Jahrhunderts, dass wir sprühende Genies wie Luca Cordero di Montezemolo und Sergio Pininfarina gewinnen konnten – und für mich als Designer, Teil des Teams sein zu können. Das wird nie wieder geschehen.

Welchen Tipp geben Sie Ihren Kunden am häufigsten?
Ich bin der „Koch" für eine gute Gestaltung. Ich stelle ein Menü zusammen, die Kunden kommen, wir reden und ich gebe ihnen sehr viel mehr als sie erwarteten, noch dazu mit einer guten Überraschung.

Was gefällt Ihnen an der Tätigkeit als Berater?
Gemeinsam mit dem Topmanagement definieren wir eine Vision für die Zukunft und die Lösungen, die uns dahinbringen werden – in strengster Vertraulichkeit. Daher arbeiten wir in jeder Branche auch nur mit einem Unternehmen. Man fühlt sich als Teil der Familie.

Simon Ong
Singapore
Singapur

Simon Ong, born in Singapore in 1953, graduated with a master's degree in design from the University of New South Wales and an MBA from the University of South Australia. He is the deputy chairman and co-founder of Kingsmen Creatives Ltd., a leading communication design and production group with 21 offices across the Asia-Pacific region, the Middle East and North America. Kingsmen has won several awards, such as the President's Design Award, Singapore Good Design Mark, SRA Best Retail Concept Award, SFIA Hall of Fame, Promising Brand Award, A.R.E. Retail Design Award and RDI International Store Design Award USA. Simon Ong is actively involved in the creative industry as chairman of the design group of Manpower, the Skills & Training Council of Singapore Workforce Development Agency. Moreover, he is a member of the advisory board of the Design Business Chamber of Singapore and Singapore Furniture Industries Council (Design). Currently, Simon Ong is a board member of the Association of Retail Environments (USA), a board director of Nanyang Academy of Fine Arts and a member of the advisory board to the School of Design & Environment at the National University of Singapore.

Simon Ong, geboren 1953 in Singapur, erhielt einen Master in Design der University of New South Wales und einen Master of Business Administration der University of South Australia. Er ist stellvertretender Vorsitzender und Mitbegründer von Kingsmen Creatives Ltd., eines führenden Unternehmens für Kommunikationsdesign und Produktion mit 21 Geschäftsstellen im asiatisch-pazifischen Raum, dem Mittleren Osten und Nordamerika. Kingsmen wurde vielfach ausgezeichnet, u. a. mit dem President's Design Award, Singapore Good Design Mark, SRA Best Retail Concept Award, SFIA Hall of Fame, Promising Brand Award, A.R.E. Retail Design Award und RDI International Store Design Award USA. Simon Ong ist als Vorsitzender der Designgruppe von Manpower, der „Skills & Training Council of Singapore Workforce Development Agency", aktiv in die Kreativindustrie involviert. Zudem ist er Mitglied des Beirats der Design Business Chamber Singapore und des Singapore Furniture Industries Council (Design). Aktuell ist Simon Ong Vorstandsmitglied der Association of Retail Environments (USA), Vorstandsvorsitzender der Nanyang Academy of Fine Arts und Mitglied des Beirats der School of Design & Environment an der National University of Singapore.

01 Twenty3
at Formula 1 2018 Singapore
Airlines Singapore Grand Prix
Scintillating action from the
race track can be caught from
full-length windows at the
restaurants at Twenty3.
Das fulminante Geschehen auf
der Rennstrecke kann durch die
raumhohen Fenster des Twenty3-
Restaurants verfolgt werden.

01

"A product that surprises me has a standout design that is simple yet well-engineered, while marrying function and aesthetics. Most importantly, it needs to be intuitive for users."

„Um mich zu überraschen, muss ein Produkt ein herausragendes Design vorweisen, das sowohl einfach als auch ausgereift ist. Gleichzeitig sollte es Funktion und Ästhetik in Einklang bringen. Am wichtigsten ist, dass es intuitiv zu benutzen ist."

What are the hallmarks of good design?
Less is more. A well-designed product that resonates with its users will let them realise that their daily lives are made better by using it whether they knew they needed it or not in the first place.

How does a product become a classic?
This status has to be earned and not claimed. The product should be able to stand the test of time amidst the changing consumer mindset and an ever increasing digitally connected world. These are products that end up representing their own category and their design becomes reason enough for users to buy the product.

Do you have a tip for young designers?
Don't lose sight that it is about the user experience (UX). You need to understand who you are designing for and how they interact and experience the product; how they use it, and the relationship the users form with the product.

Was kennzeichnet gutes Design?
Weniger ist mehr. Ein gut gestaltetes Produkt, das mit seinen Nutzern im Einklang ist, wird ihnen zeigen, dass ihr Alltag durch seine Verwendung besser wird, auch wenn sie sich vorher gar nicht bewusst waren, dass sie es brauchten.

Wie wird ein Produkt zum Klassiker?
Dieser Status will verdient sein und kann nicht einfach beansprucht werden. Das Produkt sollte sich langfristig bewähren, trotz der ständig wechselnden Einstellung der Konsumenten und der zunehmend digital vernetzten Welt. Klassiker sind Produkte, die in einer Kategorie für sich stehen und deren Design Grund genug ist, sie zu kaufen.

Haben Sie einen Tipp für junge Designer?
Nie die Benutzererfahrung (UX) aus den Augen verlieren. Sie müssen wissen, für wen sie gestalten und wie ihre Zielgruppe mit dem Produkt umgeht und es erlebt; wie sie es benutzt und welche Beziehung sie zu dem Produkt entwickelt.

Dr. Sascha Peters
Germany
Deutschland

Dr. Sascha Peters is founder and owner of the agency for material and technology HAUTE INNOVATION in Berlin. He studied mechanical engineering at the RWTH Aachen University, Germany, and product design at the ABK Maastricht, Netherlands. He wrote his doctoral thesis at the University of Duisburg-Essen, Germany, on the complex of problems in communication between engineering and design. From 1997 to 2003, he led research projects and product developments at the Fraunhofer Institute for Production Technology IPT in Aachen and subsequently became deputy head of the Design Zentrum Bremen until 2008. Sascha Peters is author of various specialist books on sustainable raw materials, smart materials, innovative production techniques and energetic technologies. He is a leading material expert and trend scout for new technologies. Since 2014, he has been an advisory board member of the funding initiative "Zwanzig20 – Partnerschaft für Innovation" (2020 – Partnership for innovation) commissioned by the German Federal Ministry of Education and Research.

Dr. Sascha Peters ist Gründer und Inhaber der Material- und Technologieagentur HAUTE INNOVATION in Berlin. Er studierte Maschinenbau an der RWTH Aachen und Produktdesign an der ABK Maastricht. Seine Doktorarbeit schrieb er an der Universität Duisburg-Essen über die Kommunikationsproblematik zwischen Engineering und Design. Von 1997 bis 2003 leitete er Forschungsprojekte und Produktentwicklungen am Fraunhofer-Institut für Produktionstechnologie IPT in Aachen und war anschließend bis 2008 stellvertretender Leiter des Design Zentrums Bremen. Sascha Peters ist Autor zahlreicher Fachbücher zu nachhaltigen Werkstoffen, smarten Materialien, innovativen Fertigungsverfahren und energetischen Technologien und zählt zu den führenden Materialexperten und Trendscouts für neue Technologien. Seit 2014 ist er Mitglied im Beirat der Förderinitiative „Zwanzig20 – Partnerschaft für Innovation" im Auftrag des Bundesministeriums für Bildung und Forschung.

01

A special area about future
food and 3D printing in the food
industry on the occasion of
"imm/LivingKitchen" trade fair in
January 2019 in Cologne
Sonderfläche zu Future Food
und 3D-Druck im Ernährungsbereich anlässlich der
„imm/LivingKitchen"-Messe im
Januar 2019 in Köln

01

"I believe the most exciting recent development to be 4D printing and the resulting potential for programmable materials. With the help of an exterior impulse, components can change their own shape."

„Der 4D-Druck und die damit zusammenhängenden Potenziale programmierbarer Materialien empfinde ich als die spannendste Entwicklung der letzten Jahre. Mithilfe eines äußeren Impulses können sich Bauteile damit selbsttätig verformen."

What are key activities of your HAUTE INNOVATION agency?

I founded HAUTE INNOVATION with the aim of speeding up the transfer of innovations in materials into marketable products. In the meantime, we have become established as a trend agency for future technologies. Our customers come from the automotive, furniture and construction industries.

What is your objective as a designer?

We don't work as classical designers, but rather carry out trend analyses for our customers and initiate innovation processes. To this end, we organise exhibitions on disruptive technology. For example, we were responsible for a special area at the "imm/LivingKitchen" trade fair in Cologne about future food and 3D printing in the food industry.

Was sind die wichtigsten Aktivitäten Ihrer Agentur HAUTE INNOVATION?

Ich habe HAUTE INNOVATION mit dem Ziel gegründet, Materialinnovationen schneller in marktfähige Produkte zu überführen. In der Zwischenzeit werden wir als Trendagentur für Zukunftstechnologien wahrgenommen und haben Kunden in der Automobil-, Möbel- und Bauindustrie.

Welches Ziel verfolgen Sie als Designer?

Wir arbeiten nicht als klassische Designer, sondern setzen für unsere Kunden Trendanalysen um und initiieren Innovationsprozesse. In diesem Zusammenhang gestalten wir Ausstellungen zu disruptiven Technologien. Hier haben wir zur „imm/LivingKitchen"-Messe in Köln beispielsweise eine Sonderfläche zu Future Food und 3D-Druck im Ernährungsbereich verantwortet.

Dirk Schumann
Germany
Deutschland

Dirk Schumann, born in 1960 in Soest, studied product design at Münster University of Applied Sciences. After graduating in 1987, he joined oco-design as an industrial designer, moved to siegerdesign in 1989, and was a lecturer in product design at Münster University of Applied Sciences until 1991. In 1992, he founded his own design studio "Schumanndesign" in Münster, developing design concepts for companies in Germany, Italy, India, Thailand and China. For several years now, he has focused on conceptual architecture, created visionary living spaces and held lectures at international conferences. Dirk Schumann has taken part in exhibitions both in Germany and abroad with works that have garnered several awards, including the Gold Prize (Minister of Economy, Trade and Industry Prize) in the International Design Competition, Osaka; the Comfort & Design Award, Milan; the iF product design award, Hanover; the Red Dot Design Award, Essen; the Focus in Gold, Stuttgart; as well as the Good Design Award, Chicago and Tokyo. In 2015, he founded Schumann&Wang in Xiamen City, the Chinese subsidiary of Schumanndesign.

Dirk Schumann, 1960 in Soest geboren, studierte Produktdesign an der Fachhochschule Münster. Nach seinem Abschluss 1987 arbeitete er als Industriedesigner für oco-design, wechselte 1989 zu siegerdesign und war bis 1991 an der Fachhochschule Münster als Lehrbeauftragter für Produktdesign tätig. 1992 eröffnete er in Münster sein eigenes Designstudio „Schumanndesign", das Designkonzepte für Unternehmen in Deutschland, Italien, Indien, Thailand und China entwickelt. Seit einigen Jahren beschäftigt er sich mit konzeptioneller Architektur, entwirft visionäre Lebensräume und hält Vorträge auf internationalen Kongressen. Dirk Schumann nimmt an Ausstellungen im In- und Ausland teil und wurde für seine Arbeiten mehrfach ausgezeichnet, u. a. mit dem Gold Prize (Minister of Economy, Trade and Industry Prize) des International Design Competition, Osaka, beim Comfort & Design Award, Mailand, dem iF product design award, Hannover, dem Red Dot Design Award, Essen, dem Focus in Gold, Stuttgart, sowie dem Good Design Award, Chicago und Tokio. 2015 gründete er mit Schumann&Wang in Xiamen City die chinesische Dependance von Schumanndesign.

01

"Good design is characterised by maximum practical value for the user, sensitive management of resources, durable design, emotion and a clear brand identification."

„Gutes Design zeichnet sich durch größtmöglichen Gebrauchswert für den Benutzer, einen sensiblen Umgang mit Ressourcen, langlebiges Design, Emotionalität und klare Identifizierbarkeit der Marke aus."

What do you design at "Schumanndesign"?

Products with sophisticated functionality for a range of industries. We have often long-standing relationship with international companies in the sanitary, medical and communication technology industries as well as in mechanical and plant engineering. The resulting products are the consequence of close, personal cooperation with customers. I particularly value the international nature of our work and the associated awareness of cultural diversity and values.

How did you come to open a branch office in Xiamen City?

It all started at the "Design Business Week", organised by Red Dot in 2013 in Xiamen, where we first made contact with companies from Xiamen City and other Chinese industrial centres. This led to concrete projects in 2015. As Xiamen is also a centre for the sanitary industry, it seemed natural for us to establish a branch office there. Our operations in southern China have also led to interesting projects and overarching activities in Beijing and Shanghai.

Was gestalten Sie bei „Schumanndesign"?

Produkte mit hohem Anspruch an ihre Funktionalität für unterschiedliche Branchen. Die oft langfristigen Kooperationen mit internationalen Unternehmen liegen in den Bereichen Sanitär, Medizin- und Kommunikationstechnik sowie Maschinen- und Anlagenbau. Die Produkte entstehen in engen, individuellen Kooperationen mit den Kunden, wobei ich die Internationalität und das damit zusammenhängende Verständnis für kulturelle Vielfalt und Werte sehr schätze.

Wie kam es dazu, dass Sie eine Dependance in Xiamen City eröffnet haben?

Der Ursprung geht letztlich auf die von Red Dot 2013 veranstaltete „Design Business Week" in Xiamen zurück, auf der es zu ersten Kontakten zu Unternehmen aus Xiamen City und anderen Industriestandorten in China und 2015 zu konkreten Projekten kam. Da auch Xiamen einen Schwerpunkt im Sanitärbereich hat, war es naheliegend, eine Dependance vor Ort zu etablieren. In der Folge unserer Tätigkeiten in Südchina haben sich auch interessante Projekte und übergreifende Aktivitäten in Beijing und Shanghai ergeben.

Prof. Song Kee Hong
Singapore
Singapur

Professor Song Kee Hong has worked with some of the world's most notable brands, including Dell, Epson, HP, Intel, Lenovo, P&G, Philips, Sanyo, Sennheiser and WelchAllyn, and he has received more than twenty international design awards for his work. His recent portfolio of cross-disciplinary design work spans diverse industries – from consumer electronics to mission-critical domains in healthcare, industrial and security for government systems. Song Kee Hong is currently a deputy head at the Industrial Design Division, National University of Singapore. He is also the design director of Design Exchange. He has over two decades of design experience, including work at global innovation consultancy Ziba and at HP.

Professor Song Kee Hong hat für einige der namhaftesten Marken der Welt gearbeitet, darunter Dell, Epson, HP, Intel, Lenovo, P&G, Philips, Sanyo, Sennheiser und WelchAllyn. Für seine Arbeit wurde er in mehr als zwanzig internationalen Designwettbewerben ausgezeichnet. Zu seinen jüngeren interdisziplinären Projekten zählen Aufträge für verschiedene Branchen von der Unterhaltungselektronik bis hin zu entscheidenden Bereichen wie dem Gesundheitswesen, der Industrie und staatlichen Sicherheitssystemen. Zurzeit ist Song Kee Hong stellvertretender Leiter der Industrial Design Division an der National University of Singapore und gleichzeitig Designdirektor von Design Exchange. Er blickt auf mehr als zwei Jahrzehnte Designerfahrung zurück, die Tätigkeiten bei der globalen Innovations-Unternehmensberatung Ziba und bei HP einschließt.

01

"Good consumer product design can be very demanding in terms of balancing stunning aesthetics with good user experience."
„Gutes Design für Konsumgüter kann sehr anspruchsvoll darin sein, beeindruckende Ästhetik mit guter Benutzererfahrung in Einklang zu bringen."

To what extent does your work as a designer in the consumer electronics industry differ from your work as a designer in the healthcare sector?
Although much of the technical process such as configuring component layout and ergonomics are similar, that's where the similarity ends. The main differences are in the user scenario and operating environment. When I designed an emergency ambulance, my team had to ride in one to real cases and understand all the critical needs of both the crew and patient; all design decisions are driven by these needs.

What do you like about being a jury member?
Besides the opportunity to view and try thousands of designs from around the world, I like to meet and share experience and insights with my peers from around the world. Always amusing to see that we're so different and yet so similar at the same time!

Inwiefern unterscheidet sich die Arbeit als Designer in der Unterhaltungselektronik von der Tätigkeit als Gestalter im Gesundheitswesen?
Obwohl ein Großteil der technischen Verfahren, z. B. die Anordnung der verschiedenen Komponenten und die ergonomische Gestaltung, sich ähneln, hört die Gemeinsamkeit da auch schon auf. Die Hauptunterschiede betreffen die Nutzungssituation und die Betriebsumgebung. Als ich dabei war, einen Notarztwagen zu gestalten, musste mein Team in einem Krankenwagen zu echten Notfällen mitfahren, um die maßgeblichen Bedürfnisse sowohl des Einsatzteams als auch der Patienten zu verstehen. Alle Designentscheidungen werden von diesen Bedürfnissen gesteuert.

Was gefällt Ihnen an Ihrer Tätigkeit als Juror?
Abgesehen von der Gelegenheit, tausende Gestaltungsprojekte aus der ganzen Welt zu sehen, gefällt mir, dass ich Kolleginnen und Kollegen aus der ganzen Welt treffen und Erfahrungen und Erkenntnisse mit ihnen austauschen kann. Es ist immer amüsant zu sehen, wie sehr wir uns unterscheiden und gleichzeitig doch ähneln!

Dick Spierenburg
Netherlands
Niederlande

Dick Spierenburg, born in 1953, studied architecture at Delft University of Technology and Interior & Product Design at the Royal Academy of Art in The Hague. He worked at the Dutch manufacturer Castelijn for over fifteen years, as managing and creative director. In 1995, he set up and managed three leading permanent interior design exhibitions in Amsterdam, NIC, Pakhuis Amsterdam and Post CS. Parallel to these activities Dick Spierenburg established KBDS with Dutch designer Karel Boonzaaijer in 2001 designing for Arco, Artifort, Castelijn, Gelderland, Hollands Licht, Minotti Italia, Montis and Moroso. In 2009, he founded his own studio. In Germany, he co-ordinated the initiative for a design and interior showroom for international brands "Design Post", and was appointed creative consultant and in 2011 creative director to imm cologne. Since 2014, Dick Spierenburg has been consulting the trade fair Orgatec, and has been focusing on the design of exhibitions such as for the MAKK museum and presentation spaces for Thonet, Linak or Oase.

Dick Spierenburg, 1953 geboren, studierte Architektur an der Technischen Universität Delft sowie Innenarchitektur und Produktdesign an der Königlichen Kunstakademie in Den Haag. Danach arbeitete er mehr als 15 Jahre als Geschäftsführer und Creative Director für den niederländischen Hersteller Castelijn. 1995 baute er drei führende permanente Innenarchitektur-Ausstellungen in Amsterdam, NIC, Pakhuis Amsterdam und Post CS, auf, die er danach auch leitete. Gleichzeitig gründete er gemeinsam mit dem holländischen Designer Karel Boonzaaijer im Jahr 2001 KBDS und gestaltete für Arco, Artifort, Castelijn, Gelderland, Hollands Licht, Minotti Italia, Montis und Moroso. 2009 eröffnete er sein eigenes Designstudio. In Deutschland organisierte er die Initiative „Design Post", ein Design- und Innenarchitektur-Showroom für internationale Marken, und wurde zum Creative Consultant benannt. 2011 wurde er Creative Director der imm cologne. Seit 2014 berät Dick Spierenburg die Fachmesse Orgatec und konzentriert sich auf die Gestaltung von Ausstellungen, u. a. für das MAKK Museum, und von Ausstellungsräumen für Thonet, Linak und Oase.

**01 Pure Editions Club
at imm cologne 2019**
The 2019 design for the Editions
Club shows an exciting contrast
between volume and lightness: a
high cross vault is suggested, but
built with paper thin walls. Only
a few materials were used to
reach the special effect of an intimate room. A stretched hospi-
tality space, serene and light,
with an impressive perspective
as scenery for seating areas.
Das Design für den Editions Club
von 2019 weist einen spannenden
Kontrast zwischen Volumen und
Leichtigkeit auf: Angedeutet wird
ein hohes Kreuzgewölbe, das aus
papierdünnen Wänden besteht. Es
wurden nur wenige Materialien
verwendet, um den besonderen
Effekt eines intimen Raumes zu
erzeugen. Ein geräumiger Hospita-
lity-Bereich, ruhig und hell, mit
einer eindrucksvollen Perspektive
als Kulisse für die Sitzecken.

01

"Next to a rational approach,
all senses should be taken in
consideration when judging a
product. Visual and tactile
aspects as well as sounds and
smells can make the difference."
„Zusätzlich zu einem rationalen
Ansatz sollten bei der Bewertung
eines Produkts auch alle Sinne
ins Spiel kommen. Optische und
haptische Aspekte, Klänge und
Gerüche können den Unterschied
ausmachen."

**With what can a piece of furniture persuade you
of its merits?**
With an innovative character: new possibilities in
use and appealing visual aspects. A new product
must earn its place with its concept, materialisation,
options for use, look & feel and sustainable qualities.

**To what extent has the "Bauhaus" movement
influenced you?**
The principles of Bauhaus have left many traces both
in my education and in my work. It is good to question
every step you take in the design process but letting
intuition speak is equally important. We should not
overestimate the influence of Bauhaus in the present
time. The world has changed in the last 100 years.
Design and architecture should lead and not follow
when it comes to societal change and development.

Womit kann ein Möbelstück Sie überzeugen?
Mit einem innovativen Charakter: neuen Möglichkeiten
der Anwendung und ansprechenden optischen Eigenschaften. Ein neues Produkt muss seinen Platz verdienen –
mit Konzept, Materialisierung, Anwendungsmöglichkeiten, Optik und Haptik und nachhaltigen Eigenschaften.

**Stichwort „Bauhaus": Inwieweit beeinflusste die
Kunstschule Sie?**
Die Bauhaus-Prinzipien haben sowohl in meiner Ausbildung als auch in meiner Arbeit nachhaltige Spuren
hinterlassen. Es ist gut, jeden Schritt, den man im Gestal-
tungsprozess macht, zu hinterfragen. Es ist allerdings
genauso wichtig, die Intuition zu Wort kommen zu lassen.
Wir sollten den Einfluss des Bauhauses allerdings nicht
überschätzen. Die Welt hat sich in den letzten 100 Jahren
verändert. Design und Architektur sollten im Wandel
der Gesellschaft und bei Entwicklungen führen und nicht
folgen.

Leon Sun
China

Leon Sun is Chief Content Officer and Editorial Director of the international home and lifestyle magazine ELLE DECORATION China. He is journalist with over a decade of experience in the interior design industry. By introducing the latest global design and trends into the Chinese market, he actively promotes the development of the domestic interior industry. Amongst others, he realised the special topics "Oriental Gene", "Asia Now" and "Rong He" at ELLE DECORATION China. Furthermore, he is judge of the EDIDA International Design Awards and Vice President of the China Gold Idea Design Award. Graduating in Visual Communication from the Shanghai Donghua University, Leon Sun started his career as Visual Director at ELLE DECORATION China in 2006. From 2011 to 2014, he was Visual Director at AD China.

Leon Sun ist Chief Content Officer und Editorial Director des internationalen Wohn- und Lifestyle-Magazins ELLE DECORATION China. Er ist Journalist mit mehr als einem Jahrzehnt Erfahrung im Sektor Inneneinrichtung. Indem er die international aktuellsten Gestaltungen und Trends auf dem chinesischen Markt vorstellt, unterstützt er die Entwicklung der heimischen Einrichtungsbranche aktiv. Unter anderem realisierte er die Themenspecials „Oriental Gene", „Asia Now" und „Rong He" bei ELLE DECORATION China. Darüber hinaus ist er Juror des EDIDA International Design Awards und Vice President des China Gold Idea Design Awards. Mit einem Abschluss in Visual Communication von der Shanghai Donghua University begann er seine Karriere 2006 als Visual Director bei ELLE DECORATION China. Von 2011 bis 2014 war er Visual Director bei AD China.

01 2019 China Interior Design Annual

ELLE DECORATION China released the 2019 China Interior Design Annual, a special selection of interior design projects. The top designers Tony Chi, Steve Leung, Alan Chan and André Fu reviewed the submitted works and leading designers like Kengo Kuma, Yabu Pushelberg, Kenya Hara and Neri&Hu Studio shared their insights on excellent China interior designs in all relevant categories.

ELLE DECORATION China ist Herausgeber des 2019 China Interior Design Annual, einer Sonderauswahl von Innenarchitekturprojekten. Die Topdesigner Tony Chi, Steve Leung, Alan Chan und André Fu haben die eingereichten Arbeiten begutachtet, während führende Designer wie Kengo Kuma, Yabu Pushelberg, Kenya Hara und Neri&Hu Studio ihre Einblicke in herausragende chinesische Innenarchitekturprojekte in allen relevanten Kategorien vermitteln.

01

"A good designer is always curious. He is an expert in exploring the unknown, creating new things and revealing his unique perspective in the way in which he interprets life and the world through his works."

„Ein guter Designer ist immer neugierig. Er ist Experte im Erforschen von Unbekanntem, im Schaffen von Neuem und im Darstellen seiner einzigartigen Sichtweise, in der er das Leben und die Welt mit seiner Arbeit interpretiert."

What constitutes good design?
Design is about solving problems and offering better services to people. Therefore, a good design is a tool that makes people's life better.

To what do you attach particular importance when judging products?
Firstly, to creativity and innovations in ideas, formats or materials; secondly, to workability and its way of solving problems and considering physical or psychological needs. Thirdly, to the look and whether it immediately catches your eye and, fourthly, to friendliness: a product needs to reflect the relationship between humans and objects and to be environmentally friendly.

Where will the design industry be ten years from now?
Our life will advance along with technological developments which allow us to dream bigger. However, design will evolve in different directions due to its diversity, interacting with technologies, culture and art.

Was macht gutes Design aus?
Bei Design geht es darum, Probleme zu lösen und Menschen einen besseren Service zu bieten. Daher ist gutes Design ein Hilfsmittel, das Menschen das Leben erleichtert.

Worauf legen Sie bei der Bewertung von Produkten ein besonderes Augenmerk?
Erstens auf die Kreativität und die Innovationen, die ein Produkt in Idee, Format und Materialien bietet; zweitens auf Praktikabilität und die Art, in der es Probleme löst und auf physische und psychische Bedürfnisse eingeht. Drittens auf den Look und ob es sofort die Augen auf sich zieht und, viertens, auf die Freundlichkeit – ein Produkt sollte die Beziehung zwischen Mensch und Objekt widerspiegeln und umweltfreundlich sein.

Wo wird die Designbranche in zehn Jahren stehen?
Unser Leben wird mit den technischen Entwicklungen voranschreiten und uns erlauben, größere Träume zu träumen. Design wird sich aufgrund seiner Vielfalt allerdings in verschiedene Richtungen entwickeln und mit Technik, Kultur und Kunst zusammenwirken.

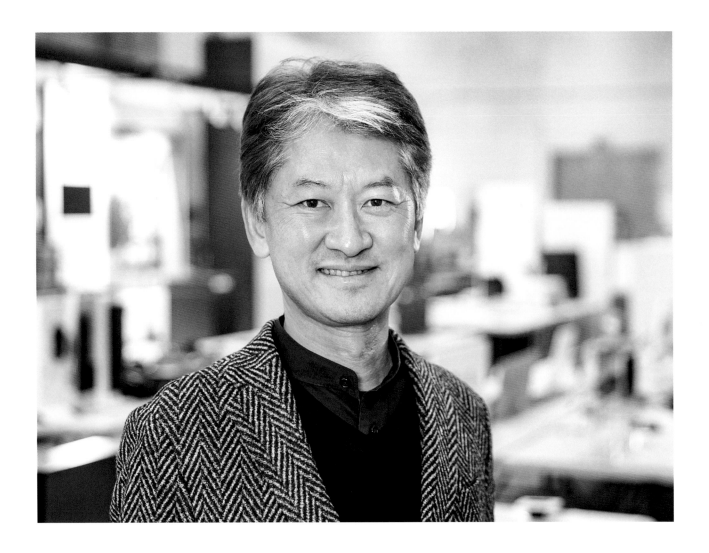

Kazuo Tanaka
Japan

Kazuo Tanaka graduated in 1983 from Tokyo University of the Arts, majored in industrial design. He is president and CEO of the GK Design Group Incorporated, a comprehensive freelance design office in Japan founded in 1952 by Kenji Ekuan. Kazuo Tanaka has been elected president of the Japan Industrial Designers Association (JIDA) and taking on many kinds of activities since 2013. In 2007, he was elected member of the board of directors of the World Design Organization (formerly Icsid) and has been active, also as a regional adviser, in many international programmes. Kazuo Tanaka has also been serving as a board member of Japan Institute of Design Promotion (JDP), and a member of the study group on the relation between industrial competitiveness and design by the Japan Patent Office (JPO) of the Ministry of Economy, Trade and Industry (METI). He also has been involved as a juror in many international design promotion activities and was awarded the Good Design Award Prime Minister Prize, the SDA Grand Prize and many other awards.

Kazuo Tanaka absolvierte sein Studium des Industriedesigns 1983 an der Tokyo University of Arts. Er ist Präsident und CEO der GK Design Group Incorporated, eines übergreifenden unabhängigen Designstudios in Japan, das 1952 von Kenji Ekuan gegründet wurde. Kazuo Tanaka wurde zum Präsidenten der Japan Industrial Designers Association (JIDA) ernannt und geht seit 2013 mehreren Tätigkeiten nach. 2017 wurde er zum Vorstandsmitglied der World Design Organization (ehemals Icsid) gewählt und ist seitdem auch auf regionaler Ebene beratend in vielen internationalen Projekten aktiv. Kazuo Tanaka ist ebenfalls als Vorstandsmitglied des Japan Institute of Design Promotion (JDP) tätig und Mitglied der Studiengruppe zur Beziehung zwischen industrieller Wettbewerbsfähigkeit und Design des Japanischen Patentbüros (JPO) des Ministeriums für Wirtschaft, Handel und Industrie (METI). Als Juror nahm er an einer Vielzahl internationaler Designwettbewerbe teil und erhielt den Good Design Award Prime Minister Prize, den SDA Grand Prize und viele weitere Auszeichnungen.

01 fugan
Fugan Suijo, shipping line of
the Toyama Prefecture, 2015
Fugan Suijo, Schifffahrtsgesell-
schaft der Toyama-Präfektur, 2015

01

"When evaluating products, I first of all prove their functionally, then their aesthetic excellence and social conviction. I then try to see if the product is pioneering by putting these views together."

„Bei der Bewertung von Produkten teste ich zuerst ihre Funktionalität, dann ihre ästhetische Qualität und soziale Überzeugung. Danach versuche ich herauszufinden, ob das Produkt bahnbrechend ist und alle diese Eigenschaften vereint."

Please describe good design:
Good design is the thing that provides excellent social, cultural and economic value. Today's design is evaluated for its comprehensiveness.

What constitutes good teamwork?
While each member has different professions and ideas, each member's deep understanding of his role in the common mission constitutes teamwork.

What does the Red Dot Award represent in your opinion?
The Red Dot Award has always been pointing towards the direction in which design should be heading in changing times. I firmly believe that it has an essential and invariable value.

How do you imagine the future of design?
New technologies and services have been changing the future of design. At the same time, the cultural nature of design, unchanged since the twentieth century, may also become more brilliant.

Beschreiben Sie bitte gutes Design:
Gutes Design ist das, was hervorragenden sozialen, kulturellen und wirtschaftlichen Wert schafft. Design wird heute nach seiner Vollständigkeit beurteilt.

Was macht gute Teamarbeit aus?
Obwohl jedes Teammitglied unterschiedliche Fachkenntnisse und Ideen hat, macht die tiefgründige Kenntnis seiner Rolle in der gemeinsamen Aufgabe die Teamarbeit aus.

Wofür steht der Red Dot Award für Sie?
Der Red Dot Award war schon immer wegweisend für die Richtung, die Design in wechselvollen Zeiten einschlagen soll. Ich bin fest davon überzeugt, dass der Red Dot Award einen maßgeblichen und konstanten Wert hat.

Wie stellen Sie sich die Zukunft des Designs vor?
Neue Technologien und Dienstleistungen beeinflussen die Zukunft des Designs. Gleichzeitig mag der kulturelle Charakter des Designs, der seit dem 20. Jahrhundert unverändert ist, noch fulminanter werden.

Nils Toft
Denmark
Dänemark

Nils Toft is the founder and managing director of Designidea. With offices in Copenhagen and Beijing, the multiple internationally awarded studio works in the key fields of sustainable energy solutions, consumer electronics, medical devices and design psychology, as well as taking on projects in business development, design strategy and exhibition design. Nils Toft graduated as an architect and designer from the Royal Danish Academy of Fine Arts in Copenhagen in 1986 and started his career as an industrial designer, joining the former Christian Bjørn Design in 1987, an internationaly active design studio in Copenhagen. Within a few years, he became a partner of CBD and, as managing director successfully ran the business until 2010. Nils Toft's work has recently been focused on understanding and measuring how people are impacted by design. By measuring physiological parameters such as heart rate, eye movements, neurological activity and electro dermal activity, it is possible to unveil a test person's emotional condition as well as their psychological reactions in relation to products, environments and services.

Nils Toft ist der Gründer und Geschäftsführer von Designidea. Mit Niederlassungen in Kopenhagen und Beijing arbeitet das international mehrfach ausgezeichnete Studio hauptsächlich in den Bereichen Erneuerbare Energien, Unterhaltungselektronik, Medizintechnik und Designpsychologie. Das Studio übernimmt ebenfalls Projekte in den Bereichen Geschäftsentwicklung, Designstrategie und Ausstellungsdesign. Nils Toft machte seinen Abschluss als Architekt und Designer 1986 an der Royal Danish Academy of Fine Arts in Kopenhagen und begann seine Karriere als Industriedesigner 1987 bei dem damaligen Christian Bjørn Design, einem international operierenden Designstudio in Kopenhagen. Innerhalb weniger Jahre wurde er Partner bei CBD und leitete das Unternehmen erfolgreich bis 2010 als Managing Director. In letzter Zeit hat Nils Toft sich in seiner Arbeit auf das Verständnis und Messen der Wirkung von Design auf Menschen konzentriert. Wenn man physiologische Parameter wie z. B. Pulsschlag, Augenbewegung, neurologische sowie elektrodermale Aktivität misst, ist es möglich, emotionale und psychologische Reaktionen der Versuchsperson auf Produkte, die Umgebung und Dienstleistungen zu erkennen.

01

01 Wittenborg 95
High-quality semi-automatic
coffee machines
Hochwertige halbautomatische
Kaffeemaschinen

01

"My professional goal is to
continually be curious, always
seeking new challenges and chasing
a continuously moving goal post."
„Mein professionelles Ziel ist es,
immer neugierig zu sein, immer
neue Herausforderungen zu suchen
und ein ständig wechselndes Ziel
zu verfolgen."

What does the "Designidea" company stand for?
Designidea is based on the philosophy that in all companies there are great ideas waiting to be discovered
and with the help of good designers can be turned
into great products.

**What, to date, has been the most exciting project
of your career?**
I have been fortunate enough to work on many different types of exiting projects and that is what has
made my career exiting. I am driven by my curiosity
and new projects – challenges are what excites me
the most.

How do you proceed when evaluating products?
I verify whether the design is of a high quality and
clearly expresses the intended idea behind the product.

With what can a designer surprise you?
I am positively surprised and full of admiration when I
see a technical product with many constraints that,
because of a great design by a talented designer,
appears so clear and obvious, that your only response
is, "of course".

Wofür steht Ihr Unternehmen „Designidea"?
Designidea basiert auf der Philosophie, dass es in allen
Unternehmen großartige Ideen gibt, die nur darauf war-
ten, entdeckt und mithilfe guter Designer in großartige
Produkte verwandelt zu werden.

**Was war das bisher spannendste Projekt Ihrer
Karriere?**
Ich habe das Glück, an vielen verschiedenen aufregenden
Projekten beteiligt gewesen zu sein. Das ist es, was meine
Karriere so spannend macht. Mich treiben Neugier und
neue Projekte an. Am aufregendsten finde ich neue
Herausforderungen.

**Wie gehen Sie bei der Bewertung von Produkten
vor?**
Ich prüfe, ob die Gestaltung qualitativ hochwertig ist und
klar die Intention hinter dem Produkt zum Ausdruck bringt.

Womit kann ein Designer Sie überraschen?
Ich bin positiv überrascht und voller Bewunderung, wenn
ich ein technisches Produkt mit vielen Features sehe, das
dank eines großartigen Gestaltungskonzepts von einem
talentierten Designer so klar und einleuchtend erscheint,
dass man nur „na klar" denken kann.

Prof. Danny Venlet
Belgium
Belgien

Professor Danny Venlet was born in 1958 in Victoria, Australia, and studied interior design at Sint-Lukas, the Institute for Architecture and Arts in Brussels. Back in Australia in 1991, Venlet started to attract international attention with large-scale interior projects such as the Burdekin hotel in Sydney and Q-bar, an Australian chain of nightclubs. His design projects range from private mansions, lofts, bars and restaurants all the way to showrooms and offices of large companies. The interior projects and the furniture designs of Danny Venlet are characterised by their contemporary international style. He says that the objects arise from an interaction between art, sculpture and function. These objects give a new description to the space in which they are placed – with respect, but also with relative humour. Today, Danny Venlet teaches his knowledge to students at the Royal College of the Arts in Ghent.

Professor Danny Venlet wurde 1958 in Victoria, Australien, geboren und studierte Interior Design am Sint-Lukas Institut für Architektur und Kunst in Brüssel. Nachdem er 1991 wieder nach Australien zurückgekehrt war, begann er, mit der Innenausstattung großer Projekte wie dem Burdekin Hotel in Sydney und der Q-Bar, einer australischen Nachtclub-Kette, internationale Aufmerksamkeit zu erregen. Seine Designprojekte reichen von privaten Wohnhäusern über Lofts, Bars und Restaurants bis hin zu Ausstellungsräumen und Büros großer Unternehmen. Die Innenausstattungen und Möbeldesigns von Danny Venlet sind durch einen zeitgenössischen, internationalen Stil ausgezeichnet und entspringen, wie er sagt, der Interaktion zwischen Kunst, Skulptur und Funktion. Seine Objekte geben den Räumen, in denen sie sich befinden, eine neue Identität – mit Respekt, aber auch mit einer Portion Humor. Heute vermittelt Danny Venlet sein Wissen als Professor an Studenten des Royal College of the Arts in Gent.

01 L-Hop 2
Toilet roll holder with integrated
light for the company Dark
Toilettenrollenhalter mit integriertem Licht für die Firma Dark

01

"Cultural exchange among designers is important to discover what other cultures have to offer and what solutions they have – in order to help us challenge our cultural dogmas."

„Der kulturelle Austausch zwischen Designern ist wichtig, um herauszufinden, was andere Kulturen zu bieten und welche Lösungen sie gefunden haben – das sollte uns helfen, unsere kulturellen Dogmen zu hinterfragen."

Is there a way of instantly recognising your designs? What are their distinguishing features?
My work is sometimes described as organic behaviouristic minimalism. Organic curves are beautiful and sensual but I believe one should use them sparingly. I am also a follower of the ideas of Wabi-Sabi, "the beauty of imperfection". I believe that the distinguishing features of my work are objects that move away from encrusted habits or customs and are therefore often behavioural change makers.

Unpretentious or grandiose – what do you prefer and why?
I would say unpretentious grandiosity would be my preference. Something is grandiose when it does not scream it out loud.

What are the essential features of a well-designed piece of furniture?
Excellence of execution, exceptional concept, emotionally capturing, elegant solution of a problem, environmentally friendly. Well-designed furniture should aim to have most of these E-factors.

Woran sind Ihre Gestaltungen zu erkennen? Was zeichnet sie aus?
Meine Arbeit wird manchmal als organisch behavioristischer Minimalismus bezeichnet. Organische Rundungen sind schön und sinnlich, doch bin ich der Meinung, dass man sie sparsam einsetzen sollte. Ich bin auch ein Anhänger der Ideen von Wabi-Sabi, „der Schönheit des Unvollkommenen". Ich glaube, dass die kennzeichnenden Merkmale meiner Arbeit Objekte sind, die sich von verkrusteten Gewohnheiten oder Gebräuchen entfernt haben und daher häufig zu „Änderungsgestaltern" des Verhaltens werden.

Schlicht oder pompös – was bevorzugen Sie und warum?
Ich würde sagen, dass ich eine Vorliebe für schlichten Prunk habe. Etwas, das pompös ist, ohne es zu laut kundzutun.

Was muss ein gut gestaltetes Möbelstück mitbringen?
Eine ausgezeichnete Umsetzung, ein herausragendes Konzept, es sollte emotional fesseln, eine elegante Lösung für ein Problem bieten und umweltfreundlich sein. Gut gestaltete Möbelstücke sollten einen Großteil dieser Eigenschaften aufweisen.

Dr.
Joseph Francis Wong
Hong Kong
Hongkong

Dr. Joseph Francis Wong joined the Hong Kong Design Institute as the Vice Principal in 2017. Prior to this, he was Associate Professor at the City University of Hong Kong, where he taught architectural design and theory for 19 years. Joseph Francis Wong received a Bachelor of Arts in Architecture from Berkeley, a Master of Architecture from MIT and a Doctor of Education from Leicester. He is a Fellow of the Hong Kong Institute of Architects, where he was part of the Board of Internal Affairs and the Board of Educational Affairs and chaired the Environment and Sustainable Design Committee. His research on open building and spatial/visual field analysis has been presented and published in many conferences and journals, including Design Studies, Habitat International, Journal of Architecture as well as Environment and Planning B. In recognition of his contribution to design education, Joseph Francis Wong was awarded the Berkeley Prize International Fellowship in 2014.

2017 trat Dr. Joseph Francis Wong dem Hong Kong Design Institute als Vice Principal bei. Zuvor war er als Associate Professor an der City University of Hong Kong tätig, wo er 19 Jahre lang architektonische Gestaltung und Theorie lehrte. Er machte einen Bachelor of Arts in Architektur in Berkeley, einen Master of Architecture am MIT und einen Doctor of Education in Leicester. Joseph Francis Wong ist Fellow des Hong Kong Institute of Architects, wo er Teil des Board of Internal Affairs und des Board of Educational Affairs war und dem Environment and Sustainable Design Committee vorsaß. Seine Forschung über offene Gebäude und räumliche/visuelle Feldanalyse wurde in vielen Konferenzen und Zeitschriften vorgestellt und veröffentlicht, so in Design Studies, Habitat International, Journal of Architecture sowie Environment and Planning B. In Anerkennung seines Beitrags zur Designlehre erhielt Joseph Francis Wong 2014 den Berkeley Prize International Fellowship.

01

"Innovation is a well-considered solution to a problem redefined through rigorous research."
„Innovation ist eine wohlüberlegte Lösung für ein Problem, das durch gründliche Recherche neu definiert wurde."

What does a product have to offer in order to persuade you of its merits?
Simplicity and user considerations. A good product does not need to attempt too much; it's more preferable to do one thing or a few things really well than too many things above average. It must also be clear and sensible about actual usage by users.

How do you proceed when evaluating products?
I would go straight for it, try to understand and use the product before reading the instructions. That's my first criterion. Next, I would correlate design intentions to the actual design itself. The product should definitely stand out in terms of elegant integration of look and feel to functionality.

Was muss ein Produkt mitbringen, um Sie zu überzeugen?
Einfachheit und eine Berücksichtigung der Nutzer. Ein gutes Produkt sollte nicht versuchen, zu viel zu leisten. Es ist besser, eine Sache oder ein paar Dinge richtig gut zu machen, als zu viele Dinge über dem Durchschnitt. Das Produkt sollte auch klar und vernünftig in Bezug auf die Anwendung durch den Nutzer sein.

Wie gehen Sie bei der Bewertung von Produkten vor?
Ich gehe ganz direkt vor und versuche, das Produkt zu verstehen und zu benutzen, bevor ich die Anleitung lese. Das ist mein erstes Kriterium. Als Nächstes versuche ich, den Zusammenhang zwischen Designintention und dem eigentlichen Design zu erkennen. Das Produkt sollte auf jeden Fall aus der Masse hervorstechen – in einer eleganten Integration von Optik, Haptik und Funktionalität.

Alphabetical index manufacturers and distributors
Alphabetisches Hersteller- und Vertriebs-Register

Shenzhen 21g Product Design Co., Ltd.
Page/Seite 203

70mai Co., Ltd.
Page/Seite 140

A

Shenzhen Accompany Tech Co., Ltd.
Page/Seite 291, 293

Aclim8
Page/Seite 178

AD Global Co., Ltd.
Page/Seite 314–315

Agrifac Machinery BV
Page/Seite 133

Akrapovič d.d.
Page/Seite 144

Amap Information Technology Co., Ltd.
Page/Seite 142

AMAZONEN-Werke
H. Dreyer GmbH & Co. KG
Page/Seite 133

Arçelik A.Ş.
Page/Seite 283

Armin Strom AG
Page/Seite 340

ASISTA Teile fürs Rad GmbH & Co. KG
Page/Seite 95

AUGLETICS GmbH
Page/Seite 167

Shenzhen Aukey E-Business Co., Ltd.
Page/Seite 228

B

Shenzhen Baojia
Battery Technology Co., Ltd.
Page/Seite 288, 297

Beijing Forbidden City
Culture Development Co., Ltd.
Page/Seite 346

belaDESIGN
Page/Seite 241

Beryl
Page/Seite 93

Beurer GmbH
Page/Seite 298

Bodyorbit Co., Ltd.
Page/Seite 168

Robert Bosch GmbH
Bosch eBike Systems
Page/Seite 89

Brembo S.p.A.
Page/Seite 143

Shenzhen Breo Technology Co., Ltd.
Page/Seite 300

BRP Inc.
Page/Seite 116–119

Burley
Page/Seite 88

C

CAKE Zero Emission AB
Page/Seite 114

Campagnolo S.r.l.
Page/Seite 90–91

Cannice
Page/Seite 256

Canyon Bicycles GmbH
Page/Seite 84

Catalyst Lifestyle
Page/Seite 318

CCILU International Inc.
Page/Seite 309

CHAPTER2
Page/Seite 85

Charles Owen
Page/Seite 158

China Mobile IOT Company Limited
Page/Seite 141

Chronoswiss AG
Page/Seite 338

CITECH
ROSE
Page/Seite 272

clearaudio electronic GmbH
Page/Seite 264–265

Cleer, Inc.
Page/Seite 239, 252–253, 258

Coleen
Page/Seite 83

Courage & Wisdom
Shenzhen Youxing Technology Co., Ltd.
Page/Seite 198–199

COWBOY
Page/Seite 80–81

Crestron Electronics, Inc.
Page/Seite 222–223, 226

CTK Cosmetics Co., Ltd.
Page/Seite 298

CWA Constructions SA/Corp.
Page/Seite 122–123

D

Dachstein Outdoor & Lifestyle GmbH
Page/Seite 175

Danke Co., Ltd.
Page/Seite 192

Tianjin Deepfar Ocean Technology
Page/Seite 163

Dell
Page/Seite 249

Dolby Laboratories
Page/Seite 246–247

Dometic
Page/Seite 182

doppler
E. doppler & Co GmbH
Page/Seite 326–327

Dots Design Studio
Page/Seite 82

Ducati Motor Holding S.p.A.
Page/Seite 110–111

E

ECCO Golf
Page/Seite 171

Ecoflow
Page/Seite 181

EM-Tech Co., Ltd.
Page/Seite 253, 272

Seiko Epson Corporation
Page/Seite 211

ESKA Lederhandschuhfabrik
Ges. m. b. H. & Co. KG
Page/Seite 157

EVBox
Page/Seite 148

F

FARE – Guenther Fassbender GmbH
Page/Seite 328–329

Federal Corporation
Page/Seite 139

Ferrari S.p.A.
Page/Seite 98–101

Fiskars Finland Oy Ab
Page/Seite 176–177

FOCUS Bikes
Page/Seite 85

FOGWARE Technology (Shenzhen) Co., Ltd.
Page/Seite 330

FRONTIER Inc.
Page/Seite 309

FUJIFILM Corporation
Page/Seite 206–207

G

August Gerstner Ringfabrik
GmbH & Co. KG
Page/Seite 347

GEWA music GmbH
Page/Seite 200–201

Gome Intelligent Technology Co., Ltd.
Page/Seite 227

Google LLC
Page/Seite 232, 239, 254

GRAMMER AG
Page/Seite 138

Great Wall Motor Company Limited
Page/Seite 107

gripmore Co., Ltd.
Page/Seite 308

Grossmann Uhren GmbH
Page/Seite 340

H

Hankook Tire
Page/Seite 139

Harman International
Page/Seite 242–243, 251, 253, 256, 258–259, 269

Harrel GmbH & Co.
Page/Seite 191

Hau Ya Co., Ltd.
Page/Seite 185

HEINZ-GLAS GmbH & Co. KGaA
Page/Seite 330

Helinox Inc.
Page/Seite 184

Helly Hansen AS
Page/Seite 308

HILLMAN
Page/Seite 174

Shanghai Himo Electric
Technology Co., Ltd.
Page/Seite 86

HMD
Page/Seite 263

HP Inc.
Page/Seite 249

Huanxing Technology (Hangzhou) Co., Ltd.
Page/Seite 280

Huawei Device (Shenzhen) Co., Ltd.
Page/Seite 296

Hutech Industry Co., Ltd.
Page/Seite 299

Hymer GmbH & Co. KG
Page/Seite 132

Hyphen Eyewear
Page/Seite 311

Hyundai Motor Company
Page/Seite 108–109

I

IDEAL Fastener (Guangdong)
Industries Ltd.
Page/Seite 306

iKamper
Page/Seite 132

IKEA of Sweden AB
Page/Seite 241

Shenzhen IMUB
Intelligent Beauty Co., Ltd.
Page/Seite 293, 296

iMuto Limited
Page/Seite 183

Guangdong Indel B Enterprise Co., Ltd.
Page/Seite 143

Infomir SA
Page/Seite 267

Iriver
Page/Seite 273

J

Shenzhen Jianyuanda
Science & Technology Co., Ltd.
Page/Seite 292

Shenzhen Jixin Technology Co., Ltd.
Page/Seite 209

JnY Archistudio
Page/Seite 194

K

K9-Sport Trade and Service LLC
Page/Seite 194

KAI Corporation
Page/Seite 281

Kia Motors Corporation
Page/Seite 104–105

KingCamp Outdoor Products Co., Ltd.
Page/Seite 185

Kingsmith
Page/Seite 167

Guangzhou Kingsons
Leather Products Co., Ltd.
Page/Seite 318

kofta
Page/Seite 320

L

Lampuga GmbH
Page/Seite 120–121, 161, 188–189

Shenzhen Lefeet
Innovation Technology Co., Ltd.
Page/Seite 163

Lenovo
Page/Seite 234, 240, 248

LG Electronics Inc.
Page/Seite 209, 212–215, 270–271, 292

LG Uplus
Page/Seite 230

Libratone
Page/Seite 256–257

Lilienthal Lifestyle GmbH
Page/Seite 340

LINDBERG
Page/Seite 312–313

LINE Corp.
Page/Seite 233, 244–245

Guangxi Liugong Machinery Co., Ltd.
Page/Seite 134

Logitech
Page/Seite 220, 240–241, 250, 257

LOVELY PLANET
Page/Seite 196

Lumileds
Page/Seite 136–137

M

MAN Truck & Bus SE
Page/Seite 128

Manfrotto
Vitec Imaging Solutions S.p.A.
Page/Seite 320

Master & Dynamic
Page/Seite 262

Maurice Lacroix SA
Page/Seite 339

Mazda Motor Corporation
Page/Seite 102–103

Medion AG
Page/Seite 270

Shenzhen Mees Tech Co., Ltd.
Page/Seite 261

MeisterSinger GmbH & Co. KG
Page/Seite 341

Alphabetical index manufacturers and distributors
Alphabetisches Hersteller- und Vertriebs-Register

Microlino AG
Page/Seite 115

MIIEGO
Page/Seite 248

MINISO Hong Kong Limited
Page/Seite 291

Shenzhen Minjun
Electronic Technology Co., Ltd.
Page/Seite 92

MIPRO Electronics Co., Ltd.
Page/Seite 203

Mobike Bike Product Center
Page/Seite 87

Mobvoi US LLC
Page/Seite 257

MODERN DAYFARER
Page/Seite 319

MOMODESIGN
Page/Seite 152–153

muli-cycles GmbH
Page/Seite 88

MYKITA
Page/Seite 310

N
NAVER Corp.
Page/Seite 233, 244–245

Hangzhou NetEase
Yanxuan Trading Co., Ltd.
Page/Seite 254

NetModule AG
Page/Seite 145

NIO GmbH
Page/Seite 146–147

Guangzhou NOME
Brand Management Limited
Page/Seite 170

North Actionsports BV
Mystic Boarding
Page/Seite 160

Nubert electronic GmbH
Page/Seite 268

O
Shenzhen Oceanwing
Smart Innovation Co., Ltd.
Page/Seite 141, 208

OnePlus Technology
Page/Seite 255

Onyx International Inc.
Page/Seite 235

OUMOS Travel
Page/Seite 321

OUTENTIC
Page/Seite 94

P
Panasonic Corporation
Page/Seite 271, 276–278, 288

Park & Diamond
Page/Seite 94

Shenzhen Qianhai Patuoxun
Network & Technology Co., Ltd.
Page/Seite 248

Peloton Interactive, Inc.
Page/Seite 166, 169, 171

Petit Pli
Page/Seite 304–305

Peugeot Deutschland GmbH
Groupe PSA
Page/Seite 107

Phiaton Corporation
Page/Seite 263

Philips
Page/Seite 278–279, 282, 288

Piuma Care S.r.l.
Page/Seite 289

Plume Labs
Page/Seite 331

Plus Eyewear (Shenzhen) Limited
Page/Seite 310

PocketBook International SA
Page/Seite 234

Polar Electro Oy
Page/Seite 170

Porsche Design Timepieces AG
Page/Seite 334–335

Prague Public Transit Co., Inc.
Page/Seite 126

Procter & Gamble Service GmbH
Page/Seite 280, 286–287

Groupe PSA
Peugeot Deutschland GmbH
Page/Seite 107

Q
Hangzhou Qingqi
Science and Technology Co., Ltd.
Page/Seite 88

QLOCKTWO Manufacture GmbH
Marco Biegert und Andreas Funk
Page/Seite 342–343

R
RAVO Group
Page/Seite 294–295

RECARO Aircraft Seating
Page/Seite 124–125

Regina Miracle International
(Holdings) Limited
Page/Seite 307

Shenzhen Renqing
Excellent Investment Co., Ltd.
Page/Seite 141

reTyre
Technium AS
Page/Seite 89

REV'IT! Sport International B.V.
Page/Seite 154–155

Revox Deutschland GmbH
Page/Seite 270

RHA Technologies
Page/Seite 260

Ride Awake AB
Page/Seite 162

Rocla Oy
Page/Seite 135

Roku
Page/Seite 240, 267

Roland Corporation
Page/Seite 203

Hangzhou Rosou Electronic
Technology Co., Ltd.
Page/Seite 283

Rottefella AS
Page/Seite 157

Ningbo Ruifu Industrial Group Co., Ltd.
Page/Seite 296

Runmi
Page/Seite 324–325

ruwido austria gmbh
Page/Seite 225

S
SACKit ApS
Page/Seite 252

Samsonite NV
Page/Seite 316–318

Sandiline d.o.o.
Page/Seite 174

Shenzhen Science Technology Co., Ltd.
Page/Seite 191

Seiko Epson Corporation
Page/Seite 211

Sennheiser Communications A/S
Page/Seite 249

Silhouette International
Page/Seite 311

Simplon Fahrrad GmbH
Page/Seite 85

Sinn Spezialuhren GmbH
Page/Seite 341

ŠKODA AUTO a.s.
Page/Seite 106

Chengdu Skywalker Technology Co., Ltd.
Page/Seite 323

Skyworth
Page/Seite 218–219

SoftBank Commerce & Service Corp.
Page/Seite 255, 260

Sonos
Page/Seite 266

Sonos Europe
Page/Seite 229

Sony Video & Sound Products Inc.
Page/Seite 236–237, 251, 259, 272

Sony Visual Products Inc.
Page/Seite 216

Stadler Rail AG
Page/Seite 127

SteelSeries
Page/Seite 250

STOWA GmbH & Co. KG
Page/Seite 336–337

Shenzhen Stylepie Lifestyle Co., Ltd.
Page/Seite 297

Suning Intelligent Terminal Co., Ltd.
Page/Seite 234

T
RS TAICHI Inc.
Page/Seite 156

TCL Corporation
Page/Seite 209, 217

Tech4home
Page/Seite 224

TechniSat Digital GmbH
Page/Seite 228

TENGA Co., Ltd.
Page/Seite 197

Thule Group AB
Page/Seite 143, 323

TiCad GmbH & Co. KG
Page/Seite 159

Sport-Tiedje GmbH
Page/Seite 169

Titan Company Limited
Page/Seite 344–345

Zhejiang Tmall Technology Co., Ltd.
Page/Seite 238, 290

Tokosha Co., Ltd.
Page/Seite 281

Tonal
Page/Seite 164–165

Torrot Electric Europa S.A.
Page/Seite 114

TPV Technology Group
MMD
Page/Seite 217

Traveler's Choice Travelware
Page/Seite 322

Shanghai Tuplus Travel
Technology Co., Ltd.
Page/Seite 324

Tupperware (China) Co., Ltd.
Page/Seite 180

Tuya Inc.
Page/Seite 227

Tweezerman International LLC
ZWILLING Beauty Group
Page/Seite 297

U
Ujet
Page/Seite 114

UMAREX GmbH & Co. KG
Page/Seite 179

UNIT 1 Gear, Inc.
Page/Seite 157

Universal Electronics
Page/Seite 221, 231

Urbanized Bikes
Page/Seite 83

Urwahn Engineering GmbH
Page/Seite 78–79

V
Vagonremmash
Page/Seite 127

VARRAM SYSTEM Co., Ltd.
Page/Seite 195

Vennskap
Christian Battel
Page/Seite 181

VF Corporation
The North Face
Page/Seite 174

Victorinox AG
Page/Seite 180

VIOMODA
Page/Seite 174

VOCIER GmbH
Page/Seite 320

Volvo Bus Corporation
Page/Seite 129

W
Wall Box Chargers S.L.
Page/Seite 149

Walnut Technology Limited
Page/Seite 190

Wataoka Co., Ltd.
Page/Seite 194

Werewoof
Sonderlust Ltd.
Page/Seite 193

Wikkelhouse
Page/Seite 130–131

Wilkinson Sword GmbH
Page/Seite 278

Wirelane GmbH
Page/Seite 149

Shenzhen Wizevo Technology Co., Ltd.
Page/Seite 283

X
X-Technology Swiss R&D AG
Page/Seite 172–173

Chengdu XGIMI Technology Co., Ltd.
Page/Seite 210

Xiaomi Inc.
Page/Seite 210

Y
Yamaha Corporation
Page/Seite 202

Yamaha Motor Co., Ltd.
Page/Seite 112–113

Yirego Corp.
Page/Seite 181

The Yokohama Rubber Co., Ltd.
Page/Seite 139

Z
Shenzhen Zhizhi
Brand Incubation Co., Ltd.
Page/Seite 301

ZTE Corporation
Page/Seite 230

ZWILLING Beauty Group GmbH
Page/Seite 284–285

Alphabetical index designers
Alphabetisches Designer-Register

8quadrat-design
Page/Seite 200–201

Shenzhen 21g Product Design Co., Ltd.
Page/Seite 203

70mai Co., Ltd.
Page/Seite 140

A

Shenzhen Accompany Tech Co., Ltd.
Page/Seite 291, 293

AD Global Co., Ltd.
Page/Seite 314–315

Yu-Jin Ahn
CITECH
ROSE
Page/Seite 272

Akrapovič d.d.
Page/Seite 144

Nigel Alcorn
Peloton Interactive, Inc.
Page/Seite 166

Benjamin Alexander
Ride Awake AB
Page/Seite 162

AMAZONEN-Werke
H. Dreyer GmbH & Co. KG
Page/Seite 133

Benjamin Amsler
NetModule AG
Page/Seite 145

Magnus Anderssen
Rottefella AS
Page/Seite 157

Arçelik A.Ş.
Page/Seite 283

Armin Strom AG
Page/Seite 340

Armis Sport Limited
Page/Seite 158

AUGLETICS GmbH
Page/Seite 167

Shenzhen Aukey E-Business Co., Ltd.
Page/Seite 228

B

Xuefeng Bai
Shenzhen Oceanwing
Smart Innovation Co., Ltd.
Page/Seite 141, 208

Jamie Baldock
Werewoof
Sonderlust Ltd.
Page/Seite 193

Haohui Bao
Ningbo Moma Industrial Design Co., Ltd.
Page/Seite 296

Shenzhen Baojia
Battery Technology Co., Ltd.
Page/Seite 288, 297

Daniel Barnes
Beryl
Page/Seite 93

Vincent Beekman
Page/Seite 130–131

belaDESIGN
Page/Seite 241

Marlon Bent
Werewoof
Sonderlust Ltd.
Page/Seite 193

Thorsten Bergmaier-Trede
MAN Truck & Bus SE
Page/Seite 128

Javier Bertani
UNIT 1 Gear, Inc.
Page/Seite 157

Beryl
Page/Seite 93

Ushio Bessho
Panasonic Corporation
Page/Seite 288

Bi Shun
belaDESIGN
Page/Seite 241

Andrzej Bikowski
ECCO Golf
Page/Seite 171

Max Blom
North Actionsports BV
Mystic Boarding
Page/Seite 160

Bodyorbit Co., Ltd.
Page/Seite 168

Robert Bosch GmbH
Bosch eBike Systems
Page/Seite 89

Matthias Böttcher
MAN Truck & Bus SE
Page/Seite 128

Bould Design
Page/Seite 240, 267

Alexis Boyer
Plume Labs
Page/Seite 331

BrandSystem GmbH
Page/Seite 145

Manfred Brassler
MeisterSinger GmbH & Co. KG
Page/Seite 341

Braun Design Team
Page/Seite 280

Brembo S.p.A.
Page/Seite 143

Jörg Brennwald
Brennwald Design
Page/Seite 249

Shenzhen Breo Technology Co., Ltd.
Page/Seite 300

Sandra Brombacher
GRAMMER AG
Page/Seite 138

BRP Inc.
Page/Seite 116–119

Daniel Brunner
Page/Seite 181

Marco Brunori
Page/Seite 115

Rick Buchter
Wikkelhouse
Page/Seite 130–131

Achim Burmeister
MAN Truck & Bus SE
Page/Seite 128

Leo Burnett-Laeufer
Page/Seite 114

Nicolas Busnel
LOVELY PLANET
Page/Seite 196

BUSSE Design+Engineering
Page/Seite 114

C

CAKE Zero Emission AB
Page/Seite 114

Campagnolo S.r.l.
Page/Seite 90–91

Cannice
Page/Seite 256

Canyon Bicycles GmbH
Page/Seite 84

Odin Cappello
Hyphen Eyewear
Page/Seite 311

Marcus Carlsson
CAKE Zero Emission AB
Page/Seite 114

Raymond Carter
Carter Design Innovation Network
Page/Seite 138

Catalyst Lifestyle
Page/Seite 318

Paolo Cattaneo
MOMODESIGN
Page/Seite 152–153

CCILU International Inc.
Page/Seite 309

Hyunbyung Cha
LG Electronics Inc.
Page/Seite 212–213

Ray Chang
AD Global Co., Ltd.
Page/Seite 314–315

CHAPTER2
Page/Seite 85

Fengming Chen
inDare Design Strategy Limited
Page/Seite 198–199, 292

Hao Chen
Guangzhou NOME
Brand Management Limited
Page/Seite 170

Hao Chen
Zhejiang Tmall Technology Co., Ltd.
Page/Seite 238

Jie Chen
Shenzhen Qifang Design Studio
Page/Seite 191

Joseph Chen
Traveler's Choice Travelware
Page/Seite 322

Lixing Chen
Skyworth
Page/Seite 219

Prof. Qing Chen
Kingsmith
Page/Seite 167

Qinglang Chen
inDare Design Strategy Limited
Page/Seite 198–199, 292

Shangping Chen
Skyworth
Page/Seite 219

Shaolong Chen
inDare Design Strategy Limited
Page/Seite 198–199, 292

Yu Chen
Mobvoi US LLC
Page/Seite 257

Yujie Chen
inDare Design Strategy Limited
Page/Seite 198–199, 292

Zhiyong Chen
Skyworth
Page/Seite 218–219

Chen Zuo
belaDESIGN
Page/Seite 241

Zhilong Cheng
Shenzhen Accompany Tech Co., Ltd.
Page/Seite 291, 293

Jack Kam Pui Cheung
Plus Eyewear Limited
Page/Seite 310

China Mobile IOT Company Limited
Page/Seite 141

Yoonyoung Cho
LG Electronics Inc.
Page/Seite 209

Yuonui Chong
LG Electronics Inc.
Page/Seite 214

Chronoswiss AG
Page/Seite 338

CITECH
ROSE
Page/Seite 272

clearaudio electronic GmbH
Page/Seite 264–265

Cleer, Inc.
Page/Seite 239, 252–253, 258

Coleen
Page/Seite 83

Jacques Colman
Lilienthal Lifestyle GmbH
Page/Seite 340

James Connors
Peloton Interactive, Inc.
Page/Seite 169

Tiago Correia
Tech4home
Page/Seite 224

Tom Cortese
Peloton Interactive, Inc.
Page/Seite 171

Mariana Couto
Tech4home
Page/Seite 224

CTK Cosmetics Co., Ltd.
Page/Seite 298

Wei Cui
Dongguan Jianghao Plastic Co., Ltd.
Page/Seite 308

Cui Yangbin
Hangzhou Teague Technology Co., Ltd.
Page/Seite 241

CWA Constructions SA/Corp.
Page/Seite 122–123

D

Luigi D'Andrea
D'Andrea & Evers Design
Page/Seite 221, 231

Dachstein Outdoor & Lifestyle GmbH
Page/Seite 175

Yuting Dan
Onyx International Inc.
Page/Seite 235

Danke Co., Ltd.
Page/Seite 192

Harald Dannert
Harrel GmbH & Co.
Page/Seite 191

Patrick David
Ujet
Page/Seite 114

Shenzhen DBK Electronics Co., Ltd.
Page/Seite 183

Pinakesh De
Panasonic Corporation
Page/Seite 276–278

Tianjin Deepfar Ocean Technology
Page/Seite 163

Dell
Dell Experience Design Group
Page/Seite 249

Chiara Delucca
Werewoof
Sonderlust Ltd.
Page/Seite 193

Tomas Deluna
Harman International
Page/Seite 269

Jasper den Dekker
REV'IT! Sport International B.V.
Page/Seite 154–155

Cole Derby
Whipsaw Inc.
Page/Seite 164–165

Designest Industrial Design Co., Ltd.
Page/Seite 170

DesignThink, Inc.
Page/Seite 88

Kebi Ding
Shenzhen Oceanwing
Smart Innovation Co., Ltd.
Page/Seite 208

Dario Distefano
Harman International
Page/Seite 243

Dolby Laboratories
Page/Seite 246–247

Dometic
Page/Seite 182

Luc Donckerwolke
Hyundai Motor Company
Hyundai Design Center
Page/Seite 108–109

Alphabetical index designers
Alphabetisches Designer-Register

Yuxiong Dong
FOGWARE Technology (Shenzhen) Co., Ltd.
Page/Seite 330

doppler
E. doppler & Co GmbH
Page/Seite 326–327

Dots Design Studio
Page/Seite 82

Fei Du
Shenzhen Breo Technology Co., Ltd.
Page/Seite 300

Ducati Motor Holding S.p.A.
Centro Stile Ducati
Page/Seite 110–111

E
ECCO Golf
Page/Seite 171

Ecoflow
Page/Seite 181

Mark Eggert
Peloton Interactive, Inc.
Page/Seite 171

Amin Einakian
Harman International
Page/Seite 269

Sander Ejlenberg
Page/Seite 130–131

EM-Tech Co., Ltd.
Page/Seite 253, 272

Seiko Epson Corporation
Page/Seite 211

ESKA Lederhandschuhfabrik
Ges. m. b. H. & Co. KG
Page/Seite 157

ESNE
University of Design, Innovation and Technology
Page/Seite 149

F
FARE – Guenther Fassbender GmbH
Page/Seite 328–329

Reyhaneh Fathollah Nouri
Ippiart Studio
Page/Seite 127

Federal Corporation
Page/Seite 139

Ferrari S.p.A.
Ferrari Design
Page/Seite 98–101

Klaus Fiorino
MOMODESIGN
Page/Seite 152–153

Fiskars Finland Oy Ab
Page/Seite 176–177

FOCUS Bikes
Page/Seite 85

FOGWARE Technology (Shenzhen) Co., Ltd.
Page/Seite 330

Oliver Forgatsch
RECARO Aircraft Seating
Page/Seite 124–125

Andreas Fredriksson
IKEA of Sweden AB
Page/Seite 241

frog design
Page/Seite 331

FRONTIER Inc.
Page/Seite 309

Dan Frykholm
Volvo Bus Corporation
Page/Seite 129

Fuchu Fu
Guangzhou Kingsons
Leather Products Co., Ltd.
Page/Seite 318

FUJIFILM Corporation
Page/Seite 206–207

Manabu Fujiki
Sony Corporation
Creative Center
Page/Seite 236–237

Masayuki Fushimi
nagahama design
Page/Seite 139

G
Sven Gaedtke
MAN Truck & Bus SE
Page/Seite 128

Wenxu Gan
Shenzhen Breo Technology Co., Ltd.
Page/Seite 300

Gao Shusan
Mobike Bike Product Center
Page/Seite 87

Yingxin Gao
Guangzhou NOME
Brand Management Limited
Page/Seite 170

Juan Garcia Mansilla
UNIT 1 Gear, Inc.
Page/Seite 157

André Gärtner
RECARO Aircraft Seating
Page/Seite 124–125

GBO Innovation Makers
Page/Seite 203

GENERATIONDESIGN GmbH
Page/Seite 278

GEO Product Creation
Page/Seite 93

Jonas Gerhardt
Sören Gerhardt
muli-cycles GmbH
Page/Seite 88

August Gerstner
Ringfabrik GmbH & Co. KG
Page/Seite 347

Marcos Gervasoni
UNIT 1 Gear, Inc.
Page/Seite 157

GK Dynamics Inc.
Page/Seite 112–113

GK Kyoto Inc.
Page/Seite 194

Prof. Justine Go
CTK Cosmetics Co., Ltd.
Page/Seite 298

Jason Gokavi
Harman International
Page/Seite 269

Gome Intelligent Technology Co., Ltd.
Page/Seite 227

David Gonzalez
CAKE Zero Emission AB
Page/Seite 114

Google LLC
Page/Seite 232, 239, 254

GRAMMER AG
Page/Seite 138

Luke Gray
Beryl
Page/Seite 93

Great Wall Motor Company Limited
Page/Seite 107

Claude Greisler
Armin Strom AG
Page/Seite 340

gripmore Co., Ltd.
Page/Seite 308

Zhiwei Guan
Hangzhou Qingqi
Science and Technology Co., Ltd.
Page/Seite 88

Bin Guo
Guangzhou NOME
Brand Management Limited
Page/Seite 170

H
Hans Haenlein
Hyphen Eyewear
Page/Seite 311

Sebastian Hahn
Canyon Bicycles GmbH
Page/Seite 84

Jillian Halbig
Tweezerman International LLC
ZWILLING Beauty Group
Page/Seite 297

David Hall
Park & Diamond
Page/Seite 94

Thibault Halm
Coleen
Page/Seite 83

Hangar Design Group
Page/Seite 289

Hankook Tire
Page/Seite 139

Dan Harden
Whipsaw Inc.
Page/Seite 164–165

Harman International
Page/Seite 242–243, 251, 253, 256, 258–259, 269

Harrel GmbH & Co.
Page/Seite 191

Hau Ya Co., Ltd.
Page/Seite 185

Jie He
Skyworth
Page/Seite 219

HEINZ-GLAS GmbH & Co. KGaA
Page/Seite 330

Helinox Inc.
Page/Seite 184

Helly Hansen AS
Page/Seite 308

Lee Hendrickson
Peloton Interactive, Inc.
Page/Seite 169

Sunghyun Heo
EM-Tech Co., Ltd.
Page/Seite 272

Christopher Herd
Canyon Bicycles GmbH
Page/Seite 84

Andreas Hess
whiteID GmbH & Co. KG
Page/Seite 268

Björn Hillesheim
TiCad GmbH & Co. KG
Page/Seite 159

HILLMAN
Page/Seite 174

Shanghai Himo Electric
Technology Co., Ltd.
Page/Seite 86

HMD
Page/Seite 263

James Ho
gripmore Co., Ltd.
Page/Seite 308

Martin Paul Hoffmann
paul martin
Page/Seite 298

Lars Hofmann
Lilienthal Lifestyle GmbH
Page/Seite 340

Stefan Hohn
Noto GmbH
Page/Seite 222–223, 226

Thomas Holm
Rottefella AS
Page/Seite 157

Shinji Honda
FRONTIER Inc.
Page/Seite 309

HP Inc.
HP Design Team
Page/Seite 249

Steve Hsu
CCILU International Inc.
Page/Seite 309

Wilson Hsu
CCILU International Inc.
Page/Seite 309

Chino Hu
Shenzhen Qianhai Patuoxun
Network & Technology Co., Ltd.
Page/Seite 248

Juan Juan Hu
Juan Juan Hu Jewellery Design
Page/Seite 346

Ave Huang
Shenzhen Mees Tech Co., Ltd.
Page/Seite 261

Chien-Hsin Huang
HMD
Page/Seite 263

Chun-Kai Huang
HMD
Page/Seite 263

Pengfei Huang
China Mobile IOT Company Limited
Page/Seite 141

Huawei Device (Shenzhen) Co., Ltd.
Page/Seite 296

David Hundertmark
MODERN DAYFARER
Page/Seite 319

Hung Shih Ming
OUMOS Travel
Page/Seite 321

Øystein Helle Husby
Page/Seite 249

Kyle Hutchison
RHA Technologies
Page/Seite 260

Hutech Industry Co., Ltd.
Page/Seite 299

Chang-Chin Hwang
Brennwald Design
Page/Seite 249

Hymer GmbH & Co. KG
Page/Seite 132

Hyphen Eyewear
Page/Seite 311

Hyundai Motor Company
Hyundai Design Center
Page/Seite 108–109

I
Idéact
Page/Seite 196

IDEAL Fastener (Guangdong)
Industries Ltd.
Page/Seite 306

IDEO
Page/Seite 149

iKamper
Page/Seite 132

IKEA of Sweden AB
Page/Seite 241

Shenzhen IMUB
Intelligent Beauty Co., Ltd.
Page/Seite 293, 296

iMuto Limited
Page/Seite 183

inDare Design Strategy Limited
Page/Seite 198–199, 292

Guangdong Indel B Enterprise Co., Ltd.
Page/Seite 143

Infomir SA
Page/Seite 267

Ippiart Studio
Page/Seite 127

Iriver
Page/Seite 273

Mikiyasu Ishikura
Panasonic Corporation
Page/Seite 276–278

J

Yonghun Jang
LG Electronics Inc.
Page/Seite 215

Byunglok Jeon
LG Electronics Inc.
Page/Seite 214–215

Seungwon Jeon
JnY Archistudio
Page/Seite 194

Christian Jeppesen
MIIEGO
Page/Seite 248

Bing Jiang
Suning Intelligent Terminal Co., Ltd.
Page/Seite 234

Dongguan Jianghao Plastic Co., Ltd.
Page/Seite 308

Chang Jin
Page/Seite 280, 283

JnY Archistudio
Page/Seite 194

Yang Ju
Hangzhou NetEase
Yanxuan Trading Co., Ltd.
Page/Seite 254

Jaeneung Jung
LG Electronics Inc.
Page/Seite 214–215

Mi-Jung Jung
CITECH
ROSE
Page/Seite 272

K

K9-Sport Trade and Service LLC
Page/Seite 194

Pooja Kabra
Titan Company Limited
Page/Seite 344–345

KAI Corporation
Page/Seite 281

Marcus Kane
Beryl
Page/Seite 93

Qian Kang
Runmi
Page/Seite 325

Seunghan Kang
UMAREX GmbH & Co. KG
Page/Seite 179

Seungkoo Kang
Hankook Tire
Page/Seite 139

Saloni Kaushik
Titan Company Limited
Page/Seite 344–345

Shigeo Kawakami
RS TAICHI Inc.
Page/Seite 156

Ke Weijia
Mobike Bike Product Center
Page/Seite 87

Roland Keplinger
Silhouette International
Page/Seite 311

Peter Kettenring
Canyon Bicycles GmbH
Page/Seite 84

Kia Motors Corporation
Kia Design Center Europe
Page/Seite 104–105

Richard John Killgren
Guangxi Liugong Machinery Co., Ltd.
Page/Seite 134

Byoungjin Kim
EM-Tech Co., Ltd.
Page/Seite 253

Hyojin Kim
Harman International
Page/Seite 242–243

Hyoungwon Kim
LG Electronics Inc.
Page/Seite 215

Jisun Kim
Iriver
Page/Seite 273

Jongchul Kim
LG Electronics Inc.
Page/Seite 214

Junki Kim
LG Electronics Inc.
Page/Seite 271

Kyungnam Kim
VARRAM SYSTEM Co., Ltd.
Page/Seite 195

Seonkyu Kim
LG Electronics Inc.
Page/Seite 212–213

Taeho Kim
LG Electronics Inc.
Page/Seite 214

Yoonsoo Kim
LG Electronics Inc.
Page/Seite 215

Young Kyung Kim
LG Electronics Inc.
Page/Seite 212–213

Yunjoo Kim
LG Electronics Inc.
Page/Seite 212–213

KingCamp Outdoor Products Co., Ltd.
Page/Seite 185

Kingsmith
Page/Seite 167

Guangzhou Kingsons
Leather Products Co., Ltd.
Page/Seite 318

Shogo Kinoshita
GK Dynamics Inc.
Page/Seite 112–113

KISKA GmbH
Page/Seite 89

Jordan Klein
Park & Diamond
Page/Seite 94

Lena Kliewer
MAN Truck & Bus SE
Page/Seite 128

Valerian Knaub
BUSSE Design+Engineering
Page/Seite 114

Wanjo Koch
Canyon Bicycles GmbH
Page/Seite 84

Konstantin Kofta
kofta
Page/Seite 320

Michael Kogelnik
VOCIER GmbH
Page/Seite 320

Martina Kögler
MAN Truck & Bus SE
Page/Seite 128

Thomas König
HEINZ-GLAS GmbH & Co. KGaA
Page/Seite 330

Holger Koos
MAN Truck & Bus SE
Page/Seite 128

Mark Kruse
Peloton Interactive, Inc.
Page/Seite 166

Dorian Kurz
Kurz Kurz Design
Page/Seite 284

Seungju Kwak
Hankook Tire
Page/Seite 139

L

Huiren La
Suning Intelligent Terminal Co., Ltd.
Page/Seite 234

Young Whan Lah
Helinox Inc.
Page/Seite 184

Andreas Läufer
Leo Burnett-Laeufer
Page/Seite 114

Le Ying Trading (Hong Kong) Limited
Page/Seite 307

Eunbong Lee
LG Electronics Inc.
Page/Seite 209

Prof. Jaehui Lee
CTK Cosmetics Co., Ltd.
Page/Seite 298

Jeongrok Lee
LG Electronics Inc.
Page/Seite 214

Minjae Lee
LG Electronics Inc.
Page/Seite 212–213

Ray Lee
Shenzhen Tianbaotong Technology Co., Ltd.
Page/Seite 183

Sangho Lee
LG Electronics Inc.
Page/Seite 270

Seoyeon Lee
LG Uplus
Page/Seite 230

Shenzhen Lefeet
Innovation Technology Co., Ltd.
Page/Seite 163

Audrey Lefort
Coleen
Page/Seite 83

Lenovo
Page/Seite 234, 240, 248

LG Electronics Inc.
Page/Seite 209, 212–215, 270–271, 292

LG Uplus
Page/Seite 230

Jianye Li
Zhejiang Tmall Technology Co., Ltd.
Page/Seite 142, 290

Messizon Li
Shenzhen Accompany Tech Co., Ltd.
Page/Seite 291, 293

Qiang Li
Skyworth
Page/Seite 219

Tong Li
Shenzhen Oceanwing
Smart Innovation Co., Ltd.
Page/Seite 141

Wentao Liang
Hangzhou NetEase
Yanxuan Trading Co., Ltd.
Page/Seite 254

Lilienthal Lifestyle GmbH
Page/Seite 340

Cheng Feng Lin
MINISO Hong Kong Limited
Page/Seite 291

Huahui Lin
inDare Design Strategy Limited
Page/Seite 198–199

Lin Jianjun
Mobike Bike Product Center
Page/Seite 87

Lanhai Lin
Dongguan Jianghao Plastic Co., Ltd.
Page/Seite 308

Siting Lin
inDare Design Strategy Limited
Page/Seite 198–199

Zhuoxi Lin
Shenzhen Renqing
Excellent Investment Co., Ltd.
Page/Seite 141

LINDBERG
Page/Seite 312–313

Prof. Andrea Lipp
MAN Truck & Bus SE
Page/Seite 128

Junting Liu
Skyworth
Page/Seite 218

Liangqiu Liu
Shenzhen Science Technology Co., Ltd.
Page/Seite 191

Min Liu
Ningbo Moma Industrial Design Co., Ltd.
Page/Seite 294–295

Wei Liu
Suning Intelligent Terminal Co., Ltd.
Page/Seite 234

Xingkang Liu
Skyworth
Page/Seite 218

Yukai Liu
Onyx International Inc.
Page/Seite 235

Zhao Liu
Zhejiang Tmall Technology Co., Ltd.
Page/Seite 238

Guangxi Liugong Machinery Co., Ltd.
Page/Seite 134

Sandi Ljutić
Sandiline d.o.o.
Page/Seite 174

Logitech
Page/Seite 220, 240–241, 250, 257

Regina Loos
ESKA Lederhandschuhfabrik
Ges. m. b. H. & Co. KG
Page/Seite 157

LOVELY PLANET
Page/Seite 196

Lauri Lumme
Polar Electro Oy
Page/Seite 170

Huide Luo
Shenzhen Zhizhi
Brand Incubation Co., Ltd.
Page/Seite 301

Jianghao Luo
Walnut Technology Limited
Page/Seite 190

Tao Luo
Chengdu XGIMI Technology Co., Ltd.
Page/Seite 210

Lv Zhiming
Mobike Bike Product Center
Page/Seite 87

David Whitney Lyndaker
IDEAL Fastener (Guangdong)
Industries Ltd.
Page/Seite 306

M

Shuai Ma
Shenzhen Oceanwing
Smart Innovation Co., Ltd.
Page/Seite 208

Ma Zheng
Shenzhen IMUB
Intelligent Beauty Co., Ltd.
Page/Seite 293, 296

Rasmus Christian Madsen
SteelSeries
Page/Seite 250

Gary Edmund Major
Guangxi Liugong Machinery Co., Ltd.
Page/Seite 134

MAN Truck & Bus SE
Page/Seite 128

Manfrotto
Vitec Imaging Solutions S.p.A.
Page/Seite 320

Flavio Manzoni
Ferrari S.p.A.
Ferrari Design
Page/Seite 98–101

Anna Marešová
anna maresova designers
Page/Seite 126

Christoph Marti
BrandSystem GmbH
Page/Seite 145

Olaf Brage Marvik
reTyre
Technium AS
Page/Seite 89

Alphabetical index designers
Alphabetisches Designer-Register

Master & Dynamic
Page/Seite 262

Maurice Lacroix SA
Page/Seite 339

Mazda Motor Corporation
Page/Seite 102–103

Samuele Meda
Dometic
Page/Seite 182

Medion AG
Medion Design Team
Page/Seite 270

Shenzhen Mees Tech Co., Ltd.
Page/Seite 261

MeisterSinger GmbH & Co. KG
Page/Seite 341

Moritz Menacher
MAN Truck & Bus SE
Page/Seite 128

Metal Sound Design
Page/Seite 273

Mettle Studio
Page/Seite 93

Microlino AG
Page/Seite 115

MIIEGO
Page/Seite 248

MINISO Hong Kong Limited
Page/Seite 291

Shenzhen Minjun
Electronic Technology Co., Ltd.
Page/Seite 92

MIPOW
Page/Seite 288, 297

MIPRO Electronics Co., Ltd.
Page/Seite 203

MNML
Page/Seite 257

Mobike Bike Product Center
Page/Seite 87

Mobvoi US LLC
Page/Seite 257

MODERN DAYFARER
Page/Seite 319

Ningbo Moma Industrial Design Co., Ltd.
Page/Seite 294–296

MOMODESIGN
Page/Seite 152–153

Michele Montemezzi
Manfrotto
Vitec Imaging Solutions S.p.A.
Page/Seite 320

So Morimoto
Sony Corporation
Creative Center
Page/Seite 259

Yujin Morisawa
Sony Corporation
Creative Center
Page/Seite 236–237

Mormedi S.A.
Page/Seite 114

Alexander Morokko
PocketBook International SA
Page/Seite 234

Federica Mucci
Samsonite NV
Page/Seite 318

Huub Mulhof
D'Andrea & Evers Design
Page/Seite 221, 231

muli-cycles GmbH
Page/Seite 88

MYKITA
Page/Seite 310

N
nagahama design
Page/Seite 139

Takahiro Nakamichi
SoftBank Commerce & Service Corp.
Page/Seite 255

NAVER Corp.
Page/Seite 233, 244–245

Dmitry Nazarov
Ippiart Studio
Page/Seite 127

Masayuki Nemoto
The Yokohama Rubber Co., Ltd.
Page/Seite 139

Neodesis Sàrl
Page/Seite 340

Hangzhou NetEase
Yanxuan Trading Co., Ltd.
Page/Seite 254

NetModule AG
Page/Seite 145

Heinke Nienstermann
AMAZONEN-Werke
H. Dreyer GmbH & Co. KG
Page/Seite 133

NIO GmbH
Page/Seite 146–147

Xiaoyu Niu
Shenzhen Oceanwing
Smart Innovation Co., Ltd.
Page/Seite 141, 208

Guangzhou NOME
Brand Management Limited
Page/Seite 170

nonobject
Page/Seite 241, 246–247

North Actionsports BV
Mystic Boarding
Page/Seite 160

Noto GmbH
Page/Seite 222–223, 226

Nubert electronic GmbH
Page/Seite 268

Jens Nybacka
Dometic
Page/Seite 182

O
Shenzhen Oceanwing
Smart Innovation Co., Ltd.
Page/Seite 141, 208

Koshi Odaira
SoftBank Commerce & Service Corp.
Page/Seite 260

Kristoffer Olsson
Dometic
Page/Seite 182

OnePlus Technology
Page/Seite 255

Onfire Design
Page/Seite 85

Onyx International Inc.
Page/Seite 235

Oral Care Design Team
Page/Seite 286–287

Elliot Ortiz
Whipsaw Inc.
Page/Seite 164–165

Jun Otsuka
KAI Corporation
Page/Seite 281

Richard Ott
GRAMMER AG
Page/Seite 138

OUMOS Travel
Page/Seite 321

OUTENTIC
Page/Seite 94

Christine Overbeck
OUTENTIC
Page/Seite 94

P
Panasonic Corporation
Page/Seite 271, 276–278, 288

Park & Diamond
Page/Seite 94

Seongyeong Park
LG Electronics Inc.
Page/Seite 209

Soon Park
iKamper
Page/Seite 132

Sooyoung Park
LG Electronics Inc.
Page/Seite 270

Sungyong Park
LG Electronics Inc.
Page/Seite 271

Sunha Park
LG Electronics Inc.
Page/Seite 292

Laurent Passini
Idéact
Page/Seite 196

Shenzhen Qianhai Patuoxun
Network & Technology Co., Ltd.
Page/Seite 248

paul martin
Page/Seite 298

Paula-D Design
Page/Seite 95

Tim Payne
Page/Seite 138

Peloton Interactive, Inc.
Page/Seite 166, 169, 171

Liyuan Peng
Skyworth
Page/Seite 218–219

Xingwei Peng
Kingsmith
Page/Seite 167

Scott Lawrence Peters
IDEAL Fastener (Guangdong)
Industries Ltd.
Page/Seite 306

Petit Pli
Page/Seite 304–305

Peugeot Deutschland GmbH
Groupe PSA
Page/Seite 107

Phiaton Corporation
Page/Seite 263

Philips Design
Page/Seite 136–137, 278–279, 282, 288

Krit Phutpim
Dots Design Studio
Page/Seite 82

Plume Labs
Page/Seite 331

Plus Eyewear Limited
Page/Seite 310

PocketBook International SA
Page/Seite 234

Polar Electro Oy
Page/Seite 170

Studio F. A. Porsche
Page/Seite 334–335

Jason Poure
Peloton Interactive, Inc.
Page/Seite 166, 169, 171

Prime Total Product Design
Page/Seite 178

Propeller Design AB
Page/Seite 80–81

Groupe PSA
Peugeot Deutschland GmbH
Page/Seite 107

Adelheid Pürstinger
ESKA Lederhandschuhfabrik
Ges. m. b. H. & Co. KG
Page/Seite 157

Q
Guohui Qian
Shanghai Tuplus Travel
Technology Co., Ltd.
Page/Seite 324

Yiran Qian
Runmi
Page/Seite 325

Zhang Qian
ZTE Corporation
Page/Seite 230

Shenzhen Qifang Design Studio
Page/Seite 191

Yeitai Qin
gripmore Co., Ltd.
Page/Seite 308

Hangzhou Qingqi
Science and Technology Co., Ltd.
Page/Seite 88

QLOCKTWO Manufacture GmbH
Marco Biegert und Andreas Funk
Page/Seite 342–343

R
Jesper Randrup
Ride Awake AB
Page/Seite 162

RBS
Page/Seite 127

RECARO Aircraft Seating
Page/Seite 124–125

Charles-Henry Regaud
OUMOS Travel
Page/Seite 321

Regina Miracle International
(Holdings) Limited
Page/Seite 307

Shenzhen Renqing
Excellent Investment Co., Ltd.
Page/Seite 141

Jonas Rentsch
HEINZ-GLAS GmbH & Co. KGaA
Page/Seite 330

reTyre
Technium AS
Page/Seite 89

REV'IT! Sport International B.V.
Page/Seite 154–155

Revox Deutschland GmbH
Page/Seite 270

RHA Technologies
Page/Seite 260

Ride Awake AB
Page/Seite 162

RISE.DESIGN
Page/Seite 309

Robin Ritter
Schweizer Design Consulting
Page/Seite 120–121, 161, 188–189

Holger Rix
MAN Truck & Bus SE
Page/Seite 128

Rocla Oy
Page/Seite 135

Roland Corporation
Page/Seite 203

Hangzhou Rosou Electronic
Technology Co., Ltd.
Page/Seite 283

Rottefella AS
Page/Seite 157

Runmi
Page/Seite 324–325

S
Doğaç Can Sağırosmanoğlu
Arçelik A.Ş.
Page/Seite 283

Natsumi Sakamoto
GK Kyoto Inc.
Page/Seite 194

Samsonite NV
Page/Seite 316–318

Sandiline d.o.o.
Page/Seite 174

Mami Sato
Yamaha Corporation
Page/Seite 202

Edwin Schaap
North Actionsports BV
Mystic Boarding
Page/Seite 160

Nicki Schäfer
IDEO
Page/Seite 149

Jörg Schauer
STOWA GmbH & Co. KG
Page/Seite 336–337

Oep Schilling
Wikkelhouse
Page/Seite 130–131

Pascal Schnell
BrandSystem GmbH
Page/Seite 145

Stephan Schönherr
MAN Truck & Bus SE
Page/Seite 128

Christoph Schürg
RECARO Aircraft Seating
Page/Seite 124–125

Steffen Schuster
MAN Truck & Bus SE
Page/Seite 128

Oliver Schweizer
Schweizer Design Consulting
Page/Seite 120–121, 161, 188–189

Shenzhen Science Technology Co., Ltd.
Page/Seite 191

Gyula Sebö
K9-Sport Trade and Service LLC
Page/Seite 194

Seiko Epson Corporation
Page/Seite 211

Jaan Selg
Propeller Design AB
Page/Seite 80–81

Patrick Senfter
Schweizer Design Consulting
Page/Seite 120–121, 161, 188–189

Cheol Hong Seo
Hutech Industry Co., Ltd.
Page/Seite 299

Baekjin Seong
Iriver
Page/Seite 273

Nicola Sgreva
Campagnolo S.r.l.
Page/Seite 90–91

Shi Hong
Hangzhou Teague Technology Co., Ltd.
Page/Seite 241

Sylvia Shih
gripmore Co., Ltd.
Page/Seite 308

Takayuki Shimizu
RISE.DESIGN
Page/Seite 309

Cheolwoong Shin
LG Electronics Inc.
Page/Seite 212–213

Ivan Shmatko
Infomir SA
Page/Seite 267

Signify Design Team
Page/Seite 136–137

Silhouette International
Page/Seite 311

Simplon Fahrrad GmbH
Page/Seite 85

Sinn Spezialuhren GmbH
Page/Seite 341

ŠKODA AUTO a.s.
Page/Seite 106

Skyworth
Page/Seite 218–219

Smartisan Technology Co., Ltd.
Page/Seite 323

Tino Soelberg
SteelSeries
Page/Seite 250

SoftBank Commerce & Service Corp.
Page/Seite 255, 260

Takashi Sogabe
Sony Corporation
Creative Center
Page/Seite 272

Wei Song
Runmi
Page/Seite 325

Sonos
Page/Seite 266

Sonos Europe
Page/Seite 229

Sony Corporation
Creative Center
Page/Seite 216, 236–237, 251, 259, 272

Jordan Spack
Ride Awake AB
Page/Seite 162

Robin Spicer
Armis Sport Limited
Page/Seite 158

Springtime Design
Page/Seite 87

Martina Stauber
Paula-D Design
Page/Seite 95

SteelSeries
Page/Seite 250

Zack Stephanchick
Whipsaw Inc.
Page/Seite 164–165

Piotr Stolarski
Yamaha Corporation
Page/Seite 202

STOWA GmbH & Co. KG
Page/Seite 336–337

René Straub
NetModule AG
Page/Seite 145

Michael Streicher
MAN Truck & Bus SE
Page/Seite 128

Markus Stridsberg
Propeller Design AB
Page/Seite 80–81

Studio SYN
Page/Seite 132

Shenzhen Stylepie Lifestyle Co., Ltd.
Page/Seite 297

Patrick Suchy
clearaudio electronic GmbH
Page/Seite 264–265

Byungjo Suh
VARRAM SYSTEM Co., Ltd.
Page/Seite 195

Congpo Sun
Designest Industrial Design Co., Ltd.
Page/Seite 170

Weizhi Sun
Shenzhen Oceanwing
Smart Innovation Co., Ltd.
Page/Seite 208

Suning Intelligent Terminal Co., Ltd.
Page/Seite 234

Swift Creatives
Page/Seite 250, 256–257

T
RS TAICHI Inc.
Page/Seite 156

Gakuto Takahashi
Panasonic Corporation
Page/Seite 271

Dengtai Tan
Guangzhou Kingsons
Leather Products Co., Ltd.
Page/Seite 318

Kunihiko Tanaka
FUJIFILM Corporation
Page/Seite 206–207

Chen Tang
Skyworth
Page/Seite 218–219

Tang Jia
belaDESIGN
Page/Seite 241

TCL Corporation
TCL Industrial Design Center
Page/Seite 209, 217

Hangzhou Teague Technology Co., Ltd.
Page/Seite 241

Tech4home
Page/Seite 224

TechniSat Digital GmbH
Page/Seite 228

TENGA Co., Ltd.
Page/Seite 197

Gianni Teruzzi
Harman International
Page/Seite 243

Mikael Thelin
Dometic
Page/Seite 182

Thule Group AB
Page/Seite 143, 323

Bo Tian
Runmi
Page/Seite 325

Chunjiang Tian
Tianjin Deepfar Ocean Technology
Page/Seite 163

Shenzhen Tianbaotong Technology Co., Ltd.
Page/Seite 183

TiCad GmbH & Co. KG
Page/Seite 159

Sport-Tiedje GmbH
Page/Seite 169

Felix Timm
BUSSE Design+Engineering
Page/Seite 114

Titan Company Limited
Page/Seite 344–345

Zhejiang Tmall Technology Co., Ltd.
Page/Seite 142, 238, 290

Tokosha Co., Ltd.
Page/Seite 281

Kris Tomasson
NIO GmbH
Page/Seite 146–147

Torrot Electric Europa S.A.
Page/Seite 114

TPV Technology Design Team
Page/Seite 217

Traveler's Choice Travelware
Page/Seite 322

Tricon AG
Page/Seite 127

Ernie Tsai
gripmore Co., Ltd.
Page/Seite 308

Yasutake Tsuchida
Mazda Motor Corporation
Page/Seite 102–103

Yusuke Tsujita
Sony Corporation
Creative Center
Page/Seite 216

Kai Tsuyama
TENGA Co., Ltd.
Page/Seite 197

Shanghai Tuplus Travel
Technology Co., Ltd.
Page/Seite 324

Tupperware Worldwide Product Innovation Team
Tupperware General Services N.V.
Page/Seite 180

Ari Turgel
Whipsaw Inc.
Page/Seite 164–165

Tuya Inc.
Page/Seite 227

Tweezerman International LLC
ZWILLING Beauty Group
Page/Seite 297

U
Ryota Uchida
Panasonic Corporation
Page/Seite 288

Ujet
Page/Seite 114

UMAREX GmbH & Co. KG
Page/Seite 179

UNIT 1 Gear, Inc.
Page/Seite 157

Urbanized Bikes
Page/Seite 83

Urwahn Engineering GmbH
Page/Seite 78–79

V
Mark van Roon
REV'IT! Sport International B.V.
Page/Seite 154–155

VanBerlo
Page/Seite 148

Vanderveer Designers
Page/Seite 133

VARRAM SYSTEM Co., Ltd.
Page/Seite 195

Shenzhen VENZO Design Co., Ltd.
Page/Seite 209

Brendon Vermillion
Ride Awake AB
Page/Seite 162

VF Corporation
The North Face
Page/Seite 174

Victorinox AG
Page/Seite 180

Gilles Vidal
Groupe PSA
Peugeot Deutschland GmbH
Page/Seite 107

Joaquín Vincent
UNIT 1 Gear, Inc.
Page/Seite 157

VIOMODA
Page/Seite 174

VOCIER GmbH
Page/Seite 320

Volvo Bus Corporation
Page/Seite 129

W
Edward Lee Wagner
Guangxi Liugong Machinery Co., Ltd.
Page/Seite 134

Annelie Waldhier-Fröhlich
August Gerstner
Ringfabrik GmbH & Co. KG
Page/Seite 347

Wall Box Chargers S.L.
Page/Seite 149

Walnut Technology Limited
Page/Seite 190

Alexander Wang
Shenzhen VENZO Design Co., Ltd.
Page/Seite 209

Anqi Wang
Gome Intelligent Technology Co., Ltd.
Page/Seite 227

Jiyong Wang
Shenzhen Qifang Design Studio
Page/Seite 191

Mingming Wang
Skyworth
Page/Seite 218–219

Neo Wang
Shenzhen Accompany Tech Co., Ltd.
Page/Seite 291, 293

Alphabetical index designers
Alphabetisches Designer-Register

Yang Wang
Shenzhen Aukey E-Business Co., Ltd.
Page/Seite 228

Mikael Warnhammar
IKEA of Sweden AB
Page/Seite 241

Prof. Jiancang Wei
Tianjin Deepfar Ocean Technology
Page/Seite 163

Shuxiao Wei
Skyworth
Page/Seite 218–219

Werewoof
Sonderlust Ltd.
Page/Seite 193

Philip Werner
Ride Awake AB
Page/Seite 162

Whipsaw Inc.
Page/Seite 164–165

whiteID GmbH & Co. KG
Page/Seite 268

Whynot Design & Innovation
Page/Seite 252

Wikkelhouse
Page/Seite 130–131

Don Wilson
Samsonite NV
Page/Seite 316–317

Shenzhen Wizevo Technology Co., Ltd.
Page/Seite 283

Sze Tung Wong
Plus Eyewear Limited
Page/Seite 310

Joshua Wright
Catalyst Lifestyle
Page/Seite 318

Changquan Wu
Skyworth
Page/Seite 219

Difei Wu
Runmi
Page/Seite 324

Guanghao Wu
Zhejiang Tmall Technology Co., Ltd.
Page/Seite 290

Yanjuan Wu
Shenzhen Renqing
Excellent Investment Co., Ltd.
Page/Seite 141

Margit Würflingsdobler
doppler
E. doppler & Co GmbH
Page/Seite 326–327

X
X-Technology Swiss R&D AG
Page/Seite 172–173

Chengdu XGIMI Technology Co., Ltd.
Page/Seite 210

Yaxun Xia
Chengdu XGIMI Technology Co., Ltd.
Page/Seite 210

Prof. Shi Xiao
Chengdu XGIMI Technology Co., Ltd.
Page/Seite 210

Xiaomi Inc.
Page/Seite 167, 210

Guo Qing Xu
KingCamp Outdoor Products Co., Ltd.
Page/Seite 185

Qing Xu
70mai Co., Ltd.
Page/Seite 140

Xu Yixin
Mobike Bike Product Center
Page/Seite 87

Tong Xue
Werewoof
Sonderlust Ltd.
Page/Seite 193

Zhichao Xue
Zhejiang Tmall Technology Co., Ltd.
Page/Seite 142

Y
Taku Yaegashi
Sony Corporation
Creative Center
Page/Seite 251

Yamaha Corporation
Page/Seite 202

Yamaha Motor Co., Ltd.
Page/Seite 112–113

Chinyun Yang
Walnut Technology Limited
Page/Seite 190

Huancan Yang
Ningbo Moma Industrial Design Co., Ltd.
Page/Seite 294–296

Masahiro Yasuda
Yamaha Motor Co., Ltd.
Page/Seite 112–113

Tomohiro Yasuda
Panasonic Corporation
Page/Seite 271

Ye Haiwei
Mobike Bike Product Center
Page/Seite 87

Wai Yung Stanley Yeung
MIPOW
Page/Seite 288, 297

Yunji Yi
JnY Archistudio
Page/Seite 194

Yige Technology (Shenzhen) Co., Ltd.
Page/Seite 181

Lingang Yin
Onyx International Inc.
Page/Seite 235

Yirego Corp.
Page/Seite 181

The Yokohama Rubber Co., Ltd.
Page/Seite 139

Hiroaki Yokota
Sony Corporation
Creative Center
Page/Seite 216

Aiko Yokoyama
GK Kyoto Inc.
Page/Seite 194

Sanghoon Yoon
LG Electronics Inc.
Page/Seite 292

Stefan Ytterborn
CAKE Zero Emission AB
Page/Seite 114

Kukil Yu
Metal Sound Design
Page/Seite 273

Sangmin Yu
Shenzhen Oceanwing
Smart Innovation Co., Ltd.
Page/Seite 141, 208

Yu Xie
Guangdong Indel B Enterprise Co., Ltd.
Page/Seite 143

Z
Farouk Zemni
Schweizer Design Consulting
Page/Seite 120–121, 161, 188–189

Terry Zeng
Shenzhen DBK Electronics Co., Ltd.
Page/Seite 183

zeug Design GmbH
Page/Seite 225

Chuang Wu Zhang
Shenzhen DBK Electronics Co., Ltd.
Page/Seite 183

Zhang Fei
belaDESIGN
Page/Seite 241

Hongzhi Zhang
Shenzhen 21g Product Design Co., Ltd.
Page/Seite 203

Lei Zhang
Suning Intelligent Terminal Co., Ltd.
Page/Seite 234

Minmin Zhang
Shenzhen Aukey E-Business Co., Ltd.
Page/Seite 228

Zhang Siyuan
Mobike Bike Product Center
Page/Seite 87

Zhang Xinwei
Shenzhen IMUB
Intelligent Beauty Co., Ltd.
Page/Seite 293, 296

Yihao Zhang
Skyworth
Page/Seite 219

Bi Zhao
Designest Industrial Design Co., Ltd.
Page/Seite 170

Weiwei Zhao
Shanghai Himo Electric
Technology Co., Ltd.
Page/Seite 86

Yaodong Zhao
Shenzhen VENZO Design Co., Ltd.
Page/Seite 209

Haiping Zheng
Shenzhen 21g Product Design Co., Ltd.
Page/Seite 203

Shenzhen Zhizhi
Brand Incubation Co., Ltd.
Page/Seite 301

Yugen Zhong
Tuya Inc.
Page/Seite 227

Yunbing Zhong
Skyworth
Page/Seite 218

Peng Zhou
Designest Industrial Design Co., Ltd.
Page/Seite 170

Zhuo Zhou
Shanghai Tuplus Travel
Technology Co., Ltd.
Page/Seite 324

ZTE Corporation
Page/Seite 230

ZWILLING Beauty Group GmbH
Page/Seite 284–285

Find additional award-winning products and designer portraits
in the separate volumes "Living", "Doing", "Working".

Weitere ausgezeichnete Produkte und Designerporträts finden Sie
in den Einzelbänden „Living", „Doing", „Working".

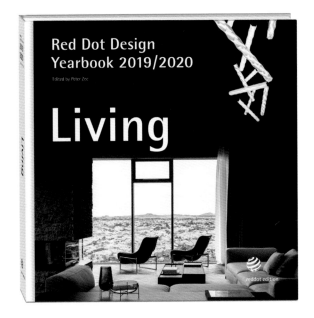

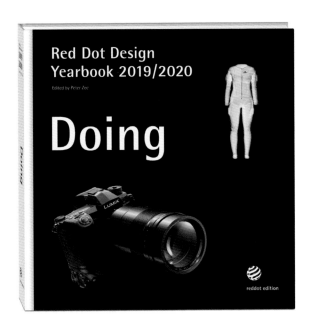

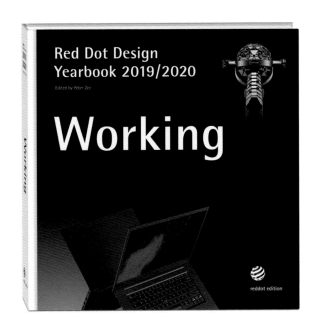

Living

Interior design
Interior Design

Living rooms and bedrooms
Wohnen und Schlafen

Kitchens
Küche

Bathrooms and sanitary equipment
Bad und Sanitär

Lighting and lamps
Licht und Leuchten

Urban design and public spaces
Urban Design und öffentlicher Raum

Doing

Babies and children
Baby und Kind

Household
Haushalt

Tableware and cooking utensils
Tableware und Kochutensilien

Garden
Garten

Tools
Werkzeuge

Cameras
Kameras

Communication
Kommunikation

Robots
Roboter

Working

Office
Büro

Computer and information technology
Computer- und Informationstechnik

**Industrial equipment, machinery
and automation**
Industriegeräte, Maschinen und Automation

Materials and surfaces
Materialien und Oberflächen

Heating and air conditioning technology
Heiz- und Klimatechnik

Life science and medicine
Life Science und Medizin

reddot edition

Editor | Herausgeber
Peter Zec

Project management | Projektleitung
Sophie Angerer

Project assistance | Projektassistenz
Theresa Falkenberg
Ekaterina Haak
Laura-Gabriela Hellbach
Anja Lakomski
Judith Lindner
Samuel Madilonga
Vivien Mroß
Louisa Mücher
Lena Poteralla
Anamaria Sumic
Sabine Wöll
Janik Zeh

Editorial work | Redaktion
Mareike Ahlborn, Essen, Germany
Jörg Arnke, Essen, Germany
Bettina Derksen, Simmern, Germany
Eva Hembach, Vienna, Austria
Karin Kirch, Essen, Germany
Karoline Laarmann, Dortmund, Germany
Bettina Laustroer, Wuppertal, Germany
Kirsten Müller, Essen, Germany
Astrid Ruta, Essen, Germany
Martina Stein, Otterberg, Germany
Corinna Ten-Cate, Wetter, Germany

"Red Dot: Design Team of the Year"
Burkhard Jacob, Krefeld, Germany

Translation | Übersetzung
Heike Bors-Eberlein, Tokyo, Japan
Patrick Conroy, Lanarca, Cyprus
Stanislaw Eberlein, Tokyo, Japan
William Kings, Wuppertal, Germany
Kocarek GmbH (Anna Krepper, Christopher Schuster,
David Lauber), Essen, Germany
Tara Russell, Dublin, Ireland
Philippa Watts, Exeter, United Kingdom
Andreas Zantop, Berlin, Germany
Christiane Zschunke, Frankfurt am Main, Germany

Proofreading | Lektorat
Klaus Dimmler (supervision), Essen, Germany
Mareike Ahlborn, Essen, Germany
Jörg Arnke, Essen, Germany
Wolfgang Astelbauer, Vienna, Austria
Dawn Michelle d'Atri, Kirchhundem, Germany
Annette Gillich-Beltz, Essen, Germany
Sonja Illa-Paschen, London, United Kingdom
Karin Kirch, Essen, Germany
Norbert Knyhala, Castrop-Rauxel, Germany
Regina Schier, Essen, Germany
Anja Schrade, Stuttgart, Germany
SPRACHENWERFT GmbH, Hamburg, Germany

Layout | Gestaltung
Lockstoff Design GmbH, Meerbusch, Germany
Nicole Slink (supervision)
Christina Jörres
Alica Kern
Alexandra Korschefsky
Alina Laase
Stephanie Marniok
Saskia Rühmkorf

Cover | Umschlag
Idea | Idee
Burkhard Jacob, Krefeld, Germany
Implementation | Umsetzung
Lockstoff Design GmbH, Meerbusch, Germany

Photographs | Fotos
Dragan Arrigler (Carefoot, juror Jure Miklavc)

Guglielmo Galliano, Responsible Grafik & Visual
of Ferrari Design (portrait of Flavio Manzoni,
Red Dot: Design Team of the Year 2019)

Altin Manaf (GENESI, juror Masayo Ave)

Peter Molick, (product photo ReThink!, USA,
Volume Working)

Jens Passoth (designer portrait photo of Kees de Boer,
Volume Working)

Singapore GP Pte. Ltd. (Twenty3, juror Simon Ong)

Swiss Krono Group (juror Katrin de Louw)

Masafumi Yamamoto (fugan, juror Kazuo Tanaka)

Jury photographs | Jurorenfotos
eventfotograf.in, Essen, Germany
Schuchrat Kurbanov
Alex Muchnik

In-company photos | Werkfotos der Firmen

Production | Produktion
gelb+, Düsseldorf, Germany
Bernd Reinkens

Lithography | Lithografie
gelb+, Düsseldorf, Germany
Bernd Reinkens (supervision)
Wurzel Medien GmbH, Düsseldorf, Germany
Jonas Mühlenweg

Printing | Druck
Dr. Cantz'sche Druckerei Medien GmbH,
Esslingen, Germany

Bookbindery | Buchbinderei
Conzella Verlagsbuchbinderei, Pfarrkirchen, Germany

Red Dot Design Yearbook 2019/2020
Living: 978-3-89939-213-5
Doing: 978-3-89939-214-2
Working: 978-3-89939-215-9
Enjoying: 978-3-89939-216-6
Set (Living, Doing, Working & Enjoying): 978-3-89939-212-8

© 2019 Red Dot GmbH & Co. KG, Essen, Germany

Publisher & worldwide distribution |
Verlag & Vertrieb weltweit
Red Dot Edition
Design Publisher | Fachverlag für Design
Contact | Kontakt
Sabine Wöll
Gelsenkirchener Str. 181
45309 Essen, Germany
Phone +49 201 81418 22
Fax +49 201 81418 10
E-mail edition@red-dot.de
www.red-dot-edition.com
Book publisher ID no. | Verkehrsnummer
13674 (Börsenverein Frankfurt)

**Bibliographic information published
by the Deutsche Nationalbibliothek**
The Deutsche Nationalbibliothek
lists this publication in the Deutsche
Nationalbibliografie; detailed bibliographic
data are available on the Internet at
http://dnb.ddb.de
Bibliografische Information
der Deutschen Nationalbibliothek
Die Deutsche Nationalbibliothek verzeichnet
diese Publikation in der Deutschen
Nationalbibliografie; detaillierte
bibliografische Daten sind im Internet über
http://dnb.ddb.de abrufbar